e Studies

William Kiffen and his World (Part 1)

Centre for Baptist History and Heritage Studies
Re-sourcing Baptist History
Seventeenth Century Series
Volume 1

William Kiffen and his World (Part 1)

Larry J. Kreitzer

Foreword by Paul S. Fiddes

Regent's Park College, Oxford

Regent's Park College is a Permanent Private Hall of The University of Oxford.

First published 2010

Centre for Baptist History and Heritage,
Regent's Park College,
Pusey Street,
Oxford,
OX1 2LB.
(Regent's Park College is a Permanent Private Hall of
the University of Oxford.)
www.rpc.ox.ac.uk

16 15 14 13 12 11 10 7 6 5 4 3 2 1

British Library Cataloguing in Publication Data
A catalogue record for this book is available from the British Library

ISBN 978–0–9539746–7–2

Front cover illustration:
The Portrait of William Kiffen (1667) which hangs in the Senior Common Room,
Regent's Park College, Oxford.
Back cover illustration by Chris Lewis. Used with permission.

Typeset by Troon & Croft
Printed and bound in Great Britain
by AlphaGraphics Nottingham
www.alphagraphics.co.uk/centres/nottingham-uk007/index.html

To Debbie

Contents

Foreword
Paul S. Fiddes ... ix

Introducing Re-sourcing Baptist History: Seventeenth Century Series ... xv

Acknowledgements of Figures ... xvii

Introduction ... 1

Chapter 1
William Kiffen's Indictments at the Surrey Assizes in March 1642 ... 6

Chapter 2
Hanserd Knollys and the Baptist Church in the Old Artillery Ground (1658–82) ... 42

Chapter 3
The Anabaptist Petitions of 1660 and 1661 ... 126

Chapter 4
'Unlawfully assembled and mett together': William Kiffen's Arrest on 24 February 1661 at the House of Robert Malbon ... 148

Chapter 5
Devonshire Square Baptist Church Membership Lists, c.1664–90 ... 177

Chapter 6
'Riotously assembled': Conventiclers arrested at the Devonshire Square Baptist Church (11 February 1686) ... 308

Chapter 7
Samuel Gleede: Master Gunner in the Commonwealth Navy ... 315

Chapter 8
Elizabeth Avery's Encounter with William Kiffen in 1647: Mis-recollection, or Mis-attribution? ... 351

Chapter 9
William Kiffen, John Locke, and the Bahama Adventurers of 1672 ... 363

Chapter 10
The Kiffen Family Wills 411

Bibliography 425

General Index 457

Foreword

For the last forty years I have, almost every day, looked into the face of William Kiffin—at least as his features are preserved in the portrait of 1667 which hangs in the Senior Common Room of Regent's Park College.[1] This has given me the sense, or the illusion, that I know this seventeenth-century merchant and Baptist minister of the City of London. How little I know him in fact is made clear in the fascinating essays which make up this book, which I highly commend. The author, Larry Kreitzer, has already established that the portrait itself is deceptive: the upraised hand, with its expensive lace around the cuff, calling for attention from the viewers, or perhaps blessing them, is probably a Victorian addition from the time when it was fashionable to show a hand.[2] But it is not just the hand which is an addition to the man: Dr Kreitzer strips away other accretions to the legend of Kiffin, while discovering many other previously unknown details, to reveal him as a man of his age, situated in the social, political and religious preoccupations of his period.

During my eighteen years as Principal of Regent's Park College, I have stood with a host of visitors in front of Kiffin's face which looks out with a sombre piety, and told them two stories which I inherited from my predecessor as Principal, the distinguished historian of the seventeenth century, Dr Barrie White. The first is one upon which Dr Kreitzer throws reasonable doubt in his Introduction. This is the account by Thomas Crosby (1738)[3] according to which Charles II, shortly after his accession, asked Kiffin for a loan of what was, for the time, the astronomical amount of £40,000. Kiffin, so the story goes, declined to make the loan but made an outright gift of £10,000, afterwards saying 'that he had saved himself thereby thirty thousand pounds' as well as earning the king's favour.

The usefulness of this story to visitors—often Anglicans—who think of Baptists either as Anabaptists or as a nineteenth-century import to England from the Southern States of America, is evident. It underlines the antiquity of Baptists and the significant part they played in seventeenth-century English society. It further neatly underlines the difference between Baptists and Anabaptists since the wealthy Kiffin was not only known at the Restoration court but had earlier accepted political office as a Member of Parliament for Middlesex, military office as a Lieutenant Colonel for the London Militia (both during the Cromwellian Protectorate), and later—though reluctantly—civil office as an Alderman of the City. The anecdote, we might also add, shows that Baptists can have a worldly shrewdness as well as piety. I shall probably now have to follow Dr Kreitzer's correction of the numbers to a loan of

[1] In this Foreword I use the customary spelling of Kiffin's name; the reasons Dr Kreitzer has for preferring 'Kiffen' are explained in Chapter 1.

[2] Larry Kreitzer, *William Kiffin: The Portrait of 1667 at Regent's Park College, Oxford* (Oxford: Centre for Baptist History and Heritage, 2006), p. 12.

[3] Thomas Crosby, *The History of the English Baptists* (4 vols; London: Printed for the Author, 1738–40), III, p. 4.

£1,000, though I suspect that I could re-shape the story to make many of the same points.

The second story I inherited, and which I often told Baptist visitors of a conservative bent, escapes deconstruction by the skilful hand of Dr Kreitzer. It is said that as a young man Kiffin listened to hyper-Calvinist preachers and could find no assurance about his election. Then he sat under a more moderate Calvinist, and even under an Arminian Puritan (John Goodwin) and found peace, remarking later that he had discovered that 'God has not tied himself to any one way of converting a sinner'.[4] Michael Haykin remarks that this freed him from being tied to any one particular method of evangelistic preaching himself.[5] It certainly did not make him any less of a fierce disputant against opinions he believed to be false, whether outside the Dissenting fold, such as Daniel Featley on the subject of infant baptism, or inside the fold, such as those holding to views of open communion or the singing of hymns.

However, even in the midst of hot disputation there appears a pleasing flexibility and irenic strain which perhaps benefits from Kiffin's early experience of seeking personal peace. In arguing against the admission to communion of those not baptized as believing disciples, he states that 'we propose our own Judgement candidly and plainly, without the least Reflection, or Prejudice to our Christian brethren that dissent from us on that point ...'.[6] Even more strikingly, although defining baptism as the 'sacrament of the new birth' and for this reason excluding those 'unbaptized' (which in his view includes those 'sprinkled' as infants)[7] from church-membership and the communion table, he hastens to deny that this means 'a total Exclusion of other Christians from our Love, Charity and *Christian-Communion*, as far as we agree...';[8] indeed, he asserts, 'we esteem them Christian Brethren and Saints'.[9] For a long time the view of Kiffin's manner in debate was coloured by the report of Elizabeth Avery, that in his disputation she found 'nothing of God there', but Dr Kreitzer is convincing (in Chapter 8) that she may well have mistaken him for another preacher, or that her comments may have been edited.

This latter example demonstrates the remarkable achievement of the essays and documents in this volume—to set Kiffin firmly in his contemporary context, and through meticulous examination of primary sources to bring historical details to light for the first time, causing us to think again about Kiffin's life and thought. Time has

---

[4] William Kiffin and William Orme, *Remarkable passages in the life of William Kiffin* (written by himself and ed. with notes and additions by W. Orme; London: n.p., 1823), p. 11.

[5] Michael A.G. Haykin, 'Kiffin, William (1616–1701)', *Oxford Dictionary of National Biography*, Oxford University Press, Sept 2004; online edn, May 2008 [http://www.oxforddnb.com/view/article/15521, accessed 4 August 2010].

[6] William Kiffin, *A sober discourse of right to church-communion: wherein is proved ... that no unbaptized person may be regularly admitted to the Lords Supper* (London: Geo. Larkin, 1681), Preface.

[7] Kiffin, *A sober discourse,* p. 9.

[8] Kiffin, *A sober discourse*, p. 19, my italics.

[9] Kiffin, *A sober discourse*, p. 6.

been well spent in exploring such resources as the National Archives, the Parliamentary Archives, the Bodleian and British Libraries, and the Archives of the Leathersellers' Company, among others, so that Dr Kreitzer has thrown fresh light on many accepted opinions of Kiffin and opened up new avenues of investigation. No previous accounts of Kiffin, for instance, have noticed that in his career as a merchant Kiffin was involved with the philosopher John Locke in the establishment of a West Indies trading company ('The Company of Adventurers to the Bahama Islands') in 1672, part of whose business included the transporting to England of goods produced by slave plantations in the Caribbean (Chapter 9). Nor have biographies previously traced the continuing relation between Kiffin and Locke in other trading ventures. As Dr Kreitzer proposes, this story provokes further reflection on the relation of Dissent both to the institution of slavery and to a notable philosopher—whose *Essay on Human Understanding*, we may add, was standard reading in the Dissenting Academies throughout the eighteenth century.[10]

I suggest that we might identify at least three significant pieces of writing by Kiffin, or shaped by him, which take on a new depth of meaning when we read them in the context of his immersion into the circumstances of his time. Theology must always be grounded in the details of daily life in society, and Dr Kreitzer has now admirably enabled us to do this with Kiffin. First, in Kiffin's early years as the pastor of a Calvinistic Baptist church he played a significant part in the development of an ecclesiology marked by the idea of the rule of Christ in the congregation. This distinctive aspect of a Baptist understanding of the church, where members together both stand under, and share in, the rule of the risen Christ alone, is clearly seen in the *Confession of Faith* (1644, often called 'The London Confession'). This influential statement, in which seven Particular Baptist churches in London set out their beliefs and practices, is generally admitted to have been written under Kiffin's guiding hand, and there are indeed traces of its ideas in Kiffin's *Observations on Hosea* (written in prison, 1642) and his *Reasons and Grounds of those People Commonly called Anabaptists* (1645). With the help of Dr Kreitzer, we can now set this critical theological development in the context of Kiffin's indictments at the Surrey Assizes in 1642 (Chapter 1) and his associated imprisonment. What may appear as mundane legal details are the moments in everyday history where the rule of Christ and the earthly rule of those who want to make laws for Christ's church come into conflict.

Second, *The humble apology of some commonly called Anabaptists* (1660), issued by thirty Baptists, headed by Kiffin, can only be read properly in the context of the two 'Humble Petitions' to the House of Lords (1660–61) and the arrest of Kiffin on 24 February 1661 for attending an 'illegal conventicle'—i.e., a meeting for worship in a private house (see Chapters 3 and 4). The petitions show Baptists distancing themselves from civil unrest and struggling for legitimacy and acceptance in the early days of the restoration of Charles II, hoping that the provisions of religious toleration contained in Charles' 'Declaration of Breda' would be applied to

[10] See Alan Sell, *Philosophy, Dissent and Nonconformity 1689–1920* (Eugene, OR: Wipf & Stock, 2009), pp. 25-26, 39-44.

law-abiding Baptists. Dr Kreitzer's careful analysis of the wording of these petitions, never before examined in such critical detail, throws light on the more theological construction of *The humble apology*, arguing as it does that the Baptist doctrine of baptism does not imply resistance to the civil government, which has a rightful authority given by God as far as worldly matters are concerned.

Third, there is the work of Kiffin I have already referred to above, *A Sober Discourse of Right to Church-Communion* (1681), denying that admission to the Lord's table can be extended to those who have not been baptized as believers. In his work he makes the most thorough defence of the 'closed communion' position in this period, opposing John Bunyan's argument in *Differences in Judgment about Water-Baptism, No Bar to Communion* (1673). I suggest that Kiffin takes the wrong side of the argument for all the right reasons: that is, he correctly appeals to both scripture and the church fathers to insist against Bunyan that baptism is a requisite for membership in the church of Christ, but (like Bunyan) simply equates infant baptism with no baptism at all. It took Baptist minds of the eighteenth century such as Daniel Turner to maintain *both* the necessity of baptism *and* open communion, through an extension of the same right of conscience claimed by Dissenters to infant-baptizers. If Christian people, argued Turner, believed they had been truly baptized as an infant, and if they found that recalling this baptism laid upon them the same 'obligations to holiness' as Baptists found their own baptism did, then they were be regarded as baptized according to their own mind, 'and, while the answer of a good conscience attends it, God will and does own [them] in it according to their own belief'; thus they should be welcomed to the same table.[11] Here, notably, Turner and others appealed to the same text as Kiffin himself had quoted in urging readers to regard infant-baptizers with 'love and affection' and in 'Christian-Communion', namely 'who art thou that judgest another man's servant?' (Romans 14.4).[12] Now, however, the injunction of the Apostle Paul that 'it is before their own Lord that they stand or fall' (Romans 14.5) became a reason for common table-fellowship.

My point here is to not to argue, against Kiffin, for the appropriateness of open communion in itself, but to remark how much more poignant Kiffin's irenic disputation becomes when set in the context of the daily life that Dr Kreitzer reveals. This is no abstract argument, but is fleshed out in the reality of the names of the members whom he lists at Kiffin's church in Devonshire Square at the time (Chapter 5), each facing difficulty and even suffering because of her or his convictions. Details that Dr Kreitzer documents throughout these essays about imprisonments, fines for failure to attend the parish church, ejectment from legally purchased land, attacks on meeting-houses, restrictions on worship and general mockery and

[11] Daniel Turner, *A Modest Plea for Free Communion at the Lord's Table; Particularly between the Baptists and Poedobaptists* (London, 1772), p. 10, and *Charity the Bond of Perfection* (Oxford, 1780), p. 23.

[12] Kiffin, *A sober discourse*, Preface. So Turner, *A Modest Plea*, pp. 5, 11; Robert Robinson, *The General Doctrine of Toleration Applied to the Particular Case of Free Communion* (Cambridge, 1781), p. 39.

contempt for 'hoax preachers' by the establishment, fill out the meaning of both 'church-communion' and 'love and affection' for other Christians in a way that the logic of argument and counter-argument cannot.

It is fitting that the portrait of William Kiffin should hang in the Senior Common Room at Regent's Park College in Oxford. Kiffin played a vital role in the development of the Particular Baptists, especially in London, in a long period spanning the reign of four English kings, including the time before and during the Protectorate of Cromwell, the Restoration of the monarchy and finally the coming of greater toleration. He gave shape and direction to the movement of Particular Baptists, and it was this group of churches in London some fifty years after his death that gave birth to this college, in its successive forms of the 'London Baptist Education Society' (1752), the Stepney Academy (1810), and Regent's Park College in London (1856) and finally in Oxford (1927). I wish that I had had at least some of the evidence gathered together by Dr Kreitzer at my finger-tips when I told my stories of William Kiffin to our visitors to the college. I will know better for the future, and so will all who read this volume and its successors, for we are promised more to come.

Paul S. Fiddes
Professor of Systematic Theology
University of Oxford
Principal, Regent's Park College, 1989–2007

Introducing Re-Sourcing Baptist History: Seventeenth Century Series

Baptist roots are firmly anchored in seventeenth-century English Separatism and we can be justly proud of such a long and established heritage. Yet as a denomination we have not always been very good about exploring those origins, certainly not with all the rigour required by modern critical historiography. This is to our own detriment, for it not only hides the distinctive role we have had within the development of Christianity over the centuries, but also blinds us as to the possible contributions we can make in the future. In fact, the opportunities for research into seventeenth-century English Baptists have never been greater. Partly this has been brought about by the internet, which means that primary source materials are much more readily accessible than they were a generation ago. The fact that Early English Books Online (EEBO) allows a researcher to download digitalized images of over 126,000 original documents to his or her own computer is an immense advantage. We are no longer at the mercy of secondary, edited versions of these texts (sometimes badly produced and misleadingly presented) but can see the originals for ourselves (though at times the transcriptions can be inaccurate). Many of the key texts essential to a study of Baptists in the period are now available for detailed investigation (and the promise of the digitalization of even more texts by EEBO in the future is eagerly awaited). In addition, many of the key resource archives now have online search engines for their holdings, which means it is much easier to locate materials for study. Especially of note in this regard is the National Archives in Kew, whose catalogue now makes available images of wills and probate records which were probated through the Prerogative Court of Canterbury. Also valuable are the search engines for the British Library in London, which enables access to the descriptions of its vast collection of manuscripts and documents, and for the London Metropolitan Archives, which is a veritable treasure trove of materials relating to the city of London itself. Oxford University Press's online *Dictionary of National Bibliography* (*DNB*) is also an extremely valuable tool for research, although there are only a few dozen seventeenth-century Baptists who have full entries within it.

Having said all that, the crying need within our denomination and the wider Christian and academic communities is a rigorous and critical study of available manuscript materials which deal with our history. Minute books and church registers of many Baptist churches are extant, but they have often not received the attention they are due. Beyond that, a vast number of sources remain virtually untouched by Baptist historians, including civic records for the various cities and towns across the land, ecclesiastical records pertaining to the courts under which Baptists and other Dissenters were tried for their non-conformity, and local parish registers which recorded baptisms, marriages and deaths. If the truth be told, these are all woefully under-used as resources for the study of seventeenth-century Baptist life and thought (no doubt partly because some of the texts are in Latin). We sometimes make the mistake of concentrating all our scholarly energies into exploring the religious dimension of Baptist figures, as if all they did was hang around the church all day, talking only to fellow church members about religious matters. In fact, much is to be gained from approaching figures within Baptist history with a conscious eye to uncovering all the various dimensions of their lives, secular as well as sacred. Knowing, for example, what a pastor's social networks were can be just as revealing as knowing what sermons he published; identifying political activity, professional associations and trade connections can be invaluable for unlocking the inner workings of the life of a Baptist minister or congregation member. Of course, advantage should be taken of the various resource aids that have been published over the years. Secondary sources, such as the Calendar of State Papers: Domestic Series (CSPD), valuable though they are as entry-level research tools, are no substitute for the original documents themselves. In fact, important factual information within the State Papers can simply be missed due to the incomplete nature of some of the descriptions contained within the Calendars. Care too must be employed in using some of the standard resources produced by Baptist historians in the past: Thomas Crosby's *The History of the English Baptists* (1738–40) is not always accurate, nor is he very comprehensive in what he does say; W.T. Whitley's *The Baptists of London* (1928) is frustratingly unreferenced; and both W.T. Whitley's *A Baptist Bibliography, Volume 1* (1916) and Edward C. Starr's *A Baptist Bibliography* (1947–76) must be used with caution, for they need updating and correcting.

The intention of this new monograph series, promoted as a vehicle of the work of the Centre for Baptist History at Regent's Park College, The University of Oxford, is to try and redress the present imbalance. It aims to offer studies which explore the riches of seventeenth-century primary sources, and to do so in a way that is helpful to the efforts of other scholars researching in the field. The focus will be on hitherto unpublished primary sources, particularly autograph letters and manuscripts (as opposed to published documents) from the period; full-text editions of published documents which are rare or difficult to access will also be covered within the series. The aim is to provide critical editions of the text of these sources, accompanied by an informative commentary and a scholarly analysis which takes advantage of the latest developments of academic research. Where necessary a transcription and translation of any Latin text will be offered (which is quite helpful for court records and the probation of wills). Thus the citation of sources will be as complete and accurate as possible, with transparency of referencing a guiding principle. The series is designed to explore material from the first century of Baptist life and witness in the hope that we might better understand the work of God in our tradition and be better equipped to continue to witness to the grace of our Lord Jesus Christ, the love of God, and the fellowship of the Holy Spirit.

Anthony R. Cross and Larry J. Kreitzer
September 2010

Acknowledgments of Figures

Unless otherwise acknowledged all photographs are by Dr Larry J. Kreitzer.

Chapter 1 – Figures 1, 2, 5, 6 are used courtesy of the National Archives, Kew; Figure 4 is used with the permission of the Leathersellers' Company, London; Figures 3 and 7 are used with the permission of The Angus Library and Archives, Regent's Park College, Oxford.

Chapter 2 – Figure 1 is used with the permission of The Angus Library and Archives, Regent's Park College; Figure 2 is used with the permission of The National Archives, Kew.

Chapter 3 – Figures 1 and 2 are used with the permission of The Parliamentary Archives, London (document numbers HL/PO/JO/10/1/283 and HL/PO/JO/10/1/306); Figure 3 is © Sara Douglass Enterprises Pty Ltd 2006 and is used with her permission.

Chapter 6 – Figures 1 is used with the permission of The London Metropolitan Archives, London.

Chapter 7 – Figure 1 is used with the permission of the Bodleian Library, Oxford; Figure 2 is from Dr Larry J. Kreitzer's private collection.

Chapter 8 – Figure 1 is used with the permission of The Angus Library and Archives, Regent's Park College.

Chapter 10 – Figure 1 is used with the permission of The National Archives, Kew.

Introduction

William Kiffen (c.1616–1701), commonly regarded as the Father of the Particular Baptists in England, may not need an introduction, but he certainly warrants a rediscovery. Baptist historians tend to take him for granted, comfortably relying on old and long-established assessments of his influence as a Baptist leader in the earliest days of the denomination. Kiffen first featured within Daniel Neal's *The History of the Puritans* (1732–1738), where he is named twice: once in connection with the publication of *The Confession of Faith* (1644), and once in connection with the publication of *The Humble Apology of Some Commonly Called Anabaptists* (1661) following Venner's Revolt.[1] Thomas Crosby's *The History of the English Baptists* (1738–40), was more ambitious, although the events of Kiffen's life discussed by Crosby were selective and not without historiographical problems.[2] Since that time Kiffen has been well-serviced by succeeding generations of historians, notably Walter Wilson's *The History and Antiquities of Dissenting Churches and Meeting Houses, Volume 1* (1808): 403-433, William Orme's *Remarkable Passages in the Life of William Kiffin* (1823), and Joseph Ivimey's *The Life of Mr William Kiffin* (1833). In addition, Kiffen was discussed in an influential entry by Alexander Gordon within the *Dictionary of National Biography* (1892), which was updated by Michael Haykin in the on-line *Oxford Dictionary of National Biography* (2004).[3] Kiffen has also figured prominently in a number of recent scholarly studies, including those of B.R. White,[4] Murray Tolmie,[5] and Stephen Wright.[6] He has also been the subject of several popular biographies, including those by B.A. Ramsbottom, Michael Haykin, and Paul Wilson.[7] Collectively these works

---

[1] Daniel Neal, *The History of the Puritans* (5 vols; 1732–38): III:160-161, IV:312-313.

[2] Kiffen is mentioned eleven times within Crosby's work, *The History of the English Baptists, Volume 3* (4 vols; London, 1738–40): I:101, 148-149, 215-216, 358; II:184, 307; III:3-8, 41, 95, 236 and 311. For an assessment of Crosby, see B.R. White, 'Thomas Crosby, Baptist Historian', *Baptist Quarterly* 21 (1965–66): 154-168 and 219-234.

[3] Alexander Gordon, 'Kiffin or Kiffen, William', in *Dictionary of National Biography, Volume 31* (London: Smith, Elder, 1892): 98-100; Michael A.G. Haykin, 'Kiffin, William (1616–1701)', *Oxford Dictionary of National Biography* (Oxford University Press, September 2004; online edn May 2008).

[4] B.R. White, 'William Kiffin—Baptist pioneer and citizen of London', *Baptist History and Heritage* 2 (1967): 91-103, 126; also see his 'Kiffin, William (1616–1701)', in Richard L. Greaves and Robert Zaller (eds), *Biographical Dictionary of British Radicals in the Seventeenth Century, Volume II: G–O* (Brighton: The Harvester Press, 1983): 155-157.

[5] Murray Tolmie, *The Triumph of the Saints: The Separate Churches of London 1616–1649* (Cambridge: Cambridge University Press, 1977).

[6] Stephen Wright, *The Early English Baptists, 1603-1649* (Woodbridge: Boydell Press, 2006).

[7] B.A. Ramsbottom, *Stranger than Fiction: The Life of William Kiffin* (Harpenden: Gospel Standard Trust Publications, 1989); Michael Haykin, *Kiffin, Knollys, and Keach:*

give us a good starting point for biographical investigations of Kiffen, but there are significant shortcomings and gaps within them.

For example, most of the modern studies are uncritically reliant upon the three nineteenth-century biographies (Wilson, Orme and Ivimey), accepting all of the information contained within them as accurate and above suspicion. However, this is not always true. A case in point is the frequent assertion that Kiffen was an apprentice of the Leveller John Lilburne (1615–57).[8] Certainly Kiffen and Lilburne knew each other, and, inasmuch as the troublesome Lilburne regarded anyone as a friend, he considered Kiffen as such; in 1652–53 he described Kiffen as 'my loving Freind' and 'my true Friend',[9] although elsewhere the mercurial Lilburne described Kiffen as 'my profest and blood thirsty enemy'.[10] But Kiffen was never appprenticed to Lilburne; the similarity in their ages alone would have precluded this as a realistic possibility. Moreover, surviving records of the Leathersellers' Company establish Kiffen's apprenticeship to a John Smith, and record his being made free by the Company on 10 July 1638.[11]

Another questionable assertion is that Kiffen was appointed an assessor of taxes for Middlesex in 1647; this is an oft-repeated idea, but I have found no evidence for it within the primary sources. Almost certainly this is a transcriptional dating error for Kiffen's appointment as an assessor for Middlesex in June of 1657; the appointment is detailed within *An Act for an Assessment* (1657), which was designed to raise money for the maintenance of the Commonwealth army and navy.[12] This later dating makes much more sense, for by this time Kiffen was well-known within the Cromwellian government and was also a member of Parliament for Middlesex.[13] As far as I can make out, Mark Noble's *Memoirs of the Protectoral-House of Cromwell* (1787) first asserted that Kiffen was appointed a tax collector for

---

Rediscovering English Baptist Heritage (Darlington: A Carey Title, 1996); and Paul Wilson, 'William Kiffin (1616–1701)', in Michael A.G. Haykin (ed.), *The British Particular Baptists 1638–1910* (3 vols; Springfield, MO: Particular Baptist Press, 1998–2003): I:65-77.

[8] Walter Wilson, *The History and Antiquities of Dissenting Churches and Meeting Houses, Volume 1* (1808): 403. Wilson was probably reliant upon Mark Noble, *Memoirs of the Protectoral-House of Cromwell, Volume 2* (London, 1787): 454, for this point. William Orme, *Remarkable Passages in the Life of William Kiffin* (London, 1823): 93-94, perpetuates the error. Roger Hayden, *English Baptist History and Heritage* (Didcot: Baptist Union of Great Britain, 2005): 78, complicates the issue further by suggesting that Kiffen and Lilburne were both apprenticed to an unnamed London brewer.

[9] John Lilburne, *As You Were* (1652): 4, and *The Banished Mans Suit for Protection* (1653).

[10] John Lilburne, *The Legall Fundamentall Liberties* (1649): 63.

[11] LCL, Register of Freemen—1630–1694 (Mem 5/1), page 15. See my article 'William Kiffen: Leatherseller and Baptist Merchant', *Leathersellers' Review 2008–09* (2009): 12-13.

[12] *An Act for an Assessment* (1657): 24. Kiffen was one of ten assessors for Middlesex.

[13] *A Perfect List of the Names of the Several Persons Returned to Serve in This Parliament 1656* (1656): 5.

Middlesex in 1647, and the suggestion has been repeated by generations of scholars ever since, apparently without any attempt to check its veracity.[14]

An even more frequently cited anecdote about Kiffen concerns his reply to Charles II when asked to lend the King the astronomical sum of £40,000. Kiffen is alleged to have offered to give the king £10,000 as a gift, explaining that 'he had saved thereby thirty thousand pounds'. The story is commonly invoked, not only to illustrate Kiffen's vast wealth as a successful London merchant, but to demonstrate his insight into the questionable character of Charles II. However, there is no evidence of which I am aware that Kiffen ever gifted the king with £10,000, although he did lend Charles II the lesser sum of £1,000 in 1670. The earliest appearance of this (apocryphal?) story was recorded by Thomas Crosby in 1738, and even he seems to have had doubts about its veracity.[15]

More importantly, there are also glaring omissions within the early biographies of Kiffen. Key details about his immediate family are missing, such as the identity of his children and grandchildren. For example, it has long been known that Kiffen alludes to the death of one of his sons, who died in Venice under suspicious circumstances while *en route* to Aleppo; in fact Kiffen believed him to have been murdered by a Roman Catholic priest.[16] But no one has ventured to identify who this son was, or when he died. In fact, the son, whom Kiffen described as 'my second eldest son', was named Joseph, and a number of intriguing documents survive about him, including an indictment dated 6 June 1669 for failure to attend his parish church,[17] and the record of him being made a freeman by the Leathersellers' Company on 29 September 1671.[18]

One of the most intriguing omissions in published biographies of Kiffen's life is the absence of any discussion of Kiffen's disastrous second marriage to Sarah Reeves in April of 1683.[19] Studies of Kiffen have tended to concentrate on the religious dimensions of Kiffen's life, notably his guiding hand in the publication of *The Confession of Faith* (1644), and his role in helping to forge the Baptists into a thriving denomination, as evidenced by *A Narrative of the Proceedings of the General Assembly* (1689). This is perfectly understandable, but it means that whole areas of Kiffen's life are left unexplored within the published studies about him. Kiffen's military career, his professional life as a glover and a member of the Leathersellers' Company, his political activities as a city of London alderman and a

---

[14] Mark Noble, *Memoirs of the Protectoral-House of Cromwell, Volume 2* (1787): 462. Wilson, *History and Antiquities*: 409-410; Orme, *Remarkable*: 112; Gordon, 'Kiffin or Kiffen, William': 99; Haykin, 'Kiffin, William (1616-1701)', all perpetuate the error.

[15] Crosby, *History of the English Baptists*: III:4.

[16] Orme, *Remarkable Passages*: 49.

[17] LMA, Sessions Roll: Sessions of the Peace Roll #1320 (5 July 1669) (MJ/SR/1370/121).

[18] LCL, Register of Freemen—1630–1694 (Mem 5/1), page 79.

[19] This is briefly discussed in my *'Seditious Sectaryes': The Baptist Conventiclers of Oxford 1641–1691* (2 vols; Studies in Baptist History and Thought, 30; Paternoster: Milton Keynes, 2006): I:153-154.

Member of Parliament for Middlesex in 1656, his work as a merchant trader with a vast network of contacts stretching from the Bahamas to Guinea and India and beyond, are all under-examined features of Kiffen's life. The various property indentures that Kiffen was involved with are also neglected features of his life, although they not only provide important information about members of his family, but also his business contacts and social networks. His treatment within the popular press, particularly as a representative Anabaptist during the early days of the Restoration, is a matter also woefully overlooked. Also under-valued is the family connection between William Kiffen and Oliver Cromwell; Kiffen's grand-daughter married Oliver Cromwell's grand-son, something which would have made Cromwell's son Henry turn over in his grave, given what we know elsewhere about his antipathy towards Anabaptists.

This volume seeks to explore several aspects of Kiffen's life which have not hitherto been given the attention they deserve, offering ten specific studies which concentrate on key primary sources. Chapter 1 focuses on Kiffen's indictment before the Surrey assizes in 1642, a crucial event in his life which established his role as a conventicler in Southwark.[20] Chapter 2 provides details of Kiffen's congregation, commonly said to be located at Devonshire Square. The membership lists of Kiffen's church are here provided, detailing the names and details of members from c.1664, 1668, 1670 and 1690. Chapter 3 explores some documents relating to the life of the Baptist congregation at Devonshire Square during the 1680s. Chapter 4 examines the connection between Kiffen and the ill-fated attempt by Hanserd Knollys to establish a Baptist church and school at the so-called Old Artillery Ground in Spitalfields in 1658, a dream which brought the Baptists into conflict with royalist interests to the contrary. Chapter 5 concentrates on two hitherto unexplored petitions submitted by the Baptists to the House of Lords in 1660 and 1661, a critical period in the life of the denomination during the early days of the Restoration. Chapter 6 provides details of Kiffen's arrest on 24 February 1661 for attending a conventicle at the house of a silk-thrower named Robert Malbon, who was later disciplined by Kiffen's church for unseemly conduct. Chapter 7 examines the life and career of Samuel Gleede, a master gunner within the Commonwealth navy, for whom Kiffen wrote a letter of recommendation in June of 1656. Chapter 8 examines the celebrated recollection of Elizabeth Avery to have heard Kiffen participate in public debates in Oxford in 1646–47, questioning whether this account should be taken at face value. Chapter 9 looks at the role that Kiffen had in helping to establish a trading company in the Bahama Islands, a venture which took him into contact with the influential philosopher John Locke (1632–1704). Chapter 10 gives details of the wills of five members of the Kiffen family, including that of William Kiffen himself, signed on 23 March 1700. These are important records for establishing family connections and composing the Kiffen family tree.

[20] This chapter was originally presented at the Second Annual Conference of The Andrew Fuller Center for Baptist Studies, delivered in August 2008, at The Southern Baptist Theological Seminary, Louisville, Kentucky.

These ten studies are offered in the hope that they might stimulate further research into the life and ministry of William Kiffen. I remain convinced that there are a host of new discoveries to be made, particularly by researchers committed to engage enthusiastically in the 'thrill of the hunt' for new documents and hitherto undiscovered primary sources. In the end, these will enable us to better understand, and more fully appreciate, the multi-faceted Baptist merchant of London, who was so instrumental in the early days of the denomination.

CHAPTER 1

William Kiffen's Indictments at the Surrey Assizes in March 1642

William Kiffen completed his *Memoirs* in 1693, when he was well into his seventies.[1] Although the *Memoirs* form the basis of any biographical study of Kiffen's life, they were never intended to be an autobiography as such. Rather they were highly selective reminiscences of Kiffen's life and thought and were meant to serve as an apology to his family and friends for his central religious beliefs. Inevitably some of the incidents Kiffen relates in the *Memoirs* are presented with a minimum amount of detail and leave us craving more information. This is especially the case when it comes to events in the late 1630s and early 1640s, when Kiffen was becoming more involved with the politics of Dissent and his commitments to the Baptist cause were being formed. However, new sources do occasionally come to the fore which shed light upon this crucial period of Kiffen's life. The purpose of this chapter is to investigate two such documents which have lain undetected, at least as far as studies of Kiffen are concerned, for over 360 years.

Within The National Archives in Kew, Surrey, there are two documents from the records of the Lent assizes for the county of Surrey in 1642 which name William Kiffen (see Documents #1 and #2).[2] These are bills of indictment, written on strips of vellum in highly formulaic, and heavily abbreviated, Latin. These indictments offer us a brief, but tantalizing glimpse into the early years of Kiffen's ministry as a dissenting minister, a period which is largely shrouded in mystery and about which there are few other primary sources available. The first of the two indictments charges Kiffen with being absent from his local parish church for a period of eleven months beginning on 10 February 1641 (Figure #1). The second indictment was more serious, and charged Kiffen, and a number of others, with holding an illegal conventicle on 13 March 1642 and there plotting political dissent against the crown (Figure #2). This chapter presents the full text and translation of these two court

[1] Walter Wilson, *The History and Antiquities of Dissenting Churches and Meeting Houses, Volume 1* (London, 1808): 403-433; William Orme, *Remarkable Passages in the Life of William Kiffin* (London, 1823); and Joseph Ivimey, *The Life of Mr William Kiffin* (1833). All had access to the original manuscript and based their studies of Kiffen upon it. Unfortunately, Kiffen's manuscript itself has not survived, although there is an early hand-written copy of it in the Congregational Library in London.

[2] TNA, ASSI 35/84/6, membrane 81, and TNA, ASSI 35/84/10, membrane 62. The first indictment is 320 x 60 mm and the second is 315 x 190 mm.

indictments, together with a number of other attendant documents which help us appreciate their significance. It will also attempt to draw out some of the implications of the indictments for our understanding of Kiffen's own commitment to the fledgling Baptist cause in London during the turbulent days of the early 1640s.

The Case of William Kiffen at the Surrey Assizes

Kiffen was tried before Justice Thomas Malet (1582–1665), who opened the court sessions in Southwark on Saturday 12 March 1642, and probably adjudicated over Kiffen's case on Monday 14 March 1642. Malet was the crown-appointed judge for the Home Circuit of assizes, which included the five counties of Hertfordshire, Essex, Surrey, Sussex, and Kent. The Home Circuit was the least popular of the six English court circuits, mainly due to the heavy work load involved. Assizes were held twice a year throughout the country, once in Lent (in March) and once in the summer (in August), with each county session generally lasting two or three days. Malet was relatively new to the job, having first been appointed to serve on the Home Circuit for the summer assizes of 1641. For the Lent assizes for 1642 Malet chose Southwark as the venue for the Surrey proceedings, and followed the standard seventeen-day schedule for the circuit as a whole.[3] In accordance with standard procedure, Malet issued a 'Judges' Precept' to John Denham, the sheriff of the county of Surrey, on 12 February 1642, indicating that the assizes were to be held in Southwark commencing on Saturday 12 March 1642.[4] The two indictment records naming Kiffen were probably written by John Eldred, the clerk of the Home Circuit assizes at the time. Eldred was a very experienced clerk, having served as clerk from the summer assizes of 1625 until his death in 1649.[5] He would have based the indictments on information provided by the local parish authorities.

So how do the two indictments fit together? It is likely that Kiffen was initially indicted to appear before the assizes court to answer charges about his failure to attend his local parish church. However, after Kiffen was caught leading the illegal conventicle the day before he was to appear at court, a second, more serious, indictment was drawn up in preparation for his trial before Judge Malet. According to the second indictment the date of the illegal conventicle that Kiffen attended was Sunday 13 March 1642, the day before his case was scheduled to be heard at the

---

[3] Malet began the assizes circuit at Hertford (Hertfordshire) on 3 March, opened the sessions at Chelmford (Essex) on 7 March, at Southwark (Surrey) on 12 March, at East Grinstead (Sussex) on 17 March, and Maidstone (Kent) on 22 March. See T.P.S. Woods, *Prelude to Civil War 1642: Mr Justice Malet and the Kentish Petitions* (Salisbury: Michael Russell, 1980): 172, for details.

[4] TNA, ASSI 35/84/10, membrane 46. Denham went on to become a poet of some note, his most celebrated work being *Coopers Hill* (1642). Denham met William Laud when the Archbishop was imprisoned in the Tower in 1641 and published an exchange that the two had about the persecuting of conventiclers (see *An Exact Copy of a Letter* (1641): 3).

[5] J.S. Cockburn, *A History of English Assizes 1558–1714* (Cambridge: Cambridge University Press, 1972): 314, summarizes his career.

assizes. This accords well with Kiffen's own brief account of his arrest and sentence in his *Memoirs*, where he says,

> [B]eing at a meeting in Southwark, I was taken and carried before some Justices of the Peace. The assizes being next day I was bound to answer there. Judge Mallett sitting as judge I was committed to White Lyon prison. Here I remained a prisoner till the judge returned home from riding the circuit out of Kent.[6]

Taken together the two indictments raise a number of interesting questions about Kiffen's life in London during the early 1640s, and they shed light on several long-standing points of historical interest about the Baptist leader. We shall consider five matters in particular.

The Spelling of Kiffen's Surname

The spelling of Kiffen's surname in the indictments is somewhat unusual: in the first of the indictments it appears as 'Cyffin' (line 1), whereas in the second it appears as 'Ciffyn' (lines 1, 13, 18 and 22). At one level this should not overly concern us, for the spelling of personal names in the seventeenth century was not regularized and it is not unusual to find divergent spellings like this. However, Kiffen himself does not ever appear to have used either of these spellings, although they have been adduced to infer his Welsh origins. In fact, I am not aware of Kiffen ever signing his name using these alternative spellings (he signed his name as either 'Kiffen' or 'Kiffin').[7] Interestingly, the only other seventeenth-century source that I know of that uses a variant of the spelling found in the indictments is Daniel Featley's celebrated tract *The Dippers Dipt* (1645) (see Figure #3).[8] This tract chronicles the public debate which took place in Southwark on 17 October 1642, and pitched Featley against four Anabaptists, including Kiffen. Interestingly, Featley consistently describes Kiffen within this book as 'Cufin', which has sometimes been taken to be a deliberate slight against the Baptist leader.[9] It is possible Featley may have derived his unusual spelling of Kiffen's surname from the indictments of the Surrey assizes.

Featley was a Justice of the Peace for the county of Surrey and in that capacity frequently sent prisoners to the various jails in and around London. He was regularly consulted by the Court of the High Commission in cases involving religious Dissenters, notably those who had reservations about the taking of *ex officio* oaths. In this regard, there is a record of him being involved in the case of Edward Barber, a General Baptist committed to Newgate prison in June of 1640.[10] Featley was also

---

[6] Orme, *Remarkable Passages*: 16.

[7] I am aware of twenty-one documents which bear Kiffen's signature, seventeen of them with the spelling *Kiffen*, and four with the spelling *Kiffin*.

[8] Daniel Featley, *The Dippers Dipt* (1645) went through six editions in as many years.

[9] Featley uses *Cufin* 26 times in *Dippers Dipt*, pages 3 (2x), 4 (7x), 5 (3x), 8 (2x), 10, 13 (3x), 17 (4x), 18 (4x).

[10] TNA, SP 16/434, page 224.

the rector of St Mary's Church in Lambeth from 1618–43, a post which also gave him unusual access to ecclesiastical circles of power (the rector of St Mary's served as a chaplain to the Archbishop of Canterbury). All of which means that the spelling of Kiffen's surname in the indictment as 'Ciffyn' or 'Cyffin' is entirely consistent with what we can deduce from Featley's book, one of the major Anglican sources for popular knowledge about Anabaptists in the early 1640s.

At the same time, Featley clearly was aware of the more traditional spelling of Kiffen's name, for he mentions Kiffen's involvement in the production of *The Baptist Confession* (1644) within a marginal comment on page 4 of his book: 'This Cufin is said to be one of the first that subscribed the Anabaptists confession'.[11] In short, the Kiffen indictments provide supportive evidence which helps make sense of Daniel Featley's account of the disputations he had with Kiffen in 1642.

Kiffen's Profession

The indictments also provide an intriguing insight into the debate about Kiffen's profession and trade associations, a matter which has been the subject of considerable debate over the years. Yet even within the indictments there is some divergence, for two different terms are used to describe Kiffen's occupation within them. In the earlier indictment Kiffen is described in line 1 as a 'yeoman', a generalized term for a freeholder under the rank of gentleman which could be applied to a person of any profession. However, in the second indictment Kiffen is described in lines 1 and 2 as a 'Brewer', which suggests that he had undergone an apprenticeship with an established master from the Guild of Brewers. This presents some difficulties, as there are no other records of Kiffen's association with the Guild of Brewers.[12] Moreover, there are documents that demonstrate Kiffen's establishment within the Leathersellers' Company. In fact, there is record of Kiffen being made a freeman of the Leathersellers' Company on 10 July 1638, after having served a seven-year apprenticeship under John Smith.[13] In addition, Kiffen had already begun to establish himself as a master leatherseller, and took on his first apprentice later in that year (Figure #4).[14] This was a young man named Francis Kelsey, the son of Thomas Kelsey from Shere in Surrey, and his seven-year

[11] *The Baptist Confession* (1644) is specifically mentioned on pages 203-204 and 219-227, although Kiffen's name is not mentioned in connection with it in either place.

[12] GLL, The Brewers' Company Minutes 1628–1634 (GL MS 5445/15), contains no mention of Kiffen being apprenticed within the company.

[13] LCL, Register of Freemen—1630–1694 (Mem 5/1), page 15.

[14] According to the records of the Leathersellers' Company, this was the first of eight apprenticeship contracts that Kiffen agreed; his last apprenticeship was dated 5 December 1663. All eight contracts are contained within the Company's Register of Apprentices—1629–1677 (Mem 7/1).

apprenticeship was agreed on 19 October 1638.[15] In other words, given that Kiffen had been established as a leatherseller in London for almost four years, it is somewhat odd to have him described as a brewer within the indictment. It may be a simple mistake on the part of the clerk of the assizes, perhaps relying upon inaccurate information supplied him by local officials. It is not unusual for such inaccuracies like this to appear in court indictments of the period.[16] However, what makes the indictment's description of Kiffen as a 'brewer' all the more intriguing is the fact that he is elsewhere associated with the Leveller John Lilburne, who was known to have been involved in a brewing company in the late 1630s.[17]

In fact it is not unusual to find biographies of Kiffen straightforwardly asserting that he was as an apprentice of the brewer Lilburne.[18] An early example is Mark Noble's *Memoirs of the Protectoral-House of Cromwell* (1787), which documented the family connections between Kiffen and Oliver Cromwell and noted in passing that Kiffen

> was put apprentice to John Lilburn, of combustible memory, who was a brewer in the city during the anarchy and confusion that the civil war produced.[19]

Another case in point is Walter Wilson's *The History of Dissenting Churches* (1808), the earliest biographical study of Kiffen himself. Wilson asserts,

> In 1629, he was put apprentice to John Lilburne, of turbulent memory, who during the reign of Charles the First, followed the profession of a brewer in London.[20]

At one level this is complete nonsense, as Kiffen and Lilburne were only about a year apart in age, which makes the chronology all wrong (apprenticeships were generally agreed when the apprentice was fourteen or fifteen, and the master would have had to be a freeman over the age of twenty-one).

So how did the association with Lilburne arise? The most likely explanation is that Kiffen and Lilburne knew each other as young apprentices, and established a

---

[15] LCL, Register of Apprentices—1629–1677 (Mem 7/1). His older brother, Thomas Kelsey Jr, was an important Parliamentarian army officer during the civil war and was made and one of Cromwell's major-generals in 1655.

[16] J.S. Cockburn, *Calendar of Assize Records: Home Circuit Indictments—Elizabeth I and James I. Introduction* (London: HMSO, 1985): 79, notes that the declarations about a trade or profession, known as 'additions', were often 'factually unreliable'.

[17] John Lilburne, *Innocency and Truth Justified* (1646): 39. Pauline Gregg, *Free-Born John; The Biography of John Lilburne* (London: Phoenix Press, 1961): 87-88, 98, and 104, discusses Lilburne's business venture as a brewer.

[18] Although Lilburne was actually apprenticed to the clothier Thomas Hewson (see John Lilburne, *The Legall Fundamentall Liberties* (1649): 20).

[19] Mark Noble, *Memoirs of the Protectoral-House of Cromwell, Volume 2* (London, 1787): 454.

[20] Wilson, *History and Antiquities*: I:403.

friendship that extended into their adulthood. Indeed, Kiffen's *Memoirs* describes his time as an apprentice in some detail, offering a chronological framework for it:

> In the year 1629, I was put apprentice to a mean calling, in which I continued till the year 1631, without any sense of the great deliverance I had obtained from the hand of God. At this time, being then at the age of fifteen years, I began to consider the condition I was in as to my outward estate, and became quite melancholy. One morning very early, I went away from my master, although without any just cause given by him. Wandering up and down the streets, and passing by St. Antholin's church, I saw people going in, which made me return and go in also. Mr. Foxley was then preaching upon the fifth commandment, and shewing the duty of servants to masters; which made me greatly wonder, as thinking he had known me, and only preached to me. It had that effect of making me immediately return to my master, without my going away being observed by any.[21]

William Orme gives an explanatory note to this passage from Kiffen's *Memoirs*:

> His master was the noted John Lilburn, who made a considerable figure during the civil wars. He was a Porter Brewer, and Cooper, in London.[22]

It is primarily through the influence of Orme's published version of Kiffen's *Memoirs* that the idea of him being an apprentice to the brewer John Lilburne gained circulation. Even the entry on Kiffen in *The Dictionary of National Biography* (1892) accepted Orme's opinion on the matter, although it did acknowledge another tradition that Kiffen served another apprenticeship as a glover:

> Kiffen was apprenticed in 1629 to John Lilburne ... then a brewer; he left Lilburne in 1631, and seems to have been apprenticed to a glover.[23]

Joseph Ivimey, in his *The Life of Mr William Kiffin* (1833), slightly altered the description of the association between Kiffen and the brewer Lilburne, suggesting not that Kiffen was an apprentice of Lilburne, but that he was employed as a clerk by him.[24] Ivimey appears to have based this on an intriguing phrase in Featley's *The Dippers Dipt*. In 'The Preface to the Reader' Featley describes public notices about preachers being displayed, such as 'On such a day such a Brewer's Clerk Exerciseth'; Ivimey took this to be a veiled reference by Featley to Kiffen, as one of his opponents in the Southwark disputations. It is also possible that Ivimey had Thomas Edwards's *Gangraena* (1645) in mind here, although he does not make specific mention of it in this regard. At one point Edwards does describes Kiffen as 'sometimes Servant to a Brewer (whose name is *John Lilburne* ...)', and this is

---

[21] Orme, *Remarkable Passages*: 2-3.

[22] Orme *Remarkable Passages*: 93-94.

[23] Alexander Gordon, 'Kiffin or Kiffen, William', in *Dictionary of National Biography, Volume 31* (London: Smith, Elder, 1892): 98.

[24] Ivimey, *Life of Mr William Kiffin*: 20.

Ivimey's essential point.[25] This is precisely the description offered by Lilburne himself in 1649, where he states that Kiffen 'was once my servant', although he does here not mention his own status as a brewer.[26] In short, the idea that Kiffen served an apprenticeship to the brewer Lilburne is almost certainly a misreading of the available evidence. What appears much more likely is that Kiffen and Lilburne first came to know each other when they were both young apprentices. Later, after both men had established themselves in their chosen careers, Kiffen agreed to help his friend Lilburne, serving as a clerk in his brewing business.[27]

Finally, it is worth noting that some pamphlets from the 1640s and 1650s describe Kiffen not as a brewer but as a glover, a trade that had a close association with the Leathersellers' Company.[28] Glovers were a subsidiary trade of the Leathersellers' Company and did not break away to form the Glovers' Company until 1638,[29] only achieving civic recognition as an independent guild in 1648. During the period that Kiffen was serving his apprenticeship glovers were in short supply in London, and special arrangements were made to allow additional apprentices to be trained and recognized professionally within the Leathersellers' Company.[30] It appears that Kiffen was a beneficiary of this situation, which explains the description of him as a glover in some literature of the time.

A case in point is the anonymous tract entitled *Tub-preachers Overturn'd* (1647). The title page lists some twenty surnames together with their professions, including 'Kiffin a Glover'; the exact same description of Kiffen is also found on page 15 of the pamphlet. There is some suggestion that the pamphlet prompted the publication of another broadsheet which satirized the professions of the sectaries. It was entitled *These Trades-Men are Preachers in and about the City of London* (1647) and contained woodcuts of twelve of the professions, including one of a glover.[31] The pamphlet *Hinc Illae Lachrymae, or the Impietie of Impunitie* (1648), similarly describes Kiffen as a glover, and further stating that he was 'a sly and sottish

---

[25] Thomas Edwards , *Gangraena* (1646): 55.

[26] Lilburne, *Legall Fundamentall Liberties*: 19 and 63.

[27] Stephen Wright, *The Early English Baptists, 1603–1649* (Woodbridge: Boydell Press, 2006): 234-235, follows a similar line of argument, although he does not offer an explanation of how Kiffen could be described as both a glover and a member of the Leathersellers' Company.

[28] Both George Unwin, *The Gilds and Companies of London* (London: Frank Cass, 4th edn, 1963): 309, 330-334; Robert Ashton, *The City and the Court, 1603–1643* (Cambridge: Cambridge University Press, 1979): 50, 56, 72-74, discuss this.

[29] Charles I granted a charter to the Worshipful Company of Glovers on 10 September 1638 (C 66/2820, part 25, no 2).

[30] The Court of Aldermen of the city of London adjudicated on this matter on 7 July 1632 (LMA, COL/CA/01/01/50, pages 300-302).

[31] Also see the related pamphlet *Mercurius Anti-mechanicus, or The Simple Coblers Boy* (1648), which discusses each of the twelve tradesmen in turn (the glover is discussed on pages 33-36). Interestingly, the connection between London and Amsterdam is noted in the discussion (page 34), perhaps recalling Kiffen's ties to the Anabaptists in Holland.

Mechanical preaching Anabaptist'.[32] The satirical broadsheet *A Declaration of the Maids of the City of London* (1659) also describes Kiffen as a glover, while mocking his sexual inadequacies ('had like even nigh to make us run mad with his Hereticall Thimble'). Moreover, the satirical pamphlet *The Life and Approaching Death of William Kiffin* (1659) describes him as 'the bounden servant of a Glover'. The prevalence of the description of Kiffen as a glover within these pamphlets is striking, particularly when he was so well established as a member of the Leathersellers' Company.

So how are we to reconcile this description of Kiffen as a glover with the records establishing his place in the Leathersellers' Company? The most likely explanation is that Kiffen's initial apprenticeship, which lasted from 1629–31, was with an unknown master in an unnamed trade, and that this was then 'turned over' into an apprenticeship with the glover John Smith. After Kiffen had completed the requisite seven-year apprenticeship with Smith he was made a freeman of the Leathersellers' Company in accordance with the arrangements in place between glovers and leathersellers at the time.

Kiffen's Parish Residence in Southwark

The two indictments offer slightly different descriptions of Kiffen's parish residence. The first indictment states that Kiffen was 'lately of the parish of Saint Olave's in the Borough of Southwark' (line 1).[33] The second indictment also contains this statement, but adds that Kiffen was 'lately of the parish of Saint Mary Matfellon, alias Whitechappel, in the County of Middlesex' (line 1). The simplest way to explain this discrepancy is to assume that at some point Kiffen had moved from Southwark to Whitechappel and that news about this relocation reached the clerk of the assizes in time to be reflected in the second indictment. Unfortunately, there is no way to know from these records precisely *when* Kiffen moved from Southwark to Whitechappel. Indeed, there is one tax record from 1638 which lists a 'Mr Kuiffen' as living in the parish of Saint Olave's, Hart Street, near Tower Hill, and it is possible that this is a reference to William Kiffen.[34] There are some indications that he may have made this move as early as the summer of 1641; there is a record of Kiffen in a poll tax collection dated to July–August of 1641, which gives his address as 'Little More fields'.[35] Curiously, there is also a record dated 1 July 1641 which

---

[32] *Hinc Illae Lachrymae, or the Impietie of Impunitie* (1648): 3, 7. The pamphlet notes that Kiffen was examined before the Committee of Complaints on 2–4 February 1647.

[33] Southwark had four parishes at this time: Saint Olave's, Saint Thomas', Saint George's, and Saint Saviour's.

[34] LPL, Cod Lambeth 282, page 282. He paid a moderated rent of £6 per annum.

[35] TNA, Poll Tax of July–August 1641—Livery Companies Records (E 179/251/22), page 185 verso. The tax was for the disbanding of the armies and was authorized by Parliament on 18 June 1641. Interestingly, Kiffen's entry does not include a record of his payment of the tax (generally 1 shilling per person of his rank and position within the company).

describes him as being from 'Stillyard in Towerhill'.[36] In any event, we can assume from the indictments that Kiffen was legally considered a resident of Saint Olave's parish in Southwark, that his offences took place there, and that he was thus under the jurisdiction of the county of Surrey.

The first indictment states that although Kiffen was a resident of the parish of Saint Olave's in Southwark he did not attend his local parish church.[37] This means that he was breaking the laws governing such attendance and was liable to censure and fines. Moreover, according to the indictment Kiffen had been absenting himself from his church for virtually the whole of the calendar year of 1641 (line 3 of the indictment notes he had not attended for eleven months, commencing from 10 February 1641).

The second indictment offers more detail about Kiffen's activities in Southwark, notably his involvement in an illegal conventicle on 13 March 1642. It also provides the names of eight others (seven men and one woman) who were also at this conventicle, and gives details of their various parish residences and professions (lines 2–8). Seven of the eight are said to have had a connection with the parish of Saint Olave's in Southwark; the one exception is Robert Warner, who is said to be from the parish of Stepney in Middlesex (line 5). The indictment also notes that the conventicle was much larger than the nine named individuals, and specifically notes that there were approximately seventy others whose names were not known to the court officials (lines 14 and 19). The connection with St Olave's is also confirmed by the list of four witnesses whose names are recorded on the reverse of the indictment. These four are collectively described as 'Constables of Saint Olave's' (lines 25–28) and their testimony was no doubt adduced to confirm the jury's verdict of the indictment as a 'True Bill' (line 29).

Saint Olave's parish in Southwark was a thriving suburb of London, with a population of around 10,000 in the late 1630s and early 1640s.[38] It is easy to see why Kiffen, the future merchant, was originally based there. In the words of Jeremy Boulton,

[36] TNA, SP 28/131, part 3, folio 7 recto. It is possible that this referred to a conventicle house 'At Tower Hill at Mrs Wilsons', where Henry Jessey and others were arrested on 21 April 1640 for holding an illegal conventicle (See ALRPCO, Benjamin Stinton, Repository of Divers Historical Matters (1712): (Stinton D/1): 8; Edward Whiston, *The Life and Death of Mr Henry Jessey* (1671): 10). Perhaps Kiffen rented from Mrs Wilson, for he does at one point describe himself as 'Meeting one Lord's day at a house on Tower-hill', where he was attacked by a stone-throwing mob (see Orme, *Remarkable Passages*: 15).

[37] There is no record of William Kiffen within the earliest parish register of Saint Olave's. However, the register only covers the years 1639–65.

[38] Jeremy Boulton, *Neighbourhood and Society: A London Suburb in the Seventeenth Century* (Cambridge: Cambridge University Press, 1987): 14-21, gives details.

> Southwark ... possessed a distinctive occupational geography in the early seventeenth century. St. Olave's in eastern Southwark was an important centre of textile manufacture.[39]

More importantly for our consideration here is the fact that Southwark was well-established as an area of dissenting activity in the 1630s and 40s.[40] For example, Henry Jessey was known to have been involved with a conventicle which met on 12 April 1640 in Tower Hill, and several several people were arrested, including two who were from Southwark.[41] The religious policies of Archbishop William Laud made him the object of particular hatred at the time. In May of 1640 a large group of apprentices and seamen from Southwark was whipped into a frenzy and attacked Lambeth Palace, hoping to catch the Archbishop at his home. Laud had evacuated the Palace under orders from Charles I, but the episode shocked him deeply.[42]

There had been a meeting of Baptists in January of 1641 which was a *cause célèbre*, and resulted in a number of the leaders being brought before the House of Lords. Records indicate that six named Baptists, led by Edmund Chillenden, appeared before Sir John Lenthall, keeper of the King's Bench prison, and were asked to answer charges pertaining to an illegal meeting held in the house of Richard Sturges at which over sixty people were present.[43] A similar meeting of conventiclers took place on 12 December 1641 when a 'great assembly of Brownists' gathered at St George's Church in Southwark, and heard a cobler preach an hour-long sermon. The authorities eventually arrived to disperse the group, who then moved to Saint Olave's Church in Southwark where another sermon was preached on the steps of the church.[44] In this sense, Kiffen's activities as a conventicler in 1641–42 are in keeping with what we know was happening elsewhere in Southwark.

---

[39] Boulton *Neighbourhood and Society*: 97.

[40] Jessica A. Browner, 'Wrong Side of the River: London's disreputable South Bank in the sixteenth and seventeenth century', *Essays in History* 36 (1994): 34-72, discusses this.

[41] LMA, MJ/SR/0873/49-52, 54. They appeared before the court on 19 May 1640 and were discharged (LMA, MJ/SB/R/007, page 112).

[42] The incident is discussed in Valerie Pearl, *London and the Outbreak of the Puritan Revolution: City Government and National Politics 1625–1643* (Oxford: Oxford University Press, 1964): 107-108; H.R. Trevor-Roper, *Archbishop Laud 1573–1645* (London: Macmillan, 2nd edn, 1962): 388-389; Steven R. Smith, 'Almost Revolutionaries: The London Apprentices during the Civil Wars', *The Huntington Library Quarterly* 42 (1979): 314-315; Keith Lindley, *Popular Politics and Religion in Civil War England* (Scolar Press: London, 1997): 4-8.

[43] TNA, SP 16/476, page 119; PA, HL/PO/JO/10/1/47; *JHL* 4 (16 January 1641): 133-134; *JHL* 4 (18 January 1641): 134. David Cressy, *England On Edge: Crisis and Revolution 1640–1642* (Oxford: Oxford University Press, 2006): 223, discusses the episode.

[44] *His Majesties Special Command under the great Seale of England* (1641): 5. Apparently the name of the cobler was Humfrey Vincent, although what he preached became the subject of an exchange of pamphlets (see *The Cobler's End* (1641); *The Coblers Sermon Cryed Down* (1641) for more on this).

How long Kiffen himself was involved in leading a church in Southwark itself is difficult to know for certain, since we do not know when the geographical focus of Kiffen's ministry was shifted to Devonshire Square near Bishopsgate Street on the north side of the River Thames. We have already noted above how Kiffen was involved in the public disputations with Dr Daniel Featley which took place in Southwark in 1642. These public debates strongly suggest that Southwark was Kiffen's geographical base of operations in the early 1640s. Moreover, it is also worth noting that the earliest record we have of Kiffen conducting a baptism is dated to February of 1644, when Luke Howard, who went on to become a Quaker, was baptized. Howard's account of his baptism records that it took place in the Neckinger river which flowed through Southwark and emptied in the Thames.[45]

Kiffen's Fellow Conventiclers

The second indictment lists eight other people as fellow conventiclers with Kiffen: John Trendall, Thomas Shelton, Francis Cooke, Robert Warner, William Rylie, John Dart, Dorothy Dart, and William Clifford (lines 2–7, 13–14 and 20). The extent of the connection between Kiffen and these eight people is not clear from the indictment itself. None of the eight named is included in the earliest surviving lists of members of Kiffen's church in Devonshire Square, which date to c.1664 and 1668.[46] Nevertheless, we can safely assume that Kiffen and the eight other conventiclers knew each other and were in regular fellowship.

One of the intriguing features of the second indictment is the prominence given to the one woman named within it, Dorothy Dart, who is described as the wife of John Dart, another of the conventiclers (lines 7, 14 and 19). The indictment states that the illegal conventicle took place in the house of John Dart, which was within the parish of Saint Olave's (line 20).[47] Interestingly, Dorothy Dart is the only one of the eight additional people named within the second indictment who also has an earlier indictment comparable to Kiffen's first indictment (see Document #3). Like Kiffen's it chronicles her absence from her parish church, although in this instance her absence is of a much shorter duration (Figure #5). She is said to have been absent for the past three months, namely from 1 December 1641 (lines 3 and 4).

However, perhaps the most interesting of the eight conventiclers is John Trendall, who is described as being a mason from the parish of Saint Olave's (line 2). It is probably no accident that John Trendall is named immediately after William Kiffen (in lines 2, 13 and 18), as there is supportive evidence for him being one of the prominent figures in the church that the younger Kiffen was leading (Trendall

---

[45] Luke Howard, *Love and Truth in Plainnesse Manifested* (1704): 7-8, 32, gives details.

[46] This is despite the fact that a number of the members of the congregation are listed as living in Southwark (GLL, Devonshire Square Baptist Church—Membership Lists 1664–1704 (GL MS 20230, pages 1-38). The membership list composed in 1668 has a total of 362 names (118 men and 244 women).

[47] Lindley, *Popular Politics and Religion*: 80, briefly notes the conventicle at Dart's house but does not note Kiffen's association with it.

was probably in his early fifties at the time, while Kiffen was about twenty-six). In fact, Trendall was known within the Anglican ecclesiastical establishment as a notorious Dissenter, and had been prosecuted for his religious activities in the past. Surviving records suggest that in early November of 1638 Trendall and his family moved from Battle Bridge in Southwark to Dover so that Trendall could work as a mason. While in Dover he became involved with conventicles meeting in the area and was arrested. He appeared before Thomas Day, the mayor of Dover, on 27–29 July 1639, and a number of affidavits were submitted to the court.[48] His failure to attend the local parish churches was documented, as were a number of his beliefs about doctrinal matters. One eye-witness described Trendall's leading of worship services at his own home on Sundays, commenting how they lasted most of the day, and that the worship included the reading of Psalms and the exposition of Christian doctrines. She also recalled that Trendall had asserted that 'such ministers that have their power from the Bishop have it by false power'.[49] By all accounts Trendall was constant in his criticism of Anglican parish ministry and believed the ministers to be unlawfully called. Such defiance was bound to attract attention and official reaction came from the highest level. Trendall's case was taken up by Archbishop William Laud and the Privy Council who, eager to promote the ideal of uniformity of religion, decided to make a public example of him.

Trendall was discussed by the Privy Council (including Laud) on 31 July 1639, and it was agreed that the Solicitor General be sent the relevant documents and asked to comment on the case.[50] On 2 August 1639 Trendall was again discussed by the Privy Council who deliberated about how best to proceed against him and whether 'a special commission be issued to tender to the said Trendall the oath of supremacie'.[51] A letter was also sent to the mayor of Dover which gave instructions that Trendall was to be kept a close prisoner, and that he was not to be allowed to have contact with anyone, either in person or in writing, until allowed by the Council.[52] The Privy Council wrote to the mayor of Dover again on 18 August 1639, instructing him to administer the oath of supremacy to Trendall.[53] They also approached Richard Neile, the Archbishop of York, for advice about how best to proceed against Trendall. Neile had experience of dealing with cases such as this, and had actually been involved in the burning of the fanatic Edward Wightman in Coventry on 11 April 1612, the last person to be so executed in England.[54] In a letter

---

[48] TNA, SP 16/432, pages 50-64.

[49] TNA, SP 16/426, page 128. This deposition, by Joan Tiddeyman, the wife of a Dover mariner, is dated 27 July 1639 and was made in the presence of Thomas Day, the mayor of Dover. Another copy is found in TNA, SP 16/432, page 55.

[50] TNA, PC 2/50, page 552.

[51] TNA, PC 2/50, pages 567-568.

[52] TNA, PC 2/50, page 571.

[53] TNA, PC 2/50, page 601.

[54] William Renwick Riddell, 'Post-Reformation Burning at the Stake of Heretics', *Journal of the American Institute of Criminal Law and Criminology* 21 (1930): 254-256, gives details.

dated 23 August 1639, Neile described Trendall as a 'blasphemous Heretick' and suggested that he should be handled in the same way that Wightman had been.[55] Meanwhile, on 24 August 1639 Mayor Day in Dover administered the Oath of Supremacy to Trendall as instructed, and sent the appropriate documentation to the Privy Council.[56]

On 6 October the Privy Council, this time with Charles I in attendance, issued orders that some spiritual provision be made for Trendall while in prison in Dover castle. They issued instructions that a Mr Reddinge, a chaplain to the Earl of Suffolk, who was the warden of the Cinque Ports, be given unlimited access to Trendall.[57] Two weeks later, on 20 October 1639, Charles I and the Privy Council again discussed Trendall's case, and decided that it was time to bring him to London, 'to be p[ro]ceeded with accordinge to his Demerrits'. They wrote to Theophilus Howard, the 2nd Earl of Suffolk, requesting him to effect Trendall's removal to London.[58] On 30 October 1639 an order was issued that Trendall be moved to the Fleete prison in London, and this was effected some time in early November.[59] He was transferred by horseback in the custody of John Reston, the keeper of the prison in Dover, who was accompanied by one guard. Reston later submitted a bill of £12 for the fifteen-week incarceration of Trendall, who is described as 'a verie poore Man … in no wise able to satisfie' his outstanding account.[60]

The examinations and affidavits concerning Trendall's case were sent to the Court of the High Commission on 9 November 1639.[61] His case was brought before the Court on 14 November, but Trendall failed to make an appearance, so he was cited for contempt.[62] At the next meeting of the Court on 21 November it was reported that Trendall refused to swear an oath *ex officio*, and it was ordered that he should appear before the Court again the next week under the custody of the keeper of the White Lion prison (to where he had apparently been moved).[63] On 28 November the Court again deliberated over Trendall's case and his refusal to take the oath *ex officio*; they agreed that if he had not taken it by the first sitting of the next court sessions, they would consider him *pro confesso*, although they did give him liberty to consult with an Anglican divine about the matter.[64] Trendall's name drops from the Court records after this, prompting H.R. Trevor-Roper to suggest that

[55] TNA, SP 16/427, page 180. Neile also wrote an earlier letter on 9 August 1639 which gave graphic details of the execution of Wightman (TNA, SP 16/432, page 63).

[56] TNA, SP 16/427, pages 183-187.

[57] TNA, PC 2/50, page 666.

[58] TNA, PC 2/50, page 683.

[59] TNA, PC 2/50, page 689.

[60] TNA, SP 16/436, pages 49-50. The request was agreed on 27 January 1640 and Reston was awarded £15 for 'keeping and bringing up Jo[hn] Trender from Dover to London' (TNA, SP 16/442, page 265).

[61] TNA, SP 16/432, pages 50-64.

[62] TNA, SP 16/432, page 115; TNA, SP 16/434, page 39 verso.

[63] TNA, SP 16/434, pages 48 recto and 49 recto.

[64] TNA, SP 16/434, page 61 recto.

'the heresy-hunt petered out with two years of custody and an apparent recantation'.[65] However, Trendall does not seem to have knuckled under the pressure quite like this, if his involvement with Kiffen's conventicle of 13 March 1642 is anything to go by. Rather, it appears that once he was back among his fellow Nonconformists in Southwark he returned to his former habits, and probably rejoined the church led by Kiffen.

Kiffen's Incarceration in the White Lion Prison

What was the outcome of the Lent assizes? We know from the annotations made by the clerk of the court upon the second indictment that Kiffen pleaded not guilty and opted for a jury trial. The fact that the clerk's annotation is made directly over Kiffen's name in line 1 of the indictment, and that no comparable plea is noted in connection with the other eight people named in the indictment, suggests that Kiffen was the focus of the indictment overall, probably because he was deemed to be the leader of the conventicle.

Generally the results of the court proceedings are recorded by the clerk in an official report known as the 'gaol delivery calendar'. This was the final document prepared by the clerk before leaving the county, effectively serving as the outer wrapping of the court documents as a whole.[66] Unfortunately, in this case the 'gaol delivery calendar' of the court is in a poor state of preservation and the statement pertaining to William Kiffen is virtually unreadable at points due to faded ink and damage to the vellum (Figure #6). Nevertheless, it can be fairly fully reconstructed, and reads as follows:

> unlawfully
> Wil[ie]l[mu]s Ciffyn Hee stands indited for being ^ p[re]sent att an unlawfull conventicle or meetinge under color of exercisinge [religion &]
> [must rema]ine in gaole [safely until deposed to] appeare at the next gaole deliv[er]ye [to prosecute]
> [his traverse] with effect upon the stat[ute] book of Indite[me]nts.[67]

Kiffen's own *Memoirs* state that he was imprisoned in White Lion prison in Southwark, one of the main gaols for the county of Surrey. The White Lion was an old converted inn, and was located on Borough High Street near to St George's Church. It had a reputation as a violent place, and in the words of one early eighteenth-century writer 'was for the Custody of Murtherers, Felons, and other

---

[65] *Archbishop Laud 1573–1645* (London: Macmillan, 2nd edn, 1962): 373.

[66] J.S. Cockburn, *Calendar of Assize Records: Home Circuit Indictments—Elizabeth I and James I. Introduction* (London: HMSO, 1985): 43-44, gives details.

[67] TNA, ASSI 35/84/6, membrane 1.

notorious Malefactors'.[68] During Kiffen's life it had become more and more used as a place of incarceration for people convicted of religious Dissent. In fact, on 20 October 1635 the custodian of the prison, Robert Bellin, petitioned the Court of High Commission at Lambeth that he might attend the trial proceedings so that 'as occasion should serve he might have now and then prisoners committed thither'. He argued that he had 'lately done some good service to the Church & State in discovering of a number of separatists and schismatics whereof divers nowe are in prison, and hopeth to doe better service in that kinde hereafter'.[69] Not surprisingly, Bellin's request was granted.

Kiffen's own account of his time in the prison confirms these descriptions of the prison as a dangerous and foreboding place, particularly for Dissenters. Within his *Memoirs* it is recorded,

> While I was there, by the malice of a prisoner, whose chamber was under mine, the prisoners in the common gaol were incensed against me, to do me a mischief; and as they themselves told me, to take away my life. Several of them had been condemned, but had obtained a reprieve, and others were in prison for great robberies. Accordingly, on a Lord's-day, in the evening, several of them came up to my chamber, my door being open, and only myself, my wife, a maid servant and child in my room. One Jackson, a noted rogue, came before them, having a great truncheon in his hand. He asked me what company I had there? To whom I replied, that I had none but what he saw. Having upon my table some Spanish tobacco, which a friend had left me; I asked him if he would accept of it. He, looking wistfully on me, and several others of his company being behind him in the room, took it and thanked me. I also asked him, if he and the rest would drink, which they did. Then this Jackson turned to them, and bid them go out of the room, and he bid me farewell and went away.
>
> The man's chamber, who had set them on, being under mine, they, finding the door shut, endeavoured to break it open; which I hearing went down and asked them what they meant to do? Jackson told me, that he was the man that had engaged them to knock me on the head; but they should do his work for him, although they should be hanged the next day. But at last, through much entreaty, they were persuaded to desist. This was a signal providence of God to me, to preserve me from such bloody men.
>
> But my neighbour that set them on, not effecting his end, had prepared a charge against me to deliver to Judge Mallet upon his return, which accordingly he did. In this charge he set forth, that several persons coming to my chamber, I had preached treasonable words against the king: which charge was very false, as God knoweth. My wife and friends applied themselves to the Judge to take bail, which he refused. Upon this I went with my keeper to speak with my Lord Brooke, who told me he would speak to the Judge in my behalf. He was then going into the house of Lords. In a little time after, he came out while I was standing in the Court of Requests, and told me he had been speaking with the Judge, but could prevail nothing. The Judge telling him he had a very high charge against me, and waited but the leisure of the house to acquaint them with it. I told my Lord, I was not conscious to myself of any such thing in the least. My Lord told me he would do the utmost he could for me when he heard what it was.

[68] John Strype, *A Survey of the Cities of London and Westminster, Volume 2* (1720): 29.
[69] TNA, SP 16/ 261, page 271.

> In the meantime, while I staid expecting further trouble, unknown to me several men were at the bar of the House of Commons as witnesses against the said Judge, for encouraging a petition during the assizes at Maidstone in his last sitting. The Commons having heard this, they esteemed what he had done of dangerous consequence. While I stood in the Court of Requests, expecting to hear what the Judge had to charge against me, the house of Commons passed through to the house of Lords; and there charged the said Judge, who was that day committed to the tower, and I was released of my imprisonment—Malet exhibiting no charge against me. Thus it pleased God to deliver me out of the hands of malicious men; causing the rage of men to praise him, and the remnant thereof he restrained.[70]

This account injects several additional figures into the overall story of Kiffen's trial and imprisonment. Three in particular are worth highlighting briefly. First, it is possible that Kiffen's fellow prisoner, the 'noted rogue' Jackson, can be further identified from other documents within the Surrey court assizes. There are three indictments naming a Walter Jackson, a labourer from Saint Olave's, who was charged in September of 1641 with 'beating, wounding and badly treating' a shipping merchant named Armiger Warner to the point that he 'despaired of his life'.[71] As a result Jackson was sent to the White Lion and his name is included in the 'gaol delivery calendar' alongside Kiffen's.[72]

Second, Kiffen's *Memoirs* note that his case was brought before the House of Lords by Robert Greville, the Second Lord Brooke (1608–43). Greville was well-known as a supporter of Parliament in its power struggle with Charles I, and he was very active in supporting the cause of religious toleration for Dissenters, including Baptists.[73] Although Kiffen only mentions Greville by name this one time within his *Memoirs*, it is very unlikely that this was their first contact. They had a number of mutual contacts, notably John Lilburne, who served as captain of a troop of foot in the regiment Lord Brook was bringing together in the summer of 1642.[74] It is possible that Kiffen and Greville were first brought together by a shared interest in the establishment of godly colonies in the Americas. In fact, Kiffen mentions in his *Memoirs* that in c.1638 he had contemplated emigrating to New England:

---

[70] Orme, *Remarkable Passages*: 16-19.

[71] TNA, ASSI 35/84/10, membranes 69, 70 and 71. Armiger Warner was a controversial figure who was involved in the shenanigans that eventually resulted in Daniel Featley himself going to jail (see John Featley, *A Succinct History of the Life and Death of the Learned and Famous Divine Doctor Daniel Featley* (1660): 48-53, for details).

[72] TNA, ASSI 35/84/6, membrane 1.

[73] Robert Greville, *A Discourse Opening the Nature of That Episcopacie* (1641): 99-100, specifically discusses two types of 'Anabaptisme', one of which he deems heretical and the other acceptable. Greville was in favour of removing bishops from the House of Lords, an opinion which many Baptists would have advocated.

[74] Lilburne fought at the battle of Edgehill, before being captured in the battle of Brentford on 12 November 1642. He was incarcerated in the royalist prison in Oxford until May of 1643 when he was released as part of an exchange of prisoners.

I joined myself to an Independent congregation, with a resolution, as soon as it pleased God to open a new way, to go to New England; being new arrived at the age of 22 years. But the providence of God prevented me …[75]

It is known that Greville was one of a group of religious progressives who considered emigrating to the Massachusetts Bay colony during the late 1630s and early 1640s. It is also possible that Henry Jessey exercised some influence in bringing Kiffen to consider emigrating to New England. During the 1630s, Jessey was in frequent contact with John Winthrop Junior, whose father was the governor of the colony.[76] In the end the group was dissuaded from doing so because of a disagreement with the leadership of the colony over the way in which citizenship was tied to church membership.[77] In any event, it seems that in Kiffen's case the 'providence of God' manifested itself through a fundamental dispute over church–state relations, and his interest in emigrating was laid aside. The *Memoirs* contain just a hint of Kiffen's interest in participating in this bold experiment in the colonies, while, at the same time, suggesting an association with Greville that predates his serving as an advocate for Kiffen within the House of Lords.

No further contact between Kiffen and Greville is known, and the possibilities of it happening were precluded by Greville's death on 2 March 1643. He was killed by a marksman stationed in Lichfield cathedral tower, and his untimely death was a shock to many supporting the parliamentary cause. A pamphlet published anonymously on 9 March entitled *Englands Losse and Lamentation* chastised the nation over his death:

O *England* consider: What hast thou lost? But why doe I ask thee? thou knowest not thine own losse; Thou art in thy stupidity: or in a slumber of carnall security, a foolish

---

[75] Orme *Remarkable Passages*: 14.

[76] See Francis J. Bremer, *John Winthrop: America's Forgotten Founding Father* (Oxford: Oxford University Press, 2003): 174, 206-7, 235, 256-257; Robert C. Black III, *The Younger John Winthrop* (New York: Columbia University Press, 1966): 80-81. Surviving records show that Jessey wrote five letters (dated 9 January 1632; 23 January 1632; ? June 1632, 12 June 1633; and 17 December 1633) to John Winthrop Junior in Boston, one letter (dated February 1635) to him when Winthrop was visiting York in England, and one letter (dated 18 August 1637) to him in New Ipswich (see *Winthrop Papers III, 1631–1637* (Boston: The Massachusetts Historical Society, 1943): 57-61, 61-63, 77-79, 126-128, 142-143, 188-189, 484-488). He also wrote one letter (dated 5 May 1629) to John Winthrop Senior in London (see *Winthrop Papers II, 1623–1630* (Boston: The Massachusetts Historical Society, 1931): 87-89), and one (dated 6 March 1647) to him in Boston (see *Winthrop Papers V, 1645–1649* (Boston: The Massachusetts Historical Society, 1947): 204-205).

[77] Karen Ordahl Kupperman, 'Definitions of Liberty on the Eve of the Civil War: Lord Saye and Sele, Lord Brooke, and the American Puritan Colonies', *The Historical Journal* 32 (1989): 17-33, offers an excellent introduction to the topic. Also see Robert E.L. Strider, *Robert Greville Lord Brooke* (Cambridge: Harvard University Press, 1958): 17-27; Thomas Hutchinson, *The History of the Colony and Province of Massachusetts Bay* (Cambridge: Harvard University Press, 1926): 410-413.

> and undiscerning nation! Thou rejecteth thy friends, and imbracest thine enemies ... Thou hast lost a Noble refreshing *Brooke*, an invaluable friend, a pearle of greate price, a *Hector* better than ever *Troy* injoyed, an *Achilles*, more valuable than ever *Greece* possessed.

Thirdly, what about the ultimate fate of Justice Malet? Kiffen states within his *Memoirs* that he was kept waiting in the White Lion prison until Malet returned from the Kent assizes. However, Kiffen was not idle during his imprisonment, and quickly put his hand to the production of his first published work, a thirty-two page pamphlet entitled *Certaine Observations Upon Hosea* (1642). The title page of the pamphlet explains the circumstances of the work, noting that the observations

> were delivered at a friends House who had broken his legg, for which meeting the Author was committed to the *White-Lyon* by Sir *Thomas Mallett* late Judge of Assize for the County where he remaineth Prisoner of Jesus Christ.[78]

In the pamphlet Kiffen included a four-page introduction entitled 'To the Reader' which is dated 25 March 1642. Within it Kiffen specifically addressed Malet as one of the Justices of the Peace responsible for putting him in prison. He noted in passing that at his trial Malet and the other judges wondered 'why I should take upon me to preach having never bin at the University, nor received orders from the Bishops'. He also offered an apology for his activities in leading a conventicle whose only purpose was 'praying for the King and Parliament and edifying one another in our most holy faith'. We do not know if Malet ever knew of or read Kiffen's pamphlet, but if he did it must have been quite an irritation to him.

Malet presided over the Kent assizes in Maidstone from 22–25 March 1642, and returned to London on Saturday 26 March 1642. According to the *Journal of the House of Lords* entry for that Saturday, an investigation was ordered into why Malet had refused to grant bail to Kiffen at the Surrey assizes two weeks before. It is likely that Robert Greville, Lord Brooke, was behind this call for an investigation, as Kiffen's *Memoirs* suggests. However, any such investigation was soon superseded by other events involving Malet. Indeed, Malet's own fortunes took a dramatic turn when he was implicated in the issuing of a pro-royalist petition which was composed by members of the Kentish grand jury.[79] This Kentish petition reached London over the weekend and was discussed by both Houses of Parliament on 28 March 1642.[80] Politically-charged deliberations continued for weeks with royalist and parliamentary factions both seeking to take advantage of the situation; in the meantime Malet was imprisoned in the Tower for his complicity in the matter. He remained there until 2 May 1642, when he was released upon payment of a £1,000 bond.

---

[78] Presumably the 'friends House' where Kiffen delivered his sermons was that of John and Dorothy Dart (as discussed above).

[79] Woods, *Prelude to Civil War 1642*, offers an in-depth study of this.

[80] *A Perfect Diurnall of the Passages in Parliament* 12 (28 March–4 April 1642): 2.

All of which is to say that Kiffen's incarceration in the White Lion at the hands of Justice Malet was forgotten as an inconsequential side-show. Once Malet himself was imprisoned in the Tower, the case against Kiffen was quietly dropped; Kiffen was released as political battle-lines were being drawn and the country prepared for civil war. Malet himself retuned to duty as a judge on the Home Circuit assizes in August 1642, but soon fell foul of Parliament again. He was arrested at Maidstone in Kent by Parliamentary order and was again imprisoned in the Tower. He remained there until October of 1644.

We turn now to consider briefly the implications of the Surrey assize indictments for discussions of Kiffen's Baptist origins.

The Surrey Assizes Indictments and the Study of Kiffen's Baptist Origins

Precise details about how and when William Kiffen joined a Baptist church, or led his Independent congregation into becoming a Baptist church, are matters of considerable scholarly debate. The primary sources which deal with this question are not very clear, and much depends upon hypothetical reconstructions of a few key paragraphs in a handful of documents, notably Kiffen's own *Memoirs*, and the so-called 'Kiffin Memorandum' within Benjamin Stinton's *Repository* (1712).[81]

The Two Theories of how Kiffen joined the Baptists

In the main there are two basic lines of interpretation, each with reputable scholarly advocates behind them, albeit with some variations of detail. The first concentrates on the 'Kiffen Memorandum' and argues that Kiffen was a member of an Independent church led by Henry Jessey, but left that church to join with John Spilsbery's Baptist congregation.[82] A short time later, after a controversy with them over the necessity of the baptism of preachers, Kiffen left to form a congregation of his own which he pastored for the rest of his life.[83]

The second focuses on Kiffen's own *Memoirs* and assumes that he joined an Independent congregation, probably that led by Samuel Eaton, in about 1638, was

---

[81] ALRPCO, Benjamin Stinton, 'Repository of Divers Historical Matters Relating to English Antipedobaptists' (1712) (D Stinton 1), pages 10-12.

[82] I am here following the spelling of Spilsbery's name signed at the end of the letter written to Oliver Cromwell, 20 January 1654, see Document #4 below), as opposed to the more frequently adopted 'Spilsbury'.

[83] Advocates include Thomas Crosby, *The History of the English Baptists, Volume 3* (4 vols; London, 1738–40): III:3-4; Wilson, *History and Antiquities*: 410; W.T. Whitley, 'Rise of the Particular Baptists in London, 1633–1644', *Transactions of the Baptist Historical Society* 1 (1908–09): 226-227, and 'The Jessey Church, 1653-1678', *Transactions of the Congregational Historical Society* 4 (1909–10): 233-239; Ernest F. Kevan *London's Oldest Baptist Church* (London: The Kingsgate Press, 1933): 58-59; Murray Tolmie, *The Triumph of the Saints: The Separate Churches of London 1616–1649* (Cambridge: Cambridge University Press, 1977): 24-27.

eventually appointed their pastor and led them to becoming a Baptist church, and served that same congregation for the whole of his life.[84] This assumes that Kiffen's church and Spilsbery's church were two separate congregations and that they were so from the time that Kiffen joined his 'Independent congregation', although both probably had roots in the Jacob-Lathrop-Jessey church.[85] Admittedly, this contradicts the testimony of Thomas Crosby, who states in no uncertain terms that Kiffen was a member of Spilsbery's church.[86] However, there are good grounds for suggesting that this is a misreading of the 'Kiffen Memorandum' on the part of Crosby.[87] This is not to suggest that Kiffen and Spilsbery were on anything other than good terms with one another. Several documents survive which illustrate the later cooperation between Kiffen and Spilsbery over a number of years. In addition, there are some revealing connections between members of the congregations led by the two men, one of the most significant being a man named William Uncles, who was arrested on 12 September 1641 for attending a conventicle led by John Spilsbery in Stepney; Uncles went on to become a member of Kiffen's church and is of the few people named in all four of the surviving membership lists (from c.1664, 1667, 1670 and 1690).[88] Perhaps the most important illustration of Kiffen and Spilsbery working together was the warning letter sent to Ireland on the subject of submission to authority; it is probably dated to early 1654 and was written in the wake of

---

[84] Advocates include B.R. White, 'Baptist Beginnings and the Kiffin Manuscript', *Baptist History and Heritage* 2 (1967): 27-37, 'How Did Kiffin Join the Baptists?', *Baptist Quarterly* 23 (1970–71): 201-207, and 'Samuel Eaton (d. 1639): Particular Baptist Pioneer', *Baptist Quarterly* 24 (1971–72): 10-21; Michael R. Watts, *The Dissenters:* Volume 1. *From the Reformation to the French Revolution* (Oxford: Clarendon Press, 1978): 361-362; and Wright, *Early English Baptists*: 77-81 and 231-235. There is a inconsistency in B.R. White's overall reconstruction of these events, for in his article 'Jessey, Henry (1601-1663)', in Richard L. Greaves and Robert Zaller (eds.) *Biographical Dictionary of British Radicals in the Seventeenth Century, Volume II: G-O* (The Harvester Press: Brighton, 1983): 140, he suggests that Kiffin was a member of Jessey's church.

[85] Some scholars think the Eaton church and the Spilsbery church were one and the same. Champlin Burrage, *The Early English Dissenters in the Light of Recent Research (1550–1641)* (2 vols; Cambridge: Cambridge University Press, 1912): I:326, suggests that John Spilsbery took over as pastor of Samuel Eaton's church following Eaton's death in August of 1639.

[86] Crosby, *History of the English Baptists*: I:149 and III.3.

[87] As White has argued in 'Baptist Beginnings and the Kiffin Manuscript', and 'How Did Kiffin Join the Baptists?'. Also see Wright, *Early English Baptists*: 77-81 and 233-234.

[88] TNA, KB, Michaelmas 1641 (KB/9/823/113). Uncles is also named in LMA, Sessions Roll: Gaol Delivery #0887 (January 1641) (MJ/SR/0887/22), where he was arrested for attending a conventicle led by the soap-boiler Thomas Lambe in Whitechapel on 17 January 1641. Uncles was a glover and no doubt had contact with Kiffen through the Leathersellers' Company. For more on his membership in Kiffen's church, see chapter 2 below. For more on Lambe, see Murray Tolmie, 'Thomas Lambe, Soapboiler, and Thomas Lambe, Merchant, General Baptists', *Baptist Quarterly* 27 (1977–78): 4-13; Geoffrey Nuttall, 'Thomas Lambe, William Allen and Richard Baxter', *Baptist Quarterly* 27 (1977–78): 139-140.

Cromwell's assumption of power as the Lord Protector on 16 December 1653 (see Document #4).[89] The letter had a calming effect on tensions between Anabaptists and Henry Cromwell in Ireland in the spring of 1654, as can be evidenced by several letters written to John Thurloe from engaged parties in Dublin.[90] Nevertheless, a distinction between Kiffen's church and Spilsbery's church in the early 1640s seems indicated by the second indictment of 14 March 1642, particularly if we assume that the conventicle described within it had Kiffen as its leader.

The Indictments as Evidence of Kiffen's Independent Conventicle

Interestingly, Dorothy Dart is *not* included among the list of women indicted to appear before the Court of High Commission on 28 April 1640 for attending a conventicle. Given that this list is headed by Magdalena Spilsbery, it is reasonable to assume that the women were members of John Spilsbery's church, and, consequently, that Dorothy Dart (and Kiffen, by extension!) were not.[91] In other words, all indications are that Kiffen was *not* a member of Spilsbery's church, and the Surrey indictments are supportive of this as a reconstruction of his Baptist origins.

It is not certain if the conventicle noted in the second indictment had self-consciously identified themselves as a Baptist (or Anabaptist) church; certainly the indictment itself does not describe them as such, although some other conventicles named in indictments were designated as Anabaptist, including the group associated with Chillenden's arrest in 1641, described above. It may be that the conventiclers associated with Kiffen had not yet reached that stage of self-identification by the spring of 1642. Indeed, there is nothing within Kiffen's first pamphlet, *Certaine Observations Upon Hosea* (written 25 March 1642), which indicates that he had come to clear Baptist convictions by then.

Moreover, there is a slight hint of uncertainty in Kiffen's theological thinking in October 1642, as is indicated within Featley's *The Dippers Dipt*. According to Featley, Kiffen's opening remarks at the public debate in Southwark were, 'I came not here to dispute, but to receive satisfaction of some doubts, which if you can resolve me in, I shall submit.'[92] Indeed, all that can be said with certainty is that

---

[89] LSA, Letters Addressed to Oliver Cromwell (SAL MS 138), pages 191-192. This letter was signed by Kiffen, Spilsbery and John Sansom. C. Eden Quainton, 'Cromwell and the Anabaptists during 1653', *The Pacific Historical Review* (1932): 164-178, discusses the Baptist antipathy to the idea of Cromwell assuming the powers of Lord Protector.

[90] Including a letter from Henry Cromwell dated 8 March 1654 (BLO, MS Rawlinson A 12, pages 169-170), and a letter from Jen[kyn] Lloyd dated 13 March 1654 (BLO, MS Rawlinson A 12, pages 300-303). These letters are printed in Thomas Birch (ed.), *A Collection of the State Papers of John Thurloe, Volume 2* (1742): 149 and 162-164.

[91] TNA, SP 16/434A, page 9 verso. The women named are Magdalena Spilsbery, Anne Pawle, Grace Dicks, Catherine Tredwell, Mary Evans, Anne Dunkley, Anne Goring, and Anne Gell.

[92] Featley, *Dippers Dipt*: 3.

Kiffen came to a firm conviction about believers' baptism some time before March 1643, when he and Hanserd Knollys were instrumental in persuading Henry Jessey to alter his position about infant baptism.[93] Indeed, a good circumstantial case can be made for suggesting that the debate with Featley in Southwark in 1642 was the catalyst for Kiffen commiting himself to the Baptist cause. Having come to that conviction by the spring of 1643, the stage is then set for Kiffen to take the leading part in the production of *The Confession of Faith* in October of 1644, arguably the most important contribution that this young, twenty-eight year old pastor was to make (Figure #7).

So we conclude our exploration into one tiny little incident in the life of a very special man, William Kiffen, who more than any other person could be justly called the Father of the Particular Baptists in England. No doubt further research among primary sources will reveal many more details of his multi-faceted life. The discovery of the Surrey court assizes alerts us to the possibilities of conducting similar research into the earliest stages of Baptist origins. This will allow us to use the lessons of the denominational past in order to make our faith come alive for the present, which in turn will enable us to face the challenges of the future with integrity and confidence.

Figures

Special thanks to the National Archives in Kew for permission to reproduce the photographs of records from the Surrey assizes of 1642 (Figures #1, #2, #5 and #6), to the Leathersellers' Company, London for permission to reproduce the illustration of Kiffen's apprenticeship from 1638 (Figure #4), and to Regent's Park College, Oxford, for permission to reproduce the illustration of books contained in The Angus Library and Archives (Figures #3 and #7).

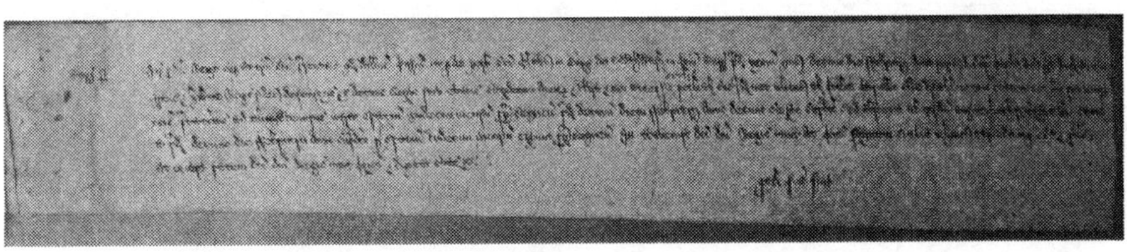

Figure #1 – First Indictment of William Kiffen – 12 March 1642

[93] W.T. Whitley, 'Debate on Infant Baptism, 1643', *Transactions of the Baptist Historical Society* 1 (1908–09): 237-245.

Figure #2 – Second Indictment of William Kiffen – 14 March 1642

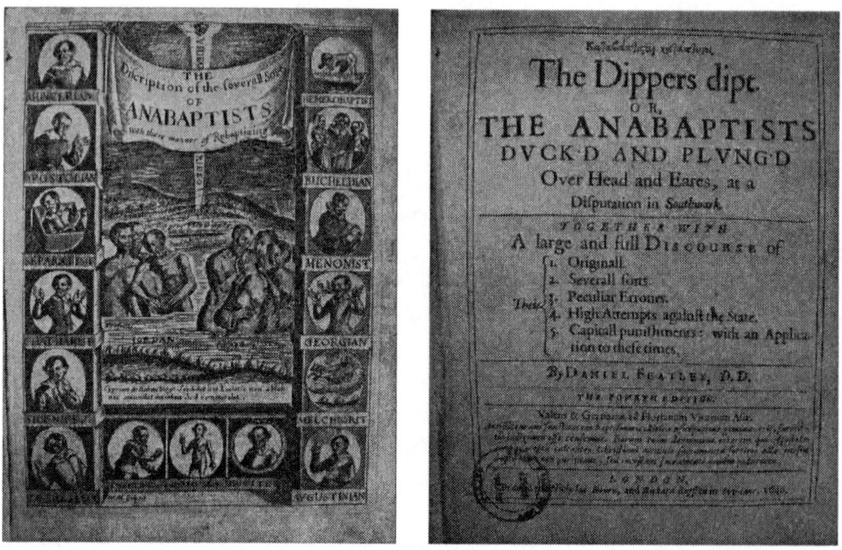

Figure #3 – Title Page of Daniel Featley's *The Dippers Dipt* (1646, second edition)

Figure #4 – Francis Kelsey's apprenticeship to William Kiffen – 19 November 1638

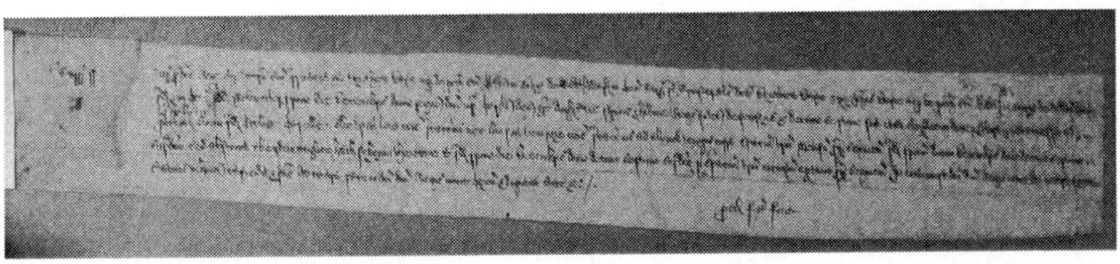

Figure #5 – Indictment of Dorothy Dart – 12 March 1642

Figure #6 – Gaol Delivery Calendar record of William Kiffen

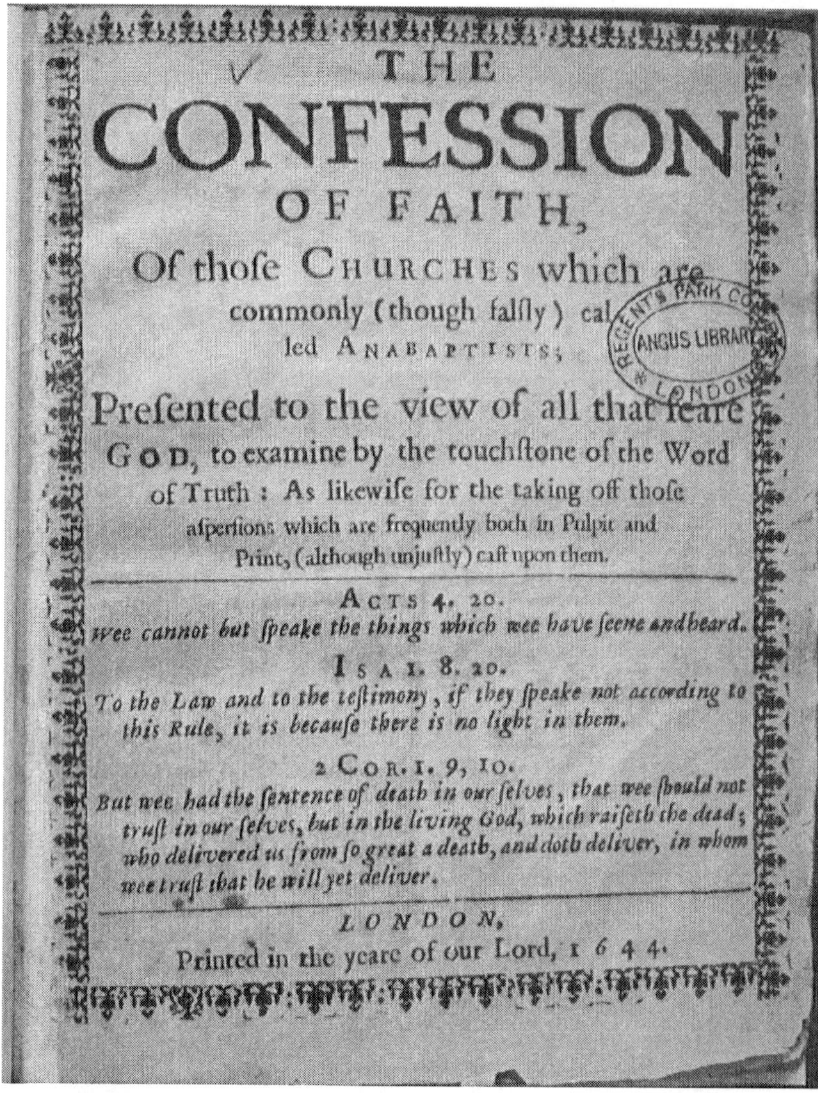

THE

CONFESSION

OF FAITH,

Of thoſe CHURCHES which are commonly (though falſly) called ANABAPTISTS;

Preſented to the view of all that feare GOD, to examine by the touchſtone of the Word of Truth: As likewiſe for the taking off thoſe aſpertions which are frequently both in Pulpit and Print, (although unjuſtly) caſt upon them.

ACTS 4. 20.

Wee cannot but ſpeake the things which wee have ſeene and heard.

ISAI. 8. 20.

To the Law and to the teſtimony, if they ſpeake not according to this Rule, it is becauſe there is no light in them.

2 COR. 1. 9, 10.

But wee had the ſentence of death in our ſelves, that wee ſhould not truſt in our ſelves, but in the living God, which raiſeth the dead; who delivered us from ſo great a death, and doth deliver, in whom wee truſt that he will yet deliver.

LONDON,

Printed in the yeare of our Lord, 1644.

Figure #7 – Title Page of *The Confession of Faith* (1644)

Documents

#1 – William Kiffen indicted for not attending his local parish church – 12 March 1642 (TNA, Surrey Assizes – Lent 1642 (ASSI 35/84/6 membrane 81):

[Text - recto]

[1] Surr[ey] S[essione]s Jur[atores] p[ro] d[omi]no Rege sup[er] Sacr[ament]u[m] suu[m] p[rae]sentant q[uo]d Wil[ie]l[m]us Cyffin nup[er] de p[ar]och[ia] Sa[ncti] Olavi in Burgo de Southwark in Com[i]t[atu] Surr[ey] p[re]d[ic]t[o], yeom[an], qui decimo die Februarii Anno Regni D[omi]ni n[ost]ri Caroli dei gra[tia] Angli[ae], Scot[iae],

[2] Franc[iae] & Hib[er]n[ia]e Regis, Fidei Defensoris, &c decimo sexto
Eccl[es]ie
fuit etatis sexdecim Annor[um] & ultra & non accessit ^ p[ar]ochial[i] suam p[re]d[ictam] nec aliqu[e] al[ie] Eccl[es]ie Capelle sive usuali loco co[mmun]is p[re]cat[i]onis nec ib[ide]m fuit temp[or]e

[3] Co[mmun]is p[re]cat[i]onis ad aliquod tempus infra spacium undecim mensiu[m] p[ro]x[ime] sequen[tium] p[re]d[ictum] decimu[m] diem Februarii Anno decimo sexto sup[ra]d[i]c[t]o sed abstinuit ab eisdem Anglice hath forborne the same
p[re]d[ictum]

[4] eo p[re]d[icto] die Februarii Anno sup[ra] p[re]d[ic]to p[er] ^ spaciu[m] undecim mensiu[m] extunc p[ro]x[ime] sequen[tium] In contempt[u] d[i]c[t]i d[omi]ni Regis nunc. Ac contra formam statut[i] hui[us]mo[di] casu edit[i] nup[er] edit[i] & p[ro]vis[i]

[5] Ac contra pacem d[ic]ti d[omi]ni Regis nunc Coron[am] & dignitat[em] suas &c.

[6] p[ro]cl[amatur] foed[a] fuit

[Text - verso]

[7] Billa Vera

[8] Exa[m]in[atio] p[res]t[it]it

[Translation - recto]

[1] Surr[ey] S[ession]s The Justices for the Lord King on their oath present that William Cyffin, lately of the parish of Saint Olave's in the Borough of Southwark in the said County of Surrey, yeoman, who on the tenth day of February [1641], in the 16th year of the Reign of our Lord Charles by the grace of God King of England, Scotland,

[2] France & Ireland, Defender of the Faith, &c, was sixteen years of age and more, & did not repair to his own said parish church or to any other church, chapel, or usual place of communal prayer, nor was he there at the time

[3] of communal prayer at any other time within the space of eleven months immediately following the said tenth day of February [1641] in the

16th year aforesaid, but abstained from the same (in English *hath forborne the same*)

[4] on the aforesaid day of February in the abovementioned year [1641] during the aforesaid space of eleven months immediately following from then, in Contempt of the said Lord King now [reigning] and against the Form of the statute published in such a matter which has lately been published and provided.

[5] And against the peace of the said Lord King now reigning, his Crown and his dignity &c.

[6] He was proclaimed [recusant] and fined

[Translation - verso]

[7] True bill

[8] The proceedings stand

#2 – William Kiffen indicted for attending an illegal conventicle – 14 March 1642 (TNA, Surrey Assizes – Lent 1642 (ASSI 35/84/10 membrane 62):

[Text - recto]

[1] Surr[ey] S[essione]s Jur[atores] p[ro] d[omi]no Rege sup[er]
po[nit] se [super patriam][94]
Sacr[ament]u[m] suu[m] p[rae]sentant q[uo]d Wil[ie]l[mu]s ^
suu[m] p[rae]sentant q[uo]d Wil[ie]l[mu]s ^ Ciffyn nup[er] de
p[ar]och[ia] S[anc]te Marie Matfellon al[ia]s Whitechappell in
Com[i]t[atu] Midd[lesex],
Brewer, al[ia]s d[ict]o no[mine] Wil[ie]l[mu]s Ciffyn nup[er]

[2] de p[ar]och[ia] Sa[ncti] Olavi in Burgo de Southwark in Com[i]t[atu]
nup[er]
Surr[ey] p[re]d[ic]t[o], Brewer, Joh[ann]es Trendall, ^ de
p[ar]och[ia] Sa[ncti] Olavi p[re]d[icta] in Burgo & Com[i]t[atu]
p[re]d[ic]t[o], Mason, Thomas Shelton nup[er] de p[ar]och[ia]
Sa[ncti]

[3] Egidii extra Cripplegate, London infra Ward[am] de Cripplegate,
London, gen[erosus] al[ia]s d[ict]o no[mine] Thomas Shelton
nup[er] p[ar]och[ia] Sa[ncti] Olavi p[re]d[icto] in Burgo &
Com[i]t[atu] Surr[ey] p[re]d[ic]t[o]

[4] gen[erosus], Franciscus Cooke nup[er] de p[ar]och[ia] Sa[ncti] Egidii
extra Cripplegate p[re]d[icta] infra Wardam p[re]d[ictam], Weaver,
al[ia]s d[ict]o no[mine] Franciscus Cooke nup[er] de p[ar]och[ia]
Sa[ncti] Olavi p[re]d[icto]

[5] Burgo & Com[i]t[atu] Surr[ey] p[re]d[ic]t[o], Weaver, Rob[er]tus
Warner nup[er] de Stepney in Com[i]t[atu] Midd[lesex], yeoman,
de p[ar]och[ia]

[94] An abbreviation for 'puts himself on the country', i.e., opts for a jury trial and pleads not guilty.

Wil[ie]l[mu]s Rylie nup[er] ^ Sa[ncti] Leonardi, Shoreditch in
Com[i]t[atu] Midd[lesex], yeoman, al[ia]s d[ict]o no[mine]
[6] Wil[ie]l[mu]s Rylie nup[er] de p[ar]och[ia] Sa[ncti] Olavi in Burgo &
Com[i]t[atu] Surr[ey] p[re]d[ic]t[o], yeoman, Joh[ann]es Dart
nup[er] de p[ar]och[ia] Sa[ncti] Olavi p[re]d[icta] in Burgo &
Com[i]t[atu] p[re]d[icto], yeoman, Wil[ie]l[m]us Cliford nup[er]
[7] de p[ar]och[ia] Sa[ncti] Olavi p[re]d[icto] in Burgo & Com[i]t[atu]
p[re]d[ic]t[o], yeom[an], & Dorothea, ux[or] Joh[ann]is Dart nup[er]
de p[ar]och[ia] Sa[ncti] Olavi p[re]d[icto] in Burgo & Com[i]t[atu]
p[re]d[ic]t[o], yeom[an], al[ia]s d[ict]o no[mine] Dorothea Dart
nup[er] de p[aro]chia Sa[ncti]
[8] Olavi p[re]d[icta] in Burgo & Com[i]t[atu] p[re]d[ic]t[o], Spinster, qui
decimo die Februarii [1642] Anno Regni D[omi]ni n[ost]ri Caroli
dei gra[tia] Angli[ae], Scot[iae], Franc[iae] & Hib[er]n[ia]e Regis,
Fidei Defensoris, &c
[9] decimo septimo fuer[unt] & quilibe[t] eor[um] fuit etat[is] sexdecim
Annor[um] & amplius p[re]d[i]c[t]o decimo die Februarii [1642]
Anno decimo septimo su[pr]a p[re]d[i]c[t]o apud d[ic]tam
p[ar]och[iam] Sa[ncti] Olavi
[10] p[re]d[icto] in Burgo & Com[i]t[atu] p[re]d[ic]t[o] obstinate
accedere
recusaver[unt] & quilibe[t] eor[um] obstinate recusavit ^ Anglice *to
repayre* ad Eccl[es]iam p[ar]ochial[em] Sa[ncti] Olavi p[re]d[icto] in
Burgo &
[11] Com[i]t[atu] p[re]d[icto] seu ad aliquam aliam Eccle[si]am Capellam
sive usual[em] locu[m] Co[mmun]is p[re]cat[i]onis ad audiend[um]
divinu[m] s[er]v[i]ciu[m] p[er] leges & Statut[a] d[omi]ne Elizabeth
nup[er] Regine Angl[ie] in hu[ius]mo[d]i
[12] casu edit[a] infra hoc Regnu[m] Angl[ie] stabilit[os] & abstinuer[unt] &
quilibe[t] eor[um] abstinuit Ang[li]ce did forbeare ad illud face[re]
p[er] spaciu[m] unius mensis p[ro]x[ime] post p[re]d[ic]tu[m]
decimu[m] diem Februarii [1642]
[13] Anno decimo septimo su[pr]a p[re]d[i]c[t]o absq[ue] l[eg]ittima causa
Q[uo]dq[ue] p[re]d[i]c[ti] Wil[ie]l[mu]s Ciffyn, Joh[ann]es Trendall,
Thomas Shelton, Franciscus Cooke, Rob[er]tus Warner,
Wil[ie]l[mu]s Rylie,
[14] Joh[ann]es Dart, Dorothea uxor eius, Wil[ie]l[mu]s Cliford &
div[er]s[ae] al[iae] p[er]son[ae] ad num[er]u[m] septuaginta
p[er]sonar[um] Jur[atoribus] p[re]d[ictis] ignot[arum] decimo tertio
die Marcii [1642] Anno decimo [septimo]
[15] su[pr]a p[re]d[i]c[t]o existen[te] die d[o]m[ini]co circa horam decimam
ante m[er]idiem eiusdem diei vi & armis &c apud d[ic]tam
p[ar]och[iae] Sa[ncti] Olavi p[re]d[icto] in Burgo & Com[i]t[atu]
Surr[ey],
[16] sese illicite assemblaver[unt] convener[unt] & conventicl[um]
illicit[um] adtunc & ib[ide]m fecer[unt] ad invenc[i]onem &
p[ro]po[s]it[um] ad denegand[um] obstand[um] & impugnand[um]

potestate[m] &

[17] authoritate[m] d[i]c[ti] d[omi]ni Regis nunc in causis Eccl[es]iasticis unit[as] & Annex[as] ad imp[er]ial[em] Coron[am] huius regni ac ad opponend[um] Regimen & gub[er]nac[i]onem

[18] d[omi]ni Regis in causis Eccl[es]iasticis infra hoc regnu[m] Angl[iae] &c ulte[r]ius q[uo]d p[re]d[icti] Wil[ie]l[mu]s Ciffyn, Joh[ann]es Trendall, Thomas Shelton, Franciscus Cooke, Rob[er]tus Warner,

[19] Wil[ie]l[mu]s Rylie, Joh[ann]es Dart, Dorothea uxor eius, Wil[ie]l[mu]s Clifford unacum p[re]d[ictis] al[iis] septuagint[a] p[er]sonis Jur[atoribus] p[re]d[ictis] ignot[is] p[re]d[icto] decimo t[er]tio die Marcii [1642] Anno decimo septimo

[20] su[pr]a p[re]d[i]c[t]o apud d[ic]tam p[ar]och[iam] Sa[ncti] Olavi p[re]d[icti] in Burgo & Com[i]t[atu] Surr[ey] p[re]d[icto] videli[cet] in domo mancional[e] p[re]d[ict]i Joh[ann]is Dart ib[ide]m de seip[s]is Ang[li]ce *of themselves* voluntarii fuer[unt] presentes &

[21] quilib[e]t eor[um] fuit p[re]sens ad easdem illicit[e] assemblat[i]ones conventic[u]l[o] & convenc[i]on[es] sub colore & p[re]textu Ang[li]ce *p[re]tence* exercicii religionis contra leges &

[22] statut[a] huius regni Angl[ie] & q[uo]d p[re]d[icti] Wil[ie]l[mu]s Ciffyn, Joh[ann]es Trendall, Thomas Shelton, Franciscus Cooke, Rob[er]tus Warner, Wil[ie]l[mu]s Rylie, Joh[ann]es Dart, Dorothea Dart, Wil[ie]l[mu]s Clifford,[95] adtunc & ib[ide]m ad invenc[i]onem & p[ro]po[s]it[um] sup[ra]dicte illicite p[er]eger[unt] exercicii religionis contra leges &

[23] statut[a] huius regni Angl[ie] in manifestu[m] contemptu[m] d[i]c[ti] d[omi]ni Regis nunc pacisq[ue] sue p[er]turbat[i]onem in malu[m] exemplu[m] ~~omna~~ omni[um] al[iorum] in c[onsimili]

[24] casu delinquen[tium] contra pacem d[ic]ti d[omi]ni Regis nunc Coron[am] & dignitat[em] suas. Ac contra formam statut[i] hu[ius]mod[i] casu edit[i] & p[ro]visi &c.

[Text - verso]

[25] John Mesiams
[26] John Stanrodd Constable of S[ain]t Olaviis
[27] John Lide
[28] Robert Wilmott

[29] Billa vera

[Translation - recto]

[1] Surrey Sessions The Justices for the Lord King on their oath present
puts himself on the country
that William ‸ Ciffyn, lately of the parish of Saint Mary Matfellon, alias Whitechappel, in the County of Middlesex, Brewer, alias by the

[95] The eight names following William Ciffyn are a superscription to the line and are indicated by a caret.

said name William Ciffyn, lately

[2] of the parish of Saint Olive's in the Borough of Southwark in the aforesaid County of Surrey, Brewer, John Trendall, lately from the parish of Saint Olave's aforementioned, the aforementioned Borough and County, Mason, Thomas Shelton, lately from the parish of Saint

[3] Giles-without-Cripplegate, London, the Ward of Cripplegate, London, gentleman, alias by the said name Thomas Shelton, lately from the parish of Saint Olave's aforementioned in the aforementioned Borough and County of Surrey,

[4] gentleman, Francis Cooke, lately of the parish of Saint Giles without Cripplegate, aforesaid, within the aforesaid Ward, Weaver, alias by the said name Francis Cooke, lately from the parish of Saint Olave's aforesaid

[5] in the aforesaid Borough and County of Surrey, Weaver, Robert Warner, lately of Stepney in the County of Middlesex, yeoman, William Riley, lately of the parish of Saint Leonard's, Shoreditch, in the County of Middlesex, yeoman, alias by the said name

[6] William Riley, lately of the parish of Saint Olave's in the aforementioned Borough and County of Surrey, yeoman, John Dart, lately of the parish of Saint Olave's aforementioned, in the aforementioned Borough and County, yeoman, William Clifford, lately

[7] of the parish of Saint Olave's aforementioned, in the aforementioned Borough and County, yeoman, and Dorothy, wife of John Dart, lately of the aforementioned parish of Saint Olave's in the aforementioned Borough and County, yeoman, alias by the said name Dorothy Dart, lately of the aforementioned parish of Saint

[8] Olave's in the aforementioned Borough and County, Spinster, who, on the 10th day of February [1642] in the 17th year of the reign of our Lord Charles, by the grace of God, King of Enlgand, Scotland, France and Ireland, Defender of the Faith &c,

[9] were all, and each of them was, of the age of 16 years and more, on the aforesaid 10th day of February [1642] in the abovementioned 17th year, in the said parish of the aforementioned Saint Olave's

[10] in the Borough and County aforementioned, obstinately refused, and each of them obstinately refused, to go (in English *to repayre*) either to the parish church of the aforementioned Saint Olave's in the aforementioned Borough and

[11] County, or to any other church, chapel, or habitual place of communal prayer in order to hear divine service in accordance with the laws and statutes of the lady Elizabeth, lately Queen of England, that were published in this type of

[12] case and established within this kingdom of England, and they abstained, and each of them abstained (in English *did forbeare*) from doing that for the period of one month immediately following the aforesaid 10th day of February

[13] in the above mentioned 17th year without legitimate cause; and that the aforementioned William Ciffyn, John Trendall, Thomas Shelton, Francis Cooke, Robert Warner, William Riley,

[14] John Dart, Dorothy his wife, William Cliford, and various other persons to the number of 70 persons unknown to the aforementioned Judges, on the 13th day of March [1642] in the abovementioned 17th year,

[15] it being a Sunday, at about the tenth hour before noon of the same day, with force and arms, in the said parish of Saint Olave's aforesaid in the Borough and County of Surrey,

[16] illegally assembled and gathered themselves and there and then formed an illegal conventicle, planning and plotting, for the purpose of denying, opposing and attacking the power and

[17] authority of the said Lord King now reigning in Ecclesiastical matters, which are united and bound up with the imperial crown of this kingdom, and for the purpose of opposing the rule and governance

[18] of the Lord King in Ecclesiastical matters within this kingdom of England, &c. Further, that the aforesaid William Ciffyn, John Trendall, Thomas Shelton, Francis Cooke, Robert Warner,

[19] William Riley, John Dart, Dorothy his wife, William Clifford, together with the aforesaid 70 other persons unknown to the aforesaid Judges, on the aforesaid 13th day of March [1642] in the 17th year

[20] mentioned above in the said parish of Saint Olave's aforesaid in the aforesaid Borough and County of Surrey, in the dwelling house, of the aforesaid John Dart, there, of themselves (in English *of themselves*) voluntarily were present and

[21] each of them was present at the same illegal assemblies, conventicles, and gatherings under the guise and pretext (in English *pretence*) of the exercise of religion, against the laws and

[22] statutes of this kingdom of England, and that the aforesaid William Ciffyn, John Trendall, Thomas Shelton, Francis Cooke, Robert Warner, William Riley, John Dart, Dorothy Dart, William Clifford, then and there for the purpose of the abovementioned planning and plotting, illegally carried out the exercise of religion against the laws and

[23] statutes of this kingdom of England in manifest contempt of the said Lord King now reigning and disturbance of his peace, to the evil example of all others offending in similar

[24] manner, against the peace of the said Lord King now reigning, his Crown and his dignity, and against the Form of the statute published and provided in such a matter &c.

[Translation - verso]

[25] John Mesiams
[26] John Stanrodd   Constables of Saint Olave's
[27] John Lide
[28] Robert Wilmott

[29] A True Bill

#3 – Dorothy Dart indicted for not attending her local parish church – 12 March 1642 (TNA, Surrey Assizes – Lent 1642 (ASSI 35/84/6 membrane 82):

[Text - recto]

[1] Surr[ey] S[essione]s Jur[atores] p[ro] d[omi]no Rege sup[er] Sacr[ament]u[m] suu[m] p[rae]sentant q[uo]d Dorothea Darte nup[er] de p[ar]och[ia] Sa[ncti] Olavi in Burgo de Southwark in Com[i]t[atu] Surr[ey] p[re]d[ic]t[o], Spinster, al[ia]s d[i]c[t]a Dorothea Darte uxor Joh[ann]is Darte nup[er] de p[ar]och[ia] Sa[ncti] Olavi p[re]d[ictaa] in Burgo de Southwark

[2] p[re]d[icto] & in Com[i]t[atu] p[re]d[icto], feltmaker, primo die Decembris [1641] Anno Regni D[omi]ni n[ost]ri Caroli dei gra[tia] Angli[ae], Scot[iae], Franc[iae] & Hib[er]n[ia]e Regis, Fidei Defensoris, &c decimo sept[im]o fuit etat[is] sexdecim Annor[um] & ultra & non accessit ad
Eccl[es]iam

[3] ^ p[ar]ochial[em] suam p[re]d[ictam] [seu alique alie] Eccl[es]ie Capelle sive usual[i] loco co[mmun]is p[re]cat[i]onis nec ib[ide]m fuit tempore co[mmun]is p[re]cat[i]onis ad aliquod tempus infra spaciu[m] triu[m] mensiu[m] p[ro]x[ime] sequen[tium] p[re]d[ictum] primu[m] diem Decembris [1641] Anno decimo septimo

[4] sup[ra]d[i]c[t]o sed abstinuit ab eisdem Anglice hath forborne the same eo p[re]d[icto] primo die Decembris Anno decimo septimo sup[ra]d[i]c[t]o
p[re]d[ictum]
p[er] ^ spacium triu[m] mensiu[m] extunc p[ro]x[ime] sequen[tium] In contempt[um] d[i]c[t]i d[omi]ni Regis nunc contra formam

[5] Statuti hu[ius]mo[di] casu edit[i] nup[er] edit[i] & p[ro]vis[i] Ac contra pacem d[i]c[t]i d[omi]ni Regis nunc Coron[am] & dignitate[m] suas &c.

[6] p[ro]cl[amatur] foed[a] fuit

[Text - verso]

[7] Billa Vera

[8] Exa[m]in[atio] p[ersti]tit

[Translation - recto]

[1] Surr[ey] S[ession]s The Justices for the Lord King on their oath present that Dorothy Darte, lately of the parish of Saint Olave's in the Borough of Southwark in the said County of Surrey, Spinster, alias the said Dorothy Dart, wife of John Darte, lately of the said parish of Saint Olave's in the said Borough of Southwark

[2] in the said County, feltmaker, on the first day of December [1641], in

the 17th year of the Reign of our Lord Charles by the grace of God King of England, Scotland, France & Ireland, Defender of the Faith, &c, was sixteen years of age and more, & did not repair
[3] to her own said parish church or to any other church, chapel, or usual place of communal prayer, nor was she there at the time of communal prayer at any other time within the space of three months immediately following the said first day of December [1641] in the 17th year
[4] aforesaid, but abstained from the same (in English *hath forborne the same*) on the aforesaid first day of December in the abovementioned 17th year [1641] during the aforesaid space of three months immediately following from then, in Contempt of the said Lord King now [reigning] and against the Form
[5] of the statute published in such a matter which has lately been published and provided. And against the peace of the said Lord King now reigning, his Crown and his dignity &c.
[6] She was proclaimed [recusant] and fined

[Translation - verso]
[7] True bill
[8] The proceedings stand

#4 – William Kiffen, John Spilsbery and Joseph Sansom write a letter to Baptists in Ireland on submission to authority – 20 January 1654(?) (LSA, Letters Addressed to Oliver Cromwell (SAL MS 138), pages 191-192):

[Folio 191 recto]

Dear Brethren London the 20 of ye 11/mo[nth] [1654?]

As there is nothing more occasions Reioycing in us then to heare of your increasse in the knowledge & love of God expressed by an humble and patient waighting for the kindgome of our Lord Jeasus Soe is theare nothing more grevious to us then to heare any thing donn by you either in word or action wich may occassion any blemish upon the Glorious profession of Christ owned by you in your visible profession of his name in the world the Lawe of that great Relation wee stand in to you as Brethren in the faith once given to the saints ingageth us as our duty to writt these fewe Lynnes unto you princi-pally occassioned from those Gennerall Romouers [Rumours?] which is in the mouths of maney that since this lawe alteration of Government in these 3 nations There is raysed up in many amongst you a Spirit of gread Dissatisfacktion and Oppossition against This present Authority in so muc as wee heare its your Resolution to make a publick protest against it to show you dislicke thereof the Report of which is in deed noe small occasion of trouble to us fearing least Therby the Glorious name of Christ will suffer, ~~Whereby~~ the hands and harts of those, who wee have cause to beleave, are strongly ingaged to lay the foundation of Justice and Righteounsness in ye 3 nations will be discoradged and ye Common inimie rejoice. Wee trust therefore that you will better consider of this manner and consult with that Blessed Rule of trust which you profess to by your Guide and then wee quistion not, but you will therby see that your Resolutions are not of god, for that Expreseth noe other things to Christians but exortations to be subject to all Civell powers they being of god, and to pray for all that are in athority that under them wee may live a godly and quiet life in all godlyness and honestie and truly it is more unlovely for us to be found contending against powers then aney others becausse wee Profess our selves to be dead with Christ Beinge Buried with him in Baptizme, and to be Raysed with him to this end that wee may walke in newness of life & as strangers & pilgrims declaring wee seeke another City even that whose builder and maker is god. the Apostle Concludes this as that which should be in every Christian Spirit in 2 Cor 10:8 that though wee are in the flesh, wee doe not warr after the flesh a Christians warefair being another thing to another end

[Folio 191 verso]

End is possile the accation of taking thesse Resolutions may arise from some misunderstandinge of the State of things heare for truly wee cannot thinke if you had bynn heare and taken an observation of ye great disesteam that all power begaine to be in by Reason of the ill manage ment of it in the handes of thosse whare it was which in an ordinary way had it bynn soe Continuwed would some have brought in a spirit of great wickedness Through the nation every man and woman, yea children, taken upon them to Judge and Contemne that Great ordinance which god hathe sett in the world to bound & restraine that great spirit of wickednesse which was licke to be amongst the sones of men, and this wee are clearly satisfied inthe proncipalls heild forth by those meeting att Blackfryers under pretence of ye first monarkie or settinge up of the kingdome of Christ to which many of these lattly in power adheared to had it bynn prosicuted would have brought as great dishoner to the name of God and shame & contempt to the whole nation as wee think could have byn imagined, for under these 2 heades the substance of all there preachings consists. i. that it was the duty of ye Maiestrat to owne there power to be received imediatly from Jeasus Christ, from this Consiquence would have unavoydablely have followed that they ware only accomptable to Christ for there actions and not to men & would not this have bynn the same with ye latte Kinge, who being perswaed by his prelats that he received his power imediatly from god was not accoumptable to the peoples representations, but the 2nd thing heild forth with great zeale by thosee frends was that ye great Rule by which they ware to act in there proseeds Towards the making of ware or peace with ye nations should arisse from a spiritt stirred up, as they say, by god to ~~god to~~ throw down potentats and powers rather then these predentiall rules of Justice & righteousness in ye doing to all men: as they would men should doe to them; wee wright not thesse things to cast a blemish upon them but to lett you see to what a condistion in an ordinary way wee ware running into that you may be sattisfied of what great necessity there was to interposse for the prevention of thesse unavoydable dangerswhich were even att the dore readied to lease upon us, & wee have ground to be confident that for ye prevention of ye dishonner which was licke to fall upon the profession of the Gospel, if things had gone one in that was, they ware a going, my Lord protector hath taken upon himthat great Burden to govern these 3 nations from whome wee may expect protecktion & shelter from all iniuries, and worship the Lord

[Folio 192 recto]

in that way our Conciennces are convinced of is most agreable to the will of god, a mercey not ussially injoyed by saints in aney age before & wee have Cause to feare not prithees [prizees] by saints, wee doe therefor beseech you for the Lords sacke, for truths sake, that it be not everll[?] spoken of men seriously by way of thesse things for surely if you Lord give us harts wee have a large advantage put into our hands to give a publicke testimoney in the face of ye world that our prencipalls are not such as they have bynn Generally Judged, by most men to be, which is, that wee deny athority & would pull downe all maiestrey and if any trouble should arisse either with you or us in the nations which might proseed to you sheddinge of blood would not all bee imputed and charged upon by babtized Churches and what greife and sorrow would be administred to us your brethren to heare ye name of god blasphemed by ungodly men through your means. this we can say, that we have not had any accassion of sorrow in this matter from any of the Churches in this nation with whome wee have Comunion, they with one hart desiringe to blesse god for there liberty and with all willingness to be subiect to your present Athority and wee trust to swere the same of you havinge latly rec'd an epistle written to us by all the Churches amoungst you pressing us to a strict walking with god & warning of us to take heed of formality ye love of this world that was slight not our mercy in ye present liberties wee injoy which wee thankfully receive from you as knowing yt such consell wee have need of and wee daly pray yt the same spiritt may be with power upon all our harts yt wee may more & more show forth ye vertues of Christ in all good Conversations & godlynes which is & shalbe the trewst prayers of

Your unfeigned Brethren in ye lord

W[illia]m Kiffen [signature]
John Spilsbery [signature]
Joseph Sansom [signature]

CHAPTER 2

Hanserd Knollys and the Baptist Church in the Old Artillery Ground (1658–82)

In October of 1658 William Kiffen and other Baptist leaders petitioned the Council of State for a ninety-nine-year lease on the Old Artillery Ground property, with the intention that it could be developed and used as a place of religious worship and teaching. A number of documents relating to this venture are found in The National Archives, the British Library, London, the Bodleian Library, Oxford, and the archives of the Honourable Artillery Company. These demonstrate that Kiffen's friend and colleague Hanserd Knollys (see Figure #1) soon assumed the initiative in the matter, and purchased the property from the Honourable Artillery Company in late 1658. He spent a considerable amount of money developing the property, and for a few short years it was used by Baptists meeting under Knollys' leadership. However, following the restoration of Charles II in May of 1660 Knollys was involved in a series of complex legal battles about ownership of the site which lasted for nearly a quarter of a century.[1] It seems that in 1661 Knollys became the victim of a vindictive royalist who ejected him from the property and took possession of it, apparently illegally. Knollys was forced to appeal to Charles II repeatedly about his treatment, and there are records of at least seven different petitions he submitted to the royal court from 1661–79.[2] Sadly, the royal court employed a stalling tactic in the matter, and Knollys' case got caught up in bureaucratic red-tape as it was passed from one official, and one administrative department, to the next. Knollys' petitions

---

[1] A brief discussion of the matter is found in F.H.W. Shepherd (ed.), *The Survey of London, Volume 27* (London: Athlone Press, 1957): 27-8. However, this contains a number of errors, and omits some key sources in the story. It also fails to include any evidence about Knollys' congregation at the Old Artillery Ground.

[2] The sources for the petitions in the TNA (and their likely dates) are as follows: Surveyor General Constat Book B—1660–1661 (CRES 6/2), pages 89-90 (from July 1661); Surveyor General Constat Book B—1660–1661 (CRES 6/2), pages 88-89 (from September 1661); SP 29/288, page 169 (from 1671); SP 29/338, page 126 verso (from 1673); Surveyor General Constat Book M—1675–1678 (CRES 6/12), page 304 (from late 1674 or early 1675); Surveyor General Constat Book M—1675–1678 (CRES 6/12), page 306 (from 1677); Surveyor General Constat Book O—1679–1682 (CRES 6/14), page 166 (from 1679). Only one of these seven (that from 1671) is an actual petition of Knollys himself, the other six are copies of his petitions which have been incorporated into other documents. A copy of the seventh petition from 1679 is also contained in TNA, Treasury Book of Out Letters 1 (T 11/5), page 126.

about the property came to nothing, and the chances of ever recovering it were finally dashed when the Old Artillery Ground was sold by the crown to property developers in 1682.

The Old Artillery Ground episode was an important one in Knollys life, and it has been briefly noted within several biographical studies of the man, but never to the extent that it perhaps should be. Some established studies on Knollys do not mention the incident at all, or make the briefest mention of it.[3] The seminal essay on Hanserd Knollys by B.R. White in 1977 has only one brief sentence and one footnote on the incident, simply concluding with the observation that 'between 1671 and 1673 Knollys was engaged in an appeal to the King for the restoration of his property'.[4] In fact, we know that the situation was much more protracted than this, and revolved around Knollys' clash with one particular royalist, Colonel William Legge. Muriel James's biographical study of Knollys from 1997 contains a bit more discussion of the incident, but incorrectly says that Knollys 'sued the army', and misunderstands some of the *State Papers* which describe the struggle over the property.[5] The most recent in-depth study of Hanserd Knollys by Dennis Bustin[6], rightly concentrates on Legge's confiscation of the Old Artillery Ground property. Unfortunately much of his discussion here is derivative, and it is overly reliant on secondary source materials, notably the *Calendar of State Papers*. This means that the complexity of Knollys' struggle over this property is unrecognized, and many of the key primary sources do not figure in scholarly discussion of the matter. This study seeks to redress that imbalance and offer a fresh investigation into Hanserd Knollys and the Baptist church in the Old Artillery Ground.

The Purchase of the Old Artillery Ground from the Honourable Artillery Company (1658)

The earliest records of the purchase of the Old Artillery Ground property by the Baptists are contained in the Minute Books of the Honourable Artillery Company (HAC). These records show that the purchase of the property was made by a Richard Wollaston (or Woollaston), who was a Baptist and was acting on behalf of Hanserd

---

[3] A case in point is Pope A. Duncan, *Hanserd Knollys: Seventeenth-Century Baptist* (Nashville: Broadman Press, 1965). James Culross, *Hanserd Knollys: A Minister and Witness of Jesus Christ (1598–1691)* (London: Alexander and Shepheard, 1895): 92, makes only a passing reference to the struggle over the property. Alexander Gordon, 'Knollys, Hanserd', in *Dictionary of National Biography, Volume 31* (London: Smith, Elder, 1892): 280, has one sentence on the incident.

[4] B.R. White *Hanserd Knollys and Radical Dissent in the 17th Century* (London: Dr Williams's Trust, 1977): 28.

[5] Muriel James, *Religious Liberty on Trial: Hanserd Knollys—Early Baptist Hero* (House Publishers, 1997): 175-177.

[6] Dennis C. Bustin, *Paradox and Perseverance: Hanserd Knollys, Particular Baptist Pioneer in Seventeenth-Century England* (Studies in Baptist Hisory and Thought, 23; Milton Keynes: Paternoster, 2006).

Knollys; it is likely that the moving force behind the sale was William Kiffen, the prominent Baptist leader from London, who was a captain within the Honourable Artillery Company.[7] The first of these purchase records is dated 17 August 1658 and is the record from a business meeting at the Court House attended by ten members of the Company (see Document #1).[8] The minute records that a Richard Wollaston, the Master Gunner of England, attended the meeting and formally agreed to the purchase of the Old Artillery Ground for the sum of £300, which was to be divided into two instalments of £150. The first of these was paid immediately and the second was to be paid on 29 September 1658. Indeed, the minute book records a receipt for the second installment of this purchase price on 29 September (see Document #2).[9] In this case it was paid to the accounts of the Honourable Artillery Company by Richard Wollaston through a Mr Peryer and received by the Clerke of the Company, James Ragge. The minute book also records a full receipt of the completed sale of the Old Artillery Ground (see Document #3).[10] This receipt notes that the Artillery Company did build upon the property by virtue of a grant from King James from 1622 (lines 27–30).

The fact that the sale was made through the then Master Gunner, Richard Wollaston, is interesting in its own right, for Wollaston was a Baptist who for many years was associated with the church led by Henry Jessey.[11] It is sometimes suggested that Wollaston and Knollys together petitioned Parliament for the abolition of tithes in 1647 and 1652.[12] The basis of this suggestion is an annotated copy of John Lewis's *A Brief History of the Rise and Progress of Anabaptism in England* (1738), which has survived in the Bodleian Library as part of the Rawlinson MSS (MS Rawl C 409). Apparently in March of 1742 Lewis was preparing a second edition of the work and made extensive notes for the volume, which he subtitled, 'The Second edition corrected with large additions and an Account of some of the

---

[7] Kiffen was admitted to the Honourable Artillery Company on 18 February 1656 (HAC, Ancient Vellum Book, folio 90). There is a record from 11 September 1657 of Captain Kiffen and the Master Gunner being summoned to appear before the Court of the Honourable Artillery Company (HAC, Minute Book of the Honourable Artillery Company—1656–1661, page 10). Although the reason for their being summoned is not specified, it is likely that it concerned the proposed sale of the Old Artillery Ground property.

[8] HAC, Minute Book of the Honourable Artillery Company—1656–1661, page 40.

[9] HAC, Minute Book of the Honourable Artillery Company—1656–1661, page 43.

[10] HAC, Minute Book of the Honourable Artillery Company—1656–1661, pages 44-45.

[11] Wollaston is identified as a witness to the healing of Sarah Wright in Henry Jessey's *The Exceeding Riches of Grace Advanced* (1647): A1. He is also named as one of the writers of a letter sent from Jessey's church in London to the Broadmead church in Bristol in June of 1671 (see E.B. Underhill, *The Records of a Church of Christ Meeting in Broadmead, Bristol* (London: The Hanserd Knollys Society, 1847): 138-140, for details).

[12] W.T. Whitley, 'Jottings by John Lewis of Margate, 1742', *Transactions of the Baptist Historical Society* 4 (1914–15): 206; Duncan *Hanserd Knollys*: 50; White *Hanserd Knollys and Radical Dissent*: 14; Bustin *Paradox and Perseverance*: 134, all note this.

first English Anabaptist Teachers'. The paragraph which brought together Wollaston and Knollys reads as follows:

> In 1647 were proposals tendred by several Elders and Brethren of Congregations of the Anabaptists to the Committee of Parliament &c. In which, among others, they proposed a repeal of all Laws, Orders and Ordinances which hinder many godly and gifted men from preaching the Gospel; That all Tithes (so farre forth as they appertayne to the maintenance of the Ministry) may be taken away: That scandalous, ungodly and ungifted Ministers throughout the Nation may be ejected from their places and Ministry: That, in lieu of Tithes, there be an equal Tax laid & brought into the publique Treasury in every County, which may be disposed to such persons and Uses as the Parliament shall think fit: That such Churches and their Elderships as are under Baptisme, being found in the Faith, may have liberty to send out such as they shall thinke fitt to preach the Gospell without coming under the Attest or Approbation of other Ministers [the Tryers] and People which refuse to joyne with them in so Brotherly a Work. This was signed by Richard Woolaston and Hanserd Knollys for them selves and others, in March 1651, renewed and enlarged, and endorsed, received March 24, 1651.[13]

In 1652 or 1653 Wollaston and Knollys submitted a proposal to the Committee for the Propagation of the Gospel, signing it 'for ourselves and others'.[14] Wollaston also appears briefly in Humphrey Brooke's *The Charity of Church-men* (1649), another example of his association with Hanserd Knollys and the circle of Baptists in London.[15] Similarly, he is one of the eighteen signatories to *A Declaration of Divers Elders and Brethren of Congregational Societies* (1651); Henry Jessey, William Kiffen, and Hanserd Knollys are also among the signatories.[16] Some other evidence of Wollaston's involvement in Baptist life at the time of the sale of the Old Artillery Ground has survived. For example, both he and Knollys are mentioned in the pamphlet *The Old Leaven Purged Out* (1658) as among the Baptist leaders contacted for advice about how to deal with a split within John Simpson's church over the Fifth Monarchy movement. In addition, Wollaston's name appears on the title page of the Quaker pamphlet *An Answer to a Declaration* (1659), written in response to the broadsheet entitled *Declaration of Several of the People called Anabaptists in and about the City of London* (1659).

Wollaston's military career is difficult to trace, although it may have begun as early as 1642 where there is record of a 'Mr Woolaston' serving as a lieutenant in

[13] BLO, MS Rawl C 409, page 60. This was intended to be an insertion to the second paragraph of page 93 of the original 1738 edition.

[14] *HMC Portland I* 637. The text of their proposal was published in Zachary Grey, *An Impartial Examination of the Fourth Volume of Mr Daniel Neal's History of the Puritans* (London, 1739): Appendix No. 81, pages 144-148.

[15] This is discussed in Murray Tolmie, *The Triumph of the Saints: The Separate Churches of London 1616–1649* (Cambridge: Cambridge University Press, 1977): 150.

[16] John Goodwin, *Peace Protected and Discontent Disarmed* (1654): 66, notes Wollaston's involvement in the pamphlet.

the Orange Company of the London militia.[17] There is a record dated 11 April 1644 which has him being re-imbursed by the navy for monies owed him, describing him as 'Captain' Richard Wollaston.[18] Certainly, by 1649 he was in place as the Master Gunner of England.[19] One of the earliest records in the *State Papers* of him serving as an ordnance officer is dated 12 November 1650, where 'out of duty by my place' he writes a recommendation for one Thomas Weekes to be a gunner aboard a naval ship; perhaps Wollaston had been involved in training Weekes in the art of ordnance at the Old Artillery Ground.[20] Weekes was himself also probably a Baptist; there is record of him being arrested for attending an illegal conventicle in November of 1662.[21] In July of 1653 Wollaston petitioned the Council of State for payment of fees owed him in connection with his duties as Master Gunner.[22] Another interesting insight into Wollaston's activities is a record dated 1 January 1654, where he submits a survey report on spare ordnance on the Tower wharf.[23] A similar record from 3 October 1655 had Wollaston submit a report about the shot and ordnance materials that were in his possession.[24] Wollaston's position as an officer in the Ordnance Office was not his only position within the government of the Nominated Parliament. He served on the committee to investigate the state of the Upper Bench prison, having been appointed by the Council of State on 29 April 1653.[25] He was

---

[17] *A List of the Names of the Severall Colonells and their Colours* (1642). In connection with the Orange Regiment there is an entry in a manuscript entitled 'Ensignes, Trayned Bands, and Auxiliaries, 1642' for a '2d Captaine—Richard Wollaston, a Wollen Draper dwelling neare ye Exchange. Fleetstreet Companye' (the manuscript is at the Royal United Services Institute for Defence and Security Studies, in Whitehall, London). For a full discussion of the document see, Harold Arthur Dillon, 'On a MS List of Officers of the London Trained Bands in 1643', *Archaeologia: or Miscellaneous Tracts Relating to Antiquity*, Second Series, Volume II (London: Society of Antiquaries of London, 1890), page 139 (article is pages 129-144).

[18] BLO, MS Rawlinson A 222, folio 20 recto.

[19] Wollaston is first named as the Master Gunner in the accounts of the Ordnance Office, where his is paid £17 10*s* for the quarter ending 31 March 1649. His wages description is 'The Master Gunner of England for his Exercise of Scholars to shoote in great Ordnance in ye Artillery Garden' (TNA, Ordnance Office—Quarter Books 1647–1650 (WO 54/17)).

[20] TNA, SP 18/58, page 170. John Barkstead also wrote a letter of reference for Weekes to have a position as a gunner on 26 September 1653 (TNA, SP 18/58, page 168). Apparently Weekes had been a gunner for a number of years; on 22 August 1643 he signed a receipt for £2, representing an advance of his monthly salary as a gunner (see TNA, SP 28/131, part 12, folio 8 recto).

[21] TNA, SP 29/67, page 4.

[22] TNA, SP 25/70, pages 4, 10 and 32.

[23] TNA, SP 18/78, page 84.

[24] TNA, SP 18/115, page 47.

[25] TNA, SP 25/69, pages 3-4. Both *A Schedule or List of the Prisoners in the Fleet* (1653) and *A List of the Prisoners in the Upper Bench Prison* (1653) name Wollaston as a member of this Committee. Also see TNA, SP 25/76, page 160, for a case involving a petition by a Richard Bedwell which Wollaston was commissioned on 4 July 1655 to investigate.

considered for an appointment as one of the judges of the Admiralty in July of 1653, but he did not receive the necessary votes in the House of Commons to obtain the position.[26] On 22 January 1656 Wollaston again petitioned the Council of State that he be paid the arrears owed him dating back to 1652;[27] the Council of State ordered on 5 February 1656 that £472 be paid to Wollaston to resolve the matter.[28] However, it is likely that, as a Baptist, Wollaston's position within the Ordnance Office became increasingly problematic during the turbulent year of 1659, and he was forced to petition the naval authorities that the Treasurer pay him £50 in a missed quarterly payment of his wages.[29] With the Restoration Wollaston was removed as Master Gunner, the post being given back to Sir James Wemyss by Charles II. He was still owed a year's salary, and sometime in 1661 he petitioned the Admiralty and Navy Commissioners for the outstanding £171 in wages owed him.[30]

William Kiffen's Petition to the Council of State for a Lease on the Old Artillery Ground (1658–59)

William Kiffen's original petition to the Council of State about the Old Artillery Ground does not appear to have survived, although a report about the petition was written by William Jessop, the Secretary to the Council, on 5 October 1658 (see Document #4).[31] It notes that the petition was presented by 'Wm Kiffin and diverse others on behalfe of themselves and ye Congregatons to which they are related' (lines 3–5). Jessop records that the matter was referred to the Commissioners of the Admiralty and the Navy and that they were asked to offer an opinion as to the feasibility of the petition. On 16 October 1658 a panel of three Commissioners requested a survey of the property from the Ordnance Office, asking them to 'returne us their opinion what thereof may be conveniently granted to Mr Kiffin and ye other petitoners for their Accomodaton without prejudice to yě State' (see Document #5, lines 8–11).

On 31 December 1658 a report about the property was sent by four officers of the Ordinance Office to the Commissioners of the Admiralty and the Navy (see Document #5).[32] However, Kiffen may have had an inside advantage in the matter, for he had long-standing personal contact with one of the three Commissioners who requested the report, Thomas Kelsey. Interestingly, there is an apprenticeship record dated 19 October 1638, which shows that Kiffen, a member of the Leathersellers' Company, had taken on Thomas Kelsey's younger brother Francis as an

[26] JHC 7 (29 July 1653): 289, 292.

[27] TNA, SP 25/76, page 488.

[28] TNA, SP 25/76, page 521.

[29] TNA, SP 18/217, page 176.

[30] TNA, SP 25/447, page 58.

[31] TNA, SP 18/183, page 6 recto.

[32] TNA, SP 18/184, pages 143-144. The four officers were Elia Palmer (Deputy Surveyor), Lewis Audeley (Clerke), John Falkener (Keeper of the Stores), and William Billers (Clerk of the Deliveries).

apprentice.[33] So certainly Kiffen knew the Kelsey family for at least twenty years prior to making the petition for the Artillery Ground property. Moreover, Thomas Kelsey participated in the Whitehall debates in January of 1649, and challenged the so-called prophetess Elizabeth Poole,[34] which may indicate another point of contact with Kiffen. Kiffen had a turbulent relationship with Elizabeth Poole, who was at one time a member of his congregation but left under a cloud of suspicion. In addition, both Kiffen and Thomas Kelsey had been elected as Members of Parliament in 1656 (Kiffen for Middlesex and Kelsey for Dover), and would have known each other from service there. In fact, in December of 1656 the two men were involved in Parliament's deliberations about the punishment to be meted out against the Quaker James Naylor (both Kiffen and Kelsey opposed the death penalty, and thought that Naylor should be offered an opportunity to repent).[35] All of which is to say, that it perhaps should come as no surprise that the petition was successful and a lease for the Old Artillery Ground was granted to the Baptists.

Hanserd Knollys Petitions for Confirmation of his Lease on the Old Artillery Ground (1660–61)

The next stage of the story sees the focus shift from William Kiffen to his friend and colleague Hanserd Knollys (1599–1691). There is a record from the Honourable Artillery Company which shows that a Court of Assistants met on 18 Juy 1660 and considered a petition submitted to them by Knollys (see Document #6).[36] Knollys related 'the greate Charge hee hath beene att in repayringe the old Armory in B[isho]ppsgate streete and that if this Co[u]rt doe not assist him hee is likely to bee turned out of it' (lines 9–12). Clearly Knollys had by this stage become aware of the opposition to his plans by Colonel William Legge. In fact, the Court decided to send a delegation of three of their members to meet with Colonel Legge and acquaint with the situation from their perspective.

The earliest document within the *State Papers* pertaining to the Old Artillery Ground which names Knollys is an order from Thomas Wriothesley, the Earl of Southampton, dated 25 September 1660 (see Document #7).[37] Lord Treasurer Southampton's order was issued to Charles Harbord (1596–1679), the Surveyor General of the Land Revenues of the Crown, and instructed him to consider Knollys' petition. In particular, Harbord was asked to suggest a rent and fee for the property, if he felt it was fit to be leased to Hanserd Knollys. Several details arise from the

[33] LCL, Register of Apprentices—1629–1677 (Mem 7/1). Kelsey was Kiffen's very first apprentice, the contract following immediately after Kiffen's admission to the Leathersellers' Company in 1638.

[34] C.H. Firth (ed.) *The Clarke Papers, Volume 2* (London: The Camden Society, 1894): 167.

[35] Thomas Burton, 'Diary of Parliament 1656–1659, Volume 1' (BLL, Add MS 15,859), folios 58 verso-59 recto.

[36] HAC, Minute Book of the Honourable Artillery Company—1656–1661, page 93.

[37] TNA, Lord Southampton's General Entry Book—1660 (T 51/1), page 152.

document, including the fact that Knollys is described in line 4 simply as a 'Clerke' (no indication of him being an Anabaptist preacher or teacher is made). Southampton's order also mentioned in passing that Knollys originally submitted a petition to Charles II sometime in early July 1660, and that the king had referred the matter on to him at the Treasury. The order also noted that Knollys had purchased the Old Artillery Ground 'from ye Company of Artillery of ye City of London' (lines 7–8), although it does not state when that purchase had been made, or who effected the sale.

Meanwhile, Knollys approached the Honourable Artillery Company again for support in his legal struggle over the property. There is a record from the Honourable Artillery Company which shows that a Court of Assistants met at the Great James Tavern on 14 October 1660 and discussed the case (see Document #8).[38] The record notes that Colonel Manby did not appear at a meeting arranged by Harbord at Denmark House, despite being summoned (lines 7–10). This put Knollys at a serious disadvantage in arguing his case, which the Honourable Artillery Company recognized. In response they agreed to have Captain Peryer and James Ragge, the Clerke of the Company, draw up a petition which was to be sent to Charles II (lines 11–13). The President (John Robinson) and Deputy-President (William Vincent) were charged with making sure that it was delivered to the king (lines 13–15).

Acting under Treasurer Southampton's orders of 25 September, Charles Harbord submitted a report to him which was dated 12 November 1660 (see Document #9).[39] Apparently Harbord had conducted an independent investigation into Knollys' personal situation and was aware that he intended to set up a Baptist church and school on the property. He reported that Knollys

> doth teach a schoole and excerise his profession as a preacher to a Congregation of p[er]sons of his owne opinion in the said Roome or Armory howse, and seemeth to be a man of a peaceable behaviour & good life, having bred up his owne sonn & others now preachers & conformable to the Church Government now established (lines 25–30).

The Surveyor General interviewed Colonel James Wemyss, the Master Gunner of England,[40] about his plans for Knollys' property. However Harbord disagreed with him about the suitability of Knollys' buildings for the storage of cannons and carriages, suggesting that other crown properties closer to the Tower were more suitable. Harbord also noted that Knollys 'would be utterly undone w[i]th his wife & family if the said howse & buildings should be taken from him' (lines 31–32).

---

[38] HAC, Minute Book of the Honourable Artillery Company—1656–1661, pages 98-99.

[39] TNA, Surveyor General Papers—1660–1662 (LR 17/2).

[40] Wemyss was Master Gunner of England from 1638–1647 and again from 1660–1666; he was succeeded by Captain Valentine Pyne who held the post until his death in 1677.

On the basis of this report Treasurer Southampton on 24 November 1660 ordered the Surveyor General to compose a constat[41] on Knollys' case, with a view to preparing a lease of twenty-one years for the property. Harbord was also instructed to consult with the Master of his Majesty's Ordnance, Sir William Compton, to obtain his views on the matter (lines 63–64). Southampton also recorded his agreement with the Surveyor General (and against the Master Gunner!) about the unsuitability of the property as a place of storage for ordnance equipment (lines 65–67).

Harbord complied promptly, producing a seven-page document (see Document #10). The Surveyor General's constat is dated 18 December 1660 and is one of the most important sources about Knollys's petition on the Old Artillery Ground for it summarizes all of the documents pertaining to the case at the time. For example, although Knollys' original petition of July 1660 does not appear to have survived, a copy of it was incorporated into Harbord's constat (lines 34–85).[42] This copy of the original petition of Knollys was accompanied by an explanatory note from Edward Nicholas, the Secretary of State (lines 86–90). According to Nicholas the petition was considered at court in Whitehall on 31 July 1660. Nicholas noted that it was referred to the Commissioners of the Treasury 'to certifie what they conceave fitt to be done herein for his Ma[jes]ties Service' (which helps explain how Treasurer Southampton first became involved in the matter).

It seems that the substance of Knollys' original petition was that he be granted a lease for ninety-nine years for the property, at a rent of £20 per annum, or whatever amount was felt appropriate. Knollys explained that he had paid £300 to the Artillery Company for the property, a transaction that was arranged through another party, namely Richard Wollaston, who held the post of the Master Gunner of England within the Ordnance Office. He also explained that he had spent a great deal of additional money in improving and repairing the property. Knollys stressed that he was seeking security for his wife and family, that they 'may not by any wayes or meanes be molested or interrupted in the posseon of the said premisses, nor hereafter be prevented in the peceable enjoym[en]t of [it]' (lines 69–72).

The Surveyor General's constat also incorporated a copy of a supplementary petition made by Hanserd Knollys, this time one sent directly to the Commissioners of the Treasury (lines 3–28).[43] In the opening lines of the petition Knollys explained why he had approached them again about the matter, saying, 'That your pet[ition]er findeing himselfe disturbed & in danger of further disturbance concerning the Tytle & poss[ess]eon of his Howse' (lines 6–7). Knollys was keen 'to assert his owne right & to sett forth before your Lo[rdshi]pps the equity of his Cause' (lines 15–16). He

---

[41] The *OED* defines a constat as 'A certificate stating what appears (*constat*) upon record touching a matter, given by the clerk of the pipe and auditors of the Exchequer at the request of a person who intends to plead or move in that court for the discharge of any matter.'

[42] TNA, Surveyor General Constat Book B—1660–1661 (CRES 6/2), pages 88-92. A copy of Knollys' original petition of July 1661 is found on pages 89-90.

[43] TNA, Surveyor General Constat Book B—1660–1661 (CRES 6/2), pages 88-89.

pleads that he is himself ignorant of what the law says in the matter, but gently suggests that the Commissioners contact men associated with the Artillery Company who knew of Knollys' purchase of the property and could vouch for him; he names six in particular: James Ragg (Clerke of the Company), Colonel Menes, Lieutenant-Colonel Hinde, Captain Prior, Captain Beast and Captain Shepard (lines 19–21). The copy of the supplementary petition is accompanied by a note from Treasurer Southampton dated 25 September 1660 (lines 29–33); this corresponds to the order from Southampton to Charles Harbord noted above (Document #7).

The Latin warrant for a lease of the Old Artillery Ground to be made out to Hanserd Knollys is also contained in the constat (lines 157–181), where it is included with a report dated 18 December 1660 of Harbord's meeting with William Compton, the Master of his Majesty's Ordnance.[44] He stated that he and the Master of his Majesty's Ordnance were of one mind about the unsuitability of Knollys' premises for the use of the crown, and that they wished 'ye s[ai]d Artillery Ground were exchanged for some other peece of Ground lyeing more neer to the Tower & more easie of accesse for his Ma[jes]t[ie]s Carriages and tryall of his Cannon' (lines 185–187). Harbord also suggested that a lease of thirty-one years[45] be granted to Knollys, with an annual rent of £20, in recognition of the large amount of money that Knollys had already expended on the property (lines 188–195). The Surveyor General concluded his constat by making further suggestions about the collection of the rent, and the upkeep of the property by the lessee (lines 197–206).

One other document pertaining to Hanserd Knollys' appeal for the Old Artillery Ground is worth noting at this point. This is a Surveyors General Land Revenue memorandum which has as its title 'Mr Knollys his Case touching the old Artillery house' (see Document #11).[46] The four-page document is anonymously written, but it does appear to be a summary memorandum compiled by Charles Harbord in preparation for the writing of the constat dated 18 December 1660. The memorandum describes how the sale of the Old Artillery Ground was made to Richard Wollaston, who was acting in trust for Knollys (lines 12–14), and notes that the documents proving the Artillery Company had the legal right to sell the property were in the possession of one Colonel William Manby, the Treasurer of the Artillery Company since 1637, who had apparently embezzeled the documents and refused to surrender them (lines 15–19). Manby died before 1661, which meant that the Artillery Company was engaged in a bitter struggle to recover their archives from his estate, something which they never managed to do. Manby's legacy to the Artillery Company is summarized in their official history:

> the ancient archives of the Regiment, which must certainly have covered the period from 1610 to 1643, and probably went back to the date of the Charter, were

---

[44] An earlier draft of both the Latin warrant and the report is found in TNA, Surveyor General Papers—1660–1662 (LR 17/2).

[45] Southampton's instruction was that the lease be for twenty-one years (line 148).

[46] TNA, Hanserd Knollys' Memorandum on the Old Artillery Ground (LR 17/8).

> irretrievably lost to posterity through the criminal stubbornness, carelessness or roguery of one individual.[47]

Interestingly, Colonel Manby, in addition to being the Treasurer of the Artillery Company, was also the Clerk of the Leathersellers' Company, and thus would have known Kiffen, also a member of that guild. In terms of Knollys' case for the property he purchased in the Old Artillery Ground, Manby's loss of the documents relating to the so-called Armoury Storehouse from the time of James I was catastrophic. It meant that Knollys had no legal basis for proving that he had purchased part of a property granted to the Honourable Artillery Company by James I in 1622.[48]

Moreover, the memorandum gives details of interviews conducted by the Surveyor General with various members of the Artillery Company following Colonel Manby's death. Significantly, it relates that Colonel Wemyss, the Master Gunner, claimed an interest in Knollys' house, arguing that it was a perk of his office. Wemyss also is recorded as arguing that Knollys' house was needed as a dry storage place for the king's gun carriages, and claimed that Sir William Compton, Master of the Ordnance, agreed with him on this point (lines 50–52). However, Compton is recorded as having some compassion for Knollys' plight in the matter, saying that

> if his Ma[jes]tie should take the Armory from Mr Knollys, then Mr Knollys had noe place to teach his scholars in, nor the Congregation had noe place to meet in & soe the poore man would suffer very much damage (lines 53–57).

The memorandum also names Colonel William Legge (1609–70), the Lieutenant of the Ordnance within the discussion. According to the memorandum Legge 'hath ye Old Artillery Ground in his Patent' and 'sent to discharge Mr Knollys out of all yt he hath bought, builded & now possess there, & also saith that the Ground & houses thereon are his' (lines 61–65). Legge was to become a significant antagonist to Knollys' plans for the property (more on him below). From the memorandum we also learn that the Surveyor General had interviewed Knollys himself, who revealed that he had spent £700 on the premises in order to prepare it for 'conveniency in teaching and boarding scholars' (lines 69–70). Interestingly, we learn that Knollys says he had earned the money to buy the property through ten years of diligent hard work as a teacher; it represented all that he had in terms of capital (lines 73–75). Understandably, Knollys sought security for his wife and three children and wanted either to have the property confirmed to him or to be reimbursed by the Artillery Company for the £700 he had expended on it. The memorandum is important because it provides additional details of Knollys and his on-going struggle to secure

---

[47] G. Goold Walker, *The Honourable Artillery Company 1537–1987* (London: The Royal Artillery Company, 3rd edn, 1986): 66.

[48] In 1631 the Honourable Artillery Company stated that the brick Armoury building had cost them £1,000 to build (TNA, PC 2/40, pages 463-464). The Honourable Artillery Company was involved in a considerable struggle with the Ordnance Office over use of the property in the spring of 1631 (see TNA, PC 2/40, pages 512-513).

rights for the property he first purchased in 1658. It identifies Colonel Legge as a prime antagonist in this regard. Yet, perhaps the most interesting feature of the report is that it includes a map of Knollys' property, complete with dimensions of the various buildings and features on it (see Figure #2).

On 5 January 1661 Lord Treasurer Southampton issued a warrant to Sir Robert Croke, the Clerk of the Pipe in the Treasury, for a lease to be made for Knollys on the Old Artillery Ground property (see Document #12). The lease was to be for thirty-one years, at an annual rent of £20; a fine of £40 was also set for the transaction. The warrant was issued promptly by Croke, and two men, John Champante of London and John Asham of Westminster, served as financial guarantors for the fees relevant to the transaction on 16 January 1661 (see Document #13). John Champante had a long-standing connection with Knollys, having worked with him in the Excise Office during the Commonwealth period.[49] At one level, the granting of this lease must have come as a great relief to Knollys (assuming that he even received news of it). However, others with competing interests also got wind of the situation and soon made things difficult for Knollys. The most significant of these figures was Colonel William Legge, the Lieutenant of Ordnance, who contacted Lord Treasurer Southampton and claimed an interest in the house that Knollys had built on the property. On 16 February 1661 Southampton wrote to Harbord, the Surveyor General, and asked him to investigate Colonel Legge's claim and, if necessary, to confer with the Attorney General about it (see Document #14). Southampton noted in passing that Legge's counterclaim described Knollys as 'a disaffected person to his Majesty' (line 6), suggesting that there was a certain animosity against the Baptist leader on the part of the royalist Legge. It is likely that there was more to the dispute between Legge and Knollys than appears at first glance. It would not be difficult to imagine that Legge's ill feeling extended to everyone associated with Baptist 'fanaticks' such as Knollys, and that the animosity had its roots much earlier in the Civil War years. Indeed, there may have been some bad blood between William Legge and Thomas Kelsey (Kiffen's friend and colleague) over their respective positions of authority as Governor of Oxford during the Civil War. Legge had been appointed Governor of Oxford on 25 December

[49] John Champante was a merchant who worked as a correspondent and bonds clerk in the Excise Office, the same place that Knollys worked as an examiner until 1655 (TNA, SP 18/109, page 99). When Knollys resigned his position to pursue other opportunities, responsibilities in the Excise Office were shuffled around and Champante was appointed as the clerk of the bonds at a salary of £20 per annum. He continued in this post throughout the Commonwealth period, and his appointment was confirmed by Charles II in July 1660 (TNA, SP 29/8, page 152: 'John Champantee, of whose fidelity and ability wee have received good utterance'), and then re-confirmed on 28 February 1661 (TNA, SP 44/11, page 32). Champante also served as the London agent for Lord William Willoughby (1615–1673), the Governor of the Caribbean Islands, from September 1665 (see TNA, CO 1/19, pages 231-232). Lillian M Penson, *The Colonial Agents of the British West Indies* (London: University of London Press, 1924): 38-47, gives some details.

1645,[50] and was succeeded by Kelsey, who served as Governor of Oxford from 1646–1650.

In any event, most intriguing is the basis upon which Legge felt he could himself claim an interest in the Old Artillery Ground property. Legge had been appointed to the post of Lieutenant of Ordnance by Charles II on 28 June 1660, and he held that his royal patent for the office included certain rights and privileges over the disputed property (see Document #15).[51] There is some substance in this claim, for lines 14–17 (in translation) record that Legge was made 'Custodian of a certain Garden commonly called Artillery Garden; to have, hold, occupy and exercise the aforesaid office and all and singular premisses by these presents granted together with the things pertaining to them'.[52] The difficulty here is that there were a number of open fields in London which were known by the name 'Artillery Garden', several of them being used for testing and firing of weapons by officers of the Ordnance Office. It is by no means clear that the property mentioned in Legge's royal patent is in fact the one that Knollys had purchased from the Honorable Artillery Company. But in one sense it did not matter; the ambiguous phrasing lent itself to Colonel Legge's purposes of dispossessing Knollys, and he was not slow to take advantage of it. Legge's claim to the Old Artillery Ground was also successful in thwarting another petition for a lease on the property. For example, there is a record dated 9 July 1661 of Charles, Lord Gerard of Brandon (c.1618–94), petitioning for a plot of two acres within the Old Artillery Ground site (see Document #16).[53] Treasurer Southampton referred this petition to Charles Harbord, the Surveyor General, asking him, 'Pray examine to whom this ground belonges' (line 6). The request apparently came to nothing, probably because it clashed with the interests of Colonel Legge, the Lieutenant of Ordnance. This is somewhat ironic, for in many respects Lord Gerard was similar to Legge. He also was a royalist military officer, a Groom of the Bed Chamber, and was resolutely Anglican in his religious sentiments.

---

[50] Samuel Clarke, *The Historian's Guide* (1690): 26.

[51] TNA, C 66/2933, Part 18, No 37.

[52] Virtually identical phrasing apears in patents granted to other Lieutenants of Ordnance, including Robert Constable in 1588 (TNA, C 66/1305, Part 2); William Heydon in 1626 (TNA, C 66/2354, Part 7, No 12); David Walter in 1670 (TNA, C 66/3121, Part 8, No 22); George Legg in 1682 (TNA, C 66/3224, Part 6, No 18); Christopher Musgrave in 1685 (TNA, C 66/3268, Part 7, No 8); Henry Tichborne in 1687 (TNA, C 66/3297, Part 7, No 8). What is most interesting about this is the fact that the established phrasing persists even after the Old Artillery Ground site was sold to property developers in 1682. In other words, the piece of land associated with the post of Lieutenant of Ordnance and described as 'the Artillery Garden' was *not* the Old Artillery Ground that Colonel Legge claimed it was. This suggests that Legge was exploiting a vague description that was contained in his royal patent, and used it to eject Hanserd Knollys from the property he purchased in 1658.

[53] BLL, Stowe MS 498, page 211.

William Legge assumes occupancy of Hanserd Knollys' property on the Old Artillery Ground (1661–70)

The period immediately following the Restoration was a difficult period for Dissenters, particularly high-profile Baptists such as Hanserd Knollys. The Venner Revolt of 7–20 January of 1661 brought great public reaction against Baptists, who were viewed as agents of violence who threatened the stability of the social order. It was no surprise that Knollys was one of the Baptist leaders arrested in the aftermath of the revolt. He was imprisoned in Newgate prison for eighteen weeks, before a general pardon was issued by the king. It is at this juncture that the confrontation with Colonel Legge over the Old Artillery Ground property took place; Knollys gives some account of this in his *Memoirs*, published by his friend William Kiffen following Knollys' death in 1692:

> After I was set at Liberty out of Prison, I went to *Holland*, and thence up into *Germany*, with my Wife and two of my Children, where we sojourned about two or three years, and in my Absence one Col. *Legge*, a Bed-chamber Man, and Lieutenant of the Ordnance, charged me in the Court of the Exchequer for keeping a House and Ground from the King, against whom I stood Suit by my Attorney: But when Col. *Legge* could not get my House from me by Law, he and some others brought several Red Coat-Souldiers, and took it by force, thrust out those persons I had left in Possession, and kept Possession by Souldiers, both of my House, Garden, and my Goods, which had cost me above 700*l.* and laid out 400*l.* more in building upon the Ground, which I had bought and paid for.[54]

Certainly Legge did not himself live in the house refurbished by Knollys; instead he resided in another property tied to his position as Lieutenant of Ordnance, the so-called Heydon House (sometimes described as the Storehouse or the Mansion House) just outside Aldgate in the Minories.[55] In 1663 Legge submitted a petition to Charles II for a sixty-year lease on this house, together with a number of other associated properties in the Minories, and the matter was discussed at court in Whitehall on 5 October 1663.[56] Sir Henry Bennet, the Secretary of State, recorded that the matter was referred to Treasurer Southampton, who in turn passed it on to the Surveyor General, Charles Harbord, the same man who dealt with Knollys' petitions from 1660. Harbord commissioned a survey to be done on the properties mentioned in Legge's petition, and reported back to his superiors on 23 March

---

[54] William Kiffen, *The Life and Death of That Old Disciple of Jesus Christ, and Eminent Minister of the Gospel, Mr Hanserd Knollys* (1692): 25. Knollys' presence in Germany in the spring of 1662[?] is also mentioned in TNA, SP 29/446, page 115.

[55] A lease granted by Charles II to William Legge's son George on 14 November 1670 describes it as 'the mansion house wherein the said William Legg lately Inhabited as belonging to his office of Lieutenant of the ordnance' (TNA, SP 29/280, page 128).

[56] TNA, SP 29/448, page 159.

1667.[57] Harbord recommended that a lease be granted to Colonel Legge, but was extremely exact in defining the property boundaries for it, carefully identifying what parts of the land and buildings were included in the lease and what parts remained with the crown. He also limited the length of the lease, reducing it from the requested sixty years to a mere thirty-one years, citing an order issued by Charles II himself in connection with such matters.[58] Perhaps the most interesting feature of William Legge's petition for these properties in the Minories is found in the report submitted by the four surveyors who actually assessed them at Harbord's request. They noted, in connection with some of the smaller properties, that 'on our knowledge Coll[onel] Legge was at great charges in the Law to recover from such as had possessed them in the Late times under pretence of ye Citties Rights'. In other words, Legge may have felt he was correcting an injustice committed against the king during the Commonwealth period. This is in keeping with what appears to have been motivating Legge in his actions over the Old Artillery Ground. Interestingly, the disputed property of Hanserd Knollys does not figure in Legge's 1663 petition to the king, and Legge appears uninterested in pursuing his claim on it any further. No doubt Legge's strategy had worked; he had friends in high places who made sure that it did. Legge had effectively blocked the grant of a lease on the Old Artillery Ground to Knollys, and he had evicted him from the property, occupying it with soldiers from the Ordnance Office. Colonel Legge had won the battle over the Old Artillery Ground and there was little that Knollys could do about it, at least as long as the Ordnance officer was still on the scene. Legge died on 13 October 1670, and all indications are that until the end of his life he steadfastly refused to budge from his opposition to Knollys' petition on the Old Artillery Ground property.

Hanserd Knollys Petitions for Reimbursement on his Lease on the Old Artillery Ground (1671–80)

Colonel William Legge's death meant that the door was now open for Hanserd Knollys to try again to recover his property. In early 1671 Knollys submitted another petition to Charles II about the matter, directing his petition to Sir Joseph Williamson (see Document #17).[59] This was Knollys' third petition about the Old Artillery Ground property, and in it he complains that he was 'obstructed in the obteyning thereof by a Caveat putt in by Colonell Legg, late Master of your Ma[jes]ties Ordnance now deceased' (lines 9–10). It seems that this petition came to nothing, which is somewhat surprising since Sir Joseph Williamson knew about Knollys and had done so for some years. Indeed, Williamson included a brief

[57] TNA, SP 29/280, pages 126 recto–127 recto. A map of the Legge properties in the Minories, probably made as part of this survey, has also survived (TNA, MPE 1/479).

[58] A lease was issued on 14 November 1670 to George Legge, the son of William (TNA, SP 44/34, pages 58-59).

[59] TNA, SP 29/288, page 169. The petition was received sometime between 1 January and 24 March 1671.

comment about Knollys within his notebook entitled 'Index of Nonconformists Ministers', dating to c.1663. Williamson's remarked in his notebook that Knollys was 'an Anabaptist Minister, a good Scholler & a teaching man, now in Amsterdam, maintained by ye Churches'.[60]

It appears that about two years passed before Knollys submitted another petition to Charles II; this was his fourth petition on the subject of the Old Artillery Ground. On 21 December 1673 Charles Cottrell, Charles II's Master of Requests, reported from the Court at Whitehall, that the king decided to refer the petition to Sir Heneage Finch, the Keeper of the Great Seal (see Document #18).[61] Finch was authorized to call all relevant parties before him and to get to the truth of the matter. He was also empowered to act 'for the pet[itioner']s releife as shall be agreeable to Justice and equity' (lines 54–55).[62] Finch wrote two reports on the case; the first is undated, but was probably issued sometime in 1673 when Finch was Attorney General,[63] while the second report was dated 22 June 1674 when he was Keeper of the Great Seal (copies of Knollys' fourth petition and the order from Charles Cottrell were included within the first report).[64] The copy of Knollys' fourth petition included within Finch's first report is especially interesting, for it includes some extra details about the situation not previously noted. For example, Knollys states that he has expended £460 (a slight increase from the figure noted elsewhere) on the premises, 'fitting the same for his Schoolehouse and dwelling house, which premisses he inhabited and enjoyed about 2 yeares' (lines 29–30). He also accused William Legge of acting 'under pretence of his Patent' (lines 31–32), and stated that Legge 'did by Force and Violence take away the s[ai]d Armory house, dwelling house and all other his out houses from your pet[ition]er' (lines 32–33). Colonel Legge's successor as Lieutenant of Ordnance, David Walter, also falls under the accusation of Knollys (lines 35–36). Knollys is bold enough to suggest that a senior member of the king's advisors be appointed to consider the case, either the Keeper of the Great Seal or the Privy Seal (line 40). Knollys concluded by appealing to the king that he is a poor and aged petitioner who had been kept out of his rightful possession for ten years (line 37), and asked either that the £760 he has expended upon the property be repaid by the responsible parties, or that he be granted a lease of ninety-nine years, paying a fine of £10 and a rate of 20*li* per annum in rent (lines 47–49).

Within his first report Finch acknowledged that 'Colo[nel] Legg did eject the pet[ition]er and hold it [the Old Artillery Ground] during his life' (line 74). Having investigated the matter Finch concluded at this point that Knollys 'be reimbursed the charge laid out upon the premisses or otherwise that he be gratified with a Lease for

---

[60] TNA, SP 9/26, page 76 recto.

[61] TNA, SP 29/338, page 126 recto.

[62] TNA, SP 29/338, page 126 verso.

[63] TNA, SP 29/338, page 127 recto.

[64] TNA, SP 29/338, page 126 recto.

yeares at some small rent to be paid your Maj[es]ty and possession be restored' (lines 78–81).

Finch notes in his second report that he had further conversations with Ordnance officers and, as a result, had changed his mind on what could realistically be offered to Knollys. Most importantly, Finch explained that 'the place in question is already granted to Mr David Walter dureing his tyme, and after him to Mr George Legge in reversion, and Soe in a manner annexed to the Office of the ordnance' (lines 13–15).[65] As a consequence Finch recommended that the only way to preserve Knollys from ruin was for the king to reimburse him the £750[66] he had spent on the property (lines 16–18). This was hardly the kind of advice that Charles II would have liked, and there is no record that he ever followed through on Finch's recommendation.

As a result of the investigation by Finch, Knollys submitted yet another petition to Charles II, his fifth on the Old Artillery Ground. A copy of this petition was incorporated in a constat compiled by the Surveyor General Charles Harbord on 16 March 1678 (Document #20), although it was probably written by Knollys in late 1674 or early in 1675. Knollys began by noting that it was now 'about 12 yeares since put out of the possession of the Armory House & buildings adjoyning' (lines 7–8). Knollys apparently had received a copy of Lord Keeper Finch's report, for he summarized the recommendations made by Finch to the king (lines 11–19). Most interestingly, Knollys relates that since he had lost the property in the Old Artillery Ground he had been forced to discontinue his vocation as a teacher, and as a consequence was in a desperate financial state (lines 20–23). He also mentions that he was now 'in his old Age (about seaventy yeares) cast into prison, without any other hope of releife then from your Ma[jes]t[ie]s Princely Compassion' (lines 24–26). He concluded by asking that Charles II would instruct the Treasurer to pay the £750 he was owed. This galvanized the king into some sort of action, for on 21 March 1675 Henry Coventry reported from the royal court in Newmarket that Charles II had referred the petition to Thomas Osborne, the Earl of Danby, the Lord High Treasurer.[67] There was some logic in asking Danby to consider the matter, for in early 1675 he was deeply involved in political debates about church–state relations and a petition from a prominent Dissenter meant he was the logical person to deal with it. Most significantly, the Treasurer supported the suppressing of Catholics and Dissenters as a means to building up a strong Anglican Church, and had urged that the licenses granted to conventicles under the *Declaration of*

---

[65] The appointment of David Walter is recorded in an order from Lord Arlington dated 19 October 1670 (TNA, SP 44/35A, page 19), and in a docquet dated 31 October 1670 (TNA, SP 38/24, page 248). An earlier draft of this appointment is found in TNA, SP 18/281, page 14.

[66] There is a discrepency of the actual amount expended here. Knollys' petition stated £760 (lines 27–28 and 45).

[67] TNA, Surveyor General Constat Book M—1675–1678 (CRES 6/12), page 304, lines 30–36.

Indulgence (1672) be revoked.[68] All of which suggests that Charles II would not have to worry very much about his Treasurer giving away anything to a disaffected Anabaptist. With this being so, it is not surprising that another lengthy delay followed in Knollys' case as the wheels of the Treasury seemingly ground to a halt.

The next document the deals with Knollys' case is a Treasury record of Knolly's request being logged in the Petitioners Entry Book by an unnamed clerk; it is undated but probably comes from the middle of 1677. The record contains a brief summary of Knollys' case, together with Treasurer Danby's resolutions about it (see Document #19).[69] It notes that previously in 1673 Sir Heneage Finch (then in his role as Attorney General) had already considered the petition and made a recommendation upon it. For himself, Danby resolved to speak with Charles Harbord about the matter. Apparently this conversation took place sometime in the middle of 1677, and there is a footnote reporting that Harbord had read the latest petition and was convinced of the equity of Knollys' case, suggesting once again that the petitioner either have the house or the £750 owed to him.

Meanwhile, Knollys' financial situation grew steadily worse. Sometime in late 1677 he wrote yet another petition, his sixth to the king; a copy of this petition was incorporated in a constat compiled by the Surveyor General Charles Harbord and dated 16 March 1678 (Document #20).[70] The tone of this petition is one of desperation, and the body contains only three short paragraphs. Knollys does not attempt to rehearse the history of his case in detail, but concentrates on the plight of himself and his family, stating that 'the Condit[i]on of himself & misserable family lye under even the pressure of Starveing without your Ma[jes]t[ie]s speedy mercy to his releife herein' (lines 93–95). On 24 December 1677 Charles Bertie, the Secretary to Treasurer Danby, reported that Danby had received Knollys' sixth petition from Charles II, along with some other supportive documents (including the forgotten fifth petition?), and that he had referred the case back to the Surveyor General Charles Harbord once again (lines 100–107). The long-suffering Harbord was asked to view the property and report back to Danby.[71]

The Surveyor General Charles Harbord's constat of 16 March 1678 once again offered a detailed report on the Knollys case. Harbord noted that he had considered several of Knollys' petitions and summarized the various administrative stages of his appeal. However, in the Surveyor General's discussion of this latest petition by Knollys a new feature appears which undermined the possibility of a lease being awarded to Knollys by the king. Ever since Harbord had first been asked to render an opinion about Knolly's case for the Old Artillery Ground in 1660, he had consistently presented the idea of a long-term lease to him as an equitable resolution

[68] Andrew Browning, *Thomas Osborne, Earl of Danby and Duke of Leeds, 1632–1712: Volume 1—Life* (Glasgow: Jackson, Son & Co., 1951): 146-184, discusses Danby's interest in ecclesiastical matters.

[69] TNA, Treasury Petitioners Entry Book—1677–78 (PRO 30/32/36), pages 12 and 62.

[70] TNA, Surveyor General Constat Book M—1675–1678 (CRES 6/12), page 304-307

[71] TNA, Surveyor General Constat Book M—1675–1678 (CRES 6/12), page 306.

of the dispute. Now, in dealing with Knollys' sixth petition, the possibility of such a lease is laid aside. The reason for this seems to be that Harbord had seen a copy of the royal patent granted by the king to his Lieutenant of Ordnance. Most importantly, lines 148–149 of Harbord's report quotes a crucial phrase found in from lines 14–15 of William Legge's patent: 'Custod[em] cuiusd[am] Gardin vulgarit[er] nuncupat[i] Artillery Gardin'. This is the only time that the actual Latin words from the patent are ever cited within the documents concerned with the Knollys case, and Harbord interpreted them to justify the opinion that the custody of the Old Artillery Ground was an integral component of the patent of the Lieutenant of Ordnance. Consequently, Harbord reported that 'the Pet[itione]r cannot have any Leave thereof without the Surrender of the said Grants, which wilbe opposed by the Office of the Ordnance' (lines 151–153). In conclusion, Harbord now agreed with the opinion of Lord Chancellor Finch (first put forward in June of 1674) that Knollys should be given the outstanding £700 for 'having been out of possession for about seaventeen yeares past' (lines 156–157). There is no indication that Harbord's recommendation to the Treasurer was acted upon, and there is every reason to believe that Danby would not have responded favourably to it (Danby and Harbord were political enemies).

Another eighteen months passed with nothing forthcoming from the Treasury, although there were administrative changes that help explain the delay. For one thing, Lord Danby was toppled from power, a victim of the hysteria surrounding the Popish Plot. He resigned from office on 25 March 1679 and was soon imprisoned in the Tower where he remained until 1684. He was replaced by a panel of Treasury Commissioners, and the changing of the guard may have inspired Knollys to try his luck one more time. He submitted another petition, his seventh, to the Lords Commissioners of the Treasury which was acknowledged by Sir Henry Guy, the new Secretary to the Treasury from the Treasury Chambers in Whitehall on 18 November 1679 (Document #21). Knollys included copies of his earlier petitions, along with the two reports of Lord Chancellor Finch on them, which were submitted to Charles II. He also noted how the king had then referred the matter to Treasurer Danby, who sent it to Charles Harbord and asked for his opinion in the matter. Knollys summarized the position:

> That upon ye whole matter as ye Case appeared before Them, they both concur yt a Satisfacton of 700*li* should be Given in money to your pet[itione]r he having been now 18 years out of possession of yt house w[hi]ch Cost him in purchase & building above 700*li* to his Great Losse and Damage & almost utter undoeing (lines 12–18).

He also stressed that the 'Conditon of himselfe & miserable distressed Family Lye under Much pressure of poverty' (lines 19–20), and, returning to the terms of his earliest petition, asked that they grant him a lease of ninety-nine years or order that the £700 he had expended be repaid to him (lines 22–24). This was the only way, he says, that they could be saved 'from utter ruine' (line 24).

Henry Guy's note on this final petition of Knollys explained that the Lords Commisioners of the Treasury wished the matter referred to the Surveyor General

William Harbord (1635–92), the son of Charles Harbord who succeeded his father as Surveyor General in May of 1679. It was also the wish of the Commissioners that Harbord consult the new Lieutenant of Ordnance, Captain George Legge, who assumed his post in April of the same year. Thus, in a bizarre twist of circumstance, Knollys' petition was to be reviewed by the sons of the very same men who first consulted over the matter nearly nineteen years before.

The new Surveyor General William Harbord responded to the Treasury order quite quickly, compiling a constat on Knollys' case which was submitted on 3 July 1680 (see Document #22). The constat not only includes a copy of Knollys' seventh petition and the order from Henry Guy dated 18 November 1679 (lines 6–30), but a copy of Harbord's own follow-up order to Colonel George Legge and the Ordnance Office dated 19 January 1680 (lines 31–39), a copy of the report from the Ordnance Office sent to Harbord dated 21 April 1680 (lines 40–56), and his own concluding recommendations on the matter (lines 58–77). Interestingly, Harbord introduced the copy of Knollys' petition with an opening heading line that does not appear in the petition itself, but one that perhaps hints at Harbord's own opinions about the case: 'The humble Petit[i]on of Hanserd Knollys a very poor & aged Minister' (line 6). A similar observation about 'this Poor man's Petit[i]on' (line 59) is included in Harbord's own concluding report.

Harbord's letter to Colonel Legge and the Ordnance Office specifically asked them to render an opinion in the matter. In order that they might make an informed decision, he sent them copies of two of Knollys' petitions to Charles II, copies of the two reports submitted by Lord Chancellor Finch, and a copy of the report of his father, Charles Harbord, on the subject dated 16 March 1678 (lines 38–40). The Ordnance Office report that was submitted to Harbord was signed by Colonel Legge and two other Ordnance officers, Edward Sherburne and Edward Conyers. Not surprisingly, their response was not very accommodating. Effectively they deferred to the opinion given by Lord Chancellor Finch in 1674, which gave the Ordnance Office full rights over the property, and denied the possibility of a lease for Knollys. The Ordnance Office even appeared to quibble over how much money Knollys had spent on the property ('the said Pet[itione]r hath disbursed (as is alledged) the best & greatest p[ar]t of his Estate in the Purchase'—lines 49-50), and suggested that the only possible way to resolve the matter lay beyond them: 'Our humble opinion is, That no better meanes can be proposed for his Compensat[i]on, Then by his Addresse (through their Lo[rdshi]ps mediat[i]on) to his Ma[jes]ty' (lines 52–53).

The Surveyor General's own recommendations on the matter do not go much beyond this. He too defers to the assessments put forward by Finch in 1674, and by his father in 1677. Some sympathy with Knollys' position of being caught in the middle between the Ordnance Office and the Artillery Company is indicated in lines 64–66: 'And the Pet[itione]r thinking he had bought a good Title of the Artillery Company w[hi]ch induced him to lay out all he had in the Purchase ye Building upon the premisses'. Harbord suggested that there was a case that Knollys be reimbursed for the money he had expended (the figures of £750 and £700 are noted in lines 68 and 70). Diplomatically, Harbord suggests that Knollys was 'a fit object for his

Ma[jes]t[ie]s Royall & Charitable Benevolence' (line 72), and appeals to 'your Lo[rdshi]ps Judgm[en]t & Compassion' (line 74) in helping to ensure that this was achieved. Despite Harbord's attempts to get financial help for Knollys, it does not appear that he ever was compensated for his loss. Perhaps the royal court was counting on the fact that the Baptist leader was now in his eighties, and would not be around much longer to irritate them with his numerous petitions about the Old Artillery Ground. In any event, in the spring of 1681 new plans for the property were beginning to be proposed which put an end to any hopes that Knollys might have had about justice being done in the matter.

The Sale of the Old Artillery Ground (1681–82)

In 1681 Charles II was facing a huge fiscal deficit, partly caused by the preparations made for the war with France in 1677–78. This meant that finances in the Ordnance Office were in a desperate state, as the Treasury struggled to pay off accumulated debts and satisfy creditors. One of the ways that Charles II tried to deal with this difficulty was by selling off crown property, and one of the properties that he decided could be sacrificed was the Old Artillery Ground in Spittlefields.[72] The first intimation of this is found in an order dated 7 April 1681 from Henry Guy, the Secretary to the Treasury, to the Ordnance Office.[73] Within it Guy noted that the sale of the Old Artillery Ground was projected to raise £3,000, although it was hoped that it might raise even more. There are several documents which relate to the sale of this property, many of them coming from the pen of Secretary Guy, who seemed to have had an active hand in the process and certainly did very well for himself out of it.

On 24 April 1681 Henry Guy wrote from the Treasury Chambers in Whitehall to Surveyor General William Harbord, asking him to view the Old Artillery Ground property and speedily submit a report to the Commissioners of the Treasury (see Document #23).[74] In particular, Harbord was asked 'what is the value of the Ground built & unbuilt, and what Improvem[en]t may be made of the same by building there upon' (lines 11–13). A survey map of the property, apparently completed in March of 1681, was sent to Harbord to assist him in his task (lines 4–7).[75] Harbord's report was done promptly and was completed on 11 May 1681, although it was not requested until 8 August 1681 when it was submitted to a Mr Aldworth (lines 89–91). Harbord reported that he had personally visited the site twice and had viewed both the ground and the houses located on it (lines 16–17). He divided the property into five separate sections and assigned values to each of them (lines 18–44). The total for the five sections came to £160 per annum, with Knollys' 'mesuage at the Southwest Corner' being valued at £30 per annum. As far as offering an opinion as

[72] H.C. Tomlinson, *Guns and Government: The Ordnance Office under the later Stuarts* (London: Royal Historical Society, 1979): 189, discusses this.

[73] TNA, Ordnance Office—Out Letters 1660–1683 (WO 46/1), folio 213 recto.

[74] TNA, Surveyor General Constat Book O—1679–1682 (CRES 6/14), pages 247-248.

[75] The map is almost certainly TNA, MPE 1/503.

to what improvements may be made upon the site by further buildings and new streets, Harbord wisely declined to answer, suggesting that the Surveyor General of the Works and other Officers under his command, who were used to working in the suburbs of the city of London, and whose daily task it was to deal with such matters, would be in a better position to say (lines 45–49).

Harbord includes in the final page of his report to the Commissioners of the Treasury a brief account of how the Old Artillery Ground had been used by the Ordnance Office, not only as the place of residence for the Master Gunner, but also as a storage site and a place for testing small weapons and training gunners in the art of warfare (lines 52–72). In passing he noted that in 1673 when his father (Charles Harbord) was Surveyor General, Lord Grandison had asked for a lease on part of the property, but that this was overruled by the needs of the Ordnance Office (lines 50–52). Harbord boldly suggested, as had his father before him, that any future grant of the property should include a proviso that the crown could, with proper compensation to the lease-holder, resume the premises if necessary (lines 75–85).

At this point it appears as if the desires of the Ordnance Office in keeping the Old Artillery Ground were overriding the aims of the Treasury in selling it off. It seemed that the only way that this could be resolved was for alternative locations to be found for the testing of military weaponry and housing the Master Gunner. On 13 November 1681 Henry Guy wrote to the Ordnance Commissioners precisely along these lines (see Document #24).[76] It seems that the Officers of the Ordnance Office had reported to their own Commissioners on 2 April 1681 that if alternative arrangements could be found they would have no objections to the sale of the property. In particular, Harbord asked the Ordnance Commissioners to confirm 'whether ye sayd Ma[ste]r Gunner be else where accomodated w[i]th another house & ground capable & fitt for the exercize of his Ma[jes]t[ie]s sayd Gunners' (lines 32–35). If so, then one of the major obstacles to the proposal was overcome and the proposed sale could go ahead. The Ordnance Commissioners must have provided the necessary assurance, for less than one month later, on 6 December 1681, Henry Guy wrote to the Sir Christopher Wren, the Surveyor General of the Works, about the proposed sale of the Old Artillery Ground property (see Document #25).[77] In this regard Guy was following up the suggestion made by William Harbord in his report of 11 May 1681. Wren was asked 'to certifie what this ground may be worth when Improved by Building and to endeavour to find out some p[er]sons to deale for building thereupon' (lines 8–10).

Sir Christopher Wren must have acted quickly, and provided the Commissioners of the Treasury with the information they requested, for less than three weeks later Henry Guy wrote to the Attorney General Sir Robert Sawyer (c.1633–92) with a specific legal question about the proposed sale (see Document #26). On 23 December 1681 Guy wrote from the Treasury Chambers to ask 'whether or no the King hath Powere to grant a Market to them that shall buy it' (lines 7–9). The

[76] TNA, Treasury Out Letter Book—1680–1682 (T 27/6), page 358.

[77] TNA, Treasury Reference Book of Applications—1680–1682 (T 4/1), page 500.

concern here was to make sure that the traditional rights of the city of London in establishing markets within the city and its environs were not being infringed upon. The Commissioners of the Treasury must have had some indication from Wren about the value of the property and some indication of interested parties, for on 23 December 1681 Guy also wrote to a number of potential buyers of the property (see Document #26). He sent letters to five people informing them of what price might be expected for the Old Artillery Ground; the five concerned were Sir William Warren, Thomas Neale, Dr Nicholas Barbon, Sir Christopher Wren and Sir William(?) Killigrew, and each probably had expressed some interest in the sale. Guy explained that 'in the Proposall for the artillery Ground, none are to bid under 400*li* without a Market, and not under 1200*li* more if a Market be obteyned and setled within two yeares after the grant is passed' (lines 13–17).

Things proceeded quickly with regard to the sale of the property. On 10 January 1682 Henry Guy wrote to Sir Robert Howard, the Auditor of the Receipt, instructing him to reserve the money paid into the Exchequer for the Old Artillery Ground to the use of the Commissioners of the Treasury (see Document #27).[78] There was almost certainly a personal incentive behind this instruction, as Guy later made sure that he received a healthy portion of the purchase price. Thus, on 20 January 1682 Guy again wrote to the Auditor of the Receipt instructing him to pay him (Guy) £500 out of the purchase money, 'For his Ma[jes]t[ie]s Secret service' (see Document #28, line 7).[79]

Meanwhile, on 18 January 1682 Charles II issued a warrant for a grant on the Old Artillery Ground property to be issued to George Bradbury and Edward Noel, two investors who were working in connection with Dr Nicholas Barbon, a well-known, if somewhat unprincipled, property speculator (see Document #29).[80] It is likely that Barbon was the driving force behind the sale, and on the same day Guy started a letter to Barbon informing him that the warrant for the property had been signed by the king (see Document #30).[81] However, this letter was never completed, or sent that day, probably because Barbon had not yet paid the money for the property. Indeed, this is not altogether surprising, for Barbon was characteristically slow to pay in money required to seal his property deals. In fact, Henry Guy had to write to Barbon on behalf of the Commissioners of the Treasury on 23 January 1682 (see Document #31),[82] telling him that they 'are informed from ye Excheq[ue]r That you have not paid in ye Purchase money for the Artillery Ground w[hi]ch they very much wonder at' (lines 4–7). He had to write a second time on 26 January 1682 (see Document #32),[83] explaining that the Treasury Commissioners were 'very Ill That you have not completed the payment of your purchase Money for the Artillery

[78] TNA, Treasury Disposition Books—1680–1684 (T 61/2), page 114.
[79] TNA, Treasury Disposition Books—1680–1684 (T 61/2), page 116.
[80] TNA, King's Warrant Book—1680–1683 (T 52/8), pages 305-307.
[81] TNA, Treasury Out Letter Book—1680–1682 (T 27/6), page 395.
[82] TNA, Treasury Disposition Books—1680–1684 (T 61/2), page 117.
[83] TNA, Treasury Out Letter Books—1680–1682 (T 27/6), page 399.

Ground' (lines 5–7). In any event, the royal warrant issued to Bradbury and Noel, who are described as 'Our Trusty and welbeloved Subjects' (Document #29, lines 9–10), stated the price to be paid for the property at £5,700 (line 11), a substantial increase on the minimum bid of £4,000 set earlier for the site without a market. A fairly full description of the property and its location is offered (lines 14–49). Interestingly, the property is described at one point as being 'formerly in the possession & occupat[i]on of Hanserd Knolls' (lines 27–28), the only time in any of the documents relating to the sale of the Old Artillery Ground that it is ever so described. Secretary Guy's letters to Nicholas Barbon produced the desired effect, for on 1 February 1682 Guy was able to write again to Sir Robert Howard, the Auditor of the Receipt, instructing him to transfer £5,200 out of the money paid for the Old Artillery Ground to the Treasurer of the Ordnance Office (see Document #33).[84]

It is not difficult to see why the Old Artillery Ground was the subject of so much interest. It was an open space that was not far outside the city walls of London, and was thus ideally located for development. The great fire of 1666 destroyed 13,000 homes and it took several decades for the city to recover from the devastation. Nicholas Barbon was a key figure in the redevelopment of London following the great fire, and thus contributed substantially to the shape of the modern city we know today.[85] Barbon was also extremely creative in the schemes he used to finance his redevelopment projects. He helped set up a property insurance scheme in 1683 which was financed in part by buildings erected on the Old Artillery Ground site. Interestingly, after the sale of the Old Artillery Ground had gone through and the area redeveloped successfully, Nicholas Barbon published *An Apology for the Builder* (1685), declaring his ideas about the economic advantages that the development of such places as Spittlefields had for the city of London at large. He argued that new developments meant an increase of trade in the area, and as a result property rents went up significantly:

> the Rents of the Houses in *Bishopsgate Street*, the *Minories*, &c are raised from fifteen or sixteen Pounds *Per Annum*, to be now worth thirty, which was by the increase of Buildings in *Spittle-Fields*, *Shadwells* and *Ratcliff-Highway* (page 21).

Barbon had a crucial role to play in the final chapter of the story of the Old Artillery Ground. The fact that he helped broker the sale of the site, effectively removing it permanently from the reach of Hanserd Knollys, means that he plays something of a villain's part in the whole process. Barbon is in many ways an enigmatic figure, and the early stages of his life are shrouded in mystery. It appears that he was awarded a medical degree from the University of Utrecht in 1661, and on this basis was named as an Honorary Fellow of the Corporation of the Kings College

---

[84] TNA, Treasury Disposition Books—1680–1684 (T 61/2), pagc 119.

[85] N.G. Brett-James, 'A Speculative London Builder of the Seventeenth Century, Dr. Nicholas Barbon', *London and Middlesex Archaeological Transactions*, New Series 6 (1929–32): 110-145, discusses his career.

of Physicians in London in 1684. But perhaps the most intriguing fact about him, at least as far as the petitions of a Baptist preacher/teacher for a plot of land outside Bishopsgate is concerned, is that Nicholas Barbon was the son of Praisegod Barbon (Barebone), who lent his name to the Nominated ('Barebones') Parliament of July–December 1653 and had close connections with many Baptist leaders. It is noteworthy that Praisegod Barbon was a member of the Leathersellers' Company, as was William Kiffen, who, as we discussed above, initiated the purchase of the Old Artillery Ground on behalf of the Baptists of London in 1658.

Hanserd Knollys' Plans for a Baptist Meeting House and School—A Dream Denied

We have already noted above that some of the documents relating to Knollys' case for the Old Artillery Ground do mention him leading a congregation on the site. What other evidence is there that Knollys' dreams for the Old Artillery Ground were ever realized? Was he able to establish a school on the site and fulfil his vocation as an educationalist? Did a Baptist congregation meet in the converted storehouse, and, if so, for how long? These are not easy questions to answer with any precision, and frequently they depend upon rather imprecise declarations about the geographical location of the congregation led by Knollys. The early Baptist historian Thomas Crosby never mentions the Old Artillery Ground site in his discussion of Knollys, although he does note that Knollys supported himself by his teaching ('the chief means of his subsistance was by teaching school'[86]). According to W.T. Whitley the church led by Hanserd Knollys from 1646–92 met in a number of places over the years, including the Old Artillery Ground. Whitley states that

> Knollys imparted a Fifth-monarchy tinge, so that the church was embroiled with the State from 1657 onwards; it then met on the *Old Artillery Ground*. After 1660 it wandered round Wapping (apparently in Shakespeare's Walk), Tower street, Artichoke lane at a house built for it, Booby lane, Broken wharf, George yard.[87]

Elsewhere, Whitley says, 'In 1676 he [Knollys] had been at Booby Lane, Wapping for apparently his lease of the old Artillery Ground had been cancelled.'[88] Curiously, Whitley also states that William Kiffen's church met in the Artillery Ground in 1669, although he does not give documentary evidence for this assertion.[89]

There are only a handful of documents from the 1660s which specifically mention Knollys as leading a church that met in the Old Artillery Ground. Several of these come from hostile sources. For example, one document, probably dating from 1660–

[86] Thomas Crosby, *The History of the English Baptists* (4 vols; London, 1738–40): I:339.

[87] W.T. Whitley, *The Baptists of London* (London: The Kingsgate Press, 1928): 107.

[88] W.T. Whitley, 'London Churches in 1682', *Baptist Quarterly* 1 (1922–23): 86. [article is pages 82-87].

[89] Whitley, *Baptists of London*: 106.

61, is entitled 'Hoax Preachers & Places'.[90] It lists fourteen Quaker and Baptist leaders, along with their places of worship, including a reference to 'Knowles neere the old Artillery ground'. A similar document, also probably from 1660–61, is entitled 'These Congregationall Ministers Preach Publiquely in or about London'.[91] It lists the names of thirty-six ministers, along with a brief description of where their churches were located. Included is an entry for 'Old Artillery- Mr Ha[n]s[erd] Knollys' (line 7). Moreover, at the bottom of the page there is a further note which reads: 'That in Petty France & by Dunstans East & at Old Artillery are large Assembling Places built of late.' This fits well with Knollys' own description of the Armory House, upon which he spent £400 making it into a church and schoolhouse (see chapter 2 for a discussion of these documents).

One other document, signed by Hanserd Knollys himself on behalf of the Baptists in London, also alludes to the Old Artillery Ground property. This is a petition submitted to the House of Lords on 4 May 1660; the petition states that the Baptist 'pet[itione]rs at theire great charge did buy and build severall howses in and about the Citty of London for theire publique meetings to worshipp the Lord in' (lines 5–6). At the time that Knollys wrote this petition Baptists were increasingly viewed with fear and suspicion, and at least one meeting house, that of William Kiffen, had been damaged by rioters. Little could Knollys imagine that in a little over a year the Old Artillery Ground property, into which he had invested so much time and money, would be lost to the denomination (see chapter 3 for more on this important document).

So where did Knollys and the Baptist congregation which he led meet after the Old Artillery Ground property was confiscated and occupied by soldiers from the Ordnance Office? Fortunately, there are one or two documents which offer some suggestions about that question. Of course we have to remember that Knollys himself was on the continent until the summer of 1663,[92] although he appears to have been in regular contact with his congregation in London. In any event, the short answer appears to be that Knollys and his fellow conventiclers met in the homes of some of their members. One such home was that of Mary Winch, a widow from the parish of Saint Giles, Cripplegate. There is record of six conventiclers being sent to Newgate prison on 10 December 1662 for a meeting which took place in Mary Winch's house. The six (including Mary Winch) were charged 'upon pretence of a religious worshipp & owne noe King, but King Jesus, and owne themselves to be Fift monarchie men'.[93] It is uncertain how long Mary and the others were detained in

---

[90] LMA, List of Hoax Preachers and Places (CLA/047/LR/02/02/001). The London Metropolitan Archives give this a tentative date of 1683, but it is more likely that it is from the early 1660s; the list also includes 'Jessey in Colemanstreete' (Henry Jessey died in 1663).

[91] TNA, SP 29/47, page 106.

[92] TNA, SP 29/79, page 146, TNA, SP 29/80, pages 31-32, SP 29/81, page 78, are ciphered reports from one of the informants of Harvey Bennet, the Secretary of State, about the activities of anti-royalists and Fifth Monarchists. Knollys is mentioned within these as having arrived in Wapping by August of 1663.

[93] TNA, SP 29/67, page 7.

Newgate prison, although it may have been as long as a month or so. There is record of an order from Charles II in Whitehall dated 13 January 1663 authorizing the release of conventiclers from Newgate, provided they were not 'dangerously seditious or seducers of others'. The order notes the king's thinking in the matter: 'Wee are willing to perswade ourselves that what they have now suffered will suffice to deterre them from falling into ye same faults again'.[94] In Mary Winch's case this was a forlorn hope, for she persisted in her involvement with Dissenters like Knollys.

The association of Mary Winch with Hanserd Knollys extended for several more years, as can be seen in a so-called 'conventicle conviction' dated 9 January 1665 (see Document #34).[95] This recounts that Hanserd Knollys and another man named Robert Siferwest, a glasier by trade, were convicted for attending an illegal meeting at the home of Mary Winch in Saint Giles, Cripplegate. The speed with which the legal process seems to have worked in this case is striking. The record suggests that the conventicle took place on Monday, the 9th of January, and that the conventiclers were brought before the two Justices of the Peace that very day. Unfortunately, Knollys' fellow convict, Robert Siferwest, remains something of a mystery; beyond the fact that he was a glasier from the parish of Saint Margaret, Westminster, nothing else is known about him. The illegal conventicle was also attended by seven other unknown people, in addition to the members of Mary Winch's family, although only Knollys and Siferwest were convicted and fined for their participation in the meeting. The two men were sentenced to three days imprisonment in Newgate prison or payment of a fine of two shillings each (lines 18–20).

This is a far cry from the dream Knollys had about opening a large meeting house and school in the Old Artillery Ground property he purchased in 1658. But the valour of Knollys' attempt shines through nonetheless, and the association of his name with the Baptist church in the Old Artillery Ground will abide as an example for all those interested in early Baptist commitments to education as an essential part of our denominational history.

---

[94] TNA, SP 29/67, page 89.

[95] LMA, Conventicle Convictions—1664–1665 (MR/R/C/001), membrane 35.

Figures

Figure #1 – Hanserd Knollys (c. 1599-1691).
Photograph courtesy of Dr Larry J. Kreitzer and used with the permission of The Angus Library and Archives, Regent's Park College

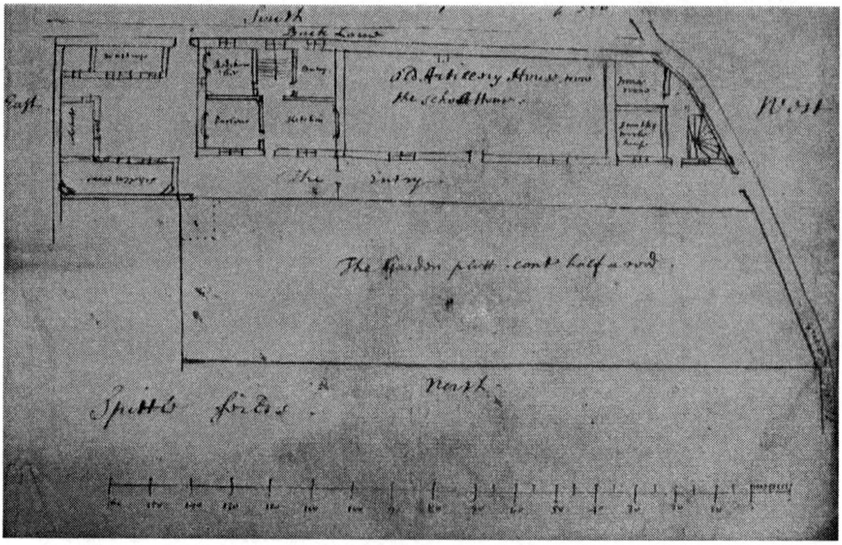

Figure #2 – Map of the Old Artillery Ground (c. 1660)

Documents

#1 – Agreement for the sale of the Old Artillery Ground by the Honourable Artillery Company to Richard Wollaston – 17 August 1658 (HAC, Minute Book of the Honourable Artillery Company – 1656–1661, page 40):

[Page 40]

Att the Co[ur]t house in the Artillery Ground ye 17th August 1658

President	Mr Wollastone beinge present assented
Treasurer	to an Agreement with the Court
Major Cruso	about the sale bargaine & sale
Lt Coll[onel] Rogers	of the Armory in the old Artillery Ground
Mr Sam[uel] Wilson	and hath appointed Mr Peryer
Lt Coll[onel] Mews	to pay to the Clerke of the Ar-
Capt Hind	tillery Company for the said
Capt Best	Companyes of the one hundred
Capt Hubland	& fifty pounds beinge p[ar]t of the
Mr Peryer	

three hundred pounds formerly agreed between ye said Company & Mr Wollastone & doth promise to pay the other hundred and fifty pounds upon the 29th of September next. The Clerke giveinge a receipt for the said monyes & to Enter ye said Agreement into this booke of orders.

#2 – Receipt on the sale of the Old Artillery Ground by the Honourable Artillery Company to Richard Wollaston – 29 September 1658 (HAC, Minute Book of the Honourable Artillery Company – 1656–1661, page 43):

[Page 43]

Mr Peryer by ye appointm[en]t of Mr Wollaston paid 150*li* to ye Clerke for ye Comp[any]

Received this 25 of August 1658 of Mr Peryer by the appointment of Mr Wollaston one hundred fifty pounds beinge p[ar]te of the 300*li* w[hi]ch the said Mr Wollaston £150 is to pay upon the Bargaine of the old Armoury say rec[eive]d for ye use of the Artillery Company

per me James Ragge Clerke

#3 – Report on the sale of the Old Artillery Ground by the Honourable Artillery Company to Richard Wollaston – 29 September 1658 (HAC, Minute Book of the Honourable Artillery Company – 1656–1661, page 5, 44-45):

[Page 44]

A Coppie of ye receipt given Mr Woollaston for 300*li* w[hi]ch hee gave to ye Company for ye Armoury in ye old Ground

The 29 Septemb[er] 1658

Received this day by the Clerke of ye Artillery Company of Mr Wollaston one hundred & fifty pounds now beinge the residue of the 300*li* from the bargaine of the Armory in the old Ground the receipt thereof being ordered to bee Entered into this booke of Orders. Received the 29th day of September, in the year of our Lord 1658, by mee James Ragge, Clerke of the Artillery Company of London, by the appointment and to the use of the said Compamy, of Richard Woollaston, of London, Esq[uire], the sume of Three hundred pounds of lawfull money of England, in full payment & sattisfacton, of & for the Ar-mory with the Co[ur]thouse, & all other the structures & buildings belongEinge to the said Company, scituate & beinge in the Old Artillery Garden, neere the Spittle, in the parish of Stepney Heath, al[ia]s Stepney, Bottolph W[i]thout Bishoppsgate, and Leonard Shoreditch, or some or any of them in the County of Midd[le]s[ex], which the said Company did heretofore Erect & build att theyre own proper Costs & Charges, by virtue of an Order graunted to the said Company by the late Kinge James and his Counsell, in the yeare of our Lord 1622. Whereby the said Company were Authorised thereunto, and to exercise armes in the said Artillery Garden: and in full payment & sattisfaction of and for all the State, right, title, interest, terme of yeares, possession, Reversion, property, clayme, & demand whatsoever of ye said Company, of, into, & out of ye said Armoury and buildings, and every part & parcel thereof, and of, in, and to all other the priviledges & advantages belongeinge to ye said Armory and buildings, graunted to the said Company by the same Order, or otherwise howsoever. To hold the said premisses unto the said Richard Woollaston, his heires, Executors, Adm[inistrat]ors, & As[igne]s, as amply to all intents & purposes whatsoever, as the said Company may, might, should, or ought to have held & enjoyed the same by any wayes or meanes whatsoever or howsoever; So that the said Company & their Successors, members of ye said Company, & every

[Page 45]

of them, of and from all challengs, claime, & demand of, into or out of ye said premisses and Every or any p[ar]t or parcell thereof, are and shall bee, by theis p[rese]nts, for ever barred & excluded; And it is promised by the said Company to the said Richard Woollaston, his heires, Exec[ut]ors, Ad[ministrat]ors, & As[sign]s, that w[i]thin one month next after the said Company, or any by theyre appointm[en]t, or to theyre use, shall receive or recover the said order (w[hi]ch is now wanteinge), and other writeings w[hi]ch concerne the premisses; the same shall be delivered to the said Richard Woollaston, his heires, Exec[ut]ors,

Ad[ministrat]ors, or Assignes. In wittness whereof, I, the said James Ragge, have hereunto sett my hand and seale, the day & yeare first above written by ye appointm[en]t and directon of ye now President, Dep[u]ty-President, Treasurer, and Co[u]rt of Assistants of the said Company, who have ordered the Registringe hereof in the booke belongeing to ye said Company, as an evidence of ye Sale of ye premisses to ye said Richard Woollaston, his heires, Exec[ut]ors, Adm[inistrat]ors, or Assignes, accordinge to the true purporte & true meaneinge hereof.

James Ragge

#4 – Report on the Petition of William Kiffen for a Lease on the Old Artillery Ground – 5 October 1658 (TNA, SP 18/183, page 6):

Tuesday 5th October 1658

By the Com[mitt]ee of ye Councell to whom the petiton of W[illia]m Kiffin and diverse others on behalfe of themselves and ye Congregatons to which they are related is referred.

Whereas the petitoners doe by their petiton pray a graunt of the ould Artillery ground with the buildings therein (except the house and place for proofe of Musketts and Liberty for the practise of ordinance in the gunrange) for the use of the said Congregations, for the terme of 99 yeares. Ordered that the Com[mission]ers of the Admiralty and Navy be desired to view or Cause to be viewed The said Artillery grounds, and buildings, and to Consider what thereof may be Conveniently graunted to the pet[ition]ers, for their accomodation, w[i]thout prejudice to the State; and to certifie their opinion in that behalfe to the Counsell.

W[illiam] Jessop S[ecretary] of ye Counsel

#5 – Report of a Survey done by Officers of the Ordinance Office – 31 December 1658 (incorporating an order by the Commissioners of the Admiralty and Navy dated 16 October 1658) (TNA, SP 18/184, pages 143-144):

[Page 143 recto]

16 October 1658

By the Com[missione]rs for ye Adm[ira]ltie and Navie

In pursuance of an order of ye Councell dated ye 5th instant, whereof ye annexed is a Coppie ordered that ye officers of ye ordinance doe forthwith view ye old Artillery Ground with ye Buildings on itt, as is directed by ye said order, and upon due consideraton amongest themselves returne us their opinion what thereof may be conveniently granted to Mr Kiffin and ye other petitoners for their Accomodaton without prejudice to ye State.

Ed[ward] Salmon John Clerke Tho[mas] Kelsey

In pursuance of your Honours orders above recited, Wee have viewed ye old Artillery Ground, with ye Buildings thereupon, A Draught whereof is herewith returned and doe humbly Certifie as followeth.

That the said Ground beinge enclosed w[i]th a Brick Wall 12 foote high, doth conteine 04 Acres 03 R[ood] 10 Poles whereof upon ye North Side is ye Gun-range 12 yards broad and 235 yards longe wherein ye Ma[st]er Gunners in tyme past did exercise their office in teaching all such persons as desired to bee disciplined in ye Art of Gunnerie, on ye South parte of this Ground is erected an Armourie and Courte house with a workehouse, all built of Brick att ye Charges of ye Pres[iden]t and Companie of Artillery of London

[Page 143 verso]

were permitted by ye late Kinge James with ye Advice of his Councell in ye yeare 1622, to exercise & practise ye Art of Drillinge All which Edifices are yett standing upon ye States Soyle, and lately Sold by ye s[ai]d Artillery Companie unto ye Petitoners.

Upon ye North wall of this Ground stands ye Ma[st]er Gunners house with a Washhouse and Stable, twoe small Stoarehouses by ye Pond and a Porters Lodge at ye Gate, all which with ye Herbage have beene in ye occupaton of ye severall M[ast]er Gunners from tyme to tyme and may bee esteemed of ye yearely value of 30*li*. Now if itt seeme meete to ye wisdome of his Highnes and Councell to grant ye pet[ition]ers A Lease of ye premisses as is desired, then wee humbly conceive and offer itt as our opinion, that ye Gunrange bee Excepted for Experim[en]ts in gr[ea]t ordinance, so often as may bee necessarie or ye State thinke fitt to make use thereof. Alsoe all yt Shedd built upon ye East wall of ye Gunrange for proofe of Hand Gunns and yt other small Structure of Brick att the East end of ye Armoury which hath beene & daily is used for ye loadeinge, Search, blowinge & viewings of Hand Guns, before and after proofe togeather with Ingresse, Egresse and Regresse to and for ye Officers of ye ordnance, and whom they shall appointe, with Carts and Horses or other Carriages, as occasion shall require for ye proofe of hand Guns and the Experiment of ordnance as afores[ai]d.

[Page 144 recto]

And yt such Lease bee made by and betweene ye Office of ye ordnance for and on ye part of his Highnes ye Lord Protector on ye one part And ye Petitioners of such as they shall nominate on ye other parte, under such Rents or quitt Rents, Services, Limitatons, Covenants and Restrictions as His Highnes and Councell shall thinke fitt.

The Counterparte of which Lease to remaine in this office upon Record to ye intent yt ye State may receive their Rights againe, when ye Lease is expired. All which wee nevertheles submitt to your Honours great wisdome, and remaine

Office of ye ordn[an]ce Your Honours most humble
31 December 1658 Servants

Elia Palmer [signature] [Lewis] Audeley [signature]
Jo[hn] Falkener [signature] Will[ia]m Billers [signature]

#6 – Hanserd Knollys petitions the Court of the Honourable Artillery Company for support in his case for the Old Artillery Ground property – 18 July 1660 (HAC, Minute Book of the Honourable Artillery Company – 1656–1661, page 93):

[Page 93]

Att a Co[ur]t of Assistants of the Artillery Company held att the Worthy &c W[illia]m Vincents Dep[ut]y President, 18 July 1660

Sir W[illia]m Vincent Dep[ut]y President

Coll[onel Owne	Captain Burkin
Lt Coll[onel] Rogers	Coll[onel] Mews
Capt[ain] Stevenson	Major Kilby
Capt[ain] Houblon	Capt[ain] Sheppeard

Mr Hansheard Knolls presented a Peticon to this Co[u]rt relateinge the greate Charge hee hath beene att in repayringe the old Armory in B[isho]ppsgate streete and that if this Co[u]rt doe not assist him hee is likely to bee turned out of it, whereupon it was resolved that 3 doe attend upon Coll Legg (viz Coll[onel] Mews, Capt[ain] Sheppeard & Capt[ain] Peryer and that they accquaint him w[i]th the Sale of the house and that the Artillery Company was att ye Charge of the buildinge of it).

#7 – Treasurer Southampton orders the Surveyor General to consider Hanserd Knollys' Petition – 25 September 1660 (TNA, Lord Southampton's General Entry Book – 1660 (T 51/1), page 152):

[Page 152)

Knollis Hanserd
Artillery Ground

September ye 25th 1660

Upon the petiton of Hanserd Knollis Clerke referred by his Ma[jes]ty ye 31th of July last praying a grant of a certaine building & parcell of ground in fee farme, scituate nere the Spittle called ye old Artillery ground purchased by ye petio[ne]r from ye Company of Artillery of ye Citty of London who hold the same from ye late King James.

I pray Mr Surveyor Gen[er]all to consider of this Petiton and to Certifie me what he conceives fit to be done therein in order to a rent & fine to be referred if it be fit to be leased.

T[reasurer] Southampton

#8 – Knollys' case for the Old Artillery Ground is discussed by the Court of the Honourable Artillery Company who agree to write to Charles II on his behalf – 14 October 1660 (HAC, Minute Book of the Honourable Artillery Company – 1656–1661, pages 98-99):

[Page 98]

Att a Co[ur]t of Assistants of the Artillery Company held att ye greate James Taverne 14th Octob[er] 1660

Sir W[illia]m Vincent Dep[ut]y Presedent

Coll[onel Crusoe	Captain Burkin
Samuell Wilson	Capt Peryer
Capt Best	Lt Coll Hind

[Page 99]

Mr Knollys informeinge this Court that Lt Coll Manby hath not made his appearance att Denmark house accordinge to ye Sumons sent to him by S[i]r Charles Herbert Surveyor Generall, it is therefore Ordered there bee a Peticon drawne by Capt Peryer & ye Clerke & directed to his Ma[jes]tie in the behalfe of ye said Mr Knollys w[hi]ch Petiton ye Presed[en]t Deputy Presed[en]t are desired to take ye Care in ye delivereinge of it.

#9 – Treasurer Southampton orders a constat for Hanserd Knollys' case – 24 November 1660 (incorporating Charles Harbord's report on Knollys' second petition dated 12 November 1660) (TNA, Surveyor General Papers – 1660–1662 (LR 17/2):[96]

[Obverse]

May it please your Lo[rdshi]p

I find that ye old Artillery ground mentoned in Mr Knollis Petiton did antiently belong to ye Crowne, & was used by the Master Gunner of England as belonging to his office for the tryall of Cannon &c. And King James in 1622 did make an Order that the Artillery Company of ye Citty should excercise their Armes there on certain dayes of ye weeke, w[hi]ch they accordingly used & built a Roome thereupon about 63 foot long and 24 foot wide & some other Roomes adjoyning fitt for that service. And having since gotten a new Artillery ground neer Moorfeilds, they have taken upon them to make sale of the said Roome & other Buildings, & of a stripe of ground for a passage to ye said buildings

[96] A copy of this document (with minor spelling variations) is contained in TNA, Lord Southampton's General Entry Book—1660–61 (T 51/2), pages 27-28.

about 10 foote wide togeather w[i]th a small yard at the East end thereof unto one Richard Wollaston, Esq[uire], for the Petitoners use for 300*li*. And the Petitoner believing it to be the right of the said Company & not his Ma[jes]ties inheritance as he professeth was induced so to purchase it & hath since layed out 400*li* more in altering & new buildings upon the premisses. And hath since obtayned leave under the late usurped Authority to inclose a small p[ar]cell of ground adjoyning containing about 20 p[er]ches p[ar]cell of the said old Artillery Ground for a Garden plott & doth teach a schoole & excerise his profession as a Preacher to a Congregation of
in the said Roome or Armory house
persons of his owne opinion ^ & seemeth to be a man of a peaceable behaviour & good life, having bred up his owne sonn & others now Preachers & conformable to the Church Governm[en]t now established as I am informed & would be utterly undone w[i]th his wife & family if the said House & buildings should be taken from him.
I have sum[m]oned those of the said Artillery Company ment[i]oned in his Petit[i]on & have heard them & ye Master

[Reverse]

Gunner touching their sev[er]all p[re]tent[i]ons to ye p[re]misses and cannot find that ye said Company had ever any Grant of ye p[re]misses or other Interest therein, then the said Order of King James in 1622. Albeit they p[re]tend to have better Evidence then they could produce, the same being imbesiled & lost as they alleaged, but the Master Gunner seemed to thinke the said great roome or Armory usefull for his Ma[jes]t[ie]s service to keepe the Carriages of his Cannon there dry & free from the weather, but I thinke they may be much better kept in the Tower or within his Ma[jes]t[ie]s yards in the Minneryes for many reasons w[hi]ch your Lo[rdshi]p may please to hear & consider w[i]th those of the Officers of the Ordnance.
If his Ma[jes]ty shall vouchsafe the Petit[i]oner a Lease of ye said House, Buildings, pasage & yard w[i]th all or p[ar]t of the said Garden I shalbe ready to make a Perticuler of the passing thereof upon your Lo[rdshi]ps warr[an]t for such terme of yeares, fine & rent as his Ma[jes]ty or your Lo[rdshi]p shall direct. All w[hi]ch I most humbly submitt to your Lo[rdshi]ps great wisdome.

C[harles] Harbord Sup[er]visor
12 No[vember] 1660
November the 24th 1660
Mr Surveyor Gennerall Make a Constat of this

Pet[ion]ers Interest in order to a Lease for 21 yeares at such Rent & fyne as you shall reasonably in his Ma[jes]tys behalfe propose, but before he doth the same, I desire him to conferr w[i]th the M[aste]r of his Ma[jes]tys Ordnance to consider whether the great Roome be usefull for that purpose it is desired. It seeming usefull to me as well as to yourself that his Ma[jes]tys stores of that nature should lye out of the Tower.

T[reasurer] Southampton

#10 – The Surveyor General's constat concerning Hanserd Knollys' Petition – 18 December 1660 (incorporating three earlier documents: Treasurer Southampton's order dated 25 September 1660 to the Surveyor General Charles Harbord asking him to consider an attached petition of Knollys; Edward Nicholas' order dated 31 July 1660 to the Commissioners of the Treasury asking them to consider an attached petition of Knollys; and Treasurer Southampton's order dated 24 November 1660 asking Harbord to compose a constat on Knollys' case) (TNA, Hanserd Knollys Petition – Surveyor General Constat Book B – 1660–1661 (CRES 6/2), pages 88-92 and 293-94):

[Page 88]

Hanserd Knollis
Artillery Yard

To ye R[igh]t Hono[ra]ble the Lords Comi[ssione]rs of ye Treasury
The humble petiton of Hanserd Knollyes Clerk

In all humility Sheweth,

That your pet[ition]er findeing himselfe disturbed & in danger of further disturbance concerning the Tytle & poss[ess]eon of his Howse p[ur]chased of the Artillery Company of London did in humble manner addresse himselfe to his most sacred Ma[jes]tie who upon consideration of his petiton and of ye Justice and merritt of his Cause therein sett forth was most gratiously pleased referr himself to your most hono[ra]ble Lo[rdshi]pps as by the petiton, and ye order of Reference thereupon hereunto annexed may appeare.

To the end therefore yt your pet[ition]er may be the better enabled to assert his owne right & to sett forth before your Lo[rdshi]pps the equity of his Cause, Hee doth most humbly pray that your Lo[rdshi]pps would be pleased to allow him ye benefitt of Councell before your Lo[rdshi]pps he being ignorant of the Law and to direct your order to James Ragg, Clarke to the said Company of

Artillery and to Coll[onel] Menes, L[ieutenan]t Coll[onel] Hinde, Capt[ain] Prior
Capt[ain] Beast and Capt[ain] Shepard, members of ye said Company
at ye time when your pet[ition[er] p[ur]chased, to appeare before your Lo[rdshi]pps
to certifie the truth of the matter contayned in the annexed

[Page 89]

petiton upon heareing whereof your petitioner does not doubt but your Lo[rdshi]pps
will deale with him according to your accustomed Justice & the Equity of
your proceedings in cases of like notice.
And your petitioner shall ever pray &c
Artillery Yard Hanserd Knollis

Sept[ember] ye 25th 1660
I pray Mr Surveyor Gen[er]all to consider of this petition & to certifie
mee what hee conceaves fitt to be done therein in Order to a Rent & Fine
to be reserved if it be fitt to be Leased.
T[reasurer] Southampton

To ye Kings most Ex[cellen]t Ma[jes]tie
The humble petition of Hanserd Knollis, Clarke

Sheweth
That your Ma[jes]ties Grandfather ~~Gen~~ King James of blessed memory did by
an Order of his most hono[ra]ble Councell give and grant unto ye Society of ye
Artillery Company of London that p[ar]cell of ground (antiently called
now called ye old artillery ground adjoyneing unto Spittle Fields of old called old porch
the Tazell Close) ^ without Bishopsgate, London for ye Exercise of Armes
there w[hi]ch ground the said Artillery Company enlarged for the conve-
niency of practice and they alsoe erected and builded an Courthouse,
Armory House ^ and other small structures in the said Ground
at ye prop[er] cost and charges of ye s[ai]d Artillery Company for the
Exercise of ye Honour of Armes.
That the said Artillery Company haveing obtayned another p[ar]cell
of ground for ye Exercise of Armes (called the new Artillery
ground on Bun-hill in Finsbery neere Moorfeilds) did sell the s[ai]d

old Armory Howse, Court howse and other Structures thereunto belonging (w[hi]ch they builded for their use at their owne prop[er] cost and charges) scituate and being at ye Southend of the s[ai]d old Artillery ground withall the Estate, Tytle, Right, Interest & Lib[er]ty w[hi]ch the said Company had or ought to have had in the said Ground unto Rich[ard] Wolaston Esq[uire] ^& his^ assignes for 300*li* (in trust for your pet[ition]er who payd the said 300*li* unto ye said Company) who hath since assigned over ye s[ai]d premisses by his Deed unto

[Page 90]

your pet[ition]er according to his trust, and your pet[ition]er is in poss[ess]eon thereof.

That your pet[ition]er since hee p[ur]chased the said premisses hath at his great cost and charges (for his conveniency of teaching schoole and boarding scholars) repaired the said Armory howse & other structures & builded a dwelling howse where ye Court howse was w[i]th two necessary sheds. And by compusition w[i]th the said Rich[ard] Wollaston hath poled & fenced in a little screed or p[ar]cell of ground for a Garden at his owne cost and charges also, for w[hi]ch he is to pay the yearly Rent of 20*li* unto the said Rich[ard] Wollaston as Ma[st]er Gunner or to his Successors.

That to the intent your pet[ition]er his wife and children may not by any wayes or meanes be molested or interrupted in the posseon of the said premisses nor hereafter be prevented in the peceable enjoym[en]t of that w[hi]ch your pet[ition]er really p[ur]chased repayred and built at his great cost and Charges but may quietly enjoy the same.

Your pet[ition]er doth most humbly pray your Ma[jes]tie to give & grant unto your pet[ition]er, his Ex[ecuto]rs and Ass[ign]es all the said Premisses & the said Garden and ground (w[hi]ch is inclosed & separated by walls Poles & buildings from ye other p[ar]te of the s[ai]d Artillery ground) in Feetfarme by patent dureing the terme of 99 yeares and ye s[ai]d Rent of 20*li* p[er] ann[um] to be payd to your Ma[jes]ties Ma[st]er Gunner or his Successors by the pet[ition]er or his Assignes, or under such yearly rent and to such p[er]son or p[er]sons as your Ma[jes]ty shall thinke fitt.

And your p[etition]er shall ever pray &c

Hanserd Knollis

At ye Court at Whitehall this 31st day of July 1660

His Ma[jes]ty is pleased to referr the consideration of this pet[ition]er to ye R[igh]t Hono[ra]ble the L[or]ds Com[ission]ers of ye Trea[su]ry to certifie what they conceave fitt to be done herein for his Ma[jes]ties Service

Edw[ard] Nicholas

[Page 91]

May it please your Lo[rdshi]p

I finde that the old Artillery Ground mentoned in Mr Knollys petiton did antiently belong to the Crowne & was used by the Ma[st]er Gunner of England as belonging to his Office for the Tryall of Common &c And King James in 1622 did make an Order that ye Artillery Company of ye Citty should exercise their Armes there on certaine days of ye weeke, w[hi]ch they accordingly used, and built a Roome thereupon about 63 foot long and 24 foot wide and some other Roomes adjoyn-ing fitt for service.

And having since gotten a new Artillery ground neer Moore fields, they have taken upon them to make Sale of the said Roome and other buildings & of a stripe of ground for a passage to ye said buildings about 10 foot wide, togeather w[i]th a small yard at ye east end thereof, unto one Richard Wollaston Esq[uire] for ye pet[ition]ers use, for 300*li*. And Pet[ition]er beleeving it to be ye right of ye said Company and not his Ma[jes]ties Inheritance as hee p[ro]fesseth was induced soe to p[ur]chase it, & hath since layd out 400*li* more in altering of new buildings upon ye premisses. And hath since obtayned leave under the late usurped Authority to incl[ose] there(?) a small p[ar]cell of ground anjoyning, rent ab[ou]t 20*li*, p[ar]cell of ye said old Artillery yard ground for a garden plott and doth teach a Schoole and exercise his p[ro]fession as a preacher to a Congregation of p[er]sons of his owne opinion in the said Roome or Armory Howse and seemeth to be a man of a peaceable behaviour and good life, having bred up his own Sonne and others now preach-ers and conformable to ye Church Governm[en]t now esta-blished as I am informed, and would be utterly undone w[i]th his Wife and family if ye said Howse & buildings shouldbee taken from him.

I have sumoned those of ye said Artillery Company ment[i]oned in his petiton & have heard them and the Ma[st]er Gunner touching their sev[er]all p[re]sentations to ye p[re]misses &

[Page 92]

cannot find, that ye said Company had ever any Great of ye p[re]misses or other Interest therein, then the said

Order of King James in 1622 albeit they p[re]tend to have better evidence then they could p[ro]duce, the same being imbesiled and lost as they alleadged, but ye Ma[st]er Gunner seemed to thinke the said Great Roome or Armory usefull for his Ma[jes]ties service to keepe the Carriages of his Cannon there dry & free from ye weather, but I thinke they may be much better kept within the Tower or within his Ma[jes]ties yards in ye mineryes, for many reasons, w[hi]ch your Lo[rdshi]pp may please to heare and consider w[i]th those of the officers of ye Ordinance.

If his Ma[jes]ty shall vouchsafe ye pet[ition]er a Lease of ye said Howse Buildings passage & yard w[i]th all or p[ar]t of ye said Garden, I shalbe ready to make a Perticuler for ye passing thereof upon your Lo[rdshi]ps war[ran]t for such terme of yeares fine and Rent as your Lo[rdshi]pp shall direct. All w[hi]ch I most humbly submitt to your Lo[rdshi]ps great wisdome.

C[harles] H[arbord] Sup[er]visor K[nigh]t gen[er]all
12 Nov[ember] 1660

[Page 293]

Nov[ember] the 24th 1660

Old Artillery Ground

Mr Surveyor Generall make a Constat of this Pet[ition]ers interest in Order to a Lease for 21 yeares at such Rent and Fine as you shall reasonably in his Ma[jes]t[ie]s behalf propose, but before hee doth the same I desire him to conferr with the M[aste]r of his Ma[jes]t[ie]s Ordinance to consider whether the great Roome be usefull tor that p[ur]pose it is desired. It seemeing unfitt to mee as well as to your selfe that his Ma[jes]t[ie]s Stores of that nature should lye out of ye Tower.

T[reasurer] Southampton

Com[itatu] Midd[lesex] Parcell[um] possession[em] D[omi]ni R[egi]s in Com[itatu] pred[icto]

Mr Knollis

Firma unius mesuag[i] sive Ten[amen]ti scituat[i] super quoddam magn[um] Gardin sive p[ar]cell[um] terr[e] incluss[um] quond[am] vocat[um] Tasell Close vel le Old Artillery Ground in vel prope spittle Feilds extra Bishoppsgate in vel prope p[ar]ochia[m] de Stepney in Com[itatu] p[re]dict[o]. Ac totius ill[ius] magne Aule ib[ide]m edificat[e] nup[er] voc[ate] le Armory Roome continen[tis] sexagint[a] tres pedes aut eo circiter in Longitudine, et circa vigint[i] quatuor pedes in Latitudine, una cu[m] quadam pecia terr[e] incluss[a] pro passagio ducen[te] ad aulam et mesuag[ium] p[re]dict[a] cont[inente[in Latitudine circa decem pedes. Ac unius parvi Gardin[i] nup[er] cu[m] paliciis incluss[i] ad boreal[em] partem dicti passagii adjungen[tis] cont[inentis] p[er] estim[ationem] vigint[i] p[er]ticas p[ar]cell[i] d[i]cti magni gardini vocat[i] ye Artillery ground existen[tis], modo in tenur[e] Hanserdi Knollis Cler[ici] vel assignator[um] suor[um] una cu[m] o[mn]ibus domibus edificiis structuris curtilagiis viis passagiis easiamentis p[ro]ficuis com[m]oditatibus et p[er]tinen[tiis] quibuscumq[ue] p[re]dict[is] messuag[io] sive ten[amen]to aut ceteris p[re]missis aliquo modo spectan[tibus] vel p[er]tinen[tibus] val[ua] p[er] ann[um]

[Page 294]

I have conferred w[i]th the M[ast]er of his Ma[jes]t[ie]s Ordinance touching ye premisses & doe not find by him that there is any great use of ye said Armory Roome for his Ma[jes]t[ie]s Service & wisheth as I doe yt ye s[ai]d Artillery Ground were exchanged for some other peece of Ground lyeing more neer to the Tower & more easie of accesse for his Ma[jes]t[ie]s Carriages and tryall of his Cannon. In case a Lease of the premisses for xxxi yeares be granted to Mr ~~Han~~ Knollis (for whome this Constant is made) I thinke it reasonable in respect of his great charge of six or seaven hundred pounds layd out in the p[ur]chase of p[ar]te of ye premisses under the late usurped authority and in new buildings & repayring the same since, that ye rent of 20*li* p[er] ann[um] being reserved according to his Ma[jes]t[ie]s Instructons as moyety of ye improved value. It maybe reasonable to take a small Fine for the same.

The rent is to be received payable at ye Anunciaton & Mich[aelm]as by equall p[or]tons. Provided if it shalbe unpayd by ye space of three monthes next after either of the said Feasts, Or if the Grant be not Inrolled w[i]th the Auditor or ye Fine payd within 6 monthes after the date the Lease to be voyd.

The Lessee is to Covenant to keepe & mainteyne ye premisses in good repayratons dureing the said terme & soe to leave it and to deliver to the Auditor a true extent of ye quantity meetes & boundaryes of ye premisses once in every 3 yeares to preserve ye knowledge thereof for his Ma[jes]t[ie]s service.

This Constat is made by Order of ye right Hono[ra]ble ye L[or]d High Trea[sure]r of England of ye 24th of Nov[ember] last.

Ex p[er] C[harles] Harbord Sup[er]visor
18 Dec[ember] 1660

The petitons ent[er]ed fol[ium] 88.

[Translation of lines 157-181]

County of Middlesex — Parcell belonging to the Lord King in the said County

Mr Knollis — Grant of a mesuage or Tenament situated overlooking a certain large Garden enclosing a piece of ground once called Tasell Close or the Old Artillery Ground in or near spittle Feilds outside Bishoppsgate in or near the parish of Stepney in the said County. And of all that large Hall built in the same place lately called the Armory Roome measuring sixty-three feet or thereabouts in Length, and around twenty-four feet in Width, together with a certain enclosed piece of ground [serving] as a passage leading to the aforesaid Hall and mesuage measuring about ten feet in Width. And of a small Garden lately enclosed with poles to the north side of the said adjoining passage consisting of approximately twenty perches parcel of the said large garden called ye Artillery ground being presently in the tenure of Hanserd Knollis, Clerk, or his assignes, together with all the houses, buildings, structures, curtilages, ways, passages, easements, profits, commodities, and advantages, whatsoever in any way regarding or pertaining to the aforesaid Mesuage or tenament or other premisses. Value per annum.

#11 – Memorandum on Hanserd Knollys' case for the Old Artillery Ground – 1660 (TNA, Hanserd Knollys' Memorandum on the Old Artillery Ground (LR 17/8):

[Page 1 recto)

Mr Knollys his Case touching the
old Artillery house &c

The Artillery Gentlemen Certify that King James did graunt them his Order to Exercise Armes & to build an House & other necessary structures for that use in the field call Tazel Close, since called the old Artillery Ground. Thereupon the Citizens of London w[hi]ch exercise the Honour of Armes builded an Armory house & other structures and enlarged the Ground for con-venience of Practice by virtue of his Ma[jes]ties Order graunted them Anno 1622 at the Cost & Charges of the said Artillery Company. Which Armory house & other structures they sold to Mr Richard Wolaston Esquire in Trust for Mr Hanserd Knollys for 300*li*. And they Certifyed Mr Surveyor Generall that they did not doubt but they had a Legall Right by his Ma[jes]ties Order to dispose of the said Houses, but the said Order & severall other writeings touching the premisses were Imbezelled & detained from them, w[hi]ch writeing they supposed were now in the handes or Custody of one Mr William Manbye or some other p[er]sons, their Executor, Executors, Administrator or Administrators of one Coll[onel] Manbye Late deceased. But they not being a Corporation were not in a Capacity to reco-ver them out of his or their Handes wherepon they desired & obtained an Order from ye Surveyor Generall to to require Mr W[illia]m Manbye or any other p[er]sons who had any writeings Concerning the Artillery Company & the Houses & Ground by them claimed to be by him p[rai]sed for his Ma[jes]ties service, and the determining ye Interests of w[hi]ch Order was given to Mr W[illia]m Manbye (by Capt James Ragge, Clarke of the Artillery Company in the p[re]sence of Mr Brome & Mr Biby) who said he would appear at the houre & place Mentioned in the said Order but he did not appeare nor send any writeings unto the Surveyor Generall. But M[aste]r Gunner of England Coll[onel] Weames did appear upon the Surveyor Generalls Order and Claimed an Interest in the said Howes as a p[er]quisite unto his Office and also told the Surveyor Generall that his Ma[jes]tie needed the said Artillery or Armory house to keep the Carrages of his Guns dry, but w[hi]ch all Confessed that none of the premisses were mentioned in his Patent.

[Page 1 verso)

Only M[aste]r Gunner said that though he had noe writeings to shew for the Ground & houses thereon yet he could prove by witnesses that both he & his predecessors always enjoyed the benefit of some houses & of all the Ground except the Armory house & other structures w[i]th the s[ai]d Artillery Company builded w[hi]ch they enjoyed, & yt now they having left it, M[aste]r Gunner said he Conceived yt it belonged to his Ma[jes]tie of right, & that both he & S[i]r W[illia]m Compton, M[aste]r of the Ordinance, judged that the Armory house would be usefull for his Ma[jes]ties service, but yet M[aste]r Gunner did say yt if his Ma[jes]tie should take the Armory from Mr Knollys, then Mr Knollys had noe place to teach his scholars in, nor the Congregation had noe place to meet in & soe the poore man would suffer very much damage for he assaid M[aste]r Gunner an honest godly man though he differ in Judgment from us in some things, and I would not prejudice him soe much for my part. But there is Coll[onel] Legge, L[ieu]t[e]n[ant] of the Ordinance who hath ye Old Artillery Ground in his Patent, that sent to discharge Mr Knollys out of all yt he hath bought, builded & now possess there, & also saith that the Ground & houses thereon are his. Mr Knollys told the Surveyor Generall that he paid 300*li* for the Intrest that ye Artillery Company had there in the houses & Ground, & also that he had laid out about 400*li* more in building & repaireing the said premisses for his use & Conveniency in teaching & boarding scholars. And unlesse it shall please his Ma[jes]tie to Confirme it to him, he and his wife and three Children, were likely to be ruined in their outward subsistance & livelihood. The said 700*li* being all that estate he had by his labour & diligent gotten this 10 years in teaching schoole. But hon[our]able Mr Knollys was willing to Lay himself & his small estate & the livelyhood of his wife & Children at his Ma[jes]ties feet most humbly begging that he might either peaceably enjoy the premisses, or be by his Ma[jes]ties Order to the Artillery Company & M[aste]r Gunner be by them, or by some other meanes reimbursed of the said 700*li* wereupon the Surveyor Generall said he would draw up a Report upon the Reference and aquaint my Lord Treasurer w[i]th it & soe know his Ma[jes]ties pleasure & Determination in this Matter.

[Page 2 recto)

The ~~Artillery~~ Armory now converted into a school is long ways 63 feet
& broad 24 & a little more of brick strong building of 5 bayes
~~of building~~ 20 feet high tassle wall plates, boarded w[i]th
daube set on end.
with an entry before this & the other building
of 10 feet wide 135 feet long
At the west end there was an house built by ye Artillery Company for
a smith to worke in, w[hi]ch Mr Knolls hath altered into 2 rooms, one
12 feet square & the other 12 & 10 foot with garretts over Head & a stayres
Upon both these buildings hee hath bested 50*li* in repayring & the paling
in ye said Entry of 10 feet wide
At the East end of the Armory huse was a Court house w[hi]ch Mr Knollys now erected
into a dwelling house about 30 feet long & 26 wide over 4 rooms of a
place & stayrecase & stayres over garretts of brick strongly & well
built.
that they open into ye Artillery yard
At the East end of this house was a yard ^ ~~w[hi]ch the Gunner~~ of 34 feet long &
36 feet broad, three sides whereof Mr Knollys hath stilled about for
washhouses, Coale houses & other necessary offfices of brick & tilled w[i]th
holland tile.
The yard or garden taken out of the Artillery yard by Mr Knollys &
10 feet high
pulled in with daube sett on end ^ & outeposts w[hi]ch is being on the south side
135 feet & 159 in the north side 159 feet & wide 39 feet and half a rod
this dwelling house, stalls & garden plott cost about 400*li*
besides the purchasing 300*li*

#12 – Lord Treasurer Southampton issues a warrant to Sir Robert Croke, the Clerk of the Pipe, for a lease to Knollys on the Old Artillery Ground property – 5 January 1661 (incorporates the constat of the Surveyor General submitted to the Treasurer dated 18 December 1660) (TNA, Lord Southampton's General Entry Book – 1660–61 (T 51/2), pages 130-131):

[Page 130]

To S[i]r Robert Croke Kn[igh]t, Clerke of ye Pipe

Com[itate] Midd[lese]x
Regis in Com[itatu] p[re]d[icto]

Parcell[um] possession[em] D[omi]ni
Firma unius Mesuag[i] sive Ten[amen]ti Scituat[i] super quoddam
magn[um] Gardin sive p[ar]cell[um] terr[e] inclus[um] quond[am] vocat[um] Tasell Close
vel Le Old Artillery ground in vel prope Spittle Fields Extra
Bishopsgate &c 20*li* p[er] ann[um]

I have conferred w[i]th the Master of his Ma[jes]ties Ordnance touching the
premisses & doe not find by him that there is any great use of the
said Armory Roome for his Ma[jes]ties service & wisheth as I doe
that the said Artillery ground were exchanged for some other peece
of ground lying more nere to the Tower & more easy of accese
for his Ma[jes]ties Carriages & tryall of his Cannon.
In case a Lease of ye premisses for one & thirty yeares be granted to Mr

[Page 131]

Knollis (for whome this Constat is made) I thinke it reasonable in respect of
his great charge of six or seaven hundred pounds laid
out in the purchase of part of ye p[re]misses under ye late usurped Authority
& in new building & repairing the same since. That ye rent of twenty pounds
p[er] ann[um] being reserved according to his Ma[jes]ties Instructons as a moyety of ye
improved value. It might be reasonable to take a small fine for ye same.
The rent is to be reserved payable at ye Annuncat[i]on & Mich[aelm]as by
equal port[i]ons Provided if it shalbe unpaid by the space of three
moneths next after either of the said Feasts or if the grant be not
Inrolled w[i]th the Auditor or the fine paid w[i]thin six monethes after the
date the lease to be voyd.

The Lesee is to Covenant to keepe & maintain the premisses
in good repairat[i]ons during the said terme & soe to leave it & to
deliver to the Auditor a true extent of the quantity meetes and
boundaryes of the premisses once in ev[er]y three yeres to preserve
the knowledge thereof for his Ma[jes]ties service.
This constat is made by order of ye right honou[ra]ble the Lo[rd] high
Trea[sure]r of England of ye 24th of November last.

Ex p[er] C[harles] Harbord Sup[er]visor

28 Decem[ber] 1660

S[i]r Robert Croke

Make a Lease of the Premisses unto [blank] Knollis or such as he shall nominate for the terme of thirty one yeres. And at the rent of twenty pounds p[er] ann[um] & the fine of forty Pounds under such Covenants & provisions as are here advised. And for soe doeing this shalbe your warr[an]t Given at South[amp]ton howse ye 5th of January 1660.

T[reasurer] Southampton

[Translation of lines 5-9]

County of Middlesex

Parcell belonging to the Lord King in the said County Grant of a Mesuage or Tenament situated overlooking a certain large Garden or enclosed piece of ground once called Tasell Close, or The Old Artillery ground, in or near Spittle Fields Outside Bishopsgate &c 20*li* per annum

#13 – Treasury warrant for a lease to Hanserd Knollys (16 January 1661) (incorporates the Treasury Record on the Old Artillery Ground dated 18 December 1660; Lord Treasurer Southampton's orders to Robert Croke, the Clerk of the Pipe, dated 5 January 1661 (TNA, Pipe Office – Warrant for Crown Lease to Hanserd Knollys (E 367/2474):

[Obverse)

Com[itatu] Midd[lesex] Parcell[um] possesion[em] D[omi]ni R[e]gis in Com[itatu] p[re]d[icto]

Firma unius Mesuag[i] sive Ten[amen]ti scituat[i] super quoddam magn[um] Gardin sive p[ar]cell[um] terr[e] inclus[um] quond[am] vocat[um] Tasell Close vel Le Old Artillary Grownd in vel prope Spittle Fields extra Bishopps gate in vel prope p[ar]ochia[m] de Stepney in Com[itatu] p[re]dict[o]. Ac totius ill[ius] magne Aule ib[ide]m edificat[e] nuper voc[ate] Le Armory Roome continen[tis] sexagint[a] tres pedes aut eo circiter in Longitudine et circa vigint[i] quatuor pedes in Latitudine una cu[m] quadam pecia terr[e] incluss[a] pro passagio ducen[te] ad aulam et Mesuag[ium] p[re]dict[a] cont[inente] in Latitudine circa decem pedes. Ac unius parvi Gardini nuper cu[m] paliciis incluss[i] ad boreal[em] partem dicti passagii adjungen[tis] cont[inentis] per estim[ationem] vigint[i] perticas parcell[i] d[i]cti magni gardini vocat[i] the Artillery grownd existen[tis] modo in tenur[e] Hanserdi Knollis Cler[ici] vel

assignator[um] suor[um] una cu[m] o[mn]ib[us] domib[us] edificiis
structuris Curtilagiis viis passagiis
easiamentis proficuis com[m]oditatib[us] et pertin[entiis] p[re]dict[is] Mesuag[io] sive ten[amen]to aut ceteris
p[re]missis
quibuscumq[ue] ^ aliquo modo spectan[tibus] vel p[er]tinen[tibus]
Val[ua] per ann[um]

[Translation of lines 1-24]

County of Middlesex   Parcell belonging to the Lord King in the said County

Grant of a Mesuage or Tenament situated
overlooking a certain large Garden or enclosed piece of ground
once called Tasell Close or The Old
Artillery Ground in or near Spittle Fields Outside
Outside Bishopps gate in or near the parish of
Stepney in the said County. And of all that large
Hall built in the same place lately called the Armory Roome
measuring sixty-three feet or thereabouts in
Length and around twenty-four feet in
Width, together with a certain enclosed piece of ground
[serving] as a passage leading to the aforesaid Hall and Mesuage
measuring about ten feet in Width. And of a
small Garden lately enclosed with poles to the
north side of the said adjoining passage consisting of
approximately twenty perches parcel of the said large
garden called the Artillery grownd being
presently in the tenure of Hanserd Knollis, Clerk, or
his assignes, together with all the houses, buildings,
structures, curtilages, ways, passages,
easements, profits, commodities, and advantages
whatsoever in any way regarding or pertaining to
the aforesaid Mesuage or tenament or other premisses.
Value per annum

I have Conferred with ye M[aste]r of his Ma[jes]ties Ordinance touching the premisse
and doe not find by him that there is any great Use of the sayd Armory
Roome for his Ma[jes]ties service and wisheth as I doe that the sayd Artillary
Grownd were exchanged for some other peece of Grownd Lying

more neere to the Tower and more easy of access for his Ma[jes]ties Carriage and Tryall of his Company.

In case a Lease of the premisses for one and Thirty yeares be granted to Mr Knollis (for whome this Constst is made) I thinke it reasonable in respect of his great Charge of six or seaven hundred pounds Layd out in the purchase of parte of the premisses under the late usurped Authority and in new building and repayring the same since, that the rent of twentie pounds per ann[um] being reserved according to his Ma[jes]ties Instruct[i]ons as a moyety of the improved value. It may be reasonable to take a smale fyne for the same.

The rent is to be received payable at ye Anunciat[i]on and Mich[aelm]as by equall port[i]ons Provided if it shall be unpaid by the space of three moneths at & after either of the sayd Feasts, or if the Grant be not Inrolled with ye Auditor or ye Fine payd within six moneths after ye Date ye Lease to bee voyd.

The Lessee is to Covenant to keepe and maintaine the p[re]misses in good reparations durieng ye sayd Terme and so to Leave it and to deliver to the Auditor a true extent of the quantity meetes and bundaryes of the p[re]misses once in every three yeares to p[re]serve ye Knowledg thereof for his Ma[jes]ties Service

This Constat is made by Order of ye right hono[ur]able ye Lord high Trea[sure]r of England of the Twenty fowerth of November Last.

Ex p[er] C[harles] Harbord Sup[er]visor
18 Dec[ember] 1660

Sir Robert Croake

Make a Lease of the premisses unto Hanserd Knollis or such as he shall nominate for the terme of thirty one yeares And at the rent of twenty pounds p[er] annu[m] & with the fyne of forty pounds under such Covenants & p[ro]visions as we have advised. And for soe doing this shalbe your warrant. Given at Southamp[ton howse ye 5th of January 1660.

T[reasurer] Southampton
Joh[ann]es Champante de London mercator et Joh[ann]es Asham de Ci[vita]te West[m]in[ster] gen[erosus] eiu manucaptor[es] invener[unt] securitat[em] Ad Solvend[um] reddit[um] & performend[um] &c
Ex p[ar]te Remendatoris D[omi]ni Regis uni[ci] Caroli S[e]c[un]di Keepe
xvi Januarii 1660

[Translation of lines 83-85]

John Champante of London, merchant, and John Asham of the City of Westminster, gentleman, his Bailsmen, have provided securities, To make the payment & perform [the necessaries] &c
On behalf of the Reconciler, the one and only Lord King Charles the Second Keepe
xvi January 1660

#14 – Treasurer Southampton notes William Legge's appeal against Hanserd Knollys' Petition and asks Charles Harbord, the Surveyor General, to investigate the matter – 16 February 1661 (TNA, Lord Southampton's General Entry Book – 1660–61 (T 51/2), page 236):

[Page 236)

Legg, Colonell Wm

February the 16th 1660

Upon the Peticon of Colonell William Legg, L[ieutenan]t of his Ma[jes]ties Ordnance who
claymeth an Interest in a howse lately erected upon the Artillery ground belonging
to the office of the Ordnance, there being a Grant lately made thereupon to
one [blank] Knollys, a disaffected person, to his Ma[jes]ty. And praying a stopp of
ye passing ye s[ai]d Grant untill he be heard to his Interest & Clayme thereunto.

I pray Mr Surveyor Gen[er]all to examine Colonell Leggs Grant & if need
be to conferr w[i]th Mr Attorney Gen[er]all in point of his right be vertue of his
patent of L[ieutenan]t of ye Ordnance. As likewise to consider the progress that hath
bin made on Mr Knollis his Lease. And upon the whole matter that Mr
Attorney & Mr Surveyor certifie me their opinions what they think reasonable

to be done thereupon.

T[reasurer] Southampton

#15 – William Legge's patent of appointment by Charles II to the office of Lieutenant of Ordnance – 28 June 1660 (TNA, Patent Roll of 12 Charles I (C 66/2993, Part 18, No. 37):

[Part 37 - Text]

S[ec]ton Will[ielm]o Legg Ar[miger]
37

Rex Om[n]ibus ad quos &c sal[u]t[e]m Sciatis q[uo]d nos de gr[ati]a n[ost]ra Sp[ec]iali ac ex c[er]ta scient[ia] et mero motu n[ost]ris assignavim[us] ordinavim[us] & constituim[us] ac p[er] p[re]sentes p[ro] nob[is] hered[ibus] et Successoribus n[ost]ris assignam[us] ordinam[us] & constituim[us] dil[igent]em & fidelem S[er]vien[tem] n[ost]r[u]m Will[ielmu]m Legg Armig[er]um un[um] Gromett[um] Camer[ae] n[ost]r[ae] Cubil[is] loc[um]tenent[em] Gen[er]al[em] om[n]i[um] & om[n]imod[arum] Ordinac[i]on[is] & munic[i]on[is] & al[iarum] rer[um] Bellicar[um] n[ost]rar[um] hered[um] & Succ[essorum] n[ost]ror[um] infra Regnu[m] n[ost]r[u]m Angl[ie] ac in villa n[ost]ra Barwici. Ac etiam de ub[er]iori gr[ati]a n[ost]ra assignavim[us] ordinavim[us] & constituim[us] ac p[er] p[re]sentes p[ro] nob[is] hered[ibus] & Successoribus n[ost]ris assignam[us] ordinam[us] & constituim[us] p[re]fat[um] Will[ielmu]m Legg Custod[em] n[ost]r[u]m tot[ius] ill[ius] mesuag[ii] sive domus manc[i]onal[is] n[ost]ri vocat[i] le Storehouse modo p[er]tinen[tis] officio n[ost]ro ordinat[i]on[is] & scituat[i] ext[ra] port[am] de Algate juxta London ac Custod[em] om[n]i[um] & Sing[u]lor[um] domor[um] edific[iorum] Custilag[iorum] hort[orum] & gardin eid[em] mesuag[o] sive domo manc[i]onal[i] Spectan[tium] sive p[er]tin[entium] ac Custod[em] cuiusd[am] Gardin vulgarit[er] nuncupat[i] Artillery Gardin h[ab]end[um] tenend[um] occupand[um] & ex[er]cend[um] offic[ium] p[re]dict[um] acetiam om[n]ia & Singula p[re]missa p[er] p[re]sentes p[re]concess[a] cum suis p[er]tinen[tiis] p[re]fat[o] Will[ielm]o Legg p[er] se vel p[er] Sufficien[tem] Deputat[um] suu[m] sive Deputat[os] suos Sufficien[tes] duran[te] vita ip[s]ius natural[e] Will[ielm]i Legg. Et ult[er]ius de ub[er]iori gr[ati]a] n[ost]ra dedim[us] & concessim[us] ac p[er] p[re]sentes p[ro] nobis hered[ibus] & Successor[ibus] n[ost]ris dam[us] & concedim[us] p[re]fato Will[ielm]o Legg p[ro] ex[er]cit[i]o[ne] & occupat[i]o[n]e eiusdem officii quand[am] an[n]uitat[em] sive an[n]ual[em] reddit[um] Cent[um] marcar[orum] leg[a]lis monete Angl[ie] Quodquid officiu[m] an[n]ual[em] reddit[um] & cet[er]a p[re]missa Joh[ann]es Heydon mil[es] defunct[us] nup[er] h[ab]uit & ex[er]cuit h[ab]end[a] gaudend[a] & an[n]uat[im] p[er]cipiend[am] p[re]dict[am] annuitat[em] sive an[n]ual[em] reddit[um] Cent[um] marcar[orum] p[re]fat[o] Will[ielm]o Legg & assign[atis] suis p[ro] & duran[te] vita sua natural[i] de Thesauro n[os]tro hered[um] & Successor[um] n[ost]ror[um] ad Recept[um] Sc[ac]c[ar]ii n[ost]ri hered[um] & Successor[um] n[ost]ror[um] p[er] man[um] Commissionar[um] p[ro] Thesauro n[ost]ro vel Thesaurar[i] & Cam[er]ar[iorum] eiusd[em] Sc[ac]c[ar]ii p[ro] temporo existen[tium] ad Festa S[anc]ti Mich[ael]is Arch[angel]i & Annu[n]ciat[i]o[n]is B[eat]e Marie Virginis p[er] equal[es] port[i]o[n]es an[n]uatim solvend[um] unacum om[n]ib[us] al[iis] vad[is] feod[is] regard[is] comoditat[ibus] p[ro]fit[is] auth[ori]tat[ibus] et p[re]heminent[ibus] quibuscunque d[ic]to officio quoquomodo Spectan[tibus] & p[er]tin[entibus] in tam amplis modo & forma p[ro] ut Rob[er]tus Constable mil[es] Georgius Du[cu]s Carew, Rog[er]us Dallison, Ric[ard]us Morrison, Wills Heydon aut p[re]no[m]i[n]at[us] Joh[ann]es Heydon mil[es] aut aliquis al[ius] sive aliqui alii offic[ium] p[re]dict[um] antehac h[ab]uit & p[er]cepit h[ab]uer[unt] vel p[er]ceper[unt] vel h[ab]ere aut p[er]cip[er]e debuit vel debuer[unt] Eo q[uo]d expressa menc[i]o &c In cuius rei &c T[este] R[ege] apud West[m]in[ster] vicesimo octavo die Junii. p[er] ip[s]u[m] Regem

[Part 37 - Translation]

S[ec]ton William Legg Esquire

37

King [Charles II] To all to whom &c Greeting. Know yee that wee of our especiall grace and out of our certain knowledge and meere motion have assigned, ordained and appointed, and by these presents, on behalf of ourselves, our heirs and Successors, do assign, ordain and appoint our diligent & faithful Servant Will[ia]m Legg, Esquire, one of the Groomsmen of our Bed Chamber, Lieutenant General of all and every kind of Ordnance and munition and other instruments of war of us, our heirs and Successors within our kingdom of England and in our castle of Berwick. And furthermore, out of our richer grace we have assigned, ordained and appointed, and by these presents, on behalf of ourselves, our heirs and Successors, do assign, ordain, and appoint the aforesaid William Legg our Custodian of all that mesuage or dwelling house of ours called The Storehouse lately pertaining to our Office of Ordnance & located outside the gate of Aldgate adjoining London; and Custodian of all and singular buildings, structures, enclosures, parks, and gardens concerning or belonging to the same mesuage or dwelling house; and Custodian of a certain Garden commonly called Artillery Garden; to have, hold, occupy and exercise the aforesaid office and all and singular premisses by these presents granted together with the things pertaining to them, to the aforesaid William Legg, by himself or by his Sufficient Deputy or Deputies for the duration of the natural life of the same William Legg. And furthermore out of our richer grace we have given & granted & by these presents, on behalf of ourselves, our heirs & Successors, we give and grant to the aforesaid William Legg for the exercising and occupying of the same office a certain annuity or annual payment of One Hundred marks of lawful English money. Whatever office, annual payment & other premisses John Heydon, Knight, deceased, lately had and exercised, are to be had and enjoyed, and the aforesaid annuity or annual payment of One Hundred marks is to be received yearly by the aforesaid William Legge and his assignes for the duration of his natural life from the Treasure of us, our heirs and Successors in the Receipt of the Exchequer of us, our heirs and successors, by the hand of the Commissioners of our Treasure or of the Treasurer & Chamberlains of the same Exchequer for the time being, at the Feast of Saint Michael the Archangel & the Annunciation of the Blessed Virgin Mary by equal portions to be paid annually, together with all other wages, fees, regards, commodities, profits, authorizations, and advantages whatsoever, howsoever regarding and pertaining to the said office, in just such a generous way and fashion as Robert Constable, Knight,

George Duke Carew, Roger Dallison, Richard Morrison, William Heydon or the aforenamed
John Heydon, Knight, or any other or any others who prior to this
had and occupied, or should have had and occupied, the aforesaid office.
Although express mention &c In [witness] thereof &c Witness the King [Charles II] at Westminster the twenty
eighth day of June. by the King

#16 – Treasurer Southampton makes a resolution on a petition by Charles Gerard, Lord of Brandon for a lease on the Old Artillery Ground – 9 July 1661 (BLL, Stowe MS 498, page 211):

[Page 211]
Charles Lord Gerard Baron of Brandon petic[i]on That there is a parcell of land contayning
two acres in the Artillery ground belonging to his Ma[jes]tie. Hee praies
to bee admitted Tenant and a Lease for xxxi yeres at the ancient Customary rents
July the 9th 1661
Mr Surveyor Generall Pray examine to whom this ground belonges
and give mee your opinion whether it bee fit to Lease and upon what termes
T[reasurer] Southampton

#17 – Hanserd Knollys' Third Petition regarding the Old Artillery Ground – 1671 (TNA, SP 29/288, page 169):

[Page 169 verso]
To Joseph Williamson

[Page 169 recto]
To the Kings most Excellent Majesty

The humble petiton of Hanserd Knollys

Sheweth
That your Petitoner having laid out a considerable sume of money upon the purchase of the old
Artillery ground in or neare Spittlefeilds and the Armory roome with thappurtenences thereunto
belonging (under the late usurped authoritie) And upon a former petiton to your Ma[jes]tie conterning the
premisses your Ma[jes]tie was graciously pleased to order

Confirmaton of the premisses unto your Petit[ion]er who was obstructed in the obteyning thereof by a Caveat putt in by Colonell Legg, late Master of your Ma[jes]ties Ordnance now deceased.

Your Pet[ition]er once more most humbly prayeth your Ma[jes]t[ie]s Confirmation to him noe person having ever enjoyed the same but your Pet[ition]er (except the aforesaid Colonell Legg) since the sale thereof made to your Pet[ition]er by the Artillery Company.

And your Petitoner shall ever pray &c.

#18 – Sir Heneage Finch's's consideration of Hanserd Knollys Petition regarding the Old Artillery Ground – 22 June 1674 (incorporating two earlier documents: a statement by Sir George Cottrell dated 21 December 1673 which referred an attached copy of Knollys' third petition for the consideration of Finch as the Keeper of the Great Seal; a copy of Attorney General Finch's first report on Knollys' case which is undated) (TNA, SP 29/338, page 126 recto-127 recto):

[Page 126 recto]

May It please yo[ur] Maj[es]ty

In obedience to this Reference I have againe Considered the Case of Hanserd Knollis whose peticon was formerly referred to me and I find as in my former Report That the man hath purchased part of the Artillery ground and built upon it and laid out 750*li* which will all be lost for want of a Title the Sayle being yo[ur] Maj[es]ties, but where in my former Report I had propose to yo[ur] Maj[es]ty that the s[ai]d Knollys might be gratified with a Lease at a small rent for his reimbursement. Now upon heareing the Officers of the ordnance I find it cannot be done partly because the place in question is affirmed to be necessary for yo[ur] Maj[es]ties Service in order to the aireing of yo[ur] Stuff in the Tower but cheifely because the place in question is already granted to Mr David Walter dureing his tyme, and after him to Mr George Legg in reversion, and Soe in a manner annexed to the Office of the ordnance. Wherefore there is noe other way left to preserve him from ruyne whose whole Estate is laid out there but by ordering him to be reimbursed the money when and where it may best Suite with yo[ur] Maj[es]ties occasions. All which as humbly submitted,

Finch &c
22 Junii 1674

[Page 126 verso]

To the Kings most Excellent Maj[es]tie
The humble peticon of Han[serd] Knollys

Humbly sheweth
That ye pet[ition]er bought the old Armory house in the Artillery ground
neere Spittle Fields London of the Artillery Company of the Citty of London who
built it, for which the pet[ition]er paid them 300*li*.
That your pet[ition]er expended 460*li* more in repaireing and building upon the
premisses fitting the same for his Schoolehouse and dwelling house, which
premisses he inhabited and enjoyed about 2 yeares.
That one Colonell Legg deceased being Lieutenant of your Maj[es]ties Ordnance under
pretence of his Patent did by Force and Violence take away the s[ai]d Armory house,
dwelling house and all other his out houses from your pet[ition]er and kept them during his
life.
That David Walters Esq[ui]re, the new Lieu[tenan]t of your Maj[es]ties Ordinance finding ye premisses
in the possession of Colo[nel] Legge when he dyed keepes the same from your pet[ition]er.
That ye poore and aged pet[ition]er hath been above 10 yeares kept out of his Right
in the premisses to the Impoverishing of himselfe and his poore Family, he having
borrowed a great part of the s[ai]d sumes of money.
May it therefore please your Maj[es]ty to appoint the L[or]d Keeper or ye L[or]d Privy Seale
or whom else your Maj[es]ty shall please to examine the contents of this petition and
call your pet[ition]er and all other p[er]sons concerned therein before him and to Report
the matter to your Maj[es]ty that if your Maj[es]ty shall see cause your Maj[es]ty will require
the Artillery Company, the Executors of Colo[nel] Legge and David Walter, Esq[ui]re to pay back
the s[ai]d 760*li* unto your poore pet[ition]er or else in consideration

that your pet[ition]er hath been out of his money soe long,

That your Maj[es]ty will be pleased to give and grant your pet[ition]er a Lease of the premisses for 99 yeares under your Maj[es]ties great Seale your pet[ition]er paying to your Maj[es]ties use 10*li* Fine and 20*li* p[er] ann[um] Rent. And &c

Att the Court att Whitehall December ye 21th 1673

His Maj[es]ty is gratiously pleased to referr this petition to the R[igh]t honourable S[i]r Heneage Finch Kn[igh]t & Barr[one]t Keeper of the great Seale of England to call all parties concerned before him and to examine the truth of ye Allegations laid downe therein and to take such order thereupon for the pet[ition]ers releife shall be agreeable to justice and equity.

Charles Cottrell

Copia vera

[Page 127 recto]

May it please your most Excellent Maj[es]ty

I have examined the matter contayned in this petiton and doe find that

The pet[ition]er is a purchaser from the Artillery Company who clayme by Colour of some orders of Councell made in the time of your Royall grandfather but never had a Legall Title that I can find.

That nevertheless the pet[ition]er who purchased about the yeare 1658 hath laid out 750*li* in building a house which is not of any necessary use to the office of the ordnance nor any hindrance to the free use of the Artillery ground

That the pet[ition]er quietly enjoyed till your Maj[es]ties returne

That the Lord Treasurer Southampton in consideration of his poverty and great charge directed a Lease to be made to him and ordered Sir Charles Harbord to prepare a Particular.

That Colo[nel] Legg did eject the pet[ition]er and hold it during his life.

That Mr David Walter pretends noe title to it other than the possession left him by Colonell Legg.

Upon the whole I conceave

That it is fitt the pet[ition]er be reimbursed the charge laid out upon the premisses or otherwise that he be gratified with a Lease for yeares at some small rent to be paid your Maj[es]ty and possession be restored.

All which is humbly submitted

Finch &c

Copia vera
1st report

#19 – Hanserd Knollys' petition is entred in the Treasury Book of Petitions and Treasurer Lord Danby (Thomas Osborn) is to consult with Surveyor General Charles Harbord about it – 1677 (TNA, Treasury Petitioners Entry Book – 1677–78 (PRO 30/32/36), pages 12 and 62):

[Page 12]

Mr Knollys

Hanserd Knollys Referr[e]d from his Ma[jes]tie sheweth that having bought a house and some Ground of the Artillery Company in London & spent 750*li* to build & repaire it he was by force put out of it by the Officers of the Ordinance & thereupon Complaining to his Ma[jes]ty he was referred to the p[re]sent L[or]d Chancelor [Finch] (then Attorney Gen[era]ll) who made report to his Ma[jes]ty that the Pet[itione]r should be restored to his house but the Officers alleging that the house was of great use for his Ma[jes]ties Service, his Ma[jes]ty was pleased to make Referrence to my L[or]d Chancelor when L[or]d Keeper who made a Second Record that the Pet[itione]r should either have his house or 750*li* w[hi]ch it Cost him Since w[hi]ch noe use is made of the s[ai]d house humbly prays to have the house or 750*li*.

S[i]r Cha[rles] Harbords since the Reading this Petiton upon Reference to him Reports that the Equity of ye Pet[itioner]s Case & Conceives it Just that the Pet[itione]r have his house or ye 750*li*

Sr Charles Harbord to be spoken with by my Lord

Treasurer
[Danby]

[Page 62]

Knollys — Mr Knollys petiton as in page ye 12 referred to
S[i]r Charles Harbord and his report upon it to
be read.

#20 – The Surveyor General's constat concerning the Hanserd Knollys case – 16 March 1678 (incorporating four earlier documents: Secretary Henry Coventry's order dated 21 March 1675 to Thomas Earle of Danby, Lord High Treasurer, asking him to consider the attached fifth petition of Knollys; Attorney General Finch's report from 1673[?] on the petition of Knollys; Sir Finch's report as Keeper of the Great Seal dated 22 June 1674 on the petition of Knollys; the statement of Charles Bertie, Secretary of the Treasury, dated 24 December 1677 to the Surveyor General Charles Harbord asking him to consider the attached sixth petition of Knollys) (TNA, Surveyor General Constat Book M – 1675-1678 (CRES 6/12), pages 304-307):

[Page 304]

Mr Hanserd Knollys for recom-
pence for his howse at the old
Artillery Garden

To the Kings Most Excellent Ma[jes]ty
The humble Petit[i]on of Mr Hanserd Knollys

Most humbly Sheweth

That your petit[i]oner being about 12 yeares since put out of the
possession of the Armory House & buildings adjoyning (w[hi]ch he purchased
of the Artillery Company of London & spent much mony in the building
thereof) did by his humble peticon repesent his Case unto your Ma[jes]ty,
which your Ma[jes]ty referred to the now Lord Keeper who made Report
unto your Ma[jes]ty that it was just your peticoner should either have £750*li*
(the mony it cost him) or a Lease of the premisses at a small rent, wher-
upon your Ma[jes]ty gave direction for a Lease to be made to your peticoner
accordingly, but it being represented unto your Ma[jes]ty by the offices of
your ordnance that the said houses were necessary for your

Ma[jes]t[ie]s service the said Lord Keeper upon a 2d Reference unto him made Report unto your Ma[jes]ty that he was humbly of opinion that the said 750*li* should be paid unto your peticoner in recompence thereof.

Now forasmuch as your peticoner by the losse of the s[ai]d Houses (w[i]thout any satisfacton) was constrained to leave his vocat[i]on (the keeping of a Schoole & Boarders) whereby he lived happily, but hath since been reduced to extreame want & poverty, and now at least in his old Age (about seaventy yeares) cast into prison, without any other hope of releife then from your Ma[jes]t[ie]s Princely Compassion.

Most humbly begs your Ma[jes]ty wilbe graciously pleased to give direction unto the Lord Treasurer for the paym[en]t of the said 750*li* to your petic[i]oner.

At the Court at Newmarket. March 21th 1674/5.
His Ma[jes]ty is graciously pleased to referr this Peticon to the Right Hono[ra]ble Thomas Earle of Danby, Lord High Treasurer of England who is desired to consider the same and Report to his Ma[jes]ty what his Lord[shi]p thinks fit to be done for the Peticoners Reliefe and then his Ma[jes]ty will declare his further pleasure.

H[enry] Coventry

L[or]d Chancellors 1st Report

May it please your Most Excellent Ma[jes]ty

I have examined the matters contained in the peticon & do find That the Petic[i]oner is a Purchasor from the Artillery Company who claime by colour of some orders of Councell made in the time of your Royall Grandfather, but never had a Legall title they can find.

[Page 305]

Mr Knollys That neverthelesse the Petic[i]oner who purchased about the yeare 1658, hath laid out 750*li* in building a House w[hi]ch is not of any necessary use to the Office of the Ordnance, nor any hindrance to the free use of the Artillery ground.

That the Petit[i]oner quietly enjoyed till your Ma[jes]t[ie]s Returne That the Lord Treas[ure]r Southampton in considerat[i]on of his poverty & great charge directed a Lease to be made to him, and ordered S[i]r Charles Harbord to prepare a p[ar]ticular.

That Coll[onel] Leg did eject the Petit[i]oner & held it during his life.

That Mr David Walter pretends no Title to it, other then the possession left him by Coll[onel] Leg

Upon the whole matter I conceive That it is fitt the Petit[i]oner be reimbursed the charge laid out upon the premisses or otherwise that he be gratified with a Lease for yeares, at some small Rent, to b paid your Ma[jes]ty & possession be restored.

All w[hi]ch is humbly Submitted

Finch C S

L[or]d Chanc[ellor]s 2d Report

May it please your Ma[jes]ty

In obedience to this Reference I have again considered the Case of Hanserd Knollys, whose petit[i]on was formerly referred to me, And find as in my former Report, That the man hath purchased P[ar]t of the Artillery ground & built upon it & laid out 750*li* w[hi]ch will all be lost for want of a Tytle, the Soyle being your Ma[jes]t[ie]s, but where in my my former Report, I had p[ro]posed to your Ma[jes]ty that the said Knollys might be gratifyed with a Lease at a small rent towards his reimbursem[en]t. Now upon hearing of the

officers of the
ordnance I find it cannot be done, p[ar]tly because the place in
question is affirmed to be necessary for your Ma[jes]t[ie]s service in
order to the Ayreing of your Stuffe in the Tower, but cheifly because
the place in question is already granted to Mr David Walter
dureing his time, & after him to Mr George Leg in Revert[i]on &
in a Manner anexed to the Office of the Ordnance. Whereforee
there is no other way left to p[re]serve Knollys from ruine,
whose whole Estate is laid out there, but by ordering him to be
reimbursed the mony, when & where it may best suite with
your Ma[jes]t[ie]s occasions.

All w[hi]ch is humbly submitted &c

Finch C S

June 22 1674

[Page 306]

Mr Knollys To the Kings most Excellent Ma[jes]tie

The humble Petit[i]on of Hanserd Knollys, a very pooree distressed and very aged Minister

Most humbly sheweth

That your petit[i]oner hath formerly by his humble
petit[i]on made his applicat[i]on to your Ma[jes]ty who was graciously pleased
to grant 2 references to the now Lord Chancellor who in obedience
thereunto made these two Reports, Coppyes whereof are hereunto
annexed.

Now forasmuch as the Condit[i]on of himself & misserable family
lye under even the pressure of Starveing without your Ma[jes]t[ie]s speedy
mercy to his releife herein.

Hee humbly therefore prayes and earnestly begs your Ma[jes]tys order
to the Lord Treasurer to pay your poor petit[i]oner the 750*li* accord-
ing to the Lord Chancellorrs Reporte anexed.

And your poore petit[i]oner shall ever pray &c

December 24th 1677

My Lord Trea[sure]r having received this Petit[i]on from his Ma[jes]ty & a former w[i]th his Ma[jes]t[ie]s Reference thereupon & hereunto anexed, is pleased to referr the same with the annexed Reports to S[i]r Charles Harbord Kn[igh]t, his Ma[jes]t[ie]s Surveyor Generall, who is desired to view the premisses & make report to his Lord[shi]p what may fitly be done for the Petit[i]oners gratificat[i]on in this Matter.

Cha[rles] Bertie

May it please your Lo[rdshi]p

I have considered the severall Petit[i]ons of Mr Hanserd Knollys and his Ma[jes]t[ie]s References thereupon, and a former Petit[i]on to my late L[or]d Trea[sure]r the Earle of Southampton and his Lo[rdshi]ps Reference & my Report thereupon, and his Lo[rdshi]ps Direct[i]on for a Constat & Lease of the Houses & Ground by him claimed, pursuant to that Report all in the year 1660. The passing whereof was stayed upon the Complaint of Colonell Legg then Lieutenant of the Ordnance, upon pretence that the said Houses & Ground were necessary to be reserved for his Ma[jes]t[ie]s service, togeather with the rest of the Houses & Ground adjoyning called the old Artillery Ground, whereupon the Petit[i]oner was soon after put out of poss[ess]c[i]on by the said Coll[onel] Legg and so continues, w[hi]ch enforced him to make these late Petit[ions] to his Ma[jes]ty where upon there have been References made to my now L[or]d Chancellor who made two severall Reports thereupon in favour of the Petit[i]oner, And by the last thereof (dated in June 1674) adviseth

[Page 307]

Mr Knollys That the Pet[itione]r may have satisfact[i]on of the Sume of seaven hundrfed and fifty pounds by him expended in the purchase &

building upon the premisses, it being affirmed to be necessary for his Ma[jes]t[ie]s service in order to the ayreing of his Ma[jes]t[ie]s Stuff in the Tower, but cheifly because the place in question is already granted to Mr David Walter during his time, and after him to Mr George Legg in Revert[i]on, and so in a Manner annexed to the Office of Ordnance, whereby the Pet[itione]r can have no Lease thereof, and therefore there is no other way left to preserve Knollys from ruin (whose whole Estate4 is layd out there) but by ordering him to be reimbursed the said Money, when and where it may best suit with his Ma[jes]t[ie]s occasions, as by the Coppyes of his Lo[rdshi]ps said Reports hereunto annexed may appear.

It did appear unto me in 1660, when upon Exa[m]i[n]at[i]on of the Petit[i]oners Complaint & Pretences, That he had really paid for the purchase of the premisses by him claimed in 1658, the sume of Three hundred pounds to the then Artillery Company, who pretended to be the rightfull owners thereof by some Grant from King James, and had disbursed four hundred pound more, in building there upon. And my late L[or]d Trea[sure]r thought fitt to grant him a Lease thereof for one and thirty yeares, at a small Rent, in Recompence of his said Purchase & Expences, but the same was stayed as abovesaid.

And it appears that the Custody of the said Artillery Ground by the name of *Custod[em] cuiusd[am] Gardin vulgariter nuncupat[i] le Artillery Garden* is now on Grant to the Lieutenant of the Ordnance, and to the said Mr George Legg in Revert[i]on for life, and so the Pet[itione]r cannot have any Leave thereof without the Surrender of the said Grants, which wilbe opposed by the Office of the Ordnance. And therefore I must agree to the said Advice of my L[or]d Chancellor for a Satisfact[i]on of the said seaven hundred pounds to be given him in mony having been out of possession for about seaventeen yeares past, to his great loss & prejudice, most humbly submitting it to your Lo[rdshi]ps wisdome.

C[harles] Harbord 16 Mar[ch 16]77

Another Petit[i]on &c

166 [Book] O

#21 – Hanserd Knollys' seventh petition regarding the Old Artillery Ground is submitted to the Commissioners of the Treasury and referred to the Surveyor General William Harbord – 18 November 1679 (TNA, Treasury Book of Out Letters 1 (T 11/5), page 126):

[Page 126 recto]

To The Com[missione]rs of ye Trea[su]ry

Mr Knollys The petition of Hanserd Knollys

Sheweth That your pet[itione]r has formerly by his humble petitons annexed applied himselfe to his Ma[jes]ty who was Graciously pleased to Grant 2 References to ye now Lord Chancellor who made two reports Thereupon to his Ma[jes]ty Coppies of both w[hi]ch are annexed.

That afterwards his Ma[jes]ty was to referre your pet[itione]r to ye Earl of Danby Then L[ord] Trea[sure]r who refered ye same to Sir Charles Harbord who did report his opinion (w[hi]ch agrees with ye advice of ye L[ord] Chancellor). That upon ye whole matter as ye Case appeared before Them, they both concur yt a Satisfacton of 700*li* should be Given in money to your pet[itione]r he having been now 18 years out of possession of yt house w[hi]ch Cost him in purchase & building above 700*li* to his Great Losse and Damage & almost utter undoeing.

Now for as much as ye Conditon of himselfe & miserable distressed Family Lye under Much pressure of poverty w[i]thout speedy money to his reliefe herein most humbly prayes your Lord[shi]ps assistance & favour either in Granting him a Lease for 99 yeares under a small rent or to order him ye s[ai]d 700*li* to save him from utter ruine.

and your pet[itione]r shall ever pray &c

Whitehall Trea[su]ry Chambers 18 Nov[embe]r 1679

The Lords Com[missione]rs of his Ma[jest]t[ie]s Trea[su]ry are pleased to refere this petiton and all ye papers anext to W[illia]m Harbord Esq[uire] his Ma[jes]t[ie]s Surveyor Gen[era]ll who is desired to Consult Coll[onel] Legge and ye rest of ye officers of ye ordnance about ye Contents thereof and then to Seale ye pet[itioner]s Case with his opinion Thereupon in a report to their Lord[shi]ps.

Hen[ry] Guy

#22 – The Surveyor General William Harbord's constat concerning Hanserd Knollys Petition – 3 July 1680 (incorporating three earlier documents: an order from Henry Guy, the Secretary to the Treasury, dated 18 November 1679 to the Surveyor General Charles Harbord asking him to consider an attached seventh petition of Knollys; an order from William Harbord to Colonel Legge and the Officers of Ordnance dated 19 January 1680 asking them to consider an attached petition of Knollys; a report from Colonel Legge and the Officers of Ordnance dated 21 April 1680 in which they offer their opinion about Knollys' case) (TNA, Surveyor General Constat Book O – 1679–1682 (CRES 6/14), pages 166-167):

[Page 166]

Hanserd Knollys
for satisfaction for
House & Ground at
the old Artillery Ground

To the R[igh]t Hono[ra]ble the L[or]ds Com[missione]rs of the Trea[su]ry

The humble Petit[i]on of Hanserd Knollys a very poor & aged Minister

Humbly Sheweth,

That ye Pet[ione]r hath formerly by his humble Petit[i]ons anexed applyed himself to his Ma[jes]t[ie]s who was graciously pleased to grant 2 References to the new L[or]d Chancellor, who made two Reports thereupon to his Ma[jes]ty, Copies of both w[hi]ch are anexed.

That afterwards his Ma[jes]ty was pleased to referr your Pet[itione]r to the Earle of Danby then L[or]d Trea[sure]r who referr'd the same to S[ir] Charles Harbord who did Report his opinion (w[hi]ch agrees with the Advice of the Chancellor) That upon the whole matter as the case appeared before them, they both conclude that a satisfact[i]on of 700*li* should be given in money to your Pet[itione]r, he having been now 18 yeares out of poss[essi]on of that House, w[hi]ch cost him in

purchase & building above 700li
to his great loss & damage & almost utter undoing.

Now forasmuch as the Condit[i]on of himself & miserable distressed family
lye under much pressure of poverty without speedy money to his Releif
herein, most humbly prayes your Lo[rdshi]ps Assistance & favour, either in
granting him a Lease for 99 years, under a small Rent or to order him
the said 700*li*, to save him from utter ruin.
And your Pet[itione]r shall ever pray &c

Whitehall Trea[su]ry Chambers 18 Nov[ember] 1679
The L[or]ds Com[missione]rs of his Ma[jes]t[ie]s Trea[su]ry are pleased to referr this Petition & all the
papers annexed to Will[ia]m Harbord Esq[uire], his Ma[jes]t[ie]s Surveyor generall, who is desired
to consult Coll[onel] Legg & the rest of the officers of the Ordnance about the Contents
thereof, and then to state the Pet[itione]rs Case with his opinions thereupon in a Report
to their Lo[rdshi]ps

Hen[ry] Guy

I desire Coll[onel] Legg & the rest of the Officers of the Ordnance to consider of this
poor mans Case, & of the papers hereunto annexed & to certify me their opinions
thereupon, That I may be the better enabled to make a Report of the State thereof
to the L[or]ds Com[missioner]s of the Trea[su]ry as I am commanded by their Reference upon this Petit[i]on

Will[iam] Harbord Sup[er]visor
19 January 1679

sent knowles 2 petit[i]ons to the K[ing] with References
thereupon, my L[or]d Chanc[ellor]s 2 Reports, & a Report
from S[i]r Ch[arles Harbord 16 March 1677

In Obedience to the Reference of the Hono[ra]ble the L[or]ds
Com[missione]rs of his Ma[jes]t[ie]s Trea[su]ry, upon
the Petit[i]on of Hanserd Knolles, whereby they are pleased to referr the said Petit[i]on
to Will[ia]m Harbord, Esq[uire] who is desired to consult Col[onel] Legg & the rest of the Offic[er]s

about the Contents thereof. We, the s[ai]d Officers of the Ordnance, who have hereunto suscribed at the instance of the said Will[ia]m Harbord Esq[uire], do humbly certify That we can make no other Return, as to the Concerns of the Pet[itione]r, then what is already made in the annexed Papers, and the Report of the R[igh]t Hono[ra]ble the L[or]d Chancellor thereupon.

But in Reguards the said Pet[itione]r hath disbursed (as is alledged) the best & greatest p[ar]t of his Estate in the Purchase & Building of the House of w[hi]ch he hath long since been dispossess'd by his Ma[jes]t[ie]s Right & Title thereto, Our humble opinion is, That no better meanes can be proposed for his Compensat[i]on, Then by his Addresse (through their Lo[rdshi]ps mediat[i]on) to his Ma[jes]ty, To whose Royall & Charitable Benevolence, we in all humility referr the Pet[itione]rs Request & Condit[i]on.

Office of Ordnance
21 April 1680 G[eorge] Legg Edw[ard] Canyon Edw[ard] Sherburne

[Page 167]

May it please your Lo[rdshi]ps

According to your Lo[rdshi]ps Reference upon this Poor man's Petit[i]on I have consulted Coll[onel] Legg and the rest of the Officers of the Ordnance upon ye Contents thereof and received their Certificate hereunto annexed, and am not able to give your Lo[rdshi]ps any better account of the State of the Pet[itioine]rs Case than is fully set forth in the Report therof made by my Father 16 March [16]77, herew[i]th sent.

And the Pet[itione]r thinking he had bought a good Title of the Artillery Company w[hi]ch induced him to lay out all he had in the Purchase ye Building upon the premisses, and my L[or]d Chancellor being clear of opinion that he cannot now be recompensed by a Lease thereof, as he should have had, but that it is just he should be reimbursed his Charges of 750*li* expended thereupon and finding by my Fathers said Response, he concurrs with my L[or]d Chancellor therein, for the Repaym[en]t of 700*li* to be given him in money (w[hi]ch he hath been out of now about 20 years) to w[hi]ch the Officers of the Ordnance have no Exception, but thinke the Pet[itione]r a fit object for his Ma[jes]t[ie]s Royall & Charitable Benevolence. I see not any object[i]on upon the whole matter to be made thereunto, but humbly submit the same to your Lo[rdshi]ps Judgm[en]t & Compassion, to give direct[i]on for such satisfact[i]on to be made to this Poor Pet[itione]r as in your Lo[rdshi]ps wisdom shall seem meet.

Will[iam] Harbor
3 July 1680

#23 – The Surveyor General William Harbord's survey of the Old Artillery Ground – 11 May 1681 (incorporating a request from Henry Guy, the Secretary to the Treasury, dated 24 April 1681 to the Surveyor General asking him to value the property and submit a report to the Commissioners of the Treasury (TNA, Surveyor General Constat Book O – 1679–1682 (CRES 6/14), pages 247-248):

[Page 247]

Old Artillery Ground
London

A Map of the old Artillery Ground neer Spittle fields in London said to be taken in M[ar]ch 1680/1 & sent to Mr Surveyor by the messenger of ye Trea[su]ry

Referred thus on the back

Whitehall Trea[su]ry Chambers Aprill the 24th 1681

The Lords Comissioners of his Ma[jes]t[ie]s Trea[su]ry are pleased to referr this Ground plott to William Harbord Esq[uire] his Ma[jes]t[ie]s Surveyor Generall, who is desired speedily to make Report to their Lo[rdshi]ps what is the value of the Ground built & unbuilt, and what Improvem[en]t may be made of the same by building there upon.

Hen[ry] Guy

I went twice & viewed the Ground & the Houses thereon &

then the Report following was made thereon.

May it please your Lo[rdshi]ps
I have p[er]used this Ground plot of ye old Artillery
Ground neer the Spittle in London, and have caused the Ground &
Houses thereupon erected to be viewed & valued, and do find That
One mesuage at the Southwest Corner thereof, togeather with a
peece of Ground poled out for a Garden to it, was purchased of
the Artillery Company of London for 300*li*, a little before his Ma[jes]t[ie]s
Restaurat[i]on by one Hanserd Knolls (who laid out 400*li* more
upon building thereupon) and was to have had a Lease thereof
in 1660, or recompence from his Ma[jes]ty for the same, being valued
30*li* at about xxx*li* a year.
Next adjoyning to this, more Eastward, is a great brick store-
house used for layhing up Match & return'd bedding, Tents & other
20*li* utensils, with a Garden to it, w[hi]ch maybe valued at xx*li* p[er] an[num].
And two other Tenem[en]ts more Eastward, with Gardens (being all
at the South End of the Ground) which maybe worth about
30*li* xxx*li* p[er] an[num].
And there is at the North end a dwelling house appropriated for the
habitat[i]on of the Master Gunner of England, with Stables, Coach-
house, Porters Lodge, & two powder houses, with a long house or
building used by the Office of the Ordnance for proving of small
Gunns, and keeping of Stores, and a charging house, all esti-
70*li* at lxx*li* p[er] an[num].
And that the Remainder of the Ground unbuilt, contayning a
few Acres, all wall'd in with a high brick wall, maybe reaso-
10*li* nably valued at x*li* p[er] an[num].
160*li* In all one hundred & sixty pound p[er] an[num]
But what further Improvem[en]t may be made of this Ground by building
it all into Tenem[en]ts & new streets, I am not so well able to

inform your
Lo[rdshi]ps as ye Surveyor Gen[er]all & Officers of his Ma[jes]t[ies] Workes
(being within the Suburbs
of ye Citie of London), whose dayly practice is in matters of ye like nature.

[Page 248]

I must inform your Lo[rdshi]ps That in 1673 when Proposalls were made
37*li* by my L[or]d Grandison to take along Lease of this Ground to build upon
& referr'd then to my Father, He then advised with the Officers of the
Ordnance, who certifyed it to be neer the value before ment[i]oned, but
they conceived that the said Storehouse, & Masters Gunners house,
with the proofe house, powder houses & charging house, were all
necessary & imployed for his Ma[jes]t[ie]s service, and arrange of the
said Ground of about 750 foot long under the East Wall, call'd
a Parke (with a great Butt to shoot at, at the North End) was used
for exercising 100 feed Gunners & trayning up of Schollars in
the Act of Gunnery, w[hi]ch the Master Gunner by his Instruct[i]ons is
bound to do once a weeke in Winter & twice in Sum[me]r
And that the Proofehouse & Buildings adjoyning to it have been
of long time used for proving his Ma[jes]t[ie]s small Gunns, and was
then lately repayr'd for that purpose, and is so fit a place for
that service, that they know not where to be provided of such
another, having constant occasion for proving great quan-
tityes there.
And that the said Storehouse was used for laying up Match
return'd Bedding &c, w[hi]ch required to be ayred & dryed in that
Ground before they were fit to be brought into the Tower, His Ma[jes]t[ie]s
Ground at Woolw[i]ch because of the distance thereof, being no way
fit for these services.

I conceive Mr Geo[rge] Legg, as Lieutenant of the Ordnance, hath the profit of such p[ar]t of the premisses, as one not used for his Ma[jes]t[ie]s immediate service during his life. And if a Grant thereof had been passed to my L[or]d Grandison, as was proposed in 1673, I find my Father in his Report then thought it necessary, That a Proviso should be inserted (as was don in the Grant of the Custom house 9 Jac[obi] & in other Grants of like nature) That if it shall appear necessary at any time hereafter to resume the premisses for the service of the Crown, the same may be resumed, giving such recompence to the then Owners or Possessors thereof as the L[or]d high Trea[sure]r of England & Chancellor of the Exchequer, or L[or]ds Comissioners of the Trea[su]ry for the time being, shall think reasonable, w[hi]ch Clause I conceive maybe as fit now to be inserted, if any new Grant should be made of the premisses, Humbly submitting the same to your Lo[rdshi]ps great Judgment.

11 May 1681 Will[iam] Harbord

This was prepared in May, but not called for till August & was delivered to Mr Aldworth 8 Aug[ust] 1681.

#24 – Henry Guy, Secretary to the Treasurer, reports to the Ordnance Commissioners about the proposed sale of the Old Artillery Ground – 13 November 1681 (TNA, Treasury Out Letter Book – 1680–1682 (T 27/6), page 358):

[Page 358]

Ordnance Com[missioner]s Gentlemen,

The L[or]ds Com[missioner]s of his Ma[jes]t[ie]s Treas[su]ry having taken into th[ei]r Considerat[i]on the sale of ye Artillery Ground, have had occasion to p[er]use the Report made to you the second of Aprill last by ye officers of the Ordnance wherein is set forth That the sayd Ground having formerly ran some hazard of being begg'd of his Maj[esti]e hath been

preserved by such arguments & reasons as were made & given for the usefullness of it in his Maj[es]t[ie]s service, especially for ye exercise of his Maj[es]t[ie]s feed Guners (the Ma[ste]r Gunner having a dwelling house there for that very purpose) & ye proof of small guns w[hi]ch have always been made there as a place most convenient, & that the L[ieutenan]t G[ene]rall of ye ordnance for the tyme being hath by his Patent ye Custody, consequently the benefit made by ye Herbage thereof & of the rent of ye other Houses thereon standing. That neverthelesse if any other convenient places can be found our for ye exercise of his Maj[es]t[ie]s sayd Gunners & the proofe of small Gunns, & that ye Lei[utena]nts of the Ordnance for the tyme being will quitt theire Interest therein as Coll[onel] Legg (the present Lei[utenan]nt), hath declared he freely will for his Maj[es]t[ie]s service, & that the Ma[ste]r Gunner for ye time being may be else where accomodated w[i]th an other dwelling house & ground Capable & fitt for ye exercise of his Ma[jes]t[ie]s feed Gunner w[hi]ch he is (*vertute oficii*) obleig'd to, Then the sayd officers are of opinion that ye sayd Artillery Ground may be diposed of as proposed without prejudice to his Ma[jest]ie. In relat[i]on to which their Lo[rdshi]pps desire to be certifyed from you whether ye sayd Ma[ste]r Gunner be else where accomodated w[i]th another house & ground capable & fitt for the exercize of his Ma[jes]t[ie]s sayd Gunners. Which by theire Lo[rdshi]pps order, I signifye to you & remaine, Gent[lemen] &c H[enry] G[uy]
13th Nov[embe]r 1681

#25 – Henry Guy, Secretary to the Treasurer, refers the proposed sale of the Old Artillery Ground to Sir Christopher Wren, the Surveyor General of His Majesty's Works – 6 December 1681 (TNA, Treasury Reference Book of Applications – 1680–1682 (T 4/1), page 500):

[Page 500]

Artillery Ground A Ground plot of ye old Artillery Ground nere ye Spittle in London together w[i]th Mr Surveyor Gen[era]ll's Report thereupon dated ye 11th of May 1681.

Whitehall Trea[su]ry Chambers 6 Dec[ember] 1681

The Lords Com[missione]rs of his Ma[jes]t[ie]s Trea[su]ry are pleased to referre this Plot to Sir Cr[ist]opher Wren, Surveyor Gen[era]ll & ye rest of ye Officers of his Ma[jes]t[ie]s Workes to certifie what this ground may be worth when Improved by Building and to endeavour to find out some p[er]sons to deale for building thereupon.

Hen[ry] Guy

#26 – Henry Guy, Secretary to the Treasurer, writes to Sir Robert Sawyer, the Attorney General, and to some interested parties about the proposed sale of the Old Artillery Ground – 23 December 1681 (TNA, Treasury Out Letter Book – 1680-1682 (T 27/6), page 368):

[Page 368]

Mr Attorney S[i]r,

The old Artillery Ground being the Kings antient Inheritance, and having been alwayes a Priviledged Place, The Lords Comm[issioner]s of his Ma[jes]tys Trea[su]ry desire you to advise them, in case the same should be sold to *(sic)* his Ma[jes]ty and prove to be within ye Lib[er]tys of the Citty, whether or no the King hath Power to grant a Market to them that shall buy it. I am, S[i]r yours &c H[enry] G[uy] 23th Dec[ember] 1681

S[i]r W[illia]m Warren S[i]r,

By Direction of the Lordes Comm[issioner]s of his Ma[jes]t[ie]s Trea[su]ry, I am to desire you to take Notice, That in the Proposall for the artillery Ground none are to bid under 400*li* without a Market, and not under 1200*li* more if a Market be obteyned and setled within two yeares after the grant is passed. And for Well Close That 20*li* p[er] Rent be reserved to the Crowne. I am &c

H[enry] G[uy]
23 Dec[ember 16]81

Mr Neale	The like L[ett]re of the like Date
Mr Barebone	The like L[ett]re of the like Date
S[i]r C[hristo]p[h]er Wrenn	The like L[ett]re of the like Date
M[iste]r Killigrew	The like L[ett]re of the like Date

w[i]th that above to S[i]r W[illia]m Warren

#27 – Henry Guy, Secretary to the Treasurer, writes to Sir Robert Howard, the Auditor of the Receipt, instructing him to reserve the money paid for the Old Artillery Ground to the use of the Commissioners of the Treasury – 10 January 1682 (TNA, Treasury Disposition Books – 1680–1684 (T 61/2), page 114):

[Page 114]

Do[cto]r Barbones
Purchase in O for
Well Close & Artill[ery]
ground

Do[cto]r Barbones S[i]r,
The Lords Com[missioner]s of his Ma[jes]t[ie]s Trea[su]ry desire that what money
shalbee paid into ye Excheq[ue]r by Doctor Barbone for ye Purchase
of Well Close and ye Old Artillery Ground be reserved for theire
Lo[rdshi]ps disposall. I am &c. H[enry] G[uy] 10 January 1681
To S[i]r Rob[er]t Howard

#28 – Henry Guy, Secretary to the Treasurer, writes to Sir Robert Howard, the Auditor of the Receipt, instructing him to pay him £500 out of the money paid for the Old Artillery Ground – 20 January 1682 (TNA, Treasury Disposition Books – 1680–1684 (T 61/2), page 116):

[Page 116]

Old
Artillery Ground
Mr Guy

S[i]r,
The Lords Com[missioner]s of his Ma[jes]t[ie]s Trea[su]ry desire That out of ye Purchase money
to be p[ai]d into ye Excheq[ue]r for the Old Artillery Ground you issue to me
For his Ma[jes]t[ie]s Secret service ye Summe of Five hundred Pounds &
that you reserve ye remainder for theire Lo[rdshi]ps
disposeal. I am &c
H[enry] G[uy] 10 January 1681
To S[i]r Rob[er]t Howard

#29 – Charles II issues a warrant for a grant on the Old Artillery Ground property to be issued to George Bradbury and Edward Noel – 18 January 1682 (TNA, King's Warrant Book – 1680–1683 (T 52/8), pages 305-307):

[Page 305]

Bradbury, Georg
&
Edward Noel
Dr Barbon

Charles R[ex]

Our will and Pleasure is that you forthwith p[re]pare a Bill for our Royall Signature to pass Our great Seale of England conteyning a Graunt to Our Trusty and welbeloved Subjects George Bradbury & Edward Noell Esq[uires], theire heires & Assignes (for & in considerat[i]on of the sum of Five Thousand seaven hundred pounds of Lawfull money of England which they are to pay into the Receipt of our Excheq[ue]r for Our use before the sayd Graunt passes under Seale), Of all yt peece or p[ar]cell of Ground comonly called or known by ye name of the Old Artillery Ground or the Old Artillery Garden or by whatsoever other name the same is called or knowne, scituate lying & being in or near the City of London, and in or near the Parish of St Buttolph Bishopsgate, upon the West Side of the fields or places comonly called Spittle fields and conteyning by admeasurement five Acres & one rood be the same more or lesse.

As ye same is now Incompassed w[i]th a Brickwall, Togeather w[i]th the sayd Brickwall, and the ground whereupon it Stands And also all that Messuage at ye southwest corner of the sayd Ground, together w[i]th the ground Paled out for a

[Page 306]

Garden to it, which were formerly in the possession & occupat[i]on of Hanserd Knolls. And also all that great brickhouse standing upon the sayd piece or p[ar]cell of ground neere to the aforesayd Messuage and which hath comonly been used by our officers of the Ordnance for laying up of stores, with the Garden belonging to ye sayd storehouse.

Two other Mesauages or Tenem[en]ts standing upon ye sayd piece or parcells of ground neare the Messuage and storehouse before mention'd, and also the two Gardens thereunto belonging, All that dwelling house which hath been comonly used for the Habitat[i]on of Our Master Gunner, likewise standing within ye aforesayd piece or p[ar]cell of Ground, and also ye stables Coach house, Porters Lodg, two Powder houses, the long house or building used by Our Officers of ye Ordnance for proving of small Gunns and keeping of stores, and also the Charging house lying contiguous to ye afores[ai]d Dwelling house, And all other Houses, Edifices and Buildings standing or being or which shall hereafter be erected or built in or upon the sayd Piece or parcell of Ground called the Old Artillery Ground or the Old Artillery Garden or in or upon any p[ar]te or p[ar]cell thereof, Together with free Liberty, Lycense and authority for them, the sayd George Bradbury and Edward Noell, theire heires and Assignes to erect, build and set up or cause to be erected, built & sett up any new houses, Edifices and Buildings in or upon the premisses. And all and singular wayes, Passages, Lights, Easiam[en]ts, Waters, Waters, Watercourses, Trees, Fences, profitts, Comoditys, Priviledges, Advantages and appurtenances whatsoever to the says piece or parcell of Ground and other the premisses or to any p[ar]te thereof belonging or in any wise apperteyning or usually accepted, reputed, or taken as p[ar]te, p[ar]cell or member of the same. And the Revert[i]on and Revert[i]ons Remaind[e]r & Remaind[e]rs, Rents, Issues & Profitts of all and singular the Premisses, And all Our Estate, right, Title, Interest, Benefit, Clayme &

[Page 307]

demand whatsoever, of in or to the same. To have and to hold for the sayd George Bradbury and Edward Noell, theire heires and Assignes, To the onely use & behoofe of the sayd George Bradbury & Edward Noell, theire heires and Assignes for ever. Of us, Our heires and Successors, as of our Manner of East Greenwich in Our County of Kent, not in Capite, or by Knights service, but in Free and common soccage, By Fealty and the rent of six shill[ing]s eight pence p[er] ann[um] to be paid into our Excheq[ue]r at Mich[aelm]as in every yeare. And you are to insert in ye sayd Bill all such Covenants, nonobstantes and other Clauses as are usuall in Grants of the like nature and such others as you shall think fitt to make the sayd Grant to ye sayd George Bradbury and Edward Noell, theire heires & Assignes, most firme, valid and effectuall, For which this shalbe your Warr[an]t. Given at Our Court at Whitehall the Eighteenth day of January in the 33th yeare of Our Reigne 1681

To our Attorney or Sollicitor G[ene]rall By his Ma[jes]t[ie]s Com[m]and

L[aurence] Hyde J[ohn] E[rnle] S[tephen] G[odolphin] S[tephen] F[ox]

#30 – Henry Guy, Secretary to the Treasurer, begins a letter to Nicholas Barbon to inform him that the warrant for the Old Artillery Ground has been signed by Charles II – 18 January 1681 (TNA, Treasury Out Letter Book – 1680–1682 (T 27/6), page 395):

[Page 395]

Barbone, Dr

S[i]r,

Your Warr[an]t for the Artillery Ground is signed by his Ma[jest]it And ye Lords of

#31 – Henry Guy, Secretary to the Treasurer, writes to Doctor Nicholas Barbon about non-payment of fee for the sale of the Old Artillery Ground – 23 January 1682 (TNA, Treasury Disposition Books – 1680–1684 (T 61/2), page 117):

[Page 117]

Do[cto]r Barebon
Artillery Ground

S[i]r,

The Lords Com[missioner]s of his Ma[jes]t[ie]s Trea[su]ry are informed from ye Excheq[ue]r That you have not paid in ye Purchase money for the Artillery Ground w[hi]ch they very much wonder at, and doe desire that you will pay the same immediately into ye Excheq[ue]r and send by this bearer when the same shalbee accordingly Paid. I am &c H[enry] G[uy] 23 Jan[uary] 1681

To Doctor Nich[olas] Barbone

#32 – Henry Guy, Secretary to the Treasurer, writes to Doctor Nicholas Barbon about non-payment of fee for the sale of the Old Artillery Ground – 26 January 1682 (TNA, Treasury Out Letter Books – 1680–1682 (T 27/6), page 399):

[Page 399]

Do[cto]r
Barebon

S[i]r,
The Lords Comm[issione]rs of his Ma[jes]t[ie]s Trea[su]ry have Commanded
me to Informe you that they take it very Ill That
you have not completed the payment of your purchase
Money for the Artillery Ground & that they expect
you pay the whole & charge the same to Morrow
without faile. I am, S[i]r, your humble Ser[van]t H[enry] Guy
Trea[su]ry Chambers 26 Jan[uary] 1681

#33 – Henry Guy, Secretary to the Treasurer, writes to Sir Robert Howard, the Auditor of the Receipt, instructing him to transfer £5200 out of the money paid for the Old Artillery Ground to the Treasurer of the Ordnance Office – 1 February 1682 (TNA, Treasury Disposition Books – 1680–1684 (T 61/2), page 119):

[Page 119]

Purchase in O[ld]
Artillery Ground

The Lords Com[missioner]s of his Ma[jes]t[ie]s Trea[su]ry you out of
ye Purchase money of ye Artillery Ground now
remaining in ye Excheq[ue]r to issue to ye Trea[sure]r of
his Ma[jes]t[ie]s Ordnance £5200
I am &c H[enry] G[uy] 1 February 1681
To S[i]r Robert Howard

#34 – Hanserd Knowles conviction for attending conventicle at the home of Mary Winch – 9 January 1665 (LMA, Conventicle Convictions 1664–1665 (MR/R/C/001), membrane 35):

[Text]

Memorand[um] q[uo]d Nono die Januarii Anno Regni D[omi]ni n[ost]ri Caroli Secundi Dei gratia
Angliae Scotiae Franciae hiberniae Regis fidei defensor[is] &c Decimo Sexto ven[er]unt Hanserd
Knowles de p[ar]ochia S[anc]ti Egidii extra Criplegate in Com[itatu]

Mid[dlesex], gener[osus], et Robertus Siferwest de
p[ar]ochia S[anc]te Margarete Westminster in Com[itatu] p[re]dict[o], Glasier, adtunc subdit[i] huius regn[i] Angl[ie] &c
Coram Riginald[o] Forster Baronet et Joh[ann]e Smith, Armiger[o], Adtunc duob[us] Justic[iariis] d[ic]ti regis
ad pacem pro Com[itatu] p[re]dict[o] conservand[am] Assignat[is] Com[itatui] Mid[dlesex] p[re]dict[o] et sup[er]inde adtunc et ib[ide]m debite
exa[m]i[n]at[i] coram Justic[iariis] p[re]dict[is] tam p[er] confession[es] ip[s]or[um] p[ro]pr[iorum] quam p[er]
notor[um] evidenc[iam] facti adtunc ib[ide]m
Justic[iariis] p[re]dict[is] manifeste appar[uit] q[uo]d p[re]dict[i] Hanserd Knowles et Robertus Siferwest et quil[i]b[e]t eor[um]
tunc existen[tes] Aet[at]is Sexdecem annor[um] et amplius et ip[s]i et eor[um] quil[i]b[e]t subdit[i] d[ic]ti regis adtunc
existen[tes] d[ic]to Nono die Januarii Anno sup[ra]d[ic]to p[re]sent[es] fuer[unt] assemblaver[unt] et illicite congregaverunt apud
dom[um] Manc[i]onal[em] cuiusdam Marie Winch vid[ue] in p[ar]ochia S[anc]ti Egidii extra Criplegate in Com[itatu] p[re]dict[o]
cum diversis aliis malefactoribus et pacis d[ic]ti d[omi]ni regis p[er]turbatorib[us] ignotis ad numerum Septem
p[er]sonarum p[re]ter p[er]sonas de familia ejusdem Marie Winch vid[ue] sub colore exercend[i] Religion[em] in alio
modo quam allocatum est p[er] Liturgiam aut usum Anglican[e] Eccl[es]ie contra pacem d[ic]ti d[omi]ni Regis
Et contra formam Statut[i] in hu[ius]mo[d]i casu edit[i] & p[ro]vis[i], Et p[re]dict[i] Hanserd Knowles et Robertus
Siferwest adtunc et ib[ide]m coram Justic[iariis] p[re]dict[is] de offens[ione] p[re]dict[a] convicti sunt & quil[i]b[e]t eor[um] convict[us]
est, Et ideo p[re]fat[i] justic[iarii] p[re]dict[os] Hanserd Knowles & Robert[u]m Siferwest die et anno sup[ra]d[ic]tis ad
Co[mmun]em Gaolam d[ic]ti d[omi]ni Regis p[ro] Com[itatu] Mid[dlesex] p[re]dict[o] p[ro] offens[ione] sup[ra]dict[a] com[m]iser[unt] ib[ide]m moratur[os] p[er]
Spacium trium dier[um] tunc p[ro]x[ime] sequen[tum] Nisi quil[i]b[e]t eorundem Hanserd et Robert[us] p[re]dict[orum] sep[ar]atim
p[ro] seip[s]is p[re]dict[is] Justic[iariis] Solveret duo Solidis p[ro] fine p[er] Justic[iarios] p[re]dict[os] tunc asses[sata] p[ro] offens[ione] p[re]dict[a]
In Cujus rei Testimon[io] Justic[iarii] p[re]dict[i] huic p[re]sen[ti] recordo manus et sigilla sua apposuer[unt] die et anno
Sup[ra]d[ic]tis.

Reginald Forster [signature]
John Smith [signature]

[Translation]

Memorandum that on the Ninth day of January in the sixteenth year of the Reign of our Lord Charles the Second, by the grace of God King of England, Scotland, France, Ireland, defender of the faith &c, Hanserd Knowles of the parish of Saint Giles without Criplegate in the County of Middlesex, gentleman, and Robert Siferwest of the parish of Saint Margaret, Westminster in the aforesaid County, Glasier, at the time subjects of this kingdom of England &c came before Riginald Forster Baronet and John Smith, Esquire, at the time two Justices of the said King Appointed to preserve the peace of the aforesaid County, in the aforesaid County of Middlesex; and moreover were then and there duly examined before the aforesaid Justices both by their own personal confessions and by the evidence of known persons about the incident. Then and there it was clearly apparent to the aforesaid Justices that the said Hanserd Knowles and Robert Siferwest, jointly and severally at the time being aged Sixteen years or more, and the same men, jointly and severally being then subjects of the said King, on the Ninth day of January in the abovementioned year were present, assembled, and unlawfully gathered at the dwelling place of a certain Mary Winch, widow, in the parish of Saint Giles without Cripplegate in the aforesaid County, with various other unknown malefactors and disturbers of the peace of the said Lord King, totalling seven persons in number beside the persons from the family of the same Mary Winch, widow, on the pretext of exercising Religion in a manner other than that which is allowed according to the Liturgy and practice of the Anglican Church, against the peace of the said Lord King And against the form of the Statute published and provided for such a case. And the aforesaid Hanserd Knowles and Robert Siferwest then and there before the aforesaid Justices were convicted of the aforesaid offense, jointly and severally, And therefore the said Justices sent the aforesaid Hanserd Knowles & Robert Siferwest on the day and year abovementioned to the Common [Newgate] Gaol of the said Lord King on behalf of the aforesaid County of Middlesex because of the abovementioned offence, and there they should remain for the space of the three days immediately following, unless either one of the same aforementioned Hanserd and Robert

individually
[20] pays, on behalf of both, two Shillings to the aforesaid Justices, as the fine assessed at the time by the aforesaid Justices for the aforesaid offence.

In Testimony thereof the said Justices have affixed their hands and seals to this present record on the day and year abovesaid.

Reginald Forster [signature]
John Smith [signature]

CHAPTER 3

The Anabaptist Petitions of 1660 and 1661

Within the Parliamentary Archives there are two petitions submitted to the House of Lords by Anabaptists in London in the early 1660s.[1] The first petition (Figure #1) bears only one signature, that of Hanserd Knollys (c.1599–1691), who signed 'by the Appointment of the rest of ye Petitioners' (lines 27-28). This petition is not internally dated, although an unknown clerk has written in the left corner of the document 'Anabaptists petition—read ye 4 May 1660'. The second petition (Figure #2) was signed by six London Baptists, most notably the Particular Baptist leader William Kiffen (1616–1701), who is, in terms of personalia, the one common denominator of the two documents. It is not specifically dated by the six signatories, although a date of 5 July 1661 was also apparently added in the upper left corner of the document by an unknown clerk.

As far as I am aware critical editions of these documents have never been published before, and as a consequence the so-called Anabaptist Petitions of 1660 and 1661 have not received the attention that they are due by Baptist historians. This is unfortunate, since they came at a critical time in the life of the denomination, struggling as it was for legitimacy and acceptance in the early days of the restoration of Charles II. The fact that within both documents the petitioners note that they are 'called Anabaptists', is an acknowledgement of the way they were popularly described at the time; it also suggests that they preferred another term of self-definition (i.e., 'Baptists'). Together the two Anabaptist petitions offer an illuminating insight of how English Baptists viewed themselves and how they were perceived by others; they also shed light on the co-operation between leaders of the General Baptists and the Particular Baptists in the face of changing political circumstances during the early 1660s. A number of interesting supplementary questions are raised by the petitions, notably the geographical location of William Kiffen's meeting house in London, and the extent to which Baptist leaders were implicated in political plots to overthrow the government by force. An investigation of these topics will invite a consideration of some additional sources from the period, documents which have been overlooked by Baptist historians.

---

[1] PA, HL/PO/JO/10/1/283 and HL/PO/JO/10/1/306.

The Anabaptist Petition of 1660

A fairly full description of the Anabaptist Petition of 1660 appeared in 1879.[2] Unfortunately, this summary description fails to record that the signatory of the petition was Hanserd Knollys. Indeed, the official description of the record in the House of Lords Archives also fails to record that Knollys was the signatory, simply describing the document as 'Petition of several people (called Anabaptists) inhabiting in and about the city of London'. The document is on a single page of parchment and contains twenty-nine lines of writing (see Document #1 for the full text).

The Anabaptist Petition of 1660 raises several interesting historical questions, not least of which is clarification as to the circumstances that gave rise to it. Clearly the immediate trigger which prompted the Baptists to petition the House of Lords as they did were the events of 1–2 May, when riots against Dissenters broke out across the city of London. These were severe enough to be recorded in *The Journal of the House of Lords*, which notes in the entry for 4 May, 'That, on Tuesday or Wednesday last, a great Riot and Violence was offered to the Persons and Estates of some Inhabitants in the City of London.'[3] The petition specifically records that within these riots one of the Baptist meeting houses was badly damaged (lines 6–8). The cost of these damages was substantial; the £200 stipulated in the petition would have the equivalent purchasing power of over £15,000 today (2009). Where these riots took place is difficult to pinpoint from the petition itself, although one contemporary account states that it involved a meeting house on St Dunstan's Hill near Thames Street:

> On Sunday night some of the rude multitude fell on the Anabaptists Church or Meeting-house on St. Dunstan's-hill, near Thames-street, pulled down the pulpit, and plucked up the seats, with many other such like insolencies.[4]

There is some evidence to suggest that this may have been the meeting house used by the congregation of William Kiffen, and some news-sheets, namely *Mercurius Publicus* and *The Parliamentary Intelligencer*, do specifically note that Kiffen's meeting house was damaged in the London riots at the beginning of May.[5] On the

---

[2] HMC, *Seventh Report of the Royal Commission of Historical Manuscripts, Part I, Report and Appendix* (London: HMSO, 1879): 80.

[3] *JHL* 11 (4 May 1660): 13.

[4] BLO, MS Carte 214, folio 99. This was published in Timothy Carte, *A Collection of Original Letters and Papers Concerning Affairs in England from the Year 1641 to 1660* (1739): 326-327.

[5] See *Mercurius Publicus* #19 (3–10 May 1660): 292, and *The Parliamentary Intelligencer* #19 (30 April–7 May 1660): 299; these reports are recorded in BLL, Thomas Rugge 'Mercurius Politicus Redivivus' (Add MS 10,116), folio 91 ('att this time the looser sort of people was very uncivill to the people called Anabaptists defaced Coll Kiffins meetinge'). Henry Jessey's *The Lords Loud Call to England* (14 August 1660): 8, similarly

strength of these news reports Tim Harris identifies the meeting house in St Dunstan's Hill as the place where the congregation of William Kiffen met (see Figure #3).[6] A few other documents from the period seem to corroborate this identification. For example, the satirical tract *The Humble Petition and Recantation of Many Dissatisfied Persons Commonly Known by the Name of Anabaptists* (1660) mentions Kiffen preaching 'in his own Synagogue near Tower-street' (St Dunstan's Hill intersected Tower Street). In addition, a list entitled 'These Congregational Ministers Preach Publiquely in or about London' notes that Kiffen's church was 'By Dunstan's East'.[7] Similarly, an undated list entitled 'Hoax Preachers & Places' specifically notes that Kiffin's meeting place was 'neere St Dunstans east' (the church of St Dunstan's-in-the-East was located between Tower Street and Thames Street).[8] In any event, it seems that the rioting in St Dunstan's was quite extensive, and lasted over several days (at least from 29 April to 2 May 1660). Such rioting and disturbance of the peace continued to be of concern to the House of Lords, who discussed the matter again on 7 May 1660 and drafted a proposal empowering civic authorities to take appropriate action to prevent further incidents.[9]

It is not clear *why* the meeting house of William Kiffen was descended upon by the rioters, although it is reasonable to assume that it had to do with a widespread public antipathy to Anabaptists, who were viewed with fear and suspicion by many at the time. The Anabaptists were also the subject of a number of satirical broadsheets in the months immediately before the riots, including *A Serious Manifesto and Declaration of the Anabaptist and Other Congregational Churches* (28 February 1660),[10] *The Humble Petition and Recantation of Many Dissatisfied*

---

notes that 'havoc was made of that Assembling house, where Mr Kiffins Friends used to meet'.

[6] Tim Harris, *London Crowds in the Reign of Charles II: Propaganda and Politics from the Restoration until the Exclusion Crisis* (Cambridge: Cambridge University Press, 1987): 52.

[7] TNA, SP 29/47, page 106. The list, which dates from c.1661, concludes with an explanatory note, 'That in Petty France, & by Dunstans East, & at Old Artillery, are large Assembling Places built of late.' This dovetails nicely with the lines 5–6 of the Anabaptist Petition of 1660, where it is stated that the Baptist petitioners 'at theire great charge did buy and build severall howses in and about the Citty of London for theire publique meetings'.

[8] LMA, List of Hoax Preachers and Places (CLA/047/LR/02/02/001). The London Metropolitan Archives give this a tentative date of 1683, but it is more likely that it is from the early 1660s; the list also includes 'Jessey in Colemanstreete' (Henry Jessey died in 1663).

[9] PA, HL/PO/JO/10/1/283 (7 May 1660). Also see the *JHL* 11 (7 May 1660): 17.

[10] William Kiffen and three other Baptists wrote a letter of protest to Thomas Allen, the Mayor of London, about it on 28 February. This was published as a broadsheet on 2 March 1660 entitled *A Letter Sent to the Right Honourable, the Lord Mayor of the City of London* (1660). The broadsheet is especially interesting for it details that Kiffen's home was searched for illegal arms, and Kiffen was imprisoned for several days before being released without charge, apparently everything taking place at the order of General Monck. This was also reported in several news-sheets (*Mercurius Politicus* #609 (23 February–1 March 1660): 1140 and 1141; *The Publick Intelligencer* #220 (27 February–5 March 1660): 1132 and

Persons Commonly Known by the Name of Anabaptists (2 March 1660), and *A Phanatique League and Covenant Solemnly enter'd into by the Assertors of the Good Old Cause* (21 March 1660). The last of these is in many ways the most interesting, for it was allegedly issued by thirty-one religious and political radicals promoting a return to the Republic; significantly, William Kiffen is named as one of the supposed subscribers.

The extent to which Kiffen was involved in such political debates of the late 1650s remains a contentious issue. According to William Allen, writing in 1659, Kiffen was opposed to Pride's Purge of Parliament in December of 1648, and was against the execution of Charles I the following month.[11] Similarly, an informant's report about the Western Association meetings in Dorchester in May of 1658 stated that Kiffen was against any association with the Fifth Monarchists and helped persuade his fellow delegates of the wisdom of such counsel.[12] On the basis of evidence such as this, Kiffen is commonly thought of as a moderate, someone who benefitted from, and was thus generally supportive of the political status quo of the Cromwellian Protectorate. It is assumed that Kiffen steered a middle course in the political currents of the day, that he was untainted by the extremes of the Fifth Monarchists in establishing the reign of Christ upon the earth, and that he was against the re-establishment of monarchial rule under Charles II.

Occasionally, however, there are documents that suggest that Kiffen may not always have held such a centrist position generally ascribed to him. For example, there is an intriguing letter dated 8 April 1660 from the disaffected General John Desborough to the publisher Livewell Chapman at his home in Pope's Head Alley, Cornhill, just opposite the Royal Exchange (see Document #2).[13] This letter has been regarded by some scholars as a contemporary forgery designed to implicate the political opponents of the Restoration in a plot to overthrow legitimate government by violent means.[14] Even if the letter is a forgery, it illustrates how certain people,

---

1133; *The Parliamentary Intelligencer* #11 (27 February–5 March 1660): 153). Kiffen discusses the incident in his *Memoirs* (William Orme, *Remarkable Passages in the Life of William Kiffen* (London, 1823): 26-27).

[11] This is contained in a letter written to Richard Baxter on 30 May 1659 (See N.H. Keeble and Geoffrey F. Nuttall, *Calendar of the Correspondence of Richard Baxter, Volume I, 1638–1660* (Oxford Clarendon Press, 1991): 393-394).

[12] BLO, MS Rawlinson A 59, pages 75-76. This was published in Thomas Birch (ed.), *A Collection of the State Papers of John Thurloe, Volume 7* (London, 1742): 138-140.

[13] TNA, SP 18/220, pages 108-109. A handwritten copy of the letter is found in TNA, SP 18/220, pages 110-112, and another copy is contained in BLL, Stowe MS 185, folios 168-170.

[14] See Louise Fargo Brown, *The Political Activities of the Baptists and Fifth Monarchy Men in England during the Interregnum* (Oxford: Oxford University Press, 1912): 198-199; Violet A Rowe *Sir Henry Vane the Younger: A Study in Political and Administrative History* (London: The Athlone Press, 1970): 218; Bernard Capp *The Fifth Monarchy Men: A Study in Seventeenth-century English Millennarianism* (London: Faber and Faber, 1972): 280, describes it as 'faked evidence of a 5th Mon[archy] plot'.

such as Chapman, were popularly conceived to be advocates of anti-establishment views. At the time of the writing of the letter Chapman was a wanted man, warrants for his arrest having been issued by the Counsel of State on 27 March and 28 April 1660.[15] Desborough writes from Llanothen in North Wales, discussing some of the plans that were being formulated to prevent the restoration of Charles II, and to ensure a return to the Republic following the resignation of Richard Cromwell and the collapse of the Protectorate. Desborough was especially critical of General Monck's involvement in these matters, railing against the 'villaine Monck' and 'his hidden workes of darkness' which threatened to undermine the aims of the Republicans. In contrast, Sir Harry Vane (1613–62) was applauded as the leader around whom revolutionary change could be effected. As Desborough says, 'Sir Harry Vane is a man that seemes to be borne for such a time as this; he will come up we hear to head us.'[16] The plans proposed recognized the possibility of a violent struggle, for Desborough states that '10,000*li* in armes' had been distributed to supporters of the cause; he also notes in passing that there was an attempt to assassinate the king ('the attempt upon Charles Stuart we heare did not succeede the way intended'). Clearly this involved a co-ordinated effort which called for ardent republicans from all around the country to converge upon the capital London and seize control of the reins of power.[17] Most importantly for our considerations here is the fact that Desborough's letter records Kiffen's involvement in these plans to force a new government:

> Mr Kiffin and Mr Cockain, Mr Hudleson, Mr M the Committeeman, Mr Feake write to us of securing the g[ene]rall [Lambert?] and ye Parliament about 6th May, to which they say all the congregations in London agree, except Mr Caryls and Mr Griffiths.[18]

---

[15] TNA, SP 25/116, pages 12 and 38. The Council of State issued a proclamation on 28 March 1660 about Chapman entitled *By the Council of State: A Proclamation* (1660). For more on Chapman, see Leona Rostenberg, *Literary, Political, Scientific, Religious & Legal Publishing, Printing & Bookselling in England, 1551–1700: Twelve Studies, Volume 1* (New York: Burt Franklin, 1965): 203-236; A. Cohen, 'Chapman, Livewell (fl.1643–d.1664)', in Richard L. Greaves and Robert Zaller (eds.), *Biographical Dictionary of British Radicals in the Seventeenth Century, Volume I: A–F* (Brighton: The Harvester Press, 1982): 136-137; Maureen Bell, 'Chapman, Livewell (*fl.*1643–1665)', *Oxford Dictionary of National Biography* (Oxford: Oxford University Press, Sept 2004; online edn, Jan 2008).

[16] Lines 51–53. Vane was popularly viewed as a supporter of religious fanaticism. A satirical pamphlet published on 11 February 1660 asserted that he had been given £300 by the Committee of Safety 'to raise a regiment of Anabaptists' (*An Exact Accompt of the Receipts and Disbursements Expended by the Committee of Safety* (1660): 9).

[17] *The Parliamentary Intelligencer* #15 (2–9 April 1660): 240, reported from Cardiff that a letter about a fanatical uprising had been intercepted.

[18] Unfortunately, the description of this letter in *CSPD* is not very accurate and it omits the reference to Kiffen.

All of which is to say that the heightened political uncertainty following the collapse of the Protectorate, combined with the perceived threat that Anabaptists intended to take power by violent means, set the scene for the riots in London. Rightly or wrongly, William Kiffen's supposed involvement in these political manoeuverings meant that his meeting house became a focal point for reactionaries. The relative degree of religious freedom enjoyed by Baptists and other sectarian groups during the Protectorate was in danger of being lost altogether. Thus, it is perfectly understandable that Hanserd Knollys addressed the Anabaptist Petition to the House of Lords.

Interestingly, the Anabaptist Petition in lines 21–24 cites from the Declaration of Breda issued by Charles II on 4 April 1660.[19] The king had issued this Declaration in anticipation of his return to English soil at the end of May 1660. It is clearly no accident that Charles II relocated to Breda in Holland before issuing the Declaration. Since his defeat at the Battle of Worcester in 1651 the king had been living in exile for eight and a half years, staying in a number of places in France, The United Provinces, and the Spanish Netherlands. From the spring of 1656 Charles II had been based in Brussels, within the Spanish Netherlands. However, once the decision was made that the time was ripe for Charles II to reclaim his throne a relocation was needed. Given the religious sensitivities of the day, and the fact that Britain had technically been at war with Spain since 1655, it was prudent that the Declaration of Breda came from a *Protestant* Holland rather than a *Catholic* Spanish Netherlands. Understandably, Charles II left Brussels, passed through Antwerp, and moved to the city of Breda before issuing the Declaration of Breda from there.[20] Charles II was in Breda from 4 April to 14 May 1660, before moving on to The Hague where plans for the journey to England were finalized.[21]

The Declaration of Breda served as a manifesto for the aims and intentions of Charles II in restoring the monarchy, and offered a proposal for resolving the matter of the so-called 'settlement of religion' which vexed the nation. Clearly on 4 May 1660 Hanserd Knollys and the petitioners were writing to the House of Lords in the hope of ensuring that these promises made for religious freedom and toleration

---

[19] The original Declaration of Breda is contained in the Parliamentary Archives (HL/PO/JO/10/1/283A). It was first read in the House of Lords on 1 May 1660, and the House immediately ordered publication of the Declaration 'for the service of the House and Satisfaction of the Kingdom' (see *His Majesties Gracious Letter and Declaration Sent to the House of Peers by Sir John Greenvil, Knight, from Breda* (1660): title page). The full text of the Declaration of Breda can also be found in Samuel Rawson Gardiner (ed.), *The Constitutional Documents of the Puritan Revolution, 1625–1660* (Oxford: Oxford University Press, 3rd rev. edn, 1906): 465-467.

[20] Thomas Gumble, *The Life of General Monck* (1671): 277, states that the advice to relocate from Brussels to Breda came from General Monck.

[21] There is evidence that Charles II was still in Brussels on 1 April 1660. A receipt signed by the king in Brussels on 1 April 1660 is contained in the archives of St John's College, Cambridge. It is bound into a Latin manuscript by Peter Barwick entitled 'Vita Ioannis Barwick (1690)' (MS St John's College H9b—James 277).

continued to be extended to Baptists. Perhaps the most interesting idea contained within the petition is found in line 13. Here the petition goes so far as to assert that there is a 'Reciprocall' social contract between the governing authorities ('the Magistrates') and the general population ('the Subjects'), so that 'there is a Stipulat[i]on betwixt them, that as Subject[i]on is due to the one, soe is protection to the other'.

One final point worth considering arises indirectly from the Anabaptist Petition of 1660, with its suggestive reference to the destruction of William Kiffen's meeting house in Thames Street on St Dunstan's Hill. This is the intriguing question: where did the congregation led by Kiffen meet after the rioters had done their damage? Presumably the damage to the meeting house could eventually be repaired so that the congregation could gather there again some time in the future, but are there any indications about where they met in the interim? There are some court records from February of 1661 that offer some insight into this question, and suggest that Baptist meetings began to take place in private homes following the destruction of Kiffen's meeting house in the riots (see chapter 4 for a full discussion of this).

The Anabaptist Petition of 1661

The Anabaptist Petition of 1661 is on a single page of parchment and contains thirty-seven lines of writing (see Document #3 for the full text). The description of the document within the House of Lords Archives gives no indication as to its signatories, simply noting that it is a 'Petition of divers persons commonly called Anabaptists'. Several interesting historical questions are raised by the petition. Chief among these is a query about what prompted the six signatories to approach the House of Lords with their concerns. Perhaps an initial hint in this regard is the fact that the petition in lines 5–6 appeals to the Declaration of Breda issued by Charles II in April 1660 (see the discussion of the Anabaptist Petition of 1660 above). It appears that the petitioners were hoping to ensure that the provisions of toleration and religious liberty contained in the Declaration of Breda were remembered and applied to peaceable and law-abiding Baptists. Indeed, a number of similar petitions presented to Charles II in early 1661 were published by Baptists eager to secure religious toleration along these lines. Included among these were *The Humble Petition and Representation* (25 January 1661), signed by four Baptists incarcerated in Maidstone prison,[22] *Sions Groans for Her Distressed* (8 May 1661), and John Sturgion's *A Plea for Tolleration* (29 March 1661). It is clear that some Baptists found themselves on the rough end of official oppressive policies and were being incarcerated for their religious beliefs. This situation is also mentioned in lines 13–14 of the Anabaptist Petition of 1661, with the statement that many 'have been disturbed and imprisoned for such the exercise of their Consciences in the worship of God'.

[22] The four prisoners were William Jeffery, George Hammon, John Reve, and James Blackmore.

Secondly, a query is raised about the circumstances surrounding the actual presentation of the petition to the House of Lords. Fortunately, the *Journal of the House of Lords* gives some details about this, recording that on Friday 5 July 1661, 'A Petition, presented from Persons calling themselves Anabaptists, was read'. It was ordered that the Anabaptist petitioners were to be heard on the following Wednesday (10 July) so that it might be considered what they shall offer to the House.[23] On 12 July the petition was discussed again and it was decided to proceed with a report from the Committee concerning Penal Laws, particularly as these concerned the restrictions imposed upon the religious liberty of Dissenters such as Baptists and Quakers. At one level it is somewhat surprising that the Anabaptists chose to present their petition to the House of Lords rather than the House of Commons. However, there is good evidence to suggest that throughout the Restoration period the upper House was in fact more favourably disposed to the plight of Protestant Dissenters than was the House of Commons.[24] In this respect, the prevailing opinion of the House of Lords in religious matters was generally closer to that of Charles II himself than was that contained in the House of Commons. There is good evidence to suggest that Charles II was personally opposed to some of the repressive policies of the House of Commons against religious Dissent and that he preferred a more accommodating line, such as that contained in the Declaration of Breda. No doubt the Baptist leaders who presented the Anabaptist Petition of 1661 could sense that there was a change in the prevailing winds of political power in Parliament, and knew that things were not blowing in their favour.

The circumstances that brought these six Baptist leaders together to make such a petition are by no means clear. That William Kiffen was among them is hardly surprising, given his prominence as a Baptist with established political connections within the Cromwellian government during the 1650s. It is understandable that he would have taken a leading role in addressing the ruling authorities at this critical point in history. There are some suggestions of co-operation among the six signatories during the late 1650s. Somewhat unusually, five of the petitioners (Kiffen, Tombes, Gosnold, Stanton and Cooper) are named in the title page of *An Answer to a Declaration* (1659), written by the Quakers Richard Hubberthorne and Edward Burroughs. There are thirty names of Baptist leaders included in the title page of this pamphlet, although where the Quaker writers got their list of names from is not known. The pamphlet was clearly written in response to the *Declaration of Several of the People Called Anabaptists in and about the City of London* (1659), but that broadsheet is anonymous and does not contain a list of its Baptist signatories. It does, however, contain some strong anti-Quaker comments within it, which helps explain why Hubberthorne and Burroughs produced the response they did.

---

[23] *JHL* 11 (5 July 1661): 299.

[24] Andrew Swatland, *The House of Lords in the Reign of Charles II* (Cambridge Studies in Early Modern British History; Cambridge: Cambridge University Press, 1996): 173-199, argues this point.

More significantly, it is likely that the heightened political circumstances following the Venner Revolt of January 1661 is what galvanized the Baptists, both General and Particular, into greater co-operation with one another. Indeed, the twenty-page pamphlet entitled *The Humble Apology of Some Commonly Called Anabaptists* (28 January 1661) was issued by a broad coalition of thirty Baptists as a direct response to the Venner fiasco. Interestingly, five of the six signatories of the Anabaptist Petition of 1661 are also listed as signatories of that published pamphlet, so there is good evidence of them working together just a few months prior to presenting their petition to the House of Lords.[25] Indeed, there are indications that some of the signatories were discussing the theological implications of religious toleration long before that. For example, a document written by an anonymous Baptist on 5 February 1658, the day after Richard Cromwell's dissolution of Parliament, mentions in passing John Tombes and William Kiffen, noting that the two men were offering Cromwell advice about how to resolve the question of the religious settlement of the nation.[26] Moreover, Tombes wrote to Richard Baxter in 1659[27] about his intention to consult with Kiffen over moves to prevent the toleration of Catholics, so clearly wider discussions about religious toleration for Dissenters were taking place.

What other indications are there that the six signatories of the Anabaptist Petition of 1661 knew each other and were working together during the waning days of the Protectorate? There are some intriguing civic and social networks that brought the signatories into contact one with another. For example, it is likely that service in the London militia was a common bond between William Kiffen and Samuel Stanton. The *Journal of the House of Commons* records that Major-General Skippon reported the names of London militia officers to Parliament on 5 August 1659, and both men are included in his list. Thus, there is record of Stanton being appointed Lieutenant in the Green Regiment, while Kiffen was appointed Lieutenant Colonel in the Red Regiment.[28]

Finally, it is worth noting that several of the six signatories of the Anabaptist Petition of 1661 went on to have some interesting collaborations in subsequent years. For example, there are indications that Christopher Blackwood (1606–70)

[25] The exception was John Tombes, whose condemnation of the Venner Revolt was published separately as *Saints no Smiters* (1664). This pamphlet denounced the Fifth Monarchists' attempts to use force in overthrowing the civic government. Tombes specifically condemned the Venner Revolt, describing it as 'a most bloody Insurrection, in a most violent audacious way not to be parallel'd' (8).

[26] The letter is among the papers of Robert Bennet (1605–83), now part of the collection of the Folger Library in Washington DC (X.d. 483 (208)). For a transcription and discussion, see David Underdown, 'Cromwell and the Officers, February 1658', *English Historical Review* 83 (1968): 101-107.

[27] The letter is dated 29 October 1659. See Keeble and Nuttall, *Calendar of the Correspondence of Richard Baxter*, Vol. 1: 417.

[28] *JHC* 7 (5 August 1659): 299. Also see *The Publick Intelligencer* #203 (14–21 November 1659): 881.

maintained contact with Kiffen. Blackwood mentions Kiffen in a letter he wrote to Samuel Jeake from Amsterdam on 4 May 1662, suggesting that Jeake arrange transfer of money through Kiffen's contacts should he decide to visit Holland.[29] Moreover, the subsequent connections between Kiffen and John Gosnold[30] are particularly interesting in that they illustrate continuing co-operation between them some ten years after the Anabaptist Petition of 1661. Both men are named in a list of Baptist leaders that was composed by an unknown writer in c.1672, in the immediate aftermath of the issuing of *The Declaration of Indulgence*.[31] Kiffen and Gosnold are also specifically named in a letter written by a group of Baptists to the Quaker leader William Penn on 15 August 1674. This was in connection with an acrimonious exchange between the Quakers and the Baptist pamphleteer Thomas Hicks. It appears that Kiffen (along with five other Baptist leaders—Hanserd Knollys, Thomas Paul, Lawrence Wise, Henry Forty and James Jones) wrote to Penn and invited him to attend a public debate with Thomas Hicks which was scheduled to take place on 28 August 1674 in John Gosnold's church in the Barbican.[32] The co-operation between Kiffen and Gosnold also extended to the inclusion of other doctrinal debates. For example, both men were among the six Baptists who intervened in the controversy between Obediah Wills and Henry Danvers over the question of paedobaptism. The six (Hanserd Knollys, William Kiffen, Daniel Dyke, John Gosnold, Henry Forty and Thomas DeLaune) published *The Baptists Answer to Mr Obed. Wills, his Appeal against Mr H. Danvers* (1675). All of which is to suggest that the six signatories of the Anabaptist Petition of 1661 shared a complex web of personal and social interests, which brought them into contact with one another on a number of key issues as the years went by. In July of 1661, however, the six men came together in pursuit of one common goal, the securing of religious

---

[29] East Sussex Record Office, Lewes – Letter of Christopher Blackwood to Samuel Jeake – 4 May 1662 (FRE 4289).

[30] Gosnold (1626–78) was the pastor of a General Baptist church in the Barbican in London. A rather negative picture of John Gosnold is portrayed in Thomas Ashton's *Satan in Samuel's Mantle* (1659). Ashton relates a visit made by Gosnold to the island of Jersey in July–September of 1659, where he served as chaplain and spiritual advisor to the newly-appointed military governor Colonel John Mason. Ashton noted that Gosnold 'seldome had the Tobaccho-pipe out of his mouth, except he were eating, drinking, riding, praying or preaching' (20). He described Gosnold as being a member of 'the bloodthirsty generation of Anabaptists' (15), accused him of plagiarizing his sermons, and says 'it was his judgment not to hear anyone preach except he were of his perswasion' (21).

[31] BLL, 'The State of the Non-conformists in England soon after the Restoration' (Stowe MS 185, folio 175 recto). The 'Cheife Teachers' are here identified as Capt Kiffen, Mr Knowles, Mr Harrison, Mr Gosnold, and Mr Northott. The full text is published in G. Lyon Turner, 'The Religious Condition of London in 1672 as Reported to King and Court', *Transactions of the Congregational Historical Society* 4 (1909–10): 192-205.

[32] The letter is printed in Thomas Hicks, *The Quakers Appeal Answer'd* (1674): A4; and reprinted in Hicks's *His Last Legacy to the Quakers* (1690): A4.

toleration and understanding for a fledgling tradition which had been badly damaged in the arena of public opinion by recent political events.

One concluding document from August 1661 serves to illustrate something of the popular fear about violent political movements involving Anabaptists; it also stands as another indication of Kiffen's involvement in, or perceived association with, such activities. This is an informer's letter, dated 27 August 1661, in which William Kiffen is named as a participant in a meeting of about thirty Fifth Monarchists which took place on 23 August 1661 in Norton Folgate outside Bishopsgate (see Document #4). The letter was written by a man named John Thedam, who described himself as a former gunner aboard the navy ship *Convertine* (lines 10–13). Kiffen's name appears within a list of twelve names which are added at the bottom of the letter (line 23). This list is written in another hand and was probably added by Sir Edward Nicholas (1593–1669), the Secretary of State; it begins with a note about Thomas Tilham (lines 14–15),[33] and seems to have been triggered by the reference to Tilham in Thedam's letter (line 8). This list concludes with the comment, 'These are now by laying plots & preparing for evill' (line 28). Once again, Kiffen is arguably implicated in anti-establishment activities, just as he was in the letter of John Desborough from April of 1660 (see above).

Summary

The two Anabaptist Petitions submitted to the House of Lords in 1660 and 1661 offer important insights into Baptists in London at a critical point in their life. They help us appreciate how Baptists perceived themselves and how they were perceived by others, as well as illustrating how they were struggling to come to grips with the implications of the restoration of Charles II to the throne. The fact that both petitions refer explicitly to Charles II's Declaration of Breda indicates that the Baptists were pinning their hopes on the promises of religious liberty and freedom of worship contained within it. The petitions point to popular antipathy towards the Baptists, and both arose in a context of heightened political and religious tension which threatened to erupt in physical violence against the Baptists. Indeed, the Anabaptist Petition of 1660 was prompted by riots directed against Baptist meeting houses, notably that of the Particular Baptist leader William Kiffen.

Meanwhile, the Anabaptist Petition of 1661, produced in the aftermath of the Venner Revolt, offers a rare insight into how the General and Particular Baptist leaders worked together to put this violent episode behind them and present themselves as loyal and peaceable subjects deserving of the religious freedom they

---

[33] Tilham was the pastor of a Seventh Day Baptist congregation in Colchester. For more on this controversial figure, see B.R. White, 'Tillam, Thomas (fl.1637–1668)', in Richard L. Greaves and Robert Zaller (eds.) *Biographical Dictionary of British Radicals in the Seventeenth Century, Volume III: P–Z* (Brighton: The Harvester Press, 1984): 240-241. See also Don A. Sanford, *A Choosing People: The History of Seventh Day Baptists* (Nashville, TN: Broadman Press, 1992), *passim.*

sought. At the same time, there is good evidence that indicates Kiffen was perceived to be involved in, or associated with, the Fifth Monarchist movement, following the Venner Revolt. In short, Kiffen's role in this critical juncture of dissenting history has been seriously underestimated and needs to be re-examined. All of which is to say that the two Anabaptist Petitions represent a unique window onto the early years of the Restoration. Baptist historians have overlooked them for too long, and future historical investigations into the period will have to take these documents into account more fully. They not only mark a new stage in Baptist life as the protection and advantages afforded by the Cromwellian Protectorate began to fade, but they also form a backdrop against which the more repressive stipulations of the so-called Clarendon Code of 1662–65 against Dissenters can be assessed.

Figures

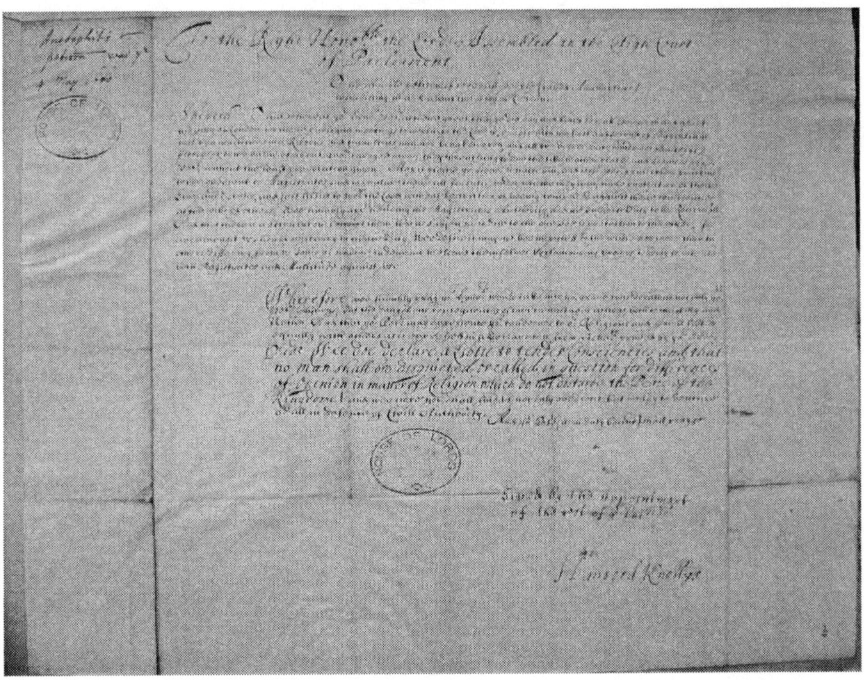

Figure #1 – The Anabaptist Petition of 1660

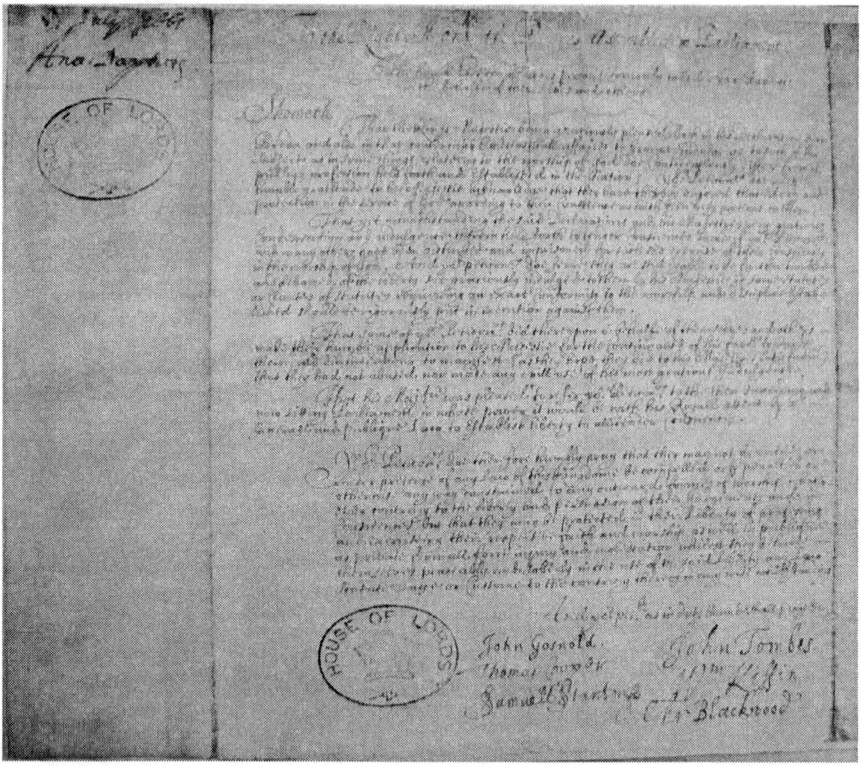

Figure #2 – The Anabaptist Petition of 1661

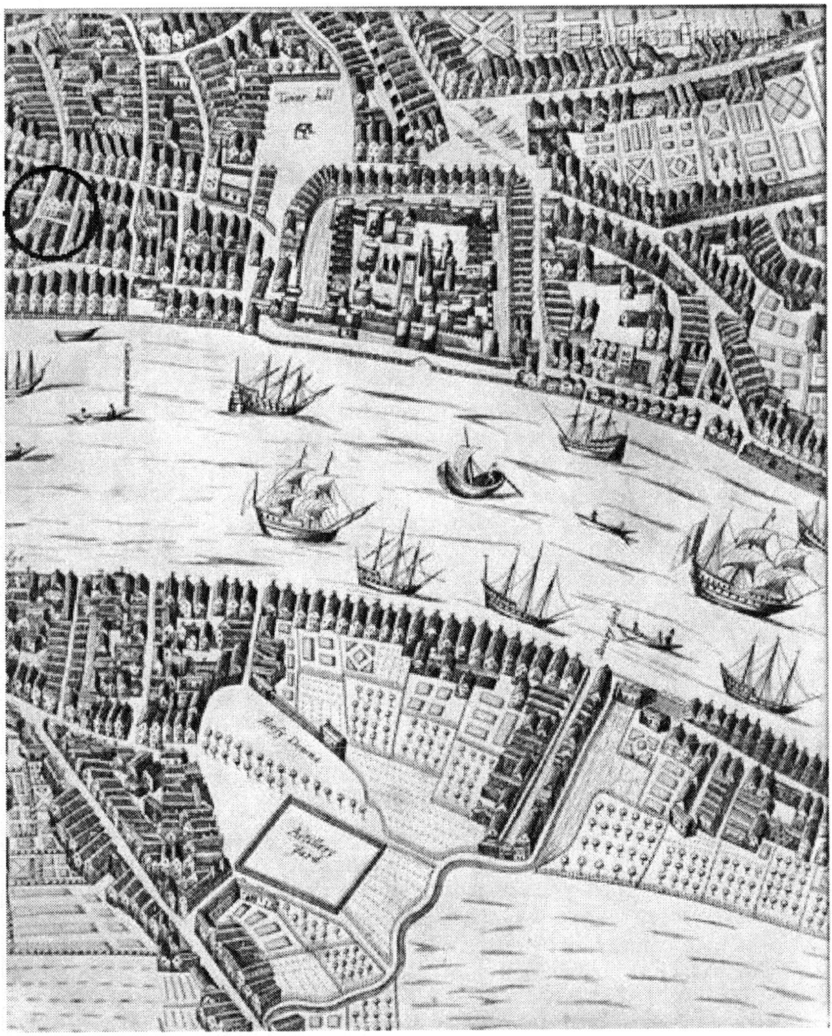

Figure #3 – Circle marks the location of St Dunstan's Hill. Detail from Richard Newcourt, *An Exact Delineation of the Cities of London and Westminster and the Surburbs and all the throughfares, highways, streets, lanes and common allies* (London, 1658). Copyright © Sara Douglass Enterprises Pty Ltd 2006 (http://www.oldlondonmaps.com/newcourtpages/newcourt32.html).Used with permission.

Documents

#1 – The Anabaptist Petition of 1660 (PA, HL/PO/JO/10/1/283):

To the Right Honorables: The Lords Assembled in the High Court of Parliament

The humble petition of severall people (called Anabaptists) inhabiting in and about the City of London.

Sheweth, That whereas your hon[ou]rs pet[itione]rs at theire great charge did buy and build severall howses in and about the City of London for theire publique meetings to worshipp the Lord in one of which the first and second of May instant was by a multitude in a Riotous and tumultuous manner broaken open and all the doores, seats, windowes, Gallerys & Floores &c to the value of about 200*li* carryed away, they threatning to doe the like to other places and howses of your pet[itione]rs, without the least provocation given. May it please your hon[ou]rs, it hath bin, and is, your pet[itione]rs principle practice to bee obedient to Magistrates, and to venture thence all for such under whome they may have protection of theire Lives and Estates, and just lib[er]ties to Wo[rshi]pp the Lord without Restriction, or beeing compelled against theire consciences at the wills of others. Wee humbly apprehending the Magistrates Authority, and the Subjects Duty to bee Reciprocall And that there is a Stipulat[i]on betwixt them, that as Subject[i]on is due to the one, soe is protection to the other. If any amongst us should miscarry in theire Duty, Wee desire it may not bee imputed to the whole noe more then to others differing from us some of whome indeavour to cleare themselves by clamouring upon us, tending to incense both Magistrates and Multitude against us.

Wherefore wee humbly pray your honours would take into your grave considerat[i]ons not only your Pet[itione]rs Injurys, but the dangerous consequences of such tumultuous actions, both to the Citty and Nation. And that your Pet[itione]rs may experience your tendernes to our Religious and Civill lib[er]ties equally with others as is oppressed in a Declarat[i]on from his Ma[jes]ty printed by your Order.
Vide Wee doe declare a Lib[er]tie to tender Consciencies and that no man shall bee disquieted or called in question for

differences of opinion in matter of Religion, which doe not disturbe the Peace of the Kingdome, and wee hope you shall find us not only obedient, but ready to venture our all in defence of Civill Authority.

And your Pet[itione]rs (as in duty bound) shall pray &c

Signed by the Appointment
of the rest of ye Pet[itio]ners

Hanserd Knollys [signature]

#2 – Letter from John Desborough to Livewell Chapman – 8 April 1660 (TNA, SP 18/220, pages 108-109):

[Page 108 recto]

Mr Chapman,

Wee count it all joy yt you are accounted worthy to suffe-re for Christ and his cause sake, and indeede there are but three things that beare up our spirits in this houre of temptations that is to come upon the earth. 1. the enraging fury of the adversary who makes it his busi-nesse to finish yt iniquity yt is not yet full. 2. the greate spirit of suffering and patience yt is dispensed out to the godly who are extraordinarily assisted to despise the suffering and shame for the prize that is set before them. 3. the great spirit of prayer that is powred out upon them together with a most lively sence of and acting faith upon the precious promises now (as wee learne by the bookes) to be accomplished. Wee have resolved upon you as the faithfullest man to conveigh our thoughts to our brethren about London. We have sent our severall messengers to our brethren over the nation. Upon the intelligence we had of there generall resolution to stand by the good old cause, once the most precious in the Eyes of saints. We have sent 3 deare brethren to south wales whence we heare yt Mr Hughes, Mr Davies, Mr Jones, Cap[t] Lloyd, Col Price with the congregations to which they belong are very forward. Dr Owen yt precious servant of Christ sent us word by one that went from him to his sinec-ure here, yt he doubted not of a good issue. Col J J is very faithfull. Capt Owen is indeede under restraint, yet hath opportu-nity to promote the businesse with Mr Wynne of Moylygte, Mr Henry Maurice, Mr Griffith Jones, Mr Jo[hn] Lloyd, Mr John Williams, Mr Will[iam] Griffith with Mr Maudrin &c are very diligent in Carnarvon-shire. Mr Rowlands, Mr Bodurda, Mr Wynne with Rice ap Evan,

John Jones, Will[iam] Morris &c have undertaken for Anglesey. Captaine Wynne, Peter Moyle, John Jones, Thomas Williams, Mr Pecke, Capt Southby, Capt Taylor, Mr Edwards of Llanvaire, Mr Jonathan Roberts &c have undertaken for Denbigh. Mr Powell &c take care for Montgomery. We hope very speedily to give you a good account, when yt discontented part of the Army we expect is come up to countenance us untill we can get together. We have laid out 10,000*li* in armes, and distributed most of them. We have raysed such a jealousy here between the cavaliers and presbyterians as were we considerable, the presbyterians would close with us, upon any termes, rather undergo an intolerable yoke under an implacable enemy. The attempt upon Charles Stuart: we heare did not succeede the way intended: But theres another way more successefull, to make it more sure. He lies very open to them whom brother Brewster mentioned in his last. When he is gone, the people will have none to dote on. The two Dukes (as they call them) being like to be otherwise secured. Mr Kiffin and Mr Cockain, Mr Hudleson, Mr M the Committeeman, Mr Feake write to us of securing the g[ene]rall and ye Parliament about 6th May, to which they say all the congregations in London agree, except Mr Caryls and Mr Griffiths. Mr Rye doeth great service in it we heare, Mr Brooks is very willing. Mr Barker is they say is indifferent. Indeed Sir Harry Vane is a man that seemes to be borne for such a time as this; he will come up we hear to head us. We shall rise first being furthest off. We have this advantage, yt by L L D &c advice a small party hath appeared at Northampton (which by designe is to be routed too). The adversary will grow soe carelesse that we may carry on what designe we will. What the divisions to be made in the house will come to we know not. This we know, that we shall be (the Lord assisting us) a moneth hence soe considerable, coming towards London, yt most of your Londoners must draw out, and then you hast your opportunity. We hope you have receaved the armes, amunition &c V A L was appoynted to bring from C to B and then to D where your carts were to meete him. What use you may make of the training dat at London, we leave to your discretion. Would wee were rid of all the carnall and selfe interested men on our side, and we doubt not but to do well. Mr Thomas the bearer hereof will tell you how farre wee prevailed upon the Irish Brigade, and pray do you tell him how farre you

[Page 108 verso]

prevailed upon your London forces. The reporte of there being to be disbanded makes much for us here; what it doth there we know not. Col Okey is very succesfull, and its beleeved his agitation may produce what may make both there eares tingle. Whether Mr Powell, Mr Mostyn, Mr Lloyd be come up to you, we heare not, when they come, we doubt not but they will put Life in the Cause. Mr Jessey with the brethren of Swan Alley, Mr Rogers, Mr Spilsbury &c are very zealous, and its good [to] be zealous in a good matter. Mr Row of Westminster hath beene very instrumentall in a late designe. The Lord strengthen the hands of such faithfull soules. I pray let us heare what the brethren of Glocestershire intend to doe. Mr Helme of Winchcombe is diligent, spending himselfe and being spent among the neighbouring congregations if they be not allready at London. Mr Helm are desired to take the comissions if they become to Mr Thomas his hands and deliver them to the officers therein named, with all speed & secrecy. Generall F M G L L G D presse very hard for something to be done by the 10th of May. See whether the churches have receaved there letters. We pray you enquire what Mr Hugh Peters hath heard from South Wales lately and know if possible his mind. It were comodious there were a day of generall fasting & seeking the Lord appointed something before the time but of this

by other more

suitable hands. We want such bookes as your *plaine english*[34] and we heare there is a piece a coming out, a character of yt watcher of villaine Monk with a discovery of the whole plott & traine of designes he hath carried on, We doubt not but god will bring to light his hidden workes of darknesse. The breath betweene the Lord Fairfax and the Yorkershire Roysters comes to nothing that Gentleman is dull and heavy, else he would not have put such things up soe much to our disappoyntment. Our first worke will be having secured the Militia and Gentry to take in the castles of Carnarvon, Denbigh, Conway, Beaumauris, Chester, &c and then advancing by the twelveth of May, we intend to be a compleatt body towards Glocester. The Glocester, Woster, Hereford shire & c brethren will meete us there and down we come untill we have tempted your generall out, (but whether your designe upon him may take, we know not. onely if you have not disposed things otherwise allready; let the quakers have the knottiest piece, for they are resolute in p[er]forming, though but rash in advising). It were to be wished the house had some bones to pick, that they might determine nothing untill 12th of May. We hope some friends will take care of that

[34] A reference to *Plain English to His Excellencie the Lord General Monck and the Officers of his Army* (1660).

we would be glad to know where the members of the Long Parliament (for that's ye only authority we have to act under) will be pleased to sit. Shrewsbury in regard of the rendesvouz there will be the safest place. We pray you conveigh the Inclosed to Col B, Al[derman] J, Al[derman] Iret[on] we would feigne heare how the Parliament proceede when they sit, whether they secure any of our agents. That we may be able to supply to goe on neverthelesse. Col W, Col R, Cap J, Cap M are gone for Ireland. The extremity of our adversaryes dealings will make an agitation there seasonable and not successelesse. Col S, Col M, M Cr, Lt. Col. Lilb[urn] are engaged for Scotland, with some others who will have tough work of it there. That country is so cunningly ordered by that crafty fellow [Monk] yt if it may be if were well all places were at once disordered by a Comon alarme, while one place is chiefly aimed at. We expect Sir Arthur [Hesilrigg] here suddenly, and when a convenient number of the old Parliament and Army are met, we declare the declaration is allready agreed on. L Col J hath by this time a draught of it. Its the equallest way of comprehending all interests ~~in the~~ that may and will be encouraged yt ever was proposed. We are apt to believe yt even honest men of all interests will acquiesce in it. Verily some Presbyterians, upon there late experience, are ready to heare and submit to the reason of it when proposed to them. The press is free enough for there being noe restraint upon that as yet.

[Page 109 recto]

Observe whether you see any of our countrey are preferred, lets know who they are, yt we may avoide them, so we have observed yet noe considerable person encouraged to act anything for our discovery or opposition. Maj[or] Wild[man] is very serviceable. The Lord remember him in that day; he with Mr H[arry] V[ane], D Bl &c Col Jo, Mr Cast & Maj Br are like to secure Berks[hire] & Oxfordshire. We would give you an account of other proceedings but you may heare of them in our expresse to the churches. We are like to have more resolves at the next meeting. We desire you to goe on speedily with the designes upon the Tower, the House and the head quarter if you hit, strike home and spare not and the Lord prosper the worke of your hands, now you have the wicked gathered together as at Armageddom by gods good providence sinne not away thy opportunity as you have done many more, if it take not soe are ready to advance as

your faithful brethren
and fellow labourers in the
Lords worke

Llanothing
the 8 of the 2d

Des[borough] Pres[ide]n[t]

moneth 1660

R. Hughes Clarke

#3 – The Anabaptist Petition of 1661 (PA, HL/PO/JO/10/1/306):

To the Right Honorables: The Peeres Assembled in Parliament

The humble Petition of divers persons comnly called Anabaptists in the behalfe of themselves and others.

Sheweth,

That the Kings Majestie being graciously pleased both in his Declaration from Breda and also in that concerning Ecclesiasticall affaires to Graunt Indulgence to such of his Subjects as in some things relateing to the worship of God doe Conscientiously differ from ye publique profession held forth and Established in the Nation. Your Petitioners doe with humble gratitude to his Majestie acknowledge that they have thereby enjoyed that liberty and protection in the service of God according to their Conscience as hath been very precious to them.

That yet notwithstanding the said Declarations and his Majestyes very gracious Condescention and indulgence therein held forth to tender Consciences some of your Petitioners and many others have been disturbed and imprisoned for such the exercise of their Consciences in the worship of God. And your petitioners doe feare they are still lyable to be further troubled and debarred of the liberty soe graciously indulged to them by his Majestie is some statutes or Clauses of Statutues requiring an exact Conformity to the worship and discipline Established should be rigorously put in ixecution against them.

That some of your Petitioners did thereupon in behalfe of themselves and others make their humble application to his Majestie for the Continuance of his favours towards them and did indeavour to manifest (as they hope they did to his Majestyes satisfaction) that they had not abused nor made any evill use of his most gracious Indulgence.

That his Majestie was pleased to refer your Petitioners to the then succeeding and now sitting Parliament in whose power it would be with his Royall assent by a

Generall and Publique Law to Establish liberty to all tender Consciences. Your Petitioners doe therefore humbly pray that they may not by virtue or under pretence of any Law of this Kingdome be compelled or by penalties or otherwise any way constrained to any outward forme of worship whatsoever contrary to the liberty and persuasion of their Judgements and Consciences but that they may be protected in their Liberty of professing and exerciseing their respective faith and worship as well in publique as private from all force, injury and molestation whilest they behave themselves peaceably and soberly in the use of the said Liberty any Law, Statute, usage or Custome to the contrary thereof in any wise notwithstanding.

And your petitioners as in duty bound shall pray &c

John Gosnold [signature] John Tombes [signature]
Thomas Cooper [signature] W[illia]m Kiffin [signature]
Samuel Stanton [signature] Chr[istopher] Blackwood [signature]

#4 – William Kiffen is named as a participant in a meeting of Fifth Monarchists which took place on 23 August 1661 in Norton Folgate – 27 August 1661 (TNA, SP 29/40, page 131):

That upon friday night the 23 of this month I was at a meting at a place called Norton folgate without bishopsgate where there were some thirty men who are most of ye opinion of the 5th monarchy men who prayed to God to strengthen them in the great worke he has in hande to pull down his enemies and the enemies of Jesus, and to strengthen the brethren from far and nere and amongst these there was one Grene who is a gunsmith by profession and workes in the Minories who produced a letter to signifie that Ludlow and Whalley and Tilham were landed in Essex in a Dutch small vessell.

John Thedam Formarle
guner to Captane bargrave
who Comanded the *convartane*
in the downs For the King

Tilham hath a house in Colchester where all the sectaries Meet & is often imployed by them beyond seas &c

D[ated] 27 Aug[ust] 1661

Coll[onel] Lockhart a wise & stout man & one of the cheifs
Coll[onel] West a Lancashire man
Lt Col[lonel] Zanchey
Coll[onel] Fitch who was lieut[enant] of the Tower
Coll[onel] Wilks or Weekes
Lt Coll[onel] Reade an actione man
Coll[onel] Kiffin

Mr Griffin their Teacher
[25] Col[lonel] Dethick
One Thompson a p[ar]l[i]am[en]t man
Mr Maile a silkeman in Chepstile
These are now by laying plots & preparing for evill

CHAPTER 4

'Unlawfully assembled and mett together': William Kiffen's Arrest on 24 February 1661 at the House of Robert Malbon

William Kiffen in his *Memoirs* makes passing reference to the difficulties he and other Baptists suffered following the tumult of the Venner Revolt in January of 1661, and records,

> A little after this, being at a meeting on a Lords-day, in Shoreditch, we were apprehended and carried before Sir Thomas Bide, and by him I was committed to the new prison with several others: but having continued there about four days, I was by him released.[1]

Fortunately some additional records pertaining to this incident have survived which allow us to fill in some of the details. They show that on 26 February 1661 Kiffen was indicted by the Middlesex Sessions of the Peace for attending an illegal conventicle on the previous Sunday (24 February) and that he gave a surety of £50 to guarantee his appearance at the next Sessions of the Peace (see Document #1). The document records that Kiffen's son-in-law Benjamin Hewling and another man named David Kinge of Lombard Street, also gave sureties of £20 each to guarantee Kiffen's court appearance. The record notes 'Mr Kiffen saith he hath taken the oath of alleigeance' (lines 10–11). An appended note by the court clerk also states that Kiffen appeared before the Sessions Court on 24 April 1661 and was discharged (line 14). Unfortunately, the indictment does not say where the illegal conventicle that Kiffen attended was held.

However, a second record dated 24 February 1661 named ten women from Kiffen's church for attending this same meeting, namely Jane wife of Richard Stanton, Ellen wife of Richard Horton, Mary wife of Nicholas Neave, Alice wife of Edmund Stout, Frances wife of George Gospright, Mary wife of Christopher Todd, Mary wife of Bartholomew Pope, Susan Lewis, Jane wife of Owen Halton, and Sarah wife of Richard Oram (see Document #2).[2] A third record dated 24 February

---

[1] The incident is briefly alluded to within Kiffen's *Memoirs* (William Orme, *Remarkable Passages in the Life of William Kiffen* (London, 1823): 32).

[2] The Hortons, Mary Neave, Alice Stout, the Gosprights, Susan Lewis, the Haltons, and Sarah Oram are all included in later membership lists of Kiffen's church (GLL, Devonshire

1661 similarly named seven women from Kiffen's church for attending this meeting, namely Mary Smith, Eleanor Simcocke, Katherine Drake, Mary Light, Susan Carnall, Hannah Lash, and Anne Graves (see Document #3).[3] A fourth record dated 8 April 1661 names one man, James Nash of Whitechapel, indicting him for attending the same meeting in February (see Document #4). These additional indictments ordered that the various persons named within them were 'To answer being taken amongst divers others persons unlawfully assembled and mett together in the house of one Robert Malbon of Shorditch'. In other words, it appears that the home of Robert Malbon (or Malban, or Malborne), who was a silk-thrower by trade, was used as a meeting place following the destruction of Kiffen's meeting house. This house was a fairly substantial property located in Holloway Street in Shoreditch.[4] For some reason, there is no corresponding indictment of Robert Malbon himself for the events of 24 February 1661, although it seems clear that he was a member of Kiffen's church. The most likely explanation of this is that Malbon was already incarcerated in the Poultrey Counter prison, having been arrested as a suspect person in the immediate aftermath of the Venner Revolt.[5] One of the earliest records of Malbon's political activism is from January of 1648, where he accompanied George Masterson at a meeting of Levellers led by John Lilburne at Well Yard in Wapping; Masterson was serving as an informant for Cromwell and reported to both the House of Commons and the House of Lords about the meeting.[6] Perhaps more significantly, Malbon appears to have been an active Fifth Monarchist and features in several documents relating to that movement.[7] In any event, Kiffen

---

Square Membership Lists (MS 20,230), pages 13, 15, 26, 28, 30, 45, 50, 55, 62, 63, 65, and 70).

[3] All, save Katherine Drake, are described in the indictment as widows. Simcocke, Drake, Light, Lash, and Graves are all included in later membership lists of Kiffen's church (GLL, Devonshire Square Membership Lists (GL MS 20,230) pages 19, 22, 24, 26, 34, 50, 56, and 62).

[4] Malborn paid tax on eight hearths in the property in the Hearth Tax for 1664 (see LMA, MR/T/H/004, membrane 5).

[5] Malbon is so named in *Mercurius Publicus* #2 (10–17 January 1661): 31. He is here described as 'a Preacher'. Also see *Londons Glory, or, The Riot and Ruine of the Fifth Monarchy Men* (1661): 16.

[6] Malbon's involvement is mentioned in *A Declaration of Some Proceedings of Lt. Col. John Lilburn* (1648): 13; George Masterson *The Triumph Stain'd* (1648): 6, 25; Jab Norris, *A Lash for a Lyar* (1648): 4.

[7] One report dated 8 March 1665 mentions how letters of secret contact were directed to 'the house of a silkthrower neer ye Church in Shoreditch, to Robert Malbone' (TNA, SP 29/114, page 151). Another document dated 22 May 1665 contains a list of disaffected people in London and gives the name of five men, including Captain Blood, who meet 'sometimes at Rob[ert] Malbones, a Silk Thrower in Shoreditch' (TNA, SP 29/121, page 175). Bernard Capp, *The Fifth Monarchy Men: A Study in Seventeenth-century English Millennarianism* (London: Faber and Faber, 1972): 254-255, offers a summary of Malbon's career, although he wrongly identifies him with a Robert Malbone who died in 1673; S.J. Stearns, 'Malban, Robert (fl.1648–1665)', in Richard L. Greaves and Robert Zaller (eds.),

and the seventeen women appeared before the Quarter Sessions court held at Hicks Hall in St John's Street on 24 April 1661; they gave evidence and were released and the bond monies put forward for them were discharged.[8] The case of the silkthrester James Nash was slightly more complicated. He also appeared before the Quarter Sessions court on 28 April 1661, although he was bailed to his kinsman Thomas Nash and required to appear at a future meeting of the court.[9]

Further light on Kiffen's case is shed by a surviving bond agreement which Kiffen signed on 20 April 1661 just prior to the appearance at the Quarter Sessions Court (see Document #5). The condition of the bond is that Kiffen 'well and truly carry & demeane himselfe and be of good behaviour towards the Kings most Excellent Ma[jes]tie' (lines 19–22). Somewhat curiously, Kiffen's address is given as 'Clapum in the County of Surrey' (line 2), the only time of which I am aware that Kiffen is said to be from the Clapham area south of the Thames. The bond is for £500 (line 8), a rather high figure which probably is an indication not only of Kiffen's wealth, but also of the potential threat that he represented to the authorities. Two friends join Kiffen in signing this bond: Nathaniel Stoner, a haberdasher from the parish of St Clement Danes, and Robert Gardyner, a silkman from Coleman Street (lines 3–5). Given the occupations of the two guarantors, it is likely that they were business associates of Kiffen. Stoner is also interesting because he was a member of Kiffen's church, appearing in the membership list of 1668, where he and his wife are said to be from Reading.[10] He died in late 1683, having signed a will on 20 October 1683 which was probated on 9 November 1683 (see Document #6). At some stage Stoner moved to the village of Agmondesham (modern Amersham), although he kept in contact with Kiffen until the end of his life. In fact, Stoner even made provision for the church within the will, leaving £20 'unto the church which Mr William Kiffin is Pastor' (lines 23–24).

However, the indictments over the Sunday services at Shoreditch were not the end of Robert Malbon's encounters with the authorities, for there is a further indictment dated 3 January 1663 which records that he offered surety of £20 for a man named Jeremie Eightshillings who had refused to take the Oath of Allegiance (see Document #7). Even more interesting is the fact that Malbon later became the subject of church discipline by Kiffen's congregation (see Document #8). There is record of him being investigated in April of 1665 following some allegations of sexual misconduct with two woman of the church, namely Eleanor Simcocke and Mary Dover; the controversial preacher and ex-army officer Paul Hobson, was also

---

Biographical Dictionary of British Radicals in the Seventeenth Century, Volume II: G–O (Brighton: The Harvester Press, 1983): 210, perpetuates the error.

[8] LMA, Middlesex Quarter Sessions Register—1660–1663 (MJ/SB/R/008), page 115.

[9] LMA, Middlesex Quarter Sessions Register—1660–1663 (MJ/SB/R/008), page 131. However, later in the year he failed to appear before the court (LMA, Gaol Delivery Record—11 December 1661 (MJ/GB/B/005/112, page 25).

[10] GLL, Devonshire Square Membership Lists (GL MS 20,230) page 28. There is record that Nathaniel Stoner was paid £15 by the Council of State on 29 August 1659 for serving as a messenger to Shrewsbury and Holland (TNA, SP 25/107, page 107).

involved. Malbon refused to appear before the church when summoned to answer these charges and was cast out of the fellowship.[11] Malbon died soon thereafter, having made his will on 3 October 1665, which was probated on 29 October 1666, with Malborn's wife Elizabeth serving as executrix (see Document #9). Curiously, both women disciplined by the church, Eleanor Simcocke and Mary Dover, were named in Malborn's will, so apparently he kept in contact with them after the excommunication orders were enforced. Mary Dover, who Malbon describes in the will as 'my welbeloved daughter' (line 19), was left £100 and Malbon's library (lines 19–23); she was also named an alternative executrix to the will should Malbon's wife Elizabeth not be able to serve as such. On the other hand, Eleanor Simcocke was bequeathed an inscribed gold ring and his Bible with silver clasps (lines 24–26), and £5 (line 40). Simcocke died in 1695, having relocated to St James's in Piccadilly. An inventory of her goods shows that she had few possessions, amounting only to £8 5s as assessed by the appraisers; the gold ring and Bible she inherited from Malbon are not listed among her belongings (see Document #10).[12] Robert Malborn remained friends with his fellow excommunicant Paul Hobson, for Malborn was named as one of the overseers of Hobson's will which was signed on 12 March 1664 and probated on 13 June 1666 (see Document #11, lines 85–86).

There are one or two further indications about the activities of Robert Malbon's widow, Elizabeth. On 3 November 1667 Elizabeth Malbon and three other women were brought before the church and asked to explain a long period of absence from fellowship (see Document #12). It appears that they had become Quakers, and the church agreed to withdraw fellowship from them, with William Kiffen himself communicating the decision about excommunication to them 'as theire mouth' (line 26). Elizabeth Malbon is also named within a list of sixty-two conventiclers indicted on 4 September 1664 for attending a meeting in Stepney.[13] It is possible that this is another indication of her widening circle of contacts with Quakers. She is described in this document as the wife of Robert Malbon, a weaver from the parish of St Leonard's, Shoreditch.

In short, Robert Malbon may have been an active member of Kiffen's church during the early days of the Restoration, but his activities within the church were divisive and controversial, and within a few short years he was disgraced and gone. However, he did step in at a critical juncture in the aftermath of the Venner Revolt to offer his house as a meeting place for the congregation of William Kiffen.

---

[11] The incident is noted in passing by W.T. Whitley, 'The Rev. Colonel Paul Hobson', *Baptist Quarterly* 9 (1938–39): 310; Richard L. Greaves, 'Hobson, Paul (d.1666)', in Richard L. Greaves and Robert Zaller (eds.), *Biographical Dictionary of British Radicals in the Seventeenth Century, Volume II: G–O* (Brighton: The Harvester Press, 1983): 97; Richard L. Greaves, *Saints and Rebels: Seven Nonconformists in Stuart England* (Macon, GA: Mercer University Press, 1985): 133-156; 'Hobson, Paul (d.1666)', *Oxford Dictionary of National Biography* (Oxford: Oxford University Press, September 2004; online edn, January 2008).

[12] LMA, Probate Inventory of Elleanor Simcocke—30 March 1695 (AM/PI(2)/1695/012).

[13] LMA, Conventicle Convictions—1664–1665 (MR/R/C/001/13).

Documents

#1: William Kiffen indicted for attending an illegal conventicle – 26 February 1661 (LMA, Sessions Roll: Sessions of the Peace #1227 (28 March 1661) (MJ/SR/1227/37):

[Text]

Memorand[um] q[uo]d Vicesimo Sexto die Februarii 1660 Annoq[ue] regni D[omi]ni n[ost]ri Caroli secundi Regis Angliae &c decimo tertio Ven[erunt] coram nobis
Thoma Byde et Ricardo Powell Ar[migeris] duobus Justic[iis] dict[i] D[o]m[ini] Regis in Pacem in dict[a] Com[itate] [Middlesex] conservand[am] assignat[is] David Kinge de
Lombard Street, London, Clothworker, et Beniamin Hewlyn de London, Mercator et manucep[erun]t pro Willielmo Kiffin de London,
Mercator[e] (vizt) uterq[ue] manucapt[or] p[re]dict[us] subpoena Viginti librar[um] et p[re]dict[us] Will[ielm]us Kiffin assumpsit pro seipso subpoena
Quadraginta librar[um], Quas concesser[unt] de bonis et catall[is]
terr[is] et tenement[is] suis ad usum dict[i] d[o]m[ini] Regis hered[itorum] et Successor[um]
suor[um] fieri et levari si dict[us] Will[ielm]us Kiffin defe[ce]r[it] in Condit[i]o[n]e Sequent[e] (vizt)
That the said William Kiffin shall p[er]sonally appeare at the next Sessions of the peace to be holden for
the said County at &c To answer for being taken at an unlawfull
meeting on the 24th day of
February, being the Sabboth day, contrary to the Kings Majesties proclamat[i]on &c

Mr Kiffin saith he hath taken
the oath of alleigeance

Tho[mas] Byde [signature]
Richard Powell [signature]

24 April[is] 1661 ven[it] et exon[erat]us

[Translation]

Memorandum that on the 26th day of February 1660, and in the 13th year of the reign of our Lord Charles the Second, King of England, &c Came before us,
Thomas Byde and Richard Powell Esquires, both Justices of the said Lord King appointed to keep the Peace in the said County [Middlesex], David Kinge of
Lombard Street, London, Clothworker, and Benjamin Hewlyn of

London, Merchant, and offered sureties for William Kiffin of London, Merchant, (vizt) each of the aforesaid manucaptors to the sum of Twenty pounds, and the said William Kiffin offered sureties for himself to the sum of Forty pounds, which they agreed would come out of their goods, chattels, lands and tenements, and be levied to the use of the said Lord King, his heirs and Successors, if the said William Kiffin should default in the following Condition (vizt) That the said William Kiffin shall p[er]sonally appeare at the next Sessions of the peace to be holden for the said County at &c To answer for being taken at an unlawfull meeting on the 24th day of February, being the Sabboth day, contrary to the Kings Majesties proclamat[i]on &c

Mr Kiffin saith he hath taken the oath of alleigeance

Tho[mas] Byde [signature]
Richard Powell [signature]

24 April[is] 1661 He came and was discharged

#2: Ten women from William Kiffen's church are indicted for attending an illegal conventicle – 24 February 1661 (LMA, Middlesex Sessions of the Peace Roll #1227 (28 March 1661) (MJ/SR/1227/39):

[Text]

Memorand[um] q[uo]d Vicesimo quarto die Februarii 1660 Annoq[ue] regni d[omi]ni n[ost]ri Caroli secundi Regis Angliae &c decimo tertio Ven[erunt] coram nobis Thoma Byde et Carolo Pitfeild Ar[migeris] duobus Justic[iis] d[ic]ti d[omi]ni ad Pacem in dict[a] Com[itate] [Middlesexiae] conservand[am] assignat[is] Thomas Cowper de p[ar]och[ia] Sancti Martini le grande, London, Mercator et Antonius Clarke de Abielane London Grocerus, et manuceper[unt] pro Jana uxore Ricardi Stanton, Ellena ux[ore] Ric[ard]i Horton, Maria ux[ore] Nicolai Neave, Alicia ux[ore] Edmundi Stout, Francisca ux[ore] Georgi Gospright, Maria ux[ore] Christopheri Todd, Maria ux[ore] Bartholomei Pope, Susanna ux[ore] Thomae Lewis, Jana ux[ore] Owenis Halton, Sara ux[ore] Ric[hard]i Oram (vizt) uterq[ue] manucapt[or] predict[us] sub pena Quadraginti librar[um] Quas concesser[unt] de bonis et catall[is] terris et tenement[is] suis ad usum dict[i] d[o]m[ini] Regis hered[itorum] et Successor[um] Suor[um] fieri et levari si

p[re]dict[ae] Janna Stanton, Ellena Horton, Maria Neave, Alicia Stout, Francisca Gospright, Maria Todd, Maria Pope, Susanna Lewis, Jana Halton, Sara Oram,

aut ear[um] altera defec[erint] in Condit[i]o[n]e Sequent[e] (vizt):

That the said Jane Stanton, Ellen Horton, Mary Neave, Alice Stout, Francis Gospright, Mary Todd, Mary Pope, Susanna Lewis Jane Halton,

and Sarah Oram and every of them shall personally appeare at the next Sessions of the peace to be holden for the said County &c

To answer being taken amongst divers other persons unlawfully assembled and mett together in the house of one Robert Malbon

of Shorditch the 24th day of February 1660 being the Sabboth day contrary to the Kinge Majesties Proclamat[i]on published for the

prohibiting of such unlawfull meetings. And in the meane time to be of the good behaviour &

Tho[mas] Byde [signature]
Charles Pitfeild [signature]

deb[i]t[a] feod[a] Cle[ri]c[o] ven[it] & exon[erat]us om[n]es

[Translation]

Memorandum that on the 24th day of February 1660, and in the 13th year of the reign of our Lord Charles the Second, King of England, &c Came before us, Thomas Byde and Charles Pitfeild, Esquires,

both Justices of the said Lord King appointed to keep the Peace in the said County [of Middlesex], Thomas Cowper of the parish of Saint Martin-the-great, London, Merchant, and Antony Clarke of Abie Lane, London,

Grocer, offered sureties for Jane the wife of Richard Stanton, Ellen the wife of Richard Horton, Mary the wife of Nicholas Neave, Alice the wife of Edmund Stout, Francis the wife of George Gospright,

Mary the wife of Christopher Todd, Mary the wife of Bartholomew Pope, Susanna the wife of Thomas Lewis, Jane the wife of Owen Halton, Sara the wife of Richard Oram (vizt) each of the aforesaid manucaptors

to the sum of Forty pounds, which they agreed would come out of their goods, chattels, lands and tenements, and be levied to the use of the said Lord King, his heirs and Successors, if the said Janna Stanton, Ellena Horton, Maria Neave, Alicia Stout, Francisca Gospright, Maria Todd, Maria Pope, Susanna Lewis, Jana Halton, Sara Oram,

or any one of them should default in the following Condition (vizt):

That the said Jane Stanton, Ellen Horton, Mary Neave, Alice Stout, Francis Gospright, Mary Todd, Mary Pope, Susanna Lewis Jane Halton,

and Sarah Oram and every of them shall personally appeare at the next Sessions of the peace to be holden for the said County &c

To answer being taken amongst divers other persons unlawfully assembled and mett together in the house of one Robert Malbon

of Shorditch the 24th day of February 1660 being the Sabboth day contrary to the Kinge Majesties Proclamat[i]on published for the

prohibiting of such unlawfull meetings. And in the meane time to be of the good behaviour &

Tho[mas] Byde [signature]
Charles Pitfeild [signature]

Fees owed to the Clerk — All came and were discharged

#3: Seven women from William Kiffen's church are indicted for attending an illegal conventicle – 24 February 1661 (LMA, Middlesex Sessions of the Peace Roll #1227 (28 March 1661) (MJ/SR/1227/38):

[Text]

Memorand[um] q[uo]d Vicesimo Quarto die Februarii 1660 Annoq[ue] regni D[omi]ni n[ost]ri Caroli secundi Regis Angliae &c decimo tertio Ven[erunt] coram nobis Thoma Byde et Carolo Pitfeild Ar[migeris] duobus

Justic[iis] ad Pacem in dict[a] Com[itate] [Middlesexiae] conservand[am] assignat[is] Thomas Cowper de p[ar]och[ia] Sancti Martini le grande, London, Mercator, et Antonius Clarke de Abie Lane, London, Grocer[us],

pro Maria Smith de Wapping, vidua, Elleanora Simcocke de Bishopsgate Street, London, vidua, Katherine Drake de p[ar]och[ia] S[anc]ti Olivi, Southwarke in Com[itate] Surr[eiae], Maria Light de

p[ar]och[ia] S[anc]ti Salvator[is], Southwarke, in dict[a] Com[itate] Surr[eiae], vidua, Susanna Carnall de Fanchurch Street, London, vidua, Hanna Lash de Wapping, vidua, et Anna Graves de Trinitie

Minorites, London, vidua, (vizt) uterq[ue] manucapt[or] praedict[us] sub pena Viginti librar[um] Et p[re]dict[ae] Maria Smith,

Elleanora Simcocke, Katherina Drake, Maria Light, Susanna Carnall,

Hanna Lash et Anna Graves assumpserunt pro sibimet ipsis sub sep[ar]alibus poenis Quadraginta librar[um] Quas concesser[unt] de bonis et catall[is] terr[is] et tenement[is] suis ad usum dict[i]

d[o]m[ini] Regis hered[itorum] et Successor[um] Suor[um] fieri et levari si p[re]dict[ae] Maria Smith, Elleanora Simcocke, Katherina Drake, Maria Light, Susanna Carnall, Hannah Lash et Anna

Graves aut ear[um] altera defec[erint] in Condit[i]o[n]e Sequent[e] (vizt)

That the said Mary Smith, Eleanora Simcocke, Katherine Drake, Mary Light, Susan Carnall, Hannah Lash, and Ann Graves, and every of them shall p[er]sonally

appeare at the next Sessions of the peace to be holden for the said County &c To answer being taken amongst divers others persons unlawfully assembled

and mett together in the house of one Robert Malbon of Shorditch the 24th day of February 1660 being the Sabboth day contrary to the Kinge Majesties

Proclamat[i]on published for the prohibiting of such unlawfull meetings. And in the meane time to be of the good behaviour &c

Tho[mas] Byde [signature]
Charles Pitfeild [signature]

ven[it] & exon[erat]us om[n]es Resp[onso]r Hanna Lash   deb[i]t[a] feod[a] Cle[ri]c[o]

[Translation]

Memorandum that on the 24th day of February 1660, and in the 13th year of the reign of our Lord Charles the Second, King of England, &c Came before us, Thomas Byde and Charles Pitfeild, Esquires, both

Justices of the said Lord King appointed to keep the Peace in the said County [of Middlesex], Thomas Cowper of the parish of Saint Martin-the-great, London, Merchant, and Antony Clarke of Abie Lane, London, Grocer,

offered sureties for Mary Smith of Wapping, widow, Elleanora Simcocke of Bishopsgate Street, London, widow, Katherine Drake of the parish of Saint Olive, Southwarke in the County of Surrey, Mary Light of

the parish of Saint Saviour, Southwarke, in the said County of Surrey, widow, Susan Carnall of Fanchurch Street, London, widow, Hannah Lash of Wapping, widow, and Anna Graves of

Trinitie Minorites, London, widow, (vizt) each of the aforesaid manucaptors to the sum of Twenty pounds, and the said Mary Smith, Elleanora Simcocke, Katherine Drake, Mary Light, Susan Carnall, Hannah Lash and Anna Graves each offered sureties separately for themselves to the sum of Forty pounds, which they agreed would come out of their goods, chattels, lands and tenements, and be levied to the use of the said Lord King, his heirs and Successors, if the said Mary Smith, Elleanora Simcocke, Katherine Drake, Mary Light, Susan Carnall, Hannah Lash and Anna Graves, or any one of them should default in the following Condition (vizt)

That the said Mary Smith, Eleanora Simcocke, Katherine Drake, Mary Light, Susan Carnall, Hannah Lash, and Ann Graves, and every of them shall p[er]sonally appeare at the next Sessions of the peace to be holden for the said County &c To answer being taken amongst divers others persons unlawfully assembled and mett together in the house of one Robert Malbon of Shorditch the 24th day of February 1660 being the Sabboth day contrary to the Kinge Majesties Proclamat[i]on published for the prohibiting of such unlawfull meetings. And in the meane time to be of the good behaviour &c

Tho[mas] Byde [signature]
Charles Pitfeild [signature]

All came and were discharged Respondent Hanna Lash

Fees owed to the Clerk

#4: James Nash arrested for attending an illegal conventicle at the home of Robert Malbon – 8 April 1661 (LMA, Middlesex Sessions of the Peace Roll #1229 (24 April 1661) (MJ/SR/1229/72):

[Text]

Memorand[um] q[uo]d Octavo die Aprilis 1661 Annoq[ue] regni D[omi]ni n[ost]ri Caroli secundi Regis Angliae &c decimo tertio Ven[erunt] coram nobis Carolo Pitfeild, Ricardo Powell Ar[migeris] duobus Justic[iis] dict[i] D[o]m[ini] Regis ad Pacem in dict[a] Com[itate] conservand[am] assignat[is] Thomas Nash de Nortonfolgate, Silkethrower, manucepit pro Jacobo Nash de Whitechappell, Labourer, sub poena Quadriginta librar[um] et dict[i] Jacobus Nash Assumpsit seipso Sub poena Quinquaginta librar[um] Quas concesser[unt] de bonis et catall[is] &c ad usum dict[i] d[o]m[ini] Regis hered[itorum] et Successor[um] suor[um] fieri et levari si ipse Jacobus Nash defecerit in Condit[i]o[n]e Sequente (vizt):

That the said James Nash shall personally appeare at the next generall quarter Sessions of the peace to be holden for the said Countie at &c To answer being taken amongst divers other persons unlawfully assembled together at the house of one Robert Malbon, in Shorditch on the 24th day of February being the Sabboth day contrary to the Kinge Majesties Proclamation and contrary to the Statute in that Proclamation ment[i]oned.

Charles Pitfeild [signature]
Richard Powell [signature]

ven[it] & trad[it]us ultra

[Translation]

Memorandum that on the Eighth day of April 1661, and in the 13th year of the reign of our Lord Charles the Second, King of England &c, Came before us, Charles Pitfeild, Richard Powell, Esquires, Justices of the said Lord King appointed to keep the Peace in the said County [of Middlesex], Thomas Nash of Nortonfolgate, Silkethrower, and offered sureties for James Nash of Whitechappell, Labourer, to the sum of Forty pounds, and the said James Nash offered sureties for himself to the sum of Fifty pounds which they agreed would come out of their goods and chattels &c, to be levied to the use of the said Lord King, his heirs and Successors, if the said James Nash should default in the following condition (vizt):

That the said James Nash shall personally appeare at the next generall quarter Sessions of the peace to be holden for the said Countie at &c To answer being taken amongst divers other persons unlawfully assembled together at the house of one Robert Malbon, in Shorditch on the 24th day of February being the Sabboth day contrary to the Kinge Majesties Proclamation and contrary to the Statute in that Proclamation ment[i]oned.

Charles Pitfeild [signature]
Richard Powell [signature]

He came & was delivered [his case being carried] further

#5: William Kiffen signs a bond for £500 promising to be of good behaviour towards the king – 20 April 1661 (TNA. SP 29/34, page 127):

[Text]

Nov[er]int universi p[er] p[rese]ntes nos Will[ielmus] Kiffen de p[ar]och[ia] Clapum de Com[itat]e Surr[e]y, Marchant et Nathan[iel] Stoner de S[an]cti Clemens Deane in Com[itate] Mid[dlese]x, Haberdasher, et Robertus Gardyner de Coleman Street London, silkman, teneri et firmiter obligari Illustrissimo domino nostro Carolo Secundo dei Grat[ia] Angl[ie] Scot[iae] Franc[iae] et Hib[er]niae Regi[s] et in Quingentis Libr[is] bone et Legal[is] monet[e] Angl[ie] Solvend[is] dicto domino Rege heredibus et Successoribus suis Ad quam quide[m] Solut[i]onem bene et fid[eli]ter faciend[am] obligamus nos utrumq[ue] nostr[um] hered[es] executor[es] et Administrator[es] n[ost]ros firm[ite]r p[er] p[rese]ntes sigillis n[ost]ris sigillat[as] Dat[as] vigissimo die Aprilis Anno Regni ~~Reg~~ dicti domini Regis Caroli Decimo tertio An[n]oq[ue] Dom[ini] 1661.

The Condit[i]on of this obligat[i]on is such that if the above bound William Kiffen shall and doe at all times hereafter well and truly Carry & demeane himselfe and be of good behaviour towards the Kings most Excellent Ma[jes]tie and all his Leige people that then this obligat[i]on to be voyd or else to Continue in full force & vertue.

William Kiffen [signature and seal]

Nath[aniel] Stoner [signature and seal]

Robert Gardyner [signature and seal]

Signed, sealed and delivered in the presence of Geo[rge] Farewell by the apointment of Mr Secretary Nicholas & in the presens of
P Snelling [signature]
Sam Batten [signature]

[Translation of lines 1–16]

Let everyone know that by these presents, we, William Kiffen of the parish of Clapham in the County of Surrey, Merchant, and

Nathaniel Stoner of Saint Clemens Deanes in the County of Middlesex, Haberdasher, and Robert Gardyner of Coleman Street, London, silkman, are bound and securely obligated to our Illustrious Lord Charles the Second, by the grace of God, King of England, Scotland, France, and Ireland, and to pay Five Hundred Pounds of good and legal money of England to the said Lord King, his heirs and Successors To the making of which payment, in good faith we obligate ourselves and each of us our Heirs, Executors and Administrators, as confirmed by these presents which are sealed with our Seals and Dated the 20th day of April in the thirteenth Year of the reign of the said Lord Charles [the Second], and in the Year of the Lord 1661.

#6: The will of Nathaniel Stoner – signed 29 October 1683; probated 9 November 1683 (TNA, PROB 11/374, pages 230 recto and verso):

[Page 230 recto]

In the name of God, Amen. the nine and twentieth day of October Anno Domini one thousand six hundred eighty and three, I, Nathaniell Stoner, of the parish of Agmondesham in the Counth of Bucks, Gent[leman], being weake in body but of good and p[er]fect memory, thanks bee given to Almighty God, doe ordaine and make this my last will and testament in manner and forme following: First and principally I commend my soule into the hands of Almighty God, my Creator, Redeemer, and Sanctifier, and my body unto the earth in sure and certaine hope of the resurrection thereof unto eternall life in the last day, and for my worldly estate that the Lord hath blessed mee with all I dispose as followeth. Item, I give and bequeath unto my Sister Anne Leake, now wife of John Leake, All that my Lease of my messuage or tenement with the appurtenances scituate in Dyattstreete, London; it is the signe of Noahs Arke. And Also all houses, edifices, buildings, barnes, stables and outhouses, orchards, gardens and backsides

[Page 230 verso]

whatsoever to the same belonging or appertaineing and now in the tenure or occupation of [blank] h[is or her] assignee or assignes To have and to hold to my said Sister Anne Leake her executors, administrators and assignes for and dureing the remainder of the said terme of Thirty and seaven yeares which is yet to come and unexpired. But in case my said sister Anne Leake shall dye before the said Lease shall bee fully ended Then my mind and Will is that my sisters daughter Mary Blundon her executors or assignes shall hold and enjoy all the remainder of the said terme that is or then shall be yet to come and unexpired of the said Lease. Item: I give and bequeath unto the church which Mr William Kiffin is Pastor to the sume of Twenty pounds. Item: I doe give and bequeath unto Elizabeth Palmer the sume of Forty pounds of lawfull money of England. Item: I doe give and bequeath unto my Sisters daughter Mary Blundon the summe of Twenty pounds. Item: I doe give and bequeath unto my couzen Moses Stoner the Summe of Tenne pounds and to my couzen Isaack Stoner the Summe of Tenne pounds. Item: I doe give and bequeath unto my brother Marke Stoner the Summe of Twenty shillings and to his sonne Marke the Summe of Twenty shillings and to his sonne Nathaniell the Summe of Twenty shillings. Item: I doe give and bequeath unto my servant maide Christian Grover the summe of five pounds all of them lawful money of England, my minde and will is And it is my true intent and meaning That all the said Legacies before ment[i]oned shall bee paid out of the two hundred pounds which is due unto mee from Thomas Wharton of Upper Winchindon in the County of Bucks, Esq[uire] and is secured unto mee by bond from him, my will is that none of the said Legacies shall bee paid untill the said two hundred

pounds bee paid, but only what I have given unto my Executrix, neither shall my
Executrix bee charged with any Legacy untill the said two hundred pounds bee paid
which is for to pay the said Legacies. And I doe make, ordaine and appoint Anne
Leake my loveing sister my sole Executris of this my last will and Testament
And all my goods and Chattells unbequeathed I doe give unto my said Executrix
And I doe revoke adnull and make void all and every other will or wills and
Testaments by mee at any time formerly made. And I doe declare and publish
this to bee my last will and Testament both in Deed and law. In witness whereof
I, the said Nathaniel Stoner, have hereunto sett my hand and seale the day
and yeare first above written. Nath[aniell] Stoner Signed sealed and published to bee my
last will and testament in the presence of Jonas Harding, Richard Bonnington,
William Chiles.
Memorandum: before sealeing I doe give unto my couzen Anne Wares
the summe of Tenn pounds, then sealed
Probatum fuit hu[ius]mo[d]i test[ament]um Londini coram ven[erabi]li viro Domino
Thoma Exton Milite legum Doctore Surr[ogat]o ven[erabi]lis et egregii viri Domini
Leolini Jenkins Militis legum etiam Doctoris Curiae Prerogativae Cantuarien[sis]
Mag[ist]ri Custod[is] sive Commissarii l[egi]time constituti Nono die mensis Novembris
Anno Domini millesimo sex[cen]tesimo octoge[si]mo tertio Juramento Anne Leake
Executricis in dicto Testamento nominat[ae] Cui Commissa fuit Administratio
omnium et singulorum bonorum jurium et creditorum dicti defuncti De bene
et fideli[te]r Administrando eadem ad Sancta Dei Evangelia Jurat

[Translation of lines 52–59]

This Will was probated in London before the venerable Lord
Thomas Exton, Knight, Doctor of Laws, and Representative of the venerable and excellent Lord
Leoline Jenkins, Knight, also Doctor of Laws, legally appointed

Master, Custodian or Commissioner of the Prerogative Court of Canterbury, the ninth day of the month of November
in the year of the Lord, One Thousand Six hundred Eighty Three on the Oath of Anne Leake,
named Executrix in the said Will, to whom was committed the Administration
of all and singular goods, rights, and credits of the said deceased, she
having sworn to the good and faithful Administration of the same on the Holy Gospels of God.

#7: Robert Malbon offers surety for Jeremie Eightshillings for his indictment for refusing to swear the Oath of Allegiance – 9 January 1663 (LMA, Middlesex Sessions of the Peace Roll #1268 (21 April 1663) (MJ/SR/1268/86).

[Text]

Mem[oran]d[um] q[uo]d Tertio die Januarii anno d[omi]ni 1662 Annoq[ue] regni d[omi]ni n[ost]ri Caroli secundi Regis Angliae &c decimo quarto
Ven[erunt] coram nobis Thoma Byde Milit[is] et Carolo Pitfeild, Ar[migeris] duobus Justic[iis] dict[i] D[o]m[ini] Regis ad Pacem in dict[a] Com[itate]
conservand[am] assignat[is] Robertus Malbon de p[ar]och[ia] S[anc]ti Leonardi Shorditch, Silkethrower et Jacobus Samwaies
de ead[em], Silkethrower et manuc[epit] pro Jeremia Eightshillings (vizt) uterq[ue] manuc[aptor] predict[us] sub poena Viginti librar[um]
Quas concesser[unt] de bonis et catall[is] terr[is] et Tenement[is] suis ad usu[m] dict[i] d[omi]ni Regis hered[itorum] et Successor[um] suor[um] fieri et levari
si ipse Jeremie Eightshillings defec[erit] in Condit[i]o[n]e Sequente (vizt):
That the said Jeremie Eightshillings shall p[er]sonally appeare at the next generall Quarter
Sessions of the peace to be holden for the said County &c To answer his refusing to take the
oath of allegeance before us being tendered unto him, and in the meane time to be of the
good behaviour.

Thomas Byde [signature]
Charles Pitfeild [signature]

[Translation]

Memorandum that on the Third day of January in the year of the Lord 1662, in the 14th year of our Lord Charles the Second, King of England &c,

Came before us Thomas Byde, Knight, and Charles Pitfeild, Esquire, both Justices of the said Lord King appointed to keep the Peace in the said County Robert Malbon of the parish of Saint Leonard, Shorditch, Silkethrower and James Samwaies of the same, Silkethrower, and offered sureties for Jeremy Eightshillings (vizt) each of the aforesaid manucaptors to the sum of Twenty pounds which they agreed would come out of their goods and chattels, lands and tenements, to be levied to the use of the said Lord King, his heirs and Successors, if the said Jeremie Eightshillings should default in the following condition (vizt): That the said Jeremie Eightshillings shall p[er]sonally appeare at the next generall Quarter Sessions of the peace to be holden for the said County &c To answer his refusing to take the oath of allegeance before us being tendered unto him, and in the meane time to be of the good behaviour.

Thomas Byde [signature]
Charles Pitfeild [signature]

#8: Robert Malbon and others disciplined by Kiffen's church – April 1665 (GLL, Devonshire Square Minute Book (MS 20228 1A), pages 3 verso – 4 verso, 5 verso):

[Page 3 verso]

Sister Elinor Simcoke & Mary Dover

5th April 1665

This day ye Crimes and misbehaviours of two sisters were given in by ye Evidence of two sober maids who declared to ye Church the substance of them: That Malborne and Hobson used very frequently to be up two p[ai]r of staires toge-ther with Mary Dover and Simcoke wh afternoones where they were very mery together and that ye s[ai]d Mary Dover and Simcoke used frequently to goe in a Coach with Hobson and Malbourne and stayed out one or two nights together and sometymes hired double horses & went out of towne.

[Page 4 recto]

That one tyme they ordered a Coach to goe to Shorditch Church empty that Mrs Hobson nor Mrs Malbourne might not take notice of it and went themselves to take Coach there, but Mrs Hobson heareing of it made haste and got to the Coach as soone as Mary Dover and Simcoke and said she would goe with them to see where there hous was upon w[hi]ch Mary Dover and Simcoke came backe againe and said if Mrs Hobson went they could not be merry.

That Mary Dover and Simcoke with Hobson and Malborne used frequently to goe to ye Riseing Sunn in More fields and carry provisions with them there to be merry and Simcoke feareing her maid would tell Mrs Hobson where they were stayed at home her selfe that in case Mrs Hobson came to Enquire after her husband shee might returne ye answer & accordingly Mrs Hobson did come to Simcokes and Enquired for her husband: Simcoke answered shee knew not where he was, shee was not her husbands keeper and soe Mrs Hobson went away and presently Mrs Simcoke went to ye Riseing Sunn to him.

That Simcoke, Mary Dover, Hobson and Malborne used to have frequently such Junckets and were often together till one of the Clocke at night.

That Mrs Simcokes hath been w[i]th Paul Hobson 3 nights together upon ye pretence of watching with him; he pretending himselfe to be sicke, although he was well att day and walked abroade; Simcokes maid telling her Mrs that these things were not for her Creditt soe to doe. Hobson thereupon came to ye maid and tolde her that if shee knew how sicke he was a nights shee would not be against her mistress watching w[i]th him, and this was further observed by Simcokes maid and others that when shee pretended to watch with him 3 nights together yet she was never observed to be sleeping a days but as fresh as if shee had beene a bed every night.

[Page 4 verso]

That Simcoke hath been heard to say that in case any came to seize Paul Hobson shee would goe to Court to him to be a Cover for him and to keepe him from being taken.

That one tyme Paul Hobson being in bedd Simcoke lay with her head upon ye pillow and at last as shee confessed tooke him by ye necke and almost pulled him out of bedd pretending herselfe to be asleep and yt shee did it in a dreame.

That Malborne with another man comeing one night to Simcokes house sent for drinke where was Mary Dover and Simcokes and as they drunk to one another kissed each other Round and soe they kissed very often.

Since ye comeing of Hobson last to ye Tower a kinswoman of his a member of Glovers hall was with her sister to vissit him finding there Mary Dover and Simcokes and having brought some Oranges to Hobson there was also a man in the Roome that was kin to Hobson& Mary Dover and Simcoke sqeezed ye oranges at one another and at ye man and ye man at them at last ye man flung Mary Dover upon ye bedd and kissed her w[hi]ch shee did not opose but continued theire Antick tricks putting sheepes tongues in his Muff the maid seeing this great boldnesse wept and her sister yt came with her being a carnall maid said shee wondered to see such things and said further shee never saw such shits in her life.

And further it was made appearfe by proof That Malborne did usuallie remaine in ye house of ye widd[ow] Simcoke till 10 0r 11 of ye Clock at night shewing himselfe to be very vaine & wanton.

And a brother comeing to Malbornes house one first day where Hobson was met to perform religious dutyes, he suddenly opening ye doore Mary Dover sitting in Malbornes lapp and his ?? very neere hers as if they had been kissing each other.

These things being charged against sister Simcoke before ye Church shee confessed p[ar]t of them were and p[ar]t of them were not w[hi]ch ye Church takeing notice of as also of ye long neglect of her ?? did Judge it meete to deliver her over to Satan. w[hi]ch accordingly was done according to ye Rule as also was Mary Dover at ye same tyme shee having refused to come before ye Church as was desired, both these sisters returned to ye Church by repentance.

[Page 5 verso]

Br[other] Malborne April 1665

The Church having had matter of charges Administered to them against Br[other] Malborne by ye testimony of severall persons given against Sister Simcocke and Mary Dover upon which ye said p[er]sons were dealt with and excommunicated ye 5th Instant as may at large appear by ye said Evidences, Relation being thereunto had. The Church did thereupon thinke fit to appoint Br[other] Cooper and Br[other] King to let Br[other] Malborne know that they expected he should come before them to answer to ye said charges soe appearing against him, to which he Replyed many impertinencyes by way of Reflection as well upon ye Rule & Authority of ye Church as perticuler members and less doubtfull whether he would come or no. It being Reported to ye Church by ye s[ai]d Messengers they were againe ye second tyme appointed to desire that he would come before them w[hi]ch being done on theire part and he refuseing, the Church did thinke it theire duty (all Circumstances considered as well those yt w[ere] his pesent State as those severall agraunted of his former miscarriages) to proceed [to] excommunicate him out of theire society Comunion w[hi]ch accordingly was done in persuance of ye Rule laid downe in Gods word for such ye like cases.

#9: The will of Robert Malbon – signed 3 October 1665; probated 29 October 1666 (TNA, PROB 11/332, pages 63 verso – 64 recto):

[Page 63 verso]

In the name of God, Amen the third day of October, In the Seaventeenth yeare of his Majesties Reigne that now is, And in the yeare of our Lord God One Thousand Six hundred Sixty and five. I, Robert Malbon, Silk Thrower, in the parish of St Leonard Shoreditch in the County of Middlesex, being in health of body and of sound mind and perfect memory, Praysed be God therefore. Yet calling to mind the uncertainty of this mortall life here on Earth and the frailty of Mankind, doe make, Publish and declare this my last Will and Testament, revoking And annulling all Will and Wills, Testament and Testaments whatsoever heretofore made by me whether by word or writing. And this onely to be taken for my last Will and Testament and none other. First, I Comend my soule unto the hands of my Faithfull and precious Redeemer Christ Jesus, trusting onely

[Page 64 recto]

And alone by the meritts of his precious death and passion to attayne exseptance with the Father of mercy and by him to enjoy eternall life and salvation in the world to come. And my body I comitt to the Earth from whence it was taken to be decently buried att the discretion of either my Executors hereafter named with and by the advice of my overseers. And for what God hath given me of this world, I dispose of all my temporall Estate as followeth. Item: I give and bequeath unto my welbeloved daughter so called Mary Dover, One hundred pounds of lawfull money of England To be paid to her within one yeare after my death (if in case shee shall live). I alsoe give unto the aforesaid Mary Dover All my Library of Books Excepting such books as writings in them of accompts. I give unto my kinswoman Barbara Leverett Forty shillings and unto Lucretia Bores, daughter to Richard Bors twenty shillings. I give to Ellin Simcock One hoope ring of gold with this motto 'Jenuah est vita', Alsoe my Bible with the silver Clasps. And all the rest of my Estate whatsoever, good Chattel, Bills Bonds, ready money, Pewter, Brasse, Bedding, Lynnen, Woolen and household stuffe and all whatsoever I give and bequeath unto my dearly beloved wife Elizabeth Malbon, whom I doe ordaine, nominate and appoint my full and whoole Executrix of this my last Will and Testament. And I doe intreate my Loveing Friend Philip Michaleborne, John Sowden, Brewer, Josias Crosley and Benjamin Knight to be Overseers of the due Execution of this my last will and Testament. And considering that many hus-bands and wives dye together, My will is further that if wee both should dye Together not else, Then I give to Ellen Malbon, my sister, That is now in

Cheshire Tenn Pounds To be paid unto her at the age of One and Twenty or day of marriage which shall first happen. And to Mary Bores, Widdow, Tenn pounds of lawfull money. And to Hannah Leverett, sister to my wife, Tenn pounds. And to Lucretia Bores, daughter to Richard Bores, Give pounds To be improved for her use till she comes to the age of One and Twenty yeares or day of marriage which shall First happen. And to Ellin Simcock Five pounds besides what before ment[i]oned This I say if my dear wife and I should dye together. And in that case I doe ordaine and appoint Mary Dover my full and whole Executrix to all intents and purposes and desire my loveing Freind abovenamed To be Assistant to see the due execution of this my last will and Testament according to the true intent and meaneing. In witness whereunto I have sett my hand and seale the day and yeare above written. And I give to each of my Overseers that shalbe alive Twenty shillings a peece To buy each of them a Ring to weare for my sake. Robert Malbon Signed, sealed, Published and declared in the Presence of us: William King, Adam Blacke, John Hall.

Probatum fuit Testamentum suprascriptum apud Aedes Exonienses in Le Strande in Comitatu Middlesexiae Coram venerabili viro Thoma Read Legum Doctore Surrogato venerabilis et Egregii viri Domini Gulielmi Merick Militis Legum etiam Doctoris Curiae Prero gativae Cantuariensis Magistri Custodis sive Commissarii legitime Constituti vicesimo Nono Die Mensis Octobris Anno Domini Millesimo Sexcentesimo Sexagesimo Sexto Juramento Elizabethae Malbon Relictae dicti defuncti et Executricis in huiusmodi Testamento nominatae Cui Commissa fuit Administrat[i]o Omnium et singulorum bonorum Jurium et Creditorum dicti defuncti de bene et fideliter Administrando ead[e]m Ad Sancta Dei Evangelia Jurat[ae].

[Translation of lines 50–60]

The abovewritten Will was probated at

the Exeter Building in Le Strande in the County of Middlesex before the venerable Thomas Read, Doctor of Laws, and Representative of the venerable and excellent Lord William Merick, Knight, also Doctor of Laws, legally appointed Master, Custodian or Commissioner of the Prerogative Court of Canterbury, The twenty-ninth day of the month of October, in the year of the Lord, One Thousand Six hundred Sixty Six, on the Oath of Elizabeth Malbon, Relict of the said deceased and named Executrix in the said Will, to whom was committed the Administration of all and singular goods, rights, and credits of the said deceased, she having sworn to the good and faithful Administration of the same on the Holy Gospels of God.

#10: Probate Inventory of Elleanor Simcock – 30 March 1695 (LMA, AM/PI(2)/1695/012):

A true and perfect Inventary of all and singular the goods, Chattels and Creditts of Elianor Simcock late of the parish of St James within the libertys of the city of Westm[inist]er in the County of Midd[lese]x, Widdow, deceased, taken, valued and appraised this thirtieth day of March Anno D[omi]ni 1695 by William Blacke and Nicholas Locke followes, viz.

In the Garrett

Imprimis one old bed, bedsted bolsters, blankett and pillow a skreen, a grate, fire irons six old chairs and lumber valued att — *li* i *s* v

One paire of staires

Item one old feather bed blankett, Rugg and pillow bolster bedsted, vallence and curtaines a Chest of Drawers, a looking Glass, Grate and fire irons, six old chaires, a table and lumber three pairs of old sheets valued att — *li* iii *s* x

In the Ground Roome Item a Presse bed and beding, 6 dishes, 12 porringers 6 plates, a warming pann, a brasse kettle, an old pott and two old skillets, three pewter potts a grate and fire irons, a table two old Truncks and Lumber and one small pockett money to the value of twenty shillings	*li* iii	*s* x
Item indesperate debts to the value of	£ x	
Suma tot[us] huius Inventarii est	£ xviii	*s* v

G. Lee

#11: The will of Paul Hobson – signed 12 March 1663; probated 13 June 1666 (TNA, PROB 11/321, pages 58 recto – 59 verso):

[Page 58 recto]

In the Name of God, Amen!

[Page 58 verso]

The Twelveth day of March 1663 and in the sixteenth yeare of the raigne of our soveraigne Lord Charles the second by the grace of God, King of England, Scotland, France and Ireland, defender of the Faith &c I, Paul Hobson, Citizen and Barber Chirurgeon of London, being sicke ad weake in body but of perfect mind and memory (praised bee Almighty god therefore) considering with my selfe the frailty of this mortall life and the incertainty thereof, And being desireous as much as in mee is so to dispose of my estate as that noe controversie may happen (after my decease) in the settling and disposeing threof do therefore make and declare That my last will and Testament in manner and forme following (That is to say) First and principally I commend my soule to God hopeing to be saved by the meritts, bitter death and passion of our Lord and Saviour Jesus Christ and by noe other meanes My doby I committ to the earth whereof it was made to be buried in such decent and Christian like manner as to my executors here in after named shalbee thought fitt and concerning the disposall of such worldly and Transitory substance as it hath pleased Almighty God of his greate bounty to bestowe on mee I doe hereby dispose thereof as followeth: First I give unto my beloved wife Hester Hobson Twenty pounds a yeare dureing her naturall life, which I purchased of Mr Samuell Wilson for her, Provided I may have a supply till I dye And I give and I give bequeath unto my sonne Paul Hobson all my right Tytle, interest, benefitt, Clayme and demand whatsoever of in and Segerston Hugh in the Bishoppricke of Durham and all the houses, Landes, Tenements, Barnes stables, prchards, gardens and other proffitts, benefitts, advantages and appurtenances whatsoever to the same belonging, Provided allwayes That when and as soon as my said sonne shall come to have possescion and enjoy the same, Then my will and meaning is And I doe hereby give and bequeath That quarter parte now in the occupaton of William Dorman unto Hester my loving wife for and during the Terme of her naturall life, which I doe give to my said wife upon conditionThat shee doth not demand her Thirde in Holdmares from my Children To whom I give it. But if she doth then this to rest in the hands of my sonne Paul hee paying for his sisters Lydia and Sara the some of Twenty pounds a peece of lawfull money the second yeare after his full possescion. And my will and mind further is That upon my said sonne his possession and enjoyment of Segerston Hugh withall the appurtenances thereunto belonging as aforesaid he shall and will demise and lett by Lease unto my sonne in lawe Henry Woolfe the seale house which I formerlie lived in w[i]th the two upper meadowes and the peece of pasture of ground being parcell of and belonging unto Sagerston Hugh aforesaid. And that to commence from our Lady next ensueing the date hereof for the Terme of fower yeares at the yearely rent of one pepper corne which was my agreement with him my said sonne in lawe at the marriage of my daughter Hester his new wife That hee should enjoye the same for soe long tyme freely without molestacon. Alsoe I give and bequeath unto my two daughters Lydia and Sara Hobson untill they shall come and attaine unto their severall ages of Eighteene yeares The rents, Issues, benefitts, profitts and advantages of and in all my houses & lands with Thappurtenances called by the name of Hold maires in the said Bishoppricke of Durham. But from and after their said severall and respective ages of eighteen yeares Then I give and demise the said house and lands with the appurtenances unto my said daughter Hester now the wife of my said sonne in law Henry Woolfen To have and to hold the same unto my said daughter Hester and to the heires of her and her said husband by her for ever. And for default of such issue Then to the right heires of the body of my

[Page 59 recto]

said daughter Hester lawfully begotten and for default of such issue then I do and demise the same unto my said sonne Paul Hobson and to his heires To have and to hold to him the said Paul his heires and assignes for ever Provided all-wayes That at the expiracion of the said Eighteene years of age of my said two daughters Lydia and Sara aforemenconed Let whomsoever the said house and lands called Hold mares come to be enjoyed by vertue of this my last will and Testament Then my will and true meaning is That my said sonne in lawe and my said daughter his wife or my said sonne Paul or one of them doe and shall well and truly pay or cause to be paid unto each of them my said two daughters Lydia and Sara one hundred pounds a peece of lawfull money of England. Alsoe I give and demise unto my daughter Reubenah and her heires for ever All my house and lands with the appurtenances called or knowne by the name of strestrups with the windmill thereupon in the Bishoppricke of Durham. And my will is that if the windill can be sold that the money may be layd out or put out for my said daughter Reubenah. Alsoe I give and bequeath unto my loveing Cousin Jeremiah Hobson my gold Watch or Twenty pounds and to my sister Anne James five pounds And to her husband a suite of my clothes. Alsoe I give and bequeath unto my Brother in law John Weedon forty shillings and my gray stuffe suite. Alsoe I give and bequeath unto my servant John Hall Twenty pounds ster-ling to bee paid unto him within six monethes after my decease Provided I doe not pay it to him before I dye together with my best suite & tayle. The rest and residue of all which is not by will and guifte disposed of before my death I doe hereby give and bequeath unto my said loving wife Hester and to my said sonne in lawe Henry Woolfe and my said belo-ved Cousin Jeremiah Hobson whom I doe make full and sole Executors of this my last will and Testament soe that they dispose of the same for and towards the payment and satisfaction of my debts and the Lega-cies herein given and bequeathed. And I doe earnestly request and desire my loveing friend Mr John Joplin of Durham and Mr Ahasueris Fromantell, Clock-maker, living at present in Colchester, And Mr Robert Malborn, Silkthrower, And Mr William Turke, Feltmaker, Cittizen of London, To bee overseers of this my last will and testament, And to bee ayding & assisting unto my said executors in the execut[i]on hereof. And for their love, paynes and care therein I doe hereby give and bequeath unto them Twenty shillings a peece to buy each of them a ring to weare in remembrance of me.

And my further order and will is That if it fall out so That I goe beyond sea before I dye That in my absence my beloved wife Hester Hobson to whome I have given a letter of Attorney To manage my affaires in my absence shall have all the profitts of Sugerston Hugh and Hold Mares and Strestrups till my Children comes to age to bring them up with suteable dyett and Clothes and learning as becomes them, Provided That she my said wife doth at my departure out of this nation or w[i]thin Two monethes after goe and live with my said Children in the Bishopricke of Durham keeping possescion for me and my children, But if she will not goe and live there but Judge it better for her owne good to live elsewhere, Then I give and bequeath all the said profitts of Segerston Hugh and Hold Mares To my daughter Hester Hobson for the bringing up of my sonne Paul and Lydia and Sarah as aforesaid till they come to age. The benefitt of Strestrupps, I bequeath to my daughter Reubenah to chase her guardians till she come to the age

[Page 59 verso]

of Twenty yeares, and then to enjoye it for her and her heires for ever. But if she dyes without heires Than I bequeath Strestrupps withall the appurtenances To my two daughters Lydia and Sarah Hobson and theire heires And if the Mill be sold as I have ordered it and the money put out for Reubenah & shee dyes, Then I bequeath that money to my sonne Paul, If my wife doe Judge him worthy or else to whome she pleaseth. And lastly I doe hereby renounce and make voyd all former wills by me made and doe publish and declare this to bee my present last will and Testament. In witness whereof I the said Paul Hobson have to this my present last will and testament conteyning five sheets of paper To each sheete thereof sett my hand and seale given the day and yeare first above writtne, Paul Hobson Signed sealed Published and declared by the said Paul Hobson to bee his last will and Testament in the presence of us Robert Topling, John Hall William Page.

Probatum fuit Testamentum suprascriptum apud London coram Surro[ga]to ven[erabi]lis viri d[omi]ni Willi[am]is Mericke milit[i]s legum D[oc]toris venerabili viro Willimo Lewin Legum doctore ^ Curia Prerogativa Cantuariensis mag[ist]ri Custodis sive Commissarii l[egi]time constituti decimo Tertio die mensis Junii Anno Domini Millimo Sextemtesimo Sexagesimo Sexto Juramento Jeremia Hobson unius executorum in huiusmodi Testamento nominat[orum] Cui commissa fuit administrat[i]o omnium et singulorum bonorum Jurium et

creditorum dicti defuncti de bene et fideliter administrand[o] eadem ad Sancta
dei Evangelia Jurat[o] Reservata potestate Similem commissionem faciendi
Hester Hobson et Henrico Woolfe inferis executoribus in huiusmodi Testamen-
to nominat[is] cum venerint eandem petitur[i].

[Translation of lines 120–129]

The abovewritten Will was probated in London before Representative of the venerable Lord William Mericke, Knight, Doctor of Laws
the venerable William Lewin Doctor of Laws, ^legally appointed Master, Custodian or
Commissioner of the Prerogative Court of Canterbury, the thirteenth day
of the month of June, in the Year of the Lord One thousand six hundred Sixty Six, On the Oath
of Jeremiah Hobson, one of named Executers of the said Will to whom
was committed the administration of all and singular goods, Rights and
credits of the said deceased, he having sworn to the good and faithful administration of the same
on the Holy Gospels of God, the power being Reserved of granting a similar Commission to
Hester Hobson and Henry Woolfe as secondary executors named in this Will
when they come to request it.

#12: Elizabeth Malbon and others disciplined by Kiffen's church – 3 November 1667 (GLL, Devonshire Square Minute Book (MS 20228 1A), pages 9 recto and verso):

[Page 9 recto]

Sister Malburne 3d November 1667
Sister Shipp
Sister Carnell
Br[other] Todd

These persons being appointed this day
to come before ye Church to give an accompt
of theire Absence from them for severall
yeares past, and thereby if possible to
Reclaime them from ye principles of the
quakers w[hi]ch they for some tyme had lived
in ye practise of, They ye s[ai]d Malburne,
Shipp and Carnell did accordingly come
who being examined severallie concerning
the neglect of theire duty in ye Church

and ye Erours w[hi]ch they held the said Malburne remained silent and gave

[Page 9 verso]

no answer but Ship and Carnell indicated what they had done & Justifyed theire opinions casting severall reflections upon ye Congregation. Whereupon ye Church considered of ye whole matter together w[i]th theire obstinancie and accordingly Agreede to withdraw from them as persons that did walk contrary to ye Doctrine of Christ w[hi]ch formerly thay had received ~~and~~ which was done by Br[other] Kiffen as theire mouth, and Br[other] Batty and Munns appointed to acquaint each of ye said persons with this sensure of ye Church against them. Br[other] Todd being also of ye same opinion living in ye same neglect and refuseing to come before ye Church, the like sensure was in like manner given against him and notice thereof sent to him as to ye rest.

CHAPTER 5

Devonshire Square Baptist Church Membership Lists, c.1664–90

Within Baptist historiography William Kiffen is generally said to be associated with the Baptist church that met in Devonshire Square outside Bishopsgate in London. Thus, Joseph Ivimey's biography of Kiffen confidently asserts on its title page that he was 'Upwards of Sixty Years Pastor of the Baptist Church, Devonshire Square, London, From 1639 to 1701'.[1] However, such claims present something of a difficulty, given the fact that the first time that Kiffen's church is specifically said to be in Devonshire Square is in *A Narrative of the Proceedings of the General Assembly* (1689).[2] In other words, the straightforward description of Kiffen's church as being located in 'Devonshire Square' is somewhat misleading, since it gives the impression of one fixed meeting place throughout the course of his long ministry. In fact, it appears that the congregation only settled in Devonshire Square toward the end of Kiffen's ministry among them, no doubt under the freedom and protection afforded by the Glorious Revolution of William III in 1688. The truth be told, it is notoriously difficult to pinpoint precisely where Kiffen's congregation met for worship prior to 1689, or to establish what rooms, or buildings or halls, were used by them. Ironically, not even the licensing procedures afforded by Charles II in his *The Declaration of Indulgence* (1672) come to help clarify the situation, for it appears that Kiffen never registered himself, or his house, as a meeting-place for the congregation he led. This is slightly odd, given that on 15 May 1672 he did support the registration of at least two other meeting-rooms in the Bishopsgate vicinity.[3]

---

[1] *The Life of Mr William Kiffin* (1833).

[2] There is a record of the Middlesex Sessions of the Peace dated 11 February 1686 which refers to an illegal conventicle in Devonshire Square. The indictment lists eight members of the conventicle who were 'riotously assembled in an unlawfull Conventicle in Devonshire Square without Bishopsgate London under Colour of Exercisen of Religion' (LMA, MJ/SP/1686/02/001). It is probable that this is William Kiffen's congregation, although he is not named within the record (see Chapter 6 for more on this record).

[3] TNA, SP 29/321, page 148. Kiffen requests licenses for Daniel Dyke at a room in the house of David Jones, and for Thomas Harrison at a room in his own house; both men were said to be of the parish of St Botolph's, Bishopsgate. Dyke and Harrison were both members of Kiffen's church and are included in membership lists of the congregation (GL MS 20,230, pages 9, 19, 33, 41, and 83).

In short, it is not historically accurate to say that Kiffen was pastor of the Baptist church in Devonshire Square from the time that he began to lead a congregation. So why did such an historical anachronism arise? In large measure it is due to the earliest biographers of Kiffen, who discussed him within what was in effect a geographical survey of London's dissenting churches. Walter Wilson's *The History and Antiquities of Dissenting Churches and Meeting Houses* (1808) is a case in point. Kiffen is discussed in volume one in a section dedicated to the Particular Baptist church at Devonshire Square, one of nineteen churches in the 'Eastern Division' of the city of London.[4] Wilson speculates that the Devonshire Square church was formed when Kiffen separated from the church of John Spilsbery in Wapping.

W.T. Whitley's *The Baptists of London* (1928) is a bit better; it notes Kiffen's leadership of a 'City' church in London commencing in 1644, but restricts the description of this church as being in Devonshire Square to the years 1685–1727.[5] Between 1644 and 1685, Whitley asserts, Kiffen's congregation met in a number of different locations:

> Met at *Cold Harbour* 1663, *Fisher's Folly* in Devonshire square, *Artillery ground* in 1669, House of *David Jones* 1672. Re-occupied *Devonshire square* 1687.

Frustratingly, Whitley does not cite any sources to back up his claims about Kiffen's congregation meeting in these places. The interested reader is left to accept Whitley's reconstruction as simple historical fact—it is asserted, unassailable and unquestionable. This is far from ideal, and it does not promote further historical investigation into the matter. There are several difficulties with Whitley's assertion. For example, where does the reference to a Cold Harbour congregation come from, and why is it tied to 1663? How is Fisher's Folly related to Devonshire Square?[6] What is the reason for asserting that Kiffen's church met in the Artillery Ground in 1669? None of these are easy questions to answer, and Whitley took his reasoning with him to the grave, or so it appears.

Occasionally there are some clues as to the geographical location of Kiffen's meeting houses, although the earliest of these do not name Devonshire Square as the site of the church. For instance, an undated list entitled 'Hoax Preachers & Places' specifically notes that Kiffin's meeting place was 'neere St Dunstans east' (line 13), whereas that of Knollys (Knowles) was 'neere the old Artillery ground' (line 12),

---

[4] Pages 400-454. Kiffen is discussed on pages 403-431.

[5] W.T. Whitley *The Baptists of London* (1928): 106, 313.

[6] Fisher's Folly was an early name for the area later designated Devonshire Square. Interestingly, Samuel Butler's *Hudibras*, Part III, Canto II (1674), lines 893-894, suggests that the newly convened Rump Parliament of 1659 represented 'no part o'th' Nation/But Fishers Folly Congregation'.

and Jessey's was 'in Colemanstreete' (line 12) (see Document #1).[7] A related document, also probably from 1660–61, is entitled 'These Congregationall Ministers Preach Publiquely in or about London' (see Document #2).[8] This single page document lists the names of thirty-six ministers, along with a brief description of where their churches were located. Included is an entry for 'By Dunstans East—Mr William Kiffen' (line 18). Moreover, at the bottom of the page there is a further note which reads, 'That in Petty France & by Dunstans East & at Old Artillery are large Assembling Places built of late.' This indicates the investment in, and importance of, Kiffen's meeting house.

The Membership Lists of the Devonshire Square Baptist Church

The Guildhall in London contains several manuscripts relating to the church of William Kiffen which eventually came to be based in Devonshire Square. One of the most important of these is a record of church members, containing four lists of names and details of people who belonged to the church in the seventeenth century. The first list is found on pages 5-9 of the manuscript. Unfortunately, the beginning pages of the list are lost and it is impossible to know when it first began to be compiled, although it was likely that it was in the early 1660s. The last dated entry in the list is from August of 1668. The second list is contained on pages 10-39 and began to be composed on 24 February 1668. The last dated entry in this list is from 1674. The third list is contained on pages 40-67 and began to be composed on 3 August 1670. The last dated entry in this list is from 1683. The fourth list is contained on pages 68-93 and began to be composed on 6 October 1690. The last dated entry in this list is from 5 January 1707. The complete text of these lists is offered here as Document #3; an alphabetical index of the member's names is also provided.

Documents

#1 – LMA, List of Hoax Preachers and Places – c.1663 (CLA/047/LR/02/02/001):

[Text]

Hoax preachers & places

Gerard Roberts in Tho[mas] Apples — The Snaile in Towerstreete
George Fox lodger there } Quakers — Mouth att Aldersgate
Margaret Fells lodger — att Roberts house
Taler a Boddiceseller at Cheapside

[7] LMA, List of Hoax Preachers and Places (CLA/047/LR/02/02/001). The London Metropolitan Archives give this a tentative date of 1683, but it is probably from the 1660s (Henry Jessey died in 1663).

[8] TNA, SP 29/47, page 106.

Cox Sopeboyler at Thamstreete } in Petty France
Waters of Whitechappell
Den att Paules
Parratt neere Baynard Castle
Jessey in Colemanstreete
Griffen teacheth att oat Balls in Bricklanee
Knowles neere the old Artillery ground
Kiffin neere st Dunstans east
Middletons in Dukes place

#2 – List of Congregational Ministers Preaching in London – 1660–61 (TNA, SP 29/47, page 106):

[Text]

These Congregationall Ministers
Preach Publiquely in, or about, London

Stepney	Mr Greenhill	Great Alhal	Mr Brag
Bednal Green	Mr Mead often	lows Thems street	Mr Jo Simson
White chappel	Mr Wallers	Pancrasse	Mr Geo Cokay
Wapping	Mr Chasey of N[?]	Trinity Lane	Mr Jo Rogers
Old Artillery	Mr Has Knollys	Broken Wharf	Mr Chr Feak
Byshopsgate	Mr Jo Simson	Brides on the	Mr Nead
		Days	
Petty France	Mr Edw Harrison	Savoy Parish	Mr Hook
within Bpgate	Mr Tobias Coniers		
Ethebens			
Dukes Place	Mr Mallery	Westminster	Mr Row
5th days at Crooked Lane		Clarkenwell	Dr Hornes
12 Days afternoon		Bartholo	Mr Gosnal
Katherines Tower	Mr Slater &	mew Close	
	Mr Kentish		
By Dunstans East	Mr W. Kiffen		
S[t] Olaves	Mr Venning	Charterhouse	Mr Griffith
Georges Southwark	Mr H. Jessey	Mary Stainings	Dr Nathaniel
		By Wood Street	Homes
Thomses Church	Mr Bearman		
at Hospitall	Mr Hancock	Coleman Street	Mr Jo Goodwin
Bridge Foot	Mr Caryll	Bartholomew	Mr Phil Nye
Fish Street Hill	Mr Tho Brooks	Lane by ye	Teacher
next above it	Mr Barker	Exchange	Mr Lodor Laster
		Crooked lane	Mr Mallery
		1st days afternoon	

That in Petty France, & by Dunstans East, & at Old Artillery
are Large Assembling Places built of late.

#3 – GLL, Devonshire Square Membership Lists – c. 1690-1707 (GL MS 20,230, folios 5-93):

[Membership List from circa 1664 (46 people – 17 men and 29 women)]

Page 5 – 10 people – 6 men and 4 women]

Bro Johnson	A weaver in Crown yard Bishopsgatestreete now in Wentworth stret	Recomended from Tibulls	
Bro West	A Brassier	at Rumford	Deceased
Bro Christopher Gough		in Leadenhall Streete Gone to ye Barbadoes	Deceased
Sr Moore	Widdow now in holborn	now in Robin hood Court in Shoe Lane	
Bro Lawrence Fayrcloath	upholster set down before	in Lothbury	
Sr Amy Laurence	widdow of Lord Lawrence Deceased	at margetts	Deceased
Sr Margrett	widdow	in gorden Land	Deceased

Tittison		at ye worlds End	
Bro Tho[mas] Buckston	a soape Boyler	in Eastsmithfeild	withdrawn from
Bro Tho[mas] Hind	a shoomaker	in grubstreette	
Sr Mary Evans	Bro[ther] Evans wife	in Bevis markes	

[Page 6 – 13 people – 4 men and 9 women]

Sr Burles	a widdow	at heeshead Down	Dyed in ye fayth
Sr An[n] Coleman	a widdow silke thrower	In three Tun alley Lane peticoate Lane	Deceased
Bro Seeleee	mariner	at Lower Shadwell gone to sea	Deceased
Sr Mary Figg now her name is Ashborn	widow at ye Sun in Clerk fayre	in Bedlam	
Bro Erpe Sr Erpe		by st martins Recomended from Ireland now at Charing Crosse	Deceased

added ye 1 March 1666	Sr Stasmoore	Living with her father	by London well	Deceased
added ye 2 March 1666	Sr Broughton	A Nurse at Bro[ther] Coopers	in Bevis markes	
	Bro Uncles Sr Uncles his wife	A Glover by plimsbery	Recomended from Bro Paul Harris	Dyed in ye fayth 1666
	Bro Patience Sr Patience		Recomended from ye church at Bristoll	Dyed in ye faith Deceased
added ye 3rd month 1666	Sr Drapes	widdowe Living with Bro[ther] Cooper	In Bevis markes	

[Page 7 – 10 people – 3 men and 7 women]

added ye 3rd month 1666	Sr Turner	A shoemakers wife Sister Stunts Daughter	in Cluck Lane	Deceased
added ye 4th month 1666	Sr Mary Baker	A Button maker with Mr Lewis now in Whitt Crosse streete	In Bullhead Court in Newgate markett	
added ye 4th month	Sr Phillis Boulton	A mayd Living at	In bell yard in	

1666		Job Boultons	Thames Streete neare Pauls wharfe gone in ye Countrey	
added ye 4th month 1666	Sr Lawrence	wife to Mr Laurence a shopkeeper	In East Smithfeild	Dyed in ye faith
	Bro Bayly	A Taylor	about Gowell Lane in hounsdich	Cast out for scandals sins & recorded
	Sr Bland	A Carpinters wife	In poplar	
	Bro Ed[ward] Eldridge	In ye Little Min-orys now in Whitt Chappel	Recomended from ye Church about abingdon	Deceased
	Sr Mary Baker now her name is Eldridge	widow now maryed to Bro[ther] Ed Eldridge	In ye Little minorys	
added ye 9th month 1666	Sr Sarah Curtisse Bro Hunters daughter	A mayd	Living in Ouldstreete with Brother Hunter	Deceased
added ye 11th month 1666	Bro John Coleman	silk threster	In 3 Tuns alley peticoate Lane	

[Page 8 – 11 people – 3 men and 8 women]

added ye 11th month 1666	Sr Legay	Brother Clarks wifes sister a mayd	in minoring Lane gone to Barbados	
	Sr Sutton	Brother Hemings his mother in law	at Stratford	
	Bro Policott Bro Tho[mas] Martin	Glassier	From ye Brethren yt were at westerhouse	
	Bro Thomas Mabbett	Living with Mr Preston A stolemaster In petty france next ye pump	Received ye 17th 1st month 1667 Came from ye people with Wanam	
added 1667	Sr Ward Bro Hunters daughter	A Brewers wife Living with Brother Hunter	In Ould streete	Deceased
	Sr Jane Cogshall	A servant with Brother Horton	Recomended from the Church at Westbury Wiltshire	
	Sr Eliz[abeth] Scott	Widow with Brother King his mother in law	In Tenter alley Little moore fields	
	Sr Bacon	A smiths wife at	Recei]ve]d by Repentance	

		ye further End of Night-ingale Lane Eastsmithfeild		
added ye 6 month 1667	Sr Wright	A Carpenters wife	In ~~gorden Lane~~ Holoway Lane	
	Sr Keyns	a Widdow In Tenter alley	with Brother Snelling	

[Page 9 – 2 people – 1 man and 1 woman]

Bro Tho[mas] Harrison	A Talow Chandler	in Whitt Chappell	withdrawn from
Sr Mary Niccoles	Brother Hunters daughter		

[Membership List from circa 1668 (362 people – 118 men and 248 women)]

[Page 10]

The Names of Those Brothers & Sisters yt have given up themselves to
The Lord to walke in his wayes In fellowship together with Bro[ther] W[illia]m Kiffin, This being
an abstract of ye former made out this 20th day of ye 12th month 1667.

[Page 11 – 16 people – 6 men and 10 women]

The names of Brothers & sisters	The place of there Habitations	there Callings & Relations	The Condition whether In Comunion or not

	Bro W[illia]m Kiffin Sr Hanah Kiffin his wife	In An alley over ag[ain]st ye new attillery row in Austin Fryers	Merchant	
	Bro Batty Sr Clement Batty his wife	at ye upper end of moore Lane widdow	A Mask maker	Brother Batte deceased
	Bro Hemings Sr Hemings his wife Sr Sutton her mayd	In phinsbury now at Stratford	merchant	
	Bro Thomas Hind	~~A shoemaker~~ In grubstreett at ye upper end	A shoemaker	
added December 1683	Bro Maurice King Sr Bridgett King his wife Sr Eliz[abeth] Scott his mother	In Tenter alley Little morre fields now in Lucon Lane	A silkman	
	Sr Negus	In Tenter alley with Brother Snelling	A widdow	
	Sr Mary Baker	In moore Lane	A Buttonmaker	

	now in playhouwse yard		
Bro Robert Amy & his wife	In forestreet	An Apothecary	Deceased Deceased
Sr Sarah Church	A shopp in ye custom under ye swan w[atc]h maker(?) now under Guild hall	sells fruite	

[Page 12 – 13 people – 3 men and 10 women]

Sr Abigail Beamon	In Redcrosse Streett	widdow	
Sr Sanders	In Redcrosse Streett Pauls alley	widow	
Sr Ireland	In Goulden Lane now in Coleman streete	widdow	
Sr Abigale Bowers	In goulden Land with Sister Ireland now in moore yard in holborn at Mr Andrews howse	a Buttonmaker	
Sr An[n] Morly	In goulden Lane now in a Court over against grubstreett now In gutter Lane	A silversmiths wife	

		in a Court by St Martins		
	Bro Tho[mas] Martin	In goulden Lane now in Ould streete	a Brewers servant	
	Bro J[oh]n Hunter Sr Hunter his wife	In Ould streette	A Brewer	
	Sr Ward Bro Hunters daughter	In Ould streett	A Brewers wife	Deceased
	Sr Mary Niccolls Sr Alice Carterson now her name is Dix	In ould streett	with her father Brother Hunter	
 added 1670	Bro Uncles Sr Uncles his wife	In ould strette blue anchor alley now in tenter alley in Little moorfeilds	A Glover	

[Page 13 – 13 people – 2 men and 11 women]

	Sr Elizabeth Biswell	about goulden Lane now in ye Countrey	A maker of silver lasse	recomended to ye Church now at wickam
	Sr Wright Sr Colemans Daughter	In Goulden Lane now in holeaway Court	A Carpenters wife	

		now in Cock Lane in Shoreditch	
	Sr Winefreed Person	In St Johns Streett now in St Martins at ye Bottles(?) now in Pauls Church yard at ye Castle	A Bottlemakers wife
	Sr Wattson now Sherman	In Bartholomew Close	A widdow maryed to Brother Sherman
	Sr Ashborn	In Cloak Fayre	A Chandlers wife
added ye 5th month 1669	Bro Rickson Sr Rickson his wife	In Longe Lane 3 Corkes	A seller of Linen
	Sr Alce Stout Sr Turner her Daughter	In Field Lane now in Southwarke	A widdow A schoomakers wife
	Sr Mary Simpson	In Shoe Lane	A Childrens Coatmaker a widow admonished
	Sr Moore	In Holborn in Whitts alley	A widdow

	Bro John Eyles Sr Sarah Eyles his wife	In Burry Streete	Merchant	

[Page 14 – 14 people – 6 men and 8 women]

	Sr Phebee Malorett	In Holborn A midwife	a victualers wife	Deceased
	Bro Policott	In Hatton garden now in Tower streete	A Glassier	Dead
added 7th month 1668	Bro Clare Sr Clare his wife Sr Kathrin Laye now servant now with Brother Rob Snelling	In St Gyles in ye fields now in ye strand	A Brewers Clarke	
	Bro Tho[mas] Atherton Sr Atherton his wife Bro Ward	In pell mell at ye sune howse	with My Lady Renulu	
	Sr Mercer	In Kings streette westminster	A shopkeeper A widdow	
	Sr Mary Kent	In Coven Garden	Tho[mas] Clarkes wife of yt p[ar]ish	

Sr An Hughes now her name Taylor	at whitt hall now in holborn	servant to ye Lady Darcy maryed to a button maker	Deceased
Bro John Johnson	at westminster	a Brewers Clarke Recomended from north howse	
Bro Stevens	at plimsbury	a Taylor	Deceased
Sr Drapes	In Chester howse Lane with her daughter mrs Davie at ye Sun	a widdow	

[Page 15 – 15 people – 2 men and 13 women]

Sr Bridgett Brown	with Mr Malbone In Shordich now in Gravell Lane hounsdich	widdow	Dyed in the fayth
Sr An[n] Popitt alias Druzie	In shordich		
Sr Creeke	In spitlefeilds	a widow	

Bro John Person Sr person his wife	In spittle In Coleman streett	Bro Pearson died 26 Sept 1668 Sr pearson Dyed in the faith	
Bro owen Halton Sr Halton his wife Sr Hanah Carter with him now her name is herne Sr Jane Sr Hanah his daughters	A Brewer In Half moone alley Bishopgatestrette now in hounsdich	A Brewer	
Sr Margett Davis	In Longe alley	A weavers wife	Dyed in ye fayth
Sr Alse Vernon	In sopers alley Bishopgatestreett	died A Calenders wife	Dyed in ye fayth
Sr Neaves	In ye sume alley	a widow	
Sr ~~Eliz~~ Hanah Stasmoore	about ye sune place	a mayd	Dyed in ye fayth
Sr Herrod	In Coleman streete a Sailors wife at greenwich		

[Page 16 – 16 people – 7 men and 9 women]

	Sr Bunkee	by ye new Churchyard In Bedlam now in bell alley in Coleman streete	A starcher	
Deceased	Bro John Hill Sr Hill alias Hutford his wife	In 3 Tun alley by London Wall	A Taylor sister Halfhead dead	Deceased Deceased
added ye first month 1670	Bro John Clements Sr Clements his wife	In Crown Court In Broadstreette	a merchant	
	Sr Angell	In ye sume Court		Deceased
	Bro Gyles Haynes Sr Haynes his wife	In Bishopsgate at ye spread Eagle now at Pauls wharfe	Stocken merchant	Deceased
added 1670	Bro Thomas Cooper Sister Cooper Sr Eyles Bro Eyles his wife	In Bury strett by Dukes place	marchants recomended to Exon	Dead
	Bro Ben Hulen Sr Hanah Hulen Bro Joseph Guicherite	In Dukes place In Coleman Streette In Dukes place	marchant	

	ther servant Sr Hanah Hulen her daughter		
	Bro Lawrence Fayrecloath	by London Wall now in	An uphoulster

[Page 17 – 12 people – 4 men and 8 women]

	Sr An[n] Hill	In Duk[e]s Place	A Nurse Keeper
	Bro Tho[mas] Lidderdale	In Duke's place	A Taylor
	Lidderdale his wife	now at Thebolds	
	Bro John Smith	In marke Len or at Dice Key	Wursinger
1664	Bro Clarke	In Seething Lane	A Barber
	Sr Leyny his sister	by Tower Hill	gone to Barbadoes
	Sr Eliz[abeth] Randale	by ye Tower	A servant
	Sr Comfort Bradshaw now her name Mabbott		a servant
	Sr Longe now her name is Jacob	by St Kathrins now in moore Lane	A widdow came from Ireland

	Bro Jacob her husband			
	Sr Christian Lan	at St Kathrins 3 maryners	A victuals wife	Dyed in ye fayth
	Bro Thomas Hix Sr Hix his wife	In the postern by aldermanbury instern	recomended from ye church at Devizes	

[Page 18 – 13 people – 6 men and 7 women]

Sr was Sr Watson	Bro Jo[hn] Sherman senior Sr Sherman his wife	In whitt Chappell wyts ye mount	A silk thwister sister Sherman is dead	
	Bro Jo[hn] Sherman junior Sr Hanah his wife	In Kathrin whele alley whitt Chappell		
	Bro Cadwell	neare him In peticote Lane in black bell alley	A weaver	Deceased
	Sr Capre	In George yard whitt chapele	A midwife widow	Deceased
	Sr Supper	In Angell Alley whitt chapele now in Katherin whele alley	A widdow	

Bro Devonshire	about ye same place in Kathrine whelle alley	working with a silke Thwister	Deceased
Sr An[n[Rochele	In whitt Chapelle now in Bedlam	widdow	
Sr Wood alias Wicke alias Gurlicke	In Kathrin whele alley whitt Chappelle	was Bro Woods wife	
Sr Edith Edwards	about ye sune place in Little minorys	wife of A Clouthwrite	Dyed in the fayth
Bro An[n] Coleman Bro John Coleman	In 3 Tun alley whitt chappele now in Kathrine whele alley	Silke thinsters	Deceased

[Page 19 – 11 people – 4 men and 7 women]

Bro Tho[mas] Harison	In whitt chappele	Talow Chandler	withdrawn from & admonished
Bro Johnson	about peticote Lane now about shordich	A weaver	
Sr Jane Bateman	In ye minorys	A Taylors wife	

	now in hounsdich		
Sr Graves	In ye minorys at ye w[hi]t Swan	an apothecary	Deceased
Sr Prisilla Smothers	In ye minorys	A flaxwoman	Deceased
Sr Janett Jones	In ye minorys	A servant	
Bro Philip Larkin Sr Larkin his wife Sr Hanah his daughter	In East smithfeild	A Translator	
Bro Tho[mas] Seaward	In East smithfeild	A Brewer	was driven from and Excluded
Sr Kath[erine] Remnant	In East smithfeild now in East cheape	wife to Bro Remnant A Bricklayer now a widdow	

[Page 20 – 11 people – 2 men and 9 women]

Bro Booth Sr Booth his wife	In East smithfeild	Seaman	Deceased

Sr Hinton	In East smithfeild	A pinmakers wife	Deceased
Sr Williams alias Herring	In East smithfeild	widow	
Sr Ruth Reade now Hinton	In East smithfeild	widow	
Sr ~~Eliz[abeth]~~ Temperance Bacon	In Nightingale Lane	A smiths wife	Deceased
Sr Eliz[abeth] Ludington	East smithfeild now in whitt Chappell	widow	
Sr Gripp	East smithfeild	widdow	Deceased
Sr Stubbs	East smithfeild	A Carpinters wife	
Sr Lambert	Ratiff his way	a widow	
Bro Seelee	at Shadwell by Ratlifts	A seaman	Deceased

[Page 21 – 11 people – 4 men and 7 women]

Sr Gibson	at Ratlift Crosse	Gone to menis	Deceased there

Sr Juncing	at poplar	a ship carpinters wife	
Sr Potts	at poplar	widow	Deceased
Sr Bocke	at poplar	widow	Deceased
Sr Bland	at poplar	A ship carpinters wife	
Bro Oeslee	at Waping	A Baker	
Bro Gaunt	at wappen	A Talowchandler	
Bro Harlem	at wappen	A Tabaconist	Cast out
Bro Algate Sr June Algate his wife	at wappen Crosse alley now in Louthbury	A seaman	Cast out Deceased
Sr Deadman	at Wappen	a widdow	Dyed in ye fayth

[Page 22 – 13 people – 4 men and 9 women]

Sr Horsley	at wappen	Nurskeeper	

added 7th month 1668	Sr Mary Arnoll Sr Eliz[abeth] Arnoll her daughter	at wappen	a widow	
	Sr Halabread her name now is Rivett	at wappen	A widow	
	Bro Rowly	at mettinghouse alley wappen	A Taylor	Deceased
	Sr An[n] Stuccee alias Wright	at or about ye same place now in holborn		~~now at~~ ~~wishbich~~
	Bro Samon Sr Samon his wife	In wappen	shipcarpinter	Sr Samon deceased
	Bro Rob[ert] Barnes	In wappen	chandler	
	Sr Abigale Hale	In wappen	A seamans wife	
	Sr Lash Sr Lash	In wappen	A widow	
	Sr Lash junior alias Blockley	In Wappen		

Bro Clare	a miller	in Eastsmithfeild	

[Page 23 – 14 people – 6 men and 8 women]

Bro Na[thanie]l Muns Sr Mary Muns his wife	In Thomas south warke by ye great maze pond	A weaver	Deceased
Bro Rumball Sr Rumball his wife	In Thomas southwark	A Talow Chandler	
Bro Corbridge Sr Corbridg his wife	now Burnebee Streett Southwark	A Castormaker	
Bro Whittman	In Tooleys streett	A Translator	Deceased
Bro Willson Sr Willson his wife	at ye Bridghowse now in gravell Lane	recomended to ye Church at Dublin In Ireland	
Sr Fortune Walton now Tarke	in Tooleys streett	widow coffee seler	
Sr Hovins	In Tooleys streett	widdow	Dead

Sr An[n] Daniele now Mills	about piclehering	wool rutter	
Bro Bonkile	about piclekherring	A Cooper	Dyed in ye fayth
Sr Little	Horsway down		

[Page 24 – 11 people – 3 men and 8 women]

Tho[mas] Watts	about Horsway down now at Redriff	Buttenmaker	
Sr Kathrin Drake	Horsway down	An Apothecary	
Bro Zachary Standard Sr Standard his wife	at Rederiff	Waterman	
Ro[bert] Tipp Sr Tipp his wife	at Rederiffe now at wappen	A shipcarpinter	
Sr Randall alias Teage	yt lived at Zusum now about Horsway down	A widdow	recomended to Bristol
Sr Eliz[abeth] Owen	In southworke	A widow	
Sr Eliz[abeth] Cramp	In southworke	A widdow	Deceased

Sr Merryseede	In southworke	A widdow	
Sr Handcocke	at ye further End of Blackman streett	A weavers wife	

[Page 25 – 13 people – 6 men and 7 women]

Bro W[illia]m Hare	In southwork	A Tanner	
Bro Jo[hn] Westley Sr Westley his wife	In ye Borough of southworke	Cast out Linen Draper	
Sr Snell	In southworke	A Tabonists wife	
Bro Stiffe Sr Stiffe his wife	In ye parke Southworke	A Carpinter	Deceased
Bro Ed[ward] Elderidg Sr Elderidg now Barber	In ye parke Southworke now by Goodmans fields	Dyed in ye fayth A Taylor	admonished withdrawn from
Bro Joseph Hodges	In ye parke now in Goodmans fields now in Castle streete	A Taylor	Deceased

Bro Ro[bert] Mabbott	with Bro Elderiges	A wrighter	gone to Bro Wise
Sr Mabbott alias Broklaw	Southworke now in Whitt Chappell		Deceased
Sr Finke	about mayd Lane	A widdow	Dyed in ye fayth
Sr Evers	In mayd Lane	A widdow	Dyed in ye fayth

[Page 26 – 10 people – 1 man and 9 women]

Sr Lewis	at ye uper end of	A waster	
Sr Light	In mayd Lane	A widdow	Deceased
Sr Patience	at Newington green	widdow	Dead
Sr Jane Cogshall	servant to her		
Sr Jane Cogshall	at Bro Snellings	a servant	
Sr Orams Daugster	Living about wickhamsted	gone to ye Quakers	
Sr Tachell	Living at Earl of Warwickes	widow	
Sr Punge	at Stratford	widow	Deceased
Sr Haray	at Stratford	a shopkeepers wife	recomended to Uxbridge at

			marlo
Bro West	at Rumsford	A Brassier	Deceased
Sr Eversy	at Hounslo now at Holbornbridge at ye kings armes	An Inkeepers wife	

[Page 27 – 11 people – 3 men and 8 women]

Bro Constable	at Greenwich beeond Black Heath	Husbandman	Deceased
Sr Dorothy Jaxon	at Greenwich		
Sr Hanah Ellis	at Greenwich		Cast out for
Sr Eliz[abeth] Banes	at Greenwich	widow	Deceased Dyed in ye fayth
Bro Tho[mas] Hunt	at Lussam	A Tanner	
Sr Kat[herine] Edmonds	at Lussam	A Tanners wife	
Sr Styles	at Lussam	A Tanners wife	
Bro Ri[chard] Barow		gone to Bro	

		Knollis Deceased	
Sr Lawrenc	at margetts	widow	Deceased
Sr Cressett	there	widow	Dead
Sr Deane	at highgate now at Bro Shermans	widow	

[Page 28 – 13 people – 1 man and 12 women]

Members of ye Congregation yt are Remote

Sr Tenter Sr Nade her daughter	at Chatham Deceased	widdow
Sr Colcott	These at Strand by Rochester	Dyed in ye fayth 1669
Sr Judith Allen		
Sr Eliz[abeth] Perons		
Sr Dorothy Fuller		
Sr Jone Countrey		

Sr Ruth Shanke		
Sr Isbell Blunt		
Sr Mary Tompson	at Quinborow	shopkeepers wife
Bro Nath[aniel] Stoner Sr Stoner his wife	at Reading	
Sr Oram	at Reading now at highgate	

[Page 29 – 13 people – 6 men and 7 women]

Members yt are remote		
Bro Aaron Jones Sr Jones his wife	at wantage	
Bro Kentish Sr Kentish his wife	about uxbridge	now returned to London in Little moorefeilds
Sr Kath[erine] Fields		
Sr Sarah Paby Sr Worsley	about Stafford at Westminster by Tutlefeilds	

Sr Evans	about Richmond		
Sr Sarah Colkins	at Ratliffe was in Plumclutch streete at a Comfitt maker		
Bro Hitts	at Harford		
Bro Cheenforth	about Kederminster	a shoemaker	
Bro Cove		a shoemaker yt was recomended from Notingam	
Bro Jo[hn] Ball	about minhead	factor	

[Page 30 – 14 people – 8 men and 6 women]

members Remote & beiond ye sea

Bro Grundee Sr Grandee his wife	at Sunderland	a seaman	Cast away deceased
Bro Tho[mas] Halett	at New England		
Bro Haray	at New England		

	Bro Christopher Gough	at Barbadoes		Deceased
	Bro George Gosfright Sr Gosfright his wife	~~In Rotterdam~~ In Lothbury	now returned	
	Bro Styles	In Amsterdam		
	Sr Ruth Prine	In Barbadoes		
	Bro Erpe Sr Erpe his wife	at Woodbridge	now about Westminster now gone to Barbadoes	
	Sr Phillis Boulton	In Cheshire		
added in ye year 1669	Sr Sarah Skellett Dr Owen his howse	gone to Deale Kent liveth with Mr Postill in Kent		
	Bro Chelensworth	a shomaker	~~In Worfesterlein~~	

[Page 31 – 14 people – 5 men and 9 women]

Member yt have left there Conversion

Sr Mary Powes	Barnabas streett	gone to ye Quakers
Bro Sum	about Kewington	
Sr Quinton		Received into Comunion
Bro Todd	A porter	Gone to ye Quakers
Sr Sarah Scott		withdrawn
Bro John Gladman Sr Gladman his wife	at Devonshire howse Deceased	recomended from Tiblods
Bro Spinagre Sr Spinagre his wife	in Southworke Deceased	recomended from Tiballs
Sr Eliz[abeth] Andrews	A factors wife in Colemanstreette	
Sr Westly alias Reeves	widdow in Southwarke at her fathers howse	
Sr Gough	Sr Gosfrights mother	

		Living with them		
	Bro Kentish Sr Kentish	In little moorefeilds upper End a Brewers Clarke		Deceased

[Page 32 – 12 people – 8 men and 4 women]

Members in and about ye Citty

added 6th month 1668	Sr Jane Best	A silk thresters wife	In ye Little Minoryes	
added ye 6th month 1668	Bro Michele Stapleton	A silke Threster	In whit Chappell	
	Bro John Wodsin	A Carpinter	working with Bro Stiff Recomended from Ireland	withdrawn from for great disorder
	Sr Pride	widdow	In Southworke in ye parke now at Mr Bankerrs in ye ould Bayley	
	Bro John Bradshaw	A Brewer	at Greenwich Rec[eiv]ed by Comendation from Scotland	

	Bro Andrew	A shoomaker	at Greenwich	Deceased
	Bro W[illia]m Warner	~~A Laborer~~ Bricklayer in Nightingale Lane	In Charter howse Lane Recommend from ye Church at Horton in Gloucestershire now in Nightingale Lane	
	Sr An[n] Standler	a servant	Recomended from y Church at Bristole Recomended Quaker Bristole	
added ye 8 month 1669	Bro John Hinton	a Translator	In Southworke	
added ye 5th month 1669	Bro Samuell Grew Sr Grew	a shomaker	Living by spitlefeilds in ye howse yt was Sr Sumers	
	Bro Gough	In spittlefeilds	formerly in Ireland	
[Page 33 – 15 people – 6 men and 9 women]				
added 2nd month 1669	Bro Dan[iel] Dike Sr Dike his wife		In gent alley Bunhill	
	Sr Mary Dutton	Living A servant	Recomended from ye Church atTibbulls	
	Sr Bridget Minns	a widdow	In Shadwell	

	Bro Rich[ard] Lateward	at Customhowse Key	Babtered in Cheshire & recomended by testimony
	Sr An[n] Bannister now heathpold	Living at Sr moore's at holborn w[h]its alley	
added 3 month 1669	Bro Bride	A Hatcher	In Blockman Street Southworke
	Bro Richard Smith Sr Eliz[abeth] Smith his wife	A Bricklayer ~~at Bro Kiffins~~ In Ouldstreet	Recomended from ye Church at Theobolds
added about ye 4th month 1669	Sr Eliz[abeth] Heming Sr Rebecca Atkinson	both servants at ye Lady Darceys Whitthall	
	Bro Tho[mas] Hethcoat	In at Crosse street at Mr Dashwood	Recomended to ye Church at Dublin
	Sr Elizabeth Hunter	In ould streete Bro Hunters sister	
	Bro J[oh]n Snelling	In Tenter alley	
	Sr Katherine Bird	In Lincoln Ins fields	

		now in Silver streete	

[Page 34 – 14 people – 3 men and 11 women]

	Sr Ann Tomson Sr horslys daughter	living at Wappin near to ye Wh[itt] Chappell now in hounsdich	
	Bro Talbott Sr Talbott his wife	In little morefeilds	recomended from ye Church at Exon
	Sr Lucas	East smithsfeild	received by repentance
added ye 24 Dec[em]ber 1669	Sr Jane Bonkill now her name Leach	servant to Mr Collett In moore fields In Dunnings Alley in Bishopsgatestreete	
	Sr Mary Power	widow	recomended from ye Church at Theobolds
	Sr Sarah Skellett alias Dowe	now with her Brother Mr Petite at Deale now at Mr Floyds at algate now in Fanchurch Streete a mealmans wife	

	Bro Robert Whaley	A Translator now Grubstreett End Criplegate	received by repentance	
	Sr Eleanoir Simcock alias Harison	Widdow in Hogg Lane	received by repentance	
	Sr Mary Fenner alias Dorie	Widdow at Tower Dich now at Irongate at ye Hart	Received by repentance	
Gone to Jamaica	Sr Argyle Sr Pocke now Whitte	at Ratliffe a widow her sister	Recomended by Bro Ward of Darby	
added 1670	Bro Cole	A shomaker in Northen for gate now in little Eastcheape	~~Recomended from~~	runaway to be dealt with all by ye Church
	Sr An[n] Maynard now Curtisie	In blue anchor alley in ould streete	widdow	

[Page 35 – 13 people – 5 men and 8 women]

	Bro W[illia]m Roper	at Westminster	a servant to an apothecary
	Bro Menlowe	shoemaker	in ye Countrey went

				away with a Letter
	Sr Culamoore	a widow at Stonbridg neare poplar		
	Sr Boulton	At Depthford		recomended from Bro Harison
added 1670	Bro Grumbridge	at Lusam a fell monger		
added 1672	Sr Eaton now Hunter	In Twisters alley Bun Hill widdow		
added 1672	Sr Mary Cowley	a servant to Mr Taylor in Clarkenwell		withdrawn from
	Sr Judith Stampers			recomended from Exon to Exon
	Bro Deane Sr Deane his wife	a shomakers Widdow	neare Lewis in Sussex	Bro Deane deceased
	Sr Sarah Drinkwater	a pewterers wife	in whitt chappell	Dyed in the fayth
	Bro John Eames	servant to a Brewer	recomended from Shaftes-	Bro Evans deceased

	Sr Emes his wife alias Mabbott	in purpoole Lane a widdow	bury	

[Page 36 – 18 people – 3 men and 15 women]

	Bro Henry Stevens	in Thames streete neare ye Custom howse	Recomended from Exon	
	Bro John Masters Sr Eliz[abeth] Masters his wife	in whitt Crosse streete Chandler	Came from Bro Knowles	
	Bro Rich[ard] Goulding	Ironmonger in Great church streete		Dyed in ye fayth
	Sr Mary Grimes	widow in Blackfriars		
added 1673	Sr Eliz[abeth] Vicars Sr Susan Bavery Sr An[n] Wrath Sr Leach	all in Long alley by the whitte ~~howse~~ neare Mr Hulets howse		
	Sr Boult	a wharfingers wife at Brookes wharf	recomended from Henly	
	Sr Richard Grigg		recomended from Theobalds	

	Sr Eliz[abeth] Pettitt Sr Archer Sr Pettits daughter		recomended from Theobalds
Gone to bristole	Sr Walker Sr Barbery fabian her sister	a Turners wife In St James	
	Sr Dorothy Hinton	servant to	recomended from Sommersetshire
	Sr Archboll	Living at Hackney with my Lord Brookes	
	Sr Beale	a Glassiers wife In little Woodstreet	

[Page 37 – 13 people – 4 men and 9 women]

1674	Sr Mary Mackrith	a widdow in Bishops gate streete by ye Spittle scoolemistriss	recomended to ye borders of Scotland
added 1674	Sr Mary Chipp	a Churgions wife by Bell savage	
added 1674	Sr Eliz[abeth] Daniele	a haberdashers wife	gone in ye Country

		in Leadenhall street	
	Sr Eliz[abeth] Wormill	a widdow of Worcestershire	withdrawn herself
added 1674	Sr Eliz[abeth] Aubrey	In frying pan alley In peticote Lane	
	Bro Gray Sr Gray his	A shomaker In Dukes place	recomended from ye church at Trofring
	Bro Delawn	at Bro Eyles	recomended from Exon
	Bro W[illia]m Shelton		
	Bro John Ward Sr Ward his wife		
	Sr Mary Monts		
	Sr Eliz[abeth] Hunt		

[Page 38 – 6 people – 0 men and 6 women]

	Sr An[n] Johnson		

Sr Francis Hunt

Sr Tuleday
survate
Sr Rogers

Sr Joans

Sr Algate

[Page 39 - Blank]

[Page 40]

The Names of the Brethren and Sisters that have given up them selves to ~~walke~~ the Lord to walke in his wayes in fellowshipp together with Bro[ther] W[illia]m Kiffin & Bro[ther] Daniele Dyke being an abstract of ye former made out the 3d August 1670.

[Page 41 – 15 people – 7 men and 8 women]

The names of Brethren & sisters	The place of ther habitation	There Callings and Relations	The Condition whether In Comunion or not
Bro W[illia]m Kiffin			

Sr Sarah[1] Kiffin his wife Sr price's sister(?)			
Bro Dan[iel] Dyke Sr Dyke his wife alias Negus	Deceased Deceased		
Bro John Johnson	Westminster	a Brewer's Clerke	Deceased
Sr Francis Mercer	In Kingstreett		
Bro W[illiam] Roper	Westminster	Apothecary	Deceased
Sr Walker	neare ye hay markett	a Tanners wife recomended Bro Harries	
Bro Atherton Sr Atherton his wife Bro Ward ~~Sr Clare~~	Deceased pell mell ~~deceas~~		
Bro Clare Sr Clare his wife	Deceased by ye new Exchange deceased		

[1] *Sarah* is written over the top of the word *Hannah* here.

	Sr Eliz[abeth] Hemings	

[Page 42 – 11 people – 2 men and 9 women]

	Sr Kent	Maiden Lane Comon Garden
	Sr Rebecca Atkinson now her name is Mainard	now in Breadstrete
	Sr Alse Girdler	In Lincoln ins fields
B F	Sr Merke	Holborn Burrs Scoolmistrisse
B F	Bro Claton & Sr Claton his wife	a Baker In Cloathfayre now in Bloomsbery
B F	Sr Bragg	In Cloyster Court Blackfryers
added 1674	Sr Margett Hill	In ye Strand a saltmans wife

added 1673	Sr Susana Alden now her name Bro her husband	servant in aldesgate streete at a wyrting m[aste]r	
added 1673	Sr Rachell Seabrooke	In Sharpes alley at Cow Crosse a widdow	

[Page 43 – 15 people – 3 men and 12 women]

	Sr Moore	Holborn st In shoe Lane	Deceased
	Sr Mabbott Bro Mabbott	Purple Lane	Deceased
	Sr Eversly	Holborn Bridge	Deceased
	Sr Drapes	at St Jones's	Deceased
	Sr Grimes	In Blackfryers	Deceased
	Sr Ashborn	Cloathfayre	
	Bro Ward Sr Ward his wife	about snowhill In Giltspriorstreete	a Taylor

	Sr Abigale Bowers	a Buttonmaker	
Came with B F	Sr An Johnson		
	Sr Meate now Stevens	Holborn burrs a scoolmistrisse	Deceased
	Bro Abraham Stevens	in mosses alley	
added 1673	Sr Thompson	widow St Johns Court in Chick Lane	
	Sr Barbera Dixon	a Butchers wife	

[Page 44 – 20 people – 5 men and 15 women]

London with in ye walls

recommended	Bro Tho Hix	
	Sr Hix his wife	In Fryday streete
	Sr Sarah her daughter	now in Crouched fryars
	Sr Jane Dyus now hatsell	In fryday street
	Sr Hanah Banister	In Bread streete
	Sr Beale	In woodstreete now in more fields

Sr Church	aldermanbury	Deceased
Bro King		
Sr King his wife		
Sr Eliz[abeth] Scott	Deceased	
Bro Ben[jamin] Hulen	Deceased	
Sr Hulen his wife	at newington green	
Sr Hanah Hulen his daughter		
Sr Kath[erine] Lane servant		
Bro Laurence faircloath		
Sr Bunkey	Bell alley	
now her nam Chess		
Sr Pride	at her howse lodger	Deceased
Bro Gough	Bell alley	
Sr Algate		
Sr Ireland	Whitts alley	Deceased

[Page 45 – 15 people – 7 men and 8 women]

Sr Andrews	Swan alley	recommended to Bro

		Barrett at Bow
Bro Gosfright	In Tokenhowse yard	
Sr Gosfright		
Sr Gough her mother	both deceased	
Sr Bateman	In peters alley	a Taylors wife
Sr Jennet Jones	by Glashowse hall at a packers	Deceased
Bro John Eyles	In St Ellens	
Sr Sarah Eyles		
Bro W[illia]m Clarke	in Tower streete	
Bro John Smith	at Dice Key	
Bro Rich[ard] Latward		Deceased
Bro Hen[ry] Stevens Sen	In moses alley	Deceased
Bro Hen[ry] Stevens jun	Whitt Chappell	
Sr Stevens his wife		
Sr Dew	a mealmans wife by Northumberland	Deceased

alley

[Page 46 – 13 people – 3 men and 10 women]

	Sr Kentish	In Northumberland alley	
	Sr Winifreed Pearson	In pauls church yard	Deceased
	Sr Boult	In Thames streete	
	Sr Collins		
	Bro Guicheritt	Dukes place	Deceased
	Bro Cray Sr Cray his wife	a shomaker Dukes place	
	Sr Dorothy Hinton now Garrett	In minorins Lane a servant to Mr Smith	Deceased
	Sr Rechard Grigg	In Buckles Bury	withdrawn from
	Sr An[n] Morley		Deceased
B F	Sr Welsh	In Whites alley	Deceased

		moorefeilds	
B F	Bro Foster Sr Foster his wife	In Crooders well alley shomaker	

[Page 47 – 15 people – 4 men and 11 women]

Ould Streett Bunhill Redcross street Moore fields &c

Bro Hunter Sr Hunter his wife	Deceased ould streete	Deceased Deceased
Sr Eliz[abeth] Hunter		
Sr Eliz[abeth] Vicars		
Bro Rich[ard] Smith Sr Smith his wife	a Bricklayer	
Sr Curtisie	In blew anchor alley	Deceased
Sr Tuladay Sr Sarah Rogers her servant	Bunhill Recommended	Deceased
Sr Alice Beaman	Deceased	

Sr Sanders	Barbican	Deceased
Mary Baker	In Towerstreet	
Bro Rob[ert] Whaley	a Translator	Deceased
Bro Hayn	a shoemaker Grubstreete	Deceased
Sr Kath[erine] Bird	In Grubstreete	

[Page 48 – 18 people – 4 men and 14 women]

Sr Clement Batty Sr Batty her daughter	Moore Lane	
Bro Jacobb Sr Jacobb his wife	Deceased moore Lane now in bell & mouth street	
Sr Prissilla Liddall	Deceased	
Sr Rachell Snelling		
Bro John Snelling Sr Negus	Little Moore fields	Deceased

	Sr Ann Snelling		
	Bro Talbott	Whitt Cross Alley	Deceased
	Sr Talbott his wife	Moore fields	Deceased
	Sr Jane Leach	Long alley	
	Sr An Wrath		
	Sr Jane Cogshall	Servant to Bro Snelling	Deceased
	Bro John Clements	In warrickshire	Deceased
	Sr Clements		
	Sr Merryseed	In Whitt Cross street	
	Sr Rochell	In Bedlam	Deceased

[Page 49 – 10 people – 1 man and 9 women]

B F	Sr Berry	In Foster Lane neare ye mile a Chandler shopp	
B F	Sr Gouge	In red Cross Streete a nurse at Mr Loudreys gone to Holland	

B F	Sr Paine	Linen draper in Barbican at ye 3 Whitte	
B F	Sr Hitton	In Chiswell Streete a Grocer	
B F	Bro Haray	In Goswell Street Glass howse yard	Deceased
B F	Sr Gosum now arch	neare Bro Hulings now arch in houders well alley a Cobler wife now in Southwarke	
B F	Sr Bertt	In Goat alley Westcross Streete	
B F	Sr Sheppard	goat alley	Deceased
B F	Sr Knight	In grub streete	
B F	Sr Willmott	servant to an apothecary In grub streete	recomended
	Sr Kathrin Brimley	In Bell alley Coleman streete	

[Page 50 – 15 people – 5 man and 10 women]

Spettlefeilds Bishoppgate without Hounsdich &c

Bro Masters Sr Masters his wife	In spitlefeilds now in goat alley	
Sr Hancock Bro Hancock her Bro		Deceased Deceased
Sr Creeke	Deceased	
Sr Drury		
Bro Johnson	Deceased	
Bro Shelton Bro Shelton his son	a brewers servant a surveyor In hounsdich	Deceased
Sr Balard	In Winford street	Deceased
Sr Awbery	In frying pan alley	
Sr Simcock	Deceased	

	Sr Fenner	Deceased
	Sr Neaves	Deceased
	Sr Mints	Cast out Sept 12 1687 for

[Page 51 – 17 people – 4 man and 13 women]

	Bro Uncles Sr Uncles his wife	without Bishopgate
added 1689	Bro Rumball Sr Rumball his wife Sr Hanah his daughter	
	Bro Gladman Sr Gladman his wife	Deceased
	Bro Rickson Sr Rickson his wife	In Housndich
	Sr Archer	Deceased
	Sr Bellars Sr Alse Bellars	In St Joness withdrawn from

	her daughter		
	Sr Anna Hill	now in mosses alley	Deceased
	Sr Pettitt	Spitelfeilds	Deceased
	Sr Eliz[abeth] Hunt now Snardale		
	Sr Francis Hunt	Deceased	
	Sr Mary MacKeith alias		

[Page 52 – 12 people – 3 man and 9 women]

	Sr Mary Barber alias Elderigge	Spitlefeilds	
	Bro John Hudleston	In angell alley	a weaver
	Sr Mary Dutton	In wholes street	Deceased
added Mar 1679	Bro Hen[ry] Stevens Junior Sr Kathrin his wife		

added 28 Sept 1680	Bro Abra[ham] Stevens		
B F	Sr Kipping	In Kingstreete Spitlefeilds towards Jarmion	
B F	Sr Fletcher	In white Lyon yard neare ye Spitle	
B F	Sr Wade	In Vine Court Sptilefeilds	Deceased
added 1683	Sr Cooper	neare Sr Wades	Deceased
added 1683	Sr Mary Knight now Shelton	Spitlefeilds	
	Sr Burwell	In Grays in Lane a mealmans wife	

[Page 53 – 10 people – 4 man and 6 women]

	Bro Addams	Recomended from Exeter	
	Bro George Ritchardson	In Eastsmithfeild	

Sr An[n] his wife		
Sr Deborah Faux	a servant	
Bro Eben[ezer] Robinson	a weaver In Spitlefeilds	
Sr Elen Bussett	In Blue ancker alley In ould streete	
Sr Joana Lightfoot	In grubstgreete	
Sr Francis	In Moon Lane ye upper end	
Sr Fuller	In Spitlefeilds	
Bro Ri[chard] Adams		

[Page 54 – 8 people – 0 men and 8 women]

Sr Susan Bauers	Easte moone alley	Deceased
Sr Eliz[abeth] Fowns now franke	Shere In Barbican	
Sr Wright	In Grand Lane	Deceased

Sr Archboll	at Hackney	Deceased
Sr Hanah Whitthead	servant at Hackney	Recomended
Sr Eliz[abeth] Cobb	In peticote Lane	
Sr Mary Boulton Sr Sarah Boulton	 Deceased	

[Page 55 – 18 people – 7 man and 11 women]

Whittchappell Minorys East Smithfeild &c

Bro Horton Sr Horton his wife Sr Hanah his daughter	
Bro John Sherman Sr Sherman his wife	Deceased Deceased
Bro Josua Sherman Sr Sherman his wife	 Kathrin whele alley
Bro Jo[hn] Coleman	Deceased

	Bro Mickell Stapleton	
	Sr Dupper	Deceased
	Sr Luddington	Deceased
	Sr Turner	Deceased
	Bro Grew	
	Sr Grew his wife	
	Bro Ed[ward] Hemings	Deceased
	Sr Hemings his wife	Mile end
		now in Winchesterstreet
		now with out aldersgate
	Sr Argile	at Bow
	Sr Whitte	now in good mans fields
	her sister	

[Page 56 – 16 people – 4 man and 12 women]

	Sr Horsley	
recommended	Sr Tompson	Minorys
	Sr Best	Deceased

Bro Larkin	East smithfeilds	Deceased
Sr Larkin his wife		Deceased
Sr Hanah Ernpij ther daughter		
Sr Herring	Deceased	
Sr Stubbly	Deceased	
Sr Hinton	Deceased	
~~now Re~~	Deceased	
Bro Bacon		Deceased
Sr Lucas	Deceased	
Sr Lash	Minorys now with Bro Laterward	Deceased
Bro W[illia]m Shelton	servant to Bro Horton	Deceased
Bro W[illia]m Shelton Junior	now in Thames Streete neare pudle Docke	
Sr Shelton his wife		
Sr An[n] Johnson	with Sr Argile now in goodmans fields	

[Page 57 – 12 people – 5 man and 7 women]

	Bro Clare Sr Clare his wife	East smithfeild a Brewers servant	
	Bro John Person	In whitt chappell	
added 12th month 1687	Bro Hezikia Farmer Sr Damaris his wife	In Castle Streete	
	Sr Jane Youndle	Recommended from Tiverton a barbers wife in Spittlefeilds	
	Bro Lawrence Rudd Sr Eliz[abeth] Rudd his Daughter	both recomended from Tiverton In Spitlefeilds	
	Sr Oakley	Reco	Recomended from ye Church of petty france
	Sr Hamden		recomended thence
	Sr Man	neare whitt chappel prisson	
	Bro Hix	In Spitle fields	

[Page 58 – 12 people – 5 man and 7 women]

	Wappen	Ratliff highway	Poplar &c
Bro Gaunt		Wappen	
Bro Barnes		Deceased	
Bro Tipp Sr Tipp his wife			
Bro Woosley		Deceased	
Bro John Warner			
Sr Lash Junior			
Sr Rivett alias Hulabren			
Sr Arnold Sr Eliz[abeth] Arnold her daughter			
Sr Abigall Hall		Deceased	
Sr Gurford now her name		Deceased	

	in Nanton		

[Page 59 – 11 people – 2 man and 9 women]

	Sr Bland	Poplar now in whitt chappell	
	Sr Janning	Deceased	
	Sr Colamoore	Deceased	
	Sr Mins	Ratliff highway	
	Sr Lambert	Deceased	
	Sr Booth		
	Bro Chelensworth	Deceased	
	Bro Samon	Wappen	Deceased
	Sr An[n] Wright formerly Stuccee	Deceased	
	Sr Kath[erine] Remnant	Wappen	
B F	Sr Patchall	In Love Lane	

Wappen

[Page 60 – 12 people – 5 man and 7 women]

	Name	Address	Remarks
	Bro Sam[uel] Reade	recomended from Corke In Christopher alley Moore fields	recomended to ye Barbadoes
B F	Sr Sarah Hilon now Drake	In Grubstreete in ouldstgreete	
B F	Sr Amy Hidgkins	In ould Jury	recommended unto ye church in Bristole
B F	Sr Abigale Gurside	with Bro Snelling a servant	recomended
B F	Bro Michael Dunwell	In Coleman street	Deceased
	Sr Desborough	In East moone alley without Bishopsgate	Deceased
	Bro Davis Sr Davis his wife	a chirugion in Jewen streete	
	Sr Anijon	In Gravell Lane	

	Bro Mountague	In Spitle fields	Silk thruster
	Sr Eliz[abeth] Dampson	In Spitle fields a Drapers wife	

[Page 61 – 5 people – 2 man and 3 women]

	Sr Simpson		
	Bro Jones	Recommended from Dublin	
	Sr Rickson		
added January 1684	Bro Ed[ward] Naroway Sr Eliz[abeth] his wife	a plasterer In ye Minorys in Hamersmith alley	

[Page 62 – 12 people – 5 man and 7 women]

Southwarke & Redriffe

	Bro Muns	Deceased	
	Bro Hinton	a Translator	
	Sr Stout	Deceased	
	Sr Owen	Deceased	

	Sr Reeves	Maryed to Bro Keiffen
	Bro Hare	
	Bro Grumbridge	Barnaby Streete
	Sr Little	
	Sr Kath[erine] Drake	Deceased
	Sr Fortune Turke	Corleys streete
	Sr Heathcoate	
added 1674	Bro Ebon	a Cloatheyer now Mary overys

[Page 63 – 16 people – 8 man and 8 women]

Bro Corbridge Sr Corbridge his wife	Southwarke
Bro Bride	Deceased
Bro Zach[ariah] Standard Sr Standard his wife	he recomended to Mr Keach Deceased

	Sr Snell	now in Litle moore fields	
	Sr Lewis	Deceased	
	Bro Spinage Sr Spinage his wife	Deceased Deceased	
	Bro Stiffe	withdrawn from	under admonition
	Bro Tho[mas] Watts	Recomended to ye Congregat[ion] with Bro	
B F	Bro Shanke Sr Shanke his wife	In Tooleys streete Linen Drapper	withdrawn from
B F	Sr Prichard	Tooleys streete	Deceased
B F	Bro Draycott Sr Draycott his wife	a Brassier on Maryetts Hill now in whitt chappell now in Tooleys streete	

[Page 64 – 12 people – 4 man and 8 women]

Debtford Greenwich Lusam

	Bro Bradshaw	Debtford	
	Sr Boulton	Debtford	
	Bro Creighton Sr Creighton his wife	withdrawn from Debtford now at Blackwall	Deceased
	Sr Jaxon	Greenwich now in wappen	
	Sr Harrod	Greenwich	Deceased
	Bro Hunt	Lussam	
	Sr Styles	Lusam	Deceased
	Sr Edmonds	Lusam	Deceased
B F	Bro Grant	a Brassier In ~~Barnabee street~~ Blackman streete now in Northumberland alley	
B F	Sr Edmonson	Blackman streete	

B F	Sr Wood	Five Fott Lane beiond horsham down	Deceased

[Page 65 – 13 people – 2 man and 11 women]

Bretheren and Sisters Remote & beiond ye Sea

Bro Styles	Deceased	
Bro Rich[ard] Stonner Sr Stonner his wife	at my Lord Deceased Deceased	
Sr An[n] Mills	about Nurding at Camberwell	
Sr Eliz[abeth] Harding	at Wickam	
Sr Haray	at Marlow	Deceased
Sr Deane	In Devonshire Court	
Sr Tenter	at Chatam	Deceased
Sr Kath[erine] Price	Barbadoes	
Sr Gibbson	at Mevis	Deceased

	Sr Tachell		Deceased
	Sr Quinton		
	Sr Orram		

Page 66 – 11 people – 0 man and 11 women]

	Sr Legay now Robinson	at Barbadoes	
	Sr Margrett Haynes	at Christchurch	Deceased
	~~Sr Chipp~~ Sr An[n] Daniell	~~at Christchurch~~ Deceased	
	Sr Chipp	at Batlebridge a Surgeons wife now at Blackwall now at Gernsey	
B F	Sr Jones	In Coperhowse Streete Redriff	Deceased
B F	Sr Stillson	a Nurskeeper Redriffe	

B F	Sr ye Lady Hartopp	Newington ~~green~~ Town	Deceased
B F	Sr Parsons	Newington	Deceased
B F	Sr Watterson	Newington	
B F	Sr Simons	Newington	
added Octo[ber] 1680	Sr Ditcham	my Lady Haripps Cochmans wife Newington	

[Page 67 – 13 people – 2 man and 11 women]

added 1681 July	Sr Helen Dutton	In bell yard Southwark a Childs Coatmaker	
	Bro Hayes	In whitt Cross streete	recommended from Ireland withdrawn from & Excluded Sept 15 1687
	Bro Hill Sr Hill his wife Sr Sands Hill his daughter	In ye way to Mile end	Recommended from Theobalds

added 1683	Bro Philip Allen	Servant to a barber in Lawrence Lane	
added 1683	Sr Kath[erine] Blackman	at newington a widow	Deceased
	Bro Fitz	at Windsor	Deceased
	Bro Colborn Sr Colborn	at Watford	
	Bro Wm Huchinson	of Ucfeild in Susses	
	Bro John Ward	In East smithfeild	

[Membership List from circa 1690 (362 people – 118 men and 248 women)]

[Page 68]

The Names of the Brethren and sisters that have given upp themselves to the Lord
for to walke in his wayes in Felloshipp together with Bro[ther] W[illia]m Kiffin and Bro[ther] Rich[ard] Adams
being an abstract of ye former made out October 6th 1690.

[Page 69 – 16 people – 5 men and 11 women]

The names of ye Brethren and sisters	The place of theire habitation	there Callings and Relations	The Condition whether in Comunion or not
Bro W[illiam] Kiffin			
Sr Sarah his wife	Excluded from Comunion		
Bro Rich[ard] Addams			Elder
~~Elizab[eth] his wife~~	dec[ease]d		
Susannah his wife			
Bro Warr	beiond Clarendon howse		
Sr Hix	dec[ease]d		
Sr Sarah her daughter			
Sr Francis Mercer	In Tuttle Streete in ye strande		
Sr Atherton	In pell mell		
Sr Alse Bellars	In ould palace yard Westminster		
Sr Kent	In Coven garden neare ye halfe moone Tavern	dec[ease]d	
Sr Eliz[abeth] Hemings	In Lincoln in Fields		
Bro Clater	In Southampton square		

Sr his wife	a Baker	
Bro Tho[mas] Mabbott	In ould southampt[on] Building	withdrawn from rec[eive]d in again
Sr Abigale Bonors	neare ye burrs in holborn	

[Page 70 – 8 people – 2 men and 6 women]

Brethren & sisters	about holborn & smithfeild charter	
Sr Barwell	a meales man wife In Graves in Lane	
Sr Sarah Tompson	In Cow Lane a whealwright by high hall	
Sr Alse Girdler	a scoolmistress there	
Sr Barbera Dixon		
Sr Pitten al[ia]s Williams		
Bro Ward	recomended to Reading	

Bro Georg Gosfright	In Clerkenwell	dead
Sr Ashborn	Cloath faire	dead

Page 71 – 11 people – 1 man and 10 women]

Names of Brothers and sisters in London within ye walls	place of aboad
Sr Bragg Sr Gough	In Blackfryers a nurs keeper
Sr Jacobb	In Bulls mouth streete
Sr An[n] Snelling	In Breadstreete
Sr Robin Maymew Colbrand	In Breedstreete
Sr Hanah Banaster ~~Colbrand~~	In Cheap side twin court
Sr	
Sr Deborah Faukes	a servant In Cheapside

Sr Jane Hatsell	In Birchin Lane a scriveners wife	
Sr Ruth Remnant	In Birchin Lane	dead
Sr Bateman	In Birchin Lane	
Bro Lawrence Faircloath	In Cheap side	cast out

[Page 72 – 19 people – 7 men and 12 women]

London within ye walls		
Bro Gough	dead	
Sr Jane a byate	In Coleman streete whitts alley	
Bro Kath Brimley	In Bell alley	
Bro S[i]r John Eyles Sr Sarah his Lady		
Bro Gray Sr his wife Bro William Gray	In Shoomaker row	

Sr Mary Ridout			
Bro W[illia]m Clarke	In Tower streete		
Sr Kath[erine] Bird	dead	In whittington Colledge	dec[ease]d
Sr Francis Clements			dec[ease]d
Bro Ri[chard] Addams	at Brewre Lane neare ye Custom howse		
Sr Paine	a midwife		
Sr Rickson	new London wall by Criplegate		
Sister Broughton	dead		
Sr Bucknall			

[Page 73 – 14 people – 1 man and 13 women]

Little Moorefeilds,	Red Cross streete Barbican		
Grub streett Jewin street	Ould streete Bunhill		
Sr Clement Batty			
Sr Batty her daughter			
Sr Austin	a pipemakers wife	dead	

Sr Francis	upper end moore Lane	
Sr Fletcher	Tenter alley	
Sr Beale	In whittes alley	
Sr Rachell Snelling Sr Mary Baker	In Crown alley in Little Moorefeilds	
Sr Snell	In moorefeilds	
Sr Hemings	by ye artillery wall	deceased
Sr Knight Sr Joana Lightfoote	In Grubstrette a nurskeeper	
Bro Maurice King Sr Bridgett his wife	In twisters alley in Bunhill	

[Page 74 – 15 people – 4 men and 11 women]

Ould streete Whitcross streete

Bro Ri[chard] Smith Sr Smith his wife	In ould streete

Bro Masters Sr Masters his wife	In grate alley	
Sr Eliz[abeth] Hunter	Witt crosse streete	
Sr Mary Knowles	there	
Sr Merrysee[illegible]	dead	
Bro Foster Sr his wife	In Jewen streete	
Bro Davis Sr Davis his wife	a Chirgion	dead
Sr Margrett Hill	withdrawn from	
Sr Eliz[abeth] Franke	In Barbycan	
Sr An[n] W[illegible]ath alias		
Sr Sarah Rogers alias		

[Page 75 – 12 people – 1 man and 11 women]

at newington green	at newington Town	

Sr Hanah Hulen	
Sr Hanah Cromwell her daughter	
Sr Waterhowse	
Sr Symonds	
Sr Dicham	
Sr Oram	at Enfeild
Sr Boote	dead
Sr Lidia Bassett	In Blue anchor alley in ould streete
Sr Sarah Hilon now Drake	
Sr Quinton	in ye fleet prison
Sr Rachell Seabrooke Snarsdale	
Bro John Pearson	dead

[Page 76 – 14 people – 6 men and 8 women]

Brethren & sisters
Bishopsgate streete and
Long alley

Bro Uncles Sr his wife	In petty france	
Bro Rumball Sr his wife dead Sr Hanah his daughter	In half moone Court	
Sr Jane ~~Bart~~ Leach Hall	In Dunings aley	dead
Bro Rickson Sr his wife	neare ye spittle	dead dead
Sr Mary Powell	at a smithsons ag[ain]st ye spittle	removed to Bro Masters
Sr Hamilton	dead	
Sr Mary Mackeith alias Griffith	about Shordich	
Bro Hix	at ye back of ye old artillery	

Bro John Hudleston	In angell alley
Bro Mountague	

[Page 77 – 15 people – 5 men and 10 women]

Brethren & sisters in and about spitlefeilds	
Bro Henry Stevens	
Sr Kath[erine] his wife	dead
Bro Rudd	
Sr Phillips	
his daughter	
Sr Palmer	removed in ye Countrey
Sr Eliz[abeth] Snarsdale	
Sr Jane Yandle	a barters wife
Sr Nipping	in Kingstreete
Bro Hezekia Farmer	
Sr his wife	

Bro Abra[ham] Stevens

Sr Eliz[abeth] Tompson a dyers wife spitlefeild

Sr Farmer

Bro Eben[ezer] Robinson a weaver
Sr his wife

[Page 78 – 15 people – 5 men and 10 women]

Brethren & sisters in
& about Whittchappel
& goodmans fields and
minorys

Bro Josua Sherman
Sr Hanah his wife dead

Sr Bland dead

Bro Hill dead
Sr his wife dead
Sr Sarah his daughter

Sr Man

Sr Collins	
Bro Grant	
Bro Michael Stapleton	dead
Sr Argyle Sr An[n] Johnson	In goodmans fields
Sr Whitte	withdrawn from
Bro Ed[ward] Naraway Sr his wife	dead a plaisterer

[Page 79 – 16 people – 4 men and 12 women]

Brethren & sisters about Eastsmithfeild & wappen &c	& Eastsmithfeild Well Closs and Ratlett highway
Bro John Ward	
Sr Hanah Erapy	
Sr Boult	
Bro George Richardson	In East smithfeild

Sr his wife

Bro Clare neare Ratlett highway
Sr his wife
Sr Mins

Sr Booth Ratlett highway

Bro Tipp in wappen dead
Sr his wife

Sr Pachell

Sr Rivett

Sr Arnold
Sr Eliz[abeth] her daughter

Sr Lash

[Page 80 – 14 people – 5 men and 9 women]

Brethren & sisters
in & about Southwarke

Bro Hinton

Bro Hare		
Bro Grambridge	Barnabystreete	dead
Sr Stillson	a nurskeeper Redrett	
Sr Little		
Sr Fortune Turke		
Sr Arch	by Battlbridge	
Bro Draycote		
Sr his wife		
Sr Elizabeth daughter		
Sr Shanke		
Sr his wife	dead	
Bro W[illia]m Gaint	removed to Bro Steed	
Sr Heathcoate		

[Page 81 – 16 people – 5 men and 10 women]

Southwarke

Bro Ebbratt & his wife	a dyer
Bro Corbridge Sr Corbridge	
Sr Edmondson	a shoomakers wife
Sr Lidia Dutton	
Bro Bradshaw Sr Boulton Mary Boulton Sr Hanah Boulton her daughter	 Debtford
Sr An[n] Criese	Debtford
Sr Mary Chipp	dead Greenwich now in Strand Thames
Bro Hunt	In Lussam
Bro John Smith	Camberwell

Bro Peter Colborn Sr his wife	In Watford	Cast out

[Page 82 – 16 people – 8 men and 8 women]

Bro Hatchman	of Ucfeild in Sussex	
Sr An[n] Mills	In Kent neare Tunbridg about narding	dead
Sr Eliz[abeth] Harding	at wickam	
Bro Nath[aniel] Greene Sr Abigail his wife		
Bro Tho[mas] Laurance	In Token house yard	
Bro John Jones	Porter	
Bro Jonas Ratcliffe	at sister Sarah Hilles house	Cast out
Sr Eliza[beth] Emerson	Pastrey lookioner ag[ains]t	

	Hard Alley in Bishopsgate streete	dead
Sr Tufnell	in Houndsitch	dead
~~Bro Tho[mas] Laurance~~	~~In token howse yard~~	
Sr Turk	In Bricklane	
Bro Harrison		
Bro Chappell Sr Chappell his wife	dead	
Bro Noble & his wife	In laslostreet dead	

[Page 83 – 26 people – 6 men and 20 women]

Bro Brannson Sr Anne his wife	Both went from the Congregation
Sr Anberry	Deceased

Sr Wright	
Sr Viccars	Dead
Bro W[illia]m Sheldon & his wife	
Bro Tho[mas] Harrisson & Joanna his wife	Dec[ease]d Dec[ease]d
Bro Chillingworth & his wife	
Sr Oakely Sr Woodrosse	dec[ease]d
Sr Jones	
Sr Horton	
Sr Jackson	
Sr Waterson	dec[ease]d
Sr Andrewes	
Sr Kentish	

Bro Sherman & his wife	dec[ease]d
Sister Sarah Hill	
Sr Abigail Rachell	dec[eas]ed
Sr Collins	dec[ease]d
Bro Mounticne	Rent from the Congregation
Sr Reynolds	

[Page 84 – 24 people – 8 men and 16 women]

Bro John Rose & Sr his wife	
Bro Jo[hn] Child & Sr his wife	Removed his Communion
Bro Bowler & Sr Bowler his wife	Removed to Lorimers Hall or the people with Brother Harrison
Sr Elii[zabeth] Kimbole	dec[ease]d

Bro Dennis	Aldersgate	
Sister Dennis his wife	Recommended to the Church with Bro Crosley	Feb 22th 1704/5
Sr Harrisson	dec[ease]d	
Sr Hannah Tompson		
Sr Anna Spencer		
Sr Consett now Deray		
Sr Uncles	Dec[ease]d	
Sr Boulton	old streete	
Sr Gren		
Sr Griffith		
Bro Hix	dec[ease]d	
Bro Huddleston	dec[ease]d	
Bro Hen[ry] Stevens	Removed to Mr Crosley	
Bro Red	Rent away	

Sr Phillips	Removed to Mr Noble
Sr Gondall	dec[ease]d
Sr Knipping	dec[ease]d

[Page 85 – 23 people – 8 men and 15 women]

Bro Farmer & Sr Damaris his wife	Rent away
Sr Carrick	dec[ease]d
Bro Nich[olas] Owen	
Sr Argyle	dec[ease]d
Sr Johnson	de[cease]d
Bro Wardcum	excluded
Sr Empy	dec[ease]d
Sr Bolt	dec[ease]d
Sr Clare	

Sr Minges	dec[ease]d
Sr Booth	dec[ease]d
Sr Tip	dec[ease]d
Sr Arnold	dec[ease]d
Sr Lash	dec[ease]d
Bro Hinton	dec[ease]d
Bro Hare	dec[ease]d
Sr Little	dec[ease]d
Bro Grant	dec[ease]d
Bro Draycott Sr Draycott Sr Eliza[beth] theire Daughter	recomended to the Church in Bro[ther] Steed
Bro Russell	dead

[Page 86 – 24 people – 7 men and 17 women]

Bro Shanke	dead
Sr Heathcott	dec[ease]d
Bro Ebbutt &	
Sr Ebbutt	
Bro Corbridge	dec[ease]d
Sr Corbridge	dec[ease]d
Sr Dutton	dec[ease]d
Sr Boulton	dec[ease]d
& her daughter	rent to ye Fr prophetts
Sr Critch	
Bro Hunt	dec[ease]d
Sr Coloume	Wattford
Bro Bagwell	
Sr Bagwell	dec[ease]d
Bro Peter Bagwell	dealt with
Bro William Hutchinson	in the Countrey

	Sussex
Sr Harding	at Wickham
Sr Tompson	in Rose & Crown Court
Sr Forrest	dec[ease]d
Sr Farmer	now Trooper Removed
Sr Barnard	dec[ease]d
Sr Mary Pitfield alias Pauforey	withdrawn from
Sr Deborah Smith	Rent from the Congregation
Sr Anne Speed	with Mr Bridg neare Merchant Taylors hall

[Page 87 – 18 people – 7 men and 11 women]

Bro Donnage	Grubstgreet
Sr Browne	at Mary bone
Sr Neale	

Sister Heffield	from the people that are with Bro Jones		
Bro Key	in Skinner Streete		
Bro John Welles	in Gray Eagle Streete	withdrawn from	
Bro John Kemble	excluded		
Bro Jabez Hill	Recommended to the Church at Newberry		
Bro John Weeden			
Anna Barrett now Smith	Petty France		
Sr Elizabeth Davis Dead	In Lamb Alley	Bishopsgate Street	Rec[eive]d in July 5, 1702
Sr Bullen	returned to the Congregation & rec[eive]d in		
Sr Ruth Fletcher			Rec[eive]d in March 7 1702/3
Sr Jiane Scott			Rec[eive]d in Jun[e] 3 1703

Sr Sparkman	in Chissell Streete	Rec[eive]d in June 3 1703
Bro Bartho[lomew] Bray & Mary his wife	in Skinners streete	Rec[eive]d in Jun 6 1703
Sr Burrell		Rec[eive]d in June 29th 1703

[Page 88 – 19 people – 6 men and 13 women]

Bro W[illia]m Cliffe		Rec[eive]d into the Congegation July 4th 1703
Sr Eliza[beth] Grace	gone to Ireland	Rec[eive]d Sept[ember] 5 1703
Sr Margaret Banks		Rec[eive]d Sept[ember] 5 1703
Sr Anne King		Rec[eive]d Sept[ember] 5 1703
Sr Mary Edwards		Rec[eive]d Sept[ember] 5
Sr Cane	in Lymehouse	Rec[eive]d Octob[er] 4

Sr Humble	In Poplar		Rec[eive]d Octob[er] 4
Sr Burges	In Poplar		Rec[eive]d Octob[er] 4
Sr Eliza[beth] Scott	in Towerstreete		Rec[eive]d Nov[ember] 4th 1703
Sr Mary Baker	from Bristoll	returned to Bristoll	Rec[eive]d 9ber
Sr Ellin Franklin	at the Lady Hortons recomended to Bro Gifford		Rec[eive]d Dec[ember] 5 1703
Bro Andrew Wilson			Rec[eive]d Dec[ember] 5 1703
Sr Brookes		Removed to	
Sr Hannah Dertiner ~~& his wife~~ Bro Ed[ward] Chamberlaine & his wife			Rec[eive]d Dec[ember] 30 1703
Bro Nath[aniel Polls			Rec[eive]d Dec[ember] 30 1703
Bro Jo[hn] Brookes			Rec[eive]d Dec[ember] 30 1703

Bro Land	for transierd locum Removed	Rec[eive]d Feb[ruary] 3 1703/4

[Page 89 – 17 people – 6 men and 11 women]

Bro Tho[mas] Priest	in Beak Lane	rec[eive]d Feb[ruary] 3 1703/4
Sr Eli[zabeth] France		Rec[eive]d Feb[ruary] 3 1703/5
Sr Ellinor Rose	Eastsmithfield	Rec[eive]d Feb[ruary] 3 1703/4
Sr Anne Butler	in Tainter Alley	Rec[eive]d April 2d 1704
Sr Esther Hartley	in Woolsack Alley	rec[eive]d eod[em] die
Sr Martha Bunker	in Woolsack Alley	rec[eive]d eod[em] die
Sr Mary Hall	in old Gravell Lane	rec[eive]d eod[em] die
Sr Hannah Heffield	Minoryes	rec[eive]d eod[em] die
Sr Isabell Jones	in Nightingale Lane	rec[eive]d eod[em] die

Bro John Hammersley & Sarah his wife	In st Martines	rec[eive]d eod[em] die
Bro Michael White	dec[ease]d	rec[eive]d June 4th 1704
Bro Sam[ue]ll Malliore		Rec[eive]d eod[em] die
Sr Eliza[beth] Cox	Sr Bunkins daughter	Rec[eive]d eod[em] die
Sr Phebe Barnes		Rec[eive]d eod[em] die
Sr Mary Lane dead	in New Lane by Horsley Down A scoolmistress	Rec[eive]d eod[em] die
Sr Baldwin Sr Peakes	In Dukes Place	Rec[eive]d eod[em] die
Bro Ward	serv[an]t to Sr Baldwine	Rec[eive]d eod[em] die
Bro Blackwell		Rec[eive]d June 2 1704

[Page 90 – 20 people – 6 men and 14 women]

Sr Chamberlayne	In Petty France	Rec[eive]d July 2d

	In pettycoate Lane	1704
Sr Mary Guy	lives with Sister Heffield	Rec[eive]d July 22d 1704
Sr Elin Hall now Dikes	in old Gravell Land	rec[eive]d eod[em] die
Bro John Reading	with Bro Gray withdrawn from for salones & Lying	rec[eive]d eod[em] die
Bro Jo[hn] Freeman Dead	in widegate Alley	rec[eive]d eod[em] die
Sr Wiffen	in wapping from Mr Elliotts	Rec[eive]d Aug[ust] 6th 1704
Bro Bond	with Sr Baldwin	Rec[eive]d eod[em] die
Sr Chillingworth	Serv[an]t	Rec[eive]d eod[em] die
Bro Humphrey Potter		Rec[eive]d eod[em] die
Sr Eliz[abeth] Heffield		Rec[eive]d eod[em] die
Sr Burrowes	Artillery Ground	Rec[eive]d Sept[ember] 4 1704

Sr Halley	in Whites y[ar]d Rosemary Lane	Rec[eive]d eod[em] die
Sr Anne Francis now Kitchin		Rec[eive]d eod[em] die
Sr Martha Hilton	In Spraces Iland	Rec[eive]d eod[em] die
Sr Hannah Roberts	Mr Bounds Maid now Millwaters in Bell Lane	Rec[eive]d eod[em] die
Bathia Hatcher Dead	in Pump y[ar]d in Kath[erines] wheele Alley in Bishopsgatestreete Dec[ease]d	Rec[eive]d eod[em] die
Sr Maulin	In Walnut Tree Court	Rec[eive]d eod[em] die

[Page 91 – 22 people – 7 men and 15 women]

Jonas Hawkes	In the Minoryes	Rec[eive]d ~~eod[em] die~~ Octo[ber] 1, 1704
Sr Su[sannah] Sanford	withdrawn from for wicked Conversation	Rec[eive]d eod[em] die
Sr Anna Rowland		Rec[eive]d eod[em] die

Sr Huddleston	in Angell Alley	Rec[eive]d eod[em] die
Sr Eliza[beth] Wolds		Rec[eive]d Nov[ember] 5th 1704
Bro Ben[jamin] Cooper		Rec[eive]d eod[em] die
Bro Nich[olas] Davis & his wife in Gin yard Moore fields both cast out for evill Conversations by Refuseing to hear the Church		Rec[eive]d Dec[ember] 3d 1704
Sister Chamberlayne		Rec[eive]d eod[em] die
Bro Boswell		Rec[eive]d Jan[uary] 6, 1704/5
Bro Loftess		Rec[eived Feb[ruary] 3d 1704/5
Bro King	at ye back side of white Chappel prision	Rec[eive]d eod[em] die
Sister Briscoe	dead	Rec[eive]d eod[em] die
Sister Rixson	neare Still Alley dead	Rec[eive]d July 1st 1705
Sr Anne Mason		Rec[eive]d eod[em] die

	Sr Martha Welles		Rec[eive]d eod[em] die
	Br Neh[emiah] Gibson		Rec[eive]d Jan[uary] 1st 1705/6
	Sister Dunbin Dead		Rec[eive]d eod[em] die
now Joles	Sr Anne Nelson		Rec[eive]d March 3d 1706
	Sr Kath[erine] Voss	now Sanderlin at Bell Wharfe	Rec[eive]d eod[em] die
	Sr Ellin Thomas		Rec[eive]d eod[em] die
	Sr Lamb	from Kirbeys	Rec[eive]d Aprill 7th 1706

[Page 92 – 20 people – 4 men and 16 women]

Sister Fisher alias Bessine	In bell Lane	Rec[eive]d May 1706
Sr Johanna Fairefield		Rec[eive]d June 1706
Sr Taylor	from Mr Piggott	Rec[eive]d eod[em] die

Br Jo[hn] Dowset		Rec[eive]d eod[em] die
Sr Durham		Rec[eive]d August 8th
Sr Sara Bradley		Rec[eive]d Dec[ember] 3
Br Rob[er]t Gibbons		Rec[eive]d Jan[uary] 5th 1706/7
Sr Mary Edmondson		Rec[eive]d eod[em] die
Sr Anne May		Rec[eive]d eod[em] die
Sr Mary Petto		Rec[eive]d eod[em] die
Bro Baggaly	at Bednall Greene Sugar loaf	
Sr Davis	in Moore fields at Bowling pins	
Sr Hunt alias Baggaly	in oldstreet square	
Bro Lyon & Sr Lyon	In Magpy y[ar]d Bishopsgatstreet now in Lamb Alley	
Sr Reest		

Sr Farmer In Haskion street

Sr Whiteseed with Sr Durham

Sr Poplar by Sr Durham

Sr Wissonman

[Page 93 – 36 people – 12 men and 24 women]

Brookes

Bro Peakes
& his wife

Sr Sarah Cowles

Sr Eliza[beth] Ward

Sr Mary Payton

Bro Humphry Cadbury

Sr Rachell Herring

Jane Jarvice
Br Lifcomb

Br W[illia]m Archer	
Br John Weaver	
Sr Yeip	
Sr Reb[ecca] Minne	
Sr Ruth Todd	
Sr Mary Johnson	
Sr Susan Wolsey	
Sr Rusteed	
Br Gordan	
Sr Anne Boulton	
Br Rich[ard] Randall	
Sr Anne Potter	
Br Joseph Cudlow	
Sr Sarah King	
Sr Wesley	petty coat Lane
Sr Sarah Collier	
Sr Cook	
Sr Han[nah] Webster	
Sr Han[nah] Larson	
Sr Anne Bankes	
Sr Anna Munday	
Br Rob[er]t Drake	
Sr Anna Collier	
Sr Mary Cooper	
Br Tho[mas] Yeast	
Br Dan[ie]l Horton	

Alphabetical Listing of Church Members

	1st List (Undated)	2nd List (1668)	3rd List (1670)	4th List (1690)
Abyate, Jane (S)			72	
Adams, Richard (B)			53	69, 72
Adams. Susannah (S)				69
Addams (B)			53	
Alden, Susana (S)			42	
Algate (B)		21		
Algate, June (S)		21		
Algate (S)		38	44	
Allen, Judith (S)		28		
Alle, Philip (B)			67	
Amy, Robert (B)		11		
Amy (S)		11		
Anberry (S)				83
Andrew (B)		32		
Andrews, Elizabeth (S)		31	45	83
Angell (S)		16		
Anijon (S)			60	
Arch (alias Gosum) (S)			49	80
Archboll (S)		36	54	
Archer, William (B)				93
Archer (S)		36	51	
Argyle (S)		34	55	78, 85
Arnoll, Elizabeth (S)		22	58	79, 85
Arnoll, Mary (S)		22	58	79
Ashborn, Mary (nee Figg)	6	13	43	70
Atherton, Thomas (B)		14	41	
Atherton (S)		14	41	69
Atkinson, Rebecca (alias Mainard) (S)			33	42
Aubrey, Elizabeth (S)			37	
Austin (S)				73
Awbery (S)			50	
Bacon, Temperance (S)		8	20	
Bacon (B)			56	
Baggaly (B)				92
Baggaly (alias Hunt) (S)				92
Bagwell, Peter (B)				86
Bagwell (B)				86
Bagwell (S)				86
Baker, Mary (S)	7	11	47	73, 88
Baker, Mary (S)	7			

Name				
Balard (S)			50	
Baldwin (S)				89
Ball, John (B)		29		
Banes, Elizabeth (S)		27		
Bankes, Anne (S)				93
Banks, Margaret (S)				88
Bannister, Hannah (S)			44	71
Bannister, Ann (S)		33		
Barber, Mary (alias Elderidge)		25	52	
Barnard (S)				86
Barnes, Phebe (S)				89
Barnes, Robert (B)		22	58	
Barow, Richard (B)		27		
Barrett, Anna (alias Smith) (S)				87
Barwell (S)				70
Bassett, Lidia (S)				75
Bateman, Jane (S)		19	45	71
Batty (B)		11		
Batty, Clement (S)		11	48	73
Batty (S)			48	73
Bauers, Susannah (S)			54	
Bavery, Susan (S)		36		
Bayly (B)	7			
Beale (S)		36	44	73
Beamon, Abigail (S)		12	47	
Bellars, Alice (S)			51	69
Bellars (S)			51	
Berry (S)			49	
Bertt (S)			49	
Bessine (alias Fisher) (S)				92
Best, Jane (S)		32	56	
Bird, Katherine (S)		33	47	72
Biswell, Elizabeth		13		
Blackman, Katherine (S)			67	
Blackwell (B)				89
Bland (S)	7	21	59	78
Blockley (alias Lash) (S)		22		
Blunt, Isabell (S)		28		
Bocke (S)		21		
Bolt (S)				85
Bond (B)				90
Bonkile (B)		23		
Bonkill, Jane (alias Leach) (S)		34		
Bonors, Abigale (S)			69	
Boote (S)				75
Booth (B)		20		
Booth (S)		20	57	79, 85

Boswell (B)				91
Boult (S)		36	45	79
Boulton, Anne (S)				93
Boulton, Phillis (S)	7			
Boulton, Mary (S)		35	54	81
Boulton, Sarah (S)			54	81, 86
Boulton, Hanah (S)				81, 86
Boulton (S)				84
Bowers, Abigale (S)		12	43	
Bowler (B)				84
Bowler (S)				84
Bradley, Sarah (S)				92
Bradshaw, Comfort (S)		17		
Bradshaw, John (B)		32	64	81
Bragg (S)		42	71	
Brannson (B)				83
Brannson, Anne (S)				83
Bray, Bartholomew (B)				87
Bray, Mary (S)				87
Bride (B)		33	63	
Brimley, (Katherine) (S)			49	72
Briscoe (S)				91
Broklaw (alias Mabbott) (S)	25			
Brookes, John (B)				88, 93
Brookes (S)				88
Broughton (S)	6		64	72
Brown, Bridgett (S)		15		
Brown (S)				87
Bucknall (S)				72
Buckston, Thomas (B)	5			
Bullen (S)				87
Bunkee (alias Chess) (S)		16	44	
Bunker, Martha (S)				89
Burges (S)				88
Burles (S)		6		
Burrell (S)				87
Burrowes (S)				90
Burwell (S)			52	
Bussett, Elen (S)			53	
Butler, Anne (S)				89
Cadbury, Humphrey (B)				93
Cadwell (B)		18		
Cane (S)				88
Capre (S)		18		
Carrick (S)				85
Carter, Alice (S)		12		
Carter, Hanah (S)		15		

Chamberlaine, Edward (B)				88
Chamberlaine (S)				88
Chamberlayne (S)				90, 91
Chappell (B)				82
Chappell (S)				82
Cheenforth (B)		29		
Chelensworth (Chillingworth) (B)		30	59	83
Chelensworth (Chillingworth) (S)				83, 90
Chess (alias Bunkee) (S)			44	
Child, John (B)				84
Child (S)				84
Chipp, Mary (S)		37	66	81
Church, Sarah (S)		11	44	
Clare (B)		22		
Clare (B)		14	41, 57	79
Clare (S)		14	41, 57	79, 85
Clarke, William (B)			45	72
Clarke (B)		17		
Clater (B)			69	
Clater (S)			69	
Claton (B)			42	
Claton (S)			42	
Clements, John (B)		16	48	
Clements, Francis (S)		16	48	72
Cliffe, William (B)				88
Cobb, Elizabeth (S)			54	
Cogshall, Jane (S)	8	26	48	
Colamoore (S)			59	
Colborn (B)			67	81
Colborn (S)			67	81
Colcott (S)		28		
Cole (B)		34		
Coleman, Ann	6	18		
Coleman, John (B)	7	18	55	
Colkins, Sarah (S)		29		
Collier, Anna (S)				93
Collier, Sarah (S)				93
Collins (S)		46	78	
Collins (S)				83
Coloume (S)				86
Consett (alias Deray) (S)				84
Constable (B)		27		
Cook (S)				93
Cooper, Benjamin (B)				91
Cooper, Mary (S)				93
Cooper, Thomas (B)		16		
Cooper (S)		16	52	

Corbridge (B)		23	63	81, 86
Corbridge (S)		23	63	81, 86
Countrye, Jone (S)		28		
Cove (B)		29		
Cowles, Sarah (S)				93
Cowley, Mary (S)		35		
Cox, Elizabeth (S)				89
Cramp, Elizabeth (S)		24		
Cray (B)			46	
Cray (S)			46	
Creeke (S)		15	50	
Creighton (B)			64	
Creighton (S)			64	
Cressett (S)		27		
Critch (S)				86
Criese, Ann (S)				81
Cudlow, Joseph (B)				93
Culamoore (S)		35		
Curtisie (S)			47	
Curtisse, Sarah (S)	7			
Dampson, Elizabeth (S)			60	
Daniel, Ann (S)		23	66	
Daniele, Elizabeth (S)		37		
Davis, Elizabeth (S)				87
Davis, Margett (S)		15		
Davis, Nicholas (B)			60	74, 91
Davis (S)			60	74, 91
Davis (S)				92
Deadman (S)		21		
Deane (B)		35		
Deane (S)		35		
Deane (S)		27	65	
Delawn (B)		37		
Dennis (B)				84
Dennis (S)				84
Deray (alias Consett) (S)				84
Dertiner, Hanah (S)				88
Desborough (S)			60	
Devonshire (B)		18		
Dew (S)			45	
Dikes, Elin (alias Hall) (S)			90	
Ditcham (S)			66	75
Dix, Alice (nee Carter) (S)		12		
Dixon, Barbara (S)			43	70
Donnage (B)				87
Dorie, Mary (alias Fenner (S)			34	
Dowe, Sarah (alias Skellett) (S)			30, 34	

Dowset, John (B)				92
Drake, Katherine (S)		24	62	
Drake, Robert (B)				93
Drake, Sarah (alias Hilon) (S)			60	75
Drapes (S)	6	14	43	
Draycott (B)			63	80, 85
Draycott (S)			63	80, 85
Draycott, Elizabeth (S)				80, 85
Drinkwater, Sarah (S)			35	
Drury (S)			50	
Druzie, Ann (nee Popitt) (S)	15			
Dunbin (S)				91
Dungster, Orams (S)		26		
Dunwell, Michael (B)			60	
Dupper (S)			55	
Durham (S)				92
Dutton, Helen (S)			67	
Dutton, Lidia (S)				81, 86
Dutton, Mary (S)		33	52	
Dyke, Daniel (B)		33	41	
Dyke (alias Negus) (S)		33	41	
Dyus, Jane (alias Hassell) (S)			44	
Eames, John (B)		35		
Eames (alias Mabbott) (S)	35			
Eaton (alias Hunter) (S)		35		
Ebbratt (Ebbut) (B)				81, 86
Ebbratt (Ebbut) (S)				81, 86
Ebon (B)			62	
Edwards, Edith (S)		18		
Edwards, Mary (S)				88
Edmonds, Katherine (S)		27	64	
Edmonson, Mary (S)			64	81, 92
Eldridge, Edward (B)	7	25		
Eldridge, Mary (nee Baker)	7			
Elderidge (S) (alias Barber)	25			
Ellis, Hanah (S)		27		
Emerson, Elizabeth (S)				82
Empy (S)				85
Erapy, Hanah (S)				79
Erpe (B)	6	30		
Erpe (S)	6	30		
Evans, Mary (S)	5			
Evans (S)		29		
Evers (S)		25		
Eversy (S)		26	43	
Eyles, John (B)		13	45	72
Eyles, Sarah (S)		13	45	72

Fabian, Barbara (S)		36		
Fairefield, John (B)				92
Farmer, Hezekia (B)			57	77, 85
Farmer, Damaris (S)			57	77, 85
Farmer (alias Trooper) (S)				77, 86
Farmer (S)				92
Faux, Deborah (S)			53	71
Fayrcloath, Lawrence (B)	5	16	44	71
Fenner, Mary (alias Dorie) (S)		34	50	
Fields, Katherine (S)		29		
Figg, Mary (S)	6			
Fink (S)		25		
Fisher (alias Bessine) (S)				92
Fitz (B)			67	
Fletcher, Ruth (S)				87
Fletcher (S)			52	73
Forrest (S)				86
Foster (B)			46	74
Foster (S)			46	74
Fowns, Elizabeth (alias Franke) (S)			54	
Francis, Anne (alias Kitchin) (S)				90
France, Elizabeth (S)				89
Francis (S)			53	73
Franke, Elizabeth (S)				74
Franklin, Ellin (S)				88
Freeman, John (B)				90
Fuller, Dorothy (S)		28	53	
Gaint, William (B)				80
Garrett, Dorothy (alias Hinton) (S)		36	46	
Gaunt (B)		21	58	
Gibbons, Robert (B)				92
Gibson, Nehemiah (B)				91
Gibson (S)		21	65	
Girdler, Alice (S)			42	70
Gladman, John (B)		31	51	
Gladman (S)		31	51	
Gondall (S)				84
Gordan (B)				93
Gosfright, George (B)[1]		30	45	70
Gosfright [Frances] (S)[2]		30	45	
Gosum (aslias Arch) (S)			49	
Gouge (S)			49	

[1] Named in LMA, Middlesex County Sessions of the Peace Roll #1227 (28 March 1661) (MJ/SP/1227/39).

[2] Named in LMA, Middlesex County Sessions of the Peace Roll #1227 (28 March 1661) (MJ/SP/1227/39).

Name				
Gough, Christopher (B)	5	30		
Gough (B)		32	44	72
Gough (S)		31	45	71
Goulding, Richard (B)		36		
Grace, Elizabeth (S)				88
Grambridge (B)				80
Grant (B)			64	78, 85
Graves [Elizabeth] (S)		19		
Gray, William (B)				72
Gray (B)		37		72
Gray (S)		37		72
Greene, Abigail				82
Greene, Nathaniel (B)				82
Gren (S)				84
Grew, Samuel (B)		32	55	
Grew (S)		32	55	
Griffith (S)				84
Grigg, Richard (B)		36	46	
Grimes, Mary (S)		36	43	
Gripp (S)		20		
Grumbridge (B)		35	62	
Grundee (B)		30		
Grundee (S)		30		
Guicherite, Joseph (B)		16	46	
Gurford (alias Nanton) (S)			58	
Gurside, Abigale (S)			60	
Guy, Mary (S)				90
Halabread (S)		22		
Hale, Abigale (S)		22		
Halett, Thomas (B)		30		
Hall, Abigail (S)			58	
Hall, Elin (alias Dikes) (S)				90
Hall, Mary (S)				89
Halley (S)				90
Halton, Hanah (S)		15		
Halton, Jane (S)		15		
Halton, Owen (B)		15		
Halton (S)		15		
Hamden (S)			57	
Hamilton (S)				76
Hammersley, John (B)				89
Hammersley, Sarah (S)				89
Hancock (B)			50	
Hancock (S)			50	
Handcocke (S)		24		
Haray (B)		30	49	
Haray (S)		26	65	

Harding, Elizabeth (S)			65	82, 86
Hare, William (B)		25	62	80, 85
Harlem (B)		21		
Harrison, Eleanoir (alias Simcock) (S)			34	
Harrison, Thomas (B)	9	19		82, 83
Harrison, Joanna (S)				83, 84
Harrod (S)			64	
Hartley, Esther (S)				89
Hartopp (S)			66	
Hassell, Jane (alias Dyus) (S)			44	71
Hatcher, Bathia (S)				90
Hatchman (B)				82
Hawkes, Jonas (B)				91
Hayes (B)			67	
Hayn (B)			47	
Haynes, Gyles (B)		16		
Haynes (S)		16		
Haynes, Margaret (S)			66	
Heathcoate (S)			62	80, 85
Heathpolch, Ann (alias Bannister)(S)		33		
Heffield, Elizabeth (S)				90
Heffield, Hannah (S)				89
Heffield (S)				87
Heming, Elizabeth (S)		33	41	69
Hemings, Edward (B)		11	55	
Hemings (S)		11	55	73
Herne, Hanah (nee Carter) (S)		15		
Herring (S)			56	
Herring, Rachell (S)				93
Herrod (S)		15		
Hethcoat, Thomas (B)		33		
Hidgkins, Amy (S)			60	
Hill, Ann (S)		17	51	
Hill, Jabez (B)				87
Hill, John (B)		16	67	78
Hill, Margett (S)			42	74
Hill (nee Hutford) (S)		16	67	78
Hill, Sands (S)			67	78
Hill, Sarah (S)				83
Hilon, Sarah (alias Drake) (S)				75
Hilton, Martha (S)				90
Hind, Thomas (B)	5	11		
Hinton, Dorothy (alias Garrett) (S)		36	46	
Hinton, John (B)		32	62	80
Hinton (S)		20	56	85
Hinton, Ruth (nee Reade) (S)		20		
Hitton (S)			49	

Hitts (B)	29		
Hix, Sarah (S)		44	69
Hix, Thomas (B)		44	84
Hix (S)		44	69
Hix (B)		57	76
Hixon, Sarah (alias Drake) (S)		60	
Hodges, Joseph (B)	25		
Horsley (S)	22	56	
Horton, Daniel (B)			93
Horton, Hanah (S)		55	
Horton [Richard?] (B)[3]		55	
Horton [Ellen?] (S)[4]		55	83
Hovins (S)	23		
Huddleston (S)			91
Hudleston, John (B)		52	76
Hudleston (B)			84
Hughes, Ann (S)	14		
Hulen, Benjamin (B)	16	44	
Hulen, Hanah (S)	16	44	75
Hulen, Hanah (alias Cromwell) (S)	16	44	75
Humble (S)			88
Hunt, Elizabeth (alias Snardale) (S)	37	51	
Hunt, Frances (S)	38	51	
Hunt, Thomas (B)	27	64	81, 86
Hunt (alias Baggaly) (S)			92
Hunter, Elizabeth (S)	33	47	74
Hunter, John (B)	12	47	
Hunter (S)	12	47	
Hutchinson, William (B)		67	86
Ireland (S)	12	44	
Jacob (B)	17	48	
Jacob (nee Longe) (S)	17	48	71
Janning (S)		59	
Jarvice, Jane (S)			93
Jaxon, Dorothy (S)	27	64	83
Joans (S)	38		
Johnson, Ann (S)	38	43, 56	78, 85
Johnson, John (B)	14	41	
Johnson, Mary (S)			93
Johnson (B) 5			
Johnson (B)	19	50	
Joles, Anne (alias Nelson) (S)			91

[3] Named in LMA, Middlesex County Sessions of the Peace Roll #1227 (28 March 1661) (MJ/SP/1227/39).

[4] Named in LMA, Middlesex County Sessions of the Peace Roll #1227 (28 March 1661) (MJ/SP/1227/39).

Jones, Aaron (B)		29		
Jones (S)		29		
Jones (S)			66	83
Jones (B)			61	
Jones, Isabell (S)				89
Jones, Janett (S)		19	45	
Jones, John (B)				82
Juncing (S)		21		
Kemble, John (B)				87
Kent, Mary (S)		14	42	69
Kentish (B)		29, 31		
Kentish (S)		29, 31	46	83
Key (B)				87
Keyns (S)	8			
Kiffin, Hanah (S)		11	41	
Kiffin, Sarah (S)		11	41	69
Kiffin, William (B)		11	41	69
Kimbole, Elizabeth (S)				84
King, Anne (S)				88
King, Bridgett (S)		11	44	73
King, Maurice (B)		11	44	73
King, Sarah (S)				93
King (B)				91
Kipping (S)			52	
Kitchin, Anne (alias Francis) (S)				90
Knight, Mary (alias Shelton) (S)			52	
Knight (S)			49	73
Knipping (S)				84
Knowles, Mary (S)				74
Lamb (S)				91
Lambert (S)		20	59	
Land (B)				88
Lane, Katherine (S)			44	
Lane, Mary (S)				89
Larkin (B)		19	56	
Larkin (S)		19	56	
Larkin, Hanah (alias Empij) (S)		19	56	
Larson, Hannah (S)				93
Lash (S)		22	56	
Lash, junior (alias Blockley) (S)		22	58	79, 85
Lateward, Richard (B)		32	45	
Laurence, Amy (S)	5			
Laurence, Thomas (B)				82
Lawrence (S)	7	27		
Laye, Katherine (S)		14		
Leach, Jane (nee Bonkill)		34	48	76
Leach (S)		36		

Legay (alias Robinson) (S)	8		66	
Lewis, {Susan] (S)[5]		26	63	
Leyny (nee Clarke) (S)		17		
Liddall, Priscilla (nee Kiffen) (S)			48	
Lidderdale, Thomas (B)		17		
Lidderdale (S)		17		
Lifcomb (B)				93
Light, [Mary] (S)		26		
Lightfoot, Joana (S)			53	73
Little (S)		23	62	80, 85
Loftess (B)				91
Longe (S)		17		
Lucas (S)		34	56	
Ludington, Elizabeth (S)		20	55	
Lyon (B)				92
Lyon (S)				92
Mabbott, Comfort (nee Bradshaw) (S)		17		
Mabbott, Robert (B)		25	43	
Mabbott (alias Broklaw) (S)		25	43	
Mabbott, Thomas (B)	8			69
Mabbott (alias Eames) (S)		35		
Mackeith, Mary (alias Griffith) (S)		37	51	76
Mainard, Rebecca (nee Atkinson) (S)			42	
Malliore, Samuel (B)				89
Malorett, Pheebee (S)		14		
Man (S)			57	78
Martin, Thomas (B)	8	12		
Mason, Anne (S)				91
Masters, Elizabeth (S)		36	49	74
Masters, John		36	49	74
Maulin (S)				90
May, Anne (S)				92
Mayhew, Robin (S)				71
Maynard, Ann (alias Curtisie) (S)		34		
Meate (alias Stevens) (S)			43	
Menlowe (B)		35		
Mercer, Francis (S)		41		69
Mercer (S)		14		
Merke (S)			42	
Merryseede (S)		24	48	74
Mills, Ann (nee Daniels) (S)	23	65	82	
Minges (S)				85
Minne, Rebecca (S)				93
Minns, Bridget (S)		33		79

[5] Named in LMA, Middlesex County Sessions of the Peace Roll #1227 (28 March 1661) (MJ/SP/1227/39).

Mins (B)			59	
Mints (S)			50	
Monts, Mary (S)		37		
Moore (S)	5	13	43	
Morly, Ann (S)		12	46	
Mountague (B)			60	76
Mounticne (B0				83
Munday, Anna (S)				93
Muns, Mary (S)		23		
Muns, Nathaniel (B)		23		
Muns (B)			62	
Nade (S)		28		
Nanton (alias Gurford) (S)			58	
Naroway, Edward (B)			61	78
Naroway, Elizabeth (S)			61	78
Neale (S)				87
Neaves (S)		15	50	
Negus (S)		11	48	
Negus (alias Dyke) (S)			41	
Nelson, Anne (alias Joles) (S)				91
Niccoles, Mary (S)	9	12		
Nipping (S)				77
Noble (B)				82
Noble (S)				82
Oakley (S)			57	83
Oeslee (B)		21		
Oram, [Sarah?](S)[6]		28	65	75
Owen, Elizabeth (S)		24	62	
Owen, Nicholas (B)				85
Paby, Sarah (S)		29		
Paine (S)			49	72
Patchall (S)			59	79
Patience (B)	6			
Patience (S)	6	26		
Payton, Mary (S)				93
Peakes (B)				93
Peakes (S)				89, 93
Pearson, Winifreed (S)			46	
Person, John (B)		15	57	75
Person (S)		15		
Persons, Elizabeth (S)		28	66	
Person, Winefreed		13		
Pettitt, Elizabeth (alias Archer) (S)		36	51	

[6] Named in LMA, Sessions Roll: Sessions of the Peace #1227 (28 March 1661) (MJ/SP/1227/39). She was arrested for attending an illegal conventicle at the home of Robert Malbon on 24 February 1661.

Petto, Mary (S)				92
Phillis (S)		30		
Phillips (nee Rudd) (S)				77, 84
Pitten (alias Williams) (S)				70
Pittfield, Mary (alias Pauforey) (S)				86
Pocke (alias Whitte) (S)		34		
Policott (B)	8	14		
Polls, Nathaniel (B)				88
Popitt, Ann (S)		15		
Poplar (S)				92
Potter, Anne (S)				93
Potter, Humphry (B)				90
Potts (S)		21		
Powell, Mary (S)				76
Power, Mary (S)		34		
Powes, Mary (S)		31		
Prasiden(?), (S)		41		
Price, Katherine (S)			65	
Prichard (S)			63	
Pride (S)		32	44	
Priest, Thomas (B)				89
Prine, Ruth (S)		30		
Punge (S)		26		
Quinton (S)		31	65	75
Rachell, Abigail (S)				83
Randale, Elizabeth (S)		17		
Randall, Richard (B)				93
Randall (alias Teague) (S)		24		
Ratcliffe, Jonas (B)				82
Reade, Ruth (S)		20		
Reade, Samuel (B)			60	84
Reading, John (B)				90
Reest (S)				92
Reeves (alias Westley) (S)		31		
Reeves (alias Kiffen) (S)			62	
Remnant, Katherine (S)		19	59	
Remnant, Ruth (S)				71
Reynolds (S)				83
Richardson, Ann (S)			53	79
Richardson, George (B)			53	79
Rickson (B)		13	51	76
Rickson (S)		13	51	76
Rickson (S)			61	72
Ridout, Mary (S)				72
Rivett (nee Halabread) (S)		22	58	79
Rixson (S)				91
Roberts, Hannah (S)				90

Robinson, Ebenezer (B)			53	77
Robinson (S)				77
Robinson (alias Legay) (S)	8		66	
Rochele, Ann (S)		18	48	
Rogers, Sarah (S)		38	47	74
Roper, William (B)		35	41	
Rose, Ellinor (S)				89
Rose, John (B)				84
Rose (S)				84
Rowland, Anna (S)				91
Rowly (B)		22		
Rudd, Elizabeth (S)			57	
Rudd, Lawrence (B)			57	77
Rudd (alias Phillips) (S)				77
Rumball (B)		23	51	76
Rumball (S)		23	51	76
Rumball, Hanah (S)			51	76
Russell (B)				85
Rusteed (S)				93
Samon (B)		22	59	
Samon (S)		22		
Sanderlin, Katherine (alias Voss) (S)				91
Sanders (S)		12	47	
Sanford, Susannah (S)				91
Scott, Elizabeth (S)	8	11	44	88
Scott, Jane (S)				87
Scott, Sarah (S)		31		
Seabrooke, Rachell (S)			42	75
Seaward, Thomas (B)		19		
Seelee (B)	6	20		
Shanke, Ruth (S)		28		
Shanke (B)			63	80, 86
Shanke (S)			63	80
Shelton, Mary (alias Knight) (S)			52	
Shelton, William (B)		37	50, 56	
Shelton, William junior (B)			50, 56	83
Shelton (S)			56	83
Sheppard (S)			49	
Sherman, Hanah (S)		18		
Sherman, John senior (B)		18	55	83
Sherman, John junior (B)		18		
Sherman, Josua (B)			55	78
Sherman, Hanah (nee Wattson) (S)		13, 18	55	78
Sherman (S)			55	83
Simcocke?, Eleanoir (alias Harrison) (S)		34	50	
Simons (S)			66	
Simpson, Mary (S)		13		

Simpson (S)			61	
Skellett, Sarah (alias Dowe) (S)		30, 34		
Smith, Anna (alias Barrett) (S)				87
Smith, Deborah (S)				86
Smith, John (B)		17	45	81
Smith, Elizabeth (S)		33	47	74
Smith, Richard (B)		33	47	74
Smothers, Prisilla (S)		19		
Snarsdale, Elizabeth (S)				77
Snell (S)		25	63	73
Snelling, Ann (S)			48	71
Snelling, John (B)		33	48	
Snelling, Rachel (S)			48	73
Sparkman (S)				87
Speed, Anne (S)				86
Spencer, Anna (S)				84
Spinagre (B)		31	63	
Spinagre (S)		31	63	
Stampers, Judith (S)		35		
Standard, Zachary (B)		24	63	
Standard (S)		24	63	
Standler, Ann (S)		32		
Stapleton, Michael (B)		32	55	78
Stasmoore (S)	6			
Stasmoore, Hanah (S)		15		
Stevens, Abraham (B)			43, 52	77
Stevens, Henry senior (B)		36	45	84
Stevens, Henry junior (B)			45, 52	77
Stevens, Katherine (S)			45, 52	77
Stevens (B)		14		
Stevens (alias Meate) (S)			43	
Stiffe (B)		25	63	
Stiffe (S)		25		
Stillson (S)			66	80
Stoner, Nathaniel (B)[7]		28		
Stoner (S)		28		
Stonner, Richard (B)			65	
Stoner (S)			65	
Stout, Alice (S)		13	62	
Stubbly (S)			56	
Stubbs (S)		20		
Stuccee, Ann (alias Wright) (S)		22	59	
Styles (B)		30	65	

[7] Named in TNA, SP 29/34, page 127, where he offers securities for Kiffen's good behaviour after his arrest on 24 February 1661. Stoner was a haberdasher from the parish of St Clement Danes.

Styles (S)		27	64	
Sum (B)		31		
Supper (S)		18		
Sutton (S)	8	11		
Symonds (S)				75
Tachell (S)		26	65	
Talbott (B)		34	48	
Talbott (S)		34	48	
Tarke, Fortune (nee Walton) (S)		23		
Taylor, Ann (nee Hughes) (S)		14		
Taylor (S)				92
Teague (alias Randall) (S)		24		
Tenter (S)		28	65	
Thomas, Ellin (S)				91
Thompson (S)		43		
Tipp, Robert (B)		24	58	79
Tipp (S)		24	58	79, 85
Tittison, Margrett (S)	5			
Todd, Ruth (S)				93
Todd (B)		31		
Tompson, Elizabeth (S)				77
Tompson, Hannah (S)				84, 86
Tompson, Mary (S)		28	56	
Tompson, Sarah (S)				70
Tomson, Ann (S)		34		
Tufnell (S)				82
Tuleday (S)		38	47	
Turke, Fortune (S)			62	80
Turk (S)				82
Turner (S)	7			
Turner (S)		13	55	
Uncles, [William] (B)[8]	6	12	51	76
Uncles (S)	6	12	51	76, 84
Vernon, Alice (S)		15		
Vicars, Elizabeth (S)		36	47	83
Voss, Katherine (alias Sanderlin) (S)				91
Wade (S)			52	
Walker (S)		36	41	
Walton, Fortune (S)		23		
Ward, Elizabeth (S)				93

[8] Named in LMA, Sessions Roll: Gaol Delivery #0887 (January 1641) (MJ/SR/0887/22), where he was arrested for attending a conventicle led by Thomas Lambe in Whitechapel on 17 January 1641. He is also named in TNA, KB, Michaelmas 1641 (KB/9/823/113), where he was arrested for attending a conventicle led by John Spilsbery in Stepney on 12 September 1641. Uncles was a glover and no doubt had contact with Kiffen through the Leathersellers' Company.

Ward, John (B)		37	43, 67	79, 89
Ward (S)		37	43	
Ward (B)		14	41	70
Ward (S)	8	12		
Wardcum (B)				85
Warner, John (B)			58	
Warner, William (B)		32		
Warr (B)			69	
Waterhowse (S)				75
Watterson (S)			66	83
Watts, Thomas (B)		24	63	
Wattson (S)		13, 18		
Weaver, John (B)				93
Webster, Hannah (S)				93
Weeden, John (B)				87
Welles, John (B)				87
Welles, Martha (S)				91
Welsch (S)			46	
Wesley (S)				93
West (B)	5	26		
Westley, John (B)		25		
Westley (alias Reeves) (S)		31		
Westley (S)		25		
Whaley, Robert (B)		34	47	
White, Michael (B)				89
Whiteseed (S)				92
Whitte (S)			55	78
Whitthead, Hanah (S)			54	
Whittman (B)		23		
Wiffen (S)				90
Williams (nee Herring) (S)		20		
Williams (alias Pitten) (S)				70
Willmott (S)			49	
Willson (B)		23		
Willson (S)		23		
Wilson, Andrew (B)				88
Wissonman (S)				92
Wodson, John (B)		32		
Wolds, Elizabeth (S)				91
Wolsey, Susan (S)				93
Wood (alias Wicke, alias Gurlicke)(S)		18	64	
Woodrosse (S)				83
Woosley (B)			58	
Wormill, Elizabeth (S)		37		
Worsley (S)		29		
Wrath, Ann (S)		36	48	74
Wright (S)	8	13		

Wright (S)		54	83
Wright, Ann (alias Stuccee) (S)	22	59	
Yeast, Thomas (B)			93
Yeip (S)			93
Youndle, Jane (S)		57	77

CHAPTER 6

'Riotously assembled': Conventiclers arrested at the Devonshire Square Baptist Church (11 February 1686)

Within the London Metropolitan Archives there is a record of the Middlesex Sessions of Gaol Delivery from February 1686 pertaining to the arrest of eight people for being 'Riotously assembled in an unlawfull Conventickell'.[1] The full text of this document is as follows:

[Folio 98 recto]

Bail[e]d	Mary Knight	Commited by the Right Honorable Sir Robert
	John Clarke	Gefferys Kn[igh]t L[or]d Mayor of the Citty of
	Tho[mas] Sutton	London, being taken Riotously assembled
	John Whitehead	in an unlawfull Conventickell in Devonsheire
[5]	Rich[ar]d Harris	Square without Bishopsgate, London under
	Peter Ken	Colour of Exercizen of Religion Contrary
	John Hedges	to Law, the 11 Day of February 1685.
Bailed	Will[iam] Teagy	

The arrest was by the order of Sir Robert Gefferys, an ironmonger by trade, who was Lord Mayor of London from 1685–86. Of the eight people named in the document, only one, Mary Knight, is clearly named in the membership lists of the Devonshire Square Baptist Church. According to the list which began to be compiled in 1670, Mary Knight joined Kiffen's church in 1683, and lived in Spittlefields. At some point, probably between 1675 and 1683, she married William Shelton. Shelton was a brewer's servant, and was also a member of the Devonshire Square church, having joined sometime in 1674.

Also contained in the London Metropolitan Archives is a series of so-called 'conventicle convictions', used by local Justices of the Peace to register the illegal attendance of Dissenters at religious meetings in their jurisdiction. These forms were pre-printed documents with formulaic phrases interspersed with blank spaces where names, dates, places, and circumstances of the attendance at the conventicle were inserted by the court officials. There are sixteen such 'certificates of conviction' which bear the name of Captain Kiffin on them, along with reference to the place of the illegal conventicle as being his house in the Devonshire buildings. These

---

[1] LMA, List of persons committed for unlawful assembly at Devonshire Square – 11 February 1686 (MJ/SP/1686/02/001), folio 98 recto.

certificates date from 26 November 1682, 3 December 1682, 10 December 1682, 17 December 1682, 24 December 1682, 31 December 1682, 7 January 1683, 14 January 1683. There are two copies for each date (all Sundays), one specifically mentioning morning meetings (*antemeridiem*) and the other afternoon meetings (*postmeridiem*); this confirms that two worship services were held each Sunday at Kiffen's church in Devonshire Square ('Devonshire buildings').[2] A representative example of one of the certificates (from 26 November 1682) is here provided (Figure #1); the text and translation, with hand-written elements given in italics, follows.

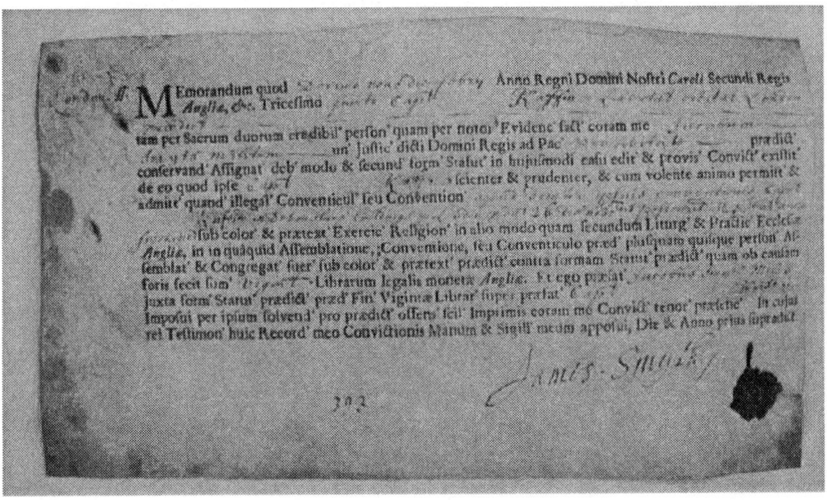

Figure #1: Certificate of Conviction for William Kiffen dated 26 November 1682

[Text obverse]

London S[ession]s Memorandum quod *Decimo nono die Febr[uari]is* Anno Regni Domini Nostri Caroli Secundi Regis

Angliae, &c Tricesimo *quinto Capt Kaffin in Libertat[ibus] Civitat[is]London*

praedict[ae]

tam per Sacrum duorum credibil[ium] person[arum] quam per notor[iam] Evidenc[iam] fact[i] coram me *Jacobum*

Smyth Militem un[um] Justic[ium] dicti Domini Regis ad Pac[em] *pro civitate* praedict[a]

[2] LMA, Certificates of Conviction (CLA/047/LR/02/02/005), folios 393-408.

conservand[am] Assignat[um] deb[ito] modo & secund[um] form[am] Statut[i] in hujusmodi casu edit[i] & provis[i] Convict[us] existit
de eo quod ipse *Capt Kaffin* scienter & prudenter, & cum volente animo permitt[it] &
admitt[it] quand[am] illegal[em] Conventicul[um] seu Convention[em] *apud domum ipsius conventionis Capt[ain]*
Kaffin in Devonshire buildings in London p[rae]dict[o] 26 die Nove[mb]ris postmerid[iem]ult[imo] praeterit[o] anno
supradict[o] sub color[e] & praetext[u] Exercic[ionis] Religion[is] in alio modo quam secundum Liturg[iam] & Practic[am] Ecclesiae
Angliae, in in quaquid Assemblatione, Conventione, seu Conventiculo praed[icto] plusquam quisque[*sic*] personae] As-
semblat[ae] & Congregat[ae] fuer[unt] sub color[e] & praetext[u] praedict[o] contra formam Statut[i] praedict[i] quam ob causam
foris fecit sum[mam] *Vigint[i]* Librarum legalis monetae Angliae. Et ego praefat[us] *Jacobus Smyth Miles*
juxta form[am] Statut[i] praedict[i] praed[ictum] Fin[em] Vigintae Librar[um] super praefat[um] *Capt[ain] Kaffin*
Imposui per ipsum solvend[um] pro praedict[a] offens[ione] scil[icet] Imprimis coram me Convict[o] tenor[e] Praesenc[e] In cujus
rei Testimon[ium] huic Record[o] meo Convictionis Manum & Sigill[um] meum apposui, Die & Anno prius supradict[is].

James Smyth [signature]

[Text reverse]

p[e]r J[ohn] Hilton

[Translation]

London Sessions Memorandum that on the Nineteenth day of February in the Thirty-fifth year of the Reign of our Lord Charles
the Second, King of England &c *Captain Kaffin in the Liberties of the aforesaid city of London*
as much by the Oath of two credible witnesses as by the notorious Evidence of the fact [presented] before me *James*
Smyth Knight one of the Justices of the said Lord King appointed to

preserve the Peace for the said city
in the approprittae manner in accordance with the form of the statute published and provided, stands convicted
in that the same *Capt[ain] Kaffin* knowingly and advisedly, & with a willing mind permitted &
allowed a certain illegal Conventicle or Convention *at the meeting-house of Captain Kaffin himself*
Kaffin in Devonshire buildings in London on the aforesaid 24th day of November in the morning of the last year gone by
aforesaid under color & pretext of the Exercise of Religion in a way other than according to the Liturgy & Practice of the Church
of England, and in which aforesaid Assembly, Convention, or Conventicle more thatn five persons were
Assembled & Congregated under the aforesaid color and praetext contrary to the form of the aforesaid Statute, for which reason
he was fined the sum of *Twenty* Pounds of legal money of England, And I the aforesaid *Jacobus Smyth Knight*
according to the form of the aforesaid Statute imposed the aforesaid Fine of Twenty Pounds upon the aforesaid *Capt[ain] Kaffin*
to be paid by him for the said offence, certainly first of all, before me having been Convicted along these Present lines. In witness of which
to this, my Record of Conviction, I have put ny Hand & Seal, on the Day & Year previously mentioned above.

James Smyth [signature]

[Translation reverse]
By means of John Hilton

Each of the certificates was signed and sealed by James Smyth (Smith), a Justice of the Peace for the city of London. His name frequently appears on documents relating to the suppression of conventicles during the 1680s, and he was a major player supporting the activities of the controversial figure John Hilton. The association of James Smyth with John Hilton can be seen within these certificates of conviction, for each one of them has the name of Hilton on its reverse ('p[e]r J[ohn] Hilton'), suggesting that the evidence for convicting Kiffen of attendance at the conventicle has come 'by means of John Hilton'. Hilton made a name for himself as the leader of a gang of thugs who were dedicated to the suppression of Dissenters.[3] In effect, Hilton was a powerful instrument for official Tory policy in its battle against the Whigs, and was thus deeply embroiled in the bitter struggle for the control of London's political scene. But so brazen was Hilton that he published a news-sheet entitled *The Conventicle Courant*, which ran for thirty numbers from 14 July 1682–14 February 1683, and chronicled his activities against Dissenters. The opening paragraph of the first number proudly heralded its aims:

> *The Conventicle Courant*: Setting forth The Daily Troubles, Dangers and Abuses that Loyal *Gentlemen* meet with, by putting the Laws in Execution against Unlawfur, and Seditious Meetings.[4]

Curiously, Hilton did not use the term *Baptist* or *Anabaptist* within *The Conventicle Courier*, even when it was discussing known Baptist conventicles. He also tended to depersonalize the Baptist Dissenters, as he does for example in discussing the octogenarian Hanserd Knollys preaching in September of 1682:

> There was lately an Old *Seditious Preacher*, who Poysoneth the Hearts of His Majesties Subjects, in a *Meeting-House* in *George-Yard* at *Broaken-Wharf*; that in a Religious manner, and like one of those that teacheth by the Spirit begun thus:
>
> *Beloved Brethren, and dear Sisters, It is now full Ten of the Clock: You know Beloved, you did promise to meet at half and Hour after Nine. You cannot tell how soon your* Teacher *may be taken from you,* (in that he was pretty right) *therefore you ought not to let slip any Time, when I appoint it.* Adding further, *The Door may also be shut up, to keep you out of this place; and then who knows, but it may be opened again to let Popery enter therein.*[5]

William Kiffen is not identified by name within any of Hilton's news-sheets, although the meeting house in Devonshire Square appears to figure at a number of points, albeit under a somewhat unusual description; Hilton generally describes it as a meeting of Independents or Presbyterians.[6] This occurs in *The Conventicle Courant* in a report on 23 September 1682:

---

[3] See Mark Goldie, 'The Hilton Gang: Terrorizing Dissent in 1680s London', *History Today* 47 (October 1997): 26-32, 'The Hilton Gang and the Purge of London in the 1680s', in Howard Nenner (ed.) *Politics and the Political Imagination in Later Stuart Britain: Essays Presented to Lois Green Schwoerer* (Rochester, NY: University of Rochester Press, 1997): 43-73.

[4] *The Conventicle Courant* No. 1 (14 July 1682).

[5] *The Conventicle Courant* No. 8 (4–10 September 1682). Also see *The Loyal Protestant and True Domestic Intelligence* No. 238 (27 February 1683), for another report on Knowles, who is described as 'an old *Anabaptist Holder-forth*'. Knowles also is mentioned in *The Loyal Protestant and True Domestic Intelligence* No. 243 (19 March 1683) in connection with two Sunday services held on 4 March 1683.

[6] Hilton's colleague Nathaniel Turner published a broadsheet entitled *A List of the Conventicles or Unlawful Meetings within the City of London* (1683), which similarly

> For Sunday, the 17th was Signed Nineteen Warrants to suppress as many, which were then to be held in the several Places, as followeth … the Presbyterians at Devonshire-House.[7].

The *Conventicle Courant* report dated 30 September 1682 stated,

> For *Sunday*, the *Twenty Fourth* day of *September*, were delivered the several Blank Warrants to Suppress the *Conventicles*, which were to be held as followeth; But it hapning (as is supposed) to be a busy time with the *Brother-hood*, in consulting about *Elections* and *Reprobations* for the Year ensuing, many of them chose rather to run the Risk of the Breach of the Laws, and the Obligation of their Duty, than be wanting at such a Time, when the Cause stands so much in need of their Assistance: An that the World may see, what Swarms of this kind of *Locusts* infest our *Horizon*, take the Names of the several Places within the Government of the City as they are here inserted. *1. Presbyterians in Devonshire-House.*[8]

Then, on 14 October 1682, *The Conventicle Courant* reported that

> For Sunday October the Eighth were delivered the several Blank warrants to Suppress as many Seditious Conventicles, which were then to be held in the several Places, within the City and Liberties of London …[9]

The news-sheet then lists twenty-two conventicle locations, including

> 13. Quakers, in Devonshire House Buildings.
> 14. Independants, or Presbyterians in the same Buildings.

Similarly, within the next edition of *The Conventicle Courant* a similar report was published:

> For *Sunday* the Fifteenth of *October*, was delivered four Warrants to as many *Constables*, to Suppress the Seditious *Conventicles*, which were then to be held, as followeth,
> 1. *The Quakers* at *the Bull and Mouth-Meeting*.
> 2. *The Quakers* at *Devonshire-House.*
> 3. *The Quakers* near *Grace-Church-street.*
> 4. *Independants*, or *Presbyterians* in the same Buildings.[10]

---

described Kiffen's Meeting House as a congregation of Independents. On this point, see W.T. Whitley, 'Thompson's List of Conventicles in 1683', *Transactions of the Congregational Historical Society* 4 (1909–1910): 49. For more on Nathaniel Turner, see Leona Rostenberg *Literary, Political, Scientific, Religious & Legal Publishing, Printing & Bookselling in England, 1551–1700: Twelve Studies, 2 Volumes* (New York: Burt Franklin, 1965): 315-343.

[7] *The Conventicle Courant* No. 10 (18–25 October 1682).

[8] *The Conventicle Courant* No. 11 (25 September–2 October 1682).

[9] *The Conventicle Courant* No. 13 (9–16 October 1682).

At this point Hilton reports his disappointment about the success of the warrant against the Independents (Baptists) in Devonshire House, noting that 'The Third and Fourth Warrants were wholly neglected by Whiggish Constables.'

[10] *The Conventicle Courant* No. 14 (16–23 October 1682)

CHAPTER 7

Samuel Gleede: Master Gunner in the Commonwealth Navy

Within the manuscripts gathered by Richard Rawlinson (1690–1755) and bequeathed to the Bodleian Library in Oxford within his will, there is one volume which contains an intriguing bundle of six letters, all relating to a petition made by a man named Samuel Gleede.[1] The bundle of letters consists of an initial petition by Samuel Gleede himself, which is undated (see Document #1), followed by five supporting letters of reference (see Documents #2, #25, #26, #27 and #28); four of the supporting letters date between 5–8 June 1656, and the fifth is undated. It seems that sometime in early June of 1656 Gleede petitioned the relevant authorities that he might be appointed as a master gunner aboard one of the ships in the Commonwealth's navy. Included within this bundle is a letter of recommendation signed by Samuel Hyland (Highland) and William Kiffen, prominent spokesmen and leaders of Separatist congregations in London.[2] Such a letter of reference indicates that Samuel Gleede had contact with Separatist churches in the city and may have even been associated with the congregation led by Kiffen (although his name does not appear in the surviving lists of members of Kiffen's church). If so, the letter provides further evidence of the involvement of Baptists within the armed forces during the Commonwealth period. The letter of reference signed by Kiffen (see Figure #1) represents one of the rare documents in the Bodleian Library which actually bears his signature, and as such the bundle is worth considering in more detail.

The fact that such a bundle of documents has survived is not altogether surprising, since the position of master gunner on board a naval vessel was such an important one. The master gunner on board a naval ship was generally a commissioned officer who held a warrant for his position. As such he was directly responsible to the captain. Needless to say the area of expertise required that the master gunner be a

---

[1] BLO, MS Rawlinson A 184, folios 56-64. The bound volume is labelled 'Pepys Papers Volume xv', although it contains many Commonwealth naval documents from the years 1650–60. No doubt Pepys incorporated these within his own papers when he assumed the position of Secretary of the Admiralty in 1673.

[2] Bernard Capp, *Cromwell's Navy: The Fleet and the English Revolution 1648–1660* (Oxford: Clarendon Press, 1989): 325, makes passing reference to the testimonial letter of Highland and Kiffen but does not provide any specific details of its contents, not even mentioning the name of the person it was supporting (Samuel Gleede).

skilled and able seaman, one who was reliable and trustworthy in the heat of battle. Several books and pamphlets from the seventeenth century discuss the importance of the position of a gunner within a sailing vessel, notably John Seller's *The Sea Gunner* (1697). This well-illustrated book explained the demands of the job and became something of a manual for gunners for many years (see Figure #2 for an illustration from it).

The petition by Gleede to be appointed as a master gunner mentions a supporting letter of recommendation by Captain John Sherwin (see Document #2). From 1651–56 Sherwin was captain of the frigate *Primrose*, the ship upon which Gleede had served. Among Samuel Pepys's papers which are contained in the library at Magdalene College, Cambridge, there is a document entitled 'A List of all the Ships, Frigates, and other Vessels belonging to the State's Navy on 1st March 1651'.[3] This document lists the frigate *Primrose* as a '5th Rate' ship and notes that she had a maximum crew of ninety men and that she carried twenty-four guns.[4] When it was that Captain Sherwin came to command the *Primrose* is not explicitly stated within the letter of reference, although we know that his appointment to command the ship was confirmed by the Council of State on 18 June 1651.[5] Orders were issued from Whitehall on 23 July 1651 that armaments and provisions were to be placed aboard the newly built *Primrose*.[6] Captain Sherwin was informed on 5 September 1651 that the ship was ready to sail and he was instructed to take her to the Downs;[7] the *Primrose* was included in the Winter Guard for 1651–52 with a station assignment of the North of Ireland and St George's Channel.[8] The ship was also part of the Summer Guard of 1652–53, and on 13 April 1652 was sent to patrol the coast of Scotland.[9] Sherwin was an experienced sea captain,[10] and by all accounts was deeply

---

[3] The list is contained within Pepys's Miscellanies, volume v, page 595. It was published in Charles Derrick, *Memoirs of the Rise and Progress of the Royal Navy* (London: H. Teape, 1806), 69-74. Also see Samuel Rawson Gardiner, *Letters and Papers Relating to the First Dutch War 1652–1654, Volume 1* (London: The Navy Records Society, 1899): 65.

[4] There are twenty ships listed within this '5th Rate' category. The *Primrose* is described as having a keel length of 86 feet, a breadth of 25 feet 1 inches, a depth of 12 feet 6 inches, and weighing 287 tonnes. The *Primrose* was built in Wapping by John Taylor. Her first master was John Humphrey who hired her to the state in June 1641 (see TNA, SP 25/118, page 123).

[5] TNA, SP 25/20, page 45. An order dated 20 August 1651 from the Committee of the Admiralty specified that twenty-four guns were to be placed on the ship (MS Rawlinson A 226, folio 6 verso).

[6] TNA, SP 25/96, page 305. Also see BLO, MS Rawlinson A 225, folio 150 verso.

[7] BLO, MS Rawlinson A 226, folio 14 verso.

[8] *JHC* 7 (30 October 1651): 32.

[9] BLO, MS Rawlinson A 226, folios, 100 verso and 118 recto; TNA, SP 25/66, page 592.

[10] He had two earlier commands aboard Commonwealth ships. The first was the *Truelove* (seventy men and twenty-four guns) from October 1648–June 1649, patrolling mainly in the Irish Sea (see TNA, SP 21/10, page 175; TNA, SP 18/1, pages 127-128; TNA SP 25/94, page 112; TNA, SP 25/113, page 41; TNA, SP 18/5, page 49). The second was the *Hind* (sixty men and eighteen guns) from December 1649–July 1651 (see TNA, SP 25/63, page 385;

committed to the Commonwealth; following the Naval Revolt in May of 1648[11] he was one of the ninety sea captains who signed a declaration addressed to the Commissioners of the Navy pledging allegiance to the Parliamentary cause.[12] Somewhat unusually, Sherwin had also served as a soldier, as can be seen within a letter he wrote from Chatham docks dated 13 April 1655 (see Document #3). Within the letter he notes that he participated in 'ye beating of ye Scotch king at Worster' (line 16), and suggests that

> itt is well known to ye Armie in ye three Nations how serviceable I have bin on Land as well as sea & have endeavr'd to ye hazarding of my Life ye readucing of all such as hath oppos'd our English Interest' (lines 17-20).

In any event, Sherwin's the letter of reference for Samuel Gleede gives the impression that the commander had had good occasion to observe his master gunner in action over the five-year period mentioned (line 6). This suggests that Gleede was probably appointed master gunner when the *Primrose* was commissioned in 1651. It is known that Sherwin was in command of the *Primrose* when she was ordered to Scotland on 13 April 1652. Gleede would have been the master gunner aboard her when she participated in a skirmish between the Commonwealth navy under Admiral Robert Blake and the Dutch navy commanded by Van Trump on 25 June 1652.[13] In

---

TNA, SP 25/123, pages 170-171, 172, 178; *JHC* 6 (2 March 1650): 375; TNA SP 18/9, page 53, BLO, MS Rawlinson A 223, page 103; TNA, SP 18/9, page 201; TNA, SP 18/12, page 86; *HMC Leyborne-Popham* 78; TNA, SP 25/96, pages 1, 188-189). The *Hind* was an old ship and in January 1651 it was decided that she was to be scrapped, and her guns moved to the *Convert* (BLO, MS Rawlinson A 225, folios 46 recto, 49 recto and verso). In the meantime, the *Hind* was still included as one of four of the Commonwealth ships on the Irish Sea as part of the Summer Guard (BLO, MS Rawlinson A 225, folio 99 verso). Unfortunately she was wrecked on the Irish coast in July 1651. Some details of Sherwin's fated second command, including the loss of six crewmen in July of 1651, can be found in BLO, MS Rawlinson A 225, folios 127 verso and 149 recto; BLO, MS Rawlinson A 226, folios 22 recto, 23 recto, 29 verso–30 recto, 197 recto. Also see Aled Eames, *Ships and Seamen of Anglesey, 1588–1918* (Greenwich: National Maritime Museum, 1981): 91-92, for a brief discussion.

[11] See J.R. Powell, *The Navy in the English Civil War* (London: Archon Books, 1962): 146-60; D.E. Kennedy, 'The English Naval Revolt of 1648', *English Historical Review* 77 (1962): 247-56; Capp, *Cromwell's Navy*, 15-41. Sherwin's second command, the *Hind*, was one of the six ships that revolted in favour of Charles I.

[12] *The Humble Tender and Declaration of Many Well-affected Mariners and Sea-men, Commanders of Ships, Members of the Trinity-house, to the Commissioners of the Navy* (1948).

[13] See *A Great Victory* (1652): 6; and *French Occurrences*, Number 8 (28 June–5 July 1652): 58, for a list of the ships engaged in the battle. There is also a Captain Sherwin who arranges the hire of the merchant ship *Richard and Benjamin* in March of 1651 and April of 1652, but this is probably a different person (see TNA, SP 18/27, pages 62 and 91). Gardiner, *Letters and Papers, Volume 1*, 191, notes this.

early October 1652 Sherwin was ordered to stay out over winter without additional provision, a matter which brought Sherwin into conflict with the Navy Commissioners. From Liverpool Sherwin wrote a letter of complaint to the Commissioners of the Navy in Tower Hill, London, asking them to persuade the Council of State to reconsider his situation. Sherwin submitted a list of needed equipment and supplies, including a number of items requested by Gleede as the ship's master gunner (see Document #4).[14] By December the *Primrose* was docked in Chester, her crew so sick with a fever they were not able to be mustered for duty.[15] Sherwin demonstrated on a number of occasions his concern for the safety and well-being of his crew.[16]

Certainly the *Primrose* was in service within the Commonwealth's navy throughout the First Dutch War, and was involved in a number of skirmishes with Dutch ships. Much of the time the *Primrose* was on patrol along the eastern coast of England and Scotland. In December 1653, Sherwin managed to capture a Dutch ship of eighteen guns after a brief battle in which five of the Dutch sailors were killed and three others injured. The prowess of Gleede and the gunners aboard the *Primrose* was evident in the exchange, and Captain Sherwin noted the 'passing of well placed

---

[14] The incident is discussed in Capp, *Cromwell's Navy*, 215.

[15] TNA, SP 18/29, page 166. The ship was ordered to Chatham on 3 August 1653 to undergo a much-needed refitting (BLO, MS Rawlinson A 227, folio 121 verso).

[16] For other letters of Sherwin aboard the *Primrose*, see BLO, MS Rawlinson A 226, folio 205 recto (22 September 1652 from Hylack in Scotland); TNA, SP 18/29, page 50 (18 November 1652 from Dublin Bay); see TNA, SP 18/29, page 68 (22 November 1652 in the Irish Sea); TNA, SP 18/30, page 10 (18 December 1652 from Chester); TNA, SP 18/45, page 81 (6 January 1653 from Liverpool); TNA, SP 18/54, page 30 (4 June 1653 from Liverpool); TNA, SP 18/54, page 290 (17 June 1653 from Liverpool); BLL, Add MS 18,986, page 84 (27 July 1653 from Plymouth); TNA, SP 18/57, page 37 (3 August 1653 from Hope); BLL, Add MS 22,546, page 139 (3 August 1653 from Hope); TNA, SP 46/115, page 115 (22 September 1653 from Chatham); TNA, SP 46/115, page 208 (29 November 1653 from Kingston upon Hull); TNA, SP 46/115, page 247 (10 December 1653 from Tinmouth); TNA, SP 18/78, page 62 (7 January 1654 from Leith Road); BLL, Add MS 22,546, page 160 (27 January 1654 from Leith Road); TNA, SP 18/81 page 79 (5 April 1654 from Leith Road); TNA, SP 18/69, page 161 (16 April 1654 from Inverness); TNA, SP 18/83, page 106 (13 June 1654 from Hull); TNA, SP 18/83, page 174 (20 June 1654 from Hull); TNA, SP 18/83, page 278 (30 June 1654 from Hull); TNA, SP 18/84, page, 167 (11 July 1654 from Hull); TNA, SP 18/85, page 70 (21 July 1654 from Whitebooth Road, Humber); TNA, SP 18/75, page 89 (26 August 1654 from Ayr); TNA, SP 18/89, page 135 (24 October 1654 from Liverpool); TNA, SP 18/90, page 139 (14 November 1654 from Liverpool); TNA, SP 18/104, page 93 (12 February 1655 from Dublin); TNA, SP 18/106, page 84 (24 March 1655 from Plymouth); TNA, SP 18/136, page 266 (26 March 1655 from Kinsale); TNA, SP 18/107, page 84 (7 April 1655 from the Downs); TNA, SP 18/107, page 172 (13 April 1655 from Chatham); TNA, SP 18/109, page 52 (20 May 1655 from Hope); TNA, SP 18/113, page 68 (7 September 1655 from Holyhead); TNA, SP 18/118, page 15 (16 December 1655); TNA, SP 18/118, page 215 (28 December 1655 from Kinsale); TNA, SP 18/135, page 208 (29 February 1656 from Kinsale).

shott in his hull between wind and water', which quickly persuaded the Dutch captain to surrender.[17]

There is evidence that the *Primrose* was back serving in the Irish Sea in 1655 with Captain Sherwin in command. For example, Sherwin wrote a letter to General John Desborough at Exeter from aboard the *Primrose* on 24 March 1655 (see Document #5). Sherwin explained that the ship had come into Plymouth harbour for repairs after delivering some military supplies to Cork in Ireland. He illustrates something of his biblical knowledge and political commitments, alluding to the biblical story of Gideon in Judges 7, as he likened the enemies of the Commonwealth to the Canaanites who surrounded the people of God, and expresses his desire that they may be destroyed 'with the power of Gidion[s] sourd' (lines 14-15). The *Primrose* was also part of a naval convoy which transported Lord Deputy Fleetwood from Chester to Ireland in September of 1655.[18]

However, on 8 March 1656 the *Primrose* was on patrol with another ship, the *Mayflower*, in the western approaches to the English Channel when disaster struck. The *Primrose* ran on to some submerged rocks near the so-called Seven Stones off the Scilly Isles and was badly damaged. The crew of the ship managed to free her from the rocks, but she quickly sank with the loss of sixteen of the company. As it happens, Captain Sherwin was consulting with the captain of the *Mayflower* about arrangements to replace a broken mast at the time of the disaster.[19] The earliest account of the incident was a report sent by Sherwin to the Commissioners of the Admiralty and Navy dated 12 March 1656 (see Document #6). A related report was submitted by Captain Peter Bowen of the *Mayflower* on 14 March 1656 from Milford Haven (see Document #7). Sherwin produced another statement about the incident for the Commissioners of the Admiralty and Navy on 14 March 1656 (see Document #8). This was sent from Plymouth where he had been transported on the ship *Bryer*, which was also soon to convey him to Portsmouth; Sherwin stressed in this statement that he was eager and willing to co-operate in the proceedings which he knew were to come.

Not surprisingly, the naval authorities quickly launched an investigation into the circumstances of the accident. On 27 March 1656 three of the Commissioners of the Admiralty and Navy, namely John Desborough, Edward Hopkins and John Clerke, issued orders to the Navy Commissioners instructing them to investigate the incident (see Document #9). As a result, the Admiralty Committee from Trinity House interviewed Captain Sherwin and the officers of the *Primrose* and sent a report dated 5 April 1656 to the Commissioners of the Admiralty and Navy which included yet another statement from Sherwin (see Document #10). Their report concluded that a

[17] SP 46/115, page 247. The captured prize was a fairly new ship out of Amsterdam and was eventually delivered to Colonel Lilburne in Scotland. It was incorporated into the English fleet and, alongside Sherwin and the *Primrose*, was sent to patrol the Scottish coast in January of 1654 (TNA, SP 18/65, page 29).

[18] TNA, SP 18/113, page 75.

[19] David J. Hepper, *British Warship Losses in the Age of Sail 1650–1859* (Rotherfield: Jean Boudriot Publications, 1994): 3.

remarkably consistent story emerged about the tragedy as a result of the interviews and they attached no blame to any crew member for the accident. A report dated 18 April 1656 and submitted by three Navy Commissioners to the Admiralty Committee at Trinity House similarly stated that the captain and crew of the *Primrose* had been interviewed, with similar conclusions being reached (see Document #11). A number of witness statements pertaining to the official investigation into the disaster survive, including an additional statement from Captain Sherwin dated 31 March 1656 explaining what had happened (see Document #12). The boatswain of the *Primrose*, Peter Rowley, submitted a statement (see Document #13), as did Edward Bason, the master of the ship (see Document #14), Henry Marven, the master's mate (see Document #15), and our master gunner Samuel Gleede (see Document #16). Further details of the incident can be gleaned from the testimony of a Plymouth merchant named William Trevitt, who happened to be a passenger aboard the *Primrose* on the fateful day. On 22 March 1656 Trevitt gave his evidence before Henry Hatsell, the Vice-Admiral of Devon, who verified Trevill's declaration by counter-signing the statement (see Document #17). Indeed, in another account of the incident, Hatsell stated that Trevitt 'was a passenger in her & swum for his life' when the *Primrose* went down.[20]

Following the official investigation into the sinking of the *Primrose* several decisions were made pertaining to the wages owed to the crew of the ship. Typically orders were issued by three of the six Commissioners for the Admiralty and Navy and directed to the Commissioners and Treasurer of the Navy in this regard. Thus, there is an order dated 22 April 1656 issued by John Desborough, John Clerke and Edward Hopkins, instructing that wages owed to the crew were to be paid, with the exception of the Captain and the Master who were to be dealt with separately (see Document #18). A related order, dated 17 April 1656 and issued by John Jones, John Clerke and Edward Hopkins, gave instructions that Joseph Scot, who served as the chaplain aboard the *Primrose*, be paid the wages owed him (see Document #19). Interestingly, this was ordered even though Scot did not have a warrant for officiating as the chaplain aboard the ship. It seems that Scot's case was supported by a letter from the Independent divine Joseph Caryll (1602–73) dated 16 April 1656 (see Document #20). Reverend Caryll explained that Scott had been persuaded to join the *Primrose* when she was in Ireland, and that he had served aboard her for six or seven months. He also made a plea that Scot be reimbursed £20 for his books and personal effects lost during the incident (lines 22–24).

Meanwhile, John Sherwin and Edward Bason, the Captain and the Master of the *Primrose*, were punished financially for their actions leading to the loss of the ship. Thus, an order by John Clerke, Edward Hopkins and Edward Salmon, dated 3 June 1656, instructed the Commissioners and Treasurer of the Navy to withhold part of their wages for their complicity in the loss of the ship (see Document #21). Half of their wages were to be 'reserved in the States hands for their neglect in p[er]formance of the duty of their places as to the losse of the said Frigott' (lines 8–

[20] TNA, SP 18/137, page 46.

11).[21] However, this was not the last word, for there is a record of another order issued on 27 April 1658 by Thomas Kelsey, Edward Salmon and Robert Beake, which overturned the order for Sherwin's garnishment of wages (see Document #22). They instructed the Commissioners and the Treasurer of the Navy to pay John Sherwin the wages due to him 'for his service as Comander of the *Primrose* Frigott notwithstanding any former Order for suspension' (lines 5–6). Clearly a naval officer as experienced as Sherwin was too valuable to be badly treated.

There are a couple of other interesting records pertaining to Sherwin, which provide extra details about his eventful, and controversial, naval career. First, there is a letter written by Samuel Windis and dated 27 July 1655 to Lieutenant Colonel Thomson, one of the Commissioners of the Admiralty and the Navy, in which complaints were lodged about the ill-treatment he received at the hands of Sherwin (see Document #23). Windis had been the navy's agent responsible for victualling the navy's ships in the port of Liverpool, but he was relieved of his post earlier in the month following a protracted dispute with the captain and crew of the *Satisfaction* over the provisions made for the ship.[22] By all accounts, Windis was an awkward individual, overly officious and insisting that the requisite paperwork all be in order before supplying anything; he also seems to have been overly protective of his wife and complained about the way she had been treated by some of the naval officers. The row between Sherwin and Windis may have been a long-standing one, probably dating back to late 1652 when Windis had served as the pursar of the *Primrose*.[23] He accused Sherwin of using the *Primrose* as a private taxi-service, ferrying unauthorized passengers and setting their fares against the pursar's accounts while pocketing the profit. Windis claimed that when he challenged Sherwin about these 'unworthy carriages', the captain tyrranically put him 'in Close imprisonment' (lines 6 and 12). No doubt Windis was bitter over his dismissal by the Commissioners of the Admiralty and Navy, after what he felt to be his six years of faithful service to the Commonwealth which had cost him and his family dearly.[24]

---

[21] Bason is also dealt with in TNA SP 18/142, page 98. According to a chart dated 24 August 1649 the captain of a 5th rate ship was paid 6 shillings per day, and the master 2 shillings and 8 pence per day (BLO, MS Rawlinson A 224, folio 101 recto).

[22] Details of this dispute can be found in TNA, SP 18/87, pages 22-23; TNA SP 18/76, pages 95-96; TNA SP 18/76, pages 142-143; TNA 18/76, page 179; TNA, SP 18/109, pages 12-14, 90-92, 153-155, 168; TNA, SP 18/42, page 313-315.

[23] TNA, SP 18/28, page 206; Windis is described here as the purser of the *Primrose*, 'an able honest man'. In a letter dated 25 September 1653, Windis also notes his long-standing contact with Captain Sherwin as purser to the *Primrose*, and before that to the *Hind* (SP 46/115, page 148). Windis was succeeded in the post by his deputy, Philip Evatt (see TNA, SP 18/112, pages 191-192; TNA SP 18/113, page 16).

[24] TNA, SP 18/99, page 121. On 2 October 1655 he applied for a new position as purser (TNA, SP 18/115, page 18). During 1657 he made several petitions for re-imbursement of money spent while employed by the Commissioners of the Admiralty and Navy (see TNA, SP 18/155, pages 59-60; TNA SP 18/157, page 62; TNA, SP 18/157, page 119).

Second, within the Rawlinson manuscripts in the Bodleian Library there is an intriguing letter written by Captain Sherwin when he was commanding the *Primrose*. The letter is undated but it probably was written sometime in May 1654 (see Document #24). It concerns an incident involving a thief and imposter named John Selby (Shelby) who was in prison in Kingston upon Hull; Sherwin has been asked to provide information about him. It seems that Selby, promoting himself as a recruit soldier bound for Ireland from Liverpool, stole the clothes, money and identity papers of a Captain Hide. He then substituted his own name on Hide's military commission before engaging, via this 'colourable pretence' (lines 9–10), in a credit swindle which took in at least five other officers. We can but speculate that Captain Sherwin and the crew of the *Primrose*, including our master gunner Samuel Gleede, had an encounter with the trickster John Selby sometime earlier. Where and when this took place is unknown, but it probably took place in Liverpool; Sherwin and the *Primrose* were in the port several times during 1653–54. Perhaps this helps explain why Sherwin disliked the Liverpool channel so much, uttering a cry of despair at the conclusion of one letter: 'For ye Lords sake, Lett me nott bee Coopt up in this Channell as it is ye fag end of ye world, butt Call mee home to spend my Life w[i]th all true-harted Englishmen'.[25] Eventually the trickster Selby was caught in Hull, and was delivered to London aboard the *Dutchy*, commanded by Captain Edmond Smyth.[26]

To return to our master gunner Samuel Gleede himself: the letter of recommendation signed by Samuel Hyland (Highland) and William Kiffen is dated 7 June 1656; it is folio 63 within the bundle of documents in the Bodleian Library (see Document #25). Obviously Hyland and Kiffen knew each other and worked together; in fact, shortly after writing the letter both Hyland and Kiffen were elected to serve as members of the second Protectorate Parliament—Hyland represented Southwark, and Kiffen represented Middlesex.[27] Of the five letters of recommendation the one that offers us the most information about the personal circumstances of Samuel Gleede is one written by Edward Ny (Nye), which is folio 64 within the bundle (see Document #26). In addition, it is the only letter which carries any indication of the person to whom it was addressed, namely 'To my h[o]n[ora]ble friend Coll[onel] Clerk'. This probably refers to Colonel John Clerke, one of the Admiralty Commissioners appointed by Parliament on 3 December 1653.[28]

The remaining two letters of recommendation offer nothing more of substance about Gleede himself, although they do provide us with the names of eight additional

---

[25] TNA, SP 18/45, page 81.

[26] This is detailed in a letter from John Jeanlett to the Secretary of State, John Thurloe, dated 21 July 1654 (BLO, MS Rawlinson A 16, folio 348). Smyth conveyed Captain Sherwin's report about Selby to Thurloe.

[27] The Second Protectorate Parliament sat from 17 September 1656 to 4 February 1658.

[28] For more on Colonel John Clerke, see Austyn Woolrych, *Commonwealth to Protectorate* (Oxford: Oxford University Press, 1982), 181-2, 199, 202, 241, 343, 382, 385, 414-15; Capp, *Cromwell's Navy*, 226.

friends willing to write on his behalf. The first of these two letters is folio 58 within the bundle; it is not dated (see Document #27). The second of these two letters is folio 62 within the bundle and interestingly includes a surgeon (a 'churgyion') among its four signatories (see Document #28).

What happened as a result of this petition by Samuel Gleede? It appears that his request to be appointed master gunner on another Commonwealth ship was successful. There are further records within another volume of the Rawlinson manuscripts which involve a charge of embezzlement of naval stores which was levelled against him while he was serving as the master gunner of the *Phoenix*. Effectively this position represents a promotion for Gleede in that the *Phoenix* was listed as a '4th Rate' ship with a maximum crew of 150 men and thirty-two guns.[29] Two letters refer to this incident of alleged embezzlement by Gleede. The first comes in the form of a certificate from officers in the Ordnance Office which is addressed to Richard Hutchinson, the Treasurer of the Navy.[30] This document is dated 20 January 1660 (see Document #29). The matter was also taken up in a further letter from four officials in the Navy Office which was sent to the Commissioners of the Admiralty and the Navy at Whitehall on 8 February 1660 (see Document #30). Clearly the certificate of 20 January 1660 was attached to this document, and although it does not mention Gleede by name, the letter gives further details of the case against him. This concerned the allegation that some of the ship's stores were being sold by the master gunner and the boatswain (lines 4–5). After examination, Gleede was cleared of these charges, the investigators declaring that 'they find noe reason why the said Guner should be suspended of his Place or Pay' (lines 13–14). .

With this letter the curtain draws over the petition of Samuel Gleede, a master gunner in the Commonwealth Navy. It is unknown how long he served aboard the *Phoenix*; perhaps it was until she was wrecked on 3 December 1664 while attempting to pass into the Atlantic through the Straits of Gibraltar.[31] If so, we do know that he survived the sinking of that ship, and indeed, progressed further in his naval career. There is a brief mention of pension payments being made to him in 1706; his superannuated payment as the master gunner of a First Rate ship was £4 per month.[32] However, he did not live long after this, for he made a will on 8 January

---

[29] Charles Derrick, *Memoirs of the Rise and Progress of the Royal Navy* (London: H. Teape), 71. The *Phoenix* is described as having a keel length of 96 feet, a breadth of 28 feet 6 inches, a depth of 14 feet 3 inches, and weighing 414 tonnes. There are thirty-one ships listed within this '4th Rate' category.

[30] Hutchinson was appointed Treasurer of the Navy in 1650. For more on him, see G.E. Aylmer, *The State's Servants: The Civil Service of the English Republic, 1649–1660* (London: Routledge & Kegan Paul, 1973), 247-50.

[31] The *Phoenix* was commanded by Captain John Chicheley and had been serving in the fleet of Sir Thomas Allin. See Hepper, *British Warship* Losses, 3

[32] TNA, Declared Accounts of the Navy – 1706 (AO 1/1726/148). The account records that Gleede was paid a total of £39 5*s* 7*d* (probably representing his pension payments for May–October 1704).

1706 which was probated on 29 April 1706 (see Document #31). Who knows what future discoveries might reveal about his connection with William Kiffen, the high-profile leader of the Baptists in London, who took time out to supply a letter of reference on his behalf?

Figures

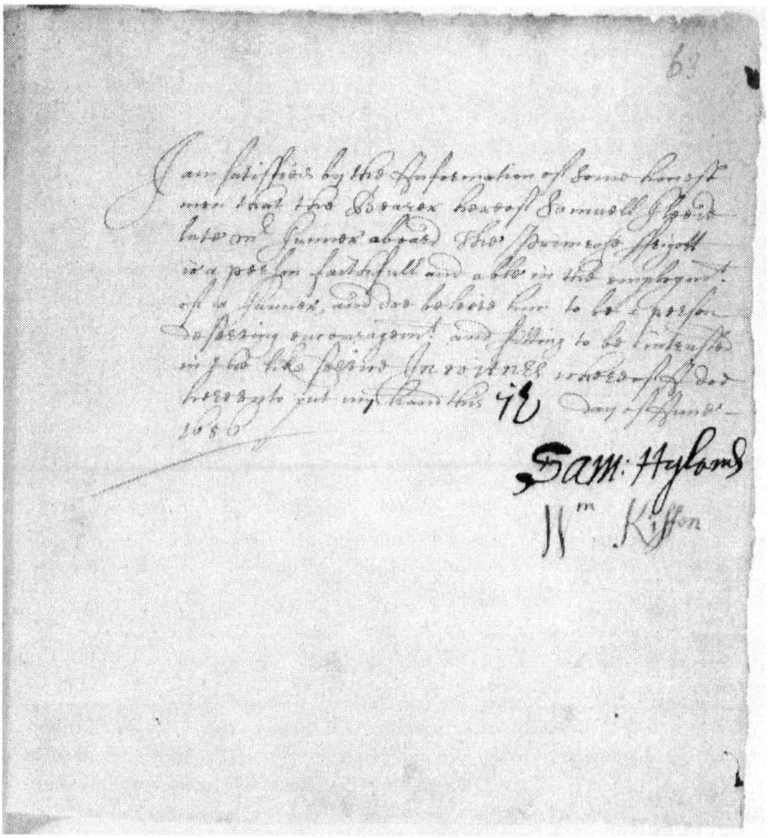

I am satisfied by the information of some honest men that the bearer hereof Samuell Gleede late [illegible] Gunner aboard the [illegible] frigott is a person faithfull and able in the employment of a Gunner, and doe beleive him to be a person deserving encouragement and fitting to be intrusted in the like service In witness whereof I doe hereunto put my hand this 7th day of June 1656

Sam: Hyland

Wm. Kiffen

Figure #1 – Samuel Hyland and William Kiffen write a letter of reference for Samuel Gleede (7 June 1656)

Figure #2 – A gun and gunner with his tools.
An engraving from John Seller's *The Sea Gunner* (1697)

Documents

#1: Petition of Samuel Gleede for a Master Gunner's position in a Commonwealth ship – undated (BLO, MS Rawlinson A 184, folio 56):

[Folio 56]

To the Right Hon[able] the Comission[ers] for the
Admiralty and Navye

The humble petition of Samuell Gleede

Sheweth

That your petitioner hath faithfully served this Comonwealth
of England the space of Five yeares as M[aste]r Gunner of

the *Primrose* Friggott Captaine Sherwin Comander as may appeare by the Certificate annexed & susteyned great Losse when the said Friggott was cast away & here by he is much Impoverished. The p^{re}mises considered and for that your petitioner is ready and willing to doe your Honores what service he may do Farre as the Lord shall enable him.

Your petitioner most humbly prayeth your Honors to Confer upon him the Gunners place in what shipp or Friggott your Honores shall think fitt and to be pleased to graunt him some allowance in consideration of his said Losse.

And your petitioner shall pray etc.

#2: Captain John Sherwin writes a letter of support for the petition of Samuel Gleede – 6 June 1656 (BLO, MS Rawlinson A 184, folio 60):

I, John Sherwin late Capt^{ne} of the *Primrose* Friggott, do certifie that the Bearer hereof Samuel Gleed was Master Gunner of the said Friggott untill she was cast away, and dureing the time of his service in the said shipp (wch was neare the space of five yeares) he demeaned himselfe as became an honest man and an able and skillfull Gunner. In witness whereof I have herewith out my hand this 6th day of June 1656.

John Sherwin [signature]

#3: Captain John Sherwin writes a letter of complaint to the Commissioners of the Navy about failure to give the *Primrose* adequate provision – 13 April 1655 (TNA, SP 18/107, page 172):

[Page 172 recto]

Right Hono[ra]ble,

I presume on your goodness assumeing ye Bouldness to trouble you w[i]th these few lines letting you know my Lord Deputy Fleetwood layd an injunction on mee to present his best respects to you & withall a L[ett]re, I have from him Directed to you enjoyning mee to Deliver itt with my hands, which shall accordingly bee Done when your honnors will Conclude mee. I would have waited on you att my first arrivall if I thought I should nott incurr your Displ[easure] att my first Comeing into this river I sent to you to signi[fy I]

expected your honnors pleasure as realating to ye frig[o]t and []
Butt I have nott heard whatt your will is att present [But I am]
expecting & hope is in mee I shall suddenly have a small
reaquest to preaferr unto you w[hi]ch I referr to your honors Considera[tion]
if I am worthy in your honnors eye to bee taken notice of to bee re[assigned]
is Destitute of a Commander as I hear shee
into ye *Pellicann* frig[o]t who ^ is Nott much better yn shee I have bin in
ever sinc I came from ye beating of ye Scotch King att Wor[ce]ster. And
itt is well known to ye Armie in ye three Nations how serviceable
I have bin on Land as well as sea & have endeavr'd to ye hazarding of
my Life ye readucing of all such as hath oppos'd our English
Interest. I Confess this is ye first tyme yt ever I writt or p[ayed for?]
one like me in my own beehalff although For ye Nien years past I
had ye Comm[an]d of severall Vessells on ye publique scoar; your Honors
may call to minde yt ye *Newcastle* frig[o]t was provided for me
and stayd some tyme in ye river. Butt my Lord Deputy reatarded
my Comeing home (in setting me on sarvice) untill my Lo[r]d Pr[otector]
Disposed of her to Capt[ain] Cobbam. I should nott have soe much enlar[ged upon this?]
Butt yt some of your officers in your regiment yt knowes mee assured
mee of your good Disposition & your Love to a faithfull souldier, w[hich]
occations my addresses to you. Generall Monck att my Departure ye
Last voyage to Scotland promised mee in Lieu of ye s[ai]d Newcastle
of those w[hi]ch wear then building Butt your honnors keeping mee
ever since (till necessity compell'd us home) hee could nott be [seen as]
farther
p[er]formanc I am unwilling to tire your patienc w[i]th using ^ arguments
Butt Committ my request to your wisdome and goodness w[hi]ch shall [end?]
and Conclude your Honnors Most assured & faithfull Sarvant att [heart]

Chatham
onbor[d] ye *Primrose* John Sherwin
ye 13 of Aprill
[16]55

#4: Captain John Sherwin writes a letter of complaint to the Commissioners of the Navy about failure to give the *Primrose* adequate provision – 5 October 1652 (TNA, SP 18/28, pages 167-168):

[Page 167 recto]

Wor[shi]pss
The last week I rec'd an order from ye Councell of State for making
Further Continuance on ye Coast (att w[hi]ch I admire) Butt fearing they are not
rightly Inform'd of ye State & Condition of ye Frig[o]t, I have this post
given them a realation, whatt impression itt will make I know nott, ye
Event I wait for & expect) p[er] ye Next, your worps (I am sure) is sencible of
our Wants. And I doubt nott butt your Care will Largely extend itt self
towards our preservation. I have hearin presented you w[i]th an Abstract
of w[ha]t is wanting onbord (nott forgetting a Little paye) to Cloath & Cherrish
a Company of sick naked men (Winter tyme Approaching). I understand our
Detention is occationd by a Company of Barking Whelps thatt mindes theyr
prey more than ye welfare of their Dam, thatt vallewes Nott if ye
Frig[o]t is lost soe yt t[hey]r self Interes is promoted & brought to Maturity.
I hope ye Lord will Direct ye Honable Councell (& if itt bee his will) Caus
them to Contradict ye last order to mee. I doe beseech you Inform mee (p[er]
next) In whatt Equipage I am like to goe to Sea. In Realation to a supply
That I may not hang like Mahometts Tombe (or between hope and dispair)
S[i]rs, I have talloweed ye Frig[o]tt & when supplyed with Cables, Stoares & Victualls
(ye Last I hope will be ready ye latter end of ye Next week) I shall be ready
to embrace ye first slant of winde to sea. I have nott els[e] butt to signify
I am your Wor[shi]ps Loving (and Reall) Sarvaunt

John Sherwin [signature]

Liverpool ye 05 of 8ber [16]52

[Page 167 verso]

For ye Service of ye State
These Present
To ye Wor[shi]pss Commisio[n]ers
of ye Navy
on Towerhill
London

[Page 168 recto]

A note of what stores is wantinge belonging to
the *Primerose*

Carpenters stores Spikes and all sortes of nailes
Pitch Tarr Oaceum
Thrumes Plankes boards
Tronells Canvas dealeboards
Leather soupboards sparrs
A bos sprit or fire sprit
Lanson Carpenter

A note of what gunners stores is wantinge aboard
the *Primerose* friggot belongeing to the Common
wealth of England

24 Barrells of powder
600 waight Threaddin
200 waight of match
100 waight of sheet lead
6 paires of buckle hookes
12 paire of tinn pinns
20 paire of fore lockes bags
500 nailes of all sortes
300 lampkins
12 paire of pulles
4 paire of heads and rammers
3 ells of Canvas
12 quire of paper Royall
50lb of Tackle
1 pottle of oyle
1 pound of starch
1 pound of thread
3 Coils of Tackles
1 Coil tard rope for brichinges
Gleed gunner

Wantinge in the Boatswaines stores

2 Cables: 11 and 12 Inch

1 horter 5 inch
1 horter for bag ropes
maine sheets and foresheetes
all other cordage is wantinge
and all such other small materialls gone
and expended
1 new Poop and lanthorne Rowley Boastwaine

#5: Captain John Sherwin writes a letter to General John Desborough from Plymouth – 24 March 1655 (TNA, SP 18/106, page 84):

[Page 84 recto]

Right honorable,
This Morning I strucke heer
Occasioned upon severall Accompts
But Especially for ye Reperation
of Sundery things, w[hi]ch In plying
up to this port hath beene out of Order
Your honor well knowes I have formerly
given you An Accompt of our proceedings
w[hi]ch have beene Cheerfully Acted by me,
In ye Midst of A Company of Murmerers
In all ye Borders Ajacent to Canaan And
at this port I am Informed yt the
Canaanuites most trouble ye Land: the
w[hi]ch party I doe desire may (w[i]th the
power of Gidion sourd) be destroyed.
I am p[er] ye first opertunity faceing
East; Alies sion ward (According to
Order) And hope suddenly to p[re]sent
ye servic of him who is
your honours most Affectionat[e]
servant whilst life

Plimouth On Bord John Sherwin [signature]
Primrose Frigg[o]tt 24th March
1654

[Page 84 verso]

These present
To ye R[igh]t hono[ra]ble
Genn[era]ll Desborough
Att Exon
hast for ye servic of ye state

#6: Captain John Sherwin writes to the Commissioners of the Admiralty and Navy about the loss of the *Primrose* – 12 March 1656 (TNA, SP 18/136, page 232):

[Page 232]

Right Hono[o]r[a]ble

From Kinsale ye ult[imo] of February last past I gave you an Acco[m]pt of my proceeding unto yt day on w[hi]chi I arrived, But when I came on shoare absolute Newes came That two of ye Spanish Friggates one of 36 ye other of 26 piece of ordinance had taken a Bristoll shipp w[i]th a Considerable quantity of money and sould her to them againe onely keepeing ye merchants on eleaven of ye Admirall Frigg[o]t for theire security untill payment. Uppon w[hi]ch true Relation I and ye *Mayflower* Capt[ain] Bowen hasted out w[i]th ye Wind at N[orth] East and East N[orth] East. The next day stretching it by ye Lands End and there plyed both for ye meeteing of our Enemy, & secureing of our friends, w[hi]ch according to Order from ye Councell It was to see about landing but on Satturday ye 8th instant betweene ye howres of 11 and 12 not perceiveing ye out breath or signe of any danger, although ye sea was high wee struck on a small Rownd sunken Rocke w[hi]ch by ye fishermen of Silly is called Seastone taken to bee one of ye 7 Stones, but distant from ye boddy of them, neare two miles to ye S[outh] East, There was not any on board mee or ye *Mayflower*, but Concluded wee were much to ye Eastwards and Southwaqrds of them, beeing by Judgm[en]t nigh fower Leagues off, Soe that some would perswade us, that wee Fowndered, and touch'd two Rockes. But to mine and others griefe, wee felt ye fatall stroakes, w[hi]ch were 3 or 4 , and they not very hard to my apprehension, Soe that I encouraged my Company to bayle and Pumpe (when wee had backed her off) in hopes to Returne her into Scilly, But noe sooner was she

Cleare of Scilly, but fell on Carigdis, Sinking imediately in 60 fathome, putting many of us to swimme for life, some naked, and otherwayes, having lost 16 of my men. And truly if ye Lord of life had not p[er] his providence ordered our affliction to bee in ye day, and one in Company w[i]th us, wee had all undoubtedly perished wee are all in a very poore Condit[i]on, some naked, others in washboates and drawers, as myself for one. But I hope your Agent Capt[ain] Hatsell, will take care for themselves when wee come to Plymouth for our supply of provision hitherto since lost. Wee have had out of ye *Mayflower*, who took us up for 4 days, But for ye future wee are all to goe on board ye Bryer, Capt[ain] Parker who carried heere yesterday, & is ye first steam of Wind to returne to Plym[outh] w[hi]ch when arrived, my Recollect[i]on is to hast in Presenteing his service to you, who is

In ye Isles of Scilly Right hono[ra]ble
March 12 [16]55

Your honours affectionate & faithfull
humble servant
John Sherwin [signature]

#7: Captain Peter Bowen writes to the Commissioners of the Admiralty and Navy about the loss of the *Primrose* – 14 March 1656 (TNA, SP 18/136, page 264):

[Page 264 recto]

Right Honor[a]ble

Being on the 3th Instant in the porte of Kinsaile takinge in of provisions where arived the *Primrose* aboute the same occasion and dureinge the tyme of our benge there I receaved Intelligence from Baltimoore of two saile of Dunkerk men of warr w[hi]ch laye plying of[f] of Cape clear, and that they had taken a vessell w[hi]ch came from Gallaway bound for Bristol as so[o]ne as the shipps weare victualled, consert ship weare made by capt[ai]n Sherwin and my selfe to goe and Cruse as is Specified by the inclosed making noe doubt but to finde them. On the sixt following wee both set sayle out of the above ment[i]oned port having the wind Esterly and the Sea beinge much growne Endeavoring to weather the ould head wee spent our Mayntopmast and on the Eight following being between the Lands End and Silly the *Primrose* strock on a Rock called the Sisteren w[hi]ch is to be seen at halfe Lyde it beares North West and by west from the Lands End neare upon two miles from the Seaven Stones and w[i]thin litle ore then halfe in Hower suncke downe most of their men betooke themselves to theire boate and to swimming. There was Sixteen men, Two women and a child Lost, the rest weare preserved by order boates and gott on board of us the wynd being Easterly wee putt the Night into Silly wheare I supplyed my selfe w[i]th a mayn topmast intending the very next opportunity that presen-ted to carry them for Plymouth, the *Brier* Friggott ariving heare and bound for the same port I desired Capt[ai]n Parker to take them on board and transport them, the which he did and on the twelve Following wee both sett sayle from thence but having a chase as high as Lundey w[hi]ch was a smale french man bound for Swansea and having spoke w[i]th him I put into this port to give your Honors this acco[mpt] where I mett w[i]th the *Basing* Friggott my intent is, god willing, to sett Saile in the morning into my Station appointed by your Honours, Soe I humbly take leave and rest

From on board the *Mayflower* Friggott in Milford Haven the 14th March 1655

Your Honors Humble and most Faithfull Sar[ve]ntt
Peter Bowen [signature]

#8: Captain John Sherwin writes to the Commissioners of the Admiralty and Navy about the loss of the *Primrose* – 14 March 1656 (TNA, SP 18/136, page 277):

[Page 277 recto]

R[igh]t Hono[ra]ble

Sinc mine from Silley of ye 12 Instant in w[hi]ch was conteyned ye sadd accompt of providentiall disposing of your ship *Primrose* and Company I am come to this place and applying my self to Capt[ain] Hatswell for our further disposall. Hee hath ordered a
vizt ye *Bryer*
Frig[o]t yt brough[t] us heer ^ to Carry us for Portsmouth to wait on ye Generalls order w[hi]ch when understood I shall use all Dilligence to give yu a more Amp-al though verball accompt then hithertoo hath Bin by your Honors Most assured faithfull Sarv[en]t

Plymouth ye 14 of March [16]55

John Sherwin [signature]

#9: The Commissioners of the Admiralty and Navy order the Navy Commissioners to investigate the loss of the *Primrose* – 27 March 1656 (TNA, SP 18/137, page 150):

[Page 150 recto]

27 March 1656

By the Com[missione]rs for the Admiralty and Navy

Whereas we have received information that on Saturday the 8th of this instant at noone the *Primrose* Frigot was cast awaynigh the Seaven Stones betweene the Landsend and Scilly in smooth water to the great coste and prejudice of the Commonwealth. It is ordered That it be referred to the Com[missione]rs for the Navy to bringe the Officers of the said frigot before them and to examine how shee came to bee lost and by whose default & to certifye their proceedings thereupon unto us.

John Desborough [signature]
Edward Hopkins [signature]
John Clerke [signature]

#10: The Admiralty Committee at Trinity House report to the Commissioners of the Admiralty and Navy that they have interviewed Captain John Sherwin and the crew of the *Primrose* – 5 April 1656 (TNA, SP 18/138, pages 267, 269):

[Page 267 recto]

Right Wor[shipfu]ll

According to your L[ett]re of the 2d instant Concerning the Examinat[i]on of the Captaine & other officers of ye Frigott *Primrose* lately cast away nigh the Seven Stones betweene Lands End & Scilley, we have had w[i]th us att a late Meeting the s[ai]d Capt[ain] and all ye Chiefe officers of that Frigott. And upon strict Exminat[i]on of them for ye discovery of ye truth of the matter of fact Concerning the Losse, wee found them all unanimously to Concur in one Relat[i]on the p[ar]ticulars whereof are Conteyned in ye Enclosed Examinat[i]on of the Captaine w[hi]ch we herewith send you. Unto w[hi]ch wee have nothing to add, but that by all wee Could discover from them wee Could not find that there was any apparent Neglect either in Officers or Company w[hi]ch wee Leave to your Considerat[i]on & Rest

Trinity House
April 5 1656

Your very loving freinds
and Servants

Maurice Thomson [signature] Thomas Scott [signature]
William Badiley [signature]

[Page 269 recto]

April 5 1656

Capt[ain] John Sherwin

Saith That ye 8th of March last, about 4 Leagues off Scilly plying w[i]th the wind att East and East & by North in Company w[i]th the *Mayflower*, Capt[ain] Peter Bowen, Hee having the weather gag & a head of him, bore up betweene ye hoare of 11 & 12 to speake w[i]th him in Order to ye obteyning a New Maine Top Mast, hee having baried one by ye board two days before, and laying his fore saile on ye Mast, the Ships way being almost lost, Struck ag[ain]st a Sunken Rock whose place of abode was not discoverable by any one on board w[i]th him or by ye *Mayflower* either before or after his Losse. Hee Comanded the Deep Sea Lead to be throwne overboard & found neare upon Sixtie fathomes water. Noe sooner did he feele ye Rock, but laid his Sailes abackstaies and gott off in hope shee had nott been soe mortally wounded, but that he might have p[re]serv'd her by aiming into Scilly, using all his Endeavours, by pumping & bayling, but yt nott availing him anie Comfort, sinking downe imediately in ye above s[ai]d Depth, Exposing him and Company to use all means by swimming or otherwise to p[re]serve their Lives (God making ye *Mayflower* instrumentall therein) on w[hi]ch ship after God had sett him on board he found ye Lands end to beare East one ½ North (by Judgm[en]t five Leauges off) so being Carried into Scilly by the *Mayflower*, Conversing w[i]th ye fishermen of ye s[ai]d Islands, they informed him yt there were 2 little Sunken Rocks yt lay to ye South East of ye body of ye 7 Stones called Pollard Sea Stone, the Southwest of w[hi]ch being ye last mentioned is neare 2 Leauges from ye s[ai]d body. upon all w[hi]ch he is willing to make Oath, when Required.

John Sherwin [signature]

#11: The Navy Commissioners report to the Admiralty Committee at Trinity House that they have interviewed Captain John Sherwin and the crew of the *Primrose* – 18 April 1656 (TNA, SP 18/138, page 265):

[Page 265 recto]

Right Hono[ra]ble

In pursuance of your Order of the 27th ult[imo], wee summoned the Captaine and Officers of the *Primrose* Frigott lately cast away nigh the Seaven Stones betweene the Lands End and Scilley. And upon strict examinat[i]on of them for the discovery of the truth of the matter of fact concerning that Losse, Wee found them all unanimously to concur in one relation. Yet for our better satisfaction wee desired the Committee of the Trinity House to reexamine these p[re]sents by whose Report unto us, as alsoe by all, wee can discover. wee doe not p[er]ceive that there was any apparent neglect either in the Officers or Company, the place where shee miscarried being a Rock not visible or described in any Plott that wee can find, w[hi]ch leaveing to your wisdome, Wee remaine

Navy Office Att your honors Commands
18 April 1656

Thomas Smith [signature] Nehemiah Bourne [signature]
Francis Willoughby [signature]

#12: Captain John Sherwin submits a report about the sinking of the *Primrose* to the Navy Commissioners – 31 March 1656 (TNA, SP 18/138, page 270):

[Page 270 recto]

The examinat[i]on of Capt[ain] Jo[hn] Sherwin late Comander of the *Primrose*, Frigott lately bcast away taken the 31st of March 1656

This Ex[aminan]t saith That upon the 8th of this Instant hee was plying w[i]th the said Frigott in company w[i]th the *Mayflower* between the Lands End & Silley, the Wind at East p[er] North by East not app[re]hending the least danger, Nor his Pilotts or any other of the Frigotts Company to the best of his observat[i]on. They supposeing themselves to be near Two leagues from the body of the Seaven Stones did unhappily strike about 12 of the Clock of the same day, the sea goding highest upon a sunken rock whereof there was not the least appearance by breaking of the Sea or otherwise where shee latiened Three or Foure knockes whereupon this Exa[minan]t caused all her Sailes to be laid abackstaies supposeing shee had not been soe dangerously bilged but that they might have recovered Silley But no sooner was the said Frigott gott cleere of the said Rock but shee imediately suncke downe in neere Threescore fathoms water The Land End beareing neere

East by North from them, hee and his Company being hard put to it to save their lives w[hi]ch through Gods mercy they all did by getting aboard the Mayflower save onely Sixteene of his Company w[hi]ch were drowned.

John Sherwin [signature]

#13: Peter Rowley submits a report about the sinking of the *Primrose* to the Navy Commissioners – 31 March 1656 (TNA, SP 18/138, page 270 verso):

[Page 270 verso]

The Examinat[i]on of Peter Rowley late Boatswaine of the *Primrose*, Frigott lately cast away taken p[er] Comm[ission]ers orders ye 31 March 1656

This Ex[aminan]t saith That upon ye 8th instant March ye *Primrose* frig[o]t being betweene ye Lands end and Silley in company w[i]th ye *Mayflower* about 11 Clocke at noone ye winde beinge then at East blowing fresh ye said frigott lying by the Lee to speake w[i]th ye *Mayflower* she having spent her Maintopmast two nights before they not p[er]ceiving any breaking of the sea or any other signe or danger ~~sea~~ ^ ~~rocke~~ did imediatley ~~rock~~ strike upon a rock some 4 leagues off of Scilley ye Capt[ain] seeing the s[ai]d frig[o]t so strike imediately ordered her sailes to be put abackstaies and comanded all to pumps and baile but she notwithstandinge suncke downe right w[i]thin halfe ~~and~~ an houre. This is all yt this examin[an]t can say.

Peter Rowley [signature]

#14: Edward Bason submits a report about the sinking of the *Primrose* to the Navy Commissioners – 31 March 1656 (TNA, SP 18/138, page 272):

[Page 272 recto]

The Exa[m]i[n]at[i]on of Edward Bason late M[aste]r of ye *Primrose*, frig[o]t taken by order of the Com[mission]ers of the Navy the last of March 1656

This Exam[inan]t saith That upon ye Sixt daie of this instant March ye said Vessell came out of Kingsale (the *Mayflower* being then her Consort and in her some of

Companie) intending to look after ~~two~~ ^ men ^ war that lay (as wee were informed) about Scilley and being come out about a league the Maintoppmast of ye *Mayflower* went by the board (shee being then a lttle to leeward ag[ains]t us) and the wind being at East north East or East south East and by East and about 8 at night in Oldhead ag[ains]t Kingsalebore on us Northwest or Northwest and by West, being about 5t leagues off and about noone ye next daie wee were about 25 leagues off on the the Oldhead aforesaid Northwest or thereabouts lyeing with our sterne East South East at w[hi]ch wee lay till about 7 at night and then backed off for feare of a danger and standing along the wind begaine to shrinke. about 8 or 9 of ye clocke or thereabouts and then wee were betwixt Scilley and the Lands End wee bore up to our consort about a mile to know what he would do do now telling him he could deep Sea and runing to leeward of him and runing ahead of him, wee did about an houre after set Maine topsaile & fore topsaile and when wee were a good distance ahead of him, about 11 or 12 a clock, wee brought our foresaile & foretopsaile to ye Mast to speake with our s[ai]dConsort and p[re]sented before our shipp had lost her way she strooke upon ye rock (there being no rock to be seene nor breach of a rock either before wee strooke upon it or after wee came off, being then 4 leagues off of Scilley

[Page 272 verso]

the 7 stones bearingoin us Northwest or thereabouts neere about 2 leagues off Crowe Sound bore of us West southwest or West and by south about 4 leagues off and the Lands end bore of us East or East and by North or thereabouts 5 Leagues off or thereabouts.

Edward Bason [signature]

#15: Henry Marven submits a report about the sinking of the *Primrose* to the Navy Commissioners – 31 March 1656 (TNA, SP 18/138, page 274):

[Page 274 recto]

The Examinat[i]on of Henry Marven late Masters Mate of the *Primrose*, Frigott taken the 31st of March 1656

This Examin[an]t saith That on the 8th of this instant March coasting
in the *Primrose* frigg[o]tt
about ye Lands end ^ the winde being at East North East wee

were comeing into ye Channell betweene the 7 Stones and the Lands end. The 7 Stones bore Northwest of us about 2 leagues & ye Tower upon St Martins Island (one of ye Isles of Scilly) bore west & by South about 4 leagues off & Crowes Sound bore West South west Westerly & the lands end bore of us East and by North about 5 leagues, our sailes being halted abackstayes to stay for our Consort (ye *Mayflower* friggott) our friggott strucke upon a rocke 2 blowes and went off againe, whereupon this Exam[inan]t heaved over ye lead and found 60 fathom water close to ye rock; that within three quarters of an hour after or lesse ye said friggott sunke. Ye Exam[inan]t and ye rest of the Company being forct to leape over board and swimm for yr lives. This Rocke is called by ye Islanders ye Sesterne but never kinown before by any of ye frigg[o]tts Company this is all he can say touching this business, & to the truth hereof hee hath sett to his hand

Henry Marven [signature]

#16: Samuel Gleede submits a report about the sinking of the *Primrose* to the Navy Commissioners – 31 March 1656 (TNA, SP 18/138, page 276):

[Page 276 recto]

The Examinat[i]on of Samuell Gleede late Gunner of the *Primrose*, Frigott taken by Order of ye Worships the Comissi[on]ers of ye Navy the 31th March 1656.

This Examinant saith yt on the Eighth Day of this month lately about Eleaven of the clocke in the foreneoon the *Primrose* Frig[o]tt being some foure leagues from ye Isle of Scilley the Lands end of England bearing East & by North, St Martins Island bearing West & by South, the said Frig[o]tt strucke on a Rocke and gave three stroakes, they backed her cleare of and then she suncke imediately and yet noe breach to be seen on ye Rocke after she was suncke and farther this Examinant saith yt he doth beleive yt ye Frig[o]tt did sincke in Fiftie fathom water and farther saith not ~~Witness~~ and to the truth hereof hath set to his hand ye day & yeare abovewritten

Samuel Gleed [signature]

#17: William Trevitt submits a report about the sinking of the *Primrose* to the Navy Commissioners – 22 March 1656 (TNA, SP 18/137, page 180):

[Page 180 recto]

The Examinat[i]on of William Trevitt of Plymouth in the County of Devon, Merchant, late a passenger on board the *Primrose* Frigott Comanded by Captaine Sherwin in the Immediate service of the Commonwealth, taken att Plymouth aforsaid before Henry Hatsell the Vice Admirall of the County of Devon, the two and Twentieth day of March 1655.

The said Examinant saith that the sixth day of this Instant moneth of march 1655 hee came in the *Primrose* Frigott Comanded by Captain John Sherwin in the Imediat service of this Comonwealth in Company with the Frigott Called the *Mayflower* In the Imediat service of this Comonwealth Comanded by Captain Bowen from Kingsale in Ireland, bounde for the Lands end of England, and that on the eighth day of this Instant March hee beinge in the said Shippe betweene the Lands end and Scilley in Company with the said other Frigott (to witt) about eight of the Clocke in the Morninge the said Captaine Sherwin in this Examinants presence demanded of the Master of the said Frigott *Primrose* whee Certen Rockes Called the Seaven Stones laye, who returned answeare that the said Stones were to the Leward of the said Frigott, and that they were past the said Stones and about three howers afterwards the said Captaine Sherwin Came upon the Decke from his Cabbinge where he had been writinge Letters to bee sent for England and Ireland advisubge that he was with the said Frigott Crusinge about the Lands end and the winde being East North East the said Captaine Sherwin having a desire to speake with the Captain of the said other Frigott about gettinge a new Maine Top mast which the said Frigott had spent two days before that gave order to beare upp to speake with him, to know what Course hee should take about gettinge a new Maine top mast and in bearing upp and bringinge the said Frigott by the lee to stay to speake with the said Captaine Bowen who was with his Frigott very neere him, the said Frigott *Primrose* stroke on two suncke Rockes about two miles distant from the seaven Stones, Called the Sistrens by the Fishermen of Scilley, lying about two miles from the seaven Stones upon which the said Frigott was bilged and drove a sterne and within halfe an hower suncke with the losse of Diverse of her seamen, this Examinant and the rest of the said Frigotts Company beinge saved by the said Captaine Bowenes Company and Carried into Scilley. Hee siath that att the tyme when the said Frigott stroke and was bilged as aforesaid itt was smooth water and hee ~~noe~~ saw noe Breach of the seas uppon the said suncke Rockes.

Henry Hatsell [signature] William Trevitt [signature]

#18: The Commissioners of the Admiralty and Navy order that the crew of the *Primrose* be paid the wages due to them– 22 April 1656 (TNA, SP 18/139, page 43):

[Page 91 recto]

22th April 1656

By the Com[missione]rs for the Admiralty and Navy

It is ordered That it be referred to the Com[missione]rs and Trea[sure]r of the Navy to pay off the wages due to the officers and Company late belonging to the *Primrose* Frigott except the Captaine and Master thereof, w[hi]ch is to be respited till further order.

John Desborough [signature]
John Clerke [signature]
Edward Hopkins [signature]

#19: The Commissioners of the Admiralty and Navy order that Joseph Scot, chaplain aboard the *Primrose,* be paid the wages due to him – 17 April 1656 (TNA, SP 18/126, page 195):

[Page 195 recto]

17 April 1656

By the Com[missione]rs for the Ad[miral]ty and Navy

It is ordered That it be referred to the Com[missione]rs and Trea[sure]r of the Navy to pay unto Mr Joseph Scot late Chaplaine of the *Primrose* frigot the wages due unto him for the time he was on board the said frigott notwithstanding he received not a warrant for officiating in that imployment. And this shall warrant thies so doeing.

John Jones [signature]
John Clerke [signature]
Edward Hopkins [signature]

#20: Joseph Caryll writes a letter supporting the case of Joseph Scot, chaplain aboard the *Primrose* – 16 April 1656 (TNA, SP 18/126, page 194):

[Page 194 recto]

Right Honor[a]ble,

The bearer hereof Mr Joseph Scot who is a Fellow of ye Colledge by Dublin in Ireland and M[aste]r in Arts there was desired by Captaine Sherwin Comander of the *Primrose* Frigot to officiate as Chaplaine in the sayd ship, beinge encouraged thereunto and approved of by the order of his Highnes Councill in Ireland as the Captaine is ready to attest in which service hee continued till the ship was unhappily cast away. And forasmuch as I have good knowledge of the person and of his abilityes for ye due discharge of the sayd place I make it my humble request to your Honors that his wages for the time he was in the service which was 6 or 7 moneths may bee speedily payd to him he being desierous to returne to his Colledge with the first occasion after he hath obteyned this favour. His poersonal Losses in Bookes and necessary provisions in the ship were to the nature of 20*li* at least, which he hopes will be considered and such repayre made as to your wisdome shall appeare equall and Just, which is also the the request of Your Honors Humble

Ap[ril] 16 [16]56 Servant

Joseph Caryll [signature]

#21: The Commissioners of the Admiralty and Navy order that half of Captain Sherwin's wages be garnished for his involvement in the loss of the *Primrose* – 3 June 1656 (TNA, SP 18/141, page 41):

[Page 91 recto]

3d April 1656

By the Com[missione]rs for the Adm[iral]ty and Navy

It is ordered That the Com[missione]rs and Trea[sure]r of ye Navy doe pay unto Captaine John Sherwin late Comander of the *Primrose*, and unto Edward Bason Master thereof the one halfe of the wages due unto them respectively for the time they served on board the said Frigott, and the other halfe is to be reserved in the States hands for thjeir neglect in p[er]formance of the duty of their places as to the losse of the said Frigott. And this shall warrant their soe doing.

John Clerke [signature] Edward Hopkins [signature]
Edward Salmon [signature]

#22: The Commissioners of the Admiralty and Navy order that Captain Sherwin's wages be restored – 27 April 1658 (TNA, SP 18/190, page 91):

[Page 91 recto]

27th April 1658

By the Com[missione]rs for the Adm[iral]ty and Navy

It is ordered That it be referred to the Com[missione]rs and Trea[sure]r of ye Navy to give direction for payment of the wages remayning due unto Captain John Sherwin for his service as Comander of the *Primrose* Frigott notwithstanding any former Order for suspension of the same, And for soe doing this shalbee their warrant.

Thomas Kelsey [signature]
Edward Salmon [signature]
Robert Beake [signature]

#23: Samuel Windis writes a letter to the Commissioners of the Admiralty and Navy complaining about the conduct of Captain Sherwin aboard the *Primrose* – 27 July 1655 (TNA, SP 18/111, page 154):

[Page 154 recto]

S[i]r,

My service presented to you I had thought to have waited one you at your owne howse to have related my Condition to you both as Pursar & Clerke of the *Primerose*. When I was in the former Condition I never knew how to have a livinge by reason of the unworthy carriages of Captain Sherwin who allwayes charged mee by multitudes of Passengers of all sorts for his owne private ends so that to compleate what the shipp wanted I was ever out of purse & could have noe Sattisfaction without wayes neither safe nor warrantable & to speake to him was to noe purpose whose tyrrany I fellt by Close imprisonment for demanding an accompt of my steward only; soe that purposinge to give over that imployment by wayes & meanes unthought of god graciously handed another to free mee from that gaole, yett soe as that I have Continued to the time the shipp was paid though to my charge was ever made all good & the party Mr Evatt whom I allwayes imployed the last voyadge hath her[e] in forms mee Cleared the accompt for the last voyadge & I have buy mee the other as cleare since the first of Jannuary 1652 & in regard this younge man is heare detained in expectation of some more mony then he hath received for his disbursements for sicke men & for his paines as Clerke I humbly desire that I may have a Tickett signed for that time as he served as defaced by mee; whatsoever informations you have had by any insinuatinge to baes humane frailetyes excepted your servant desires to keepe the mistery of the faith in a poore Conscience soe prays hee for all the Grace of god beinge

your ser[ven]t as any opportunitie
tenders Samuell Windis [signature]

Grave Morrice in Leaden
hall streete, London
27 July 1655

S[i]r, havinge a Corne cutt which bled beinge advised to favor itt, the bearer Mr Shott doth attend your answere

#24: Captain John Sherwin of the *Primrose* writes a letter about the thief and imposter John Selby – May 1654 (BLO, MS Rawlinson A 14, folio 590 recto):

An Acco[un]^{t} given by Capt John Sherwin Comand^{er} of y^{e} *Prime-Rose* Frigott concerning John Selby, prisoner at Kingstowne upon Hull

As for ye man entitled Capt[ai]^{n} Shelby I never saw him in Ireland, only by Capt Hide (a gent of Creditt) that ye said Shelby going as a recruite Sold^{ier} for Ireland ran away w[i]th his Captaines horse & Portmantau, wherein was his Clothes, money & Comission and that he rased his Capt[ai]^{ns} name out, and in stead thereof inserted his owne, soe became a supposed Captaine, by meanes of which Colourable p^{re}tence hee borrowed of Coll[one]^{ll} Birtch eight halfe Crownes, of Majo^{r} Fenwick, Coll[one]^{ll} Fenwick's Brother, twenty pounds [in] half Crownes, of Mr Browne a watch worth five pounds, and of Mr Roe a Rapier & paire of Cuffs w[hi]^{ch} he never hitherto (as I know of) hath restored back and I believe never will.

Postscript

This Selby is as you relate a black spare man in fare but midle stature, his apparell a Shammoy dubblett & Scarlett breeches w[hi]^{ch} were (as Capt Hide informeth) his Captaines Clothes when he as in Liverpoole.

#25: Samuel Hyland and William Kiffen write a letter of support for the petition of Samuel Gleede – 7 June 1656 (BLO, MS Rawlinson A 184, folio 63):

I am satisfied by the Information of some honest men that the Bearer hereof Samuell Gleede late Mr Gunner aboard The *Primrose* Friggott is a person faithfull and able in the employm^{t} of a Gunner, and doe believe him to be a person deserving encouragem^{t} and fitting to be intrusted in the like service. In witness whereof I do hereunto put my hand this 7th day of June 1656.

Sam Hyland [signature]
Wm Kiffen [signature]

#26: Edward Ny writes a letter of support for the petition of Samuel Gleede – 8 June 1656 (BLO, MS Rawlinson A 184, folio 64):

To my h[o]n[ora]ble friend
Coll[onel] Clerke
There present

S[i]r,
The bearer hereof Samuell Gleed is the person on whose behalfe (at the desire of some fearing God) I took the boldnes to move you at Wallingford house, he was Mr Gunner of The *Primrose* frigott until she was lost, his humble desire is to doe the like service in one of the new frigotts, his wife I have knowne for some ~~tyme~~ yeares & I judge she fears God, & truly I heare well of him, & hope he may be very serviceable, otherwise I should not give you this trouble, w[hi]ch I pray excuse from

S[i]r,

yo^ur friend & servant

Edw Ny [signature]

Marybone
8 June [16]56

#27: Four others write a letter of support for the petition of Samuel Gleede – undated (BLO, MS Rawlinson A 184, folio 58):

I am satisfied by the Information of some honest Men that the Bearer hereof Samuell Gleede late Mr Gunner Abored the *Primrose* Friggott is A person faithfull and Able in the Employment of A gunner and do beleave him to be A person deservin Encouragement & Fitting to bee intrusted in the like Service. In witness hereof I do hereunto putt my hand.

Rob[ert] Thompson [signature]
Tho[mas] Henson(?) [signature]
Henry Spurston [signature]
Henry Coope [signature]

#28: Four others write a letter of support for the petition of Samuel Gleede – 5 June 1656 (BLO, MS Rawlinson A 184, folio 62):

Whereas I am credibly Informed by honest &

Good men that the Bearer hereof Samuell Gleede late Mr Gunner of the *Primrose* Frigott is a Person honest, ably and every way sufficient for the Employment of a Gunner. I thought it good to certifie this much hereby to all whom it shall any way concerne. And do beleeve that hee the said Samuell Gleede is a person deserving Encouragement and fitt to bee employed in the like service. In witness whereof I have herewith put my hand this fifth day of June 1656.

Tho[mas] Sandforde [signature]
Polycarpus Engeham, Ch[u]rg[yion] [signature]
Ed[ward] Bourne [signature]
John Jacobs [signature]

#29: Certificate from officers in the Ordnance Office about the actions of Samuel Gleede aboard the *Phoenix* – 20 January 1660 (BLO, MS Rawlinson A 187, folio 221 recto):

For our honorable friend Rich[ar]d Hutchinson Esq[uire] Trea[sure]r for ye Navy

Mr Trea[sure]r,

Wee have received ye Accompts of Samuell Gleede Ma[ste]r Gunner of y^{e} *Phenix* f[riggo]t, and have taken examination of ye matters alledged ag[ains]t him, and do neverthelesse Certifie you as before, that hee hath delivered in his remaines of Stores togeather with an Accompt of ye Expence, and yt no reason doth appeare unto us why ye said Ma[ste]r Gunner should be suspended of his place or Pay. Wee are

Sir,

Office of ye ordn[an]ce
20 Jan[uary] 1659

Your affectio[nate] Freinds

Elia Palmer [signature]
[Lewis] Audeley [signature]
Will[ia]m Billers [signature]

#30: Letter from officers in the Ordnance Office about the actions of Samuel Gleede aboard the *Phoenix* – 8 February 1660 (BLO, MS Rawlinson A 187, folio 219 recto):

Right Hono[ra]ble

In pursuance of an Order from the late Comiss[ion]ers of the Admiralty^{y} and Navy of the 14th of 10ber lasst grounded upon a Letter from Capt[ai]n Bun Comander of the *Phenix* Frig[o]tt touching severall of the States Stores thereby informed to be sould by her Guner and Boatsw[ai]n. As to that p[ar]te of the Order which relates to the Gun^{ers} trust, wee thought it most proper to be examined by the Officers of the Ordnance, into whose more immediate cognizance that action referrs, and in order thereunto transmitted the same Order and Capt[ai]n Buns Letter to them to be examined accordingly. Thereupon they have since returned to us the inclosed Certificate directed to the Trea[sure]r of the Navy, Intimating that they have viewed the Guners Acc[oun]t and examined the matters alleadged against him, yet nevertheless certifie that they find noe reason why the said Guner should be suspended of his Place or Pay. And as to the other parte of the Order w[hi]ch concernes the Boatswaine, his Acc[oun]ts are now under examination, and as soon as they are finished wee shall likewise returne s[ai]d reports thereon. All w[hi]ch wee leave to your wisdome And remaine

Att your honores Comands

Navy Office
8 Febr[uary] 1659
Rob: Thomson [signature] Fr[ancis] Willoughby [signature]
Peter Pett [signature] N[ehemiah] Bourne [signature]

#31: Will of Samuel Gleed – signed 8 January 1706; probated 26 April 1706 (TNA, PROB 11/487, folios 312 recto and verso).

[Folio 312 recto]

I, Samuel Gleed, of the parish of St Olave in Southwark in the County of Surrey, Mariner, being sick and weak in body but praised be Almighty God of perfect sound disposing mind and memory For the settlement of that small Estate God in his mercy hath been pleased to bestowe upon me and preventing any trouble or controversy that may arise for want thereof Do make this my last Will in manner and forme following (that is to say): First an principally, I commend my Soul unto the hands of Almighty God that gave it. My body I commit to the earth from when it came to be decently interred at the discretion of my Executrix hereinafter named, And touching my worldly Estate I do dispose thereof as followeth (that is to say) I devise and give to my Nephew Samuel Adams, to his sons Samuell and Thomas, to his daughter to his daughter [*sic*] Sarah and her Husband and Children, to Sarah and Mary Adams, Daughters of my late dead Nephew Thomas Adams to my Niece Rose Waxon and to Martha and Mary Cox and Elizabeth Waxon her daughter, and to all and every other of my near Relations or Kindred that may or might say any rightfull claim to my Estate or any part of it to each and every of them twelve pence a peece in case it be lawfully demanded. Item: I devise and give to Elizabeth Simcock the Trundle Bed and Bed belonging to it, two Pillowes and a Bolster, two paires of sheets and the great Sauce pan. Item: I devise and give to Sarah Gibbins the Red Bed and all that belongs to it a Back, the Brass in the Chimney, a small Table, three Cane Chaires, a paire of Brass Candlesticks and a little Chest with Drawers. Item: I devise and give to Elizabeth Harding, my Servant Maid, the Bed and Furniture of the Upper Chamber, three Chests, a great Chest with Drawers, a Cupboard, a spice Box, the Grates and Iron Work in the Chimney, a Pottage Post, one halfe of my Pewter and one halfe of my Linnen, three Cane Chaires and a Table. Item: I devise and give to Alice Adams, Relict of my late deceased Nephew Thomas Adams All that my pent[i]on and Sallery that shall be due to me at the time of my decease and all my trades money, Goods, chattles, Estate reall and personall of what nature, kind, and quality; the same is, or may be found, at the time of my decease or which I shall be possessed of, interested in, or any way intituled to after my aforesaid Legacies and Funerall Expences are paid and discharged. To have and hold to the foresaid Alice Adams, her Executors, Administrators and Assignes to her and their own use and behoofe freely and absolutely for ever. And I doe hereby nominate and appoint the said Alice Adams sole Executrix of this, my Will, Revoking all others publishing these presents to be and contain all my whole mind and will. In witness whereof I have hereunto sett my hand and seal this Eighth day of January Anno D[omi]ni 1705 And in the Fourth year of the Reigne of our Sovereign Lady Queen Anne over England &c Samuell Gleed Signed, Sealed, published and declared by the Testator as his last Will in presence of the marke of Richard Bell Richard Wilkings John Allen Not[arius] Publ[icus] on Roderife Wall Probatum fuit hu[ius]mo[d]i Testamentum apud London Coram ven[erabi]li viro Johanne Exton Legum Doctore

Surrogato ven[erabi]lis et egregii viri D[omi]ni Richardi Raines Militis
Legum etiam Doctoris Curiae Praerogat[ivae] Cantuarien[sis] Magistri
Custodis sive Com[missa]rii legitime constitut[i] Vicesimo nono Die
mensis Aprilis Anno D[omi]ni Mill[es]imo septinge[ntes]imo sexto Juram[en]to
Aliciae Adams viduae Executricis unicae in dicto Testamento
nominat[ae] Cui commissa fuit Administratio omnium et
singulorum bonorum jurium et creditorum dicti defuncti de
bene et fideliter administrand[o] eadem ad Sancta Dei Evangelia
juratae. Exam[inatum]

[Translation of lines 53-63]

This will was probated in
London before the venerable John Exton, Doctor of Laws,
Representative of the venerable and esteemed Lord Richard Raines, Knight,
also Doctor of Laws, legitimately appointed Master, Custodian and Commissary of
the Prerogative Court of Canterbury, on the Twenty ninth Day
of the month of April in the year of the Lord One Thousand seven hundred six, on the Oath of
Alice Adams, widow, named sole Executrix in the said Will,
To whom was committed administration of all and
singular goods, rights, and credits of the said deceased,
she having sworn to the good and faithful administration of the same on the Holy
Gospels of God. [The will] was Examined

CHAPTER 8

Elizabeth Avery's Encounter with William Kiffen in 1647: Mis-recollection, or Mis-attribution?

It has been suggested that William Kiffen participated in public debates that took place in Oxford in late 1646 or early 1647. No pamphlets or tracts of the proceedings of such debates involving Kiffen are extant, although one intriguing allusion to his participation in them has survived. This comes in the form of a testimonial by Elizabeth Avery, first published within John Rogers's *Ohel or Beth-shemesh* (see Figure #1).[1] John Rogers (1627–71?) was a well-known Fifth Monarchist and the pastor of an Independent church which met at Christ Church Cathedral, Dublin. Elizabeth Avery joined this congregation sometime in the early 1650s, giving her testimony before the assembled church.[2] Details of the life of this self-styled prophetess are sketchy, although her place as a minor figure among women writers of the period now seems secure, and she has an entry in the new *Dictionary of National Biography*.[3] Avery's reputation is due primarily to the publication of her *Scripture-Prophecies Opened* (1647), consisting of three separate chapters, or letters, which are given over to millenarian themes. Not surprisingly, Avery was preoccupied with the awaited second coming of Christ and offered interpretations of key apocalyptic texts (notably Daniel and Revelation), which she applied to the life of England in the turbulent years at the end of the Civil War.[4] The pamphlet was cited within several Presbyterian tracts published in 1647–48, which saw it as part of a sectarian conspiracy designed to undermine the Solemn League

---

[1] John Rogers, *Ohel or Beth-shemesh, A Tabernacle for the Sun* (1653): 402-406.

[2] D. Bruce Hindmarsh, *The Evangelical Conversion Narrative: Spiritual Autobiography in Early Modern England* (Oxford: Oxford University Press, 2005): 47, notes Avery's testimony as an example of the practice in Rogers's church in Dublin.

[3] Jane Baston, 'Avery, Elizabeth (fl. 1614–1653)', *Oxford Dictionary of National Biography* (Oxford University Press, 2004; online edn, 2008). Avery is noted in Nigel Smith, *Perfection Proclaimed: Language and Literature in English Radical Religion 1640–1660* (Oxford: Oxford University Press, 1989): 43-44; Patricia Crawford, *Women and Religion in England 1500–1720* (London: Routledge, 1993): 142; Susan Wiseman, *Conspiracy and Virtue: Women, Writing, and Politics in Seventeenth-Century England* (Oxford: Oxford University Press, 2006): 204; Crawford Gribben, *The Puritan Millennium: Literature and Theology, 1550–1682 (Revised Edition)* (Milton Keynes: Paternoster, 2008): 194-99.

[4] At one point Avery, *Scripture-Prophecies Opened* (1647): 15, notes 'the violence done to the Saints: remember *March* and *April, Anno Dom. 1647*'.

and Covenant of 1643.[5] The pamphlet also prompted a public rebuke by her brother Thomas Parker (1595–1677) who sought to put the lid on what he deemed to be her 'heretical opinions' by publishing a small pamphlet entitled *The Copy of a Letter* (1650). Here Parker betrayed his own patriarchial attitudes by suggesting that his sister was the victim of the 'Pride of Women',[6] and asserting 'your printing of a Book, beyond the custom of your Sex, doth rankly smell'.[7]

In any event, it is Elizabeth Avery's later testimony from 1653 that concerns us here, and within it she reveals that she suffered the loss of several of her children during the Civil War. Their deaths traumatized her greatly and contributed to a desperate search for spiritual comfort.[8] Following the surrender of Oxford in June of 1646 she received an invitation from Colonel John Lambert, the military governor of the city.[9] It is in replying to this invitation that Avery mentions in passing that she had encountered William Kiffen (whom she calls Kiffith):

> A while after this, Colonel Lambert desired me to go to Oxford, and when I was to go, I made ready my self, packt up my cloaths and all, and rid away; most with desire for communion with godly people there, for (as yet) I could see no further ---. I heard their disputes between Master Kiffith and others, very hot, but saw nothing of God there, and was troubled at it, and could not after that hear him or others (lines 71–78).

Avery clearly states that the desire for 'communion with godly people' was one of the reasons why she headed for Oxford. Instead, what she found there were public disputes and personal disappointments. According to Avery, Kiffen was in the city, and his reputation as a controversial speaker must have preceded him, for she states that he was engaged in 'very hot' public debates. Avery, writing with the advantage of hindsight, says that she 'saw nothing of God there', and hints that the experience robbed her of any desire for future contact with Kiffen, or any of the others involved in the disputations. She goes on to explain that she did meet with Colonel Lambert later and reported her experiences to him, and that he did offer some words of advice and comfort. In any event, despite the best attempts of Lambert to help her, Avery testified that her spiritual distress continued throughout her brief stay in Oxford.

---

[5] *A Testimony to the Trueth of Jesus Christ and to our Solemn League and Covenant* (1648): 20-21; *A Glasse for the Times* (1648): 5; *The Joint Testimonie of the Ministers of Devon* (1648): 20-21.

[6] Thomas Parker, *The Copy of a Letter* (1650): 12.

[7] Parker, *Copy of a Letter*, 13.

[8] Phyllis Mack, *Visionary Women: Ecstatic Prophecy in Seventeenth-Century England* (University of California Press, CA: Berkeley, 1992): 92-93, notes Avery's loss of her children had a profound effect upon her development as a prophetic voice. She argues, p. 93, that such women 'saw, and were taught to see, moral and spiritual significance in childbirth and in the mother/child relationship'. Mack also notes that many women in John Rogers's church converted after the death of a child.

[9] Lambert was appointed governor of Oxford in early July 1646 (see *The Moderate Intelligencer* #70 (2–9 July 1646): 528).

What are we to make of this tantalizingly brief reference to Kiffen's presence in Oxford, and his participation in public debates that took place there in 1646–47? Does further investigation substantiate the declaration made by Elizabeth Avery? Or should we look at her narrative in another way? In the main, the tendency among scholars has been to accept Avery's testimony as a straightforward account of historical events. Brief though it is, her recollection of hearing Kiffen in Oxford is generally taken at face value. Nevertheless, attempts have been made to fill out the details of the incident. For example, in a recent full-bodied study of John Lambert, David Farr argued that the primary person Lambert encouraged Elizabeth Avery to hear preach in Oxford was the controversial William Erbury (1604–54).[10] Farr noted that by 1646 Erbury, a noted military chaplain, had established something of a reputation as a controversial figure, and his presence in Oxford invited public disputations with the Presbyterians clerics that dominated the city at the time. Moreover, on the basis of Avery's testimony cited above, Farr also argued that William Kiffen was somehow associated with William Erbury in these high-profile debates which, in the end, left Elizabeth Avery so unimpressed. In Farr's view Erbury and Kiffen were 'the two most prominent preachers there [in Oxford] at the time'.[11] Both aspects of this interpretation of Elizabeth Avery's testimony warrant further investigation.

William Erbury and the Public Disputations in Oxford (1646–47)

First, what of the suggestion that Colonel Lambert encouraged Elizabeth Avery to go and hear William Erbury in Oxford? At first glance, there is much to commend this as a proposal. It is likely that in late 1646 Lambert would have been personally acquainted with Erbury as a religious leader and army chaplain. Indeed, Erbury went on to serve as a chaplain in Lambert's regiment in Oxfordshire from January to April 1647, which suggests that Lambert had confidence in his abilities.[12] More importantly, there was a series of debates in 1646–47 between William Erbury and the Presbyterian ministers appointed as Parliamentary Visitors to Oxford.[13] These culminated in two high-profile confrontations which took place in the University Church of St Mary the Virgin on 11 December 1646 and 11 January 1647.[14] It is

---

[10] David Farr, *John Lambert, Parliamentary Soldier and Cromwellian Major-General, 1619–1684* (Woodbridge: The Boydell Press, 2003): 174.

[11] David Farr, 'The Militia and Political Career of John Lambert, 1619–57' (PhD thesis, Cambridge University, 1996): 182. Farr suggests that Avery approached Lambert in Oxford because she was from the nearby town of Newbury in Berkshire.

[12] Anne Laurence, *Parliamentary Army Chaplains, 1642–1651* (Woodbridge: Boydell Press, 1990): 124, discusses Erbury's military career.

[13] The six Parliamentary Visitors were Henry Wilkinson, Francis Cheynell, Henry Langley, Henry Cornish, Robert Harrys, and Edward Reynolds.

[14] Five different pamphlets were issued between November 1646 and February 1647 which described these public disputations: *A True Relation of the Late Conference Held at Oxford Between Presbyterians and Independents* (1646); Robert Waring, *A Publike*

quite likely that Lambert had these disputations in mind when he made his recommendations to Elizabeth Avery. No doubt he hoped that Erbury would be a comfort to her, although how is not entirely clear. Erbury's conduct during the debates was controversial, to say the least, and his antics prompted negative comments from a number of observers. One oft-repeated criticism made by the Presbyterians was the way in which he used his army connections to intimidate his clerical opponents in the debates. For example, Francis Cheynell reported that Erbury brought a company of soldiers with him to the first public disputation and severely disrupted the order and dignity of the proceedings.[15] Thomas Edwards similarly vilified Erbury as a fanatic who only dared to challenge the Presbyterians in Oxford ('our Ministers') because he had sectarian soldiers accompanying him.[16]

However, it is by no means clear within Avery's testimony from 1653 that Erbury was the person Lambert suggested she should go and hear in order to strengthen her faith. Farr's supposition about this is perfectly plausible, but his case is entirely circumstantial in nature. Perhaps the most serious weakness of it is that Avery's account does not explicitly mention William Erbury by name. What is even less certain, however, is Farr's suggestion that Kiffen was somehow associated with Erbury in these debates. By this time Kiffen was becoming increasingly well known as a leader of the Baptists in London; his guiding hand in the issuing of *The Confession of Faith* (1644), and its re-issue in 1646, made sure of that. Yet it is remarkable that none of the five pamphlets issued in 1646–47 in connection with these public disputations mentions Kiffen by name even once. Moreover, the collection of Erbury's published works, put together by his disciple John Webster and published in 1658 following Erbery's death, does not mention Kiffen as participating in the Oxford disputations.[17]

Conference Betwixt the Six Presbyterian Ministers and Some Independent Commanders at Oxford, 12 November 1646 (1646); Francis Cheynell, *Truth Triumphing over Errour and Heresie* (1647); William Erbury, *Nor Truth nor Error nor Day nor Night* (1647); Francis Cheynell, *An Account Given to the Parliament by the Ministers Sent by Them to Oxford* (1647).

[15] Cheynell, *An Account Given*, 13.

[16] Thomas Edwards, *Gangraena (Part Three)* (1646): 250. This was issued at the end of December 1646.

[17] Kiffen's name appears at only one point in the whole book of 338 pages; this is a satirical comment about Captain Kiffin in a tract from 1652 entitled *The Woman Preacher* (see John Webster, *The Testimony of William Erbery* (1658): 150). B.R. White, 'William Erbury and the Baptists', *Baptist Quarterly* 23 (1969–70): 114-125, lists three meetings between Erbery and Baptists, all in 1652–53; none of these involved William Kiffen. However, it is worth noting that Erbury was one of the church leaders consulted by the congregation of Henry Jessey on 27 March 1644 when they were debating the question of infant-baptism; William Kiffen was involved in these debates (ALRPCO, Benjamin Stinton, 'Repository of Divers Historical Matters Relating to English Antipedobaptists' (1712) (ALRPCLO, D Stinton 1): 25-28).

One would have thought that others familiar with, or interested in, the Oxford disputations would have mentioned Kiffen's participation in them. But is this ever the case? It appears not. The Oxford antiquarian Anthony Wood (1632–95) gives an account of the debates in *The History and Antiquities of the University of Oxford*, but he does not mention Kiffen in connection with them.[18] Similarly, although Kiffen is one of the main targets of Thomas Edwards's *Gangraena* (1646), the Baptist leader is not mentioned in the treatment of the Oxford debates between Erbury and the Presbyterians. In 1678 Thomas Long wrote a brief account of the public debates in Oxford, but again there is no mention of Kiffen's involvement.[19] Perhaps most significantly, Kiffen's own autobiography omits any reference to public debates in Oxford in 1646–47.[20] In fact, outside of Elizabeth Avery's testimony there is no evidence that marks Kiffen as a participant in the Oxford debates. All of which means that one has to wonder if Kiffen participated in these public debates in the way that Avery suggests. Is it possible that her account confuses the Oxford debate with another public debate, and inadvertently transplants Kiffen to a time and place where he was not? After all, there were two celebrated debates, one in 1642 and one in 1646, in which Kiffen did participate.

William Kiffen and the Public Disputations in Southwark (1642) and Coventry (1646)

Baptists were engaged in a number of public disputations in the seventeenth century, many of them focusing on the place of re-baptism in the life of the church; such debates were an important part of the process of self-definition for the denomination.[21] Perhaps the most famous of these disputations took place in Southwark on 17 October 1642. The main antagonist on this occasion was Daniel Featley, who immortalized the occasion with the publication of his *The Dippers Dipt* (1642), a best-selling pamphlet which went through six editions in as many years.

---

[18] Anthony Wood, *The history and antiquities of the University of Oxford, in two books: by Anthony à Wood, ... Now first published in English, from the original MS in the Bodleian Library: by John Gutch, Volume 2* (Oxford, 1792–96): 489-500. Neither is Kiffen mentioned in Wood's discussion of Erbury in *Athenae Oxonienses, Volume 2* (1692): 103-105.

[19] Thomas Long, *Mr Hales's Treatise of Schism Examined and Censured* (1678): 133-34. Interestingly Long does name Colonel John Hewson, the regicide, as one of the soldiers who accompanied Erbury to the debates. This represents an intriguing connection to Elizabeth Avery, for, like her, Hewson is known to have joined John Rogers's church in Dublin in c.1651 while he was serving as military governor of the city (see Rogers, *Ohel or Beth-shemesh*, 395-396).

[20] William Orme, *Remarkable Passages in the Life of William Kiffin* (London, 1823).

[21] Arthur S. Langley, 'Seventeenth Century Baptist Disputations', *Transactions of the Baptist Historical Society* 6 (1918–19): 216-243, catalogues 109 debates between 1641 and 1698.

William Kiffen (whom Featley calls Cufin) was one of four Baptists who participated in this debate.[22]

Moreover, Kiffen is known to have participated in a number of other public disputations. Indeed, in 1918 Arthur S. Langley suggested Kiffen participated in *five* other debates following the meeting with Featley at Southwark, although the primary sources for these is not provided within his article.[23] These other debates are: 1. a debate between Hanserd Knollys, Henry Jessey and Kiffen in London in 1643;[24] 2. a debate between Edward Barber, Thomas Lambe, Thomas Patient and Kiffen in Kent in 1644;[25] 3. a debate between John Bryan, Obadiah Grew, Hanserd Knollys and Kiffen at Trinity Church, Coventry in 1646;[26] 4. a debate between Peter Chamberlen and Kiffen in London on 6 November 1653;[27] 5. a debate between the Quakers William Penn, George Whitehead, Stephen Crisp, George Keith, and the Baptists Jeremiah Ives, Thomas Hicks, Thomas Plant, Robert Ferguson and Kiffen on 9 October 1674.[28] In addition, we should note that Kiffen was scheduled to participate

[22] Featley uses *Cufin* 26 times in *The Dipper Dipt* (1645); pages 3 (2x), 4 (7x), 5 (3x), 8 (2x), 10, 13 (3x), 17 (4x), 18 (4x).

[23] Langley 'Seventeenth Century Baptist Disputations', 223, 224.

[24] See ALRPCO, Benjamin Stinton 'Repository of Divers Historical Matters Relating to English Antipedobaptists' (1712) (ALRPCLO, D Stinton 1): 25-28; Thomas Crosby, *The History of the English Baptists, Volume 3* (London, 1740): 311.

[25] Perhaps an echo of this is recorded in an anonymous report dated 6 July 1646 by Edwards, *Gangraena (Part Three)*, 78 ('I heard last week at an open ordinary in presence of two of our Deputy Lieutenants, that since *Kiffen* and *Lamb* have been here re-baptizing, now there's a third man come that contradicts them both, and re-baptizes again').

[26] Crosby, *History of the English Baptists, Volume 3*, 5; John Ley, *A Discourse* of *Disputations* (1658): 7, 47, 74-75; Nathaniel Stephens, *A Precept for the Baptisme of Infants* (1651): A3.

[27] See *A Discourse Between Cap. Kiffin and Dr. Chamberlain about Imposition of Hands* (1654).

[28] This public debate sparked off a pamphlet war between Quakers and Baptists. Included were *The Quakers Last Shift Found Out* (1674); William Penn, *Naked Truth Needs No Shift* (1674); Thomas Plant, *A Contest for Christianity* (1674); Thomas Rudyard, *The Anabaptists Printed Proposals* (1674); William Mead, *A Brief Account of the Most Material Passages Between those Called Quakers and Baptists* (1674); William Penn, *William Penn's Answer to John Faldo's Printed Challenge* (1674); William Penn, *William Penn's Return to John Faldo's Reply* (1674); William Penn and George Whitehead, *The Christian-Quaker and his Divine Testimony Vindicated* (1674); William Penn, *The Counterfeit Christian Detected; and the Real Quaker Justified* (1674); William Penn, *Libels No Proof* (1674); Thomas Hicks, *A Rebuke to Tho. Rudyard's Folly and Impertinencies* (1674); Thomas Hicks, *The Quakers Appeal Answer'd* (1674); Thomas Rudyard, *An Answer to a Scandalous Paper* (1674); Thomas Rudyard, *The Barbican Cheat Detected* (1674); George Whitehead, *The Timorous Reviler Sleighted* (1674); George Whitehead, *A Serious Search into Jeremy Ives's Questions to the Quakers* (1674); George Whitehead, *The Quakers Plainness Detecting Fallacy* (1674); George Keith, *Vindication from the Forgeries & Abuses of T. Hick & W. Kiffin* (1674); Henry Hedworth, *Quakers Quibbles* (1674); William Penn, *More Work for George Keith* (1696). According to Thomas Plant, *A Contest for Christianity* (1674): 104, Kiffen also participated

in a debate with Edward Calamy in Aldermanbury, London on 3 December 1645, but the license for this was controversially revoked by the Mayor of London.[29]

Finally, one other possible way of understanding Elizabeth Avery's testimony about her encounter with William Kiffen needs to be noted. It should not be forgotten that Avery's recollection about Kiffen comes down to us as part of John Rogers's collection of testimonies in *Ohel or Beth-shemesh, A Tabernacle for the Sun*, which inevitably means that her testimony has gone through the editorial filter of Rogers himself.[30] It may well be that what we are seeing in Avery's testimony is a reflection of Rogers's own contest with Kiffen and his particular ideas about congregational life. Rogers's *Ohel or Beth-shemesh* is a forceful apology for the church's practice of an open-membership and open-communion policy. Intriguingly, this was in contrast to the practice of Kiffen's own church. One cannot help but wonder if Avery's negative comments about Kiffen have ostensibly been put on her lips by Rogers, and thus have a more complicated story than is often recognized.

---

in a follow-up debate between Quakers and Baptists held at the home of Thomas Rudyard on 20 October 1674. On the follow-up debates, see William Mead, *A Brief Narrative of the Second Meeting Between the People Called Quakers and Baptists* (1674).

[29] *The Lord Mayors Farewell* (1646); Edward Barber, *A Declaration Concerning the Publike Dispute* (1648).

[30] Gribben, *Puritan Millennium*, 195, has a good discussion of this, noting how Rogers controls and manipulates the Oxford narrative to his own purposes. Also, see his *God's Irishmen: Theological Debates in Cromwellian Ireland* (Oxford: Oxford University Press, 2007): 158-173, where her life is discussed.

Figure

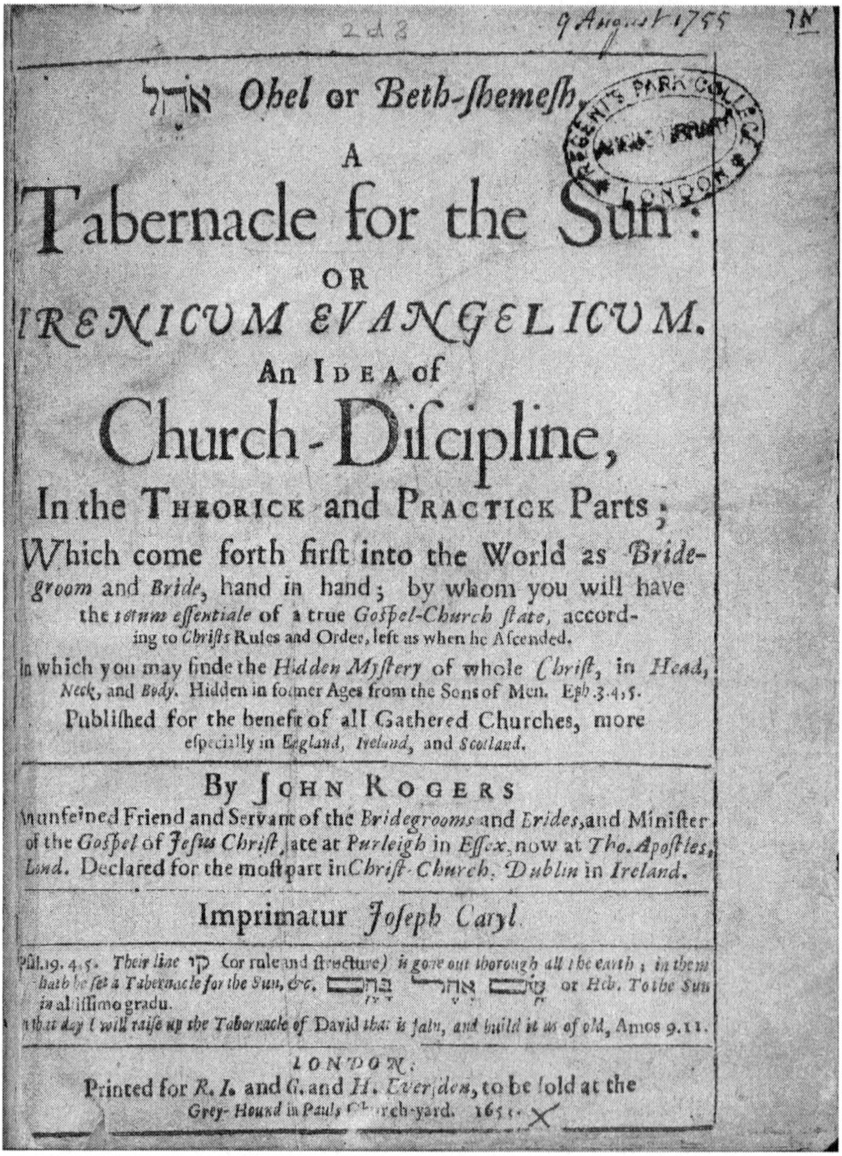

9 August 1755

אהל Ohel or Beth-shemesh.

A

Tabernacle for the Sun:

OR

IRENICUM EVANGELICUM.

An IDEA of

Church-Discipline,

In the THEORICK and PRACTICK Parts;

Which come forth first into the World as *Bride-groom* and *Bride*, hand in hand; by whom you will have the *totum essentiale* of a true *Gospel-Church state*, according to *Christs* Rules and Order, left as when he Ascended.

In which you may finde the *Hidden Mystery* of whole *Christ*, in *Head*, *Neck*, and *Body*. Hidden in former Ages from the Sons of Men. Eph.3.4,5.

Published for the benefit of all Gathered Churches, more especially in *England*, *Ireland*, and *Scotland*.

By JOHN ROGERS

an unfeined Friend and Servant of the *Bridegrooms* and *Brides*, and Minister of the *Gospel* of *Jesus Christ*, late at *Purleigh* in *Essex*, now at *Tho. Apostles*, *Lond.* Declared for the most part in *Christ-Church*, *Dublin* in *Ireland*.

Imprimatur *Joseph Caryl*.

Psal.19.4,5. *Their line* קו (or rule and structure) *is gone out thorough all the earth; in them hath he set a Tabernacle for the Sun, &c.* לשמש שם אהל בהם or *Heb. To the Sun in altissimo gradu.*

In that day I will raise up the Tabernacle of David that is faln, and build it as of old, Amos 9.11.

LONDON:

Printed for *R. I.* and *G.* and *H. Everfden*, to be sold at the *Grey-Hound* in *Pauls* Church-yard. 1653.

Figure #1 – Title Page of John Rogers's Ohel *Ohel or Beth-shemesh* (1653)

Document

#1: John Rogers, *Ohel or Beth-shemesh, A Tabernacle for the Sun* (1653): 402-406.

[Page 402]

A *fuller* Testimony *as it was taken from* Elizabeth Avery, *out of her own mouth, and declared by her self to the whole Church.*

In this *society* I see much of God, and have a great desire to be one with you. From my *childhood* I have lived un-

[Page 403]

der *good education*; my *Father was a godly man*. I was always tender and consciencious, but my *conversion* was *wonderful*. On one *Sabbath-day* I was playing, but I was soon and soundly *checked* for it in my *spirit*; and went home, but I was a great while troubled, and lay under *bondage* all along: And I was much *distracted* and confused for sin a long time, till about *sixteen years* of age; and then I began to be very *strick*, and so retired in my *life*, that many wondered at it: I had an entire *love* to the *preaching of the Gospel;* O how I longed after it! but alas! we had then no good *Preaching-Ministery* to be had or heard about us: and yet my heart lon ged a long time after it, till I casme to be *married*. But alas! I was yet under the *Law*, and *Works*, until *God* called me out of *Egypt*; and I could not tell how I was once wrapt in a *light*, and *hearing* something spoken of *Free-grace*, then I melted. Yet for all these, I had *great afflictions*, and amongst others, by the loss of my *children*, *Gods rod* was laid *heavy* upon me, insomuch, That he struck *three* of them together; and one *childe* above all, a most aweet *childe*, and one, that I least thought of them all would have died, was very ill; and we were talking (I, my Husband, and some Friends,) together of comfortable *things*, and amongst others of *David*, when he said of his *childe* (dead) *I shall go to it, it shall not return to me*. Ay sayes one, that is to the *grave*; which word *wounded* me; and I went into the *Garden* to *wail* and *moan* my self; but soon after, my *Husband* came and told me my *childe* was dying; at which I was left in an *horror*, as if I were in *Hell*, none would comfort me, nothing could *satisfie* me, no *Friends*, nothing; then it was sad indeed to me, a *Hell* indeed. I sent for the Doctor and others, but to no purpose. Yet after this the Lord wrought on me much; and one, a *Minister of Christ*, that had *power* from *God* to do me good, gave me much *satisfaction* by a *Letter* of his: And after that, me

thoughts, I was content to part with all, and to let all go; then God tryed me, and took away another *childe* from me, and I could bear it very well, and was not *troubled*, but rather did rejoyce within me to be thus *tryed*. No cross,

[Page 404]

nor loss could trouble me then, and I continujed in this *strength* (I praise God) pretty long. But after this I was like to have died, and then, to adde to by *great sorrow*, the good *Minister* that did me *so much good*, left the place, and went away, and my friends slighted me, and one thing added to another, made me begin to *despair* again; but then I know not how God *quieted* me again, which I wondered at, and was much *comforted*, and *confident*, that *God* would do me *good*, and I hoped and looked for it: And the very *next morning* as I was at *prayer*, God *wonderfully appeared*; and then was it, that *Christ* was *manifested* to my *spirit*, and I was as in a *trance* for a while, but after I awaked *full of joy*; and yet for all this, I was somewhat under *bondage* (me thoughts,) but the *Word* and *Means* of *Grace* did *confirm me*, and *comfort me*. In the times of the *Wars* in England. I was brought out of *Egypt* into the *Wilderness*. O! I was *much refreshed* by the *Lord* two or three years, and was much *contented*, and had his *teachings within me*, yea, and (many times) *without* his *outward instruments*; for I had his *Spirit*, *his voice* speaking *within me*, and *God* alone was with me, and no *strange god*. But when the *wars* began to cease, my *greatest trouble*, and that at which I took offence was, That we were so without the *means*, and without able *Ministers*; for now I could not be *satisfied*, but even *doted* on them, and could not *wait* with *patience*; for I had forgot now how *God* had *taught* me within before, and without them. Yet I *followed* and *hunted* after my *lovers*, having *mens persons in admiration*; and thus *God suffered me* for a while to go after them. A while after this, Colonel *Lambert* desired me to go to *Oxford*, and when I was to go, I made ready my self, packt up my cloaths and all, and rid away; most with *desire* for *communion* with *godly people* there, for (as yet) I could see no further ---. I heard *their disputes* between Master *Kiffith* and others, very hot, but saw nothing of *God* there, and was troubled at it, and could not after that hear *him* or others; but I went into a *Garden* alone my self mourning, and sat so a while under a *Wall*, and by and by came three men to me

[Page 405]

(passing that way) and *wondered* to see me so; they asked

me many *questions* ---. But a little after I *recovered* my self out of that *passion*, and went and told Colonel *Lambert* how it was with me; but he told me, I should not onely be taken off of *Ordinances*, but off of *believing* too, within a while, at which I was troubled, and went away *unsatisfied.* I was troubled to hear any *Preach*, and being once got to go to the *publick place*, I was so *tormented* that I could not bear it; for I could not *joyn with them*, nor *hear*, nor *pray*, nor had no *rest*, nor *comfort*, nor *ease*, nor could I *eat* or *drink*, but went (as I was wont) to bewail in a *Garden*, where I was mourning, when there came *one* unto me, and presently told me, That I was under the *opening* of the *fifth seal*, and very near the *sixth*, in the condition which I was in, and should be in.

Being thus afflicted, I desired to go home again from *Oxford,* and writ to my *Husband*, but the *Letter* was burnt; but I was in such a condition to see *Gods wrath* in every thing against me, as is not to be *expressed*; I was left in *all kindes of troubles* (as it were) at once, but here was all the *comfort* that was left me, and it was my *Heaven* in my *Hell*, that God would be glorified by my destruction: And so long I found some *ease*, and *content* (me thought,) and it did *joy* me at my *heart* to think, That all things should *go well* with the *Saints*, and they should be *happy*; though I had no *share with them*, yet these *things* did me *good*. And indeed, I dare boldly say when *my faith was gone*, and *hope gone*, and *all gone*, and *flew from me*, and could not be *seen* in me that I had any; yet love remained, and might be seen, and *was not gone*; noe, though I were to be cast presently *into Hell*; yet I could *love God*, and *was glad* he was to be *glorified*, though I *were* to be *ruined*; and so *I was glad* at the *welfare* of *Gods people*.

Thus *I was* three quarters of a year, and did not *now care for my self*, what became of me, for the *reasons* I said before; but it appeared *my deliverance was near at hand*, though (as yet) I had no assurance of salvation; yet at last I was carried out with a great confidence, that *light* was near at *hand*,

[Page 406]

And yet I met *with terrible* shakings for all that, which lit altogether upon *the flesh*, for the *spirit was free*: So that some *three years* agone, *God* came in upon my *spirit*, and gave me *full assurance*, and I heard a *voice* say ---, *And sorrow thou shalt see no more*. Then I *writ down* what *God* had *done* for me, and *writ* about to *my friends*; but yet I was *struck* in the *flesh* again, *which I wonder at;* and then I heard the *voice* again say, *It was sin that was suffering in me, and* the *flesh as the punishment of sin*; and so I *found* it was, for the *destruction of the flesh*; and ever after that *I found Christ in me*, ruling and reigning, and taking *all power to himself*, and he hath caught the *man-childe* up to God, which I brought forth. *i.e. The flesh*, (by his *incarnation*) and *I have found* in me (and do yet) his *judgement-seat sit*, to *judge* and *sentence sin*, and *lust*, and *corruption*, and his *throne* is there for *himself* to *sit*, and to *rule* by his own *Laws*: And thus it continues with me at this day, and the *Lord* leads me on, *higher and higher* in himself; and for that I see so much of him here in the *midst* of this *Church*, I desire to be *one also with you.*

CHAPTER 9

William Kiffen, John Locke, and the Bahama Adventurers of 1672

In the British Library in London there is an intriguing volume among the John Locke manuscripts whose title page reads 'Articles and Orders of the Company of Adventurers to the Bahama Islands, 1672'.[1] What is most significant about this manuscript for our considerations is that it records the involvement of the Baptist leader William Kiffen, along with ten others, including the philosopher John Locke (1632–1704), in the establishment of a West Indies trading company, part of whose business included the transporting to England of goods produced by the various slave plantations in the Caribbean. The manuscript has figured prominently in scholarly discussions about John Locke's attitudes to slavery, particularly as it seems contradictory to the philosophical arguments he put forth in his *Second Treatise of Civil Government* (1690), which condemned slavery as a institution incompatible with human freedom.[2] However, the manuscript also provides clear evidence of the Baptist merchant's involvement with the commercial side of the slave plantations, and, as far as I am aware, it has never been noted by biographers of Kiffen. Moreover, the manuscript invites a fresh consideration of Kiffen's contacts with the philosopher John Locke, something which has not been recognized by Baptist historians.

The purpose of this chapter is twofold. First, to provide the full text of two of the key documents relating to the establishment of the Bahama Adventurers Company, namely the charter of the Bahama Islands granted by Charles II in 1670 (Document #1), and the Bahama Adventurers manuscript itself (Document #2), and to offer some comments about the activities of the trading company and Kiffen's relationship with others associated with the enterprise. Several supplementary primary source documents will be included within this discussion, particularly as they pertain to the trading ship used by the Adventurers, namely the *Bahama Merchant* (Documents #3–4). Second, to note some of the subsequent contacts between William Kiffen and John Locke, which suggest that the two men remained in contact for several years after their joint involvement in the establishment of the Bahama Islands Company of Adventurers.

---

[1] BLL, Add MS 15,640. The manuscript appears to have marginal annotations in the hand of John Locke himself.

[2] Wayne Glausser, *Locke and Blake: A Conversation across the Eighteenth Century* (Gainesville, FL: University Press of Florida, 1998): 62-67, has a good discussion of this.

The Charter of the Bahama Islands (1670), and the British Library Manuscript of the Company of Adventurers to the Bahama Islands (Add MS 15,640)

In 1670 Charles II issued a charter granting the Bahama Islands to the Lords Proprietors of Carolina, six of his friends and supporters: Christopher, Duke of Albemarle,[3] William, Earle of Craven,[4] John Lord Berkeley,[5] Anthony Lord Ashley,[6] Sir George Carteret,[7] and Sir Peter Colleton.[8] The charter was recorded in Letters Patent C 66/3122, part 9, although it was also published as a sixteen-page pamphlet (see Document #1). Clearly the charter followed the basic pattern of most of Charles II's colonial charters, treating the geographical area as if it were a medieval fiefdom, with powers and authority being handed down to his feudal tenants-in-chief (that is, the Proprietors).[9] The six Proprietors of the Bahamas had full rights and possession of all of the Bahama Islands, and were charged with the establishment of 'good and happy Government' (line 101) there, including building churches, setting up law courts and creating a social infrastructure conducive to commerce. As far as the trading activities were concerned, the charter contains several interesting clauses which describe the rights and responsibilities of the Proprietors. For example, they had fishing and whaling rights, and mineral rights to all precious metals (notably gold and silver), and precious stones and gems found on the islands (lines 33–42). The Proprietors were obliged to pay the king one quarter of all gold and silver ore found in the Bahamas, and to deliver to him one pound of fine silver should he ever happen to visit the island personally (lines 80–87). In order to encourage the development of the colony as a trading centre the charter granted free license to transport to the Bahama Islands any goods and merchandise deemed necessary (lines 250–258).

On the basis of this charter the Proprietors of the Bahama Islands entered into a business agreement with a newly-established trading company known as the Bahama Adventurers. The British Library manuscript recounts the establishment of the Bahama Adventurers Company in 1672. The manuscript contains thirty-two pages of text, divided into three main sections: articles of agreement between the Lords Proprietors of the Bahama Islands and the Bahama Adventurers (pages 1-12);

---

[3] Monck (1653–88), the son of General George Monck, was an army officer and colonial governor.

[4] Craven (c.1608–97) was an army officer and royal servant.

[5] Berkeley (c.1607–78) was an army officer and courtier, who served as Lord-Lieutenant of Ireland from 1670–72, and as an ambassador to France from 1675–77.

[6] Cooper (1621–83) was president of the Council of Trade and Foreign Plantations from 1672–76, he was appointed Lord Chancellor on 17 November 1672 and under-treasurer of the Exchequer in April 1672. He served as Lord Chancellor until 9 November 1673. E.E. Rich, 'The First Earl of Shaftesbury's Colonial Policy', *Royal Historical Society Transactions*, 5th Series 7 (1957): 47-70, discusses his role as a colonial proprietor.

[7] Carteret (1610–80) was a naval officer and civil administrator.

[8] Colleton was Deputy-Governor of Barbados from 1673–74.

[9] Michael Craton and Gail Saunders, *Islanders in the Stream: A History of the Bahamian People* (Athens, GA: The University of Georgia Press, 1992): 93-94, discuss the charter.

articles of agreement between the Bahama Adventurers for the running of their company (pages 15-27); minutes of four business meetings of the Bahama Adventurers held during September-November 1672 (pages 29-32) (pages 13, 14 and 28 are blank).[10]

The Articles of Agreement between the Lords Proprietors of the Bahama Islands and the Bahama Adventurers (pages 1-12)

The manuscript records that on 4 September 1672 these Lords Proprietors of Bahama Islands established a trading company of Merchant Adventurers consisting of eleven wealthy investors: Richard Kingdon,[11] William Kiffen, Edward Thornburgh,[12] John Mapletoft,[13] John Baynes, Henry Aldrich, John Locke, Thomas Stringer,[14] John Darrell,[15] Richard Davy and Peter Jones (lines 1–37).

The articles of agreement between these two groups contain eight numbered sections. In the first section the details of the arrangements for the first subscription were outlined and provisions made for the increase of investment and additional stock by the eleven subscribers, should they so be inclined (lines 38–116). The basic idea was that the eleven Adventurers collectively were to raise between £1,600–£2,000 before 29 September 1672 in order to establish the trading company (lines 59–63), and then share the profits proportionally once it became successful. The manuscript later records that various amounts were committed by the eleven subscribers; John Locke, and William Kiffen both invested £100 (lines 713–715 and 719–721), although Locke soon took over the £100 investment of his friend John Mapletoft (lines 780–781).[16] The second section established a thirty-one year lease for each of the subscribers on land within the Bahama Islands, namely 12,000 acres on the island of New Providence (modern Nassau) and 12,000 acres of land on one or more of the other islands in the Bahamas. They were to pay a rent of one peppercorn per year for the period of twenty-one years for this land, and after the expiration of the twenty-one years to pay a rent of one penny per acre (lines 117–

[10] Several pages at the end of the volume were used as a ledger for the household accounts of Anne King, the wife of Locke's cousin Peter King.

[11] Kingdon was a Commissioner of Excise from 1665–77.

[12] Thornburgh was the London-based secretary to the Gentlemen Planters of Barbados from February 1671–77.

[13] Mapletoft (1631–1721) was a physician and a Church of England clergyman.

[14] Stringer (c.1639–72) was a steward to the Anthony Cooper, the Earle of Shaftesbury, and lived in Exeter House, along with Shaftesbury and John Locke.

[15] Darrell (or Dorrell) had lived and worked in Bermuda for a number of years. He and Hugh Wentworth wrote a letter to the Lords Proprietors of Carolina on 17 February 1670 originally encouraging the establishment of a colony in the Bahama Islands. See PRO 30/24/48/55, pages 4, 6. Alan Burns, *History of the British West Indies* (London: George Allen & Unwin, 2nd edn, 1965): 358-60, discusses Wentworth's career.

[16] Maurice Cranston, *John Locke: A Biography* (Oxford: Oxford University Press, 1985): 155.

175). Section three set out conditions and arrangements for the Adventurers to have rights and royalties on natural commodities found on or around the islands, including gold, silver, minerals, gems, ambergrice, whales, pearls, and shipwrecks. These conditions were to be in effect for thirty-one years (lines 176–215). Ambergrice in particular was much sought after in the Bahamas, as is evidenced by a letter sent by Richard Lilburne to the Bahama Adventurers on 9 August 1674.[17] He notes that following a storm coasters go in search of ambergrice around the Bahamas and 'travell some 100 miles upon the bays before they finde any'. Section four similarly granted to the Adventurers rights and royalties on timber resources on the islands, notably on brasiletto wood and cedar. A price of £5 per tonne, payable to the Adventurers, was set on all timber harvested on the islands (lines 216–267). Section five relieved the Adventurers from having to pay capital rents and duties on their property, with the exception of a levy of one-quarter of all gold and silver ore found on the islands which remained payable to the king (lines 268–291). Section six put in place provision for paying a proprietory governor of the Bahama Islands. His salary was set at the rate of ten per cent of the original subscription raised, although provision was made for agreed increases and penalties put into place should the Lords Proprietors of the Bahamas refuse to hand over the governor's share out of the subscription monies they had received (lines 292-347). Section seven makes provision for the Adventurers to use the company stock to supply the inhabitants of the Bahama Islands with necessary merchandise and to limit their profits in so doing to no more than 25% of expenditure (lines 347–361). Section eight allowed the Lords Proprietors to nominate one additional person to have an equal share in the management of the company as the eleven subscribers had (lines 362–371). The articles of agreement were then signed by five of the six Lords Proprietors of the Bahama Islands, with eleven other men signing as witnesses of the transaction (lines 371–390). The one Lords Proprietor who did not sign the agreement was Sir Peter Colleton, but his absence was no doubt due to the fact that he was serving as Deputy-Governor in Barbados at the time.

The Bahama Island venture was by no means a financial certainty; by its very nature the establishment of the trading company was risky business. Indeed, the islands had proven economically unviable in the recent past and the number of people available to work the plantations was not large. Indeed, one census of the Bahamas from 1671 recorded that the total population resident in New Providence was 903, 403 out of which were slaves.[18] Even some of the men deeply committed to the Bahama venture advised caution about the best way to establish plantations on the islands. Perhaps the best example of this is contained in a letter written to Locke by Sir Peter Colleton on 28 May 1673. Colleton, who had much experience living and working in the Caribbean, wrote,

---

[17] TNA, PRO 30/24/49, page 58.

[18] A. Talbot Bethell, *The Early Settlers of the Bahama Islands* (Norfolk: Rounce & Wortley, 1930): 63-71. Michael Craton, *A History of the Bahamas* (London: Collins, 1968): 70, discusses the figures.

> I find I am your partner in the Bahama trade which will turne to accompt if you meddle not with planting, but if you plant otherwise then for provizion for your factor you will have your whole stock drowned in a plantation and bee never the better for it, planting is my trade and I thinke I may without vanity say I understand it as well as most men, and I am sure I am not deceived in this particular, if other men will plant there, I mean the Bahamas, hinder them not, they improve our province, but I would neither have you nor my lord [Shaftesbury] engage in it.[19]

Articles of Agreement for the Running of the Bahama Adventurers Company (pages 15-27)

The articles of agreement between the eleven men who made up the Bahama Adventurers is dated 4 September 1672 (lines 395–396) and opens with a listing of the eleven, together with an indication of the social ranking of each and some description of where they lived (lines 401–423). The legal relationship between the Proprietors of the Bahama Islands and the Bahama Adventurers is summarized, including the need to raise between £1,600-£2,000 in stock to establish the company (lines 424–467). The articles of agreement themselves are then set out in twelve numbered sections.

The first section allows the company to elect its treasurer and governor from among their number once the subscription costs have been successfully raised (468–475). The second section spells out that whatever amount any of the subscribers pledged to the scheme would not come oblidgeing until the overall total of between £1,600-£2,000 was achieved (lines 476–483). The third section deals with arrangements for the subscribers to have their money refunded should the requisite total fail to be reached (lines 484–506). The provision for an alternative subscriber to be enlisted is also explicitly mentioned (lines 493–495). Section four sets out how the subscribers, by a majority vote, may choose to increase the stock (lines 507–547). Subscribers were to pay to the treasurer their proportionate share increase within fourteen days, or be liable for a penalty amounting to £2 per hundred per month. Any subscriber who failed to meet his proportionate share obligations in this regard was barred from holding one of the offices of the company or voting in the business meetings (lines 534–539). Section five deals with voting rights for the subscribers, giving each of them in financial good standing one vote for each £100 invested. A subscriber in good standing was allowed to stand for the office of treasurer or governor (lines 548–554). Section six sets out provisions for business meetings to be held in the company (lines 555–579). Business meetings were to take place twice and were called by either the treasurer of governor. The first business meeting was to take place on the first Saturday in April, where officers were to be elected and a full financial declaration about the state of the company was to be produced. The second business meeting was to take place on the first Saturday in

[19] TNA, PRO 30/24/48, No 90 (published in E.S. De Beer (ed.), *The Correspondence of John Locke, Volume One* (Oxford: Clarendon Press, 1976): 379-380).

September, where any matters pertaining to the good management of the company were discussed. The governor or treasurer was empowered to call an additional business meeting if it was thought necessary. Section seven gave authority to a duly-called meeting of at least half of the members of the company to make rules and orders for the management of its stock and trade; these rules and orders were to be binding upon all the Adventurers (lines 580–590). Section eight set out provisions for the payment of a dividend from the profits and proceeds of the stock whenever this was felt appropriate by a general meeting of the company (lines 591–596). The Adventurers are also reminded here of their responsibility in paying a fine of one penny per acre to the Lords Proprietors for their land holdings in the Bahama Islands (lines 596–601). Section nine set out arrangements for the distribution of profits and proceeds owned by the company once the thirty-one year contract had expired (lines 602–621). These were to be equally divided to the Adventurers, or in whatever arrangements were agreed at a business meeting attended by a majority of the members. Section ten provided for the full benefits and profits owed to an Adventurer to be passed on to his heirs should he die. The inheritors had to declare their desire to be included in these arrangements, and thereby did accept the benefits, and risks, of the company (lines 622–642). Section eleven allowed for an Adventurer to dispose of his stock in the company, and gave whoever received it full rights as an Adventurer (lines 643–651). Section twelve made provision for any disagreements that might arise between the Adventurers to be resolved within the company itself and without recourse to law courts. If needed an arbitrator or arbitrators would be appointed whose decision was binding upon all parties (lines 652–692).

The Business Meetings of the Bahama Adventurers (pages 29-32)

The first business meeting took place on 9 September 1672 at Exeter House. Significantly, this was the residence of Sir Anthony Cooper, the Earl of Shaftesbury, one of the Proprietors of the Bahama Islands. It was also the home of John Locke, Shaftesbury's private secretary and colonial administrator, who lived with his employer from 1667–75. Six of the eleven Adventurers were present at this meeting; Kiffen was not among them (lines 752–762).

The second business meeting took place on 23 October 1672, again at Exeter House. Eight of the eleven Adventurers were present at this meeting; again Kiffen was not among them (lines 782–798). The third business meeting took place on 8 November 1672, on board a trading ship named *Bahamas Merchant*. This time only five of the original eleven Adventurers was present, although it is probably significant that Captain John Darrell, who was an experienced sea captain in the West Indies, was among them. It is probable that the business meeting took place upon the ship because it was one of the ships in use by the Adventurers and was being prepared for a voyage to the Bahama Islands. It seems that the ship was classified as a brigantine, a two masted ship of about 200 tons and eighty feet in length, with 10–12 guns and a crew of up to 100 men. According to a petition submitted by John Baynes to the Privy Council in Whitehall on 29 January 1675, the ship was purchased by the Bahama Adventurers in July 1672 (see Document #3). Their aim was to refit the ship and use it for trade in the Bahamas. Interestingly, the ship was bought from a George Potts who purchased it from the Commissioners of Prizes for the Port of London for £400.[20] The ship was originally named *Old Abraham*, out of Amsterdam, and it had been captured with a load of grain on board in April of 1672 (Britain had declared war against the Dutch on 7 April).[21] Indeed on 29 April the Treasury Lords, led by the Earl of Shaftesbury, wrote to the Customs Commissioners about the need to sell the grain aboard the *Old Abraham* as quickly as possible, so that it not spoil, and gave instructions about taxing the merchandise appropriately.[22] Now, two and a half years later, Baynes and his fellow Bahama Adventurers were petitioning the Privy Council for assistance in the difficulties that they were having using the ship in their trade; apparently some port authorities did not regard the *Bahama Merchant* as a free ship and were levying extra taxes upon her. Charles II and the Privy Council referred the matter to the Lord High Treasurer to see what may be done with respect to the *Bahama Merchant*. The success of the petition seems to have been successful, which is hardly surprising given that two of the Proprietors of the Bahama Islands (the Earl of Craven, and Lord Berkeley) were members of the Privy Council in attendance at the time.

One or two details about the activities of the *Bahama Merchant* have survived. For example, the ship is mentioned in a letter dated 16 December 1673 written by Samuel Pepys to Colonel Piper, the governor of Plymouth, instructing him to release a crewman from the *Bahama Merchant* who had been impressed for service aboard another navy vessel.[23] Pepys mentions that he had been in contact with Sir George Carteret, one of the Lords Commissioners of the Admiralty about the *Bahama Merchant*, which was docked at Plymouth.[24] Pepys also describes the ship as 'a ship of value, and not yet come to her port of unladling', presumably London. No doubt Sir George Carteret also had, as one of the Proprietors of the Bahama Islands, a vested interest in ensuring that the ship be allowed to complete her journey to London with whatever her cargo was, as soon as possible. We also learn from Pepys' letter that the master of the *Bahama Merchant* at the time was named Thomas Fasted.

---

[20] Potts was apparently an employee of the Prize Office and took advantage of his position to obtain prize ships at bargain prices (see TNA, SP 29/220, page 62).

[21] A letter from Silas Taylor in Harwich to Joseph Williamson, the Secretary of State, dated 9 April 1675 states, 'a prize called the *old Abraham* of Amsterdam was comeing in hither & ran upon the Andrews, where with strong help I got her off & send her up to London, she is 200 tun, laden with Barley & Rye of w[hi]ch I have wrote at Large to ye Prize office' (TNA, SP 29/305, page 125).

[22] TNA, T 51/43, page 346.

[23] J.R. Tanner (ed.), *Naval Manuscripts in the Pepysian Library at Magdalene College, Cambridge, Volume II, Admiralty Letters* (Publications of the Naval Records Society Volume 27; London: Navy Records Society, 1904): 173. The document is Letter 893.

[24] TNA, SP 29/338, page 107, records that two vessels from the Barbados arrived at Plymouth on 12 December 1673. It is likely that one of these was the *Bahama Merchant*.

The *Bahama Merchant* is also mentioned in two letters written from the West Indies to John Locke. The first is from Sir Peter Colleton in Barbados and dates from sometime in October 1673.[25] It is especially interesting because Colleton notes that the *Bahama Merchant* had recently arrived 'whom Captain Dorrell hath luckily sent here to seek a fraught and I hope he will make upwards of 1000ld: fraught of what he takes in here'. Moreover, Colleton goes on to argue that shipping brasiletta wood from the Bahamas to England was a loss-making exercise, and suggests that sugar loaded from Barbados would be a much more lucrative business. Indeed, Dorrell may have even been on the *Bahama Merchant* for her first voyage to the West Indies; he was in London in November 1672 (see below), but was in the West Indies by early 1673. The second letter is from Locke's Quaker friend Isaac Rush in New Providence and is dated 10 August 1674.[26] Rush records that he had received Locke's letter which had been sent via the *Bahama Merchant*, clearly indicating that the ship of the Bahama Adventurers was being used to carry mail between England and those involved in the West Indies themselves.

In addition, there is record within the official reports of the harbourmaster, Captain Philip Lanyon, detailing that the *Bahama Merchant* docked in Plymouth on 20 January 1677. This entry misnames the ship as the *Bohemian Merchant* of London, but notes that her master was William Fowle, and that the ship had arrived from New Providence and was carrying brasiletta wood.[27]

In connection with this report, there is also a letter from the harbourmaster Philip Lanyon to Joseph Williamson, the Secretary of State, dated 21 January 1677 (see Document #4). This letter states that in addition to its cargo the ship transported the disgraced governor of the Bahama Islands, John Wentworth, as a prisoner to England.[28] Apparently the ship had sailed from England to America the year before, transporting the new proprietory governor of the Bahama Islands, Charles Chillingworth, to New Providence in the process. The intention was that the ship first called at Jamestown in Virginia and take on a load of tobacco to be brought back to England before calling in at the Bahama Islands on the return leg. However, the *Bahama Merchant* arrived in Jamestown in September of 1676 just after a rebellion led by Nathaniel Bacon had disrupted the colony. This revolt meant that alternative arrangements had to be made and the ship sailed from Virginia without the tobacco, and arrived at New Providence where she took on board a load of Brasiletto wood before setting sail for England.

The *Bahama Merchant* was also involved in another celebrated incident in 1698. This took place while Nicholas Webb was the proprietory governor of the Bahama

---

[25] BLO, MS Locke c6, pages 215-216 (published in De Beer (ed.), *Correspondence of John Locke, Volume One*, 392-396).

[26] TNA, PRO 30/24/49, pages 60-61 (published in De Beer (ed.), *Correspondence of John Locke, Volume One*, 407-408).

[27] TNA, SP 29/390, page 169.

[28] TNA, SP 29/390, page 160. Wentworth had served as proprietory governor from December of 1671–76, but was frequently in trouble with the Proprietors of the Bahama Islands.

Islands and was attempting to deal with the rampant activity of pirates in the West Indies. It seems that Webb appointed a mulatto named Read Elding to head a task force of five ships to track down and capture a notorious pirate named Kelly. Elding never caught up with Kelly, but he did capture the *Bahama Merchant*, which he claimed he found deserted (the crew of the ship feared they were being chased by pirates and fled ashore).[29] Later, however, the owner of the ship, a John Edwards, made a complaint about this incident and accused Webb and Elding of outright piracy. Bizarrely, the lost crew of the *Bahama Merchant* reappeared in February of 1699 and the matter was summarily dealt with in the Admiralty Court in Nassau.[30] It is unlikely that the ship was by this stage still in active use by the Bahama Adventurers.

The fourth business meeting of the Bahama Adventurers took place on 11 November 1672, this time at Austin Fryers. Here six of the original eleven Adventurers were present, and William Kiffen is listed among them. Indeed, it is highly likely that the meeting took place at Kiffen's home (he lived in Austin Fryers from about 1668 until at least 1682); the fact that his name is listed as the first of the members attending suggests that he may have hosted the meeting. Two matters were decided at this business meeting. First, it was decided that the identifying mark for goods transported by the Adventurers should be a stylized capital 'B' (lines 825–827). Second, it was agreed that Peter Jones was to be appointed the accountant and clerke of the Adventurers (lines 828–829)

It is uncertain what happened to the Bahama Adventurers Company, or how long William Kiffen remained an active member of it. It is likely that the fall of the Earl of Shaftesbury from power in 1675 meant that interest in the company waned among Shaftesbury's network of supporters and fellow investors. There is some suggestion that John Locke sold his stock in the Bahama Adventurers in 1677,[31] and it is quite likely that Kiffen did the same.

---

[29] The incident is noted in a report from Edward Randolph to the Lords of Trade dated 16 March 1699 (*Edward Randolph: Letters and Papers from the New England, Middle and Southern Colonies in America, with other Documents relating Chiefly to the Vacating of the Royal Charter of the Colony of Massachusetts Bay, 1676–1703, Volume 5* (Boston, MA: The Prince Society, 1899): 199); in a letter from Randolph to the Board of Trade dated 27 May 1700 (*Edward Randolph: Including his Letters and Official Papers from the New England, Middle, and Southern Colonies in America, and the West Indies, 1678–1700, Volume 7* (Boston, MA: The Prince Society, 1909): 627).

[30] TNA, CO 5/1259, pages 395-408; and TNA, CO 5/1288, pages 56-61, discuss the incident.

[31] Maurice Cranston, *John Locke: A Biography* (Oxford: Oxford University Press, 1985): 115, states 'The £100 stock he bought in the Bahama Adventurers in 1675 he sold the following year for £127 10s.'

William Kiffen and John Locke—An Acquaintance Extended

Finally, one or two other contacts between William Kiffen and John Locke are worth noting, for they demonstrate an on-going relationship between the two men following the contact afforded by the Bahama Adventurers episode. For example, there is a letter dated 22 May 1678 from a Robert Huntington writing from Aleppo in Syria to John Locke.[32] Interestingly, the letter is addressed 'For Mr John Locke at Mr Kiffins a Merchant in Austin Friers in London'. Huntingdon was chaplain to the Levant Company's factory in Aleppo from 1671–81, and it is likely that he knew of Kiffen through the Baptist's mercantile contacts (Kiffen's son Henry and his son-in-law Benjamin Hewling were both agents of the Levant Company in Aleppo in the early 1680s).

Even more significant are the journal entries Locke made while travelling around France in 1675–79. Locke mentions Kiffen by name at four points within his journals; three of the entries also note the involvement of Thomas Stringer, who was, along with Kiffen and Locke, one of the eleven Bahama Adventurers. The first of these is dated 17 March 1676 while Locke was in Montpellier and involves him sending some grape vines to London which were to be picked up by Kiffen. Locke records,

> Tues[day] Mar[ch] 17
> Rain I sent ye bill of ladeling for the vines
> to ~~Englan~~ Mr Stringer. They were shipd at
> Bourdeaux 5 March by Pierre Rocaure
> on the ship *James* of Yarmouth, Master
> Tho: Paris, consigned to Mr Kiffin at
> London. Freight five shillings.[33]

The second entry is similar and is dated 24 March 1676. It records that Locke sent some oranges to London, again consigning them to Kiffen:

> Tues[day] Mar[ch] 24
> Sent the bill of Loading for the oranges
> to Mr Stringer. Shipped by Pierre Rocaure
> on ye *Recovery* of Yarmouth at Borde
> aux, Nathaniel Locke, Master, consignd
> to Mr Kiffin at London, 13 Mar[ch] [16]76. Freight 8
> s[hillings].[34]

---

[32] BLO, MS Locke c 11, folio 247-248 (printed in De Beer (ed.), *Correspondence of John Locke, Volume One*, 571).

[33] BLO, MS Locke f1, page 152 (printed in John Lough, *Locke's Travels in France 1675–79* (Cambridge: Cambridge University Press, 1953): 56). Lough was apparently unaware of Kiffen's role as a wealthy trading merchant. He suggested that Kiffen was a member of Shaftesbury's household.

[34] BLO. MS Locke f1, page 159 (printed in Lough, *Locke's Travels in France*, 60).

The third entry is dated 10 May 1677 and records that Locke turned to Kiffen and asked his assistance in making some credit transfer arrangements. The entry apparently shows Locke replacing his financial agent in London, Sir Patience Ward, with Kiffen. It reads,

> Munday May 10
> I received of Mr Tho Arundell at
> Bourdeaux 255£ or 85 escus upon a
> ~~bill~~ letter of credit of S[i]r Patience Wards
> for 20li sterling, & according to the direction
> of the letter & Mr Arundell's demands who
> writ the bills, signed two bills upon S[i]r Pati
> ence Ward himself, but however writ
> away the same day to Mr Kiffin to desire him
> to repay the 20li to S[i]r Patience Ward &
> take his discharge.[35]

The fourth entry shows Kiffen continuing to act as Locke's financial agent. This is written 9 June 1677 while Locke was in Paris and it reads,

> Wed[nesday] Jun[e] 9
> Recd of Mr Peletier upon a bill of Mr
> Kiffin's of 13 7ber 1676 £315-15-9 for
> 25li sterling (v. leger, p. 89) p[ai]d by Mr Stringer.[36]

Kiffen is also named in a number of entries within Locke's account books which were kept by Thomas Stringer. For example, a page headed 'Received for Mr Lock' has an entry dated January 1678 which reads,

Janu[ary 23	Rec of Mr Kiffen for Silks	£120	19s 03 ¼ d
	Rec more for Silks	50	00 00
31	Rec more for Silks	66	10 $8^{3}/_{4}$[37]

Similarly, a page headed 'Money disbursed for Mr Lock' has an entry dated 14 September 1676 which reads,

> Sept 14 P[ai]d Mr Kiffen to returne to Paris £25 00 00[38]

[35] BLO, MS Locke f2, page 133 (printed in Lough, *Locke's Travels in France*, 142). BLO, MS Locke b1, page 25, records that Thomas Stringer paid £100 to Sir Patience Ward for a bill of exchange on 7 January 1676, and £20 to him for a bill of exchange on 4 June 1677.

[36] BLO, MS Locke f2, page 151 (printed in Lough, *Locke's Travels in France*, 149).

[37] BLO, MS Locke b1, page 24.

[38] BLO, MS Locke b1, page 25.

This is a difficult entry to pin down. On the surface it suggests that Kiffen had arranged Locke's journey from London to Paris which he made in November 1675, and that Kiffen was thus being reimbursed for arranging Locke's second visit to the city (his first visit to Paris was in 1672). However, the date of the entry seems too late for this. Alternatively, it could be read as Locke paying Kiffen £25 for him [Kiffen] to return to Paris. However, there is no other record of Kiffen making such a journey to France. Thus, it is more likely that the entry is a reference not to the city of Paris but to Thomas Paris, the Master of the ship *Recovery* on which Locke had sent a load of grape vines back to London in March of 1676 (see above). In effect, it appears that Kiffen was paid £25 to help settle a debt Locke had with the master of the ship.

Finally, there is also an entry for September 1678 which reads,

Sept 3	pd Mr Kiffen's man mo[ney] he disbursed			
	for a letter	£0	01	00

All of which suggests that Locke was still in contact with Kiffen during his long stay in France, at least six years after the two men had joined in the Bahama Adventurers Company.

Finally, it is perhaps important to note that the involvement of William Kiffen with the Bahama Adventurers was not his only excursion into the world of the West Indian colonies. There is record of Kiffen petitioning the Council of State on 31 May 1655 for a warrant to send thirty horses and 600 pair of shoes to the plantations in Barbados.[39] At the time Jamaica and the West Indies was a favourite Cromwellian interest, and Kiffen was generally supportive of the Lord Protector in his foreign policy, particularly when it had a religious motivation as a rationale. Interestingly, the petition of Kiffen specifically mentions that 'Without releife from England the Island of Barbados and plantations belonging to England are not able to subsist.' Kiffen is described as a merchant within these documents, stressing the commercial dimension of his involvement.

Documents

#1: *The Charter of the Bahama Islands* (1670)

[Page 1]

The
Charter
of the

[39] TNA, CO 1/12, page 110. Also see TNA, SP 25/76, page 110; and TNA, SP 25/112, page 160, where warrants were issued allowing Kiffen to transport the horses to 'the Barbados and other plantations in America'.

Bahama Islands

Charles the Second, by the Grace of God, King of *England, Scotland, France*, and *Ireland*, Defender of the Faith, &c. To All to whom these presents shall come greetings.

Know Yee that We for divers good Causes and Considerations, us hereunto especially moving, of our especial Grace, certain Knowledge, and meer Motion: Have Given and Granted, and by these Presents, for us, our Heirs and Successors, Do Give and Grant unto our Right truly and Right intirely Beloved Cosen *Christopher* Duke of *Albemarle*, our Right truly and Right Well-beloved Cozen and Councellour *William* Earl of *Craven*, our Right trust and Well-beloved Councellours, *John* Lord *Berkeley*, *Anthony* Lord *Ashley*, Chancellour and Under-Treasurer

[Page 2]

of our Exchequer; Sir *George Carterett* Knight, and Baronet, Vice-Chamberlain of our Houshold; and our Trusty and Well-beloved Sir *Peter Colleton* Baronet, their Heirs and Assigns. All those Islands called *Bahama, Clentheria, Vtanis, Providence, Inagua*, and all other those Islands lying in the Degrees of Twenty and Two, to Twenty and seven North Latitude, commonly known by the Name of the *Bahama Islands*, or the Islands of the *Lucayes*.

Together with all and singular Ports, Harbours, Bays, Rivers, and Islets belonging unto the Islands aforesaid; with the Fishing of all Sorts of Fish; Whales, Sturgeons, and all other Royal Fishes in the Sea, Bays, Islets, and Rivers within the Premises; and the Fish therein taken: Together with the Royalty of the Sea upon the Coast within the limits aforesaid.

And moreover, All Vains, Mines, and Quarries, as well discovered as not discovered, of Gold, Silver, Gems, precious Stones, and all other whatsoever, be it of Stones, Mettals, or any other thing whatsoever found, or to be found within the Islands and Limits aforesaid.

And furthermore, The Patronage and Avowsons of all the Churches and Chapels (which as Christian Religion shall increase) within the Islands, Isles, Islets, and Limites aforesaid shall happen hereafter to be Erected; together with License and Power to Build and Found Churches, Chapels, and Ortories in convenient and fit Places within the said Bounds and Limits, and to cause them to be Dedicated and Consecrated according to the Ecclesiastical Laws of our Kingdom of *England:* Together with all and singular the like, and as ample Rights, Jurisdictions, Priviledges, Prerogativ es, Royalties Liberties, Immunities, and Franchises of what kind soever with in the Islands, Isles, Islets, and Limits aforesaid

To Have, Use, Exercise and Enjoy: the same as amply fully, and in as ample manner as any Bishop of *Durham* in our Kingdom of *England*, ever heretofore Held, Used, or Enjoyed; or of Right ought or could Have, Use, or Enjoy.

And them, the said *Christopher* Duke of *Albemarle*, *William* Earl of *Craven*, *John* Lord *Berkeley, Anthony*

[Page 3]

Lord *Ashley*, Sir *George Carterett,* and Sir *Peter Colleton,* their Heires and Assigns.

We do by these Presents for us, our Heires and Successors, Make, Create, and Constitute the true and absolute Lords and Proprietors of the said Islands; and of all other, the Premises, saving always the Faith, Allegiance, and Sovereign Dominion due to us, our Heires and Successors, for the same.

To Have and to Hold, Possess, and Enjoy the said Islands, Isles, Islets, and all and singular other the Premises, unto them the said *Christopher* Duke of *Albemarle*, *William* Earl of *Craven*, *John* Lord *Berkeley*, *Anthony* Lord *Ashley*, Sir *George Carterett*, and Sir *Peter Colleton*, their Heires and Assigns for ever.

To be Holden of us, our Heires, and Successors, as Tenure of our Mannor of *East-Greenwich* in our County of *Kent*, in free and common Soccage, and not *in Capite*, or by Knights-service: Yielding and paying yearly to us, our Heirs and Successors for the same, the Fourth part of all Gold and Silver Oar, which within the Limits hereby granted, shall from time to time happen to be found. And also Yeilding and paying to us, our Heirs and Successors as often as we or they shall happen to come or enter in to the said Islands, one Pound of fine Silver.

And forasmuch as we have Made and Ordained the aforsaid *Christopher* Duke of *Albemarle*, *William* Earl of *Craven*, *John* Lord *Berkeley*, *Anthony* Lord *Ashley*, Sir *George Carterett*, and Sir *Peter Colleton*, their Heirs and Assigns, the True Lords and Proprietors of the

Islands aforesaid: Know ye therefore moreover that we reposing especial Trust and Confidence in their Fidelity, Wisdom, Justice, and Provident Circumspection for us, our Heires and Successors. Do Grant full and absolute Power by Vertue of these Presents, to them the said *Christopher* Duke of *Albemarle*, *William* Earl of *Craven*, *John* Lord *Berkeley*, *Anthony* Lord *Ashley*, Sir *George Carterett*, and Sir *Peter Colleton,* and their Heires and Assigns, for the good and happy Government of the said Islands, full Power and Authority to Erect, Constitute, and make several Counties, Baronies, and

[Page 4]

Colonies, of, and within the aforesaid Islands, Lands, and Hereditaments, in, and by these Presents granted, or mentioned to be granted as aforesaid, with several and distinct Jurisdictions, Power, Liberties and Priviledges: And also to Make, Ordain, and Enact, and under their Seals to publish any Laws and Constitutions whatsoever, either appertaining to the Publick Estate of the said Islands, or of any distinct or particular County, Barony, or Colony, of or within the sme, or to the private Utility of particular Persons, according to their best Discretion, by and with the Advice, Assent and Approbation of the Free-Men of the same Islands, or of the Free-Men of the County, Barony, or Colony for which such Laws or Constitution shall be made, or of the greater part of them, or of their Delegates or Deputies, whom for Enacting of the said Laws, When, and as often as need shall require. We Will, that the said *Christopher* Duke of *Albemarle*, *William* Earl of *Craven*, *John* Lord *Berkeley*, *Anthony* Lord *Ashley*, Sir *George Carterett*, and Sir *Peter Colleton*, and their Heires and Assigns, shall from time, to tikme, Assembled in such Manner and Form as to them shall seem best; and the same Law duely to Execute upon the People within the said Islands, County, Barony, or Colony, and the Limits thereof for the time being, or which shall be Constituted under the Power or Government of them, or any of them; wither failing towards the said Islands, or returning from thence towards *England*, or any other of ours or Forreign Dominions, by Imposition of Penalty, Imrpisonment, or any other Punishment. Yea, if it shall be needful, and the quality of the Offence require it, by taking away Member and Life, either by them the said *Christopher* Duke of *Albemarle*, *William* Earl of *Craven*, *John* Lord *Berkeley*, *Anthony* Lord

Ashley, Sir *George Carterett*, and Sir *Peter Colleton,* and their Heires, or by them or their Deputies, Lieutenants, Judges, Justices, Magistrates, Officers and Ministers to be Ordained or Appointed according to the Tenor and true intention of these Presents. And likewise to Erect and mane any Court or Courts whatsoever or Judicature or otherwise, as shall be requisite; and to

[Page 5]

Appoint and Establish any Judges, or Justices, Magistrates, or Officers whatsoever, as well within the said Islands as at Sea, in such Manner and Form as unto the said *Christopher* Duke of *Albemarle*, *William* Earl of *Craven*, *John* Lord *Berkeley*, *Anthony* Lord *Ashley*, Sir *George Carterett*, and Sir *Peter Colleton*, or their Heires shall seem most convenient: Also to Remit, Release, Pardon and Abolish, either before Judgment or after, all Crimes and Offences whatsoever against the said Laws, and to do all and every othr thing and things which unto the compleat Establishment of Justice unto Courts, Sessions, and Forms of Judicature and Manners of proceedings therein do belong, although in these Presents express Mention is not made therof, and by Judges by him or them delegated to Award, Process, hold Pleas, and determine in all the said Courts and Places of Judicature, all Actions, Suits, and Causes whatsoever, as well Criminal as Civil, Real, Mixt, Personal, or of any other kind or nature whatwoever; which Laws so as aforesaid to be Published. Our will and pleasure is, and we do enjoyn, require and command, shall be absolute, Firm, and Available in Law; and that all the Leige People of us, our Heirs and Successors within the said Islands; to observe and keep the same inviolably in those Parts so far as they concern them, under the Pains and Penalties therein expressed, or to be expressed: Provided nevertheless that the said Laws be consonant to Reason, and as near as may be conveniently agreeable to the Laws and Custome of this our Kingdom of *England*.

And because such Assemblies of Free-holders cannot be so suddainly called as there may be occasion to require the same: We do therefore by these Presents, Give and Grant unto the said *Christopher* Duke of *Albemarle*, *William* Earl of *Craven*, *John* Lord *Berkeley*, *Anthony* Lord *Ashley*, Sir *George Carterett*, and Sir *Peter Colleton;* their Heires and Assigns by themselves or their Magistrates in that behalf lawfully Authorized, full Power and

Authority from time to time, to make and ordain fit and wholsome Orders and Ordinances within the aforesaid Islands, or any County, Barony or Province, of

[Page 6]

or within the same, to be kept and observed as well for the keeping of the Peace, as for the better Government of the People there abiding, and to publish the same to All to whom it may concern, which Ordinance we do by these Presents strictly Charge and Command to be inviolably observed within the said Islands under the Penalties therein expressed, so as such Ordinances be reasonable and not repugnant or contrary, but as near as may be agreeable to the Laws and Statues of this our Kingdom of *England*, and so as the same Ordinances do not extend to the binding, charging or taking away of the Rights or Interest of any Person or Persons, in their Free hold, Goods, or Chattels, whatsoever.

And to the end, the said Islands may be the more happily encreased by the multitude of People resorting thither, and may likewise be the more strongly defended from the Incursions of *Salvages* and other *Enemies, Pirates* and *Robbers*: Therefore, we for us, our Heirs, and Successors, do Give and Grant by these Presents, Power, License, and Liberty unto all the liege People of us, our Heirs, and Successors, in our Kingdom of *England* or elsewhere within any other our Dominions, Islands, Colonies, or Plantations, (excepting those who shall be especially forbidden) to transport themselves and Families into the said Island with convenient Shipping and fitting Provisions, and there to settle themselves, Dwell, and Inhabit any Law, Act, Statute, Ordinances, or other Thing to the contrary in any wise notwithstanding.

And we will also and of our more especial Grace, for us, our Heirs, and Successors, do strictly Enjoyn, Ordain, Constitute and Command, that the said Islands, shall be of our Allegiance, and that all and singular the Subjects and Liege People of us, our Heirs and Successors, transported, or to be transported into the said Islands, and the Children of them, and such as shall descend from them, there born, or hereafter to be born, be, and shall be Denizons and Leiges of us, our Heirs, and Successors, of this our Kingdom of *England*, and be in all things Held, Treated, and Reputed as the liege faithful People of us, our Heirs and Successors, born within this

[Page 7]

our said Kingdom, or any other of our Dominions, and may inherit, or otherwise purchase and receive, take, have, hold, buy and possess any Lands, Tenements, or Hereditaments within the said Places, and them may Occupy, and Enjoy, Give, Sell, Alien, and Bequeath: As likewise, all Liberties, Franchises, and Priviledges, of this our Kingdom of *England*, and of other our Dominions aforesaid, may freely and quietly have, Possess, and Enjoy, as our liege People, born within the same, without the molestation, lett, vexation, trouble or grievance, of us, our Heirs and Successors, any Statute, Act, Ordnance, or Provisions to the contrary notwithstanding.

And farthermore, that our Subjects of this or said Kingdom of *England*, and other our Dominions, may be the rather incouraged to undertake this Expedition, with ready and cheerful mind; Know Yee, That we of our especial Grace, certain Knowledg, and meer Motion, do Give and Grant by vertue of these Presents, as well as to the said *Christopher* Duke of *Albemarle*, *William* Earl of *Craven*, *John* Lord *Berkeley*, *Anthony* Lord *Ashley*, Sir *George Carterett*, and Sir *Peter Colleton,* and their Heirs, as unto all others as shall from time to time repair unto the said Islands, with a purpose to inhabit there, or to trade with the Natives thereof, free Liberty and License to Lade and Fraight in any Ports whatsoever, of us, our Heirs and Successors and into the said Islands, by them then Servants and Assigns, to transport all and singular their Goods, Wares, and Merchandizes; as likewise all sorts of Grain whatsoever, and any other Thing whatsoever, necessary for their Food and Cloathing (not prohibited by the Laws and Statutes of our Kingdoms and Dominions to be carried out of the same without any lett, or molestation of us, our Heirs and Successors, or of any other our Officers and Ministers whatsoever) saving also, to us, our Heirs and Successors, the Customs, and other Duties and Payments due for the said Wares and Merchandizes, according to the several Rates of the Places from whence the same shall be Transported.

[Page 8]

We will also, and by these Presents, for us, our Heirs and Successors, do give, and grant icense by this our Charter, unto the said *Christopher* Duke of *Albemarle*, *William* Earl of *Craven*, *John* Lord *Berkeley*, *Anthony*

Lord *Ashley*, Sir *George Carterett*, and Sir *Peter Colleton,* their Heirs and Assigns, and to all the Inhabitants and Dwellers in the Islands aforesaid, both present and to come, full Power, and absolute Authority to import or unlade by themselves, or their Servants, Factors, or Assigns, all Merchandizes and Goods whatsoever that shall arise of the Fruits and Commodities of the said Islands, either by Land, or Sea, into any the Ports of us, our Heirs and Successors, in our Kingdom of *England*, *Scotland*, and *Ireland*, or otherwise to dispose of the said Goods in the said Ports; and if need be, within one Year next after the unlading to lade the said Merchandizes and Goods again into the same, or other Ships, and to Export the same into any other Countries, either of our Dominions or Forreign, (being in Amity with us, our Heirs and Successors) so as they pay such Customs, Subsidies, and other Duties for the same, to us, our Heirs and Successprs, as the rest of the Subjects of this our Kingdom for the time being shall be bound to pay, beyond which, we will not that the Inhabitants of the said Islands shall be any way Charged: *Provided* nevertheless, and out Will and Pleasure is, and we have further for the considerations aforesaid, of our especial Grace, certain Knowledg, and meer Motion, given and Granted, and by these Presents, for us, our Heirs and Successors, Do Give and Grant unto the said *Christopher* Duke of *Albemarle*, *William* Earl of *Craven*, *John* Lord *Berkeley*, *Anthony* Lord *Ashley*, Sir *George Carterett*, and Sir *Peter Colleton:* their Heirs and Assigns, full and free License, Liberty, Power, and Authority at any time or times, from and after the Feast of St. *Michael the Archangel*, next ensuing, the date hereof to Export and carry out of any of our Dominions into the said Islands Custom free, all Sorts of Tools which shall be usefull and necessary for the Planters there in the Accommodation and Improvement of the Premises, any thing before in these Presents contained,

[Page 9]

or any Law, Act, Statute, Prohibition, or othr Matter or Thing heretofore Had, Made, Enacted, or Provided; or hereafter to be Had, Made, Enacted, or Provided, or the contrary in any wise Notwithstanding.

And Furthermore, of our more ample and especial Grace, certain Knowledg, and meer Motion, we do for us, our Heirs and Successors, Grant unto the said *Christopher* Duke of *Albemarle*, *William* Earl of *Craven*,

John Lord *Berkeley*, *Anthony* Lord *Ashley*, Sir *George Carterett*, and Sir *Peter Colleton;* their Heirs and Assigns, full and absolute Power and Authority to Make, Erect, and Constitute within the said Islands, and the Isles and Islets aforesaid, such and so many Sea Ports, Harbours. Creeks, and other Places for discharge and Unlading of Goods and Merchandizes out of Ships, Boats, and other Vessels; and for lading tghem in such and so many Places, and with such Jurisdictions, Priviledges, and Franchises unto the said Ports belonging as to them shall seem most expedient: And that all and singular the Ships, Boats, and other Vessels, which shall come for Merchandizes and Trade into the said Islands, or shall depart out of the same, shall be laden and unladen at such Ports only as shall be Erected and Constituted by the said *Christopher* Duke of *Albemarle*, *William* Earl of *Craven*, *John* Lord *Berkeley*, *Anthony* Lord *Ashley*, Sir *George Carterett*, and Sir *Peter Colleton*, their Heirs and Assigns, and not elsewhere any Use, Custom, or any thing to the contrary in any wise Notwithstanding.

And we do furthermore Will, Appoint and Ordain, and by these Presents for us, our Heirs and Successors, do Grant unto the said *Christopher* Duke of *Albemarle*, *William* Earl of *Craven*, *John* Lord *Berkeley*, *Anthony* Lord *Ashley*, Sir *George Carterett*, and Sir *Peter Colleton*; their Heirs and Assigns. That they the said *Christopher* Duke of *Albemarle*, *William* Earl of *Craven*, *John* Lord *Berkeley*, *Anthony* Lord *Ashley*, Sir *George Carterett*, and Sir *Peter Colleton;* their Heirs and Assigns, may from time to time for ever, have and enjoy the Customs and Subsidies in the Ports, Harbours, Creeks, and other places within the aforesaid Islands, payable for Goods, Merchandizes, and Wares there

[Page 10]

laded, or to be laded, or ulnaded, the said Customs to be reasonably Assessed upon any occasion by themselves, and by and with the consent of the Free People there, or the greater part of them as aforesaid. To whom we give Power by these Presents, for us, our Heirs and Successors, upon just Cause and in due proportion to Assess and Impose the same.

And further, of our especial Grace, certain Knowledg, and meer Motion, we have Given, and Granted, and by these Presents for us, our Heirs and Successors, do Give, Grant, unto the said *Christopher* Duke of *Albemarle*, *William* Earl of *Craven*, *John* Lord

Berkeley, *Anthony* Lord *Ashley*, Sir *George Carterett*, and Sir *Peter Colleton*; their Heira and Assigns, full and absolute License, Power and Authority. That they the said *Christopher* Duke of *Albemarle*, *William* Earl of *Craven*, *John* Lord *Berkeley*, *Anthony* Lord *Ashley*, Sir *George Carterett*, and Sir *Peter Colleton;* their Heirs and Assigns, from time to time hereafter for ever at his, and their Will and Pleasure, may Assign, Alien, Grant, Demise, or Enfeoff the Premises or any part or parel thereof, to him or them, that shall be willing to purchase the same, and to such Person, and Perons as they shall think fit, To have and to hold to them the said Person, or Persons, their Heirs and Assigns in Fee Simple, or Fee Tail, or for Term of Life, or Lives, or Years, to be held of them the said *Christopher* Duke of *Albemarle*, *William* Earl of *Craven*, *John* Lord *Berkeley*, *Anthony* Lord *Ashley*, Sir *George Carterett*, and Sir *Peter Colleton*; their Heirs and Assigns, by such Rents, Services, and Customs, as shall seem fit to the said *Christopher* Duke of *Albemarle*, *William* Earl of *Craven*, *John* Lord *Berkeley*, *Anthony* Lord *Ashley*, Sir *George Carterett*, and Sir *Peter Colleton*; their Heirs and Assigns; and not immedittely of us, our Heirs and Successors: And to the same Person, or Persons, and to all and every of them, we do Give and Grant by these Presents for us, our Heirs and Successors, License, Authority, and Power, that such Person, or Persons may have and take the Premises, or any

[Page 11]

Parcel thereof, of the said *Christopher* Duke of *Albemarle*, *William* Earl of *Craven*, *John* Lord *Berkeley*, *Anthony* Lord *Ashley*, Sir *George Carterett*, and Sir *Peter Colleton*; their Heirs and Assigns, and the same to hold to themselves, their Heirs or Assigns, in what Estate of Inheritance soever, in Fee Simple, or in Fee Tail, or otherwise, as to them, the said *Christopher* Duke of *Albemarle*, *William* Earl of *Craven*, *John* Lord *Berkeley*, *Anthony* Lord *Ashley*, Sir *George Carterett*, and Sir *Peter Colleton*; their Heirs and Assigns shall seem ecpedient: The Statute in the Parliament of *Edward* Son of King *Henry*, heretofore king of *England*, our Predessor, commonly called the Statute of *Quia emptores terrarum*, or any other Statute, Act, Ordinance, Use, Law, Custom, or any other Matter, Cause, or thing heretofore

Published or Provided to the contrary, in any wise notwithstanding: And because many Persons born or inhabiting in th said Island for their Perfect and Services, may expect and be capable of Marks of honour and Favour, which is respect of the great Distance cannot conveniently be conferred by us. Our Will and Pleasure therefore is, and we do by these Presents, Give, and Grant, unto the said *Christopher* Duke of *Albemarle*, *William* Earl of *Craven*, *John* Lord *Berkeley*, *Anthony* Lord *Ashley*, Sir *George Carterett*, and Sir *Peter Colleton*; their Heirs and Assigns, full Power and Authjority to Give, and Confer unto, and upon such of the Inhabitants of the said Islands, as they shall think, do, or shall Merit the same, such Marks of Favour and Titles of Honour be not the same as are enjoyned by, or conferred upon any the Subjects of this our Kingdom of *England*.

And further, also we do by the Presents, for us, our Heirs and Successors, Give, and Grant, License to them the said *Christopher* Duke of *Albemarle*, *William* Earl of *Craven*, *John* Lord *Berkeley*, *Anthony* Lord *Ashley*, Sir *George Carterett*, and Sir *Peter Colleton*; their Heirs and Assigns, full Power, Liberty, and License to Erect, Raise, and Build within the said

[Page 12]

Islands and Places aforesaid, or any Part, or Parts thereof, such and so many Forts, Fortresses, Castles, Cities, Boroughs, Towns, Villages, and other Fortifications whatsoever; and the same or any of them to fortifie and furnish with Ordinance, Powder, Shot, Armour, and all other Weapons, Amunition, and Habiliments of War, both Offensive, and Defensive, as shall be thought fit and convenient for the safety and welfare of the said Islands, or any part thereof, and the same or any of them from time to time, as occasion shall require to Dismantle, Disfurnish, Demolish and pull down. And also to Place, Constitute, and Appoint, in, or over all or any of the said Castles, Forts, Fortifications, Cities, Towns, and Places aforesaid; Governours, Deputy-Governours, Magistrates, Sheriffs, and other Officers, Civil, and Millitary, as to them shall seem meet. And to the said Cities, Boroughs, Towns, Villages, or any other Place, or Places within the said Islands, to Grant Letters or Charters of Incorporation; with all Liberties, Franchises and Priviledges requisite and usual, or to, or within any Corporations within this our Kingdom of *England*, granted or belonging, and in the same Cities, Boroughs, Towns, and other Places, to Constitute, Erect, and Appoint such, and so many Markets, Marts, and Fairs, as shall in that behalf be thought fit and necessary.

And further, also to Erect and Make in the Islands aforesaid, or any part thereof, so many Mannors with such Seigniories as to them shall seem meet and convenient, and in every of the said Mannors *To Have* and hold a Court Baron, wth all things whatsoever, which to a *Court-Baron* do belong. And *To Have* and to hold *Viewes of Franck-Pledge* and *Court-Leet* for the Conservation of the Peace, and better Government of those Parts with such Limits, Jurisdictions, and Precincts as by thye said *Christopher* Duke of *Albemarle*, *William* Earl of *Craven*, *John* Lord *Berkeley*, *Anthony* Lord *Ashley*, Sir *George Carterett*, and Sir *Peter Colleton*; or their Heirs shall be Appointed for that purpose, with all things whatsoever, which

[Page 13]

to a *Court-Leet*, or *View of Franck-Pledge* do belong, the same Courts to be Holden by Stewards to be deputed and Authorized by the said *Christopher* Duke of *Albemarle*, *William* Earl of *Craven*, *John* Lord *Berkeley*, *Anthony* Lord *Ashley*, Sir *George Carterett*, and Sir *Peter Colleton*; or their Heirs, or by the Lords of the Mannors and Leets for the time being, when the same shall be Erected; and because that, in so remote a Country, and scituate among so many barbarous Nations, the Invasions as well of *Salvages* or other *Enemies*, *Pirats*, and *Robbers*, may probably be feared: Therefore we have given, and for us, our Heirs and Successors, do give Power by these Presents, unto the said *Christopher* Duke of *Albemarle*, *William* Earl of *Craven*, *John* Lord *Berkeley*, *Anthony* Lord *Ashley*, Sir *George Carterett*, and Sir *Peter Colleton*; their Heirs and Assigns by themselves, or their Captains, or other Officers, to Leavy, Muster, and Train all sorts of Men, of what Condition soever, or wheresoever born, whether in the said Islands or elsewhere for the time being; and to make War, and to pursue the *Enemies* aforesaid, as well by Sea as by Land; Yea, even without Limits of the said Islands, (and by Gods assistance) to vanquish and take them, and being taken, to put them to Death by the Law of War, and to save them at their pleasure, and to do all and every other thing which to the Charge and Office of a Captain General or any Army belongeth, or hath accustomed to beloing, as fully and freely, as any Captain General of an Army hath ever had the same.

Also, our Will and Pleasure is, and by this our Charter, we do give unto the said *Christopher* Duke of *Albemarle*, *William* Earl of *Craven*, *John* Lord *Berkeley*, *Anthony* Lord *Ashley*, Sir *George Carterett*, and Sir *Peter Colleton*; their Heirs and Assigns, full *Power*, *Liberty*, and *Authority*, in case of *Rebellion*, *Tumult*, or *Sedition*, (if any should happen, which God forbid), or upon the *Main Sea*, in making a Voyage thither, or returning from thence, by him and themselves, their Captains, Deputies, or Officers, to be

[Page 14]

authority under his, or their Seals for that purpose. To whom also, for us, our Heirs and Successors, we do Give and Grant by these Presents, full Power and Authority to Exercise Martial Law against mutinous and seditious Persons of those parts, such as shall refuse to submit themselves to their Government, or shall refuse to serve in the Wars, or shall fly to the Enemy, forsake their Colours, or Ensigns, or be Loyterers, or Straglers, or otherwise howsoever offending against Law, Custom, or Discipline Military, as freely, and in as ample manner and form, as any Captain General of any Army by vertue of his Office, might, or hath accustomed to use the same.

And our further pleasure is, and by these Presents, for us, our Heirs and Successors: We do Grant unto the said *Christopher* Duke of *Albemarle*, *William* Earl of *Craven*, *John* Lord *Berkeley*, *Anthony* Lord *Ashley*, Sir *George Carterett*, and Sir *Peter Colleton*; their Heirs and Assigns, and to the Tenants and Inhabitants of the said Islands, boith present and to come, and to every of them, that the said Islands, and the Tenants and Inhabitants thereof shall not from henceforth be held or reputed any Member or Part of any Colony whatsoever, in *America*, or elsewhere, now Transported or made, or hereafter to be Transported or made; nor shall be depending on, or subject to their Government in any thing, but be absolutely seperated and divided from the same: And our Will and Pleasure is, by these Presents that they be seperated, and that they be subject immediately to out Crown of

England, as depending thereof for ever.

And that the Inhabitants of the said Islands nor any of them shall at any time hereafter be compelled or compellable, or by any ways subject or liable to appear or answer to any Matter, Suit, Cause, or Plaint whatsoever out of the Islands aforesaid, in any other of our Islands, Colonies, or Dominions in *America* or elsewhere, other than in our Realm of *England*, and Dominion of *Wales*. And because it may happen that some of the People and Inhabitants of the said Islands, cannot in their private Opinions Conform to the Pub-

[Page 15]

lick Exercise of Religion according to the Liturgy, Forms, and Ceremonies of the Church of *England*, or take or subscribe the Oaths and Articles made and established in that behalf; and for that the same by reason of the remote Distances of these Places, will as we hope, be no Breach of the Unity and Uniformity Established in this Nation. Our Will and Pleasure therefore is, and we do by these Presents, for us, our Heirs and Successors, Give and Grant unto the said *Christopher* Duke of *Albemarle*, *William* Earl of *Craven*, *John* Lord *Berkeley*, *Anthony* Lord *Ashley*, Sir *George Carterett*, and Sir *Peter Colleton*; their Heirs or Assigns, full and free License, Liberty, and Authority by such ways and means as they shall think fit to Give and Grant to such Person and Persons inhabiting and being within the said Islands hereby, mentioned to be Granted as aforesaid, or any part thereof, such Indulgencies and Dispensations in that behalf, for, and during such time and times, and with wuch Limitations and Restrictions as they the said *Christopher* Duke of *Albemarle*, *William* Earl of *Craven*, *John* Lord *Berkeley*, *Anthony* Lord *Ashley*, Sir *George Carterett*, and Sir *Peter Colleton*; their Heirs and Assigns, shall in their discretion think fit and reasonable: And that no Person or Persons unto whom such Liberty shall be given, shall be any way molested, Punished, disquieted, or called in question for any differences in Opinion, or Practice in matters of Religious Concernment, who do not actually disturb the Civil Peace of the Island, County, or Colony, that he or they shall make their Aboad in. But all and every such Person or Persons may from time to time and at all times, freely and quietly have and enjoy hir and their Judgments and Consciences in Matters of Religion throughout all the said Islands, they behaving themselves peaceably, and not using the Liberty to Licentiousness, nor to the Civil Injury nor outward disturbance of others; any Law, Statute, or Clause contained, or to be contained, Usuage or Custom of our Realm of *England* to the contrary hereof in any wise notwithstanding. And in case it shall happen that any Doubt

[Page 16]

or Question should arise concerning the true Sense and Understanding of any Word, Clause, or Sentence contained in our present Charter.

We will Ordain and Command, That at all times, and in all things, such Interpretations be made thereof, and allowed in all and every of our Courts whatsoever as lawfully may be adjudged most advantageous and favourable to the said *Christopher* Duke of *Albemarle*, *William* Earl of *Craven*, *John* Lord *Berkeley*, *Anthony* Lord *Ashley*, Sir *George Carterett*, and Sir *Peter Colleton*; their Heirs and Assigns.

Although express mention of the true yearly Value, or certainty of the Premises, or of any of them, or of any other Gifts or Grants, by us, or by any of our Progenitors or Predecessors heretofore made by the said *Christopher* Duke of *Albemarle*, *William* Earl of *Craven*, *John* Lord *Berkeley*, *Anthony* Lord *Ashley*, Sir *George Carterett*, and Sir *Peter Colleton*; in these Presents is not made, or any Statute, Act, Ordinance, Proviso, Proclamation, or Restriction heretofore Had, Made, Enacted, Ordained or Provided, or any other Matter, Cause, or Thing whatsoever, to the contrary hereof in any wise notwithstanding.

In Witness, whereof we have caused these our Letters to be made Patents. Witness our Self at *Westminister*, the first Day of *November*, In the two and twentieth Year of our Reign.

By Writ of Privy Seal.

PIGGOTT

#2: The Articles and Orders of the Company of Adventurers to the Bahama Islands (1672) (BLL, Add MS 15,640)

[Title Page]

Articles and

Orders of the
Co[m]pa[ny] of Adventurers
to ye Bahama
Islands 1672

[Page 1]

Articles of agreement Indented made and concluded upon ye 4th day of Sept[e]mber in ye Fower and twentieth yeare of ye Raigne of our Soveraigne Lord Charles ye Second by ye Grace of God of England, Scotland, France, and Ireland, King, defender of ye Faith &c Annoque Dom[ini] 1672 Betweene Christopher Duke of Albemarle, William Earle of Craven, Anthony Earle of Shaftesbury Chancellor and undertreasurer of the Exchequer, John Lord Berkeley, Sir George Carteret Kn[igh]t and Barronet vice Chamberlaine of his Maj[es]ties Household & Sir Peter Colleton, Bar[o]net, being Lords and Proprietors of ye Bahama Islands in America of ye one parte, And Richard Kingdon of Hackney in ye County of Midlesex Esq[uire], William Kiffen of London Esq[uire] Edward Thornburgh of Augustin Fryers London Esq[uire], John Mapletoft Doctor in Physsick, John Baynes of Westminster gent[leman], Henry Aldrich of St Martins in the Fields, gent[leman], John Lock of ye p[ar]ish of St Clements Danes in ye County of Midlesex, Gent[leman], Thomas Stringer of St Clements Danes aforesaid, Gent[leman], John Darrell of Bermudas, Marchant, Richard Davy of St Martins in the Fields, Gent[leman], And Peter Jones of St Clements Danes aforesaid Gent[leman], being Adventurers to and for the said Bahama Islands of ye other part in manner following.

[Page 2]

1 Whereas his said Majesty by his Gracious Letters Pattent bearing date ye first day of November in ye two and twentieth yeare of his s[ai]d Maj[es]ties Raigne for ye Considerations and under the Reservations, Covenants & agreements therein mentioned was pleased to Grant to ye s[ai]d Christopher Duke of Albemarle, William

Earle of Craven, John Lord Berkeley, Anthony Lord Ashley now Earle of Shaftes bury, Sr George Carteret, & Sr Peter Colleton and their heires & Assignes All these Islands called by ye name of Bahama Islands or ye Islands of ye Lucayes in America w[i]th such Rights, Jurisdictions, Priviledges & Royal tys thereby Granted as in & by ye said Letters Pattents may more fully appeare And whereas it hath bin judged necessary in pursuance of ye s[ai]d Letters Pattents and for ye better carrying on ye Plantation in the s[ai]d Bahama Islands for ye Inlargem[en]t of his s[ai]d Maj[es]ties Dominions in America That a sufficient stock not under ye Sum of one thousand six hundred pounds nor exceeding ye sum of two thousand pounds sterling be at present advanced Raised and mannaged according to ye Provisions Conditions and agreements herein after mentio ned. It is therefore concluded and agreed by and between all ye said p[ar]tyes And ye said Adventurers to & for ye said Bahama Islands Doe in consideration of ye setlements, Priviledg es and Imunityes hereby Conveyed & Granted

[Page 3]

or agreed to be Convey'd and Granted to and upon them the said Adeventurers for and dureing the times and in such manner as is herein after mentioned and of ye p[er]formance thereof and of what else is herein agreed to be done and p[er]formed by ye s[ai]d Lords and Propriet[or]s of ye s[ai]d Islands Severally Covenant & Agree for themselves their respective heires, Executors, Administrators and Assignes, & not the one or ye Heires Executors & Administrators of any one for the other or for ye Heires Executors and Adm[inistrat]ors of ye other, That each and every of them their respective Heires, Executors and Adm[inistrat]ors shall and will subscribe towards ye Stock afore said before ye 29th day of September next ensue ing the date hereof, Such sums of money as shall be intended and agreed by them under their hands severally to be subscribed by one Instru ment and Writeing Indented made and Executed betweene the s[ai]d Severall Adventurers bearing even date w[i]th theise p[re]sents for ye purposes afores[ai]d. Provided always & soe, as no subscr iption of any of ye s[ai]d Adventurers nor any Covenant herein, for & concerning ye same or ye matters herein contained on their parts to be performed be binding to or any Advantage taken thereof against them their Heires, Execut[or]s Adm[inistrat]ors or assignes untill and unlesse there be ye sum of One thousand sixe hundred pounds at ye least there First Subscription unto subscribed for ye ends afores[ai]d. And it is Covenanted & agreed by and betweene the partys afores[ai]d that if ye Greater p[ar]te of ye s[ai]d Adventurers their Executors, Administrators or Assignes

[Page 4]

Increase shall thinke fitt to increase he s[ai]d Stock above the Sum first subscribed, That ye s[ai]d Adventurers shall have power to encrease the same according ly. And ye s[ai]d Adventurers shall and doe hereby Covenant and agree to and w[i]th he said Lords Proprietors to pay to ye Treasurer of the s[ai]d Adventurers fo ye time being their respec tive parts of such increase or Additionall stocks w[i]thin ye space of Fourteene days after notice Given by the s[ai]d Treasurer to him of them for the payment thereof Provided alwayes that ye Additionall Stock or increase soe to be paid be not greater to each Adventurer then what he did at first subcribe.

2. Alsoe it is concluded and agreed by and betweene all ye said p[ar]ties, and the said Christopher Duke of Albemarle William Earle of Craven Anthony Earl of Shaftesbury John Lord Berkeley, Sr George Carteret and Sr Peter Colleton Doe Covenant and agree for them and every of them their & every of their Heires, Executors, Adm[inistrat]ors and Assignes to and w[i]th the s[ai]d Adventurers and every of them their & every of their Heires, Executors, Administrators & Assignes That ye s[ai]d Christopher Duke of Albemarle William Earle of Craven Anthony Earle of Shaftesbury, John Lord Berkeley, Sir George Carteret & Sr Peter Colleton their Heires and Assignes for and in consideration of ye subscrip tions afores[ai]d shall & will at ye Request of the s[ai]d Adventurers or ye Major part of them from time

[Page 5]

to time at any time w[i]thin the space of the One and Thirty yeares herefter mentioned Assume Grant and Setle in due forme of Law to and upon ye s[ai]d Adventurers their Heires, Executors, Adm[inistrat]ors & Assignes respectively in such manner as shall be in that behalfe by ye Councell of the s[ai]d Adventurers reasonably advised All those the severall acres and quantitys of Land here after mentioned that is to say the full quan tity and Contents of Twelve Thousand acres of Land according to ye measure of acres in England used, lying scituate & being in ye Island of New Providence, And alsoe ye full quantity and Contents of Twelve Thousand acres of Land more, lying scituate & being in any other one or more of ye Bahama Islands or such part of ye s[ai]d Twelve Thousand and Twelve Thousand acres as ye s[ai]d Adventurers at any time & from time to time shall choose so as such Grant and Setlement of ye said Twelve Thousand acres in New Providence and the s[ai]d Twelve Thousand acres in any of ye rest of ye Bahama Islands or any part there of be only of Land not Granted to or taken up by any others at any time before ye said Adventurers shall come to desire or take up the same. To have and hould the s[ai]d Severall acres and quantitys of Land and premisses to the said Severall Adventurers subscribeing, sealing & Executing theise presents & to their Heires & Assignes for ever, Yeilding & Paying there fore yearly And the s[ai]d Adventurers are in & by the s[aid] Grants & Setlements to Covenant and

12000 acres in providence

12000 acres in any other of ye Bahamas

[Page 6]

Agree to pay yearely dureing ye space of One and Twenty yeares next Imediately ensueing the date of ye s[ai]d Respective Setlements Corne at ye Feast of St Michaell ye ArchAngell yearely if it be lawfully demanded And from & after ye expiration of the s[ai]d term of One and Twenty yeares the yearely Rent of One penny for ever for every acre of Land to be setled upon and posest by the s[ai]d Adventurers as aforesaid.

Rent

One Pepper

3. Alsoe it is Concluded and agreed by and between the said partys And ye s[ai]d Christopher

Royalty for 31 years

Duke of Albemarle, William Earl of Craven, Anthony Earle of Shaftesbury, John L[or]d Berkeley Sir George Carteret and Sr Peter Colleton Doe by theise presents in Consideration of ye Subscriptions afores[ai]d Grant, Assigne and Transferr & Covenant and Agree for them their Heires & Assignes That they will further upon reasonable request Grant, Assigne, Transferr, and Confirme unto the s[ai]d Adventurers All the Rights, Interest, Royaltyes, Priviledges & Imunitys of the said Lords and Proprietors to them Granted by ye said Letters Pattents of and in all Gould, Silver and other Mines & Minneralls, Gems, Ambergreece, Whales Whalefishing, Pearle fishing and Wracks and the haveing, obtaining & getting thereof in any of ye s[ai]d Bahama Islands To have and to hould the s[ai]d Royaltys & Priviledges of Gould and Silver Mines & other Minneralls, Gemms, Ambergrees, Whales, Whalefishing, Pearlefishing & Wracks, to ye s[ai]d Adventurers their Executors, Administrators, and Assignes for ye terme and space of One and Thirty yeares from henceforth Fully to be

[Page 7]

Compleate and Ended And that noe other p[er]son or p[er]sons dureing the time aforesaid shall fish for Whales or Pearls or dig or worke any Mine of Coast for any of the s[ai]d Royaltys & Priviledges not take and dispose of any Ambergreece, Wracks, Mines, Minneralls, Gems in any part whatsoever of any of ye s[ai]d Bahama Islands Save only the siad Adventurers & such as shall by any authority or Interest derived from them, have power, Lycence or Liberty for ye same Yeilding and Paying therefore dureing the s[ai]d terms of One and thirty yeares to ye s[ai]d Lords and Proprietors their Heires and Assignes on ye Feast of St Michaell ye Arch angell One Pepper Corne yearely if ye same be lawfully Demanded.

Alsoe it is Concluded & agreed by and 4
betweene the said partys and the said Christopher Duke of Albemarle William Earle of Craven, Anthony Earle of Shaftes bury, John Lord Berkeley, Sir George Carteret, & Sr Peter Colleton Doe by theise presents in Consideration of ye s[ai]d Subscriptions, Grant

Assigne and Transferr and Covenant and Agree That they will further upon reasonable request Grant, Assigne, Transferr, & Confirme unto ye s[ai]d Adventurers All ye Rights, Interest, Royaltys, Priviledges, & Imunitys of ye said Lords and Proprietors to them Granted by the said Letters Pattents of and in Brasiletto Wood Brasiletto, Cedar & Cedar, and any other Timber & the having, Obtaining and cutting & disposing thereof in any of the s[ai]d Bahama Islands, Soe as this Grant of

[Page 8]

Brasiletto Wood, Ceder, and other timber extend not any further nor otherwise to ye possession of any other planter then that all ye owners of Land and plantations by any Grant thereof heretofore made or hereafter to be made from ye s[ai]d Lords and Proprietors shall be & are intended hereby to be obleidged to sell all their Brasiletto Wood they shall cutt or dispose of upon or from any of their possessions dureing the terme of One & Thirty yeares from ye date hereof unto ye s[ai]d Adventurers
5li their Executors, Adm[inistrat]ors, & Assignes at ye rate of
per tun five pounds p[er] tunn & noe more To have & hould the s[ai]d Brasiletto Wood, Ceder and Timber [i]th ye having, obtaineing, cutting & disposing thereof in manner aforesaid to ye s[ai]d Adventurers their Executors, Adm[inistrat[ors, and Assignes for ye Terme & Space of One and Thirty yeares from hence forth fully to be compleat and ended And that noe p[er]son or p[er]sons dureing the time afores[ai]d besides the s[ai]d Adventurers shall cutt downe or dispose of any Brasiletto Wood, Ceder, or other Timber in and upon the said Islands or any part thereof w[hi]ch are not or shall not be in ye Propriety or possession of any private Planters by Grant from ye s[ai]d Lords Proprietors thereof Formerloy or hereafter to be made save only the s[ai]d Adventurers or such as by any Interest Lycence or Authority derived from them shall have liberty for the same Yeilding and Paying therefore yearely dureing the said Terme of One and thirty yeares to the said Lords and Proprietors their Heires & Assignes the

[Page 9]

yearely Rent of One Pepper Corne at the

Feast of St Michaell the Archangell if the same be lawfully demanded.

5 Provided alwayes and it is Concluded and Agreed upon by & between the said Partys And ye s[ai]d Christopher Duke of Albemarle, William Earle of Craven, Anthony Earle of Shaftesbury, John Lord Berkeley, Sir George Carteret & Sif Peter Colleton Doe Covenant & Grant for them their Heires & Assignes to & w[i]th the s[ai]d Adventurers their Heires, Executors, Adm[inistrat[ors, & Assignes That the s[ai]d Adventurers their Heires, Executors, Adm[inistrat]ors & Assignes for & dureing their respec tive Interest & Estates of & in any the s[ai]d Lands Royaltys, Priviledges, & Premisses are and shall be at all times & from time to time freed & discharged by the s[ai]d Lords & Proprietors their Heires & Assignes of & from all Rents & Dutys whatsoever reserved by the s[ai]d Letters Pattents & now or hereafter thereby due and payable to his Maj[es]tie his Heires & Successors Excepting one quarter of all Gould and Silver Oare w[hi]ch dureing the time afores[ai]d shall be by them or any deriveing power of Interest under them found in & upon ye p[re]misses or any part thereof.

Discharged from rent capitall

1/4 gold & silver oar

6. Also it is Concluded & Agreed upon by and betweene the s[ai]d Partys And the said Christopher Duke of Albemarle, William Earle of Craven, Anthony Earle of Shaftesbury, John Lord Berkeley, Sir George Carteret and Sir Peter Colleton Doe Covenant & agree for

[Page 10]

themselves their Heires & Assignes and w[i]th the s[ai]d Adventurers their Heires Executors, Adm[inistrat]ors & Assignes that they the s[aid] Christopher Duke of Albemarle William Earl of Craven, Anthony Earl of Shaftesbury, John L[or]d Berkeley, Sir George Carteret and Sir Peter Colleton shall and will w[i]th in Eight days after ye date hereof add & pay unto ye Treasurer for he s[ai]d Adventurers soe much money as shall amount unto one Ninth part of ye Stock subscribed by ye s[ai]d Adventurers for ye purposes afores[ai]d And that when the Greater part of ye s[ai]d Adventurers shall judge it Convenient to encrease ye present Stocke afores[ai]d to a greater sum & shall accordingly Order ye Increase thereof the s[ai]d L[or]ds Proprietors shall & will pay unto the Treasurer of the Adventurers for the time being their One Tenth part or proportion of such increase or Aditionall Stock w[i]thin Fourteene days after notice Given by the s[ai]d Treasurer to ye p[er]son by the Lords Proprietors nominated to manage their share of ye s[ai]d stock and for want of such nomination to any one of the s[ai]d Lords Proprietors for ye time being, upon Penalty that if they the s[ai]d Lords Proprietors shall faile to pay their s[ai]d share or proportion of the Additional Stock as afores[ai]d they shall be lyable to & Charged w[i]th & accordingly pay unto the s[ai]d Treasurer ye sum of Two pounds p[er] Cent p[er] mensem for their s[ai]d proportions soe unpaid to be reckoned from ye Failer thereof untill they shall fully satisfye & pay unto the

[Page 11]

said Treasurer their s[ai]d Proportions of the increase or Additionall Stock together w[i]th ye s[ai]d Pennalty of Two pounds p[er] Cent as afores[ai]d or untill ye whole money formerly by them paid in & by ye proceed or effects there of in ye Joynt Stock be fully thereby extingui shed as ye major parte of ye s[ai]d Adventurers whose payments shall be fully paid in shall determine the same It being declared & agreed by all ye s[ai]d partyes that ye Growing profitts & proceeds of ye s[ai]d Ninth parte being one Tenth part of ye whole is to belong to & upon all Dividends to be made, be duely from time to time, be paid to ye Governor or Governors of ye s[ai]d Bahama Islands for ye time being to & for his owne use & benefitt w[i]thout any account rendering for the same.

Governors share

7

Alsoe it is concluded and agreed by and between all ye s[ai]d Partyes & the said Adventurers Doe severally Covenant & Agree for themselves their Severall Heires Executors & Administrators and not one for the other that they shall & will from time to time Imploy the said Stock in a Trade unto ye s[ai]d Islands for a supply of the Inhabitants of ye Islands with necessary Marchandize & make noe greater profitt upon sale thereof then what shall amount to ye vallew of 25li p[er] Cent above all charges & reprizes for & concerning the same, or under that rate. 25 p[er] C

[Page 12]

8 Provided and it is lastly agreed and declared by & betweene all ye s[aid] partyes That the said Lords Proprietors their Heires & Assignes shall have power from time to time to nominate one person who (soe as the s[ai]d One Tenth parte payable by the Lords Proprietors be duely paid in) shall have the same & like powers, shares & priviledges in ye management of the Stock that any one of the s[ai]d Adventurers proportion ably hath. In witness whereof of the severall partyes hereunto as well Proprietors as Adven turers have hereunto their hands & seales Interchangeably putt, the day & yeare first above written.

Albemarle Craven Shaftesbury Jo[hn] Berkeley
Geo[rge] Carteret

Sealed & delivered by ye w[i]thin named William Earle of Craven & Anthony Earle of Shaftesbury in the p[re]sence of Thomas Browne Bartholomew Fillingham
Anthony Shepherd

Sealed & delivered by the w[i]thin named Christopher Duke of Albemarle in ye p[re]sence of William Peirson
John Limbery Ralph Egerton

Sealed & delivered by ye w[i]thin named Lord Berkeley in the presence of Ellis Leighton
Rowland Powell James Worrall

Sealed & delivered by the w[i]thin named Sir George Carteret in ye presence of John Richards
James Allerdice

Exam[inatur] p[er] P J

[Pages 13 and 14 are blank]

[Page 15]

Articles of agreement Inden ted Made & ~~Punctually~~ Mutually Concluded and Agreed upon ye Fowerth day of September in ye Fower & Twentieth yeare of the Raigne of our Soveraigne Lord Charles ye Second by ye Grace of God off England, Scotland, France , & Ireland, King, Defender of ye Faith &c annoque Dom[ini] 1672 Betweene Richard Kingdon of Hackney in ye County of Midlesexe Esquire on ye First part, William Kiffen of London, Esq[ui]r[e] of ye second part, Edward Thornburgh of Austin Fryers London Esq[ui]r[e] of ye third parte John Mapletoft Doctor in Phisick of ye Fowereth part, John Baynes of Westminster, gent[leman], of ye Fifth part, Henry Aldrich of St Martins in ye Fields, gent[leman], of ye Sixth part, John Locke of ye p[ar]ish of St Clements Danes in ye County of Midlesex gent[leman of the Seventh part, Thomas Stringer of

[Page 16]

St Clements Danes afores[ai]d gent[leman] of the Eighth part John Darrell of Bermuda, Marchant, of the ninth part, Richard Davy of St Martins in ye Fields gent, of the Tenth part, and Peter Jones of St Clements Danes afores[ai]d gent[leman] of ye Eleaventh part being all of them Adventurers to & for ye Bahama Islands in America and severally hereunder Writeing their subscriptions.

Whereas for ye better carrying on the Plantacon in the Bahama Islands & for the Inlargement of his Maj[es]ties Dominions in America It hath bin Judged necessary by ye Lords & Proprietors of ye s[ai]d Islands in pursuance of his Maj[es]ties Gracious letters Pattents to them Granted bearing Date ye first day of November in ye Two & Twentieth yeare of his s[ai]d Majestys Raigne In consideracon of a present stock of between One thousand six hundred poundes and Two thousand poundes to be Advanced & Mannaged according to & under such provi sions proposalls & Covenants as are Contained in certaine Articles of Agreement bearing even Date w[i]th theise presents made between the said Lords Proprietors of the other part Thereby to Grant and setle or Covenant and Agree upon the termes and conditions.

[Page 17]

therein Exprest for Encouragement to be Adventurers to & for the s[ai]d Islands To Grant and setle upon the s[ai]d Adventurers their Heires, Executors, Administrators or Assignes such Quantitys of Lands & such Royaltys, Priviledges & Imunitys as are herein Contained. Now therefore wittness theise present Articles of Agreement that the said Adventurers for ye better Regula tion & Improvement of ye s[ai]d Stock by them Subscribed or to be subscribed for the more orderly & due mannagem[en]t of all the Affaires touching the s[ai]d Islands & the Trade thereunto belonging so farr as the said Adventurers shall be therein concerned. Doe for and amongst themselves, and for their severall Heires, Ex[ecuto]rs, Adm[inistrat]ors and Assignes and not any one for ye other or for ye Heires Ex[exuto]rs. Adm[inistrato]rs, or Assignes of ye other by theise presents, Covenant, Conclude & Agree to & w[i]th each other their severall Heires, Ex[ecuto]rs, Adm[inistrato]rs & Assignes wll & truly to observe, Fulfill & performe ye severall Articles, Clauses & Agreements & in such manner as ye same are herein after mentioned, That is to say

Imprimis That when the sum of One Thousand six hundred pounds shall be

[Page 18]

subscribed some one p[er]son of the subscribers shall be chosen by the subscribers to be ye p[re]sent Treasurer for ye s[ai]d Adventurers And the s[ai]d subscribers shall & may then alsoe as they see cause choose a present Governor of the s[ai]d Society from amongst themselves.

2 Item That what Sum soever anyone of the s[ai]d Adventurers shall subscribe the same shall not be oblidgeing to him his Heires, Executors, Adm[inistrato]rs or Assignes nor he or they oblidged to pay in the same nor be lyable to or charged w[i]th any Covenants herein contained untill & unless the full sim of One Thousand Six hund

red pounds be fully subscribed.

3 That what sum any of ye s[ai]d Adventurers shall subscribe either fore or after ye said sum of One Thousand Six hundred pounds is subscribed as aforesaid shall be carefully paid into ye Treasurer for ye Time being w[i]th in Seaven days after ye said subscription soe that the whole subscription amount be One Thousand Six hundred pounds or more & for want of payment thereof w[i]thin that time Such subscription shall be voyd & it shall be Lawfull for ye rest of ye s[ai]d Adventurers to admitt whom they shall thinke fitt to make up ye s[ai]d subscription And in case any of ye s[ai]d Adventurers have paid in to ye s[ai]d Treasurer any of ye Sums of money by them subscribed & the whold money pain in to

[Page 19]

him w[i]thin Thirty days shall not amount unto ye s[ai]d sum of One Thousand Six hundred pounds Each of them respectively who hath paid in his money as afores[ai]d shall have Liberty to Demand his money againe & the s[ai]d Treasurer upon his Demand of ye same shall repay it unto him, his Executors or Administrators accordingly.

That when ye greatest parte of the 4
s[ai]d Adventurers shall Judge it Convenient to Encrease ye p[re]sent Stock afores[ai]d to a Greater sum & shall accordingly Order the Increase thereof each Adventurer shall pay in their respective Proportion of the Additionall Stock or increase to be new Raised, to ye Treasurer w[i]thin Fowerteene days after such Order made upon Penalty.

That if having paid his or their first subscription he or they shall faile to pay any such Following share or Proportion he or they shall be Lyable to & Charged w[i]th and accordingly pay unto ye Treasurer of the s[ai]d Stock the sum of Two pounds p[er] Cent p[er] mensem for his or their respective propor tions soe unpaid to be Reckoned from ye failer thereof untill he or they shall fully sattisfye & pay unto ye s[ai]d Treasurer his & their proportion of ye s[ai]d Increase or Additional

[Page 20]

Stocke together w[i]th ye Pennalty of Two pounds p[er] Cent p[er] mensem as afores[ai]d or untill the whole money by him or them formerly subscribed and the proceed & effects thereof in the joynt stock be fully thereby extinguished as ye Major parte of the s[ai]d Adventurers whose payments shall be fully paid shall determine ye same, & Moreover every person soe failing to pay his s[ai]d subscrip tion shall be thereby uncapable to be chosen into any Government or Mannagement of the s[ai]d Stock or Company or to Give any vote at any Meeting concerning the same or Relateing thereunto untill & unless he shall pay or sattisfye for his s[ai]d subscription by ye Penalty of Two pounds p[er] Cent for each Month as aforesaid Provided & soe ye whole Additionall Stock to be soe raised by ye severall Adventurers be not Greater to each Adventurer then the sume first Subscribed by him & soe as the s[ai]d Recited Articles of Agreem[en]t Concerning such non payment be in all things therein likewise observed.

5 That every Adventurer not fayling to make payment as afores[ai]d who shall be present at any meeting of ye s[ai]d Adventurers for every Hundred pounds by him subscribed shall have the Priviledge of One vote & be Capeable of being chosen Governor or Treasurer for ye better Mannagement of ye Stock of ye s[ai]d Adventurers

[Page 21]

6 That a Generall Meeting shall be Sumoned Twice every yeare by the Governor or Treasurer for ye time being One upon ye first Satterday in April at w[hi]ch time after ye first Choice of such Officers made as afores[ai]d The Governor Treasurer & any other officer that shall be judged necessary shall be chosen & ye State of ye Company Stock by an Exact Balance of the amounts & an Indifferrent valluation of all remaining effects shall then alsoe be produced that thereby the Adventurers may know the true Condit[i]on of their Stock & Trade and if any Officer shall dye, a new one shall be Chosen at ye next meeting after such death if they thinke fitt. And the

other Generall meeting shall be upon the first Satterday in September yearly for ye considering of & determinint any matters requisite for ye good mannagement of ye s[ai]d Stocke & if often or at other times other meetings shall be necessary the same shall be sumoned at such times as ye Gover nour or Treasurer shall finde occasion for the same.

That one halfe or more & noe Fewer 7
of the s[ai]d Adventurers shat have votes and

[Page 22]

are in and about ye Citty of London or West minster all being duely sumoned shall have power to make Rules & Orders for manageing of ye s[ai]d Stock & Trade of ye s[ai]d Company or any thing Relateing thereunto w[hi]ch Rules & Orders shall be observed by all ye Adventurers and by every p[er]son & p[er]sons deriveing any Autho rity or Interest in or Concerning premises by from or under them or any of them.

8 That a Devidend shall be made in money of ye profitts & proceed of ye Stock of ye said Adventurers as often as ye Adventurers at a Gennerall Meeting or any other meeting at w[hi]ch the greater part of all ye Adventurers are present shall thinke fitt And that ye said Adventurers & Every of them shall & will from time to time & at all times pay, beare & allow his share & proportion of ye s[ai]d Rent of one penny an acre payable unto ye Lords Proprietors as aforesaid.

9 That at ye Expiration of other Determina tion of ye time & space of One & Thirty yeares to beginn fron ye Date hereof and being ye Terme in and by the s[ai]d Recited Articles Covenanted to be Granted of ye Royaltys therein mentioned An Equall Devidend shall be made of all ye Land and Stock profitts & proceed of ye same what soever in such manner as shall be agreed upon

[Page 23]

(at a Gennerall Meeting or such other mee ting at wh[hi]ch ye Greater part of all ye Adventu rers are present) by ye Majority of the Adventurers present. And alsoe of all profitts Advantages whatsoever of Roy altys priviledges & Imunitys, Granted and Setled or Covenanted to be Granted and Setled by ye s[ai]d Recited Articles to the said Adventurers And w[hi]ch during that time have binn or shall be made by ye said Adven turers or any of them in any kind or manner of way whatsoever.

That noe advantage or bennefitt 10
shall be at any time had & made by and amongst ye s[ai]d Adventurers their Heires, Ex[ecut]ors, Adinistrat]ors or Assignes by way of Survivorship but in case that any of them dye the Heires, Executors, or Adm[inistrat]ors respectively of him or them soe dying from time to time shall have ye whole bennefitt & Advantage of the share & Interest of him or them soe dying they bearing their Equall share of any Charge & Losses proportionable to their Interest, any thing herein contained to ye Contrary notwith standing. And that such Heires, Executors, or Adm[inistrat]ors of ye party soe dyeing doe signifye to ye Governor or Treasurer for ye time being that they desire to be admitted ~~accordingly~~

[Page 24]

amongst ye Adventurers And in such cases they shall be received & admitted accordingly upon ye same Termes & Conditions that ye party soe deceased was to have binn continued if he had lived.

11 That upon leave obteyned from ye Adven turers & not otherwise at any meeting of the Adventurers any one of ye Adventurers shall have power to Assigne his share in ye Stock or any p[ar]te thereof unto any other p[er]son & thereupon such p[er]son shall be admitted to ye profitts & privi ledges of the said share, upon ye same termes & Condicons that ye Assigner did or ought to enjoy the same.

12 Lastly It is mutually agreed & severally Cove nanted, Agreed & Concluded by ye s[ai]d Adven turers for themselves, their severall Heires, Executors, Adm[inistrat]ors & Assignes to & w[i]th each other & ye Heires, Executors, Adm[inistrat]ors & Assignes of each other that if any Differrence or Controversy shall at any time hereafter arise or happen

betweene and amongst them or any of them their Heires, Ex[ecut]ors, Adm[inistrat]ors or Assignes touching & Concerning ye s[ai]d Stock & Trade or any their shares & proportions therein or dut to or from the same or touching any other matter or thing relateing thereunto or to ye premises that in such case w[i]th out seeking other Remedy in any Courts of Law or Equity they & every of them therein

[Page 25]

concerned shall & will consenbt to referr and submitt ye full & final detrmination of all such differrences or controversys to some p[er]son or p[er]sons to be chosen Arbitrator or Arbuitrators or Umpire thereof Indifferrently betweene them & shll & will bind themselves their Heires, Ex[ecut]ors & Adm[inistrat]ors in Bonds or other Engadgem[en]ts w[i]th such reasonable Pennaltys therein, as shall be then agreed on betweene them or as ye s[ai]d Arbitrator or Arbitrators or umpire shall determine the same to be for ye submitting standing to observeing and p[er]forming the Sentence, Award, Arbitrament or Umpirage of such Arbitrator & Arbitra tors or umpire respectively w[i]thout any appeale from the same or any wise seeking to evade the due & just p[er]formance thereof according to ye true intent & meaning of ye Arbitrator or Arbitrators or umpire exprest therein. And for the due performance of this last Article & Covenant they the s[ai]d Adventurers doe mutually & severally bind themselves their severall Heires, Ex[ecut]ors and Administrators to each other & to the Executors & Adm[inistrat]ors of each other in the Pennalty of one hundred pounds sterling In witness wereof ye said Adventurers

[Page 26]

who have likewise hereunder written their subscriptions have hereunto their hands & seales putt the day & yeare first above written.

I Richard Kingdon doe subscribe according to ye above ~~written~~ Articles 200li

Ri[chard] Kingdon

I Rich[ard] Davy doe subscribe according
to ye above written Articles 200li
Rich[ard] Davy

I Henery Aldwich doe subscribe according
to ye above written Articles ye sume of 200li
Henery Aldwich

I Thomas Stringer doe subscribe accor
ding to ye above written Articles 300li
Tho[mas] Stringer

I Edward Thornburgh doe subscribe
according to ye above written Articles 200li
Edw[ard] Thornburgh

I John Lock doe subscribe according
to ye above written Articles 100li
John Locke

I John Darrell doe subscribe accor
ding to ye above written Articles 100li
John Darrell

I William Kiffen doe subscribe accor
ding to ye above written Articles 100li
W[illia]m Kiffen

I John Mapletoft doe subscribe
according to ye above written Articles 100li
John Mapletoft

I John Baynes doe subscribe
according to ye above written Articles 200li
John Baynes

I Peter Jones doe subscribe accor
ding to ye above written Articles 200li
Peter Jones

[Page 27]

Sealed & del[ivered] by ye w[i]thin named W[illia]m Kiffen
in ye p[re]sence of us Tho[mas] Hasted
Wal[ter] Bayly
J[oh]n Wiseman

Sealed & delivered by the within named Rich[ard] Kingdon, Tho[mas] Stringer, J[oh]n Maplecost Henery Aldrich, Richard Davy, John Lock John Darrell & Peter Jones in ye p[re]sence of

Charles Morgan
Edward Rogers
John Young

Sealed & delivered by ye w[i]thin mentioned Edward Thornburgh in ye p[re]sence of

Thomas Ditchfield
J[oh]n Thornburgh

Sealed & del[ivered] by ye w[i]thin named John Baynes in ye p[re]sence of

Edward Clarke
J[oh]n Baynes

Copia Vera

Ex[amine]d L J

[Page 28 is blank]
[Page 29]

Exeter House Sept[emb]er 9th 1672

Att a meeting of ye Adventurers to ye Bahama Islands being present

Mr Richard Kingdon
Mr Henery Aldrich
Mr John Lock
Mr Thomas Stringer
Mr John Maplecost
Mr Richard Davy
Captn John Darrell
Mr Peter Jones

It was agreed that ye above named Thomas Stringer should be Treasurer for ye s[ai]d Adventurers
That Peter Jones should be Clarke to ye Adventurers & have ye Custody of ye Writeings that concerne them.
That Five hands or more of any of the Adventurers be ye Authority by w[hi]ch the Treasurer shall make all payments out of their stocke in his hands.

That the Receipt ye Treasurer shall give to ye Adventurers for such money as they from time to time doe pay him shall be of this forme Received of A B the sum of being in full or p[ar]te of his subscription to ye stock of Adventu rers to ye Bahama Islands to be issued only by an Order under ye hands of any 5 or more of ye s[ai]d Adventurers.

That Doctor John Mapletoft might Assigne over to Mr John Lock his Interest in ye s[ai]d Stock.

[Page 30]

Exeter House ye 23d October 1672

At a meeting of ye Adventurers to the Bahama Islands being present

Mr Richard Kingdon
Mr John Locke
Mr Henery Aldrich
Mr Richard Davy
Captn John Darrell
Mr Peter Jones It was agreed

That Doctor John Mapletoft having Assigned to Mr John Lock his Interest in ye Stock of ye Adventurers to ye Bahama Islands And the s[ai]d John Lock having accepted thereof That he be accordingly admitted thereto and he is accordingly admitted to as full a right therein to all intents & purposes as ye s[ai]d Doctor J[oh]n Maplecost ever had or enjoyed.

[Page 31]

November ye 8th 1672

At a meeting of ye Adventurers on Board ye ship *Bahama Merchant* present

Mr John Baynes
Mr John Locke
Mr Richard Davy
Captn John Darrell
Mr Peter Jones It was agreed

Noe bill or account of mony due is to be paid before it hath ye hand of ye Clarke or Accountant to it. Nor is ye Clerke or accountants hand to be sett thereto untill (1st) it be owned by some one of the

Company to be according to contract (2ly) It be acknowledged to be received well conditioned (3ly) till he hath Examined whether it be right cast up.

[Page 32]

Austin Fryers November 11th 1672

At a meeting of ye Adventurers to the Bahama Islands being present
Mr William Kiffen
Mr John Locke
Mr John Baynes
Mr Richard Davy
Captn John Darrell
Mr Peter Jones It was agreed

That ye Gennerall marke for all Goods belonging to ye Adventurers should be ye Letter B.
That Mr Peter Jones should be both Accomptant & Clerke to ye Adventurers.

#3: Record of a Petition by the Bahama Adventurers to the Privy Council that their ship the *Bahama Merchant* be made free for trading purposes – 29 January 1675 (TNA, PC 2/64, page 361):

[Page 361]

John Baynes & others about making ye *Bahama Merchant* a Free Ship

Upon reading this day at the Board the humble Petition of John Baynes Esq[uire] on behalfe of himselfe and others his Ma[jes]ties Subjects Merchants Adventurers to the Bahama Islands in the West Indies, Setting forth, That the Pet[ition]ers did in the Moneth of July 1672 buy of Mr George Potts a certain Ship for the carrying on their Trade aforesaid, which Ship was One of his Ma[jes]ties Prizes called by the name of the *Old Abraham* & was sold by his Ma[jes]ties Com[missione]rs of Prizes for the Port of London upon the 17th of the same July unto the said Mr George Potts for the sume of

400 li. That the Pet[ition]ers did at their Charge repaire & fitt the said Ship for Sea, & sent her by the name of the *Bahama Merchant* upon a voyage to the said Islands. That the Pet[itione]rs are obstructed in their Trade with the said Ship upon [re]tence that she is not a Free Ship, whereas the Pet[itione]rs did suppose that shee having once been his Ma[jes]ties propriety shee could not in reason be afterwards reputed Forreigne, having never since been other then the propriety of his Ma[jes]ties Native Subjects of England. And praying his Ma[jes]ties Order for the making Free the said Ship, It was Ordered by his Ma[jes]tie in Councill That it be & hereby it is Referred to the Right Hon[ora]ble the Lord High Treasurer of England to Examine the Matters contayned in the said Petition & Report to his Ma[jes]tie what may be fitt to be done thereupon.

#4: Record from Philip Lanyon in Harwich to Sir Joseph Williamson that the *Bahama Merchant* had arrived in Plymouth with a load of brasiletta wood from the Bahamas – 21 January 1677 (TNA, SP 29/390, page 160)

[Page 160]

Plym[outh] Janua[ry] 21th 1676

Right hon[ora]ble

Friday last at night heer arrived the shipp *Bahama Merchant* from the Iland of new providence Hee Carted out with him a New governor for the said Ilands & hath brought home with him the old governor, Capt Wentworth Prisoner. When he went out of Englanf he went for Virginia he arrived in James River about the 22th of 7ber last past. the day before he arrived Bacon had burnt James Towne. The Governor S[i]r William Barklaye with what Company he had with him was about 100 to a 150 most or all the considerable persons with what soldiers the governor had were one board the shipps and sloops in James River. The Comander of this ship William Fowle further Reports that Bacon's forces are about 4 to 500 men, amongst whome is not one considerable person. he sayes that Bacon doth great spoyle where he comes. This Comander Remained in James River tenn days, from thence he sayled to New Providence, sayeing that the governor was resolved in a very short time after his departure to sayle for Rapahanacke or Yorke, this shipp was to Retourn from New Providence to Virginia to load tobacco for England, but, considering the danger he should be in by goeing there, and that he had noe hopes to purchase tobacco, made him to alter his design and load Brazelletta wood at New Providence for England this being far present the Needfull. I most humblye subscribe my selfe

Right hon[oura]ble
Your honours most humble servant
Philip Lanyon [signature]
1676

CHAPTER 10

The Kiffen Family Wills

Within the National Archives in Kew there are transcriptions of several wills of the Kiffen family recorded in the *Prerogative Court of Canterbury and Related Probate Jurisdictions: Will Registers 1384–1858.* In addition, William Kiffen's actual will itself has survived, although it is creased and torn and not in the best of conditions (see Figure #1). These documents not only provide crucial dating information, but also contain other important biographical details about the family, as well as providing insight into the social circumstances of the persons concerned (occupations, how much money they acculumated, etc). Within this chapter we shall offer the full text and translation of the wills of five members of the Kiffen family, beginning with that of William Kiffen himself:

Figure

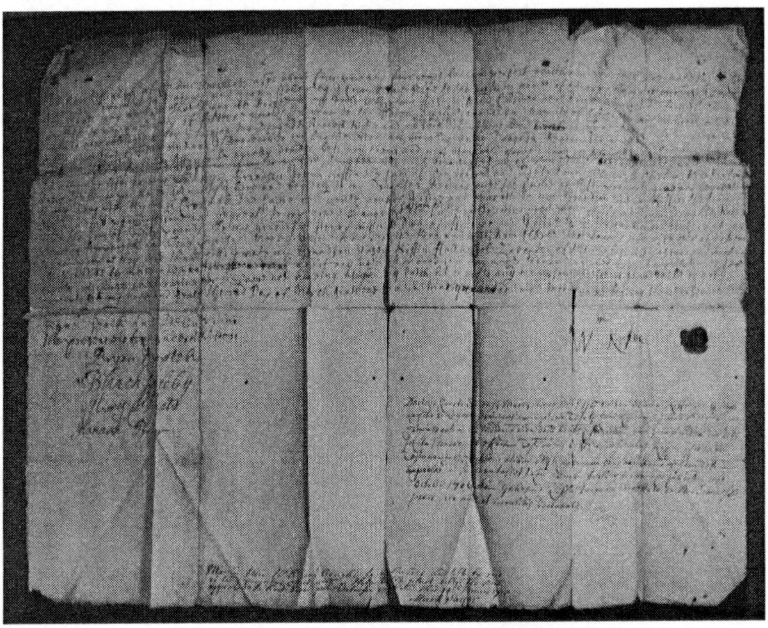

Figure #1 – The Will of William Kiffen

Documents

#1: The Will of William Kiffen – signed 23 March 1700; probated 14 March 1716 (TNA, PROB 10/1532); a copy of the will is also found into the Will Register of the Prerogative Court of Canterbury (TNA, PROB 11/551, folios 51 verso-52 recto).

William Kiffen was born in circa 1616 and died on 29 December 1701; he was buried in Bunhill Fields. His grandson, also named William Kiffen, was granted a commission to administer his goods, rights and credits on 2 October 1706, although this was apparently never carried out.[1] A subsequent commission was granted to another of William Kiffen's grandchildren, Susan Kiffen, on 14 March 1716.

[Recto]

I, William Kiffin, Esq[uire], of London, Merchant, aged about four score and four years, being in perfect health and Memory, Doe make this my Last Will and Testament in Manner and forme following: I Committ my selfe to the Earth in hopes of a happy Resurrection. First, I desire My Debts may be paid That I may be Buryed in my Vault where my first Wife and Children were Buryed. Whereas I did formerly Oblidge my selfe to pay an Annuity of Fifteen pounds P[er] Annum to the Widdow Sarah Oram, which said Annuity of Fifteen pounds my Grandson William Kiffin is now obliged to pay, I having my Daughter Rachell Kiffin and my said Grandson William Kiffin's Bond therein having made over Land to him, the said William Kiffin upon that Consideration. Next, I Bequeath to my daughter Hannah Hewling and my daughter Rebecca Hayes All my household Goods that are in my house in Whites Alley, to be equally devided between them, and what Household Goods I have at Bexwell, I give to my Grand daughter Susan Kiffin. I further give to my said daughter Hannah Hewling the Su[m]me of ten pounds as also twenty pounds p[er] Annum During her life, having paid to my Grandson Joseph Kiffin the Sum[m]e of One hundred and Eighty pounds, thereby to oblidge Him the said Joseph Kiffin to pay the said Annuity. I give and bequeath to my Daughter Rebecca Hayes the Sum[m]e of Fifty pounds. I give and bequeath to my Daughter Hannah Cromwell the Sum[m]e of Twenty pounds. I give and bequeath to my Grandson William Kiffin the Sum[m] of One hundred pounds. I give and bequeath to my Grand Daughter Susan Kiffin the sum[m]e of One Hundred pounds. To my Granddaughter Rachel

[1] TNA, PROB 6/82, page 142.

Kiffin the Sum[m]e of Fifty pounds. To my Grandson Henry Kiffin the sum of Fifty pounds. I give to my Servant Richard Hudson all my Wearing Apparrell and Five pounds in money. I give to Mr Morrice King and Mr William Clerke Ten pounds to be disposed of by them to such poor as they shall thinke fitt. I make my Grandson Joseph Kiffin Full and sole Executor of this my Last Will Testament revokeing all other Wills formerly made. ~~In witnesse hereof~~ and if any note, bill or bond is in being under the hand or Signed by my daughter Hayes, I doe freely discharge and forgive her the same not having assigned any such bill or bond to any one person whatsoever. In witnesse hereof I hereunto Sett my hand and seale this 23d day of March sixteene hundred ninety and nine, Monday next begining the yeare seventeene hundred. W[illia]m Kiffin [signature and seal]

Signed, Sealed and Delivered in
the presence of us underwritten.
Brian Appleby [signature]
Blanch Appleby [signature]
Mary Wright [signature]
Hannah Porter [signature]

Decimo Quarto die mensis Martii Anno D[omi]ni 1715 em[anavi]t Com[missi]o Susanna Kiffin Solutae Nepoti ex filis et Legatariae Principali nominat in Test[ament]e Gulielum Kiffin nup[er] paro[chi]ae S[anc]ti Aegidii Cripplegate in Com[itatu] Midd[lese]xiae Vidui def[unc]ti h[ab]entis &c Ad ad[mini]strand[um] bona jura et credita dicti def[unc]ti juxta tenorem et effectum Test[ament]i ipsius def[unc]ti (Eo quod Josephus Kiffin Ex[ecu]tor in d[ic]to Test[ament]o nominat mortem etiam obijt antequam onus Executionis ejusdem Test[ament]i expresse in se acceptasset) L[itte]ris Administrationis bonorum &c dicti def[unc]ti Mense Octobris 1706 cuidam Gulielmo Kiffin tanquam abintestato deceder[it] concessis prius pro nullis et invalidis declaratis.

[Translation of lines 26-33]

On the Fourteenth day of the Month of March in the Year of the Lord 1715, There was published a Commission to Susan Kiffin, Unmarried filial Granddaughter and Principal Legatee named in the Will of William Kiffin formerly of the parish of St Giles, Cripplegate in the County of Middlesex, Widdower, having died &c To administer the goods, rights and credits of the said deceased according to the intent and meaning of the Will of the dead man himself

(The reason being that Joseph Kiffin, the Executor named in the said Will, passed away, and died before he had expressly taken upon himself the duty of Execution of the same Will); the Letters of Administration of the goods &c of the said deceased that were granted in the month of October 1706 for a certain William Kiffin as if he had died intestate first having been declared null and void.

M[emoran]dum: This Will was brought to my hands and left be me in the Prerogative Office with a Hole in the place where the seal appeared to have been put. Witnesse my hand this 14th March 1715

Mark Sayer [signature]

[Verso]

The Last Will and Testament
of W[illia]m Kiffin Esq[uire] Dated the
23d March 1699/1700

#2: The Will of Henry Kiffen – signed 29 July 1698; probated 1 March 1699 (TNA, PROB 11/449, folio 342 verso-343 recto)

Henry Kiffen was William Kiffen's son and was granted his freedom as a leatherseller on 9 October 1673. He married Rachel Dashwood, the daughter of the financier William Dashwood, on 11 March 1675. He died on 8 December 1698 at the age of forty-four.

[Folio 342 verso]

In the Name of God, Amen.

I, Henry Kiffin of London, Merchant, being weak and indisposed in body but of sound and perfect mind and memory (praised be God for the same) and considering the uncertainty of this transitory life, do make and declare this my last Will and Testament in manner following. And first I comend my soul into the hands of Almighty God my Creator and preserver and of Jesus Christ my blessed Saviour and Redeemer, my body I comit to the earth from whence it is to be decently buried according to the discret[i]on of my Executors hereafter named. And as for such worldly Estate as God of his goodness hath been pleased to intrust and bless me withall, I give, devise, bequeath and Dispose of the same in manner and form following, that is to say, Imprimis

[Folio 343 recto]

I give and bequeath unto my deat and loving wife Rachell, her Executors, Admin[istrat]ors and assignes, All that my two Messuages or Tenements with their appurt[enance]s scituate in or near Austin Fryars, London, and the Lease by which I hold the same and all my Interest and term therein, she and they from time to time paying the ground rent to grow due therefore from and after my decease. Item: I give and bequeath unto my said wife Rachell and her assignes for and during the term of her naturall life all these my three messuages or Tenements with their appurten[an]ces situate and being in Loathbury, London and the Rents and profits thereof chargeable nevertheless with the paym[en]t of One Annuity of Fifty pounds per ann[um] by four quarterly payments unto my son William Kiffin during the life time of her my said wife and from and imediately after the decease of my said wife Rachell I do give and devise the said three messuages in Loathbury and all the rents and profits thereof unto my said son William Kiffin and his heirs forever. Item: I give and devise unto my said son William Kiffin and his heirs forever, all those three Farms with the Lands and appurten[an]ces thereunto belonging now held by John Saywell, Goodman Batsfeild and Thomas Cork situate and being in Baddow and Mowsom in the County of Essex chargeable neverthelesse and I do hereby charge the said three Farms and the rents and profits thereof with the payment of Nine hundred and seventy pounds principall money and the interest to grow due for the same into Mr Joseph Masters in discharge of One Bond wherein my said son stands bound with me for the payment thereof. Item: I give and devise unto my son Joseph Kiffin all those my Lands and Estate whatsoever of Boxwells and high Elmes in the said County of Essex, To hold unto him, my said son Joseph and his heires in such manner as is limited and prescribed in a Deed of Settlement formerly made of the said Lands and premises. Item: I give and devise unto my said wife Rachell and to my Brother-in-Law Robert Liddell, Esq[uire] and their heirs all those my two Farms and Lands whatsoever with their appurten[an]ces situate and being at Hornechurch in the said County of Essex and all my Copyhold Mesuages, Lands and Tenements whatsoever and wheresoever in Trust nevertheless and to the intent that they, my said wife and Brother or the survivor of them, his or her heirs, shall with all convenient speed sell and dispose of the said Farmes, Lands and premises and every of them to the best advantage they can reasonably make of the same, and by and out of the money to be raised thereby to pay and satisfye all such just Debts as I shall owe and be indebted upon any amount at my Decease (the aforesaid debts to the said Joseph Masters excepted together with my funerally charges and what reasonable expences they may be at in executing this trust and afterwards to pay and equally divide the remainder of the said moneys unto and between my daughter Rachel Kiffin and my son Henry Kiffin share and share alike. Item: I doe give to my Brother Robert Liddell Twenty pounds for mourning. Item: all the rest and residue of my goods, chattells, moneys, plate, Jewells, Bedding, Linnen, Debts and Estate whatsoever I give and bequeath unto my said loving wife Rachell and I do hereby make name and appoint her my said wife Rachell and my said Brother Robert Liddell full and joint Executors of this my Will and do revoake all former and other wills by me at any time heretofore made and declare this only to be my last Will and Testament. In witness whereof I have hereunto set

my hand and seale to twenty nineth day of July Anno D[omi]ni 1698 and in the
tenth yeare of the reign of our soveraign Lord King William the third of
England &c. Henry Kiffin Signed, sealed published and declared by the

[Folio 343 verso]

said Henry Kiffin the Testator for and as his last Will and Testament in the
presence of Thomas Gouge, David Jameson, John Owen.

Probatum fuit huiusmodi Testamentum apud London
coram ven[erabili]li viro Johanne Cooke, Legum Doctore Surrogato ven[erabi]lis et
egregii viri D[omi]ni Richardi Raines Militis legum etiam Doctoris Curiae
Prerogativae Cantuar[iensis] Magistri Custodis sive Comissarii l[egi]time constituti
Primo die mensis Martii Anno D[omi]ni (Stylo Angliae) Millesimo Sexcentesimo
nonagesimo octavo Juramento Rachaelis Kiffin Relictae dicti defuncti et
unius Executor[um] in dicto Testamento nominat[orum] Cui com[m]issa fuit admin[istra]t[i]o omniu[m]
et singulor[um] bonor[um] jur[ium] et creditor[um] dicti defuncti de bene et fidelit[er] administrando
eadem ad Sancta dei Evangelia Jurat[ae] Reservata potestate similem
Comit[i]onem faciendi Roberto Liddell alteri Executorum in dicto Testamento
nominat[orum] Cum venerit eandem petitur[us]. Ex[aminatu]r

[Translation of lines 66-76]

This will was probated in London
before the venerable gentleman John Cooke, Doctor of Laws and Representative of the venerable and
excellent Lord Richard Raines, Knight, also Doctor of Laws, legally appointed
Master, Custodian or Commissioner of the Prerogative Court of Canterbury,
The first day of the month of March, in the year of the Lord (English Style) One Thousand Six hundred
ninety eight, on the Oath of Rachael Kiffin, Relict of the said deceased and
one of the Executors named in the said Will, to whom was committed the administration of all
and singular goods, rights, and credits of the said deceased, she

having sworn to the good and faithful administration of the same on the Holy Gospels of God, the power having been reserved to make a similar Commission to Robert Liddell, the other Executor named in the said Will, when he comes and petitions for it.

#3: The Will of Rebecca Hayes – signed 17 June 1703; probated 5 August 1703 (TNA, PROB 11/471, folio 148 verso)

Rebecca Hayes was William Kiffen's daughter and was born in 1652. She married Joseph Hayes on 12 March 1671.

[Folio 148 verso]

In the Name of God, Amen.

I, Rebecca Hayes, Widdow of Joseph Hayes, deceased, doe make this my last Will and Testament and doe make Joseph Appleby, son of Bryan Appleby my onely Executor to my all my goods and chattells and what is due to me on my Annuity from Mr Robert Sidersin. I give and bequeath to my servant Mary White my Chest of Drawers and all my wearing Apparrell and what is due to her from me. In Witness whereof I hereunto set my hand and the marke of Rebecca Hayes. Witness Blanche Appleby Betty May Bryan Appleby

Quinto die Mensis Augusti Anno D[omi]ni Mill[es]imo Septinge[si]mo tertio Emanavit Com[missio] Mariae Wright Solutae Matertae et Curatrici legitime assignatco Josepho Appleby Executori nominato in Testamento Rebecca Hayes nup[er] paroc[hial]e Sanctae Mariae Whitechappell in Com[itate] Midd[lese]x viduea defunctae h[ab]entis &c ad Adm[ini]strand[o] bona jura et credita dictae defunctae juxta tenorem et effectum Testamenti ipsius defuncti in usum et beneficium d[ic]ti Executoris et doner decimum septimum aetatis Annum alligevit de bene et fidel[ite]r Adm[ini]strando eadem ad Sancta Dei Evangelia Jurat[ae] Ex[aminatu]r

This 17 of June 1703

[Translation of lines 9-17]

On the Fifth day of the month of August in the year of the Lord One Thousand Seven hundred three, There was published a Commission to Mary Wright, Unmarried Maternal Aunt and legally appointed Guardian to Joseph Appleby, named Executor in the Will of Rebecca Hayes, formerly of the parish of Saint Mary, Whitechappell in the County of Middlesex, widow, she having died &c To administer the goods, rights and credits of the said deceased according to the intent and meaning of the Will of the dead woman herself to the use and benefit of the said Executor and until he attains the age of seventeen years of age, she having sworn to the good and faithful Administration of the same on the Holy Gospels of God. It is Examined.

This 17 of June 1703

#4: The Will of Benjamin Hewling – signed 16 April 1684; probated 7 June 1684 (TNA, PROB 11/376, folio 206 verso-207 verso)

Benjamin Hewling was William Kiffen's son-in-law, having married Kiffen's daughter Hannah in c.1661. Benjamin Hewling is known to have been a trader in Aleppo in 1680–81(see SP 110/14 folios 107–139).

[Folio 206 verso]

In the Name of God, Amen. I, Benjamin Hewling of London, Merchant, being infirme and weake of body but of sound minde (through the goodnesse of God unto mee, Doe make this my last will and testament and dispose of that worldly estate where with God hath bin pleased to blesse mee as followeth. Impri[mi]s: I give and bequeath unto my sonn Benjamin Hewling the sume of one thousand four hundred pounds to be paid him as soone as conveniently it can be raised. Item: I give and bequeath unto my sonne William Hewling the summe of one Thousand pounds to be paid unto him when he shall attaine to the age of one and Twenty yeares. Item: I give and bequeath unto my Daughter Hannah the summe of twelve hundred pounds to be paid unto her when and as soon as the same can be raised and gotten in out of my estate. Item: I give and bequeath unto my daughter Rebecca the sume of eight hundred pounds when shee shall attaine to the age of one and twenty yeares or bee married which shall first happen. Item: I give and bequeath unto my daughter Elizabeth the sume of six hundred pounds when shee shall attaine the like age of one and twenty yeares or day of marriage which shall first happen. Item: I give and bequeath unto my daughter Priscilla the summe of Five hundred pounds at her age of one and twenty yeares or day of marriage first happening. Item: I give and bequeath unto my daughter Henrietta the summe of Five hundred pounds at er age of one and twenty yeares or day of marriage which shall first happen. And if it shall happen that my said sonne William shall die before hee attaine his age of one and twenty yeares or that any of my said daughters Rebecca, Elizabeth, Priscilla or Henrietta shall dye

[Folio 207 recto]

before they attaine their respective ages of one and Twenty yeares or bee married which shall first happen. Then I give the legacy and portion or legacies and port[i]ons of him, her or them so dieing to and amongst all the rest of my surviveing Children as well these of full ages, married as those under age or not married, equally to bee divided amongst them and to come and be paid unto them respectivelie at the respective times and in manner before appointed for payment of their respective portions or legacies herein before perticularly bequeathed to them. And my will and meaning is that the severall legacies and portions herein before given and I bequeathed unto my said sonne William and unto my daughters Rebecca, Elizabeth, Priscilla and Henrietta shall be disposed of and laid out by my Executrix herein after named, either in purchasing of Lands or put out at Interest by her or in any otherwise improved by my Executrix for the benefitt of my said sonne and daughters respectively untill they shall respectively attaine their respective ages of one and twenty yeares or be married as aforesaid, but my mind is that such disposition, putting out, or improvement shall not bee at the hazard or loss of my

Executrix hereafter named but at my childrens respective hazards as to their respective portions. And my further will and minde is that out of the improvem[en]t increase and profitt of each of my said Childrens portions they shall bee in the first place respectively maintained and educated by my Executrix and the residue of the improvement thereof shall goe towards the increasing of the said respective portions. Item: I give and devise unto my deare and beloved wife Hannah Hewling and her heires, the house wherein I now live and inhabitt, scituate in Coleman Streete, London, and my two houses or tenements adjoyneing thereunto one of which has two Tenements is scituate on the one side of the Gateway of my said dwelling house in Coleman streete aforesaid and the other of the said two houses is scituate on the other side of the said Gate of my said house, and also all other my houses, Lands and Tenements whatsoever, and wheresoever, To have and to hold the said Three messuages or dwelling houses with thappurtenances and all other my lands and tenements unto my said deare wife, her heires and assignes forever and to noe other use whatsoever. Item: I give unto Mr Morrice King the summe of Tenne pounds by him to be disposed to and amongst such poore Christians and in such manner as hee shall see cause. Item: I give unto my nephew John Pearson the summe of Tenne pounds to be opaid to the hands of some friend for his use. Item: I give unto my Neece Hannah Pearson the summe of Tenne pounds as a token of my love and to muy mourning if shee please. Item: I also give and bequeath unto my said deare wife all my household goods, plate, jewells and all and singular my Leases and revertions. Item: I likewise give my said wife all the rest and residue of my goods, chatells and other my personall estate whatsoever the port[i]ons and legacies before bequeathed being satisfied. And I doe hereby make, ordaine and appoint my said wife my sole Executrix of this my last will and testament and my expresse will and desire is that my wife and children, all of them, acquiese and be satisfied in this my will without insisting upon any right or custome whatsoever, and my further expresse will is that if my wife or any my children shall not be satisfied herein but endeavour to alter the same, The respective legacies or gifts of such dissatisfied person or persons hereby willed shall not goe to him, her or them respectively soe dissatisfied. And I desire my most Honoured father-in-law William Kiffin, Esq[uire], Mr John Smith, Merchant, and my brother-in-law Mr Henry Kiffin, to bee overseers of this my last will and to assist my deare wife in the execution thereof, w[hi]ch I know they will readily take upon themselves the trouble to doe. And lastly, I doe hereby revoke all former wills by mee at any time heretofore made, declaring this to be my last will and Testament. In witness whereof I have to this my last will

[Folio 207 verso]

and testament contained in three sheetes of paper, vizt, to each sheete thereof sett my hand and seale this Sixteenth day of April, Anno Domini, one thousand six hundred eighty foure. Benja[min] Hewling Signed, Sealed published and declared (the words *and her heires* in the second Sheete, being first interlined by the said Benjamin Hewling) to be his last will and testament in the presence of Jo[hn] Greene Tho[mas] Prince, George Poinder, Letitia Jaque.

[Text]

Probatum fuit hu[ius]mo[d]i test[a]m[en]t[um] Londini coram ven[erabi]li viro D[omi]no Nich[ola]o Lloyd, Milite, legum D[oc]tore Surrogato venerabilis et egregii viri D[omi]ni Leolini

Jenkins, Militis, legum etiam D[oc]toris Curiae Praerogativae Cantuariensis mag[ist]ri Custod[is] sive Commissarii le[gi]time constituti Septimo die mensis Junii Anno D[omi]ni Mill[es]imo sexcen[tesi]mo octoge[si]mo quarto Juramento Hannae Hewling, Relictae dicti defuncti et Executricis in dicto testamento nominat[ae] Cui Commissa fuit Administratio omnium et singulorum bonorum iurium et creditorum dicti def[unc]ti de bene et fidel[ite]r Ad[mini]strando eadem ad S[an]cta Dei Evangelia Jurat[ae]. Ex[aminatu]r

[Translation of lines 81-88]

This will was probated in London before the venerable Lord Nicholas Lloyd, Knight, Doctor of Laws, Surrogate of the venerable and esteemed Lord Leoline Jenkins, Knight, also Doctor of Laws, legitimately appointed Master, Custodian or Commissary of the Prerogative Court of Canterbury, on the Seventh day of the month of June in the year of the Lord One Thousand six hundred eighty four, on the Oath of Hannah Hewling, Relict of the said deceased, and named Executrix in the said will, to whom was Committed the Administration of all and singular goods, rights, and credits of the said deceased, she having sworn to the good and faithful Administration of the same on the Holy Gospels of God. It is Examined.

#5: The Will of Hannah Cromwell – signed 9 March 1732; probated 7 February 1733 (TNA, PROB 11/656, folio 262 recto)

Hannah Cromwell was William Kiffen's grand-daughter, the daughter of Hannah and Benjamin Hewling. She was born in 1662 and married Henry Cromwell (the grandson of Oliver Cromwell) on 11 May 1686. She died 26 March 1732.

[Folio 262 recto]

In the Name of God, Amen.

I, Hannah Cromwell of the parish of St Andrews Holborn in the County of Middlesex, Widdow, doe make this my last Will and Testament in man[n]er following: I give and bequeath unto my dear Son William Cromwell, his Heires, Executors and Administrators respectively All my Estate both real and personal whatsoever and wheresoever and I doe make my said Son Executor of this my last Will and Testament and I doe hereby revoke all former Wills by me made. In Wittnes whereof to this my last Will and Testament I have set my hand and affixed my Seal the Ninth day of March, Anno Domini 1731 H[annah] Cromwell Signed, Sealed, Published and declared by the said Testatrix Hannah Cromwell to be her last Will and Testament in the presence of us who subscribe our Names as Wittnesses hereto in her presence Mary Webber Eli[zabeth] Nash

Probatum fuit huiusmodi Testamentum apud London coramVenerabili Viro Gulielmo Straham Legum Doctore Surrogato Venerabilis et Egregii Johannis Bettesworth Legum Doctoris Curiae Praerogativae Cantuariensis Magistri Custodis sive Commissarii legitime Constituti Septimo die Mensis Februarii Anno Dominis Millessimo Septingentesimo Tricesimo Secundo Juramento Gulielmi Cromwell filii et Executoris unici in dicto Testamento Nominato Cui commissa fuit administratio omnium et singulorum bonorum jurium et Creditorum dicti defuncti de bene et fideliter administrando eadem ad Sancta Dei Evangelia Jurat[o]. Ex[aminatu]r

[Translation of lines 15-24]

This will was probated in London before the Venerable William Strahan, Doctor of Laws, Representative of the Venerable and Esteemed John Bettesworth, Doctor of Laws, legitimately appointed Master, Custodian and Commissary of the Prerogative Court of Canterbury on the Seventh day of the Month of February in the Year of the Lord One thousand Seven hundred and Thirty Two on the Oath of William Cromwell, son and named sole Executor in the said Will, To Whom was committed administration of all and singular goods, rights, and Credits of the said deceased, he having sworn to the good and faithful administrations of the same on the Holy Gospels of God. It is Examined.

Bibliography

Whenever possible manuscripts are entered under the catalogue reference numbers assigned by the library or institution; in principle this enables easy access for ordering the manuscript via the on-line search engines of The National Archives, The British Library, The London Metropolitan Archives, etc. The publication dates of materials contained in the Thomason collection are given where known and are indicated by a 'T' (for example, 1 January 1661T); these dates are adjusted to reflect modern dating of January 1-25 March of the calendar year. Thomason reference numbers, or Wing reference numbers, are also provided, which will make access to the document in Early English Books Online (EEBO) easier. References to the printed *Calendars* of the State Papers within the National Archives are deliberately avoided, mainly because of their inadequacies, notably the tendency to use document numbers rather than page numbers. Here references are to the acual page numbers stamped on the documents, giving a much more precise means to find the source needed.

Manuscripts in Libraries and Special Collections

Historical Manuscripts Commission Volumes (HMC)

The Manuscripts of His Grace The Duke of Portland Preserved at Welbeck Abbey, Volume I (London: HMSO, 1891): 637 = Proposal from Hanserd Knollys and Richard Wollaston to the Committee for the Propagation of the Gospel (between 10 February 1652 and 11 February 1653).

Report on the Manuscripts of F.W. Leyborne-Popham (London: Historical Manuscripts Commission, 1899): 78 = Letter of John Sherwin to Colonel Deane and Colonel Popham at Whitehall while aboard the *Hind* with an account of his actions against pirates in the Irish Sea (22 November 1650 from Liverpool).

Seventh Report of the Royal Commission of Historical Manuscripts, Part I, Report and Appendix (London: HMSO, 1879): 80 = description of the Anabaptist Petition of 1660.

Angus Library, Regent's Park College, Oxford (ALRPCO)

Stinton, Benjamin 'Repository of Divers Historical Matters Relating to English Antipedobaptists' (1712) (D Stinton 1), pages 10-12 = The so-called Kiffen Memorandum.

Stinton, Benjamin 'Repository of Divers Historical Matters Relating to English Antipedobaptists' (1712) (D Stinton 1): pages 25-28 = Debates about Infant-Baptism in 1644.

Bodleian Library, Oxford (BLO)

MS Carte 214, folio 99 = Report of destruction of Anabaptist meeting house in the riots of May 1660.

MS Locke b1, page 24 = Accounting record showing John Locke received money from Kiffen for silks (January 1678).

MS Locke b1, page 25 = Accounting record showing that Thomas Stringer paid monies to Sir Patience Ward on (7 January 1676, and 4 June 1677).

MS Locke b1, page 25 = Accounting record showing that John Locke paid William Kiffen £25 to settle a debt (14 September 1676).

MS Locke b1, page 25 = Accounting record showing that John Locke paid William Kiffen's man for a letter (3 September 1676).

MS Locke c 6, pages 215-216 = Letter from Sir Peter Colleton in Barbados to John Locke noting that the *Bahama Merchant* had arrived there (October 1673).

MS Locke c 11, folio 247-248 = Letter from Robert Huntington in Aleppo to John Lock at William Kiffen's house in Austin Friers (22 May 1678).

MS Locke f 1, page 152 = Entry in John Locke's travel journal about grape vines sent to Kiffen in London (17 March 1676).

MS Locke f 1, page 159 = Entry in John Locke's travel journal about oranges sent to Kiffen in London (24 March 1676).

MS Locke f 2, page 133 = Entry in John Locke's travel journal requesting Kiffen to make credit transfer arrangements (10 May 1677).

MS Locke f 2, page 151 = Entry in John Locke's travel journals about a money transfer (9 June 1677).

MS Rawlinson A 12, pages 169-170 = Letter from Henry Cromwell in Dublin to John Thurloe which mentions the letter from Kiffen, Spilsbery and Sansom about Oliver Cromwell assuming Lord Protectorate powers (8 March 1654).

MS Rawlinson A 12, pages 300-303 = Letter from Jen[kyn] Lloyd in Dublin to John Thurloe which mentions the letter from Kiffen, Spilsbery and Sansom about Oliver Cromwell assuming Lord Protectorate powers (13 March 1654).

MS Rawlinson A 14, folio 590 recto = Captain John Sherwin of the *Primrose* writes a letter about the thief and imposter John Shelby (May 1654).

MS Rawlinson A 16, folio 348 recto = Letter from John Jeanlett to the Secretary of State John Thurloe giving details of the transport of John Selby to London (21 July 1654).

MS Rawlinson A 59, pages 75-76 = Informant's report about the Baptist meeting at Dorchester in May 1658 at which Kiffen advised against association with the Fifth Monarchists.

MS Rawlinson A 184, folio 56 = Petition of Samuel Gleede for a Master Gunner's position in a Commonwealth ship (undated).

MS Rawlinson A 184, folio 58 = Four others write a letter of support for the petition of Samuel Gleede (undated).

MS Rawlinson A 184, folio 60 = Captain John Sherwin writes a letter of support for the petition of Samuel Gleede (6 June 1656).

MS Rawlinson A 184, folio 62 = Four others write a letter of support for the petition of Samuel Gleede (5 June 1656).

MS Rawlinson A 184, folio 63 = Samuel Hyland and William Kiffen write a letter of support for the petition of Samuel Gleede (7 June 1656).

MS Rawlinson A 184, folio 64 = Edward Ny writes a letter of support for the petition of Samuel Gleede (8 June 1656).

MS Rawlinson A 187, folio 219 recto = Letter from officers in the Ordnance Office about the actions of Samuel Gleede aboard the *Phoenix* (8 February 1660).

MS Rawlinson A 187, folio 221 recto = Certificate from officers in the Ordnance Office about the actions of Samuel Gleede aboard the *Phoenix* (20 January 1660).

MS Rawlinson A 222, folio 20 recto = Captain Richard Wollaston is paid £165 13*s* 10*d* owed him by the Navy (11 April 1644).

MS Rawlinson A 223, page 103 = The *Hind* included in a list of ships for the winter guard (16 August 1650).

MS Rawlinson A 224, folio 101 recto = Chart of rates of pay for naval officers (24 August 1649).

MS Rawlinson A 225, folio 46 recto = Report about the *Hind* noting she was 'old and crazy' and due to be sold, her guns transferred to the *Convert* (7 January 1651).

MS Rawlinson A 225, folio 49 recto and verso = Report about the *Hind* noting she was 'old and defective and unserviceable for the States use' (11 January 1651).

MS Rawlinson A 225, folio 99 verso = Captain Sherwin on the *Hind* is included as part of the Summer Guard on the Irish Sea (24 April 1651).

MS Rawlinson A 225, folio 127 verso = Captain Sherwin on the *Hind* is ordered to take supplies to Ireland (10 June 1651).

MS Rawlinson A 225, folio 149 recto = Captain Sherwin on the *Hind* is ordered to escort provisions to Scotland and patrol there (19 July 1651).

MS Rawlinson A 225, folio 150 verso = Orders issued to fit out the *Primrose* as soon as possible (22 July 1651).

MS Rawlinson A 226, folio 6 verso = Order from the Committee of the Admiralty for 24 guns on the *Primrose* (20 August 1651).

MS Rawlinson A 226, folio 14 verso = Captain Sherwin on the *Primrose* is ordered to the Downs (5 September 1651).

MS Rawlinson A 226, folios 22 recto and verso and 23 recto = Four petitions from families of lost crew of the *Hind* which was cast away when Sherwin was Captain (29 September 1651).

MS Rawlinson A 226, folios 29 verso and 30 recto = Petition from the widow of a lost crewman of the *Hind* which was killed on the Isle of Man when Sherwin was Captain (15 October 1651).

MS Rawlinson A 226, folio 100 verso = The *Primrose* under Captain Sherwin is included in the list of ships for the Summer Guard of 1652 (14 January 1652).

MS Rawlinson A 226, folio 118 recto and verso = The *Primrose* under Captain Sherwin is sent to patrol the coast of Scotland (13 April 1652).

MS Rawlinson A 226, folio 194 recto = A petition from the widow of a crewmember of the *Hind* which was cast away when Sherwin was Captain (8 September 1652).

MS Rawlinson A 226, folio 203 recto = Report of a letter from Captain Sherwin to the Committee of the Admiralty requesting repairs and supplies for the *Primrose* in anticipation of her service in the Winter guard (22 September 1652).

MS Rawlinson A 227, folio 121 verso = Captain Sherwin and the *Primrose* are ordered from Hope to the docks in Chatham for refitting (4 August 1653).

MS Rawlinson C 409, page 60 = Manuscript addition about Knollys and Wollaston inserted into copy of John Lewis's *A Brief History of the Rise and Progress of Anabaptism in England* (1738).

British Library, London (BLL)

Add MS 10,116, folio 91 = Thomas Rugge's, 'Mercurius Politicus Redivivus', note on defacement of Kiffen's meeting-house.

Add MS 15,640 = Articles and Orders of the Company of Adventurers to the Bahama Islands (1672).

Add MS 15,859, folios 58 verso-59 recto, Thomas Burton, 'Diary of Parliament 1656-1659, Volume 1' = Kiffen's opposition to the death penalty being inflicted on James Naylor (December 1656).

Add MS 18,986, page 84 = Captain Sherwin aboard the *Primrose* (27 July 1653 from Plymouth).

Add MS 22,546, page 139 = Captain Sherwin aboard the *Primrose* (27 January 1654 from Leith Road).

Stowe MS 185, folios 168-170 = Letter of John Desborough to Livewell Chapman (8 April 1660).

Stowe MS 185, folio 175 recto = 'The State of the Non-conformists in England soon after the Restoration', identifies Capt Kiffen, Mr Knowles, Mr Harrison, Mr Gosnold, and Mr Northott as Baptist leaders.

Stowe MS 498, page 211 = Treasurer Southampton's resolution on Old Artillery Ground petition (9 July 1661).

The Guildhall Library, London (GLL)

MS 20,228 1A, folios 3 verso-5 verso, Devonshire Square Minute Book = Robert Malbon and others disciplined by Kiffen's church (April 1665).

MS 20,228 1A, folio 9 recto and verso, Devonshire Square Minute Book = Elizabeth Malbon and others disciplined by Kiffen's church (3 November 1667).

MS 20,230, folios 5-93, Devonshire Square Membership Lists – c. 1664-1690.

MS 5445/15, The Brewers' Company Minutes 1628-1634 = No record of Kiffen's apprenticeship to John Lilburne.

Lambeth Palace Library (LPL)

Cod Lambeth 272, page 282 = tax record of 'Mr Kuiffen' paying tax on a property in Hart Street, Saint Olave's, near Tower Hill which rented for £6 per annum (1638).

The London Metropolitan Archives, London (LMA)

AM/PI(2)/1695/012, Probate Inventory of Elleanor Simcock (30 March 1695).

CLA/047/LR/02/02/001, List of Hoax Preachers and Places (circa 1663).

CLA/047/LR/02/02/005, folios 393-408, Certificates of Conviction = Convictions involving William Kiffen in Devonshire Square (November 1682-January 1683).

COL/CA/01/01/50, pages 300-302 = Court of Aldermen discuss Leathersellers Company (7 July 1632).

MJ/GB/B/005/112, page 25 = James Nash fails to appear before the Quarter Sessions court (11 December 1661).

MJ/SB/R/007, page 112 = Henry Jessey and seven others from his church appear before the Middlesex Quarter Sessions court and are discharged (19 May 1640).

MJ/SB/R/008, page 115 = William Kiffen and fifteen women from his church appear before the Middlesex Quarter Sessions court and are discharged (24 April 1661).

MJ/SB/R/008, page 131 = James Nash appears before the Middlesex Quarter Sessions court and is ordered to return to a later court session (28 April 1661).

MJ/SP/1686/02/001, folio 98 recto = List of persons committed for unlawful assembly at Devonshire Square (11 February 1686).

MJ/SR/0873/50-52, Sessions Roll: Sessions of the Peace #0873 (19 May 1640) = Indictments of members of Henry Jessey's conventicle in Southwarke (12 April 1640).

MJ/SR/0887/22, Sessions Roll: Gaol Delivery #0887 (29 January 1641) = William Uncles's indictment for attending an illegal conventicle led by Thomas Lambe (17 January 1641).

MJ/SR/1227/37, Sessions Roll: Sessions of the Peace #1227 (28 March 1661) = William Kiffen's indictment for attending an illegal conventicle (26 February 1661).

MJ/SR/1227/38, Sessions Roll: Sessions of the Peace #1227 (28 March 1661) = Indictment of seven women from Kiffen's church for attending an illegal conventicle (24 February 1661).

MJ/SR/1227/39, Sessions Roll: Sessions of the Peace #1227 (28 March 1661) = Indictment of ten women from Kiffen's church for attending an illegal conventicle (24 February 1661).

MJ/SR/1229/72, Sessions Roll: Sessions of the Peace #1229 (24 April 1661) = Indictment of James Nash from Kiffen's church for attending an illegal conventicle (8 April 1661).

MJ/SR/1268/86, Sessions Roll: Sessions of the Peace #1268 (27 April 1663) = Robert Malbon offers surety for Jeremie Eightshillings for his indictment for refusing to swear the Oath of Allegiance (9 January 1663).

MJ/SR/1370/121, Sessions Roll: Sessions of the Peace #1320 (5 July 1669) = Joseph Kiffen indicted for failing to attend his local parish church (6 June 1669).

MR/R/C/001, membrane 35, Conventicle Convictions – 1664-1665 = Hanserd Knollys' conviction for attending conventicle at the home of Mary Winch (9 January 1665).

MR/R/C/001/13, membrane 13, Conventicle Convictions – 1664-1665 = Elizabeth Malbon named in Stepney congregation conviction (4 September 1664).

MR/T/H/004, membrane 5, Hearth Tax for 1664 = Robert Malborne pays tax on a property containing eight hearths (1664).

Library of Society of Antiquaries, London (LSA)

Letters Addressed to Oliver Cromwell (SAL MS 138), pages 191-192 = Letter of William Kiffen, John Spilsbery and Joseph Sansom to Ireland on submission to authority – 20 January 1654(?).

The National Archives, London (TNA) – alphabetically arranged by catalogue reference numbers

AO 1/1726/148, Declared Accounts of the Navy – 1706 = Pension pay Samuel Gleede for May-October 1704.

ASSI 35/84/6, membrane 1, Surrey Assizes – Lent 1642 = Gaol delivery calendar of assizes of 12 March 1642.

ASSI 35/84/6, membrane 81, Surrey Assizes – Lent 1642 = William Kiffen indictment of 12 March 1642.

ASSI 35/84/6, membrane 82, Surrey Assizes – Lent 1642 = Dorothy Dart indictment of 12 March 1642.

ASSI 35/84/10, membrane 46, Surrey Assizes – Lent 1642 = Judges Precept for assizes of 12 March 1642.

ASSI 35/84/10, membrane 62, Surrey Assizes – Lent 1642 = William Kiffen indictment of 14 March 1642.

ASSI 35/84/10, membrane 69, Surrey Assizes – Lent 1642 = Walter Jackson indictment of 14 March 1642

ASSI 35/84/10, membrane 70, Surrey Assizes – Lent 1642 = Walter Jackson indictment of 14 March 1642

ASSI 35/84/10, membrane 71, Surrey Assizes – Lent 1642 = Walter Jackson indictment of 14 March 1642

C 66/1305, Part 2, Patent Roll of 30 Elizabeth I = Robert Constable's patent of appointment to the office of Lieutenant of Ordnance (1588).

C 66/2354, Part 7, No 12, Patent Roll of 1 Charles I = William Heydon's patent of appointment to the office of Lieutenant of Ordnance (16 March 1626).

C 66/2820, Part 25, No 2, Patent Roll of 14 Charles I = Charter for the Worshipful Company of Glovers (10 September 1638).

C 66/2933, Part 18, No 37, Patent Roll of 12 Charles II = William Legge's patent of appointment to the office of Lieutenant of Ordnance (28 June 1660).

C 66/3121, Part 8, No 22, Patent Roll of 22 Charles II = David Walter's patent of appointment to the office of Lieutenant of Ordnance (15 November 1670).

C 66/3224, Part 6, No 18, Patent Roll of 33 Charles II = George Legg's patent of appointment to the office of Lieutenant of Ordnance (28 January 1682).

C 66/3268, Part 7, No 8, Patent Roll of 1 James II = Christopher Musgrave's patent of appointment to the office of Lieutenant of Ordnance (2 April 1685).

C 66/3297, Part 7, No 8, Patent Roll of 3 James II = Henry Tichborne's patent of appointment to the office of Lieutenant of Ordnance (1 August 1687).

CO 1/12, page 110 = William Kiffen's petition for license to export horses to Barbados (31 May 1655).

CO 1/19, pages 231-232 = John Champante serving as London agent for Lord Willoughby in the Caribbean (2 September 1665).

CO 5/1259, pages 395-408 = Court records of the capture of the *Bahama Merchant* in 1699.

CO 5/1288, pages 56-61 = Court records of the capture of the *Bahama Merchant* in 1699.

CRES 6/2, pages 88-92 and 293-94, Surveyor General Constat Book B – 1660-1661 = The Surveyor General's constat concerning Hanserd Knollys' Petition (18 December 1660).

CRES 6/12, pages 304-307, Surveyor General Constat Book M – 1675-1678 = The Surveyor General's constat concerning the Hanserd Knollys case (16 March 1678).

CRES 6/14, pages 166-167, Surveyor General Constat Book O – 1679-1682 = The Surveyor General William Harbord's constat concerning Hanserd Knollys Petition (3 July 1680).

CRES 6/14, pages 247-248, Surveyor General Constat Book O – 1679-1682 = The Surveyor General William Harbord's survey of the Old Artillery Ground (11 May 1681).

E 179/251/22), page 185 verso, Poll Tax of July-August 1641 – Livery Companies Records = entry for William Kiffen.

E 367/2474, Pipe Office – Warrant for Crown Lease to Hanserd Knollys = Treasury warrant for a lease to Hanserd Knollys (16 January 1661).

KB 9/823/113, Michaelmas 1641 = William Uncles's indictment for attending an illegal conventicle led by John Spilsbery (15 September 1641).

LR 17/2, Surveyor General Papers – 1660-1662 = Treasurer Southampton orders a constat for Hanserd Knollys' case (24 November 1660).

LR 17/8, Hanserd Knollys' Memorandum on the Old Artillery Ground (LR 17/8).

MPE 1/479 = Map of St James's Park (1667).

MPE 1/503 = Map of Old Artillery Ground (1681).

PC 2/40, pages 463-464 = The Honourable Artillery Company state that the Old Artillery Ground Armoury building cost £1,000 to build (1631).

PC 2/40, pages 512-513 = Privy Council discusses the use of the Old Artillery Ground property (18 May 1631).
PC 2/50, page 552 = The Privy Council discusses the case of John Trendall (31 July 1639).
PC 2/50, pages 567-568 = The Privy Council discusses the case of John Trendall (2 August 1639).
PC 2/50, page 571 = The Privy Council discusses the case of John Trendall (2 August 1639).
PC 2/50, page 601 The Privy Council orders Oath of Supremacy to be administered to John Trendall (18 August 1639).
PC 2/50, page 666 = Privy Council orders a chaplain for Trendall in Dover prison (6 October 1639).
PC 2/50, page 683 = Privy Council orders Trendall to be brought to London (20 October 1639)..
PC 2/50, page 689 = Privy Council orders Trendall be moved to the Fleete prison in London (30 October 1639).
PC 2/64, page 361 = Record of a Petition by the Bahama Adventurers to the Privy Council that their ship the *Bahama Merchant* be made free for trading purposes (29 January 1675).
PRO 30/24/48/55, pages, 4, 6 = Hugh Wentworth letter to the Lords Proprietors of Carolina about the establishment of a colony in the Bahama Islands (17 February 1670).
PRO 30/24/49, page 58 = Letter from Richard Lilburne to the Bahama Adventurers about ambergrice (9 August 1674).
PRO 30/24/49, pages 60-61 = Letter from Isaac Rush to John Locke with news of the *Bahama Merchant* (10 August 1674).
PRO 30/24/48, No 90 = Letter from Sir Peter Colleton to John Locke with news about the life in the Caribbean, (28 May 1673).
PRO 30/32/36, pages 12 and 62, Treasury Petitioners Entry Book – 1677-78 = Hanserd Knollys' petition on the Old Artillery Ground (1677).
PROB 6/82, page 142 recto = Commission granted to William Kiffen to administer the goods of his grandfather William Kiffen (2 October 1706).
PROB 10/1532 = The Will of William Kiffen (signed 23 March 1700; probated 14 March 1716).
PROB 11/321, pages 58 recto-59 verso = The will of Paul Hobson (signed 12 March 1663; probated 13 June 1666).
PROB 11/332, pages 63 verso-64 recto = The will of Robert Malbon (signed 3 October 1665; probated 29 October 1666).
PROB 11/374, pages 230 recto and verso) = The will of Nathaniel Stoner (signed 29 October 1683; probated 9 November 1683).
PROB 11/376, folio 206 verso-207 verso = The Will of Benjamin Hewling (signed 16 April 1684; probated 7 June 1684).
PROB 11/449, folio 342 verso-343 recto = The Will of Henry Kiffen (signed 29 July 1698; probated 1 March 1699).

PROB 11/471, folio 148 verso = The Will of Rebecca Hayes (signed 17 June 1703; probated 5 August 1703).

PROB 11/487, folios 312 recto and verso = Will of Samuel Gleed (signed 8 January 1706; probated 26 April 1706).

PROB 11/551, folios 51 verso-52 recto = The Will of William Kiffen (signed 23 March 1700; probated 14 March 1716).

PROB 11/656, folio 262 recto = The Will of Hannah Cromwell (signed 9 March 1732; probated 7 February 1733).

PROB 11/782, folio 182 verso = The Will of Susannah Kiffen (signed 9 August 1750; probated 6 September 1750).

SP 9/26, page 76 recto, Joseph Williamson's Index of Nonconformist Ministers – 1663 = Note on Hanserd Knollys.

SP 16/261, page 271 = Prison custodian Robert Bellin, petitions the Court of High Commission at Lambeth (20 October 1635).

SP 16/426, page 128 = Testimony of Joan Tiddeyman in Case of John Trendall (27 July 1639).

SP 16/427, page 180 = Archbishop Neile's letter about the heretic Trendall (23 August 1639).

SP 16/427, pages 183-187 = Trendall administered the Oath of Supremacy (24 August 1639).

SP 16/432, pages 50-64 = Case of John Trendall before Thomas Day (27-29 July 1639).

SP 16/432, page 63 = Archbishop Neile's account of the execution of Edward Wightman (9 August 1639).

SP 16/432, page 55 = Testimony of Joan Tiddeyman in Case of John Trendall (27 July 1639). .

SP 16/432, page 115 = John Trendall case before Court of High Commission (14 November 1639).

SP 16/434, page 39 verso = John Trendall case before Court of High Commission (14 November 1639).

SP 16/434, pages 48 recto and 49 recto = John Trendall case before Court of High Commission (21 November 1639).

SP 16/434, page 61 recto = John Trendall case before Court of High Commission (28 November 1639).

SP 16/434, page 224 = Edward Barber committed to Newgate prison in June of 1640.

SP 16/434A, page 9 verso = Eight women indicted for a conventicle (28 April 1640).

SP 16/436, pages 49-50 = Jailer John Reston's bill for transferring John Trendall from Dover (20 December 1639).

SP 16/442, page 265 = Jailer John Reston paid for transporting John Trendall to London (27 January 1640).

SP 16/476, page 119 = Baptists led by Edmund Chillenden, appear before Sir John Lenthall for an illegal meeting in the house of Richard Sturges on 13 January 1641

SP 18/1, pages 127-128 = Council of State orders Captain Sherwin to patrol in the Irish Sea aboard the *Truelove* (24 April 1649).

SP 18/5, page 49 = Accounting record of the victualling of Captain Sherwin aboard the *Truelove* (14 June 1649).

SP 18/9/page 53 = Orders for Captain Sparling aboard the *President* and Captain Sherwin aboard the *Hind* to seek out pirates in the Irish Sea and the Isle of Man (9 April 1650).

SP 18/9/page 201 = Orders to resupply Sherwin aboard the *Hind* at Chester for service in the Irish sea (20 August 1650).

SP 18/12, page 86 = Note that Captain Sherwin aboard the *Hind* successfully transported money to pay the army in Ireland (23 September 1650).

SP 18/27, page 62 = Captain Sherwin commissions the hire of the *Richard and Benjamin* (12 March 1651).

SP 18/27, page 91 = Captain Sherwin commissions the hire of the *Richard and Benjamin* (12 April 1652).

SP 18/28, pages 167-168 = Captain John Sherwin writes a letter of complaint to the Commisioners of the Navy about failure to give the *Primrose* adequate provision (5 October 1652).

SP 18/28, page #206 = Samuel Windis aboard the *Primrose* as purser (26 October 1652).

SP 18/29, page 50 = Captain Sherwin aboard the *Primrose* (18 November 1652 from Dublin Bay).

SP 18/29, page 68 = Captain Sherwin aboard the *Primrose* (22 November 1652 in Irish Sea).

SP 18/29, page 166 = Crew of the *Primrose* sick with fever (17 December 1652).

SP 18/30, page 10 = Captain Sherwin aboard the *Primrose* (18 December 1652 from Chester).

SP 18/42, page 313-315 = Samuel Windis explains his side of the dispute about victualling the *Satisfaction* (23 September 1654).

SP 18/45, page 81 = Captain Sherwin aboard the *Primrose* (6 January 1653 from Liverpool).

SP 18/54, page 30 = Captain Sherwin aboard the *Primrose* (4 June 1653 from Liverpool).

SP 18/54, page 290 = Captain Sherwin aboard the *Primrose* (17 June 1653 from Liverpool).

SP 18/57 page 37 = Captain Sherwin aboard the *Primrose* (3 August 1653 from Hope).

SP 18/58, page 170 = John Barkstead recommendation for Thomas Weeks (26 September 1653).

SP 18/58, page 170 = Master Gunner Richard Wollaston recommendation for Thomas Weeks (12 November 1650).

SP 18/65, page 29 = Sherwin and *Primrose* sent to guard Scottish coast (10 January 1654)
SP 18/69, page 161 = Captain Sherwin aboard the *Primrose* (16 April 1654 from Inverness).
SP 18/75, page 89 = Captain Sherwin aboard the *Primrose* (26 August 1654 from Ayr).
SP 18/76, pages 95-96 = Samuel Windis explains his side of the dispute about victualling the *Satisfaction* (23 September 1654).
SP 18/76, pages 142-143 = Samuel Windis explains his side of the dispute about victualling the *Satisfaction* (6 October 1654).
SP 18/76, page 179 = Samuel Windis explains his side of the dispute about victualling the *Satisfaction* (21 October 1654).
SP 18/78, page 62 = Captain Sherwin aboard the *Primrose* (7 January 1654 from Leith Road).
SP 18/78, page 84 = Richard Wollaston's report on ordnance in the Tower wharf (1 January 1654).
SP 18/81 page 79 = Captain Sherwin aboard the *Primrose* (5 April 1654 from Leith Road).
SP 18/83, page 106 = Captain Sherwin aboard the *Primrose* (13 June 1654 from Hull).
SP 18/83, page 174 = Captain Sherwin aboard the *Primrose* (20 June 1654 from Hull).
SP 18/83, page 278 = Captain Sherwin aboard the *Primrose* (30 June 1654 from Hull).
SP 18/84, page 167 = Captain Sherwin aboard the *Primrose* (11 July 1654 from Hull).
SP 18/85, page 70 = Captain Sherwin aboard the *Primrose* (21 July 1654 from Whitebooth Road Humber).
SP 18/87, pages 22-23 = Samuel Windis explains his side of the dispute about victualling the *Satisfaction* (19 August 1654).
SP 18/89, page 135 = Captain Sherwin aboard the *Primrose* (24 October 1654 from Liverpool).
SP 18/90, page 139 = Captain Sherwin aboard the *Primrose* (14 November 1654 from Liverpool).
SP 18/99, page #121 = Samuel Windis complains about his dismissal (13 July 1655).
SP 18/104, page 93 = Captain Sherwin aboard the *Primrose* (12 February 1655 from Dublin).
SP 18/106, page 84 = Captain John Sherwin aboard the *Primrose* writes a letter to General John Desborough (24 March 1655 from Plymouth).
SP 18/107, page 84 = Captain Sherwin aboard the *Primrose* (7 April 1655 from the Downs).
SP 18/107, page 172 = Captain Sherwin aboard the *Primrose* writes a letter of complaint to the Commissioners of the Navy about failure to give adequate provision (13 April 1655 from Chatham).

SP 18/109, pages 12-14 = Captain Nutton explains his side of the dispute about victualling the *Satisfaction* (18 May 1655).

SP 18/109, page 52 = Captain Sherwin aboard the *Primrose* (20 May 1655 from Hope).

SP 18/109, pages 90-92 = Captain Nutton explains his side of the dispute about victualling the *Satisfaction* (22 May 1655).

SP 18/109, page 99 = Hanserd Knollys resigns his post at the Excise Office (23 May 1655).

SP 18/109, pages 153-155 = Captain Nutton and crew of the *Satisfaction* submit their complaints about the conduct of Samuel Windis (28 May 1655).

SP 18/109, page 168 = Captain Nutton explains his side of the dispute about victualling the *Satisfaction* (29 May 1655).

SP 18/111, page 154 = Samuel Windis writes a letter to the Commissioners of the Admiralty and Navy complaining about the conduct of Captain Sherwin aboard the *Primrose* (27 July 1655).

SP 18/112, pages 191-192 = Petition of Philip Evatt for his supplying the *Primrose* (28 August 1655).

SP 18/113, page 16 = Order to pay Philip Evatt for his supplying the *Primrose* (28 August 1655).

SP 18/113, page 68 = Captain Sherwin aboard the *Primrose* (7 September 1655 from Holyhead).

SP 18/113, page 75 = Captain Sherwin and the *Primrose* help escort Lord Deputy Fletwood to Ireland (8 September 1655).

SP 18/115, page 18 = Samuel Windis petitions for post as a purser noting his service aboard the *Primrose* (2 October 1655).

SP 18/115, page 47 = Richard Wollaston's report of shot and ordnance in his possession (3 October 1655).

SP 18/118, page 15 = Captain Sherwin aboard the *Primrose* (16 December 1655).

SP 18/118, page 215 = Captain Sherwin aboard the *Primrose* (28 December 1655 from Kinsale).

SP 18/126, page 194 = Joseph Caryll writes a letter supporting the case of Joseph Scot, chaplain aboard the *Primrose* (16 April 1656).

SP 18/126, page 195 = The Commissioners of the Admiralty and Navy order that Joseph Scot, chaplain aboard the *Primrose,* be paid the wages due to him (17 April 1656).

SP 18/135, page 208 = Captain Sherwin aboard the *Primrose* (29 February 1656 from Kinsale).

SP 18/136, page 232 = Captain John Sherwin writes to the Commissioners of the Admiralty and Navy about the loss of the *Primrose* (12 March 1656).

SP 18/136, page 264 = Captain Peter Bowen writes to the Commissioners of the Admiralty and Navy about the loss of the *Primrose* (14 March 1656).

SP 18/136, page 266 = Captain Sherwin aboard the *Primrose* (26 March 1655 from Kinsale).

SP 18/136, page 277 = Captain John Sherwin writes to the Commissioners of the Admiralty and Navy about the loss of the *Primrose* (14 March 1656).

SP 18/137, page 46 = Report of William Trevitt swimming for his life when the *Primrose* sank (21 March 1656).

SP 18/137, page 150 = The Commissioners of the Admiralty and Navy order the Navy Commissioners to investigate the loss of the *Primrose* (27 March 1656).

SP 18/137, page 180 = William Trevitt submits a report about the sinking of the *Primrose* to the Navy Commissioners (22 March 1656).

SP 18/138, page 265 = The Navy Commissioners report to the Admiralty Committee at Trinity House that they have interviewed Captain John Sherwin and the crew of the *Primrose* (18 April 1656).

SP 18/138, pages 267, 269 = The Admiralty Committee at Trinity House report to the Commissioners of the Admiralty and Navy that they have interviewed Captain John Sherwin and the crew of the *Primrose* (5 April 1656).

SP 18/138, page 270 = Captain John Sherwin submits a report about the sinking of the *Primrose* to the Navy Commissioners (31 March 1656).

SP 18/138, page 270 verso = Peter Rowley submits a report about the sinking of the *Primrose* to the Navy Commissioners (31 March 1656).

SP 18/138, page 272 = Edward Bason submits a report about the sinking of the *Primrose* to the Navy Commissioners (31 March 1656).

SP 18/138, page 274 = Henry Marvin submits a report about the sinking of the *Primrose* to the Navy Commissioners (31 March 1656).

SP 18/138, page 276 = Samuel Gleede submits a report about the sinking of the *Primrose* to the Navy Commissioners (31 March 1656).

SP 18/139, page 43 = The Commissioners of the Admiralty and Navy order that the crew of the *Primrose* be paid the wages due to them (22 April 1656).

SP 18/141, page 41 = The Commissioners of the Admiralty and Navy order that half of Captain Sherwin's wages be garnished for his involvement in the loss of the *Primrose* (3 June 1656).

SP 18/142, page 98 = Order to pay Edward Bason half of his wages owed for his part in the loss of the *Primrose* (16 July 1656).

SP 18/155, pages 59-60 = Petition of Samuel Windis for reimbursement for victualling the *Primrose* (22 May 1657).

SP 18/157, page 62 = Petition of Samuel Windis for reimbursement for victualling the *Primrose* (21 October 1657).

SP 18/157, page #119 = Petition of Samuel Windis for reimbursement for victualling the *Primrose* (31 October 1657).

SP 18/183, page 6 = Council of State report about William Kiffen's petition on the Old Artillery Ground (5 October 1658).

SP 18/184, pages 143-144 = Report of a Survey of the Old Artillery Ground done by Officers of the Ordinance Office (31 December 1658).

SP 18/190, page 91 = The Commissioners of the Admiralty and Navy order that Captain Sherwin's wages be restored (27 April 1658).

SP 18/217, page 176 = Richard Wollaston petitions the Naval authorities for a missed quarterly payment (1659).

SP 18/220, pages 108-109 = Letter from John Desborough to Livewell Chapman (8 April 1660).

SP 18/220, pages 110-112 = Copy of the letter from John Desborough to Livewell Chapman (8 April 1660).

SP 18/281, page 14 = Appointment of David Walter as Lieutenant of Ordnance (31 October 1670).

SP 21/10, page 175 = Captain Sherwin aboard the *Truelove* is sent to Dublin (24 October 1648).

SP 25/20, page 45 = Council of State confirms John Sherwin as Captain of the *Primrose* (18 June 1651).

SP 25/63, page 385 = Captain Sherwin appointed to command the *Hind* (12 December 1649).

SP 25/66, page 592 = Captain Sherwin to have the *Primrose* victualled and fitted and to sail to Scotland (13 April 1652).

SP 25/69, pages 3-4 = Richard Wollaston appointed by Council of State on committee to investigate prisons (29 April 1653).

SP 25/70, pages 4, 10 and 32 = Council of State records of petitions by Richard Wollaston for salary owed him (July 1653).

SP 25/76, page 110 = Warrant for William Kiffen to export horses to Barbados (31 May 1655).

SP 25/76, page 160 = Petition by Richard Bedwell which Richard Wollaston was commissioned to investigate (4 July 1655).

SP 25/76, page 488 = Richard Wollaston petitions the Council of State that he be paid the arrears owed him (22 January 1656).

SP 25/76, page 521 = Council of State order that £472 be paid to Richard Wollaston (5 February 1656).

SP 25/94, page 112 = Captain Sherwin aboard the *Truelove* to patrol the Irish Sea (24 April 1649).

SP 25/96, page 1 = Council of State orders for the *Hind* to carry money to pay the army in Ireland (18 February 1651).

SP 25/96, pages 188-189 = Capotain Shertwin aboard the *Hind* captures the pirate Captain Bradshaw (19 May 1651).

SP 25/96, page 305 = Council of State order the *Primrose* armed and supplied (23 July 1651).

SP 25/107 #107, page 107 = The Council of State pays Nathaniel Stoner £15 for serving as a messenger to Shrewsbury and Holland (29 August 1659).

SP 25/112, page 160 = Warrant for William Kiffen to export horses to Barbados (31 May 1655).

SP 25/116, page 12 = Warrant for the arrest of Livewell Chapman (27 March 1660).

SP 25/116, page 38 = Warrant for the arrest of Livewell Chapman (28 April 1660).

SP 25/118, page 123 = John Humphrey, Master of the *Primrose*, is paid £130 for his first months after the ship was hired by the Navy (21 June 1649).

SP 25/123, page 41 = Captain Sherwin aboard the *Truelove* to be paid for three months extra service (26 April 1649).

SP 25/123, page 170 = Captain Sherwin appointed to be Captain of the *Hind* (12 December 1649).

SP 25/123, page 171 = Captain Bowen to surrender the *Hind* to Captain Sherwin (12 December 1649).

SP 25/123, page #172 = The *Hind* to serve on convoy duty (13 December 1649).

SP 25/123, page #178 = Captain Sherwin aboard the *Hind* to report to the Downs (18 December 1649).

SP 25/447, page 58 = Richard Wollaston petition to the Admiralty and Navy Commissioners for wages owed him (1661).

SP 28/131, part 3, folio 7 recto = William Kiffen pledges a horse to the Parliamentary cause (1 July 1642).

SP 28/131, part 12, folio 8 recto = Thomas Weekes signs a receipt for his monthly salary as a gunner (22 August 1643).

SP 29/8, page 152 = John Champante's appointment in the Excise Office confirmed by Charles II (July 1660).

SP 29/34, page 127 = William Kiffen signs a bond for £500 promising to be of good behaviour towards the king (20 April 1661).

SP 29/47, page 106 = List of Congregational Ministers Preaching in London – 1660-61.

SP 29/67, page 4 = Thomas Weekes arrested for attending an illegal conventicle (2 November 1662).

SP 29/67, page 7 = Mary Winch and six others arrested for being Fifth Monarchists (10 December 1662).

SP 29/67, page 89 = Charles II in Whitehall authorizes the release of conventiclers from Newgate prison (13 January 1663).

SP 29/79, page 146 = Ciphered report to Harvey Bennet about activities of anti-royalists and Fifth Monarchists; includes mention of Knowles in Wapping (28 August 1663).

SP 29/80, pages 31-32 = Informant's report to Harvey Bennet about activities of anti-royalists and Fifth Monarchists, including Hanserd Knollys (4 September 1663).

SP 29/81, page 78 = Ciphered report to Harvey Bennet about activities of anti-royalists and Fifth Monarchists (9 October 1663).

SP 29/114, page 151 = report of how secret communications were directed to the home of Robert Malborne in Shoreditch (8 March 1665).

SP 29/121, page 175) = a list of disaffected people in London who meet at the home of Robert Malborne in Shoreditch (22 May 1665).

SP 29/220, page 62 = Letter from Richard Bower to Joseph Williamson complaining that George Potts purchased prize ships from the Commissioners of Prizes for the Port of London at knock-down prices (17 October 1667).

SP 29/280, pages 126 recto-127 recto = Charles Harbord reports on William Legge's petition for a property in the Minories (23 March 1667).

SP 29/280, page 128 = Grant of a lease on the Minorites property to Captain George Legge (14 November 1670).

SP 29/288, page 169 = Hanserd Knollys petition for Old Artillery Ground (1671).

SP 29/305, page 125 = Letter from Silas Taylor to Joseph Williamson about selling grain on the *Old Abraham* (9 April 1675).

SP 29/321, page 148 = William Kiffen applies for meeting-house licenses under provisions of the *Declaration of Indulgence* (15 May 1672).

SP 29/338, page 107 = Report that two vessels (one the *Bahama Merchant*?) from the Barbados arrived at Plymouth on (12 December 1673).

SP 29/338, page 126 recto-127 recto = Sir Heneage Finch's consideration of Hanserd Knollys Petition regarding the Old Artillery Ground (22 June 1674).

SP 29/390, page 160 = Record from harbourmaster Philip Lanyon in Harwich to Sir Joseph Williamson that the *Bahama Merchant* had arrived in Plymouth with a load of brasiletta wood from the Bahamas (21 January 1677).

SP 29/390, page 169 = Record from harbourmaster Philip Lanyon in Harwich that the *Bahama Merchant* had arrived in Plymouth with a load of brasiletta wood from the Bahamas (21 January 1677).

SP 29/446, page 115 = Spies report on Knollys' presence in Germany in the spring of 1661[?].

SP 29/448, page 159 = William Legge's petition on the Minories property discussed in court at Whitehall (5 October 1663).

SP 38/24, page 248 = Appointment of David Walter as Lieutenant of Ordnance (31 October 1670).

SP 44/11, page 32 = John Champante's appointment in the Excise Office re-confirmed by Charles II (28 February 1661).

SP 44/34, pages 58-59 = George Legg lease on a property in the Minories (14 November 1670).

SP 44/35A, page 19 = Lord Arlington records appointment of David Walter as Lieutenant of Ordnance (19 October 1670).

SP 46/115, page 115 = Captain Sherwin aboard the *Primrose* (22 September 1653 from Chatham).

SP 46/115, page 148 = Samuel Windis' letter about his service as purser to the *Primrose* and the *Hind* (26 September 1653).

SP 46/115, page 208 = Captain Sherwin aboard the *Primrose* (29 November 1653 from Kingston upon Hull).

SP 46/115, page 247 = Captain Sherwin aboard the *Primrose* reports that he has captured a Dutch ship (10 December 1653 from Tinmouth).

T 4/1, page 500, Treasury Reference Book of Applications – 1680-1682 = Henry Guy refers the proposed sale of the Old Artillery Ground to Sir Christopher Wren (6 December 1681).

T 11/5, page 126, Treasury Book of Out Letters 1 = Hanserd Knollys seventh petition on the Old Artillery Ground (1679).

T 27/6, page 358, Treasury Out Letter Book – 1680-1682 = Henry Guy reports to the Ordnance Commissioners about the proposed sale of the Old Artillery Ground (13 November 1681).

T 27/6, page 368, Treasury Out Letter Book – 1680-1682 = Henry Guy writes to Sir Robert Sawyer and to some interested parties about the proposed sale of the Old Artillery Ground (23 December 1681).

T 27/6, page 395, Treasury Out Letter Book – 1680-1682 = Henry Guy begins a letter to Nicholas Barbon to inform him that the warrant for the Old Artillery Ground has been signed by Charles II (18 January 1681).

T 27/6), page 399, Treasury Out Letter Books – 1680-1682 = Henry Guy again writes to Doctor Nicholas Barbon about non-payment of fee for the Old Artillery Ground (26 January 1682).

T 51/1, page 152, Lord Southampton's General Entry Book – 1660 = Treasurer Southampton orders the Surveyor General to consider Hanserd Knollys' Petition (25 September 1660).

T 51/2, pages 27-28, Lord Southampton's General Entry Book – 1660-61 = Copy of Treasurer Southampton's order for a constat on Hanserd Knollys' case (24 November 1660).

T 51/2, pages 130-131, Lord Southampton's General Entry Book – 1660-61 = Treasurer Southampton's warrant for a lease to Knollys on the Old Artillery Ground property (5 January 1661).

T 51/2, page 236, Lord Southampton's General Entry Book – 1660-61 = Treasurer Southampton notes William Legge's appeal against Hanserd Knollys' Petition and asks Charles Harbord, the Surveyor General, to investigate (16 February 1661).

T 51/43, page 346 = Treasury Lords instruct the Customs Commissioners about grain on the *Old Abraham* (21 April 1671).

T 52/8, pages 305-307, King's Warrant Book – 1680-1683 = Charles II issues a warrant for a grant on the Old Artillery Ground property (18 January 1682).

T 61/2, page 114, Treasury Disposition Books – 1680-1684 = Henry Guy writes to Sir Robert Howard instructing him about money paid for the Old Artillery Ground (10 January 1682).

T 61/2, page 116, Treasury Disposition Books – 1680-1684 = Henry Guy writes to Sir Robert Howard instructing him to pay him £500 out of the money paid for the Old Artillery Ground – (20 January 1682).

T 61/2), page 117, Treasury Disposition Books – 1680-1684 = Henry Guy writes to Doctor Nicholas Barbon about non-payment of fee for the Old Artillery Ground (23 January 1682).

T 61/2), page 119, Treasury Disposition Books – 1680-1684 = Henry Guy writes to Sir Robert Howard instructing him to transfer £5200 out of the money paid for the Old Artillery Ground to the Treasurer of the Ordnance Office (1 February 1682).

WO 46/1, folio 213 recto, Ordnance Office – Out Letters 1660-1683 = Order from Henry Guy to the Ordnance Office about the proposed sale of the Old Artillery Ground (7 April 1681).

WO 54/17, Ordnance Office – Quarter Books 1647-1650 = Richard Wollaston's wages record for 1649.

The Leathersellers' Company, London (LCL)

Register of Apprentices – 1629-1677 (Mem 7/1) = Records of Kiffen's eight apprenticeship contracts.

Register of Freemen – 1630-1694 (Mem 5/1), page 15 = Kiffen made a freeman on 10 July 1638.

Register of Freemen – 1630-1694 (Mem 5/1), page 79 = Joseph Kiffen made a freeman on 29 September 1671.

The Honourable Artillery Company, London (HAC)Ancient Vellum Book, folio 90 William Kiffen admitted to the Honourable Artillery Company (18 February 1656).

Minute Book of the Honourable Artillery Company - 1656-1661, page 10 = William Kiffen summoned before the Court of the Honourable Artillery Company (11 September 1657).

Minute Book of the Honourable Artillery Company - 1656-1661, page 40 = Agreement for the sale of the Old Artillery Ground by the Honourable Artillery Company to Richard Wollaston (17 August 1658).

Minute Book of the Honourable Artillery Company - 1656-1661, page 43 = Receipt on the sale of the Old Artillery Ground by the Honourable Artillery Company to Richard Wollaston (29 September 1658).

Minute Book of the Honourable Artillery Company - 1656-1661, pages 44-45 = Report on the sale of the Old Artillery Ground by the Honourable Artillery Company to Richard Wollaston (29 September 1658).

Minute Book of the Honourable Artillery Company - 1656-1661, page 93 = Hanserd Knollys petitions the Court of the Honourable Artillery Company for support in his case for the Old Artillery Ground property (18 July 1660).

Minute Book of the Honourable Artillery Company - 1656-1661, pages 98-99 = Knollys' case for the Old Artillery Ground is discussed by the Court of the Honourable Artillery Company who agree to write to Charles II on his behalf (14 October 1660).

The Parliamentary Archives, London (PA) (including published Journals)

HL/PO/JO/10/1/283 = Anabaptists' Petition (7 May 1660).

HL/PO/JO/10/1/306 = Anabaptists' Petition (5 July 1661).

HL/PO/JO/10/1/283A = Charles II's Declaration of Breda – 1660.

HL/PO/JO/10/1/47 = Record of Anabaptists in court (16 January 1641).

JHC 6 (2 March 1650): 375 = Captain Sherwin appointed to the *Hind*.

JHC 7 (5 August 1659): 299 = William Kiffen and John Westley appointed officers in the London militia.
JHC 7 (29 July 1653): 289, 292 = Richard Wollaston is considered for position as judge of the Admiralty.
JHC 7 (30 October 1651): 32 = The *Primrose* appointed to Winter Guard in 1651-2.
JHL 4 (16 January 1641): 133-134 = Record of Southwark Anabaptists in court.
JHL 4 (18 January 1641): 134 = Record of Southwark Anabaptists in court.
JHL 4 (26 March 1642): 672 = Sir Thomas Mallet ordered to explain his actions in not granting William Kiffen bail.
JHL 11 (4 May 1660): 13 = Record of riots against Anabaptist meeting houses.
JHL 11 (7 May 1660): 17 = Record of preventative measures being taken against further rioting and destruction of property.
JHL 11 (5 July 1661): 299 = Record of Anabaptists presenting petition to the House of Lords.

Royal United Services Institute for Defence and Security Studies, Whitehall, London

'Ensignes, Trayned Bands Bands, and Auxiliaries, 1642'

Magdalene College, Cambridge

Samuel Pepys, Miscellanies, volume v, page 595 = List of Vessels belonging to the State's Navy on 1st March 1651'.

St. John's College, Cambridge

'Vita Ioannis Barwick (1690)' (MS St John's College H9b – James 277).

East Sussex Record Office, Lewes

Letter of Christopher Blackwood to Samuel Jeake – 4 May 1662 (FRE 4289).

The Folger Library, Washington D.C.

Letter of Anonymous Baptist to Robert Bennet – 5 February 1658 (X.d. 483 (208)).

Newssheets

The Conventicle Courant No. 1 (14 July 1682) = announces the aims and intentions of the news-sheet to chronicle suppression of conventicles.
The Conventicle Courant No. 8 (4-10 September 1682) = Reports on Hanserd Knollys preaching at Broken Wharf in September of 1682.
The Conventicle Courant No. 10 (18-25 October 1682) = Reports on arrest warrants for Presbyterians meeting at Devonshire-buildings.

The Conventicle Courant No. 11 (25 September – 2 October 1682) = Reports on arrest warrants for Presbyterians meeting at Devonshire-buildings.

The Conventicle Courant No. 13 (9-16 October 1682) = Reports on arrest warrants for Independents or Presbyterians meeting at Devonshire-buildings.

The Conventicle Courant No. 14 (16-23 October 1682) = Reports on arrest warrants for Independents or Presbyterians meeting at Devonshire-buildings.

French Occurrences, Number 8 (28 June-5 July 1652) = Report of *Primrose* participating in a sea battle between Commonwealth navy under Adrmiral Robert Blake and the Dutch navy commanded by Van Trump (25 June 1652).

The Loyal Protestant and True Domestic Intelligence No. 238 (27 February 1683) = reports on Hanserd Knowles, who is described as 'an old *Anabaptist Holder-forth*', preaching at George-Yard in Broken-Wharf.

The Loyal Protestant and True Domestic Intelligence No. 243 (19 March 1683) = reports on Hanserd Knowles preaching at two Sunday services held on 4 March 1683.

Mercurius Politicus #609 (23 February-1 March 1660): 1140 and 1141 = Report that William Kiffen was released from prison by order of General Monck (29 February 1660).

Mercurius Publicus #2 (10-17 January 1661): 31 = Robert Malborn incarcerated in Poultrey Counter prison following the Venner revolt (16 January 1661).

Mercurius Publicus #19 (3-10 May 1660): 292 = Report that William Kiffen's meeting house was defaced in riots (1-2 May 1660).

The Moderate Intelligencer #70 (2-9 July 1646): 528 = Reports that John Lambert was appointed governor of Oxford.

The Parliamentary Intelligencer #11 (27 February-5 March 1660): 153 = Report that William Kiffen was released from prison by order of General Monck (29 February 1660).

The Parliamentary Intelligencer #15 (2-9 April 1660): 240 = Report that a letter about a fanatical uprising had been intercepted (April 1660).

The Parliamentary Intelligencer #19 (30 April-7 May 1660): 299 = Report that William Kiffen's meeting house was defaced in riots (1-2 May 1660).

A Perfect Diurnall of the Passages in Parliament 12 (28 March – 4 April 1642): 2 = reports that the Kentish petition had reached London and was discussed by both Houses of Parliament on 28 March.

The Publick Intelligencer #203 (14-21 November 1659): 881 = William Kiffen appointed officer in the London militia (16 November 1659).

The Publick Intelligencer #220 (27 February-5 March 1660): 1132 and 1133 = Report that William Kiffen was released from prison by order of General Monck (29 February 1660)

Seventeenth-Century Publications
(all published in London unless otherwise noted)

An Act for an Assessment (26 June 1657T). [Wing E995E]

An Answer to a Declaration (1659). [Wing H3219]
Ashton, Thomas *Satan in Samuels Mantle* (1659). [Wing A3992B]
Avery, Elizabeth *Scripture-Prophecies Opened* (1647). [Wing A 4272]
The Baptist Confession (1644). [Wing C5790]
The Baptists Answer to Mr Obed. Wills, his Appeal against Mr H. Danvers (1675). [Wing K705]
Barber, Edward *A Declaration Concerning the Publike Dispute* (1648). [E.313[22]]
Brookes, Humphrey *The Charity of Church-men* (1649). [Wing B4903A]
Butler, Samuel *Hudibras* (1674). [Wing B6311]
By the Council of State: A Proclamation (29 March 1660T). [669 f.24[47]]
The Charter of the Bahama Islands (1670). [Wing C3724aA]
Cheynell, Francis *Truth Triumphing over Errour and Heresie* (15 January 1647T). [E 371[7]]
________ *An Account Given to the Parliament by the Ministers Sent by Them to Oxford* (26 March 1647T). [E 382[1]]
Clarke, Samuel *The Historian's Guide* (1690). [Wing H2094D]
The Cobler's End (1641). [Wing C4783]
The Coblers Sermon Cryed Down (1641). [Wing V398A]
The Confession of Faith (1644). [Wing C5790]
A Declaration of Divers Elders and Brethren of Congregational Societies (1651). [Wing G1850]
Declaration of Several of the People called Anabaptists in and about the City of London (1659). [Wing D619]
A Declaration of Some Proceedings of Lt. Col. John Lilburn (14 February 1648T). [E 427[6]]
A Declaration of the Maids of the City of London (1659). [Wing D710]
Declaration of Several of the People Called Anabaptists in and about the City of London (1659) [Wing D619]
Denham, John *An Exact Copy of a Letter* (1641). [Wing A2]
________ *Coopers Hill* (1642). [Wing D993]
A Discourse Between Cap. Kiffin and Dr. Chamberlain about Imposition of Hands (1654). [Wing K424]
Edwards, Thomas *Gangraena (Three Parts)* (1646). [Wing E229; E235; E237]
Englands Losse and Lamentation (1643). [Wing E2992]
Erbury, William *Nor Truth nor Error nor Day nor Night* (1647). [Wing E3234]
An Exact Accompt of the Receipts and Disbursements Expended by the Committee of Safety (1660). [E.1079[3]]
Featley, Daniel *The Dippers Dipt* (1645). [Wing F586]
Featley, John *A Succinct History of The Life and Death of the Learned and Famous Divine Doctor Daniel Featley* (20 December 1660T). [E.1937[2]]
A Glasse for the Times (29 July 1648T). [E.455[10]]
Goodwin, John *Peace Protected and Discontent Disarmed* (11 April 1654T). [E.732[27]]

A Great Victory (1 July 1652T). [E.669[1]]

Greville, Robert *A Discourse Opening the Nature of That Episcopacie* (1641). [E.177[22]]

Gumble, Thomas *The Life of General Monck* (1671). [Wing G2230]

Hedworth, Henry *Quakers Quibbles* (1674). [Wing T1012]

Hicks, Thomas *A Rebuke to Tho. Rudyard's Folly and Impertinencies* (1674). [Wing H1924A]

________ *The Quakers Appeal Answer'd* (1674). [Wing H1924]

________ *His Last Legacy to the Quakers* (1690).

Hinc Illae Lachrymae, or the Impietie of Impunitie (30 January 1648T). [E.540[16]]

His Majesties Gracious Letter and Declaration Sent to the House of Peers by Sir John Greenvil, Knight, from Breda (1660). [Wing C3015]

His Majesties Special Command under the great Seale of England (1641). [Wing C2772]

The Humble Apology of Some Commonly Called Anabaptists (28 January 1661T). [E.1057[1]]

The Humble Petition and Recantation of Many Dissatisfied Persons Commonly Known by the Name of Anabaptists (1660). [Wing T1730bA]

The Humble Petition and Representation (25 January 1661). [Wing H3444]

The Humble Tender and Declaration of Many Well-affected Mariners and Sea-men, Commanders of Ships, Members of the Trinity-house, to the Commissioners of the Navy (June 23 1948T). [669.f.12[53]]

Jessey, Henry *The Exceeding Riches of Grace Advanced* (1647). [Wing J687]

________ *The Lords Loud Call to England* (1660). [Wing J694]

The Joint Testimonie of the Ministers of Devon (1648): 20-21. [E.450[1]]

Keith, George *Vindication from the Forgeries & Abuses of T. Hick & W. Kiffin* (1674). [Wing K229]

Kiffin, William, *Certaine Observations Upon Hosea* (1642). [Wing K423A]

A Letter Sent to the Right Honourable, the Lord Mayor of the City of London (2 March 1660T). [669.f.23[72]]

Ley, John *A Discourse of Disputations* (13 April 1658T). [E.938[1]]

The Life and Approaching Death of William Kiffin (1659). [Wing L1989]

The Life and Death of That Old Disciple of Jesus Christ, and Eminent Minister of the Gospel, Mr Hanserd Knollys (1692). [Wing K715]

Lilburne, John *Innocency and Truth Justified* (6 January 1646T). [E.314[21]]

________ *The Legall Fundamentall Liberties* (4 August 1649T). [E.567[1]]

________ *As You Were* (May 1652T). [Wing L2084]

________ *The Banished Mans Suit for Protection* (15 June 1653T). [669.f.17[16]]

A List of the Conventicles or Unlawful Meetings within the City of London (1683). [Wing L2418]

A List of the Names of the Severall Colonells and their Colours (1642). [669.f.6[8]]

A List of the Prisoners in the Upper Bench Prison (1653). [Wing L2418]

Locke, John *Second Treatise of Civil Government* (1690). [Wing L2766]

Londons Glory, or, The Riot and Ruine of the Fifth Monarchy Men (15 January 1661T). [E1874[3]]

Long, Thomas *Mr Hales's Treatise of Schism Examined and Censured* (1678). [Wing L2974]

The Lord Mayors Farewell (23 September 1646T). [E.355[6]]

Masterson, George *The Triumph Stain'd* (10 February 1648T). [E.426[18]]

Mead, William *A Brief Account of the Most Material Passages Between those Called Quakers and Baptists* (1674). [Wing M1565]

__________ *A Brief Narrative of the Second Meeting Between the People Called Quakers and Baptists* (1674). [Wing M1565A]

Mercurius Anti-mechanicus, or The Simple Coblers Boy (1648). [E.470[25]]

A Narrative of the Proceedings of the General Assembly (1689). [Wing N216]

Norris, Jab *A Lash for a Lyar* (1648). [E.428[8]]

The Old Leaven Purged Out (1658). [Wing O205]

Parker, Thomas *The Copy of a Letter* (1650). [Wing P475]

A Perfect List of the Names of the Several Persons Returned to Serve in This Parliament 1656 (September 1656T): 5. [E.498[5]]

Penn, William *Naked Truth Needs No Shift* (1674). [Wing P1324]

________ *William Penn's Answer to John Faldo's Printed Challenge* (1674). [Wing P1254A]

________ *William Penn's Return to John Faldo's Reply* (1674). [Wing P1355]

________ *Jeremy Ives's Sober Request* (1674). [Wing P1306]

________ *Libels No Proofs* (1674). [Wing P1322A]

________ *The Counterfeit Christian Detected; and the Real Quaker Justified* (1674). [Wing P1271]

________ (and George Whitehead) *The Christian-Quaker and his Divine Testimony Vindicated* (1674). [Wing P1266]

________ *More Work for George Keith* (1696). [Wing P1323]

A Phanatique League and Covenant Solemnly enter'd into by the Assertors of the Good Old Cause (21 March 1660). [Wing F395]

Plain English to His Excellencie the Lord General Monck and the Officers of his Army (1660). [Wing P2359]

Plant, Thomas *A Contest for Christianity* (1674). [Wing P2377]

The Quakers Last Shift Found Out (1674). [Wing Q26]

Rogers, John *Ohel or Beth-shemesh, A Tabernacle for the Sun* (1653). [Wing R1813]

Rudyard, Thomas *The Anabaptists Printed Proposals* (1674). [Wing R2174]

________ *An Answer to a Scandalous Paper* (1674). [Wing R2176]

________ *The Barbican Cheat Detected* (1674). [Wing R2177]

A Schedule or List of the Prisoners in the Fleet (1 June 1653T). [E.698[13]]

Seller, John *The Sea Gunner* (1697). [Wing S2487]

Sions Groans for Her Distressed (8 May 1661). [Wing S3870A]

Stephens, Nathaniel *A Precept for the Baptisme of Infants* (10 February 1651T). [E.623[9]]

Sturgion, John *A Plea for Tolleration* (29 March 1661). [Wing S6093]

A Testimony to the Trueth of Jesus Christ and to our Solemn League and Covenant (1648). [E.423[3]]

These Trades-Men are Preachers in and about the City of London (1647). [Wing T883]

Tombes, John *Saints no Smiters* (1664). [Wing T1816]

A True Relation of the Late Conference Held at Oxford Between Presbyterians and Independents (26 November 1646T). [E.363[6]]

Tub-preachers Overturn'd (1647). [Wing T3207]

Waring, Robert *A Publike Conference Betwixt the Six Presbyterian Ministers and Some Independent Commanders at Oxford, 12 November 1646* (26 November 1646T). [E.363[4]]

Webster, John *The Testimony of William Erbery* (1658). [Wing E3239]

Whiston, Edward *The Life and Death of Mr Henry Jessy* (1671). [Wing W1679]

Whitehead, George *The Timorous Reviler Sleighted* (1674). [Wing W1965]

________ *A Serious Search into Jeremy Ives's Questions to the Quakers* (1674). [Wing W1958]

________ *The Quakers Plainness Detecting Fallacy* (1674). [Wing W1949]

Winter, Samuel *The Summe of Diverse Serons Preached in Dublin* (Dublin, 1656).[Wing W3089]

Wood, Anthony *Athenae Oxonienses, 2 Volumes* (1691-92). [Wing W3382 and W3383A]

Other Publications (1700-2009)

Ashton, Robert *The City and the Court, 1603-1643* (Cambridge: Cambridge University Press, 1979).

Aylmer, G.E. *The State's Servants: The Civil Service of the English Republic, 1649 – 1660* (London: Routledge & Kegan Paul, 1973).

Baston, Jane, 'Avery, Elizabeth (*fl.* 1614–1653)', *Oxford Dictionary of National Biography* (Oxford University Press, Sept 2004); online edn, Jan 2008 [http://ezproxy.ouls.ox.ac.uk:2117/view/article/69074, accessed 15 July 2010]

Bell, Maureen, 'Chapman, Livewell (*fl.* 1643–1665)', *Oxford Dictionary of National Biography* (Oxford University Press, Sept 2004); [http://ezproxy.ouls.ox.ac.uk:2117/view/article/67700, accessed 15 July 2010]

Bethell, A. Talbot *The Early Settlers of the Bahama Islands* (Norfolk: Rounce & Wortley, 1930).

Birch, Thomas (ed.), *A Collection of the State Papers of John Thurloe, 7 Volumes* (London, 1742).

Black, Robert C. III *The Younger John Winthrop* (New York: Columbia University Press, 1966).

Boulton, Jeremy *Neighbourhood and Society: A London Suburb in the Seventeenth Century* (Cambridge: Cambridge University Press, 1987).

Bremer, Francis J. *John Winthrop: America's Forgotten Founding Father* (Oxford: Oxford University Press, 2003).

Brett-James, N.G., 'A Speculative London Builder of the Seventeenth Century, Dr. Nicholas Barbon', *London and Middlesex Archaeological Transactions,* New Series 6 (1929-32): 110-145.

Brown, Louise Fargo *The Political Activities of the Baptists and Fifth Monarchy Men in England during the Interregnum* (Oxford: Oxford University Press, 1912).

Browner, Jessica A., 'Wrong Side of the River: London's disreputable South Bank in the sixteenth and seventeenth century', *Essays in History* 36 (1994): 34-72.

Browning, Andrew *Thomas Osborne, Earl of Danby and Duke of Leeds, 1632-1712: Volume 1 - Life* (Glasgow: Jackson, Son & Co., 1951).

Burns, Alan *History of the British West Indies* (London: George Allen & Unwin, 1965, 2nd edition): 336-337, 358-363.

Burrage, Champlin *The Early English Dissenters in the Light of Recent Research (1550-1641), Volume 1,* (Cambridge: Cambridge University Press, 1912).

Bustin, Dennis C. *Paradox and Perseverance: Hanserd Knollys, Particular Baptist Pioneer in Seventeenth-Century England* (Milton Keynes: Paternoster Press, 2006).

Capp, Bernard *The Fifth Monarchy Men: A Study in Seventeenth-century English Millennarianism* (London: Faber and Faber, 1972).

________ *Cromwell's Navy: The Fleet and the English Revolution 1648-1660* (Oxford: Clarendon Press, 1989).

Carte, Timothy *A Collection of Original Letters and Papers Concerning Affairs in England from the Year 1641 to 1660* (1739).

Cockburn, J.S. *A History of English Assizes 1558-1714* (Cambridge: Cambridge University Press, 1972).

________ *Calendar of Assize Records: Home Circuit Indictments –Elizabeth I and James I. Introduction* (London: HMSO, 1985).

Cohen, A., 'Chapman, Livewell (fl. 1643-d. 1664)', in Richard L. Greaves and Robert Zaller (eds.) *Biographical Dictionary of British Radicals in the Seventeenth Century, Volume I: A-F* (Brighton: The Harvester Press, 1982): 136-137.

Cranston, Maurice *John Locke: A Biography* (Oxford: Oxford University Press, 1985).

Craton, Michael *A History of the Bahamas* (London: Collins, 1968).

________ (and Gail Saunders) *Islanders in the Stream: A History of the Bahamian People* (Athens, Georgia: The University of Georgia Press, 1992).

Crawford, Patricia *Women and Religion in England 1500-1720* (London: Routledge, 1993).

Cressy, David *England On Edge: Crisis and Revolution 1640-1642* (Oxford: Oxford University Press, 2006).

Crosby, Thomas *The History of the English Baptists, 4 Volumes* (London, 1738-40).

Culross, James *Hanserd Knollys: A Minister and Witness of Jesus Christ (1598-1691)* (London: Alexander and Shepheard, 1895).

De Beer, E.S. (ed) *The Correspondence of John Locke, Volume One* (Oxford: Clarendon Press, 1976).

Derrick, Charles *Memoirs of the Rise and Progress of the Royal Navy* (London: H. Teape, 1806).

Dillon, Harold Arthur, 'On a MS List of Officers of the London Trained Bands in 1643', *Archaeologia: or Miscellaneous Tracts Relating to Antiquity*, Second Series, Volume II (London: Society of Antiquaries of London, 1890): 129-144.

Duncan, Pope A. *Hanserd Knollys: Seventeenth-Century Baptist* (Nashville: Broadman Press, 1965).

Eames, Aled *Ships and Seamen of Anglesey, 1588-1918* (Greenwich: National Maritime Museum, 1981).

Farr, David *John Lambert, Parliamentary Soldier and Cromwellian Major-General, 1619-1684* (The Boydell Press: Woodbridge, 2003).

Firth, C.H. (ed.) *The Clarke Papers, Volume 2* (London: The Camden Society, 1894).

Gardiner, Samuel Rawson (ed.) *Letters and Papers Relating to the First Dutch War 1652-1654, Volume 1* (London: The Navy Records Society, 1899).

________ *The Constitutional Documents of the Puritan Revolution, 1625-1660* (Oxford: Oxford University Press, 1906, third edition revised).

Gibbon, Crawford *The Puritan Millennium: Literature and Theology, 1550-1682* (Milton Keynes: Paternoster, 2008).

Glausser, Wayne *Locke and Blake: A Conversation across the Eighteenth Century* (Gainesville, Florida: University Press of Florida, 1998).

Goldie, Mark, 'The Hilton Gang: Terrorizing Dissent in 1680s London', *History Today* 47 (October 1997): 26-32.

________ 'The Hilton Gang and the Purge of London in the 1680s', in Howard Nenner (ed.) *Politics and the Political Imagination in Later Stuart Britain: Essays Presented to Lois Green Schwoerer* (Rochester, New York: University of Rochester Press, 1997): 43-72.

Gordon, Alexander, 'Kiffin or Kiffen, William', in *Dictionary of National Biography, Volume 31* (London: Smith, Elder & Co., 1892): 98-100.

________ 'Knollys, Hanserd', in *Dictionary of National Biography, Volume 31* (London: Smith, Elder & Co., 1892): 279-281.

Greaves, Richard L., 'Hobson, Paul (d. 1666)', in Richard L. Greaves and Robert Zaller (eds.) *Biographical Dictionary of British Radicals in the Seventeenth Century, Volume II: G-O* (Brighton: The Harvester Press, 1983): 95-97.

________ *Saints and Rebels: Seven Nonconformists in Stuart England* (Macon: Mercer University Press, 1985).

________ 'Hobson, Paul (*d.* 1666)', *Oxford Dictionary of National Biography* (Oxford University Press, Sept 2004); online edn, Jan 2008 [http://ezproxy.ouls.ox.ac.uk:2117/view/article/37554, accessed 15 July 2010]

Gregg, Pauline *Free-Born John; The Biography of John Lilburne* (London: Phoenix Press, 1961).

Grey, Zachary *An Impartial Examination of the Fourth Volume of Mr Daniel Neal's History of the Puritans* (London, 1739).

Gribben, Crawford *God's Irishmen: Theological Debates in Cromwellian Ireland* (Oxford: Oxford University Press, 2007).

________ *The Puritan Millennium: Literature and Theology, 1550-1682* (Milton Keynes: Paternoster, 2008).

Harris, Tim *London Crowds in the Reign of Charles II: Propaganda and politics from the Restoration until the exclusion crisis* (Cambridge: Cambridge University Press, 1987).

Hayden, Roger *English Baptist History and Heritage* (Didcot: Baptist Union of Great Britain, 2005).

Haykin, Michael A.G., *Kiffin, Knollys and Keach: Rediscovering English Baptist Heritage* (Leeds: Reformation Today, 1996).

________ 'Kiffin, William (1616–1701)', *Oxford Dictionary of National Biography* (Oxford University Press, Sept 2004); online edn, May 2008 [http://ezproxy.ouls.ox.ac.uk:2117/view/article/15521, accessed 15 July 2010]

Hepper, David J. *British Warship Losses in the Age of Sail 1650-1859* (Rotherfield, East Sussex: Jean Boudriot Publications, 1994).

Hindmarsh, D. Bruce *The Evangelical Conversion Narrative: Spiritual Autobiography in Early Modern England* (Oxford: Oxford University Press, 2005).

Howard, Luke *Love and Truth in Plainnesse Manifested* (1704).

Hutchinson, Thomas *The History of the Colony and Province of Massachusetts Bay* (Cambridge: Harvard University Press, 1926).

Ivimey, Joseph *The Life of Mr William Kiffin:* (1833).

James, Muriel *Religious Liberty on Trial: Hanserd Knollys – Early Baptist Hero* (Franklin, Tennessee: Providence House Publishers, 1997).

Johnson, Ronald Angelo, 'The Peculiar Ventures of Particular Baptist Pastor William Kiffin and King Charles II of England', *Baptist History and Heritage* 44 (2009): 60-71,

Keeble, N.H. (and Geoffrey F. Nuttall) *Calendar of the Correspondence of Richard Baxter, Volume I, 1638-1660* (Oxford Clarendon Press, 1991).

Kennedy, D.E., 'The English Naval Revolt of 1648', *English Historical Review* 77 (1962): 247-256;

Kevan, Ernest F. *London's Oldest Baptist Church* (London: The Kingsgate Press, 1933): 58-59;

Kreitzer, Larry J. *'Seditious Sectaryes': The Baptist Conventiclers of Oxford 1641-1691, 2 Volumes* (Studies in Baptist History and Thought #30; Paternoster Press: Milton Keynes, 2006).

________ 'William Kiffen: Leatherseller and Baptist Merchant', *Leathersellers' Review 2008-09* (2009): 12-13.

Kupperman, Karen Ordahl, 'Definitions of Liberty on the Eve of the Civil War: Lord Saye and Sele, Lord Brooke, and the American Puritan Colonies', *The Historical Journal* 32 (1989): 17-33.

Langley, Arthur S., 'Seventeenth Century Baptist Disputations', *Transactions of the Baptist Historical Society* 6 (1918-9): 216-243.

Laurence, Anne *Parliamentary Army Chaplains, 1642-1651* (Boydell Press: Woodbridge, 1990).

Lindley, Keith, *Popular Politics and Religion in Civil War England* (Scolar Press: London, 1997).

Lough, John *Locke's Travels in France 1675-79* (Cambridge: University Press, 1953).

Mack, Phyllis *Visionary Women: Ecstatic Prophecy in Seventeenth-Century England* (University of California Press: Berkeley, 1992).

Neal, Daniel *The History of the Puritans, 4 Volumes* (London, 1732-1738).

Noble, Mark *Memoirs of the Protectoral-House of Cromwell, Volume 2* (London, 1787).

Nuttall, Geoffrey, 'Thomas Lambe, William Allen and Richard Baxter' *The Baptist Quarterly* 27 (1977-78): 139-140.

Orme, William *Remarkable Passages in the Life of William Kiffin* (London, 1823).

Pearl, Valerie *London and the Outbreak of the Puritan Revolution: City Government and National Politics 1625-1643* (Oxford: Oxford University Press, 1964).

Penson, Lillian M. *The Colonial Agents of the British West Indies* (London: University of London Press, 1924).

Powell, J.R. *The Navy in the English Civil War* (London: Archon Books, 1962).

Quainton, C. Eden, 'Cromwell and the Anabaptists during 1653', *The Pacific Historical Review* (1932): 164-178.

Ramsbotton, B.A. *Stranger Than Fiction: The Life of William Kiffin* (Harpenden: Gospel Standard Trust, 1989).

Randolph, Edward *Edward Randolph: Letters and Papers from the New England, Middle and Southern Colonies in America, with other Documents relating Chiefly to the Vacating of the Royal Charter of the Colony of Massachusetts Bay, 1676-1703, Volume 5* (Boston: The Prince Society, 1899).

________ *Edward Randolph: Including his Letters and Official Papers from the New England, Middle, and Southern Colonies in America, and the West Indies, 1678-1700, Volume 7* (Boston: The Prince Society, 1909).

Rich, E.E., 'The First Earl of Shaftesbury's Colonial Policy', *Royal HistoricalSociety Transactions*, 5th Series 7 (1957): 47-70.

Riddell, William Renwick, 'Post-Reformation Burning at the Stake of Heretics', *Journal of the American Institute of Criminal Law and Criminology* 21 (1930): 254-256.

Rostenberg, Leona *Literary, Political, Scientific, Religious & Legal Publishing, Printing & Bookselling in England, 1551-1700: Twelve Studies, 2 Volumes* (New York: Burt Franklin, 1965).

Rowe, Violet A. *Sir Henry Vane the Younger: A Study in Political and Administrative History* (London: The Athlone Press, 1970).

Sanford, Don A. *A Choosing People: The History of Seventh Day Baptists* (Nashville, TN: Broadman Press, 1992).

Shepherd, F.H.W. (ed.) *The Survey of London, Volume 27* (London: Athlone Press, 1957).

Smith, Nigel *Perfection Proclaimed: Language and Literature in English Radical Religion 1640-1660* (Oxford: Oxford University Press, 1989).

Smith, Steven R., 'Almost Revolutionaries: The London Apprentices during the Civil Wars', *The Huntington Library Quarterly* 42 (1979): 314-315.

Stearns, S.J., 'Malban, Robert (fl. 1648-1665)', in Richard L. Greaves and Robert Zaller (eds.) *Biographical Dictionary of British Radicals in the Seventeenth Century, Volume II: G-O* (Brighton: The Harvester Press, 1983): 210.

Strider, Robert E.L. *Robert Greville Lord Brooke* (Cambridge: Harvard University Press, 1958).

Strype, John *A Survey of the Cities of London and Westminster, Volume 2* (1720).

Swatland, Andrew *The House of Lords in the Reign of Charles II* (Cambridge Studies in Early Modern British History; Cambridge: Cambridge University Press, 1996).

Tanner, J.R. (ed), *Naval Manuscripts in the Pepysian Library at Magdalene College, Cambridge, Volume II, Admiralty Letters* (Publications of the Naval Records Society Volume 27; London: Navy Records Society, 1904).

Tolmie, Murray *The Triumph of the Saints: The Separate Churches of London 1616-1649* (Cambridge: Cambridge University Press, 1977).

________ 'Thomas Lambe, Soapboiler, and Thomas Lambe, Merchant, General Baptists', *The Baptist Quarterly* 27 (1977-78): 4-13.

Tomlinson, H.C. *Guns and Government: The Ordnance Office under the later Stuarts* (London: Royal Historical Society, 1979).

Trevor-Roper, H.R. *Archbishop Laud 1573-1645* (London: Macmillan, 1962, second edition).

Turner, G. Lyon, 'The Religious Condition of London in 1672 as Reported to King and Court', *Transactions of the Congregational Historical Society* 4 (1909-10): 192-205.

Underdown, David, 'Cromwell and the Officers, February 1658', *English Historical Review* 83 (1968): 101-107.

Underhill, E.B. *The Records of a Church of Christ Meeting in Broadmead, Bristol* (London: The Hanserd Knollys Society, 1847).

Unwin, George *The Gilds and Companies of London* (London: Frank Cass & Company, 1963 fourth edition).

Walker, G. Goold *The Honourable Artillery Company 1537-1987* (London: The Royal Artillery Company, 1986, third edition).

Watts, Michael *The Dissenters from the Reformation to the French Revolution* (Oxford: Clarendon Press, 1978).

White, B.R., 'Baptist Beginnings and the Kiffin Manuscript', *Baptist History and Heritage* 2 (1967): 27-37.

________ 'William Kiffin – Baptist Pioneer and Citizen of London', *Baptist History and Heritage* 2 (1967): 91-103, 126.

________ 'William Erbury and the Baptists', *The Baptist Quarterly* 23 (1969-70): 114-125.

________ 'How Did Kiffin Join the Baptists?', *The Baptist Quarterly* 23 (1970-71): 201-207.

________ 'Samuel Eaton (d. 1639): Particular Baptist Pioneer', *The Baptist Quarterly* 24 (1971-72): 10-21.

________ *Hanserd Knollys and Radical Dissent in the 17th Century* (London: Dr Williams's Trust, 1977).

________ 'Jessey, Henry (1601-1663)', in Richard L. Greaves and Robert Zaller (eds.) *Biographical Dictionary of British Radicals in the Seventeenth Century, Volume II: G-O* (Brighton: The Harvester Press, 1983): 140-141.

________ 'Kiffin, William (1616-1701)', in Richard L. Greaves and Robert Zaller (eds.) *Biographical Dictionary of British Radicals in the Seventeenth Century, Volume II: G-O* (Brighton: The Harvester Press, 1983): 155-157.

Whitley, W.T., 'Debate on Infant Baptism, 1643', *Transactions of the Baptist Historical Society* 1 (1908-09): 237-245.

________ 'Rise of the Particular Baptists in London, 1633-1644', *Transactions of the Baptist Historical Society* 1 (1908-09): 226-236.

________ 'Thompson's List of Conventicles in 1683', *Transactions of the Congregational Historical Society* 4 (1909-1910): 49-53.

________ 'The Jessey Church, 1653-1678', *Transactions of the Congregational Historical Society* 4 (1909-10): 233-239.

________ 'Jottings by John Lewis of Margate, 1742', *Transactions of the Baptist Historical Society* 4 (1914-15): 206.

________ 'London Churches in 1682', *The Baptist Quarterly* 1 (1922-23): 82-87.

________ *The Baptists of London* (The Kingsgate Press, London, 1928).

________ *A Baptist Bibliography, Volume 1 1526-1776* (The Kingsgate Press, London, 1936).

________ 'The Rev. Colonel Paul Hobson', *The Baptist Quarterly* 9 (1938-39): 307-310.

Wilson, Paul F., 'William Kiffin (1616-1701)', in Michael A.G. Haykin (ed.), *The British Particular Baptists 1638-1910, Volume 1* (Particular Baptist Press: Springfield, Missouri, 1998): 64-77.

Wilson, Walter *The History and Antiquities of Dissenting Churches and Meeting Houses, Volume 1* (London, 1808).

Winthrop, John *Winthrop Papers II, 1623-1630* (Boston: The Massachusetts Historical Society, 1931).

________ *Winthrop Papers III, 1631-1637* (Boston: The Massachusetts Historical Society, 1943).

________ *Winthrop Papers V, 1645-1649* (Boston: The Massachusetts Historical Society, 1947).

Wiseman, Susan *Conspiracy and Virtue: Women, Writing, and Politics in Seventeenth-Century England* (Oxford: Oxford University Press, 2006).

Wood, Anthony *The history and antiquities of the University of Oxford, in two books: by Anthony à Wood, ... Now first published in English, from the original MS in the Bodleian Library: by John Gutch, ... Vol. 2.* (Oxford, 1792-96).

Woods, T.P.S. *Prelude to Civil War 1642: Mr Justice Malet and the Kentish Petitions* (Michael Russell: Salisbury, 1980).

Woolrych, Austyn *Commonwealth to Protectorate* (Oxford: Oxford University Press, 1982).

Wright, Stephen *The Early English Baptists, 1603-1649* (Woodbridge: Boydell Press, 2006).

Theses and Unpublished Studies

Farr, David 'The Militia and Political Career of John Lambert, 1619-57' (PhD thesis, Cambridge University Press, 1996).

General Index

(The membership lists of the Devonshire Square Baptist Church are *not* included within this index; however, a full alphabetical list of the members is contained on pages 289-307.)

Adams, Alice 349, 350
Adams, Mary 349
Adams, Samuel 349
Adams, Samuel Jr 349
Adams, Sarah 349
Adams, Thomas 349
Adams, Thomas Jr 349
Aldrich, Henry 365, 389, 398, 406, 407
Aldworth, Mr 62
Allen, John 349
Allen, Thomas 128
Allen, William 129
Allerdice, James 397
Allin, Thomas 323
Ann I 349
Appleby, Blanch 413, 418
Appleby, Brian 413, 418
Appleby, Joseph 418
Arundell, Thomas 373
Asham, John 53, 93
Ashton, Robert 12
Ashton, Thomas 135
Audeley, Lewis 47, 75, 347
Avery, Elizabeth 4, 351-362
Aylmer, G E 323

Bacon, Nathaniel 370, 409
Badiley, William 335
Barber, Edward 8, 356, 357
Barbon, Nicholas 64, 65, 117, 118, 119, 121, 123
Barbon, Praisegod 66
Barker, Mr 142, 180
Barwick, Peter 131
Bason, Edward 320, 321, 337, 338, 343
Baston, Jane 351
Batsfeild, Goodman 415
Batten, Samuel 159
Batty, Brother 176
Bayly, Walter 405
Baynes, John 365, 368, 369, 389, 398, 405, 406, 407, 408 .
Baxter, Richard 129, 133
Beake, Robert 321, 344
Bearman, Mr 18
Beast (Best), Captain 51, 76, 80
Bedwell, Richard 46
Bell, Maureen 130
Bell, Richard 349
Bellin, Robert 20
Bennet, Henry (Lord Arlington) 55, 58, 67
Bennet, Robert 134
Berkeley, John (Lord Berkeley) 364, 369, 375, 376, 377, 378, 380, 381, 382, 383, 384, 385, 386, 387, 388, 389, 390, 391, 393, 395, 397
Berkeley (Barklaye), William 409
Bertie, Charles 59, 102, 106
Best, Captain 70
Bethell, A Talbot 366
Bettesworth, John 424
Biby, Mr 86
Bide, Thomas 148, 152, 153, 154, 155, 156, 157, 158, 163, 164
Billers, William 47, 75, 347
Birch, Thomas 26, 129
Birtch, Colonel 345
Black, Robert C 22
Blacke, Adam 169
Blacke, William 170
Blackmore, James 132
Blackwood, Christopher 134, 135, 146
Blake, Robert 317
Blood, Thomas 149
Blunden, Mary 161
Bodura, Mr 141
Bonnington, Richard 162
Bores, Lucretia 168
Bores, Mary 168

Bores, Richard 168, 169
Boulton, Jeremy 14, 15
Bourne, Edward 347
Bourne, Nehemiah 336, 347, 348
Bowen, Peter 319, 331, 332, 333, 335, 30, 341
Bradbury, George 64, 119, 120, 121
Brag, Mr 180
Breda, The Declaration of 131, 132, 133, 136, 140, 145
Bremer, Francis J 22
Brett-James, N.G. 65
Brewster, Mr 142
Brome, Mr 86
Brooke, Humphrey 45
Brooks, Mr 142
Brooks, Thomas 180
Brown, Louise Fargo 129
Browne, Mr 345
Browne, Thomas 397
Browner, Jessica A 15,
Browning, Andrew 59
Bryan, John 356
Burkin, Captain 76, 77
Burns, Alan 365 Edward 133
Burton, Thomas 48
Bustin, Dennis 43
Butler, Samuel 178

Calamy, Edward 357
Capp, Bernard 129, 149, 315, 317, 318, 322
Carew, George 95, 97
Carnall, Susan 149, 155, 156, 157, 175
Carte, Timothy 128
Carteret, George 364, 369, 375, 376, 377, 378, 380, 381, 382, 383, 384, 385, 386, 387, 388, 389, 390, 391, 393, 395, 397
Caryll, Joseph 130, 142, 180, 320, 342, 343
Certaine Observations Upon Hosea (1642) 23, 26
Chamberlen, Peter 356
Champante, John 53, 93
Chapman, Livewell 129, 130, 141
Chicheley, John 323
Clarendon Code, The 137
Charles I 12, 15, 18, 21, 34, 35, 36, 37, 38, 129, 130, 317
Charles II 3, 42, 47, 49, 53, 54, 55, 56, 57, 58, 59, 60, 61, 62, 63, 64, 68, 77, 94, 95, 97, 98, 119, 121, 126, 129, 130, 131, 132, 133, 136, 177, 309, 310, 363, 364, 369
Chasey, Mr 180
Cheynell, Francis 353, 354
Chiles, William 162
Chillenden, Edmund 15, 26
Chillingworth, Charles 370
Clarke, Anthony 153, 155, 156, 157
Clarke, Edward 406
Clarke, John 308
Clarke, Samuel 54
Clerke, John 74, 319, 320, 322, 334, 341, 342, 343, 346
Clerke, William 413
Clifford, William 16, 33, 34, 35, 36
Cockain, George 130, 142, 180
Cockburn, J.S, 7, 10, 19
Cohen, A 130
Colleton, Peter 364, 366, 370, 375, 376, 377, 378, 380, 381, 382, 383, 384, 385, 386, 387, 388, 389, 390, 391, 393, 395
Compton, William 50, 51, 52, 87
Confession of Faith, The (1644) 1, 3, 9, 27, 30, 354
Coniers, Tobias 180
Constable, Robert 54, 95, 96
Conyers (Canyon), Edward 61
Cooke, Francis 16, 32, 33, 34, 35, 36
Cooke, John 417
Coope, Henry 346
Cooper, Anthony Ashley 364, 365, 368, 369, 371, 375, 376, 377, 378, 380, 381, 382, 383, 384, 385, 386, 387, 388, 390
Cooper, Thomas 133, 146, 153, 155, 156, 157, 167
Cork, Thomas 415
Cornish, Henry 353
Cottrell, Charles 57, 98, 100
Coventry, Henry 58, 102, 103
Cox, Martha 349
Cox, Mary 349

Cox, Mr 180
Cranston, Maurice 365, 371
Craton, Michael 364, 366
Craven, William (Earl of Craven) 364, 369, 375, 376, 377, 378, 380, 381, 382, 383, 384, 385, 386, 387, 388, 389, 390, 391, 393, 395, 397
Crawford, Patricia 351
Cressey, David 15
Crisp, Stephen 356
Croke, Robert 53, 88, 90, 92
Cromwell, Hannah 4, 412, 423, 424
Cromwell, Hannah Jr 4408
Cromwell, Henry 4, 26, 423
Cromwell, Henry Jr 4, 423
Cromwell, Oliver 4, 10, 24, 26, 38, 39, 129, 133, 137, 149, 423
Cromwell, Richard 130, 134
Cromwell, William 423, 424
Crosby, Thomas 1, 3, 24, 25, 66, 356
Crosley, Josias 168
Cruso, Major 70, 77
Culcross, James 43

Dallison, Roger 95, 97
Danvers, Henry 135
Darrell (Dorrell), John 365, 368, 370, 389, 398, 405, 406, 407,
Dart, Dorothy 16, 23, 26, 29, 33, 34, 35, 36, 37
Dart, John 16, 23, 33, 34, 35, 36, 37
Dashwood, Rachel 414
Dashwood, William 414
Davies, Mr 141
Davy, Richard 365, 389, 398, 405, 406, 407, 408
Day, Thomas 17, 18
De Beer, E S 367, 370, 372
Declaration of Indulgence, The (1672) 58, 135, 177
DeLaune, Thomas 135
Denne, Henry 180
Denham, John 7
Derrick, Charles 316, 323
Desborough, John 129, 130, 136, 141, 144, 319, 320, 330, 334, 341
Dethick, Colonel 147
Dicks, Grace 26
Dillon, Harold Arthur 46
Ditchfield, Thomas 406
Dorman, William 172
Dover, Mary 150, 164, 165, 166, 167, 168, 169
Drake, Katherine 149, 155, 156, 157,
Duncan, Pope A. 43, 44
Dunkley, Anne 26
Dyke, Daniel 135, 177

Eames, Aled 317
Eaton, Samuel 24, 25
Edwards, Mr 142
Edwards, John 371
Edwards, Thomas 11, 12, 354, 355, 356
Egerton, Ralph 397
Eightshillings, Jeremy 163, 164
Elding, Read 371
Eldred, John 7
Engeham, Polycarpus 347
Erbury, William 353, 354, 355
Ernle, John 121
Evans, Mary 26
Evans, Rice 141
Evatt, Philip 321, 344
Exton, John 349, 350
Exton, Thomas 162

Falkener, John 47, 75
Farewell, George 159
Farr, David 353, 354
Fasted, Thomas 369
Feake, Christopher 130, 142, 180
Featley, Daniel 8, 9, 11, 16, 21, 26, 27, 28,
Featley, John 21
Fells, Margaret 179
Fenwick, Colonel 345
Ferguson, Robert 356
Fillingham, Bartholomew 397
Finch, Heneage 57, 58, 59, 60, 61, 98, 99, 100, 101, 102, 104, 105
Firth, C.H. 48
Fitch, Colonel 146
Fleetwood, Charles 319, 32
Forster, Reginald 123, 124, 124
Forty, Henry 135
Fowle, William 370, 409

Fox, George 179
Fox, Stephen 121
Foxley, Mr 11
Fromantel, Ahasuerus 173

Gardiner, Samuel Rawson 131, 316, 317
Gardyner, Robert 150, 159, 160
Gell, Anne 26
Gerard, Charles 54, 97
Gibbins, Sarah 349
Glausser, William 363
Gleede, Samuel 4, 315-350
Godolphin, Stephen 212
Goldie, Mark 312
Goodwin, John 45, 180
Gordon, Alexander 1, 3, 11, 43
Goring, Anne 26
Gosnold, John 133, 135, 146, 180
Gospright, Frances 148, 153, 154, 155
Gospright, George 148, 153, 154
Gouge, Thomas 417
Grandison, Lord 63, 115
Graves, Anne 149, 155, 156, 157,
Greaves, Richard L 151
Greene, John 422
Greenhill, Mr 180
Gregg, Pauline 10
Grene, Mr 146
Greville, Robert (Lord Brooke) 20, 21, 22, 23
Grew, Obadiah 356
Grey, Zachary 45
Gribben, Crawford 351, 357
Griffin, Mr 147, 180
Griffith, William 141
Griffiths, Mr 142, 180
Grove, Christian 161
Gumble, Thomas 131
Guy, Henry 60, 62, 63, 109, 112, 115, 116, 117, 118, 121, 122

Hall, John 169, 173, 174
Halton, Jane 148, 153, 154, 155
Halton, Owen 148, 153, 154
Hammon, George 132
Hancock, Mr 180
Harbord, Charles 48, 49, 50, 51, 52, 53, 54, 55, 56, 57, 58, 59, 60, 61, 63, 76, 77, 78, 79, 80, 83, 85, 87, 89, 92, 93, 100, 101, 102, 104, 106, 108, 109, 110, 111
Harbord, William 61, 62, 63, 64, 65, 110, 111, 112, 115
Harding, Elizabeth 349
Harding, Jonas 162
Harris, Richard 308
Harris, Tim 128
Harrison, Edward 180
Harrison, Mr 135
Harrison, Thomas 177
Harrys, Robert 353
Hasted, Thomas 405
Hatsell, Henry 320, 332, 340, 341
Hayden, Roger 2
Hayes, Joseph 418
Hayes, Rebecca 412, 413, 418
Hedges, John 308
Hedworth, Henry 356
Helm, Mr 143
Henson, Thomas 346
Hepper, David J 319, 323
Haykin, Michael 1, 3
Hesilrigg, Arthur 143
Hewling, Benjamin 148, 162, 372, 419, 422, 423
Hewling, Benjamin Jr 419
Hewling, Elizabeth 419, 420
Hewling, Hannah 412, 421, 423
Hewling, Hannah Jr 419, 423
Hewling, Henrietta 420
Hewling, Priscilla 420
Hewling, Rebecca 419, 420
Hewling, William 419
Hewson, John 355
Hewson, Thomas 10
Heydon, John 95, 96, 97
Heydon, William 54, 95, 97
Hicks, Thomas 135, 356
Hilton, John 310, 311, 312
Hind, Captain 70, 77, 80, 345
Hinde, Lieutenant-Colonel 51, 77
Hindmarsh, D. Bruce 351
Hobson, Hester 165, 172
Hobson, Hester, Jr 172, 173, 174, 175
Hobson, Jeremiah 173
Hobson, Lydia 172, 173, 174

Hobson, Paul 150, 151, 164, 165, 166, 171, 172, 173, 174, 175
Hobson, Paul Jr 172, 173, 174
Hobson, Reubenah 173, 174
Hobson, Sara 172, 173, 174
Horton, Ellen 148, 153, 154, 155
Hobson, Jeremiah 173, 174, 175
Homes, Nathaniel 180
Hook, Mr 180
Hopkins, Edward 319, 320, 334, 341, 342, 343
Hornes, Dr 180
Horton, Richard 148, 153, 154
Howard, Luke 16
Howard, Robert 65, 118, 122
Howard, Theophilus 18
Hubberthorne, Richard 133
Hubland, (Houblon) Captain 70, 76
Hudleston, Mr 130, 142
Hudson, Richard 413
Hughes, Mr 141
Hughes, R 145
Humble Apology of Some Commonly Called Anabaptists, The (1661) 1, 134
Humphrey, John 316
Huntington, Robert 372
Hutchinson, Richard 323, 347
Hutchinson, Thomas 22
Hyde, Laurence 121
Hyland (Highland), Samuel 315, 322, 324, 345

Ireton, Alderman 143
Ives, Jeremiah 356
Ivimey, Joseph 1, 2, 6, 11, 12

Jackson, Walter 21
Jacob, Henry 25,
Jacobs, John 347
James I 52, 72, 74, 76, 78, 80, 82, 83, 86, 107
James, Anne 173
James, Muriel 43
Jameson, David 417
Jaque, Letitia 422
Jeake, Samuel 135
Jeanlett, John 322
Jeffery, William 132
Jenkins, Leoline 162, 422, 423
Jessey, Henry 14, 15, 22, 24, 25, 27, 44, 45, 67, 127, 128, 143, 179, 180, 354, 356
Jessop, William 47, 73
Jones, David 177
Jones, Griffith 141
Jones, James 135
Jones, John 142, 320, 342
Jones, Mr 141
Jones, Peter 365, 371, 389, 398, 405, 406, 407, 408
Joplin, John 173

Keeble, N.H. 129, 134
Keith, George 356
Kelly (pirate) 371
Kelsey, Francis 9, 29, 47
Kelsey, Thomas 9, 10
Kelsey, Thomas Jr 10, 47, 48, 53, 54, 74, 321, 344
Ken, Peter 308
Kennedy, D E 317
Kentish, Mr 180
Kevan, Ernest F 24
Kiffen, Henry (William Kiffen's son) 372, 414, 417, 422
Kiffen, Henry (William Kiffen's grandson) 413
Kiffen, Joseph 3
Kiffen, Joseph (William Kiffen's grandson) 412, 413, 416
Kiffen, Rachel 412, 415, 416, 417
Kiffen, Susan 412, 413
Kiffen, William (William Kiffen's grandson) 412, 415
Kilby, Major 76
Killihrew, William 64, 117
King, Anne 365
King, Maurice 167, 413, 421
King, Peter 365
King, William 169
Kingdon, Richard 365,
Kinge, David 148, 152
Knight, Benjamin 168
Knight, Mary 308
Knollys, Hanserd 4, 27, 42-125, 126, 127, 131, 135, 141, 178, 180, 312

Kreitzer, Larry J 2, 3
Kupperman, Karen Ordahl 22

Lambe, Thomas 25, 305, 356
Lambert, John 130, 352, 353, 354, 360, 361
Langley, Arthur S 355, 356
Langley, Henry 353
Lanson, Mr 329
Lanyon, Philip 370, 409, 410
Lash, Hannah 149, 155, 156, 157
Laster, Lodor 180
Lathrop, John 25,
Laud, William 7, 9, 15, 17389, 398, 404, 406, 407,
Laurence, Anne 353
Leake, Anne 160, 161, 162
Leake, John 160
Lee, G. 171
Legge, George 55, 56, 58, 61, 98, 105, 106, 107, 108, 110, 111, 115, 116
Legge, William 43, 48, 52, 53, 54, 55, 56, 57, 60, 76, 87, 93, 94, 95, 96, 98, 99, 100, 106, 109, 111
Leighton, Ellis 397
Lenthall, John 15
Leverett, Barbara 168
Leverett, Hannah
Lewin, William 174, 175
Lewis, John 44
Lewis, Susan 148, 153, 154, 155
Lewis, Thomas 148, 153, 154
Ley, John 356
Liddell, Robert 416, 417, 418
Lide, John 34, 36
Light, Mary 149, 156, 157,
Lilburne, Robert 143, 319, 366
Lilburne, John 2, 10, 11, 12, 21, 149
Lilburne, Richard 366
Limbery, John 397
Lindley, Keith 15, 16
Lloyd, Jenkyn 26
Lloyd, John 141
Lloyd, Mr 141, 143
Lloyd, Nicholas 422, 423
Locke, John 4, 363, 365, 366, 367, 368, 369, 370, 371, 372, 373, 374, 398, 405, 407, 408
Locke, Nathaniel 372
Locke, Nicholas 170
Lockhart, Colonel 146
Long, Thomas 355
Lough, John 372
Ludlow, Edmund 146

Mack, Phyllis 352
Maile, Mr 147
Malbon, Elizabeth 150, 165, 168, 169, 170, 175
Malbon, Ellen 168
Malbon, Robert 4, 148, 149, 150, 151, 154, 155, 156, 157, 158, 163, 164, 165, 166, 167, 168, 173, 301
Malet, Thomas 7, 21, 23, 24
Mallery, Mr 180
Manby, William 49, 51, 52, 77, 86
Mapletoft, John 365, 389, 398, 405, 407
Marven, Henry 320, 338, 339
Mason, John 135
Masters, Joseph 415
Masterson, George 149
Maudrin, Mr 141
Maurice, Henry 141
May, Betty 418
Mead, Mr 180
Mead, William 356, 357
Menes, Colonel 51, 80
Merick, William 169, 170, 174, 175
Mesiams, John 34, 36
Mews, Lieutenant-Colonel 70, 76
Michaelborne, Philip 168
Middletons, Mr 180
Monck, Christopher (Duke of Albemarle) 364, 375, 376, 377, 378, 380, 381, 382, 383, 384, 385, 386, 387, 388, 389, 391, 392, 393, 395, 397
Monck, George 128, 130, 131, 143, 327, 364
Morgan, Charles 406
Morris, William 142
Morrison, Richard 95, 97
Mostyn, Mr 143
Moyle, Peter 142
Munns, Brother 176
Musgrave, Chrisopher 54

Narrative of the Proceedings of the General Assembly, A (1689) 3, 177
Nash, Elizabeth 424
Nash, James 149, 150, 157, 158
Nash, Thomas 150, 157, 158
Naylor, James 48
Nead, Mr 180
Neal, David 1, 45
Neale, Thomas 64, 117
Neave, Mary 148, 153, 154, 155
Neave, Nicholas 148, 153, 154
Neile, Richard 17
Newcourt, Richard 139
Nicholas, Edward 50, 79, 82, 159
Noble, Mark 2, 3, 10
Noel, Edward 64, 119, 120, 121
Norris, Jab 149
Northott, Mr 135
Nuttall, Geoffrey 25, 129, 134
Ny (Nye), Edward 322
Nye, Philip 180

Okey, John 143
Oram, Richard 148, 153, 154
Oram, Sarah 148, 153, 154, 155, 412
Orme, William 1, 2, 3, 6, 8, 11, 14, 21, 22, 129, 148, 355
Osborne, Thomas (Earl of Danby) 58, 59, 60, 101, 102, 103, 108
Owen, Captain 141
Owne, Colonel 76
Owen, John 141, 417

Page, William 174
Palmer, Elia 47, 75, 347
Palmer, Elizabeth 161
Paris, Thomas 372, 374
Parker, Captain 332, 333
Parker, Thomas 352
Parratt, Mr 180
Patient, Thomas 356
Paul, Thomas 135
Pawle, Anne 26
Pearl, Valerie 15
Pearson, Hannah 421
Pearson, John 421
Pecke, Mr 142
Peirson, WIlliam 397
Penn, William 135, 356
Penson, Lillian M 53
Pepys, Samuel 315, 316, 369
Peters, Hugh 143
Pett, Peter 348
Piper, Colonel 369
Pitfeild, Charles 153, 154, 155, 156, 157, 163, 164
Plant, Thomas 356
Poinder, George 422
Poole, Elizabeth 48
Pope, Bartholomew 148, 153, 154
Pope, Mary 148, 153, 154, 155
Porter, Hannah 413
Potts, George 369, 408
Powell, J.R. 317
Powell, Mr 142
Powell, Richard 152, 152, 153, 157, 158
Powell, Rowland 397
Powell, Vavasour 143
Price, Colonel 141
Prince, Thomas 422
Pride's Purge 129
Prior, Captain 51, 80
Puryer (Peryer), Mr 44, 49, 70, 71, 77
Pyne, Valentine 49

Quainton, C. Eden 26

Ragge, James 44, 49, 51, 71, 73, 79, 86
Raines, Richard 350, 417
Ramsbottom, B.A. 1
Rawlinson, Richard 315, 323
Read, Thomas 169, 170
Reade, Lieutenant-Colonel 146
Reddinge, Mr 18
Reston, John 18
Reve, John 132
Reynolds, Edward 353
Rich, E.E. 136
Richards, John 397
Riddell, William Renwick 17
Roberts, Gerard 179
Roberts, Jonathan 142
Robinson, John 49
Rocaure, Pierre 372
Roe, Mr 345
Rogers, Edward 406

Rogers, John 143, 180, 351, 352, 355, 357, 358, 359
Rogers, Lieutenant-Colonel 70, 76
Rostenberg, Leona 130, 313
Row, Mr 143, 180
Rowe, Violet A 129
Rowlands, Mr 141
Rowley, Peter 320, 330, 337
Rudyard, Thomas 356, 357
Rugge, Thomas 127
Rush, Isaac 370
Rye, Mr 142
Rylie, William 16, 33, 34, 35, 36

Salmon, Edward 74, 321, 343, 344
Samwaies, James 163, 164
Sandforde, Thomas 347
Sanford, Don A 136
Sansom, John 26, 38, 39, 41
Saunders, Gail 364
Sawyer, Robert 63, 117
Sayer, Mark 414
Saywell, John 415
Scot, Joseph 320, 342
Scot, Thomas 225
Selby (Shelby), John 322, 345
Seller, John 316, 325
Shelton, Thomas 16, 32, 33, 34, 35, 36
Shelton, William 308
Shepherd, Anthony 397
Shepherd, Captain 51, 76, 80, 80
Shepherd, F.H.W. 42
Sherburne, Edward 61, 111
Sherwin, John 316, 317, 318, 319, 320, 321, 322, 326, 327, 328, 330, 331, 332, 333, 334, 335, 336, 337, 340, 342, 343, 343, 345
Shipp, Sister 175
Shott, Mr 344
Siferwest, Robert 68, 123, 124
Simcocke, Eleanor 149, 150, 151, 155, 156, 157, 164, 165, 166, 167, 168, 169, 170
Simcock, Elizabeth 349
Simpson, John 45, 180
Skippon, Philip 134
Slater, Mr 180
Smith, James 309, 310, 311
Smith, John 2, 9
Smith, John 124, 125, 422
Smith, Mary 149, 155, 156, 157
Smith, Nigel 351
Smith, Steven R 15
Smith, Thomas 336
Smyth, Edmond 322
Snelling, P 159
Southby, Captain 142
Sowden, John 168
Spilsbery, John 24, 25, 26, 38, 39, 41, 143, 178, 305
Spilsbery, Magdalena 26
Spurston, Henry 346
Stanrodd, John 34, 36
Stanton, Jane 148, 153, 154, 155
Stanton, Richard 148, 153, 154
Stanton, Samuel 133, 134, 146
Stearns, S.J. 149
Stephens, Nathaniel 356
Stevenson, Captain 76
Stinton, Benjamin 14, 24, 354, 356
Stoner, Isaac 161
Stoner, Mark 161
Stoner, Moses 161
Stoner, Nathaniel 150, 159, 160, 162, 304
Stout, Alice 148, 153, 154, 155
Stout, Edmund 148, 153, 154
Strahan, William 424
Strider, Robert E.L. 22
Stringer, Thomas 365, 372, 373, 389, 398, 405, 406
Strype, John 20
Sturges, Richard 15
Sturgion, John 132
Sutton, Thomas 308
Swatland, Andrew 133

Taler, Mr 179
Tanner, J R 369
Taylor, Captain 142
Taylor, John 316
Taylor, Silas 369
Teagy, William 308
Thedam, John 136, 146
Thomas, Mr 142, 143
Thompson, Mr 147

Thompson, Robert 346
Thomson, Lieutenant-Colonel 321
Thomson, Maurice 335
Thomson, Robert 348
Thornburgh, Edward 365, 389, 398, 405, 406
Thornburgh, John 406
Thurloe, John 26, 129, 322
Tichborne, Henry 54
Tiddeyman, Joan 17
Tilham, Thomas 136, 146
Todd, Brother 175, 176
Todd, Christopher 148, 153, 154
Todd, Mary 148, 153, 154, 155
Tolmie, Murray 1, 24, 25, 45
Tombes, John 133, 134, 146
Tomlinson, H.C. 62
Topling, Robert 174
Tredwell, Catherine 26
Trendall, John 16, 17, 18, 19, 32, 33, 34
Trevitt, William 320, 340, 341
Trevor-Roper, H.R. 15, 18
Turke, William 173
Turner, G. Lyon 135
Turner, Nathaniel 312

Uncles, WIlliam 25, 305
Underdown, David 134
Underhill, E.B. 44
Unwin, George 12

Vane, Henry 129, 142, 144
Van Trump, Admiral 317
Venner Revolt 1, 55, 134, 136, 137, 148, 149, 151
Venning, Mr 180
Vincent, Humfrey 15
Vincent, William 49, 76, 77

Walker, G. Goold 52
Wallers, Mr 180
Walter, David 54, 57, 58, 98, 99, 100, 104, 105, 107
Ward, Patience 373
Wares, Anne 162
Waring, Robert 353
Warner, Armiger 21
Warner, Robert 14, 16, 32, 33, 34
Warren, William 64, 117
Waters, Mr 180
Watts, Michael R. 25
Waxon, Elizabeth 349
Waxon, Rose 349
Webb, Nicholas 370, 371
Webber, Mary 424
Webster, John 354
Weedon, John 173
Weekes, Thomas 46
Wemyss, James 47, 49, 52
Wentworth, Hugh 365
Wentworth, John 370, 409
West, Colonel 146
Whalley, Edward 146
Wharton, Thomas 161
Whiston, Edward 14
White, B.R. 1, 25, 43, 44, 136, 354
White, Mary 418
Whitehead, George 356
Whitehead, John 308
Whitley, William T. 24, 27, 44, 66, 151, 178, 313
Wightman, Edward 17, 18
Wildman, Major 144
Wilkings, Richard 349
Wilkinson, Henry 353
Wilks (Weekes), Colonel 146
William III 177
Williams, John 141
Williams, Thomas 142
Williamson, Joseph 56, 57, 97, 369, 370, 409,
Willoughby, Francis 336, 348
Willoughby, William 53
Wills, Obediah 135
Wilmott, Robert 34, 36
Wilson, Walter 1, 2, 3, 6, 10,
Wilson, Mrs 14
Wilson, Paul 1
Wilson, Samuel 70
Wilson, Walter 1, 2, 3, 6, 10, 24, 178
Winch, Mary 67, 68, 122, 123, 124
Windis, Samuel 321, 344
Winthrop, John Jr 22
Winthrop, John Sr 22
Wise, Lawrence 135
Wiseman, John 405

Wiseman, Susan 351
Wollaston, Richard 43, 44, 45, 46, 47, 50, 51. 70, 71, 72, 78, 81, 82, 86
Wood, Anthony 355
Woods, T.P.S. 7, 23
Woolfen, Henry 172, 173, 175
Woolrych, Austyn 322
Worrall, James 397
Wren, Christopher 63, 64, 116, 117
Wright, Mary 413, 418
Wright, Sarah 44
Wright, Stephen 1, 12, 25
Wriothesley, Thomas (Earl of Southampton) 48, 50, 51, 53, 54, 55, 76, 77, 79, 80, 83, 85, 88, 90, 93, 97, 100, 104,
Wynne, Captain 142
Wynne, Mr 141

Young, John 406

Zanchey (Sankey), Jerome 146

The Centre for Baptist History and Heritage
Regent's Park College, Oxford

Aims

The aims of the Centre are:

- to deepen an awareness and appreciation of Baptist history and theology
- to develop research and scholarship in these areas
- to relate Baptist history and theology to Baptist life and principles today

The Centre pursues these aims by:

- providing College membership for students studying for research degrees in related areas
- offering research facilities to visiting scholars
- organizing lecture series, seminars and consultations of international significance and publishing these in an appropriate form
- exploiting the facilities of the Angus Library at the highest academic level
- appointing leading specialists as advisors to develop an international network of distinguished Baptist historians and theologians
- appointing Fellows and Research students of the Centre
- developing publications in cooperation with others to forward these aims

For further information contact:
Rev. Dr Anthony R. Cross,
Director of the Centre for Baptist History and Heritage,
Regent's Park College,
Pusey Street,
Oxford,
OX1 2LB,
United Kingdom
College Main Office: +44 (0)1865 – 288120
anthony.cross@regents.ox.ac.uk
or
visit the College's website, www.rpc.ox.ac.uk

The Angus Library and Archives

The Angus Library and Archive is the leading world-class collection for Baptist and Nonconformist history and heritage. It comprises over 70,000 printed books, including pamphlets, journals, church and association records, church histories, manuscript letters and other artefacts. These items date from the late fifteenth century onwards and many of these items are only found in the Angus Library.

The Revd Dr Joseph Angus
(President of Regent's Park College, 1849–93)

Collections

Joseph Angus Collection
Joseph Angus collected items relating to Baptist and Nonconformist history, many of which are only held in this collection providing a unique insight into Baptist life.

Journal Collection
There are over 300 journal titles held dating back to the eighteenth century with the main focus being Baptist and Nonconformist life, development and history.

Angus Archive
The papers of many leading Baptist figures from the eighteenth to twentieth centuries are held here such as, C.H. Spurgeon, Joseph Angus, the Steele and Whitaker families, E.A. Payne, G. Henton Davies and J.H. Rushbrooke. Alongside the minutes, papers and other Baptist archival material.

Baptist Missionary Society Collection
The BMS collection holds comprehensive papers for many missionaries such as William Carey and his family, Andrew Fuller, Joshua Marshman, William Ward, Timothy Richard and William Knibb. It also holds

photographs, minutes, correspondence, and other documents covering mission fields such as China, India, Congo and the West Indies from the commencement of BMS in 1792.

Church Records
The church records and minutes from many older and historically significant Baptist churches and chapels dating from the mid seventeenth century are held in this collection.

Hymnbook Collection
This collection has over 4,000 items ranging from Sunday School anniversary booklets to denominational hymnbooks, from the late eighteenth century to the present day.

John Bunyan
John Bunyan was a key Baptist figure and as such we have many of his publications, including over forty versions of *The Pilgrims Progress*, starting with the eighth edition.

The Angus Library, London

Using the Library

Information regarding the use of the Angus is as follows:
Hours: Monday – Friday 9:30am–4:30pm (closed from 1pm–2pm).
The Library is also closed for all of August.
For further information contact:
Email: angus.library@regents.ox.ac.uk
Phone: +44 (0)1865 288 120
Fax: + 44 (0)1865 288 121

Regent's Park College

Regent's Park College is a Christian foundation in the University of Oxford, which focuses on achieving excellence in undergraduate and graduate studies, ministerial formation and academic research. Our mission is to create an exceptional community of learning and research made up of individuals from a broad range of backgrounds and life experience.

Regent's Park College was originally founded as The Baptist Academical Institution (BAI) in Stepney, in the East End of London, in 1810. When the BAI moved to Regent's Park in 1857 the Institution was renamed Regent's Park College. The name was then retained when the College relocated to Oxford in 1927. In 1957, after thirty years in the city, the College became a Permanent Private Hall of the University of Oxford.

As part of the University of Oxford, the College has approximately 200 students in total and admits in the region of thirty undergraduates per year to read for BA (Hons) degrees in Theology, English, Law, History, Geography, Modern Languages, Classics and PPE (Politics, Philosophy and Economics).

Regent's is affiliated to the Baptist Union of Great Britain and a significant proportion of the student body is engaged in training for the ordained ministry among Baptist churches in Great Britain and overseas.

For further information contact:
Regent's Park College,
Pusey Street,
Oxford,
OX1 2LB,
United Kingdom.
Email: postmaster@regents.ox.ac.uk
Tel: (+44) 01865 288120
Fax: 01865 288121
Website: www.rpc.ox.ac.uk
To order any College publications visit www.rpc.ox.ac.uk and select 'Publications'.

Centre for Baptist History and Heritage Studies

Anthony R. Cross and Nicholas J. Wood (eds)
Exploring Baptist Origins
Vol. 1
The 400th anniversary of the origins of the Baptists in Amsterdam in 1609 is here celebrated by Baptist historians and theologians. Originally presented as a lecture series at Regent's Park College, University of Oxford, in the autumn of 2009, these fuller versions of the papers examine various aspects of Baptist beginnings in the light of the latest research and seek to explore some of their implications for today. Subjects discussed are the adoption of believer's baptism, whether Baptists are a church or sect, Thomas Helwys' *The Mystery of Iniquity*, William Kiffen and the Anabaptist Petitions of 1660 and 1661, Baptists and millennialism, the dangers of 'just' reading the Bible, and Baptists and Anabaptists. Contributors are Anthony R. Cross, Paul S. Fiddes, Brian Haymes, Larry J. Kreitzer, Crawford Gribben, Stephen R. Holmes, and Keith G. Jones.
Anthony R. Cross is Director of the Centre for Baptist History and Heritage and a Research Fellow of Regent's Park College, University of Oxford.
Nicholas J. Wood is Director of the Oxford Centre for Christianity and Culture at Regent's Park College, and Fellow in Religion and Culture, University of Oxford.
2010 / ISBN 978–0–9539746–6–5

Paul W. Goodliff
Ministry, Sacrament, and Representation
Ministry and Ordination in Contemporary Baptist Theology, and the Rise of Sacramentalism
Vol. 2
This study in the surprising rise in a sacramental understanding of ministry amongst ministers of the Baptist Union of Great Britain is the result of empirical research which compares the conciliar statements about ministry and ordination, and the wider literature, that together comprise the formal understanding of ministry amongst Baptists for the past seventy years, with the actual beliefs of over 300 ministers surveyed in 2007. Sacramental views have seen a remarkable resurgence amongst the more recently trained, and this study explores the reasons for this rise amongst both ecclesial factors and wider cultural processes These include changes in the character of Evangelicalism, the widespread impact of charismatic renewal, the acceptance of ecumenism and a kind of 'demotic' post-liberal theology now mainstream for British Baptists. The study also places these developments within a MacIntyrean framework, especially in the rejection of two models of ministry: the therapeutic and the managerial.
Paul W. Goodliff is currently Head of the Department of Ministry for the Baptist Union of Great Britain, a tutor in Christian doctrine for the Open Theological College and an Associate Research Fellow of Spurgeon's College.
2010 / ISBN 978–0–9539746–8–9

Darrell Jackson
'As we are gathered ...': Membership and Belonging in Contemporary Baptist Congregations
Vol. 3
Statistics show a decline in membership and an increase in regular church attendance. This timely work observes practices and theologies of both membership and belonging emerging from local congregations. It examines theological writing about membership, constitutional resources for membership, and the language of church members and non-members. Jackson concludes that these three emphases–covenantal, denominational, and relational–fail to connect, producing popular understandings that will prove problematic in the long term. His solution prioritises the congregation as a site of theological production and outlines a post-foundational theology of belonging and membership that understands the church as the body of Christ, catholic, and covenantal. A process for achieving this is located in the discussion and adoption of a sixth 'Core Value'–relational communities.
Darrell Jackson has ministered in a local church, an Association, the Baptist Union of Great Britain, the Conference of European Churches, and is now the Director of the Nova Research Centre and Lecturer in European Studies at Redcliffe College.
2011 / ISBN 978–0–9539746–9–6

Andy Goodliff
'To such as these': The Child in Baptist Thought
Vol. 4
This study examines what British Baptists have written about and prayed for in regard to children in the twentieth century. Beginning with the Baptist liturgical practice of infant dedication or presentation, it explores the use of scripture, in particular Mark 10.13-16; the theology of sin and salvation; the relationship of children to the church, with a focus on baptism and eucharist; and who the child is as gift, agent and made in the image of God. A final chapter argues that Baptists must root and display a theology of the child in infant presentation.
Andy Goodliff trained for ministry at Regent's Park College, University of Oxford.
2010 / ISBN 978–1–907600–03–6

Peter J. Morden
'Communion with Christ and his people': The Spirituality of C.H. Spurgeon
Vol. 5
Charles Haddon Spurgeon (1834-92) was the most famous Baptist minister of his generation. For such a significant figure, he has received surprisingly little scholarly coverage. This present work seeks to make a contribution to Spurgeon studies by examining him through the lens of his 'spirituality'. A wealth of primary material, much of it previously untapped, is used to build up a picture of Spurgeon's spiritual life. Whereas older and more recent interpretations of Spurgeon have a tendency to be one-dimensional, examination of Spurgeon's spirituality reveals him to be a complex figure, one who was moulded by a diverse range of factors. Despite this

complexity, a unifying theme for Spurgeon's spirituality is traced and fresh light is shed on the foremost popular preacher of the Victorian age.
Peter J. Morden is tutor in church history and spirituality at Spurgeon's College, London, and a fellow of the Centre for Baptist History and Heritage, Regent's Park College, Oxford.
2010 / ISBN 978-1-907600-04-3

Brian Talbot
A Man sent from God: The Life and Ministry of John T. Hamilton 1916–1999
Vol. 7
John Hamilton was a locally successful Baptist minister in the middle years of the twentieth century. This book explores his life and work from the time of his theological training in South Wales and at Spurgeon's College in London, together with his short earlier pastorates in Coggeshall and Basingstoke. In addition to service as an RAF Chaplain in the 1940s, he held distinguished pastorates in Barnsley, Liverpool, Cleveleys, Morecambe and Caton between 1951 and 1994. This study sets these ministries in their social context and where appropriate in relation to the work of other Christian churches in these particular communities.
Brian Talbot is Minister of Broughty Ferry Baptist Church, Dundee, and a Fellow of the Centre for Baptist History and Heritage at Regent's Park College, University of Oxford. His published works include: *Search for a Common Identity: The Origins of the Baptist Union of Scotland, 1800–1870* (2003) and *'Standing on the Rock' A History of Stirling Baptist Church 1805–2005* (2005).
2011 / ISBN 978-1-907600-06-7

John H.Y. Briggs (ed.)
Baptists and the World: Renewing the Vision
Papers from the Baptist Historical Society Conference, Prague, Czech Republic, July 2008
Vol. 8
Here are essays on theology, history and vision, traced first in the story of British Baptists, and then in the recent history of Europe, East and West whilst a final section addresses the issues in global dimensions. Mission and evangelism, religious liberty, and relationships within community which respect the kingdom values of justice, peace and the God-created world in which we live, play their part as Baptists, always a biblical people, wrestle with the meaning of scripture for discipleship in today's world. The hope is that, whilst this volume celebrates 100 years of history, it may nourish faith in such a way that today's Baptists may develop the vision to discern the missionary task in the modern world—not just for discussion, but as a spur to decisive action. In this way history may become the inspiration for the living of tomorrow's story, as vision is realised in action.
John H.Y. Briggs is President of the Baptist Historical Society in the United Kingdom; Director Emeritus of the Baptist History and Heritage Centre, Regent's Park College, University of Oxford; Visiting Research Professor, the International Baptist Theological Seminary, Prague; a Trustee of Keston College; Emeritus

Professor in the University of Birmingham; and Senior Deacon Highgate Baptist Church, Birmingham.
2010 / ISBN 978-1-907600-05-0

Jonathan W. Arnold
The Reformed Theology of Benjamin Keach
Vol. 9
Taking into account the totality of Benjamin Keach's theological thought and writings, *The Reformed Theology of Benjamin Keach* places the seventeenth-century Particular Baptist theologian in his larger theological tradition. After re-creating the theologian's social networks, this work examines the impact of those networks on the often dogmatic and polemical stances espoused by this second generation Particular Baptist leader. In the process, this work highlights the uniquenesses in Keach's theology—especially within the Baptist community—and demonstrates that his legacy pertains to more than the oft-cited hymn-singing controversy.
Jonathan W. Arnold recently graduated from the University of Oxford with a DPhil in Ecclesiastical History undertaken at Regent's Park College. He is also an ordained Baptist minister.
2010 /

Re-sourcing Baptist History: Seventeenth Century Series

Larry J. Kreitzer
William Kiffen and his World (Part 1)
Vol. 1
The London merchant William Kiffen (c.1616–1701) is commonly regarded as one of the founding fathers of the Particular Baptists in London. For over sixty years Kiffen played a significant role in the complex world of the 17th century, with its volatile mix of religion, politics and commerce. He established himself in the early 1640s as the leader of a Baptist congregation, became an important contact for the Cromwellian Commonwealth and Protectorate, and was intimately involved in the political manoeuvrings of the royal courts of Charles I, Charles II, James II and William III. This volume seeks to explore several aspects of Kiffen's life which have not hitherto been given the attention they deserve, and offers ten specific studies which concentrate on key primary sources.
Larry J. Kreitzer is Tutor of New Testament and Tutor for Graduates at Regent's Park College, Oxford. He holds a Research Lectureship within the Faculty of Theology, University of Oxford, and is a member of the Society of New Testament Studies
2010 / ISBN 978–0–9539746–7–2

Centre for Baptist History and Heritage Studies Occasional Papers

Anthony R. Cross
Should we take Peter at his word (Acts 2.38)?
Recovering a Baptist Baptismal Sacramentalism
In his inaugural lecture, Dr Anthony R. Cross, Director of the Centre for Baptist History and Heritage, Regent's Park College, Oxford, challenges the widely held assumption, not least among Baptists, that baptism is merely symbolic, a believer's testimony to what God *has* done in the past. Cross examines this position biblically, theologically and historically and finds it wanting. Restating an understanding more faithful to biblical and early Baptist teaching he argues that baptism always has been an integral part of becoming a Christian and that it was always faith-baptism. Cross also contends for an evangelical use of the term sacrament, as he affirms what God *does* in baptism in the present. This restatement of a key Baptist conviction is an important contribution to Baptist thought and practice and to ecumenical debates. It is particularly addressed to all who claim scripture as their rule of faith and practice, urging the necessity of reform of both the theology and practice of baptism in the contemporary church. The lecture concludes by outlining seven ways in which such reform might be realized.
Anthony R. Cross is Director of the Centre for Baptist History and Heritage, a Research Fellow of Regent's Park College, and a Member of the Faculty of Theology, University of Oxford.
2010 / ISBN 978-1-907600-02-9

Regent's Study Guides

General Editor:
Paul S. Fiddes
Regent's Study Guides is a series characterized by the concern of the College to integrate careful theological thinking with the practice of pastoral care and service in society. The Guides are designed especially for those engaged in Christian pastoral ministry, whether as ordained ministers or lay leaders in the congregation, and it is hoped that they will also be of help to other church members who are willing to invest time and serious thought in reading them. Covering areas of biblical study, Christian doctrine, and spirituality, the Guides relate their subject to current affairs, modern literature, the arts, science, and a Christian life-style for the present age.

Larry Kreitzer
The Gospel According to John
Vol. 1
This volume explores the distinctive character of John's Gospel as a 'spiritual Gospel' which is grounded in history. After opening chapters which alert the reader to the faith and intention of the evangelist, Dr Kreitzer finds the portrayal of the

relationship between Jesus and John the Baptist to be a challenge about the sacrificial nature of Christian ministry. The last five chapters explore such major themes of the Gospel as eternal life, the Paraclete, sacramentalism, the 'I am' sayings, and Jesus as 'Son of God'.
Larry Kreitzer, Tutor of New Testament and Tutor for Graduates, Regent's Park College, and a Member of the Faculty of Theology of the University of Oxford
1990 / ISBN 978–0–9518104–0–8

Rex Mason
Old Testament Pictures of God
Vol. 2
Rex Mason invites us to walk with him around the 'portrait gallery' of the Old Testament to look at the many pictures of God that the writers present. Images of God as Redeemer, Craftsman, Father, King, Judge, Shepherd, warrior, and Lover are surveyed, together with 'human' and 'feminine' characteristics ascribed to God. The author's approach is to enable us actually to 'view' the pictures by providing us with substantial amounts of text to read, woven into a lovely commentary that uses the best literary and historical-critical tools to 'restore' the pictures to the freshness and colour that they had in Ancient Israel.
Rex Mason, Fellow and Tutor in Old Testament at Regent's Park College, University of Oxford (1975–90).
1993 / ISBN 978–0–9518104–1–5

John David Weaver
In the Beginning God: Modern Science and the Christian Doctrine of Creation
Vol. 3
John Weaver works out his belief that modern discoveries in science, especially in cosmology and geology, have given new life to the old arguments for design and purpose in the universe. While not proving the existence of God, such features as the 'fine tuning' of the origin of the universe, the 'Anthropic Principle', and the non-computable nature of the human mind show the reasonableness of belief in a Creator God. They also prompt theological reflection on the nature of God, opening up a vision of a God who is deeply involved in his creation, guiding the development of life from within and suffering with its pains. The author thus ventures, in a bold way, to integrate science and faith while not ignoring the differences between them.
John D. Weaver, Principal of South Wales Baptist College, Cardiff.
1994 / ISBN 978–0–9518104–2–2

Paul S. Fiddes (ed.)
Reflections on the Water: Understanding God and the World through the Baptist of Believers
Vol. 4
This is a timely book about baptism. The first six chapters are all by British Baptists whose main aim is not to repeat well-worn arguments between advocate of believers'

and infant baptism. Rather, they show how the act of believers' baptism can help us understand the creative activity of God in the natural world, human society, political life, and the Christian community. Above all, the baptism of believers leads us to contemplate the nature of the triune God who calls people into relationships. As the contributors reflect on the central place that the dramatic act of baptism has in Christian faith and practice, they find the image of God and many aspects of the world reflected on the waters of the baptismal pool. The books ends with an extended response to these essays by the Anglican New Testament scholar, Professor Christopher Rowland. This is a fresh approach both to ecumenical conversation and Baptist identity.
Paul S. Fiddes, Director of Research, Regent's Park College, and Professor of Systematic Theology, University of Oxford.
1996 / 978–0–9518104–3–9

Michael I. Bochenski
Theology from Three Worlds: Liberation and Evangelization for the New Europe
Vol. 5
This study sets out to transfer some key principles of liberation theology, as they emerged in Latin America, into the very different context of contemporary Europe. Secondly, in conversation with the Bible, it aims to make clear the links between liberation and evangelism, two concepts that are often fostered in quite separate theological camps. Finally, it asks the church to face the challenges of the New Europe developing within the European Union and the collapse of old-style Communism. This study will help readers understand how the local church, wherever it is in the world, can develop an evangelism that is truly liberating.
Michael I. Bochenski, former Rector of the Warsaw Baptist Theological Seminary, Poland, and Minister of Rugby Baptist Church.
1997 / ISBN 978–0–9518104–4–6

Timothy Bradshaw
Praying as Believing: The Lord's Prayer and the Christian Doctrine of God
Vol. 6
Pastoral leaders who take courses in theology to prepare for their ministry are bound to meet the thoughts, for example, of the great Swiss-German theologian Karl Barth, or the British theologian John Macquarrie, or the American School of Process Theology. How shall we assess what they have to say about the being and acts of God? Why should it matter to members of a local congregation anyway? This book sets out to answer these questions by bringing recent developments in Christian theology up against the test of prayer, and especially against the challenge of the master-prayer of Christians, the Lord's Prayer. The author sets out to consider how 'talk *about* God' (theology) might help us to talk *to* God in prayer. Conversely he considers what the great prayer of Jesus tells us about the very nature of God.

Timothy Bradshaw, Senior Tutor and Tutorial Fellow, Regent's Park College, University of Oxford.
1998 / ISBN 978–0–9518104–5–3

G. Henton Davies and J.E. Morgan-Wynne
The Last Seven Days: The Story of Jesus and Holy Week
Vol. 7
This book follows the story of Holy Week as told by the writers of the four Gospels. While it aims to examine the particular ways that each evangelist tells the story, it also sets out to uncover the main features of that story as it happened in that crucial week. The authors believe that there is both a story of history and a story of faith, and that the two intertwine in the story of the Gospels. The main part of the book traverses the days of Holy Week one by one, before moving in the final part to draw out the theological meaning which the Gospel writers find there.
G. Henton Davies, former Professor of Old Testament, University of Durham, and Principal of Regent's Park College, Oxford (1958–72).
John E. Morgan-Wynne, former Principal of Bristol Baptist College (1987–93) and Minister of Ilkley Baptist Church.
1999 / ISBN 978–0–9518104–6–0

Michael Ball
The Radical Stories of Jesus: Interpreting the Parables Today
Vol. 8
Michael Ball shows how shocking, disturbing and even subversive Jesus' parables must have seemed to those who first heard them. They are not bedtime stories or moralistic example stories, rather, he suggests, they are designed to get under the guard of our minds and make us see new truths from new perspectives, pointing to the reality of God and his kingdom. Drawing on illustrations from novels, poems and sermons, his aim is that the authentic voice of Jesus may be heard as clearly as possible.
Michael Ball, Minister of Llanishen Baptist Church, Cardiff.
2000 / ISBN 978–0–9518104–7–7

Paul S. Fiddes (ed.)
Faith in the Centre: Christianity and Culture
Vol. 9
This volume explores the many ways in which Christian faith and human culture have been related to each other in the past and how they interact with each other in the present. In particular, it asks how we can tell the Christian story in the midst of a postmodern culture, marked as it is by a rejection of all large-scale explanations of the world, by relativizing truth and by the loss of a memory of Christian images. Special attention is given to the experience of women—theologians, poets and artists—in the meeting between gospel and culture.

Paul S. Fiddes, Director of Research, Regent's Park College, and Professor of Systematic Theology, University of Oxford.
2001 / ISBN 978–0–9518104–8–4

Anthony Clarke
A Cry in the Darkness: The Forsakenness of Jesus in Scripture, Theology, and Experience
Vol. 10
The dying cry of Jesus, 'My God, my God, why have you forsaken me?', has puzzled and inspired Christian thinkers and preachers through the ages. In the past it has raised questions about the historicity of the events of the cross, the identity of Jesus, and the meaning of atonement. In the present this cry has taken a central place in grappling with the problems of human suffering and in exploring the idea of the suffering of God. Clarke's exegesis of the text and the way it has been used by Moltmann, Sölle, Jüngel and von Balthasar, leads him to conclusions about the vulnerability and justice of God which begin to meet the challenge of doing theology after the Holocaust. He also draws practical implications about hope for both the Godless and the Godforsaken.
Anthony Clarke, Tutorial Fellow in Pastoral Studies and Community Learning
2002 / ISBN 978-0–9518104–9–1

Richard Kidd and Graham Sparkes
God and the Art of Seeing: Visual Resources for a Journey of Faith
Vol. 11
The authors of this book invite us to accompany them in walking around an imaginary gallery which exhibits the work of six artists—Munch, Chagall, Spencer, O'Keeffe, Lawrence and Van Ggh. Along the way they draw widely on their own experience, essentially one of joy in the presence of visual forms—pictures, sculptures, landscapes, seascapes and city–scapes, and other memorable art-objects. Their conviction is that too much Western Christianity, with its strong emphasis on words, creeds and doctrines, has forgotten just how important the visual form can be for human development.
Richard Kidd, Principal of Northern Baptist College, Manchester.
Graham Sparkes, Head of the faith and Unity Department for Ecumenical Engagement, Public Issues and Social Justice, Baptist Union of Great Britain.
2003 / ISBN 978–0–9518104–0–3

Anthony J. Clarke and Paul S. Fiddes (eds)
Flickering Images: Theology and Film in Dialogue
Vol. 12
Studies of the relationship between film and Christian theology are growing in number and this collection of essays has the special aim of offering help to those who want to draw on current films in church services or small study groups. Questions of theory are kept in mind, especially in the first part of the book which

explores theological, existential and ideological approaches to film. The second part of the book then aims to model a variety of ways of holding the dialogue between film and theology, while the third reflects on a film in a group context. The popular culture of film provides rich material for theological and spiritual reflection.
Anthony Clarke, Tutorial Fellow in Pastoral Studies and Community Learning
Paul S. Fiddes, Director of Research, Regent's Park College, and Professor of Systematic Theology, University of Oxford.
2005 / ISBN 978–0–9539746–1–0

John Weaver
Outside-In: Theological Reflections on Life
Vol. 13
John Weaver argues for a radical reversal in thinking about the church and the world, urging us to stop looking form the 'outside-in' and to let God's activity in society and human lives outside the church make an impact upon worship and Christian teaching. The direction must be 'outside-in'. He believes it is 'time for the church to stop playing games' and aims to provide ways in whcih church members can relate their faith to their actual daily work and to the tough and sometimes brutal world in which they spend their lives. This guide for congregational leaders sets out a method for exploring experience and for moving through reflection to action.
John D. Weaver, Principal of South Wales Baptist College, Cardiff.
2006 / ISBN 978–0–9539746–2–7

Paul S. Fiddes (ed.)
Under the Rule of Christ: Dimensions of Baptist Spirituality
Vol. 14
In this book the Principals of the six Baptist Colleges in Great Britain explore Baptist spirituality. They propose that the spirituality of Baptists, in all its diversity, is characterized by living 'under the rule of Christ'. While all Christian spiritual traditions affirm this truth, they suggest that there is a particular sense of being under Christ's rule which has been shaped by the story of Baptists and by their way of being church through the centuries. Elaborating the main theme, chapters explore various dimensions of spirituality: giving attention to God and to others; developing spirituality through suffering; having spiritual liberty within a community; living under the rule of the Word of Christ and scripture; integrating the Lord's Supper with the whole of life; and engaging in the mission of God from an experience of grace. Together, the writers present an understanding of prayer and life in which Christ is both the final authority and the measure of all things.
Paul S. Fiddes, Director of Research, Regent's Park College, and Professor of Systematic Theology, University of Oxford.
2008 / ISBN 978–0–9539746–4–1

Laurie Guy
Making Sense of the Book of Revelation
Vol. 15
As the author of this study remarks, the Book of Revelation stirs powerful emotions. It can fascinate, inspire and mystify, while it can also repel the reader with its images of violence. Competing voices today cry out for us to accept their interpretation. Some claim the book is a road map for future events, others that it is a plea for justice for the oppressed. The author sets out to provide a guide for the perplexed, setting the book in the context of its time and showing that it remains an encouragement for Christians facing opposition and hostility in any age. In a straightforward way the author explores the colourful and often puzzling imagery of the book, tracing its origins in the Old Testament and other literature, and highlighting the message that Christ is the Lord of the world who will overcome all evil. In an exceptionally clear style, the author roots the book in history, finds its message for today, and opens up its assurance of hope for the future.
Laurie Guy has taught at Carey Baptist College, Auckland, New Zealand, for nearly twenty years. He is currently Vice-Principal (Academic) at the College.
2009 / ISBN 978–0–9539746–5–8

Baptist Historical Society

What this Society does

We are here to help Baptists understand their heritage and history. We provide an appropriate academic opportunity for those who wish to study life of Baptist churches, people and ideas, so that Baptists can 'articulate and discover the faith by which we all live' (Brian Haymes). We are interested in collecting primary Baptist information for the national Baptist collection in The Angus Library and Archives, Regent's Park College, Oxford (www.rpc.ox.ac.uk), and finding such resources in local churches, Record offices and any in the possession of private individuals.

Series

History of the English Baptists

A full history of English Baptists is within the 'century' volumes listed below.

B.R. White
The English Baptists of the 17th Century
Enlarged revised edition 1994, 176pp
ISBN 0980903166218

Raymond Brown
The English Baptists of the Eighteenth Century
1986, viii + 187pp
ISBN 0980903166107

J.H.Y. Briggs
The English Baptists of the Nineteenth Century
1994, 432pp
Paperback ISBN 0980903166188

Ian M. Randall
The English Baptists of the Twentieth Century
2005, xxvi + 600pp
Paperback ISBN 9780903166356

English Baptist Records
Series Editor: Roger Hayden

Transcribed by L.G. Champion
No. 1. The Chesham, Bucks
1985, xiv + 166pp
Paperback ISBN 0903166097

Transcribed by L.G. Champion and K.A.C. Parsons
No. 2. Church Book: St Andrews Street Baptist Church, Cambridge 1720–1832
1991, xl +196pp
Paperback ISBN 0903166143

Transcribed and edited by S.L. Copson
No 3. Association Life of the Particular Baptists of Northern England 1699–1732
1991, x + 153pp
Paperback ISBN 0903166151
A set of volumes 1 to 3 is available for £25

Individual Volumes

Geoffrey R. Breed
Particular Baptists in Victorian England and their Strict Communion Organizations
2003, xiv + 348pp
Paperback ISBN 0903166348
[Only available from the Revd Dr Roger Hayden—see below]

Sharyl Corrado and Toivo Pilli (Eds)
Eastern European Baptist History: New Perspectives
International Baptist Seminary, Prague, 2007,
Paperback ISBN 80-87006-02-X
[Only available from the Revd Dr Roger Hayden—see below]

Kenneth Dix
Strict and Particular
English Strict and Particular Baptists in the Nineteenth Century
2001, xii + 337pp
Paperback ISBN 9780903166317
[Only available from the Revd Dr Roger Hayden—see below]

Stephen Greasley
Recording your Church's History
2009, 12pp
[Only available from the Revd Dr Roger Hayden—see below]

Bernard Green
Crossing the Boundaries: A History of the European Baptist Federation
1999, xiv + 243pp
Paperback ISBN 0903166291

Bernard Green
European Baptists and the Third Reich
2008, xii + 270pp
Paperback ISBN 9780903166386
[Only available from the Revd Dr Roger Hayden—see below]

Bernard Green
Tomorrow's Man: A Biography of James Henry Rushbrooke
1997, 228pp
Paperback ISBN 978090366294
Hardback ISBN 0903166275

Roger Hayden
Continuity and Change: Evangelical Calvinism among 18th century Baptist Ministers trained at Bristol Baptist Academy, 1690-1791.
2006, xiv + 273pp
Paperback ISBN 139780903166379
[Only available from the Revd Dr Roger Hayden—see below]

Roger Hayden
English Baptist History & Heritage (Second Edition)
Published by Baptist Union of Great Britain, 2005, xvi + 286pp
Paperback ISBN 0901472794
[Only available in UK, for overseas and trade orders visit the Baptist Union of Great Britain's website, see below]

Susan J. Mills
Exploring History
Probing the Past: A Toolbox for Baptist Historical Research.
2009, 199pp
Paperback ISBN 978-0-903166-39-3
[Only available from the Revd Dr Roger Hayden—see below]

Michael Walker
Baptists at the Table: The Theology of the Lord's Supper amongst English Baptists in the Nineteenth Century
1992, xii + 212pp
Paperback ISBN 9780903166164

W.M.S. West
Baptists Together
2000, vi + 143pp
Paperback ISBN 0903166305
[Only available from the Revd Dr Roger Hayden—see below]

Baptist Quarterly
The journal of the Society contains articles on history, theology and general topics, together with reviews of recent books. Published four times a year, each issue being around 52pp, and an index is produced alternate years.
ISSN 0005 – 576X
Sent free to members.

Cumulative Indices
The updated CD Rom is now available. It contains

- *Transactions of the Baptist Historical Society* Vols 1–7
- *Baptist Quarterly* Vols 1–41

All these in ASCII txt format and volumes 40 and 41 are also in Rich Text Format.

Web: http://www.baptisthistory.org.uk/

To order any Baptist Historical Society Publications
Retail sales in Great Britain:
Baptist Union Publications Department,
Baptist House
PO Box 44
129 Broadway
Didcot
Oxon
OX11 8RT
www.baptiststore.co.uk

Trade and Overseas Sales:
Revd Dr Roger Hayden,
15 Fenhurst Gardens,
Long Ashton,
Bristol.
BS41 9AU. UK
rogerhayden@tiscali.co.uk

For information on membership of the Baptist Historical Society contact:
Steve Langford: adm@baptisthistory.clara.co.uk